BRITAIN

1994

AN OFFICIAL HANDBOOK

Prepared by the Central Office of Information
London: HMSO

© Crown Copyright 1993
Applications for reproduction should be made to HMSO
First published 1993

ISBN 0 11 7017590

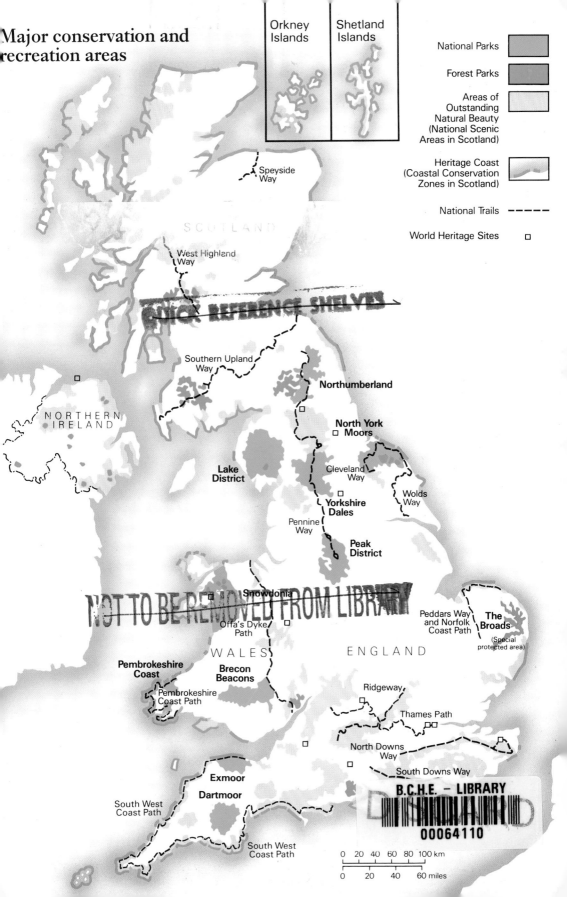

Major conservation and recreation areas

Orkney Islands

Shetland Islands

National Parks

Forest Parks

Areas of Outstanding Natural Beauty (National Scenic Areas in Scotland)

Heritage Coast (Coastal Conservation Zones in Scotland)

National Trails

World Heritage Sites □

Speyside Way

SCOTLAND

West Highland Way

Southern Upland Way

NORTHERN IRELAND

Northumberland

Lake District

North York Moors

Cleveland Way

Wolds Way

Yorkshire Dales

Pennine Way

Peak District

Snowdonia

Offa's Dyke Path

Peddars Way and Norfolk Coast Path

The Broads (Special protected area)

WALES

ENGLAND

Pembrokeshire Coast

Brecon Beacons

Pembrokeshire Coast Path

Ridgeway

Thames Path

North Downs Way

South Downs Way

Exmoor

Dartmoor

South West Coast Path

South West Coast Path

0 20 40 60 80 100 km

0   20   40   60 miles

BRITAIN
1994
AN OFFICIAL HANDBOOK

Contents

List of Illustrations

Photographs

Acknowledgments for use of photographs appear on p. 520

Foreword

Britain 1994 is the 45th in the series of Handbooks prepared by the Central Office of Information (COI). Drawing on a wide range of official and other authoritative sources, it provides a factual overview of Government policy and developments in Britain.

The Handbook is widely recognised as an established work of reference, not only in Britain but overseas, where it is an important element of the information service provided by British diplomatic posts. It is sold by HMSO and its agents throughout the world.

New Features

The text has, of course, been fully updated and revised. The structure has been altered and chapters are now grouped in sections. Other new features introduced, some at the suggestion of readers, include:

- a list of Charters produced under the Government's Citizen's Charter initiative;
- a brief reading list at the end of most chapters; and
- a guide to the contents of each chapter at the head of the chapter itself.

Coverage

Every effort is made to ensure that the information given in the Handbook is accurate at the time of going to press. The text, generally, is based on information available up to September 1993.

As far as possible, the Handbook presents information that applies to Britain as a whole. However, this is not always possible. Care should be taken when using the Handbook to note whether the information given refers to:

- Britain, formally the United Kingdom of Great Britain and Northern Ireland;

- Great Britain, which comprises England, Wales and Scotland;
- England and Wales, which are grouped together for many administrative and other purposes; or, in some instances,
- England alone.

Aspects of Britain

COI also produces the Aspects of Britain series of paperbacks, which covers in depth Britain's political, economic and social structure, and its place in the international community. Some titles are extended versions of the chapters in the Britain Handbook, but most are completely new texts. Appropriate titles are given in the list of further reading at the end of most chapters and a selection is listed on the back cover. For further information please write to COI Reference Services or phone 071 261 8310.

Acknowledgments

The Handbook has been compiled with the co-operation of around 250 organisations, including other government departments and agencies. The editor would like to thank all those who have contributed their comments.

Readers' Comments

We welcome readers' comments and suggestions on the Britain Handbook. These should be sent to:

The Editor
Britain: An Official Handbook
Reference Services
Central Office of Information
Hercules Road
London SE1 7DU

Britain and its People

1 Introduction

Britain comprises Great Britain (England, Wales and Scotland) and Northern Ireland, and is one of the 12 member states of the European Community (EC). Its full name is the United Kingdom of Great Britain and Northern Ireland.

Physical Features

Britain constitutes the greater part of the British Isles. The largest of the islands is Great Britain. The next largest comprises Northern Ireland and the Irish Republic. Western Scotland is fringed by the large island chain known as the Hebrides and to the north east of the Scottish mainland are Orkney and Shetland. All these have administrative ties with the mainland, but the Isle of Man in the Irish Sea and the Channel Islands between Great Britain and France are largely self-governing, and are not part of the United Kingdom.

With an area of some 242,000 sq km (93,000 sq miles), Britain is just under 1,000 km (some 600 miles) from the south coast to the extreme north of Scotland and just under 500 km (some 300 miles) across in the widest part.

The climate is generally mild and temperate. Prevailing winds are south-westerly and the weather from day to day is mainly influenced by depressions moving eastwards across the Atlantic. The weather is subject to frequent changes. In general, there are few extremes of temperature, with the temperature rarely above 32°C (90°F) or below -10°C (14°F).

In recent years, however, there have been some notable extremes of weather, including:

- the highest temperature officially recorded in Britain—37.1°C (98.8°F) at Cheltenham (Gloucestershire) in August 1990;

- the great storm of October 1987, which in southern England resulted in about 15 million trees being blown down; and

- a long period of low rainfall in the southern and eastern areas of England, which ended in 1992—in January 1992 London experienced its driest January since records began in 1838.

The average annual rainfall is more than 1,600 mm (over 60 inches) in the mountainous areas of the west and north but less than 800 mm (30 inches) over central and eastern parts. Rain is fairly well distributed throughout the year, but, on average, March to June are the driest months and September to January the wettest. During May, June and July (the months of longest daylight) the mean daily duration of sunshine varies from five hours in northern Scotland to eight hours in the Isle of Wight; during the months of shortest daylight (November, December and January) sunshine is at a minimum, with an average of an hour a day in northern Scotland and two hours a day on the south coast of England.

Historical Outline

The name 'Britain' derives from Greek and Latin names probably stemming from a Celtic original. Although in the prehistoric timescale the Celts were relatively late arrivals in the British Isles, only with them does Britain emerge into recorded history. The term 'Celtic' is often used rather generally to distinguish the early inhabitants of the British Isles from the later Anglo-Saxon invaders.

After two expeditions by Julius Caesar in 55 and 54 BC, contact between Britain and the Roman world grew, culminating in the Roman invasion of AD 43. Roman rule was

3

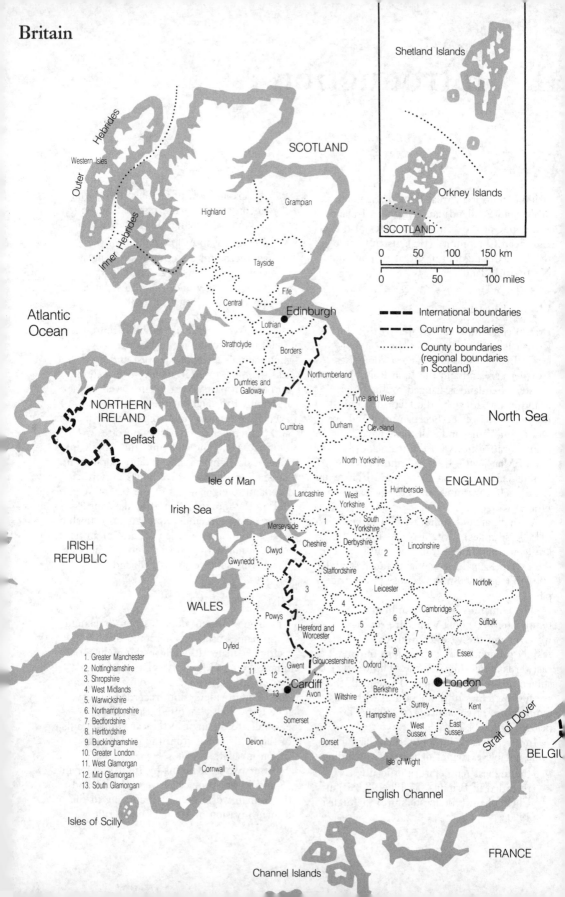

Britain

Shetland Islands

SCOTLAND

Orkney Islands

SCOTLAND

| 0 | 50 | 100 | 150 km |
| 0 | | 50 | 100 miles |

━ ━ ━ International boundaries
━ ━ Country boundaries
· · · · · County boundaries
(regional boundaries
in Scotland)

Hebrides

Western Isles

Outer

Inner Hebrides

Atlantic
Ocean

Highland

Grampian

Tayside

Central

Fife

Lothian

Edinburgh

Strathclyde

Borders

Dumfries and
Galloway

Northumberland

NORTHERN
IRELAND

Belfast

Cumbria

Durham

Cleveland

Tyne and Wear

North Sea

North Yorkshire

Isle of Man

ENGLAND

Irish Sea

Lancashire

West
Yorkshire

Humberside

IRISH
REPUBLIC

Merseyside

1

South
Yorkshire

Cheshire

Derbyshire

2

Lincolnshire

Clwyd

Gwynedd

Staffordshire

Leicester

3

Norfolk

WALES

4

Cambridge

Suffolk

Powys

5

6

Hereford and
Worcester

7

Dyfed

Gloucestershire

9

8

Essex

11

12

Gwent

Oxford

10

London

Cardiff

Avon

Berkshire

13

Wiltshire

Surrey

Kent

Somerset

Hampshire

West
Sussex

East
Sussex

Strait of Dover

BELGIU

Devon

Dorset

Isle of Wight

Cornwall

English Channel

1. Greater Manchester
2. Nottinghamshire
3. Shropshire
4. West Midlands
5. Warwickshire
6. Northamptonshire
7. Bedfordshire
8. Hertfordshire
9. Buckinghamshire
10. Greater London
11. West Glamorgan
12. Mid Glamorgan
13. South Glamorgan

Isles of Scilly

FRANCE

Channel Islands

gradually extended from south-east England to include Wales and, for a time, the lowlands of Scotland. The final Roman withdrawal in 409 followed a period of increasing disorder during which the island began to be raided by Angles, Saxons and Jutes from northern Europe. It is from the Angles that the name 'England' derives. The raids turned into settlement and a number of small English kingdoms were established. The Britons maintained an independent existence in the areas now known as Wales and Cornwall. Among these kingdoms more powerful ones emerged, claiming overlordship over the whole country, first in the north (Northumbria), then in the midlands (Mercia) and finally in the south (Wessex). However, further raids and settlement by the Vikings from Scandinavia occurred, although in the tenth century the Wessex dynasty defeated the invading Danes and established a wide-ranging authority in England.

Some of the main dates in present day Britain's history are given on p. 6. The early histories of England, Wales, Scotland and Northern Ireland are included in Chapters 2 to 5, which also deal with the main aspects of their social, economic and political life. Additional material is included on the political situation in Northern Ireland. Table 1.1 gives a selection of some of the main statistics for each of the four lands.

Channel Islands and Isle of Man

Although the Channel Islands and the Isle of Man are not part of the United Kingdom, they have a special relationship with it. The Channel Islands were part of the Duchy of Normandy in the 10th and 11th centuries and remained subject to the English Crown after the loss of Normandy to the French. The Isle of Man was under the nominal sovereignty of Norway until 1266, and eventually came under the direct administration of the Crown in 1765. Today the territories have their own legislative assemblies and systems of law. The British Government is responsible for their defence, their international relations and, ultimately, their good government.

Table 1.1: General Statistics

	England	Wales	Scotland	Northern Ireland	United Kingdom
Population (mid-1991) ('000)	48,208	2,891	5,107	1,594	57,801
Area (sq km)	130,423	20,766	77,080	13,483	241,752
Population density (persons per sq km)	370	139	66	118	239
Gross domestic product (£ per head, 1991)	8,680	7,365	8,234	6,567	8,516
Employees in employment ('000, June 1992)	18,359	942	2,005	542	21,848
Percentage of employees (June 1992) in:					
services	72.4	69.0	71.5	72.1	72.1
manufacturing	20.8	22.2	18.4	18.8	20.6
construction	4.0	4.5	5.9	4.4	4.2
energy and water supply	1.7	2.3	2.9	1.3	1.8
agriculture, forestry and fishing	1.2	2.0	1.3	3.5	1.3
Unemployment rate (per cent, seasonally adjusted, June 1993)	10.3	10.3	9.6	14.0	10.4

Sources: *Regional Trends*, Office of Population Censuses and Surveys, Department of Employment.

Significant Dates

55 and 54 BC: Julius Caesar's expeditions to Britain

AD **43**: Roman conquest begins under Claudius

122–38: Hadrian's Wall built

c409: Roman army withdraws from Britain

450s onwards: foundation of the Anglo-Saxon kingdoms

597: arrival of St Augustine to preach Christianity to the Anglo-Saxons

664: Synod of Whitby opts for Roman Catholic rather than Celtic church

789–95: first Viking raids

832–60: Scots and Picts merge under Kenneth Macalpin to form what is to become the kingdom of Scotia

860s: Danes overrun East Anglia, Northumbria and eastern Mercia

871–99: reign of Alfred the Great in Wessex

1066: William the Conqueror defeats Harold Godwinson at Hastings and takes the throne

1215: King John signs Magna Carta to protect feudal rights against royal abuse

1301: Edward of Caernarvon (later Edward II) created Prince of Wales

1314: battle of Bannockburn ensures survival of separate Scottish kingdom

1337: Hundred Years War between England and France begins

1348–49: Black Death (bubonic plague) wipes out a third of England's population

1381: Peasants' Revolt in England

1455–87: Wars of the Roses between Yorkists and Lancastrians

1477: first book to be printed in England by William Caxton

1534–40: English Reformation; Henry VIII breaks with the Papacy

1536–42: Acts of Union integrate England and Wales administratively and legally and give Wales representation in Parliament

1547–53: Protestantism becomes official religion in England under Edward VI

1553–58: Catholic reaction under Mary I

1558: loss of Calais, last English possession in France

1558–1603: reign of Elizabeth I; moderate Protestantism established

1588: defeat of Spanish Armada

c1590–c1613: plays of Shakespeare written

1603: union of the two crowns under James VI of Scotland

1642–51: Civil Wars between King and Parliament

1649: execution of Charles I

1653–58: Oliver Cromwell rules as Lord Protector

1660: restoration of the monarchy under Charles II

1688: Glorious Revolution; accession of William and Mary

1707: Act of Union unites England and Scotland

c1760s–c1830s: Industrial Revolution

1761: opening of the Bridgewater Canal ushers in Canal Age

1775–83: American War of Independence leads to loss of the Thirteen Colonies

1793–1815: Revolutionary and Napoleonic Wars

1801: Act of Union unites Great Britain and Ireland

1825: opening of the Stockton and Darlington Railway, the world's first passenger railway

1829: Catholic emancipation

1832: First Reform Act extends the franchise

1914–18: First World War

1921: Anglo-Irish Treaty establishes the Irish Free State; Northern Ireland remains part of the United Kingdom

1939–45: Second World War

1952: accession of Elizabeth II

1973: Britain enters European Community

2 England

England is predominantly a lowland country, although there are upland regions in the north (the Pennine Chain, the Cumbrian mountains and the Yorkshire moorlands) and in the south west, in Cornwall, Devon and Somerset. Central southern England has the downs—low chalk hill ranges. The greatest concentrations of population (see Table 2.1) are in London and the South East, the West Yorkshire and north-west industrial cities, the Midlands conurbation around Birmingham, the north-east conurbations on the rivers Tyne and Tees, and along the Channel coast.

Early History

In 1066 the last successful invasion of England took place. Duke William of Normandy defeated the English at the Battle of Hastings. Normans and others from France came to settle. French became the language of the nobility for the next three centuries and the legal and, to some extent, social structure was influenced by that prevailing across the Channel. The English language, which descended from the German tongue spoken by the Anglo-Saxons in the fifth and sixth centuries, was transformed with the Norman Conquest. English re-emerged as a literary language in the 14th century, and it became the universal tongue for all segments of English society—although strong regional variations continued to flourish.

With the final loss of the English Crown's possessions in France during the late Middle Ages, and the union of England and Scotland in 1707, England's position as the most populous part of the nation state was established.

Government

England has no government minister or department exclusively responsible for its central administration in domestic affairs, in contrast to Wales, Scotland and Northern Ireland. Instead, there are a number of government departments, whose responsibilities in some cases also cover aspects of affairs in Wales and Scotland.

There are 524 Members of Parliament for England in the House of Commons. In September 1993 England had 317 Conservative Members of Parliament, 194 Labour, 12 Liberal Democrat and the Speaker of the House of Commons. Conservative support is to be found particularly in suburban and rural areas and the Conservatives have a large majority of the parliamentary seats in the southern half of England and in East Anglia. The Labour Party derives its main support from urban industrialised areas.

Local government is mainly administered through a two-tier system of counties (see map, p. 4) subdivided into districts.

Table 2.1: Population and Population Density Mid-1991

	Population	People per sq km		Population	People per sq km
North Region	**3,091,700**	**201**	**South East Region**	**17,636,800**	**648**
Cleveland	559,700	938	Bedfordshire	532,400	431
Cumbria	489,200	72	Berkshire	753,000	598
Durham	605,800	249	Buckinghamshire	639,100	340
Northumberland	306,700	61	East Sussex	715,600	399
Tyne and Wear	1,130,400	2,093	Essex	1,546,900	421
Yorkshire and Humberside Region	**4,982,800**	**323**	Greater London	6,889,900	4,366
Humberside	877,300	250	Hampshire	1,581,900	419
North Yorkshire	719,100	87	Hertfordshire	988,700	603
South Yorkshire	1,301,900	835	Isle of Wight	126,300	332
West Yorkshire	2,084,500	1,025	Kent	1,536,100	411
East Midlands Region	**4,035,400**	**258**	Oxfordshire	580,900	223
Derbyshire	943,100	359	Surrey	1,033,600	616
Leicestershire	894,400	351	West Sussex	712,300	358
Lincolnshire	591,000	100	**South West Region**	**4,717,800**	**198**
Northamptonshire	586,600	248	Avon	964,900	724
Nottinghamshire	1,020,200	472	Cornwall	474,100	133
East Anglia Region	**2,081,900**	**166**	Devon	1,038,700	155
Cambridgeshire	668,700	197	Dorset	660,500	249
Norfolk	759,400	141	Gloucestershire	539,400	203
Suffolk	653,800	172	Somerset	468,400	136
West Midlands Region	**5,265,500**	**405**	Wiltshire	571,800	164
Hereford and Worcester	685,400	175	**North West Region**	**6,396,100**	**871**
Shropshire	411,600	118	Cheshire	966,100	414
Staffordshire	1,049,800	387	Greater Manchester	2,570,500	1,999
Warwickshire	489,200	247	Lancashire	1,409,900	459
West Midlands County	2,629,400	2,925	Merseyside	1,449,700	2,213
			England	**48,208,100**	**370**

Source: Office of Population Censuses and Surveys.

However, there are some single-tier authorities—32 boroughs in London and 36 metropolitan districts in other conurbations. The Local Government Commission has begun its review of the structure of local government in England (see p. 69).

The English legal system comprises on the one hand a historic body of conventions known as 'common law' and 'equity', and, on the other, parliamentary and EC legislation. In the formulation of common law since the Norman Conquest, great reliance has been placed on precedent. Equity law derives from the practice of petitioning the King's Chancellor in cases not covered by common law.

The Church of England, which was separated from the Roman Catholic Church at the time of the Reformation, is the Established Church; the Sovereign must always be a member of the Church and appoints its two archbishops and 42 other diocesan bishops.

The Economy

Considerable changes in the economy of England have occurred during the 20th century. In the second half of the century, jobs in service industries have grown and now account for over two-thirds of employees in employment, with expansion having been particularly noticeable in financial and business services. Services account for over three-quarters of gross domestic product (GDP) in London and the South East, and over 20 per cent of people in Greater London work in banking and finance.

London is one of the world's leading centres of banking, insurance and other financial services. It is also the main English media centre; the national press is published there, and the national radio and television networks have their headquarters there. After London and the South East, the South West has the next highest concentration of service industries.

Manufacturing, although declining as a proportion of the employment base, remains important in a number of areas. It is most significant in the West Midlands (where manufacturing accounted for 29 per cent of

the region's GDP in 1991) and the North.

East Anglia has been the fastest-growing English region in terms of both population and employment since the 1960s. Although largely agricultural, high-technology industry has in recent years developed in the region.

In agriculture, dairying is most common in the west of England; sheep and cattle are reared in the hilly and moorland areas of the North and South West. Arable farming, pig and poultry farming and horticulture are concentrated in the east and south. Horticulture is also important in the West Midlands. The principal fishing ports are on the east coast and in the South West.

England has plentiful energy resources in its coalfields and has access to offshore oil and gas reserves. Important mineral deposits include sand, gravel and crushed rock used by the construction industry; industrial minerals include clay, salt from the North West, china clay from Cornwall and gypsum from the Midlands, North and South East.

Transport

The motorway network comprises four long-distance routes linking London and the cities of the Midlands, the North and North West, and the South West, the London orbital route (M25), and over 30 shorter motorways.

On the railways a major development will be the inauguration of services through the Channel Tunnel in early 1994. The tunnel will link Britain with the European rail system and also provide a vehicle shuttle service on specially designed trains. The major airports are Heathrow (the busiest international airport in the world) and Gatwick, both serving London; and Manchester, Birmingham, Stansted and Luton.

Tourism

Tourism and the leisure industries have expanded in recent years. Over half the expenditure by overseas visitors in Britain takes place in London. The South West is the most popular region for domestic tourism. Of the many tourist attractions in England, the most popular of those charging for admission in 1992 were Alton Towers (Staffordshire), Madame Tussaud's waxworks in London, and the Tower of London, with 2.5, 2.3 and 2.2 million visitors respectively.

Cultural and Social Life

London has a concentration of cultural features, including four major art galleries and many renowned museums, together with theatrical, opera, ballet and concert venues. Other major cities and towns also have a broad range of cultural interests. Many theatres outside London are used for touring by the national theatre, dance and opera companies. Many regions and towns have associations with great English writers and artists, such as William Shakespeare (Stratford-upon-Avon), William Wordsworth (Lake District), Arnold Bennett (Stoke-on-Trent), the Brontë sisters (Yorkshire), Thomas Hardy (Dorset) and John Constable (Essex and Suffolk).

Despite the relatively high population density and degree of urbanisation, there are still many unspoilt rural and coastal areas. There are seven National Parks, six forest parks, 34 designated 'areas of outstanding natural beauty', 16 environmentally sensitive areas, almost 200 country parks approved by the Countryside Commission, over 6,000 conservation areas, 800 km (500 miles) of designated heritage coastline, and about 2,000 historic buildings and some 3,600 gardens open to the public. There are also safari and wildlife parks, and 'theme' parks, all offering family activities and entertainment.

Further Reading

Regional Trends, annual report. HMSO.

3 Northern Ireland

About half of the 1.5 million people in Northern Ireland are settled on the eastern seaboard, the centre of which is Belfast, with a population of some 287,100. Most industry is situated in this eastern part of the province. Agriculture is one of the most important sectors of the economy.

Just under two-thirds of the population are descendants of Scots or English settlers who crossed to north-eastern Ireland mainly in the 17th century; most are Protestants, British by culture and tradition and committed to maintaining the constitutional link with the British Crown. The remainder, just over a third, are Roman Catholics, Irish by culture and history, and favour union with the Irish Republic.

Early History

During the tenth century Ireland was dominated by the Vikings.

In 1169 Henry II of England launched an invasion of Ireland. He had been granted its overlordship by the English Pope Adrian IV, who was anxious to bring the Irish church into full obedience to Rome. Although a large part of the country came under the control of Anglo-Norman magnates, little direct authority was exercised from England during the Middle Ages.

The Tudor monarchs showed a much greater tendency to intervene in Ireland. During the reign of Elizabeth I, a series of campaigns was waged against Irish insurgents. The main focus of resistance was the northern province of Ulster. With the collapse of this resistance and the flight of its leaders in 1607, Ulster was settled by immigrants from Scotland and England.

The English civil wars (1642–51) led to further risings in Ireland and these were crushed by Cromwell. There was more fighting after the deposition of James II in 1688.

During most of the 18th century there was an uneasy peace; towards its end various efforts were made by British governments to achieve stability. In 1782 the Irish Parliament (dating from medieval times) was given legislative independence; the only constitutional tie with Great Britain was the Crown. The Parliament only represented the privileged Anglo-Irish minority and Catholics were excluded from it. An abortive rebellion took place in 1798, and in 1801 Ireland was unified with Great Britain.

The Irish question was one of the major problems of British politics during the 19th century. In 1886 the Liberal Government introduced a Home Rule Bill designed to give an Irish Parliament authority over most internal matters while reserving control over external affairs to Britain. This led to a split in the Liberal Party and the failure of the

Bill. In 1914 Home Rule was enacted by the Government of Ireland Act. Its implementation was prevented by the threat of armed resistance on the part of the Protestant majority in Ulster and by the outbreak of the First World War.

Although a nationalist rising in Dublin in 1916 was suppressed, a guerrilla force known as the Irish Republican Army (IRA) began operations against the British administration at the end of the First World War. The Government of Ireland Act 1920 provided for the establishment of two Home Rule parliaments, one in Dublin and the other in Belfast. The Act was implemented in 1921 in Northern Ireland, when six of the nine counties of the province of Ulster received their own Parliament and remained represented in, and subject to the supreme authority of, the British Parliament. In the South the IRA continued to fight for independence from the British administration. After the signature of a truce in June 1921, the Anglo-Irish Treaty of December 1921 established the Irish Free State, which became a republic in 1949.

For 50 years from 1921 Northern Ireland had its own devolved Parliament in which the mainly Protestant Unionists consistently formed the majority and therefore constituted the Government after successive elections. Nationalists resented this domination and their effective exclusion from political office.

An active and articulate civil rights movement emerged during the late 1960s. Although reforms were made in response (see p. 13), sectarian disturbances developed and this required the introduction of Army troops in 1969 to support the police in keeping order. Subsequently, sectarian divisions were exploited by the actions of terrorists from both sides, but most notably by the Provisional Irish Republican Army, who claimed to be protecting the Roman Catholic minority.

Despite the reform programme, the inter-communal violence continued, leading to a decision by the British Government to take over responsibility for law and order in 1972. The Northern Ireland Government resigned in protest against this decision and direct rule from Westminster began.

Geography

Northern Ireland is at its nearest point only 21 km (13 miles) from Scotland. It has a 488-km (303-mile) border in the south and west with the Irish Republic. At its centre lies Lough Neagh, Britain's largest freshwater lake (381 sq km, 147 sq miles). Many of the principal towns lie in valleys leading from the Lough, including the capital, Belfast, which stands at the mouth of the river Lagan. The Mourne Mountains, rising sharply in the south-east, include Slieve Donard, Northern Ireland's highest peak (852 m, 2,796 ft).

Government

Northern Ireland continues to be governed by direct rule under legislation passed in 1974. This allows the Parliament in Westminster to approve all laws for Northern Ireland and places its government departments under the direction and control of the Secretary of State for Northern Ireland, who is a Cabinet minister (see p. 500).

Northern Ireland returns 17 members to the United Kingdom Parliament. In the most recent general election in April 1992 the Ulster Unionists won 9 seats, the Democratic Unionists 3, the Ulster Popular Unionists 1 and the Social and Democratic Labour Party 4. The Alliance Party, set up to offer an alternative to unionist and nationalist parties, did not obtain a seat.

Efforts to Achieve Devolved Government

Legislation passed in 1973 provided for a measure of devolved government in Northern Ireland. This was implemented in January 1974 following agreement between Northern Ireland political parties to form a power-sharing Executive. The Executive, however, collapsed in May 1974 as a result of a protest strike by 'loyalists'.

Attempts have been made by successive British governments to find a means of restoring a widely acceptable form of devolved government to Northern Ireland. A 78-member Assembly was elected by proportional representation in 1982. Four years later this was dissolved after it ceased to discharge its responsibilities to make proposals for the resumption of devolved government and to monitor the work of the Northern Ireland government departments. One of the reasons for the Assembly's dissolution was in part the Unionists' reaction to the Anglo-Irish Agreement between the British and Irish governments in November 1985.

The objectives of the Agreement are to:

● promote peace and stability in Northern Ireland;

● create a new climate of friendship and co-operation between the peoples of Britain and the Irish Republic; and

● improve co-operation in fighting terrorism.

It commits both governments to the principle that Northern Ireland shall remain part of Britain for as long as that is the wish of a majority. It recognises that at present a majority there wishes to remain part of Britain. Both governments have undertaken that, should a majority in Northern Ireland formally consent to the establishment of a united Ireland, they would introduce and support the necessary legislation. The Agreement binds Britain and the Irish Republic to these commitments in international law.

The Agreement also established an Inter-governmental Conference through which the Irish Government can put forward views and proposals on specified matters affecting Northern Ireland affairs. This only applies if these matters are not the responsibility of a devolved administration in Northern Ireland and where cross border co-operation can be promoted in the interests of both countries. Each government retains sovereignty and full responsibility for decisions and administration within its own jurisdiction.

The British Government remains committed to the principle of a locally accountable administration acceptable to, and enjoying the support of, both sections of the community. Following lengthy consultations with the four main constitutional parties—the Ulster Unionists, Democratic Unionists, Alliance Party and Social Democratic and Labour Party—the Northern Ireland

Secretary announced in March 1991 that agreement had been reached on a basis for formal political talks.

The talks, which took place in 1991 and 1992, had as their aim the achievement of a political accommodation taking into account the three sets of relationships relevant to the Northern Ireland problem: those within Northern Ireland, within the island of Ireland, and between the two governments. The British and Irish governments also made clear that they were prepared to consider a new and more broadly based Anglo-Irish Agreement if one could be arrived at through direct discussion and negotiation between all the parties concerned. Although the talks ended in November 1992 without full agreement, all the parties agreed that further dialogue was necessary and desirable.

Human Rights

The Government is committed to the protection of human rights.

From 1969 the Northern Ireland Government enacted a number of reforms aimed at securing the minority's right to an effective voice on public bodies. These reforms included:

● the creation of a police authority representative of all sections of the community;

● the appointment of commissioners to investigate complaints of maladministration, including discrimination, against government departments and local authorities; and

● the creation of a central housing executive with responsibility for all public sector house-building and for allocating housing according to need.

Legislation passed in 1973 outlaws discrimination by public bodies, including the Government, on the grounds of religious belief or political opinion. It also set up the independent Standing Advisory Commission on Human Rights, which advises the Government on the effectiveness of anti-discrimination legislation and on other human rights issues. In 1987 a central community relations unit was established within the Government to advise on the impact of government policies and programmes on community relations and to bring forward ideas on future action.

Direct and indirect discrimination in employment by public and private employers is also illegal. Legislation passed in 1976 made discrimination on the grounds of religion or politics unlawful and established a Fair Employment Agency to promote equal opportunities and work towards the eradication of discrimination.

New laws came into effect in 1990. These strengthened the 1976 measures by requiring employers to:

- monitor the religious affiliations of their workforce and job applicants;

- take firm action, where necessary, to provide for a fair distribution of jobs between the two communities; and

- review their employment practices every three years.

Employers found guilty of bad practice can be fined and economic sanctions can be imposed.

The Fair Employment Agency was renamed as the Fair Employment Commission, which has increased powers and resources to enable it to investigate employment practices, prescribe affirmative measures and offer advice and guidance. The Fair Employment Tribunal deals with individual complaints of alleged discrimination and appeals by employers against directions of the Commission. The effectiveness of the legislation has to be reviewed after five years.

Security Policy

While terrorism continues, certain emergency powers are in force. These include special powers of arrest in respect of certain serious crimes, non-jury courts to try certain terrorist offences (see p. 85), and the banning of terrorist organisations (see p. 77). Terrorists are tried for the criminal offences they commit, and not for political beliefs. The powers are balanced by specific safeguards; the measures are temporary, need annual renewal by Parliament, and are subject to annual independent review.

The Government has restricted the broadcasting on television and radio of direct statements made by representatives of terrorist organisations or their supporters.

The security forces are accountable to the law; if they break it, their members are liable to prosecution like any other members of the community. An independent police complaints commission supervises police investigations into more serious complaints and, at its discretion, the investigation of others. Northern Ireland's legal system, and the safeguards it enshrines, are broadly similar to those in England and Wales (see Chapter 8).

The use of violence has been condemned by the overwhelming majority of people living in Northern Ireland and, although terrorism continues, the overall level of violence is lower than in the early 1970s. Since 1969 over 3,000 people have been killed as a result of terrorist campaigns.

The police are responsible for maintaining law and order, and are assisted by the Army.

The Economy

Northern Ireland had a gross domestic product of some £10,470 million in 1991 and a working population of some 722,000 in June 1992. Trends in output, employment and unemployment tend to reflect overall trends in Britain. Almost half of manufacturing output is sold to the rest of Britain and a quarter is sold locally.

In the 1980s employment fell in manufacturing and rose in services. Unemployment is higher than in the rest of Britain and reached 14 per cent in June 1993, compared with 10.3 per cent in Great Britain.

An economic development strategy published by the Government in 1990 concluded that long-term growth could only be generated by improvements in international competitiveness led by the private sector. Its main features include:

- helping companies to identify and remove obstacles to growth;

- an intensified drive for inward investment;

- building up management and workforce skills;

- stimulating the development of an enterprise culture;

- giving a new impetus to support for innovation and for research and development;

- increasing the contribution made by tourism to economic development; and

- targeting programmes, where necessary, on areas of social and economic deprivation and on the needs of long-term unemployed people.

Industrial development policy is carried out by five agencies associated with the Department of Economic Development:

- the Industrial Development Board deals with companies with more than 50 employees and with inward investment;

- the Local Enterprise Development Unit promotes enterprise and the development of small businesses employing up to 50 employees;

- the Training and Employment Agency is responsible for training the workforce;

- the Northern Ireland Tourist Board promotes tourism; and

- the Industrial Research and Technology Unit provides advice and assistance to encourage research and development and technology transfer.

Considerable public expenditure is devoted to urban renewal in Belfast and Londonderry. The Department of the Environment has a grant scheme which has generated over £256 million of private investment at a private/public funding ratio of over 3:1. In addition, under the Making Belfast Work programme for the period from 1988 to 1994, over £100 million is being used to promote jobs and businesses, improve training, and make improvements to the environment and living conditions. There is also a government and private sector scheme designed to redevelop the banks of the river Lagan in the heart of the city. In Londonderry there is a town centre development programme as well as community action to create more jobs.

Northern Ireland has parity with England, Scotland and Wales on taxation and services. The British Government makes a contribution (£3,300 million in 1992–93) to maintain social services at the level of those in Great Britain, to meet the cost of security measures and to compensate for the natural disadvantages of geography and lack of resources. Resources are focused on those suffering the highest level of social and economic disadvantage.

In 1986 the British and Irish governments established the International Fund for Ireland to promote social and economic advance. Some three-quarters of the Fund is spent in Northern Ireland, the rest going to border areas in the Republic. Programmes financed by the Fund cover business enterprise, tourism, community relations, urban development, agriculture and rural development. Donors include the United States, the European Community, Canada and New Zealand.

Cultural and Social Life

Northern Ireland's heritage is preserved and portrayed by the Ulster Museum in Belfast and the Ulster Folk and Transport Museum in County Down, and by a number of smaller museums and interpretive centres. The Ulster–American Folk Park in Omagh specialises in the history of Irish emigration to America; it is developing an extensive computer database on emigrants which will be available to the public.

Local arts festivals are an important feature of the arts calendar, the highlight being the Belfast Festival, based at Queen's University. The Ulster Orchestra is a major musical force. Government support for the arts is channelled through the Northern Ireland Arts Council, which gives financial help and advice to opera and drama companies, orchestras and festivals, arts centres, writers and artistic groups; the Council has its own gallery in Belfast.

The Government funds local district councils, which provide leisure facilities including 50 centres and 40 swimming pools. It finances the Sports Council for Northern Ireland, which promotes sport and physical recreation.

Health and personal social services correspond fairly closely to those in the rest of Britain, although the administrative system is different.

Although publicly maintained schools must be open to children from all religions, in practice Roman Catholic and Protestant children are mainly educated in separate schools. There are 21 integrated schools providing education for some 3,500 Protestant and Roman Catholic children and this process is being encouraged by the Government. A common curriculum applicable to all publicly financed schools is being introduced (see p. 409).

In the last ten years the housing stock has increased by about 12 per cent and owner-occupation from 54 per cent to 65 per cent. The Housing Executive is the sole public housing authority and allocates homes to those in greatest need.

Local television and radio programmes are broadcast and there is a local press (see p. 454). National television and radio broadcasts are also received and the national press is sold widely.

Further Reading

Expenditure Plans and Priorities Northern Ireland: The Government's Expenditure Plans 1993–94 to 1995–96. Cm 2216. HMSO, 1993.

Northern Ireland. Aspects of Britain series, HMSO, 1992.

4 Scotland

Three-quarters of the population of Scotland and most of the industrial towns are in the central lowlands. The chief cities are Edinburgh (the capital), Glasgow, Aberdeen and Dundee. However, just over half of Scotland consists of the sparsely populated highlands and islands in the north.

Scotland contains large areas of unspoilt and wild landscape, and the majority of Britain's highest mountains—nearly 300 peaks over 913 m (3,000 ft). The highest are the Grampians in the central highlands, with Ben Nevis (1,343 m, 4,406 ft) the tallest peak.

The predominant Church of Scotland is a Protestant church which is Presbyterian in form; it is governed by a hierarchy of church courts, each of which includes lay people.

Table 4.1: Population June 1991

	Population	Population density (people per sq km)
Regions		
Borders	104,100	22
Central	272,900	104
Dumfries and Galloway	147,700	23
Fife	349,400	267
Grampian	515,600	59
Highland	204,100	8
Lothian	751,000	428
Strathclyde	2,298,200	170
Tayside	392,500	52
Islands		
Orkney Islands	19,560	20
Shetland Islands	22,540	16
Western Isles	29,400	10
Scotland	**5,107,000**	**66**

Source: General Register Office for Scotland.

Early History

At the time of the Roman invasion of Britain, what is now Scotland was mainly inhabited by the Picts. Despite a long campaign by the governor Julius Agricola, Roman rule was never permanently extended to most of Scotland. In the sixth century, the Scots from Ireland settled in what is now Argyll, giving their name to the present-day Scotland. Lothian was populated by the Angles, while Britons moved north to Strathclyde. In the ninth century parts of Scotland were subject to raids by the Vikings; a united Scottish kingdom dated from that era. The powerful monarchy which existed in England threatened Scottish independence in the Middle Ages, particularly under Edward I, and war between the two kingdoms was frequent. There were also, however, strong links with England; several Scottish kings held land and titles in England and there was intermarriage between the Scottish and English royal families. Cultural influences on Scotland were also strong. Despite reverses such as the defeat of William Wallace's uprising in 1298, Robert the Bruce's victory over Edward II of England at Bannockburn ensured the survival of a separate kingdom of Scotland.

The two crowns were eventually united when Elizabeth I of England was succeeded in 1603 by James VI of Scotland (James I of England), who was her nearest heir. Even so, England and Scotland remained separate political entities during the 17th century, apart from an enforced period of unification under Oliver Cromwell in the 1650s. Religiously, too, the two kingdoms had developed in different directions, with England retaining an Episcopalian church and Scotland embracing a Presbyterian system. In 1707 both countries, realising the benefits of closer political and economic union, agreed on a single parliament for Great Britain. Scotland retained its own system of law and church settlement. The union became strained during the reigns of the Hanoverians George I and George II, when Jacobite risings in 1715 and 1745 attempted to restore the Stuart line.

Government

There are special arrangements for the conduct of Scottish affairs within the British system of government and separate Acts of Parliament are passed for Scotland where appropriate. There are 72 Scottish seats in the House of Commons. The General Election in April 1992 resulted in the election of 49 Labour Members of Parliament, 11 Conservative, 9 Liberal Democrat and 3 Scottish Nationalist.

Scottish administration is the responsibility of the Secretary of State for Scotland, a member of the Cabinet, working through The Scottish Office, which has its headquarters in Edinburgh and an office in London.

Review of Scottish Government

In March 1993 the Government issued a White Paper, *Scotland in the Union: A Partnership for Good,* which set out its conclusions following a wide-ranging examination of Scotland's place in Britain and the role of Parliament in Scottish affairs. A series of initiatives was announced to improve the parliamentary arrangements for handling Scottish business. This would involve the widening of the range of business to be handled by the Scottish Grand Committee (which consists of all 72 Scottish MPs), meeting in Scotland as well as at Westminster; improved scrutiny of Scottish legislation through special standing committees; and greater accountability of Scottish Office ministers through parliamentary question time (see p. 55).

Other proposals include a number of changes in the responsibilities of the Secretary of State and The Scottish Office. For example, from April 1994 responsibility for training policy in Scotland, within the framework of the Government's overall policy on training, will be transferred to the Secretary of State and responsibility for the Scottish Arts Council will be transferred from the Department of National Heritage to The Scottish Office. A more accessible Scottish Office is planned through establishing a series of information points and a central enquiry unit. Opportunities for a broader spread of Scottish Office activities around Scotland will be investigated.

Local Government

Local government generally operates on a two-tier basis broadly similar to that in England and Wales. The three islands councils (for Orkney, Shetland and the Western Isles) are single-tier authorities.

In July 1993 the Government issued its proposals for the reform of local government. The main proposal envisages the creation of a single-tier structure of 28 councils. Existing regional and district councils would be replaced by 25 new councils, while the three islands councils would be unchanged. Each of the four cities of Edinburgh, Glasgow, Dundee and Aberdeen would have its own single-tier council. The new councils would be required to devise plans for decentralisation to increase the involvement of local people in council activities. Subject to the passage of the necessary legislation, it is envisaged that the existing councils would be wound up on 31 March 1996, with the new authorities assuming full control on 1 April 1996.

Legal System

The principles and procedures of the Scottish legal system differ in many respects from those of England and Wales. These differences stem, in part, from the adoption of elements of other European legal systems, based on Roman law, during the 16th century. One difference is in the verdicts which a jury may give—in Scotland a jury can give a verdict of 'not proven' when, as with a 'not guilty' verdict, the accused is acquitted.

The Economy

Scotland has experienced the same pressure on its traditional industries as the north of England and Wales. However, since 1987 economic growth in Scotland has been greater than in Britain as a whole and it has been less affected by the recent recession than other areas.

The most significant economic development has been the impact since the early 1970s of the discovery of oil and gas under the North Sea. Up to about 100,000 jobs are estimated to have arisen directly or indirectly as a result of North Sea activities.

Industry

As traditional industries, such as coal, steel and shipbuilding, have declined, there has been growth in industries such as chemicals, electronic engineering and lighter forms of mechanical and instrument engineering. The electronics industry, which includes many of the world's leading companies in this field, provides 13 per cent of jobs in manufacturing and about 20 per cent of manufacturing output and investment. By 1991 over 200 plants were employing some 44,300 workers, one of the biggest concentrations of the electronics industry in Western Europe. Scotland accounts for more than half of Britain's output of integrated circuits and for over 10 per cent of European output.

Some traditional industries, such as high-quality tweeds and other textiles, and food and drink products, remain important. There are over 100 whisky distilleries, mostly in the north-east. Whisky exports, valued at over £1,800 million in 1991, represent about one-fifth of Scotland's exports of manufacturing.

Services

A marked expansion has occurred in services, which now employ about 70 per cent of the workforce. Financial services are of growing importance, and over 200,000 people are now employed in the sector. There are four Scottish-based clearing banks and they have limited rights to issue their own banknotes. About one-third of investment funds in Britain are managed from Scotland, which is also a base for a large number of insurance companies. Tourism and leisure also make a significant contribution to the economy, directly providing over 180,000 jobs. In 1992, 10.8 million visitors spent some £1,750 million in Scotland.

Industrial Developments

Government measures have helped to attract firms to Scotland, and investment by overseas companies has helped to make a significant contribution to the growth of modern technologically based industries. In 1992 about 81,400 people were employed in overseas-owned manufacturing units, representing almost 25 per cent of manufacturing employment in Scotland.

Recent changes to the mechanism for government support for enterprise and training led in 1991 to the creation of Scottish Enterprise and Highlands and Islands Enterprise, which both have general functions in economic development, training and environmental improvement in the Scottish lowlands and the Highlands and Islands respectively. They contract with 22 Local Enterprise Companies (led by the private sector), which arrange the provision of training and business support.

Agriculture, Forestry and Fishing

About 80 per cent of the land area of Scotland is devoted to agriculture. Hill and upland farms account for about two-thirds of the agricultural area. Much of this is rough grazing (including common grazing) for cattle and sheep. Scotland's cattle industry has a worldwide reputation, both for the quality of meat and for pedigree breeds. Arable farms are highly productive, and the principal crop is barley, which is used in the making of whisky and beer.

> Scotland accounts for nearly half of Britain's forest area and for over one-third of timber production. The bulk of new planting in Britain takes place in Scotland, mostly in the upland and mountain areas.

Fishing remains an important activity, particularly in the north-east and the islands. Scottish boats land about 70 per cent by weight and over 60 per cent by value of total landings of fish in Britain by British vessels.

Energy and Water Resources

Nuclear and hydroelectric generation supply a higher proportion of energy than in any other part of Britain. About 40 per cent of Scotland's electricity comes from nuclear power, with hydro-power and other renewables contributing a further 10 per cent.

With abundant rainfall, there is an extensive supply of water from upland sources. Water supply is currently the responsibility of the regional and islands councils, although the Government plans to create three public water authorities which would own and operate the water and sewerage services. They would be able to attract private capital to help to fund major investment projects.

Transport

Communications, both domestic and international, have improved in many parts of Scotland. The electrification scheme of the Edinburgh to London rail line was completed in 1991. The A74 road linking Glasgow and Carlisle is being upgraded to provide a northward extension of the M6 motorway, while the Central Scotland motorway network is to be completed.

Environment

Scotland's countryside contains a rich variety of wildlife, with some species not found elsewhere in Britain. There are 71 national nature reserves and over 1,300 Sites of Special Scientific Interest. Four regional parks and 40 national scenic areas have been designated, covering 13 per cent of the land surface. Four of the 11 forest parks in Great Britain are in Scotland, and a fifth spans the border between Scotland and England.

Housing and Urban Regeneration

The tenure pattern is somewhat different from that in the rest of Britain. Home ownership is increasing but, at 53 per cent, is still lower than in other areas of Britain. Some 38 per cent of housing is rented from the public sector, compared with 22 per cent for Britain as a whole. Some areas, particularly peripheral housing estates and inner city areas, have been affected by urban deprivation. A number of projects are in hand to tackle the problems, including a series of partnerships between The Scottish Office and other groups, including local communities and the private sector.

Cultural and Social Life

One of the major contributions to the arts is the annual Edinburgh International Festival, one of the world's leading cultural events. Held annually in August and September, it is the largest of its kind in the world. Since 1982 Glasgow has also held its own international arts festival, the Mayfest, which is now the second largest festival in Britain. Scotland possesses a number of major collections of the fine and applied arts such as the Burrell Collection in Glasgow. A new Museum of Scotland is to be built in Edinburgh to house the National Museums' Scottish collection.

Gaelic, a language of ancient Celtic origin, is spoken by some 80,000 people; the greatest concentration of Gaelic speakers is in the islands of the Hebrides.

An active press includes six national daily morning newspapers, six local evening newspapers and four national Sunday newspapers. Television programmes are produced by BBC Scotland and by three independent companies, covering the highland, lowland and border regions. BBC Radio Scotland covers most of the population.

The concept of universal education was accepted in Scotland as early as the 16th century. The Scottish education system has a number of distinctive features, for example, in examinations. There are 12 universities, of which four—St Andrews, Glasgow, Aberdeen and Edinburgh—were established in the 15th century, four in the 1960s and four were accorded university status in 1992–93. Many Scots have achieved eminence in arts and sciences.

The sport of golf originated in Scotland, and there are over 400 golf courses, including St Andrews, Gleneagles, Turnberry, Muirfield, Troon and Prestwick, which are internationally renowned. A wide range of outdoor activities, such as mountaineering and hill walking, and fishing, are also pursued. Winter sports are becoming increasingly popular in the Cairngorm Mountains, Glencoe and a number of other areas.

Further Reading

Scotland. Aspects of Britain series, HMSO, 1993.

Scotland in the Union: A Partnership for Good. Cm 2225. HMSO, 1993.

Serving Scotland's Needs: The Government's Expenditure Plans 1993–94 to 1995–96. Departments of the Secretary of State for Scotland and the Forestry Commission. Cm 2214. HMSO, 1993.

5 Wales

Two-thirds of the population of Wales live in the southern valleys and the lower-lying coastal areas. The chief urban centres are Cardiff (with a population of nearly 300,000), Swansea, Newport and Wrexham. However, much of Wales is hilly or mountainous. The highest mountains are in Snowdonia and the tallest peak is Snowdon (1,085 m, 3,560 ft).

Wales is a principality; Prince Charles, the heir to the throne, was invested by the Queen with the title of Prince of Wales at Caernarfon Castle in 1969, when he was 20. The Welsh name of the country is Cymru.

Early History

After the collapse of Roman rule in Britain (see p. 5), Wales remained a Celtic stronghold, although often within the English sphere of influence. For much of the period, it was divided into a number of separate principalities, and unity was achieved only sporadically. In 1267 Llywelyn ap Gruffudd, who had achieved control over a large portion of Wales, was recognised as Prince of Wales by the English. However, on his death in 1282, Edward I launched a successful campaign to bring Wales under English rule. The series of great castles that he built in north Wales remain among Britain's finest historic monuments

Table 5.1: Population Mid-1991

	Population	Population density (people per sq km)
Clwyd	413,500	170
Dyfed	350,000	61
Gwent	448,500	326
Gwynedd	239,300	62
Mid Glamorgan	541,800	533
Powys	118,600	23
South Glamorgan	408,600	982
West Glamorgan	371,000	452
Wales	2,891,500	139

Source: Office of Population Censuses and Surveys.

(see p. 348). Edward I's eldest son—later Edward II—was born at Caernarfon in 1284 and was given the title Prince of Wales, which continues to be borne by the eldest son of the reigning monarch to this day.

Continued strong Welsh national feeling was indicated by the rising led by Owain Glyndŵr at the beginning of the 15th century. The Tudor dynasty, which ruled England from 1485 to 1603, was of Welsh ancestry. The Acts of Union of 1536 and 1542 united England and Wales administratively, politically and legally.

Language

At the 1991 census Welsh speakers made up 19 per cent of the population. Welsh speakers are concentrated in the rural north and west, where Welsh remains the first language of most of the population. Welsh has equal validity with English in law courts; bilingual education in schools is encouraged, and there has been an extended use of Welsh for official purposes and in broadcasting. Since the 1960s both the Government and voluntary groups have taken steps to revive the use of Welsh. There are now many more bilingual publications than previously, and most road signs are bilingual. A Welsh Language Board advises on matters relating to the Welsh language.

The Government has reaffirmed its commitment to enhancing Welsh culture and developing greater use of the Welsh language. The Welsh Language Bill, now being considered by Parliament, would ensure that Welsh speakers are able to use Welsh when dealing with public authorities. The Welsh Language Board would be placed on a statutory basis and would have wide-ranging advisory powers. Its function would be to promote the Welsh language. The Bill would also remove legal obstacles to the use of Welsh and amend legislation which has been seen as granting a lesser status to Welsh than to English in Wales.

Religion

There is no established church, the Anglican church having been disestablished in 1920 following decades of pressure from adherents of the Methodist and Baptist churches. Methodism in particular spread rapidly in Wales in the 18th century, assuming the nature of a popular movement among Welsh speakers and finding strong support later in industrial communities.

Government

The country returns 38 Members of Parliament. For the last 60 years the industrial communities have tended to support the Labour Party in elections, ensuring a Labour majority of seats. Following the 1992 General Election, Wales has 27 Labour Members of Parliament, 6 Conservative, 4 Plaid Cymru (Welsh Nationalist) and 1 Liberal Democrat. Special arrangements exist for the discussion of Welsh affairs in the Welsh Grand Committee, whose function is to consider matters relating exclusively to Wales and Bills referred to it at second reading stage (see p. 55).

The Secretary of State for Wales, who is a member of the Cabinet, has wide-ranging responsibilities relating to the economy, education, welfare services and the provision of amenities. The headquarters of the administration is the Welsh Office in Cardiff, which also has an office in London.

Local government is exercised through a system of elected authorities similar to that in England, and the legal system is identical with the English one. Fundamental changes in the structure of local government were announced in 1992 and in March 1993 a White Paper was published. A Bill is planned to implement the reorganisation. The plans involve replacing the existing eight county councils and 37 district councils by a single tier of authorities from April 1995; elections for these authorities would be held in 1994.

The Economy

Recent decades have seen fundamental changes in the basis of the Welsh economy. The most notable features have been expansion in service industries and the development of a more diverse range of manufacturing industries, including many at the forefront of technology. For example, Wales is now an important centre for electronics, information technology, automotive components, chemicals and materials, and new high-technology businesses in related industries have been established. The traditional industry of steelmaking remains important, and Wales accounts for about a third of steel production in Britain.

In services (which account for two-thirds of employment) the most marked growth has been in financial and business services, and leisure services. Tourism is estimated to employ some 95,000 people, with annual earnings of about £1,300 million. The National Garden Festival Wales, a major national tourism and leisure event, was held at Ebbw Vale in spring and summer 1992, and attracted 2 million visitors.

Although south Wales remains the principal industrial area, new industries and firms have been introduced in north-east Wales and light industry attracted to the towns in the rural areas of mid- and north Wales.

The Government has recently established a Welsh Economic Council, chaired by the Secretary of State. It is looking at a range of economic issues, including training, inward investment, exports, creation of an enterprise culture, and diversification and expansion of the economy.

Inward Investment

Wales has been particularly successful in attracting investment by overseas companies. In recent years it has regularly obtained about 20 per cent of overseas inward investment into Britain. Some 200 new projects were secured from abroad and the rest of Britain in 1992–93 and are expected to lead to nearly 14,000 new jobs and £950 million of capital investment.

Economic Development

The economic programmes of the Welsh Office are complemented by the work of the Welsh Development Agency, which has wide powers to promote industrial and

environmental change. Its budget in 1993–94 is £171 million. One of its main areas of activity is providing accommodation for business, increasingly in partnership with the private sector. It has also undertaken the largest land reclamation programme in Europe, and all the significant remaining industrial dereliction in Wales is expected to have been removed by 1997.

The south Wales valleys is one of the main areas to have been affected by the decline in traditional industries. The Programme for the Valleys was the most extensive programme of economic and urban regeneration undertaken in Wales. In April 1993 this was succeeded by a new five-year Programme for the Valleys. The emphasis of the new programme will move away from centralised initiatives towards local partnerships, and greater emphasis will be placed on links with Europe.

As well as the extensive clearance of derelict land, achievements of the original Programme for the Valleys included:

● **additional private sector investment of nearly £700 million, involving 24,000 jobs;**

● **the creation of 240,000 sq m (2.6 million sq ft) of new industrial floorspace; and**

● **the improvement of over 7,000 homes.**

A development corporation has been set up to stimulate the regeneration of the Cardiff Bay area and its proposals include a new barrage across the harbour mouth. The regeneration is expected to attract over £1,200 million of private investment and to create over 23,000 new jobs.

Agriculture and Forestry

Agriculture occupies nearly 80 per cent of the land area. The main activities are sheep and cattle rearing in the hill regions and dairy farming in the lowlands. About 12 per cent of Wales is covered by woodland.

Transport

Improvements to road and rail links, such as the upgrading of the north Wales coast road, have helped the Welsh economy in recent years. In the south there are motorway links across the Severn Bridge to southern England and the Midlands, and high-speed rail services to a number of destinations in England. A second major motorway crossing of the Severn is under construction, with completion planned in 1996. Work on motorway links to the new bridge started in early 1993.

Environment

There are extensive areas of picturesque hill, lake and mountain country, and the countryside supports a variety of plants and wildlife. There are three National Parks (Snowdonia, the Brecon Beacons and the Pembrokeshire Coast), five Areas of Outstanding Natural Beauty and two national trails as well as 31 country parks and large stretches of heritage coast. There are about 50 National Nature Reserves and over 800 Sites of Special Scientific Interest. Nearly all of the rivers and canals are classified as having water of good or fair quality, and a significant improvement has been achieved in the quality of bathing waters.

Cultural and Social Life

Welsh literature is one of the oldest and richest in Europe, and there is a national library. The Welsh people also have strong musical traditions; the country is well known for its choral singing and the Welsh National Opera has an international reputation. Special festivals, known as *eisteddfodau*, encourage Welsh literature and music. The largest is the annual Royal National Eisteddfod, consisting of competitions in music, singing, prose and poetry entirely in Welsh. Artists from all over the world come to the town of Llangollen for the annual International Musical Eisteddfod. A major expansion scheme at the National Museum of Wales, in Cardiff, has been completed and the galleries were opened in October 1993.

An active local press includes a number of Welsh language publications. The fourth television channel, Sianel Pedwar Cymru (S4C), broadcasts most of its programmes in Welsh during peak viewing hours and is required to see that a significant amount of programming is in Welsh.

The education system is similar to that in England. Welsh and English are both used as media of instruction in a number of schools. Most Welsh-medium schools are situated in the traditionally Welsh-speaking, largely rural, areas. There are also designated bilingual schools in the anglicised, mainly industrial areas to cater for children whose parents want them to be educated through the medium of both languages. Welsh is a core subject in Welsh-speaking schools and a foundation subject elsewhere under the National Curriculum. The collegiate University of Wales, founded in 1893, comprises six member institutions.

Among many sporting activities, there is particular interest in rugby union football, which has come to be regarded as the Welsh national game. The provision of sports facilities, such as indoor sports halls and swimming pools, has increased.

Further Reading

The Government's Expenditure Plans 1993-94 to 1995-96. A report by the Welsh Office. Cm 2215. HMSO, 1993.

Wales. Aspects of Britain series, HMSO, 1993.

6 The Social Framework

Among the main social changes during the second half of the 20th century are longer life expectancy, reflected in a growing proportion of elderly people; a lower birth rate; a higher divorce rate; wider educational opportunities; technological progress and a higher standard of living.

POPULATION

According to mid-1991 estimates, Britain's population is 57.8 million. It ranks 17th in the world in terms of population. Statistics are derived from the census of population (taken every ten years), with allowance for subsequent births and deaths (obtained from compulsory registration), and migration.

The 1991 census counted 54.9 million people as resident in Great Britain. Some 98.5 per cent lived in private households and the number of such households totalled 21.9 million. The most densely populated region was the North West, with 8.5 people per hectare, and the least densely populated was Scotland, with 0.6 people per hectare. Some 20 per cent were children (aged under 16) and nearly 19 per cent were of pensionable age—60 and over for women and 65 and over for men.

The population has been growing slowly since the early 1980s. On mid-1991-based projections, the population in Britain is forecast to rise to 59.7 million in 2001 and 61.1 million in 2011.

Birth Rates

In 1992 there were 781,000 live births, slightly fewer than in 1990 or 1991, compared with 634,200 deaths. The total period fertility rate (an indication of the average family size) remains below 2.1, the level leading to the long-term replacement of the population, although it is projected to increase from 1.8 in 1989 to 2 for women born in or after 1980.

Contributory factors to the relatively low birth rate in recent years (13.5 live births per 1,000 population in 1992) include:

- the trends towards later marriage and towards postponing births, which have led to an increase in the average age of women having children—27.9 years in England and Wales in 1992 compared with 26.8 in 1981;
- the current preference for smaller families than in the past, which has led to a significant decline in the proportion of families with four or more children. In 1991, 66 per cent of families consisted of a married couple with one or two dependent children, compared with 15 per cent of families consisting of a married couple with three or more dependent children; and

● more widespread and effective contraception, making it easier to plan families. Voluntary sterilisation for men and women has also become more common.

Mortality

At birth the expectation of life for a man is about 73 years and for a woman 78 years, compared with 49 years for men and 52 years for women in 1901. There has been only a small increase in life expectancy in the older age groups.

The general death rate has remained roughly the same for the past 40 years, at about 12 per 1,000 population, although in recent years it has been nearer to 11 per 1,000 population. There has been a decline in mortality at most ages, particularly among children. The infant mortality rate (deaths of infants under one year old per 1,000 live births) was 6.6 in 1992; neonatal mortality (deaths of infants under four weeks old per 1,000 live births) was 4.3 in 1992; and maternal mortality is about 0.07 per 1,000 total births. The decline in mortality reflects better nutrition, rising standards of living, the advance of medical science, the growth of medical facilities, improved health measures, better working conditions, education in personal hygiene and the smaller size of families.

Deaths caused by circulatory diseases (including heart attacks and strokes) now account for nearly half of all deaths, and mortality from heart disease in England and Wales remains high compared with that of other developed countries. The next largest cause of death is cancer, which is responsible for nearly one-quarter of deaths.

Cigarette smoking is the greatest preventable cause of illness and death in Britain. However, there has been a significant decline in the prevalence of smoking, with 31 per cent of adult males and 29 per cent of adult females smoking cigarettes in 1990, as against 52 and 41 per cent respectively in 1972. In 1992 the Government set out strategies in England and Scotland for continuing the overall improvement in health, emphasising disease prevention and health promotion.

The Government is pursuing a comprehensive strategy against drug misuse in Britain. Initiatives are aimed at reducing both the supply of, and demand for, drugs. A number of government priorities, aimed at supporting the overall goals of improving the country's health and providing high-quality care for those who need it, have been listed.

Marriage and Divorce

Britain has one of the highest marriage and divorce rates in the European Community. In 1991 there were 340,500 marriages in Great Britain, of which 37 per cent were remarriages of one or both parties. Some 35 per cent of marriages in 1991 were remarriages where one or both parties had been divorced. Of the population aged 16 or over in England and Wales in 1991, 58 per cent were married, 27 per cent single, 9 per cent widowed and 7 per cent divorced. The average age for first marriages in England and Wales is now about 27.5 for men and 25.5 for women.

In 1991 about 13 decrees of divorce were made absolute for every 1,000 married couples in England and Wales. The rates are lower in Scotland and Northern Ireland. In 1991, 158,700 divorces were granted in England and Wales. The average age of people at the time of divorce in England and Wales is now about 38.5 for men and 36 for women.

Another feature, common to many other Western European countries, has been an increase in cohabitation. Some 23 per cent of non-married women aged 18–49 were cohabiting in 1991, compared with 11 per cent in 1979. Cohabitation is particularly high (30 per cent) among divorced women, but recently the largest increase has been for single women.

There is some evidence of a growing number of stable non-married relationships. Half of all births outside marriage (which now account for 31 per cent of live births in Britain) are registered by both parents giving a single address as their place of residence.

Age and Sex Structure

The most significant changes in the age structure of the population have been the growing numbers of elderly people and the decline in the proportion of young people. The proportion of young people aged under 16 fell from 25.5 per cent in 1971 to 20.3 per cent in 1991. During the same period the proportion of elderly people (those aged 65 and over) increased from 13.2 to 15.7 per cent. Some 18.3 per cent of the population were over the normal retirement ages (65 for men and 60 for women), compared with 14.7 per cent in 1961.

There is a ratio of about 105 females to every 100 males. There are about 3 per cent more male than female births every year. Because of the higher mortality of men at all ages, there is a turning point, at about 50 years of age, beyond which the number of women exceeds the number of men. This imbalance increases with age so that there are many more women among the elderly.

Distribution of Population

The population density is about 239 inhabitants per sq km, which is well above the EC average of about 146 per sq km. Of the four lands, England is the most densely populated, with 370 people per sq km. Scotland is the least densely populated, with 66 people per sq km. Wales and Northern Ireland have 139 and 118 people per sq km respectively.

Since the 19th century there has been a trend, especially in London, for people to move away from congested urban centres into the suburbs. Between 1981 and 1991 all metropolitan counties (with the exception of West Yorkshire) experienced small decreases in population, the largest being in Merseyside (5 per cent). There has also been a geographical redistribution of the population, away from Scotland and the northern regions of England. The regions with the highest rates of increase in population between 1981 and 1991 were East Anglia (10 per cent) and the South West (8 per cent). Retirement migration is also a feature of population movement, the main recipient areas (where in

some towns the retired constitute over one-quarter of the population) being the south coast of England and East Anglia.

The population of the main urban areas in mid-1991 was:	
Greater London	6,889,900
Birmingham	1,006,500
Leeds	717,400
Glasgow	688,600
Sheffield	529,300
Liverpool	480,700
Bradford	475,400
Edinburgh	439,700
Manchester	438,500
Bristol	397,000
Coventry	305,600
Cardiff	293,600
Belfast	287,100

Migration

From 1988 to 1992 some 1.1 million people left Britain (excluding the Channel Islands and the Isle of Man) to live abroad and about 1.2 million came from overseas to live in Britain, so that net immigration increased the population by about 75,500. (These figures exclude migration to and from the Irish Republic.)

In 1992 the total inflow of people intending to stay in Britain was 215,900, some 20 per cent less than in 1991. The outflow of people leaving to live abroad, at 227,000, was 5 per cent lower than in 1991.

Of the 227,000 departing residents in 1992:

- 30 per cent for other EC countries;

- 20 per cent left for Australia, Canada or New Zealand;

- 10 per cent for other Commonwealth countries;

- 20 per cent for the United States;

- 10 per cent for the Middle East; and

- 2 per cent for South Africa.

Of the 215,900 new residents in 1992:

- 20 per cent came from Australia, Canada or New Zealand;

- 20 per cent from other Commonwealth countries;
- 30 per cent from other EC countries;
- 8 per cent from the United States;
- 3 per cent from the Middle East; and
- 3 per cent from South Africa.

Nationality

Under the British Nationality Act 1981 there are three main forms of citizenship:

- British citizenship for people closely connected with Britain, the Channel Islands, and the Isle of Man;
- British Dependent Territories citizenship for people connected with the dependent territories (see p. 292); and
- British Overseas citizenship for those citizens of the United Kingdom and Colonies who did not acquire either of the other citizenships when the 1981 Act came into force.

British citizenship is acquired automatically at birth by a child born in Britain if his or her mother or father is a British citizen or is settled in Britain. A child adopted in Britain by a British citizen is a British citizen. A child born abroad to a British citizen born, adopted, naturalised or registered in Britain is generally a British citizen by descent. The Act safeguards the citizenship of a child born abroad to a British citizen in Crown service, certain related services, or in service under an EC institution.

British citizenship may also be acquired:

- by registration for certain children, including those born in Britain who do not automatically acquire such citizenship at birth or who have been born abroad to a parent who is a citizen by descent;
- by registration for British Dependent Territories citizens, British Overseas citizens, British subjects under the Act, British Nationals (Overseas) and British protected persons after five years' residence in Britain, except for people from Gibraltar, who may be registered without residence;

- by registration for stateless people and those who have previously renounced British nationality; and
- by naturalisation for all other adults aged 18 or over.

Naturalisation is at the Home Secretary's discretion. It requires five years' residence or three years if the applicant's spouse is a British citizen. Other requirements include good behaviour and sound mind. Those who are not married to a British citizen are also required to have a sufficient knowledge of English, Welsh or Scottish Gaelic; they must also intend to have their main home in Britain or be employed by the Crown, by an international organisation of which Britain is a member, or by a company or association established in Britain.

Legislation passed in 1983 conferred British citizenship on Falkland Islanders who did not acquire it under the 1981 Act. Special arrangements covering the status of British Dependent Territories citizens connected with Hong Kong when the territory returns to the People's Republic of China in 1997 are made by the Hong Kong (British Nationality) Order 1986. Under this, such citizens are entitled, before 1997, to acquire a status known as British National (Overseas) and to hold a passport in that status. In addition, the British Nationality (Hong Kong) Act 1990 made provision for the registration as British citizens before 30 June 1997 of up to 50,000 people who are able to meet certain criteria and who are recommended by the Governor.

In 1992, 42,000 people acquired British citizenship by naturalisation or registration in Britain.

Immigration

Immigration into Britain is controlled under the Immigration Rules made in accordance with legislation passed in the 1970s and 1980s, and the Asylum and Immigration Appeals Act 1993. These set out the requirements to be met by those, excluding British citizens, who seek entry to or leave to remain in Britain. British citizens and those Commonwealth citizens who had the right of abode before 1 January 1983 maintain the right of abode and are not subject to immigration control.

Under the Immigration Rules nationals of certain specified countries or territorial entities must obtain a visa before they can enter Britain. Other nationals subject to immigration control require entry clearance when coming to work or settle in Britain. Visas and other entry clearances are normally obtained from the nearest or other specified British diplomatic post in a person's home country.

In accordance with Britain's obligations under the Treaty of Rome, EC nationals do not require entry clearances, nor are they subject to restrictions on their freedom to take or seek work in Britain. Britain similarly respects its obligations under the United Nations Convention and Protocol relating to the Status of Refugees. These provide that refugees lawfully resident in a contracting state should enjoy treatment as least as favourable as that accorded to other foreign nationals in similar circumstances.

In 1992, 9.2 million foreign and Commonwealth nationals (excluding EC nationals) were admitted to Britain. Some 53,000 people were accepted for settlement.

ETHNIC AND NATIONAL MINORITIES

For centuries people from overseas have settled in Britain, either to escape political or religious persecution or in search of better economic opportunities.

The Irish have long formed a large

section of the population. Jewish refugees who came to Britain towards the end of the 19th century and in the 1930s were followed by other European refugees after 1945. Substantial immigration from the Caribbean and the South Asian sub-continent dates principally from the 1950s and 1960s. There are also sizeable groups from the United States and Canada, as well as Australians, Chinese, Greek and Turkish Cypriots, Italians and Spaniards. More recently people from Latin America, Indo-China and Sri Lanka have sought refuge in Britain.

The 1991 census included for the first time a question on ethnic grouping. This found that 94.5 per cent of the population belonged to the 'white' group, while just over 3 million people (5.5 per cent) described themselves as belonging to another ethnic group (see Table 6.1). Members of other ethnic groups were heavily concentrated in industrial and urban areas, and over half lived in the South East. The highest proportion was in the London borough of Brent: nearly 45 per cent of the population. Ethnic minority groups also accounted for over a third of the population in the London boroughs of Newham, Tower Hamlets and Hackney.

Outside London the main concentrations were in Leicester, Slough, Bradford, the West Midlands and the Pennine conurbation. Regional concentrations varied among the ethnic groups. About three-fifths of people from black ethnic groups lived in London, compared with about two-fifths of Indians and 18 per cent of Pakistanis, who were concentrated in other metropolitan areas such as West Yorkshire.

According to the results of the Labour Force Survey, nearly half of ethnic minority groups were born in Britain. A higher proportion is under 16 than for the white group, but a much lower proportion (4 per cent) is over pensionable age. Economic activity rates for men of working age in Great Britain tend to be similar to those for the white groups. In spring 1993 they were 76 per cent for the black and Indian groups, 73 per cent for the white population and 69 per cent for the

Table 6.1: Proportion of Population by Ethnic Group 1991

	per cent
White	94.5
Other groups:	5.5
of whom:	
Black	1.6
Indian	1.5
Pakistani	0.9
Bangladeshi	0.3
Chinese	0.3
Other	0.9

Source: Office of Population Censuses and Surveys.

Pakistani/Bangladeshi group. The variations are much greater for women: 62 per cent of those from the black ethnic group were economically active, compared with 57 per cent in the Indian group, 53 per cent in the white group and only 23 per cent in the Pakistani/Bangladeshi group.

Alleviating Racial Disadvantage

Although many members of the black and Asian communities are concentrated in the inner cities, where there are problems of deprivation and social stress, progress has been made over the last 20 years in tackling racial disadvantage in Britain.

Many individuals have achieved distinction in their careers and in public life, and the proportion of ethnic minority members occupying professional and managerial positions is increasing. There are at present six ethnic minority Members of Parliament, and the number of ethnic minority councillors in local government is growing. There has also been an expansion of commercial enterprise, and numerous self-help projects in ethnic minority communities have been established. Black competitors have represented Britain in a range of sporting activities (such as athletics and football), and ethnic minority talents in the arts and in entertainment have increasingly been recognised.

The principal means of combating disadvantage is through the economic, environmental, educational and health programmes of central government and local authorities. There are also special allocations, mainly through Home Office grants and the Urban Programme, which channel extra resources into projects of specific benefit to ethnic minorities. These include, for example, the provision of specialist teachers for children needing English language tuition, business support services, and measures to revive local economies and improve the inner city environment. Cultural and recreational schemes and the health and personal social services also take account of the particular needs of ethnic minorities.

The Government is promoting equal opportunities for ethnic minorities through training programmes, including greater provision for unemployed people who need training in English as a second language.

In recognition of the tensions that can arise between the police and ethnic minorities, there is statutory consultation between the police and the community. Liaison work is also undertaken in schools.

Race Relations Act 1976

The Race Relations Act 1976 strengthened previous legislation passed in the 1960s. It makes discrimination unlawful on grounds of colour, race, nationality or ethnic or national origin in the provision of goods, facilities and services, in employment, in housing and in advertising. The 1976 Act also gave complainants direct access to civil courts and, for employment complaints, to industrial tribunals.

It is a criminal offence to incite racial hatred under the provisions of the Public Order Act 1986.

Commission for Racial Equality

The Commission for Racial Equality was established by the 1976 Act. It has power to investigate unlawful discriminatory practices and to issue non-discrimination notices, requiring such practices to cease. It has an important educational role and has issued codes of practice in employment, education, health care and housing. It also provides the main advice to the general public about the Race Relations Act and has discretion to assist individuals with their complaints about racial discrimination. In 1992 the Commission registered 1,557 applications for assistance and handled successfully 113 litigation cases. It can also undertake or fund research.

The Commission supports the work of over 80 racial equality councils. These are autonomous voluntary bodies set up in most areas with a significant ethnic minority population to promote equality of opportunity and good relations at the local level. It helps pay the salaries of the racial equality officers employed by the councils, most of whom also receive funds from their local authorities. It also gives grants to ethnic minority self-help groups and to other projects run by or for the benefit of the minority communities.

THE ECONOMIC AND SOCIAL PATTERN

Marked improvements in the standard of living have taken place during the 20th century. According to a United Nations report on human development published in 1993, Britain ranked tenth out of 173 countries on a human development index that combines life expectancy, education levels and basic purchasing power.

Britain has also performed well economically. Growth between 1980 and 1990 was higher than in all other major EC countries except Spain.

In the early 1990s Britain and many other industrialised countries were affected by recession, but Britain has been one of the first countries to experience recovery from the recession. Gross domestic product in Britain declined by 0.4 per cent in 1992, but there are signs of a recovery in 1993, with an increase in manufacturing output and growth in retail sales. Inflation levels have recently been below 2 per cent.

Income and Wealth

Earnings from employment remain the main source of household income for most people, although the proportion of household income (58 per cent in 1991) has been declining. Sources which have become more important are income from self-employment (10 per cent in 1991) and private pensions and annuities (9 per cent), as the numbers of self-employed and the elderly respectively have grown.

The distribution of pre-tax income has

Availability of Certain Durable Goods

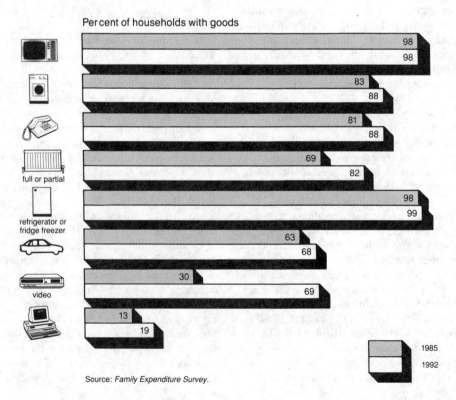

Per cent of households with goods

	1985	1992
television	98	98
washing machine	83	88
telephone	81	88
central heating full or partial	69	82
refrigerator or fridge freezer	98	99
car	63	68
video	30	69
home computer	13	19

Source: *Family Expenditure Survey.*

remained relatively stable over a long period, the lower 50 per cent of income earners accounting for some 22 to 26 per cent of pre-tax income since 1949. The combined effect of the tax system and the receipt of benefits is to redistribute incomes on a more equal basis.

Wealth is less evenly distributed, with the richest 1 per cent of the population aged 18 or over owning 18 per cent of marketable wealth in 1991, and the richest 10 per cent having 50 per cent. The inclusion of 'non-marketable' rights in occupational and state pension schemes reduces these shares substantially, to 11 and 36 per cent respectively. Since the mid-1970s there has been little change in the distribution of marketable wealth.

A growing proportion of personal wealth— 36 per cent in 1989—is in dwellings. The proportion of net wealth held in shares declined up to 1984, but has since increased. The Government's privatisation programme has contributed to the growth in share ownership. In early 1992 over one-fifth of the adult population in Great Britain owned shares, compared with one in 13 people in 1979.

Eating and Drinking Habits

The general level of nutrition remains high. There has been a significant shift in eating patterns over the last decade, reflecting greater emphasis on convenience foods and processed products. Changes in household consumption of selected foods between 1982 and 1992 are shown in the diagram on p. 34. Consumption of several items, such as packet sugar, eggs, fresh potatoes and fresh green vegetables, has declined substantially. Other changes include:

- a decline in consumption of beef, lamb and pork, which has been partly offset by a continuing increase in poultry consumption, which is now at a record level;

- an increase in purchases of semi-skimmed milk, so that skimmed milks now constitute half of the total household consumption of liquid milk;

- a rapid rise in consumption of vegetable and salad oils and of low fat and dairy spreads, while consumption of butter, margarine and lard has been declining substantially;

- a trend away from consumption of some fresh green vegetables such as cabbages and beans towards leafy salads and cauliflowers;

- a large increase in purchases of fruit juice; and

- a switch in fish consumption away from fresh white fish towards canned fish and shellfish.

Average mineral and nutrient intakes are generally above the daily amounts recommended by the Department of Health. There has been a steady fall in fat intakes, and a small increase in the intake of fibre. There is some evidence that health considerations influence food consumption, as in the move away from whole milk and the growth in wholemeal bread consumption. The Government encourages the widest availability of wholesome food, while giving high priority to consumer safety.

There has been an increase in the number of meals eaten away from home, for example, in restaurants or at work, and a growth in the consumption of food from 'take-away' and 'fast-food' shops.

There has been little change in alcohol consumption in recent years. Beer and lager (now estimated to account for over half of beer sales) are the most popular drinks among male drinkers, whose overall consumption is significantly higher than that of women. The largest consumers of alcohol are those aged 18 to 24, with consumption generally declining with age. Consumption of table wine has grown, although there has been little change in the consumption of higher strength wines such as sherry and port. The pattern of spirits consumption has also been changing, with a decline in whisky and gin, and higher consumption of some other spirits.

A high proportion of beer is drunk in public houses ('pubs'), a traditional social centre for many people, and in clubs. The Licensing Act 1988 relaxed restrictions on the opening hours of public houses, but this has

Changes in Average Household Food Consumption 1982-1992

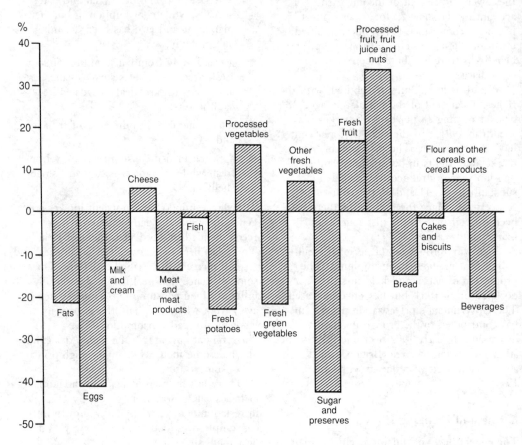

Source: *National Food Survey*, MAFF.

not resulted in a significant increase in consumption. There are signs that they are becoming more popular with families: more meals are being served and the consumption of non-alcoholic drinks is increasing.

Households

The average size of households in Great Britain has fallen from over four people in 1911 to 3.09 in 1961 and 2.48 in 1992. The fall reflects a greater number of people living on their own (11 per cent of adults in 1991), or in one-parent families, the increasing number of old people (more of whom are living alone) and the preference for smaller families.

A large proportion of households, 67 per cent, own or are buying their own homes. Owner-occupation is higher among married couples than for single, divorced or widowed household heads. The number of owner-occupied dwellings rose from over 4 million in 1951 to nearly 16 million in 1992. Four-fifths of British households live in houses rather than flats.

Transport and the Environment

An important influence on the planning of housing and services has been the growth of car ownership; in 1991, 67 per cent of households had the use of at least one car or van, including 23 per cent with the use of two or more. Greater access to motorised transport and the construction of a network of modern trunk roads and motorways have resulted in a considerable increase in personal mobility and changed leisure patterns. Most detached or semi-detached houses in new suburban estates have garages. Out-of-town shopping centres, often including large supermarkets and do-it-yourself stores, are usually planned with the motorist in mind.

Although the growth in car ownership has brought benefits, there have been a number of problems, notably, in many towns and cities, increased congestion, noise and air pollution arising from motor vehicle emissions. Cars, taxis and motor cycles accounted for 87 per cent of all passenger transport in Great Britain in 1992, compared with 55 per cent in 1961. To relieve road congestion, the Government regards carefully targeted improvements to the road system as essential.

Women

The economic and domestic lives of women have been transformed in the 20th century. These changes are due partly to the removal of much of sex discrimination in political and legal rights. A major feature has been the rise in the number of women, especially married women, at work. With later marriages and the availability of effective contraception there has been a decline in family size. Women are involved in childbearing for a shorter time and this, together with technological advances which have made some tasks, such as housework, less onerous and time-consuming, has made it possible for women with children to combine child-rearing with paid employment. The growth of part-time and flexible working patterns, and training and retraining schemes, allows more women to take advantage of employment opportunities.

Women make up more than two-fifths of the workforce. Over two-thirds of non-married working women aged 16–59 work full time, compared with half of married women. Married women are most likely to be in ful-time work if they are aged 16 to 29 with no children. More than two-fifths of all women in employment work part time, representing almost nine-tenths of all part-time workers.

Although equal pay legislation was intended to narrow the gap, there is still a difference between men's and women's earnings. In 1993 women's average hourly earnings were 79 per cent of men's. Women's wages remain relatively low because they tend to work in the lower-paid sectors of the economy and work fewer hours than men (the latter because of their domestic commitments). A major reform in the taxation of women came into effect in 1990, when their earnings began to be taxed separately rather than being treated as part of their husbands' income for tax purposes.

In April 1992 the Department of Employment assumed responsibility for co-ordinating policy and strategy on women's issues. The Secretary of State set up a working group to advise on practical measures to extend equal opportunities for women in the workplace and elsewhere.

In 1993 the Department launched 'New Horizons for Women', a programme of regional events. The objectives include:

- raising awareness of the opportunities available to women in employment, training, and public and community life;
- encouraging employers to be flexible in their working practices to enable women to contribute fully in the workplace; and
- highlighting priority areas of government policy.

One of these areas is a new childcare initiative introduced to provide out-of-school and holiday childcare. The Government is to spend £45 million to help set up over 50,000 out-of-school childcare places in Great Britain over the next three years.

In October 1991 the Government, as an employer, joined the 'Opportunity 2000' campaign, an employer-led initiative to increase the quantity and quality of women's participation in the workforce. Membership stands at some 200 employers, with organisations employing nearly a quarter of the workforce being committed to the campaign.

Equal Opportunities

The Sex Discrimination Acts 1975 and 1986 make discrimination between men and women unlawful, with certain limited exceptions, in employment, education, training and the provision of housing, goods, facilities and services. Discriminatory job recruitment advertisements are also unlawful. Complaints of discrimination concerning employment are dealt with by industrial tribunals; other complaints are taken before county courts in England and Wales or the Sheriff Court in Scotland. Under the Equal Pay Act 1970, as amended in 1984, women in Great Britain are entitled to equal pay with men when doing work that is the same or broadly similar, or work which is rated as equivalent or work which is of equal value. Parallel legislation on sex discrimination and equal pay is in operation in Northern Ireland.

The Equal Opportunities Commission, set up in 1975 (1976 in Northern Ireland under separate laws), has powers to enforce some parts of the Sex Discrimination and Equal Pay Acts. Its statutory duties are to work towards the elimination of sex discrimination, to promote equality of opportunity, and to keep legislation on sex discrimination and equal pay under review, submitting proposals for amending it to the Government. The Commission may advise people of their rights under the Acts and may give financial or other assistance to help individuals conduct a case before a court or tribunal. It is empowered to carry out formal investigations and issue notices requiring discriminatory practices to stop. The Commission also keeps sex discrimination and equal pay legislation under review and submits proposals for amending it to the Government.

Voluntary Organisations

There is a long tradition in Britain of voluntary service to the community, and partnership between the voluntary and statutory sectors is encouraged by the Government. It has been estimated that about half of all adults take part in some form of voluntary work during the course of a year.

There are hundreds of thousands of voluntary organisations, ranging from national bodies to small local groups. 'Self-help' groups have been the fastest expanding area over the last 20 or so years. Examples include bodies which provide playgroups for pre-school children, or help their members to cope with a particular disability. Groups representing ethnic minorities and women's interests have also developed in recent years. Many organisations belong to larger associations or are represented on local or national co-ordinating councils or committees. Organisations may be staffed by professional and/or voluntary workers.

A large proportion of volunteers are involved in work which improves the quality of life in their communities or more widely, giving their time to help organise events or groups in the arts and sport. A very large number of volunteers are involved in activities to protect or improve the environment, working, for example, for the National Trust, which has over 2 million members (see p. 342). Voluntary organisations are also important partners as providers of government-supported employment and training services for unemployed people.

The Home Office Voluntary Services Unit co-ordinates government interests in the voluntary sector throughout Britain.

Funding

Voluntary organisations receive income from several sources, including contributions from individuals, businesses and trusts; central and local government grants; and earnings from commercial activities and investments. They also receive fees (from central and local government) for those services which are provided on a contractual basis. In 1991–92 direct grants to voluntary organisations from government amounted to £490 million.

Tax changes in recent budgets have helped the voluntary sector secure more funds from industry and individuals. The Gift Aid scheme, introduced in 1990, provides tax relief on gifts of more than £250 in any one year. By the end of 1992 charities had received donations of more than £351 million under the scheme and had claimed tax repayments of £117 million on them. Employees can now make tax-free donations to charity from their earnings. The Payroll Giving scheme provides tax relief on donations of up to £900 a year.

Charities

There are over 170,000 charities registered in England and Wales with the Charity Commission. The Commission also gives advice to trustees of charities on their administration. Organisations may qualify for charitable status if they are established for purposes such as the relief of poverty, the advancement of education or religion, or the promotion of certain other purposes of public benefit. These include good community relations, the prevention of racial discrimination, the protection of health and the promotion of equal opportunity. Legislation was passed in 1992 to strengthen the Charity Commissioners' powers of investigation and supervision, and increase the public accountability of charities.

The Charities Aid Foundation, an independent body, is one of the main organisations that aid the flow of funds to charity from individuals, companies and grant-making trusts.

Umbrella Organisations

The National Council for Voluntary Organisations is the main co-ordinating body in England, providing close links between voluntary organisations, government departments, local authorities, the European Commission and the private sector; around 650 national voluntary organisations are members. It also protects the interests and independence of voluntary agencies, and

provides them with advice, information and other services. Councils in Scotland, Wales and Northern Ireland perform similar functions. The National Association of Councils for Voluntary Service is another umbrella organisation providing resources, with over 230 local councils for voluntary service throughout England encouraging the development of local voluntary action, mainly in urban areas. The rural equivalent is Action with Communities in Rural England, representing 38 rural community councils.

Leisure Trends

Some 15 per cent of total household expenditure went on leisure goods and services in 1992. The most common leisure activities are home-based, or social, such as visiting relatives or friends. Television viewing is by far the most popular leisure pastime, and nearly all households have a television set, with 95 per cent in 1991 having a colour set. Average viewing time is about 26 hours a week. Television viewing has been declining slightly, but there has been a significant increase in watching video cassettes. Some 69 per cent of households now have at least one video recorder, compared with 30 per cent in 1985.

Listening to radio has been increasing, and averages over 10 hours a week. Purchases of compact discs have risen very rapidly, and in 1992 for the first time exceeded the sales of audio cassettes. The proportion of households with a compact disc player has grown considerably, from 15 per cent in 1989 to 27 per cent in 1991.

Other popular pursuits include: reading, do-it-yourself home improvements, gardening and going out for a meal, for a drink or to the cinema. About half of households have a pet, the most common being dogs and cats, of which there are thought to be roughly 7 million of each in Britain.

Holidays

In 1991, over 90 per cent of full-time manual employees were entitled to more than four weeks paid holiday and 30 per cent to five weeks; in 1961, 97 per cent were entitled to only two weeks. In 1992, 59 per cent of the adult population took at least one long holiday of four or more nights away from home. The number of long holidays taken by British residents was nearly 54 million in 1992 (compared with 48 million in 1978), of which 32 million were taken in Britain. The most frequented free attraction in 1992 was Blackpool Pleasure Beach (Lancashire), with 6.5 million visitors. The most popular destinations for summer holidays are the West Country, Scotland, and Wales.

In 1992 the most popular destinations for overseas holidays by British residents were:
- Spain (24 per cent);
- France (13 per cent);
- Greece (9 per cent); and
- the United States (8 per cent).

In all, British residents took nearly 22 million holidays overseas in 1992, of which 60 per cent involved 'package' arrangements. About 77 per cent of all holidays abroad are taken in Europe. The proportion of adults taking two or more holidays a year was 15 per cent in 1992.

Further Reading

Ethnic Minorities. Aspects of Britain series, HMSO, 1991.
Immigration and Nationality. Aspects of Britain series, HMSO, 1993.
Women in Britain. Aspects of Britain series, HMSO, 1991.

Annual Reports
Family Spending. HMSO.
General Household Survey. HMSO.
Social Trends. HMSO.
Women and Men in Britain. Equal Opportunities Commission.

Government and
Administration

7 Government

The system of parliamentary government in Britain is not based on a written constitution, but is the result of gradual evolution over many centuries. The monarchy is the oldest institution of government, dating back to at least the ninth century. Parliament is one of the oldest representative assemblies in the world. In government one of the most significant recent developments has been the establishment of the Citizen's Charter, designed to raise the standards of public service.

Development of the British System of Government

The growth of political institutions in England can be traced back to the period of Saxon rule, which lasted from the fifth century AD until the Norman Conquest in 1066 (see p. 15). This period saw the origins of the institution of kingship, and of the idea that the king should seek the advice of a council of prominent men.

The period of Norman rule after 1066 saw a considerable strengthening of royal control. However, the monarchy eventually experienced difficulties in controlling the growing machinery of government. The actions of King John (1199–1216) led to opposition from feudal barons and leading figures in the Church. In 1215 the barons forced the King to agree to a series of concessions embodied in a charter which became known as Magna Carta. The charter, which provided for the protection of the rights of feudal proprietors against the abuse of royal power, came to be regarded as the key expression of the rights of the community against the Crown.

The term 'Parliament' was first officially used in 1236 to describe the gathering of feudal barons and representatives of counties and towns which the king summoned if extraordinary taxation was required. By the 15th century Parliament had acquired the right to make laws (see p. 46).

A clash between the monarchy and Parliament led to the outbreak of the Civil War in 1642. Following the defeat of the royalist armies and the execution of King Charles I in 1649, the monarchy and the House of Lords were abolished and the country was proclaimed a republic. However, the republican experiment came to an end in 1660, two years after the death of the 'Lord Protector', Oliver Cromwell. Charles I's son was restored to the throne as King Charles II.

Charles II's successor, King James II (1685–88), attempted to rule without the consent of Parliament. As a result, in 1688 a group of leading men invited William of

Orange (a grandson of Charles I and the husband of Mary, James II's eldest daughter) to 'secure the infringed liberties' of the country. James II fled into exile. Following the success of the revolution of 1688, Parliament in 1689 passed the Bill of Rights, which made it impracticable for the Sovereign to ignore the wishes of Parliament. To enable the Sovereign and Parliament to work together, a group of ministers, or cabinet, became the link between the executive and the legislature. Although the ministers were appointed by the Sovereign, they had to have sufficient support in the House of Commons to enable them to persuade Parliament to pass legislation and vote for taxation.

A few years after the accession to the throne of George I in 1714, the monarch ceased to attend Cabinet meetings and none of his successors did thereafter. Instead, the Cabinet was presided over by the First Lord of the Treasury, who came to be known as the Prime Minister. After that the individual influence of the monarch in exercising executive power declined with a corresponding increase in that of the Cabinet as a whole. Sir Robert Peel, Prime Minister from 1841 to 1846, was probably the first holder of his office to perform a role similar to that of a modern Prime Minister. Since the mid-19th century the Prime Minister has normally been the leader of the party with a majority in the House of Commons.

The Reform Act 1832 reformed the system of parliamentary representation, which dated from medieval times. It also standardised the qualifications for the right to vote. The Act started a train of events which led to all adults (with a few exceptions—see p. 49) receiving the vote and direct popular control over the House of Commons, a process which was completed early in the 20th century.

The British Constitution

The British constitution is to a large extent a product of the historical events described above. Unlike the constitutions of most other countries, it is not set out in any single document. Instead it is made up of statute law, common law and conventions. (Conventions are rules and practices which are not legally enforceable but which are regarded as indispensable to the working of government.)

The constitution can be altered by Act of Parliament, or by general agreement. The constitution is thus adaptable to changing political conditions.

The organs of government overlap but can be clearly distinguished. Parliament is the legislature and the supreme authority. The executive consists of:

● the Government—the Cabinet and other ministers responsible for national policies;

● government departments, responsible for national administration;

● local authorities, responsible for many local services; and

● public corporations, responsible for operating particular nationalised industries or other bodies, subject to ministerial control.

The judiciary (see Chapter 8) determines common law and interprets statutes.

The Monarchy

The monarchy is the oldest institution of government, going back to at least the ninth century. Queen Elizabeth II is herself directly descended from King Egbert, who united England under his rule in 829. The only interruption in the history of the monarchy was the republic, which lasted from 1649 to 1660 (see p. 41).

Today the Queen is not only head of State, but also an important symbol of national unity. The royal title in Britain is: 'Elizabeth the Second, by the Grace of God of the United Kingdom of Great Britain and Northern Ireland and of Her other Realms and Territories Queen, Head of the Commonwealth, Defender of the Faith'.

In the Channel Islands and the Isle of Man the Queen is represented by a Lieutenant-Governor.

The Commonwealth

Although the seat of the monarchy is in Britain, the Queen is also head of state of a

The Royal Family from the Reign of Queen Victoria to August 1993

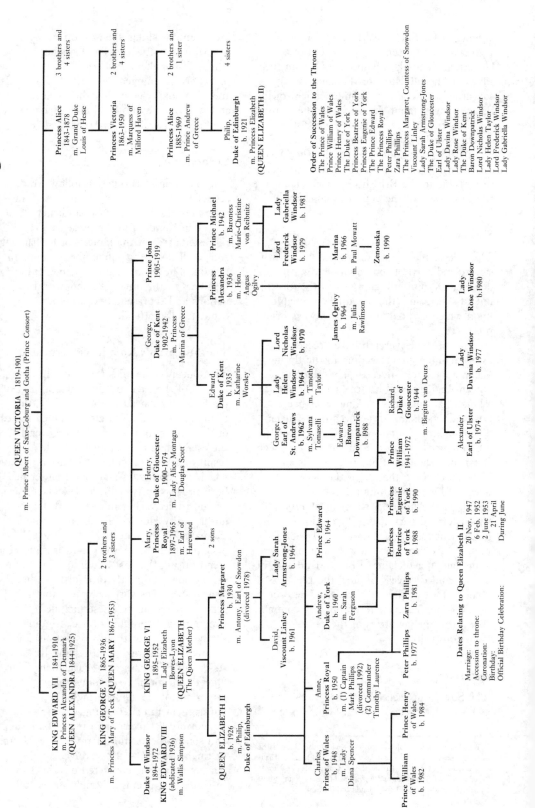

QUEEN VICTORIA 1819–1901
m. Prince Albert of Saxe-Coburg and Gotha (Prince Consort)

KING EDWARD VII 1841–1910
m. Princess Alexandra of Denmark
(QUEEN ALEXANDRA 1844–1925)

2 brothers and 3 sisters

Duke of Windsor
1894–1972
KING EDWARD VIII
(abdicated 1936)
m. Wallis Simpson

KING GEORGE V 1865–1936
m. Princess Mary of Teck (QUEEN MARY 1867–1953)

KING GEORGE VI
1895–1952
m. Lady Elizabeth
Bowes–Lyon
(QUEEN ELIZABETH
The Queen Mother)

Mary,
Princess
Royal
1897–1965
m. Earl of
Harewood

2 sons

Henry,
Duke of Gloucester
1900–1974
m. Lady Alice Montagu
Douglas Scott

George,
Duke of Kent
1902–1942
m. Princess
Marina of Greece

Prince John
1905–1919

QUEEN ELIZABETH II
b. 1926
m. Philip,
Duke of Edinburgh

Princess Margaret
b. 1930
m. Antony, Earl of Snowdon
(divorced 1978)

David,
Viscount Linley
b. 1961

Lady Sarah
Armstrong–Jones
b. 1964

Prince William
1941–1972

Richard,
Duke of
Gloucester
b. 1944
m. Birgitte van Deurs

Alexander,
Earl of Ulster
b. 1974

Lady
Davina Windsor
b. 1977

Lady
Rose Windsor
b. 1980

Edward,
Duke of Kent
b. 1935
m. Katharine
Worsley

George, Earl of
St. Andrews
b. 1962
m. Sylvana
Tomaselli

Edward,
Baron
Downpatrick
b. 1988

Lady
Helen
Windsor
b. 1964
m. Timothy
Taylor

Lord
Nicholas
Windsor
b. 1970

Princess
Alexandra
b. 1936
m. Hon.
Angus
Ogilvy

James Ogilvy
b. 1964
m. Julia
Rawlinson

Marina
b. 1966
m. Paul Mowatt

Zenouska
b. 1990

Prince Michael
b. 1942
m. Baroness
Marie–Christine
von Reibnitz

Lord
Frederick
Windsor
b. 1979

Lady
Gabriella
Windsor
b. 1981

Charles,
Prince of Wales
b. 1948
m. Lady
Diana Spencer

Prince William
of Wales
b. 1982

Prince Henry
of Wales
b. 1984

Anne,
Princess Royal
b. 1950
m. (1) Captain
Mark Phillips
(divorced 1992)
(2) Commander
Timothy Laurence

Peter Phillips
b. 1977

Zara Phillips
b. 1981

Andrew,
Duke of York
b. 1960
m. Sarah
Ferguson

Princess
Beatrice
of York
b. 1988

Princess
Eugenie
of York
b. 1990

Prince Edward
b. 1964

Princess Alice
1843–1878
m. Grand Duke
Louis of Hesse

3 brothers and
4 sisters

Princess Victoria
1863–1950
m. Marquess of
Milford Haven

2 brothers and
4 sisters

Princess Alice
1885–1969
m. Prince Andrew
of Greece

2 brothers and
1 sister

Philip,
Duke of Edinburgh
b. 1921
m. Princess Elizabeth
(QUEEN ELIZABETH II)

4 sisters

Order of Succession to the Throne
The Prince of Wales
Prince William of Wales
Prince Henry of Wales
The Duke of York
Princess Beatrice of York
Princess Eugenie of York
The Prince Edward
The Princess Royal
Peter Phillips
Zara Phillips
The Princess Margaret, Countess of Snowdon
Viscount Linley
Lady Sarah Armstrong–Jones
The Duke of Gloucester
Earl of Ulster
Lady Davina Windsor
Lady Rose Windsor
The Duke of Kent
Baron Downpatrick
Lord Nicholas Windsor
Lady Helen Taylor
Lord Frederick Windsor
Lady Gabriella Windsor

Dates Relating to Queen Elizabeth II

Marriage:	20 Nov. 1947
Accession to throne:	6 Feb. 1952
Coronation:	2 June 1953
Birthday:	21 April
Official Birthday Celebration:	During June

number of Commonwealth states.[1] In each such state the Queen is represented by a Governor-General, appointed by her on the advice of the ministers of the country concerned and completely independent of the British Government. In each case the form of the royal title varies. Other member states are republics or have their own monarchies.

In British dependent territories the Queen is usually represented by governors, who are responsible to the British Government for the administration of the countries concerned.

Succession

The title to the Crown is derived partly from statute and partly from common law rules of descent. Despite interruptions in the direct line of succession, the hereditary principle upon which it was founded has always been preserved.

Sons of the Sovereign have precedence over daughters in succeeding to the throne. When a daughter succeeds, she becomes Queen Regnant, and has the same powers as a king. The consort of a king takes her husband's rank and style, becoming Queen. The constitution does not give any special rank or privileges to the husband of a Queen Regnant, although in practice he fills an important role in the life of the nation, as does the Duke of Edinburgh.

Under the Act of Settlement of 1700, which formed part of the Revolution Settlement following the events of 1688 (see p. 42), only Protestant descendants of a granddaughter of James I of England and VI of Scotland (Princess Sophia, the Electress of Hanover) are eligible to succeed. The order of succession can be altered only by common consent of the countries of the Commonwealth.

Accession

The Sovereign succeeds to the throne as soon as his or her predecessor dies: there is no interregnum. He or she is at once proclaimed at an Accession Council, to which all members of the Privy Council (see p. 61) are summoned. The Lords Spiritual and Temporal (see p. 48), the Lord Mayor and Aldermen and other leading citizens of the City of London are also invited.

Coronation

The Sovereign's coronation follows the accession after a convenient interval. The ceremony takes place at Westminster Abbey in London, in the presence of representatives of the Houses of Parliament and of all the great public organisations in Britain. The Prime Ministers and leading members of the other Commonwealth nations and representatives of other countries also attend.

The Monarch's Role in Government

The Queen personifies the State. In law, she is head of the executive, an integral part of the legislature, head of the judiciary, the commander-in-chief of all the armed forces of the Crown and the 'supreme governor' of the established Church of England. As a result of a long process of evolution, during which the monarchy's absolute power has been progressively reduced, the Queen acts on the advice of her ministers. Britain is governed by Her Majesty's Government in the name of the Queen.

Within this framework, and in spite of a trend during the past hundred years towards giving powers directly to ministers, the Queen still takes part in some important acts of government. These include summoning, proroguing (discontinuing until the next session without dissolution) and dissolving Parliament; and giving Royal Assent to Bills passed by Parliament. The Queen also formally appoints many important office holders, including government ministers, judges, officers in the armed forces, governors, diplomats, bishops and some other senior clergy of the Church of England. She is also involved in pardoning people convicted of crimes; and in conferring peerages, knighthoods and

---

[1] The other Commonwealth countries of which the Queen is head of state are: Antigua and Barbuda, Australia, Bahamas, Barbados, Belize, Canada, Grenada, Jamaica, New Zealand, Papua New Guinea, Saint Christopher and Nevis, Saint Lucia, Saint Vincent and the Grenadines, Solomon Islands and Tuvalu.

other honours.[2] An important function is appointing the Prime Minister: by convention the Queen invites the leader of the political party which commands a majority in the House of Commons to form a government. In international affairs the Queen, as head of State, has the power to declare war and make peace, to recognise foreign states and governments, to conclude treaties and to annex or cede territory.

With rare exceptions (such as appointing the Prime Minister), acts involving the use of 'royal prerogative' powers are now performed by government ministers, who are responsible to Parliament and can be questioned about particular policies. Parliamentary authority is not required for the exercise of these prerogative powers, although Parliament may restrict or abolish such rights.

The Queen continues to play an important role in the working of government. She holds Privy Council meetings, gives audiences to her ministers and officials in Britain and overseas, receives accounts of Cabinet decisions, reads dispatches and signs state papers. She must be consulted on every aspect of national life, and must show complete impartiality.

Provision has been made to appoint a regent to perform these royal functions should the Queen be totally incapacitated. The regent would be the Queen's eldest son, the Prince of Wales, then those, in order of succession to the throne, who are of age. In the event of the Queen's partial incapacity or absence abroad, the Queen may delegate certain royal functions to the Counsellors of State (the Duke of Edinburgh, the four adults next in line of succession, and the Queen Mother). However, Counsellors of State may not, for instance, dissolve Parliament (except on the Queen's instructions), nor create peers.

Ceremonial and Royal Visits

Ceremonial has always been associated with the British monarchy, and, in spite of changes in the outlook of both the Sovereign and the people, many traditional ceremonies continue to take place. Royal marriages and royal funerals are marked by public ceremony, and the Sovereign's birthday is officially celebrated in June by Trooping the Colour on Horse Guards Parade. State banquets take place when a foreign monarch or head of State visits Britain; investitures are held at Buckingham Palace and the Palace of Holyroodhouse in Scotland to bestow honours; and royal processions add significance to such occasions as the state opening of Parliament.

Each year the Queen and other members of the royal family visit many parts of Britain. Their presence at events of national and local importance attracts considerable interest. They are also closely involved in the work of many charities. The Queen pays state visits to foreign governments, accompanied by the Duke of Edinburgh. She also tours the other countries of the Commonwealth. Other members of the royal family pay official visits overseas, occasionally representing the Queen, or often in connection with an organisation with which they are associated.

Royal Income and Expenditure

Until 1760 the Sovereign had to provide for payment of all government expenses, including the salaries of officials and the expenses of the royal palaces and households. These were met from hereditary revenues, mainly income from Crown lands, and income from some other sources granted to the monarch by Parliament. The income from these sources eventually proved inadequate and in 1760 King George III turned over to the Government most of the hereditary revenue. In return he received an annual grant (Civil List) from which he continued to pay the royal expenditure of a personal character and also the salaries of government officials and certain pensions. The latter charges were removed from the Civil List in 1830.

Present Arrangements

Today the expenditure incurred by the Queen in carrying out her public duties is financed from the Civil List and from

---

[2] Although most honours are conferred by the Queen on the advice of the Prime Minister, a few are granted by her personally—the Order of the Garter, the Order of the Thistle, the Order of Merit and the Royal Victorian Order.

government departments (which meet the cost of, for example, the Royal Yacht and the aircraft of the Queen's Flight). All such expenditure is approved by Parliament. In 1991 Civil List payments were fixed at £7.9 million a year for ten years. About three-quarters of the Queen's Civil List provision is required to meet the cost of staff. These deal with, among other things, state papers and correspondence and the organisation of state occasions, visits and other public engagements undertaken by the Queen in Britain and overseas. The Queen's private expenditure as Sovereign is met from the Privy Purse, which is financed mainly from the revenue of the Duchy of Lancaster;[3] her expenditure as a private individual is met from her own personal resources.

Since April 1993 the Queen has voluntarily paid income tax on all her personal income and on that part of the Privy Purse income which is used for private purposes. The Queen also pays tax on any realised capital gains on her private investments and on the private proportion of assets in the Privy Purse. Inheritance tax will not, however, apply to transfers from one sovereign to his or her successor, although any personal bequests other than to the successor will be subject to inheritance tax. In line with these changes the Prince of Wales pays income tax on the income from the Duchy of Cornwall to the extent that it is used for private purposes.

Under the Civil List Acts, other members of the royal family also receive annual parliamentary allowances to enable them to carry out their public duties. The Prince of Wales, however, receives no such allowance, since as Duke of Cornwall he is entitled to the income of the estate of the Duchy of Cornwall. Each year the Queen pays the Government a sum equivalent to that provided by Parliament for all members of the royal family except the Queen Mother and the Duke of Edinburgh.

Parliament

Origins of Parliament

The medieval kings were expected to meet all royal expenses, private and public, out of their own revenue. If extra resources were needed for an emergency, such as a war, the Sovereign would seek to persuade his barons, in the Great Council—a gathering of leading men which met several times a year—to grant an aid. During the 13th century several kings found the private revenues and baronial aids insufficient to meet the expenses of government. They therefore summoned not only the great feudal magnates but also representatives of counties, cities and towns, primarily to get their assent to extraordinary taxation. In this way the Great Council came to include those who were summoned by name (those who, broadly speaking, were to form the House of Lords) and those who were representatives of communities—the commons. The two parts, together with the Sovereign, became known as 'Parliament' (the term originally meant a meeting for parley or discussion).

Over the course of time the commons began to realise the strength of their position. By the middle of the 14th century the formula had appeared which in substance was the same as that used nowadays in voting supplies to the Crown—that is, money to the Government—namely, 'by the Commons with the advice of the Lords Spiritual and Temporal'. In 1407 Henry IV pledged that henceforth all money grants should be approved by the House of Commons before being considered by the Lords.

A similar advance was made in the legislative field. Originally the King's legislation needed only the assent of his councillors. Starting with the right of individual commoners to present petitions, the Commons as a body gained the right to submit collective petitions. Later, during the 15th century, they gained the right to participate in giving their requests—their 'Bills'—the form of law.

---

3 The Duchy of Lancaster is an inheritance which, since 1399, has always been enjoyed by the reigning Sovereign. It is kept quite apart from his or her other possessions and is separately administered by the Chancellor of the Duchy of Lancaster.

The subsequent development of the power of the House of Commons was built upon these foundations. The constitutional developments of the 17th century (see p. 42) led to Parliament securing its position as the supreme legislative authority.

The Powers of Parliament

The three elements which make up Parliament—the Queen, the House of Lords and the elected House of Commons—are constituted on different principles. They meet together only on occasions of symbolic significance such as the state opening of Parliament, when the Commons are summoned by the Queen to the House of Lords. The agreement of all three elements is normally required for legislation, but that of the Queen is given as a matter of course to Bills sent to her.

Parliament can legislate for Britain as a whole, or for any part of the country. It can also legislate for the Channel Islands and the Isle of Man, which are Crown dependencies and not part of Britain. They have local legislatures which make laws on island affairs.

As there are no legal restraints imposed by a written constitution, Parliament may legislate as it pleases, subject to Britain's obligations as a member of the European Community. It can make or change any law, and overturn established conventions or turn them into law. It can even prolong its own life beyond the normal period without consulting the electorate.

In practice, however, Parliament does not assert its supremacy in this way. Its members bear in mind the common law and normally act in accordance with precedent. The House of Commons is directly responsible to the electorate, and in this century the House of Lords has recognised the supremacy of the elected chamber. The system of party government helps to ensure that Parliament legislates with its responsibility to the electorate in mind.

The European Community

As a member of the European Community, Britain recognises the various types of Community legislation and wider policies. It sends 81 elected members to the European Parliament (see pp. 290–1).

The Functions of Parliament

The main functions of Parliament are:

- to pass laws;
- to provide, by voting for taxation, the means of carrying on the work of government;
- to scrutinise government policy and administration, including proposals for expenditure; and
- to debate the major issues of the day.

In carrying out these functions Parliament helps to bring the relevant facts and issues before the electorate. By custom, Parliament is also informed before all important international treaties and agreements are ratified. The making of treaties is, however, a royal prerogative exercised on the advice of the Government and is not subject to parliamentary approval.

The Meeting of Parliament

A Parliament has a maximum duration of five years, but in practice general elections are usually held before the end of this term. The maximum life has been prolonged by legislation in rare circumstances such as the two world wars. Parliament is dissolved and writs for a general election are ordered by the Queen on the advice of the Prime Minister.

The life of a Parliament is divided into sessions. Each usually lasts for one year— normally beginning and ending in October or November. There are 'adjournments' at night, at weekends, at Christmas, Easter and the late Spring Bank Holiday, and during a long summer break starting in late July or early August. The average number of 'sitting' days in a session is about 160 in the House of Commons and about 145 in the House of Lords. At the start of each session the Queen's speech to Parliament outlines the Government's policies and proposed legislative programme. Each session is ended by prorogation. Parliament then 'stands prorogued' for about a week until the new session opens. Prorogation brings to an end nearly all parliamentary business: in particular, public Bills which have not been passed by the end of the session are lost.

The House of Lords

The House of Lords consists of the Lords Spiritual and the Lords Temporal. The Lords Spiritual are the Archbishops of Canterbury and York, the Bishops of London, Durham and Winchester, and the 21 next most senior diocesan bishops of the Church of England. The Lords Temporal consist of:

- all hereditary peers and peeresses of England, Scotland, Great Britain and the United Kingdom (but not peers of Ireland);
- life peers created to assist the House in its judicial duties (Lords of Appeal or 'law lords');[4] and
- all other life peers.

Hereditary peerages carry a right to sit in the House provided holders establish their claim and are aged 21 years or over. However, anyone succeeding to a peerage may, within 12 months of succession, disclaim that peerage for his or her lifetime. Disclaimants lose their right to sit in the House but gain the right to vote and stand as candidates at parliamentary elections. When a disclaimant dies, the peerage passes on down the family in the usual way.

Peerages, both hereditary and life, are created by the Sovereign on the advice of the Prime Minister. They are usually granted in recognition of service in politics or other walks of life or because one of the political parties wishes to have the recipient in the House of Lords. The House also provides a place in Parliament for people who offer useful advice, but do not wish to be involved in party politics.

Some peers with a writ of summons to the House of Lords never claim it. (In mid-1993 there were 85 peers without writs.) Nor do all peers with writs regularly attend the sittings. Peers who attend the House (the average daily attendance is some 375) receive no salary for their parliamentary work, but can claim for expenses incurred in attending the House (for which there are maximum daily rates) and certain travelling expenses. Some peers (86 in mid-1993) apply for Leave of Absence, indicating that they do not intend to come to the House at all.

Officers of the House of Lords

The House is presided over by the Lord Chancellor, who takes his place on the woolsack[5] as ex-officio Speaker of the House. In his absence his place is taken by a deputy. The first of the deputy speakers is the Chairman of Committees, who is appointed at the beginning of each session and normally chairs most committees. The Chairman and the Principal Deputy Chairman of Committees are the only Lords who receive salaries as officers of the House.

In mid-1993 there were 1,183 members of the House of Lords, including the two archbishops and 24 bishops. The Lords Temporal consisted of 760 hereditary peers who had succeeded to their titles, 15 hereditary peers who had had their titles conferred on them (including the Prince of Wales), and 382 life peers, of whom 19 were 'law lords'.

The Clerk of the Parliaments is responsible for the records of proceedings of the House of Lords and for the text of Acts of Parliament. He is the accounting officer for the cost of the House, and is in charge of the administrative staff of the House, known as the Parliament Office. The Gentleman Usher of the Black Rod, usually known as 'Black Rod', is responsible for security, accommodation and services in the House of Lords' part of the Palace of Westminster.

---

[4]The House of Lords is the final court of appeal for civil cases in Britain and for criminal cases in England, Wales and Northern Ireland.

[5]The woolsack is a seat in the form of a large cushion stuffed with wool from several Commonwealth countries; it is a tradition dating from the medieval period, when wool was the chief source of the country's wealth.

The House of Commons

The House of Commons is elected by universal adult suffrage (see below) and consists of 651 Members of Parliament (MPs). At present there are 60 women, three Asian and three black MPs. Of the 651 seats, 524 are for England, 38 for Wales, 72 for Scotland, and 17 for Northern Ireland.

General elections are held after a Parliament has been dissolved and a new one summoned by the Queen. When an MP dies or resigns,[6] or is given a peerage, a by-election takes place. Members are paid an annual salary of £30,854 (from January 1993) and an office costs allowance of up to £40,380. There are also a number of other allowances, including travel allowances, a supplement for London members and, for provincial members, subsistence allowances and allowances for second homes. (For ministers' salaries see p. 59.)

Officers of the House of Commons

The chief officer of the House of Commons is the Speaker, elected by MPs to preside over the House. Other officers include the Chairman of Ways and Means and two deputy chairmen, who act as Deputy Speakers. They are elected by the House on the nomination of the Government but are drawn from the Opposition as well as the government party. They, like the Speaker, neither speak nor vote other than in their official capacity. Overall responsibility for the administration of the House rests with the House of Commons Commission, a statutory body chaired by the Speaker.

Permanent officers (who are not MPs) include the Clerk of the House of Commons, who is the principal adviser to the Speaker on its privileges and procedures. The Clerk's departmental responsibilities relate to the conduct of the business of the House and its committees. The Clerk is also accounting officer for the House. The Serjeant-at-Arms, who waits upon the Speaker, carries out

certain orders of the House. He is also the official housekeeper of the Commons' part of the building, and is responsible for security. Other officers serve the House in the Library, the Department of the Official Report (*Hansard*), the Finance and Administration Department and the Refreshment Department.

Parliamentary Electoral System

For electoral purposes Britain is divided into constituencies, each of which returns one member to the House of Commons. To ensure that constituency electorates are kept roughly equal, four permanent Parliamentary Boundary Commissions, one each for England, Wales, Scotland and Northern Ireland, keep constituencies under review. They recommend any adjustment of seats that may seem necessary in the light of population movements or other changes. The Government has introduced legislation to shorten the intervals at which reviews are carried out. Elections are by secret ballot.

Voters

British citizens, together with citizens of other Commonwealth countries and citizens of the Irish Republic resident in Britain, may vote provided they are aged 18 or over, included in the annual register of electors for the constituency and not subject to any disqualification. People not entitled to vote include members of the House of Lords, patients detained under mental health legislation, sentenced prisoners and people convicted within the previous five years of corrupt or illegal election practices. Members of the armed forces, Crown servants and staff of the British Council employed overseas (together with their wives or husbands if accompanying them) may be registered for an address in the constituency where they would live but for their service. The Representation of the People Act 1989 extended the right to vote for British citizens living abroad by increasing from 5 to 20 years the period during which they may apply to be registered to vote.

---

[6] An MP who wishes to resign from the House can only do so by applying for an office under the Crown as Crown Steward or Bailiff of the Chiltern Hundreds, or Steward of the Manor of Northstead.

Voting Procedures

Each elector may cast one vote, normally in person at a polling station. Electors whose circumstances on polling day are such that they cannot reasonably be expected to vote in person at their local polling station—for example, electors away on holiday—may apply for an absent vote at a particular election. Electors who are physically incapacitated or unable to vote in person because of the nature of their work or because they have moved to a new area may apply for an indefinite absent vote. People entitled to an absent vote may vote by post or by proxy, although postal ballot papers cannot be sent to addresses outside Britain.

Voting is not compulsory; 76.9 per cent of a total electorate of 43.3 million people voted in the general election in April 1992. The simple majority system of voting is used. Candidates are elected if they have more votes than any of the other candidates (although not necessarily an absolute majority over all other candidates).

Candidates

British citizens and citizens of other Commonwealth countries, together with citizens of the Irish Republic, may stand for election as MPs provided they are aged 21 or over and are not disqualified. Those disqualified include undischarged bankrupts; people sentenced to more than one year's imprisonment; clergy of the Church of England, Church of Scotland, Church of Ireland and Roman Catholic Church; peers; and holders of certain offices listed in the House of Commons Disqualification Act 1975. The latter include holders of judicial office, civil servants, some local government officers, members of the regular armed forces, police officers, some members of public corporations and government commissions, and British members of the legislature of any country outside the Commonwealth. A candidate's nomination for election must be proposed and seconded by two electors registered as voters in the constituency and signed by eight other electors.

Candidates do not have to be backed by a political party. A candidate must also deposit £500, which is returned if he or she receives 5 per cent or more of the votes cast.

The maximum sum a candidate may spend on a general election campaign is £4,330 plus 3.7 pence for each elector in a borough constituency, or 4.9 pence for each elector in a county constituency. Higher limits have been set for by-elections in order to reflect the fact that they are often regarded as tests of national opinion in the period between general elections. The maximum sum is £17,323 plus 14.7 pence for each elector in borough seats, and 19.4 pence for each elector in county seats. A candidate may post an election address to each elector in the constituency, free of charge. All election expenses, apart from the candidate's personal expenses, are subject to the statutory limit.

The Political Party System

The party system, which has existed in one form or another since the 18th century, is an essential element in the working of the constitution. The present system depends upon the existence of organised political parties, each of which presents its policies to the electorate for approval. The parties are not registered nor formally recognised in law, but in practice most candidates in elections, and almost all winning candidates, belong to one of the main parties.

For the last 150 years a predominantly two-party system has existed. Since 1945 either the Conservative Party, the origins of which go back to the 18th century, or the Labour Party, which emerged in the last decade of the 19th century, has held power. A new party—the Liberal Democrats—was formed in 1988 when the Liberal Party, which could trace its origins to the 18th century, merged with the Social Democratic Party, which was formed in 1981. Other parties include two nationalist parties, Plaid Cymru (founded in Wales in 1925) and the Scottish National Party (founded in 1934). In Northern Ireland there are a number of parties. They include the Ulster Unionist Party, formed in the early part of this century; the Democratic Unionist Party, founded in 1971 by a group which broke away from the Ulster Unionists; and the Social Democratic and Labour Party, founded in 1970.

Since 1945 eight general elections have been won by the Conservative Party and six by the Labour Party; the great majority of members of the House of Commons have belonged to one of these two parties. The number and percentages of votes cast for the main political parties in the last general election of April 1992 and the resulting distribution of seats in the House of Commons are shown in Table 7.1.

The party which wins most seats (although not necessarily the most votes) at a general election, or which has the support of a majority of members in the House of Commons, usually forms the Government. By tradition, the leader of the majority party is asked by the Sovereign to form a government. About 100 of its members in the House of Commons and the House of Lords receive ministerial appointments (including appointment to the Cabinet—see p. 60) on the advice of the Prime Minister. The largest minority party becomes the official Opposition, with its own leader and 'shadow cabinet'.

The Party System in Parliament

Leaders of the Government and Opposition sit on the front benches of the Commons with their supporters (the backbenchers) sitting behind them.

Similar arrangements for the parties also apply to the House of Lords; however, Lords who do not wish to be associated with any political party may sit on the 'cross-benches'.

The effectiveness of the party system in Parliament rests largely on the relationship between the Government and the opposition parties. Depending on the relative strengths of the parties in the House of Commons, the Opposition may seek to overthrow the Government by defeating it in a vote on a 'matter of confidence'. In general, however, its aims are to contribute to the formulation of policy and legislation by constructive criticism; to oppose government proposals it considers objectionable; to seek amendments to government Bills; and to put forward its own policies in order to improve its chances of winning the next general election.

Government business arrangements are settled, under the direction of the Prime Minister and the Leaders of the two Houses, by the Government Chief Whip in consultation with the Opposition Chief Whip. The Chief Whips together constitute the 'usual channels' often referred to when the question of finding time for a particular item of business is discussed. The Leaders of the two Houses are responsible for enabling the Houses to debate matters about which they are concerned.

Outside Parliament, party control is exercised by the national and local organisations. Inside, it is exercised by the

Table 7.1: Results of the 1992 General Election

Party	Members elected	Number of votes cast	% of votes cast
Conservative	336	14,094,116	41.9
Labour	271	11,557,134	34.4
Liberal Democrats	20	5,998,446	17.8
Scottish National	3		
Plaid Cymru (Welsh Nationalist)	4		
Ulster Unionist (Northern Ireland)	9	1,960,703	5.9[a]
Democratic Unionist (Northern Ireland)	3		
Ulster Popular Unionist (Northern Ireland)	1		
Social Democratic and Labour (Northern Ireland)	1		
Total	651	33,610,399	100.0

[a]These figures include votes for other parties whose candidates were unsuccessful.

Chief Whips and their assistants, who are chosen within the party. Their duties include keeping members informed of forthcoming parliamentary business, maintaining the party's voting strength by ensuring members attend important debates, and passing on to the party leadership the opinions of backbench members. The Whips indicate the importance their party attaches to a vote on a particular issue by underlining items of business (once, twice or three times) on the notice sent to MPs. Failure to comply with a 'three-line whip' (the most important) is usually seen as a rebellion against the party. Party discipline tends to be less strong in the Lords than in the Commons, since Lords have less hope of high office and no need of party support in elections.

The formal title of the Government Chief Whip in the Commons is Parliamentary Secretary to the Treasury. Of the other Government Whips, three are officers of the Royal Household (one of these is Deputy Chief Whip), five hold titular posts as Lords Commissioners of the Treasury and five are Assistant Whips. The Opposition Chief Whips in both Houses and two of the Opposition Assistant Whips in the Commons receive salaries. The Government Whips in the Lords hold offices in the Royal Household; they also act as government spokesmen.

Financial Assistance to Parties

Annual assistance from public funds helps opposition parties carry out parliamentary work at Westminster. It is limited to parties which had at least two members elected at the previous general election or one member elected and a minimum of 150,000 votes cast. The amount is £2,550 for every seat won at the previous general election, plus £5.10 for every 200 votes.

Parliamentary Procedure

Parliamentary procedure is based on custom and precedent, partly codified by each House in its Standing Orders. The system of debate is similar in both Houses. Every subject starts off as a proposal or 'motion' by a member. After debate, in which each member may

speak only once, the Speaker or Chairman 'puts the question' whether to agree with the motion or not. The question may be decided without voting, or by a simple majority vote. The main difference of procedure between the two Houses is that the Speaker or Chairman in the Lords has no powers of order; instead such matters are decided by the general feeling of the House.

In the Commons the Speaker has full authority to enforce the rules of the House and must guard against the abuse of procedure and protect minority rights. The Speaker has discretion on whether to allow a motion to end discussion so that a matter may be put to the vote and has powers to put a stop to irrelevance and repetition in debate, and to save time in other ways. In cases of grave disorder the Speaker can adjourn or suspend the sitting. The Speaker may order members who have broken the rules of behaviour of the House to leave the Chamber or he or she can initiate their suspension for a period of days.

The Speaker supervises voting in the Commons and announces the final result. In a tied vote the Speaker gives a casting vote, without expressing an opinion on the merits of the question. The voting procedure in the House of Lords is broadly similar.

Financial Interests

The Commons has a public register of MPs' financial interests. Members with a financial interest in a debate in the House must declare it when speaking. To act as a disqualification from voting the interest must be direct, immediate and personal. In other proceedings of the House or in dealings with other members, ministers or civil servants, MPs must also disclose any relevant financial interest.

There is no register of financial interests in the Lords, but Lords speaking in a debate in which they have a direct interest are expected to declare it. Lords by custom speak 'on their honour'.

Public Access to Parliamentary Proceedings

Proceedings of both Houses are normally

public. The minutes and speeches (transcribed verbatim in *Hansard*) are published daily.

The records of the Lords from 1497 and of the Commons from 1547, together with the parliamentary and political papers of a number of former members of both Houses, are available to the public through the House of Lords Record Office.

The proceedings of both Houses of Parliament may be broadcast on television and radio, either live or, more usually, in recorded or edited form. Complete coverage is available on cable television.

The Law-making Process

The law undergoes constant reform in the courts as established principles are clarified or reapplied to meet new circumstances. Fundamental changes are the responsibility of Parliament and the Government through the normal legislative process.

Draft laws take the form of parliamentary Bills. Most are public Bills involving measures relating to public policy. Public Bills can be introduced, in either House, by a government minister or by an ordinary ('private' or 'backbench') member. Most public Bills that become law are sponsored by the Government.

Before a government Bill is drafted, there may be consultation with professional bodies, voluntary organisations and other agencies interested in the subject, and interest and pressure groups which seek to promote specific causes. Proposals for legislative changes are sometimes set out in government 'White Papers', which may be debated in Parliament before a Bill is introduced. From time to time consultation papers, sometimes called 'Green Papers', set out government proposals which are still taking shape and seek comments from the public.

Bills must normally be passed by both Houses. Government Bills likely to raise political controversy usually go through the Commons before being discussed in the Lords, while those of a technical but non-political nature often pass through the Lords first. A Bill with a mainly financial purpose is nearly always introduced in the Commons,

and a Bill involving taxation must be based on resolutions agreed by that House, often after debate, before it can be introduced. If the main object of a Bill is to create a public charge (that is, new taxation or public spending), it must be introduced by a government minister in the Commons or, if brought from the Lords, be taken up by a government minister. This gives the Government considerable control over financial legislation.

Private Members' Bills

At the beginning of each session private members of the Commons ballot (or draw lots) for the opportunity to introduce a Bill on one of the Fridays specially allocated; the first 20 are successful. Private members may also present a Bill after question time (see p. 56). They may also seek to introduce a Bill under the 'ten minute rule'. This allows two speeches, one in favour of and one against the measure, after which the House decides whether to allow the Bill to be brought in. These Bills often do not proceed very far, but a few become law each session. Private members' Bills do not often call for the expenditure of public money; but if they do they cannot proceed to committee stage unless the Government decides to provide the necessary money resolution. Private Peers' Bills may be introduced in the House of Lords at any time, but when they come to the Commons they do not proceed further unless taken up by a private member. They must then take their turn behind private members' Bills which have already obtained a second reading in the Commons.

Passage of Public Bills

The process of passing a public Bill is similar in both Houses. On introduction, the Bill receives a first reading, without debate, and is printed. After between one day and several weeks, depending on the nature of the Bill, it is given a second reading after a debate on its general principles. In the Commons a non-controversial Bill may be referred to a second reading committee for its second reading debate. After a second reading in the

53

Commons, a Bill is usually referred to a standing committee for detailed examination (see p. 55). If the House so decides, the Bill may be referred to the whole House sitting in committee. The committee stage is followed by the report stage in the whole House, during which further amendments may be considered.

At the third reading a Bill is reviewed in its final form and may be debated again. The House may vote to limit the time devoted to examining a Bill by passing a government timetable motion, commonly referred to as a 'guillotine'.

After the third reading a Commons Bill is sent to the Lords. After the second reading in the Lords, a Bill is considered by a committee of the whole House, unless the House takes the rare decision to refer it to a Public Bill Committee. It is then considered on report and read a third time. At all these stages amendments may be made.

A Bill which starts in the Lords and is passed by that House is then sent to the Commons for all its stages there. Amendments made by the second House must generally be agreed by the first, or a compromise reached, before a Bill can become law.

Royal Assent

When a Bill has passed through all its parliamentary stages, it is sent to the Queen for Royal Assent, after which it is part of the law of the land and known as an Act of Parliament. Royal Assent takes the form of an announcement rather than any signature or mark on a copy of the Bill. The Royal Assent has not been refused since 1707. A list of the main public Bills receiving Royal Assent since autumn 1992 is given on pp. 503–4.

Limitations on the Power of the Lords

Most government Bills introduced and passed in the Lords pass through the Commons without difficulty, but a Lords Bill which was unacceptable to the Commons would not become law. The Lords, on the other hand, do not generally prevent Bills insisted upon by the Commons from becoming law, though they will often amend them and return them for further consideration by the Commons. By convention the Lords pass Bills authorising taxation or national expenditure without amendment. Under the Parliament Acts 1911 and 1949, a Bill that deals only with taxation or expenditure must become law within one month of being sent to the Lords, whether or not they agree to it, unless the Commons directs otherwise. If no agreement is reached between the two Houses on a non-financial Commons Bill the Lords can delay the Bill for a period which, in practice, amounts to at least 13 months. Following this the Bill may be submitted to the Queen for Royal Assent, provided it has been passed a second time by the Commons. The Parliament Acts make one important exception: any Bill to lengthen the life of a Parliament requires the full assent of both Houses in the normal way.

The limits to the power of the Lords, contained in the Parliament Acts, are based on the belief that nowadays the main legislative function of the non-elected House is to act as a chamber of revision, complementing but not rivalling the elected House.

Delegated Legislation

In order to reduce unnecessary pressure on parliamentary time, primary legislation often gives ministers or other authorities the power to regulate administrative details by means of 'delegated' or secondary legislation. To minimise any risk that delegating powers to the executive might undermine the authority of Parliament, they are normally only delegated to authorities directly accountable to Parliament. Moreover, the Acts of Parliament concerned usually provide for some measure of direct parliamentary control over the delegated legislation, by giving Parliament the opportunity to affirm or annul it. Certain Acts also require that certain organisations affected must be consulted before rules and orders can be made.

A joint committee of both Houses reports on the technical propriety of these 'statutory instruments'. In order to save time on the floor of the House, the Commons uses standing committees to debate the merits of instruments; actual decisions are taken by the House.

Private Legislation

Private Bills are promoted by people or organisations outside Parliament (often local authorities) to give them special legal powers. They go through a similar procedure to public Bills, but most of the work is done in committee, where procedures follow a semi-judicial pattern. The promoter must prove the need for the powers sought and the objections of opposing interests are heard. Both sides may be legally represented. Hybrid Bills are public Bills which may affect private rights. As with private Bills, the passage of hybrid Bills through Parliament is governed by special procedures which allow those affected to put their case.

Parliamentary Committees

Committees of the Whole House

Either House may pass a resolution setting itself up as a committee of the whole House to consider Bills in detail after their second reading. This permits unrestricted discussion: the general rule that an MP or Lord may speak only once on each motion does not apply in committee.

Standing Committees

House of Commons standing committees debate and consider amendments to public Bills at the committee stage and, in certain cases, discuss them at the second reading stage. They include two Scottish standing committees, and the Scottish and Welsh Grand Committees. Ordinary standing committees do not have names but are referred to simply as Standing Committee A, B, C, and so on; a new set of members is appointed to them to consider each Bill. Each committee has between 16 and 50 members, with a party balance reflecting as far as possible that in the House as a whole.

The Scottish Grand Committee comprises all 72 Scottish members (and may be convened anywhere in Scotland). It may consider the principle of Scottish Bills referred to it at second reading stage. It also debates Scottish estimates and other matters concerning Scotland only which may be referred to it. Under government proposals announced in March 1993, there would be provision for more debates by the Scottish Grand Committee, meeting at locations other than London or Edinburgh, and from time to time sessions of questions to Scottish Office ministers would be held in the Committee. It might also occasionally be appropriate for statements to be made by Scottish Office ministers to the Committee. In addition, a new procedure would enable the Committee to invite the Scottish Office Minister in the House of Lords and the Lord Advocate to give evidence before it on matters within their fields of responsibility.

The Welsh Grand Committee, with all 38 Welsh members and up to five others, considers Bills referred to it at second reading stage, and matters concerning Wales only.

There is also provision for a Northern Ireland committee to debate matters relating specifically to Northern Ireland.

The Lords' equivalent to a standing committee, a Public Bill Committee, is rarely used; instead the committee stage of a Bill is taken by the House as a whole.

Select Committees

Select committees are appointed to examine a subject and to report their conclusions and recommendations. A select committee may be appointed for a Parliament, or for a session, or for as long as it takes to do its job. To help Parliament with the control of the executive by examining aspects of public policy and administration, 15 committees have been established by the House of Commons to examine the work of the main government departments. The Foreign Affairs Committee, for example, 'shadows' the work of the Foreign & Commonwealth Office. The committees are constituted on a basis which is in approximate proportion to party strength in the House.

Other regular Commons committees

include those on Public Accounts, European Legislation, Members' Interests, and the Parliamentary Commissioner for Administration (the 'Parliamentary Ombudsman'—see p. 58). 'Domestic' select committees also cover the internal workings of Parliament. On rare occasions a parliamentary Bill is examined by a specially appointed select committee, in addition to the usual legislative process: this occurs, for example, every few years for the Armed Forces Bill.

In their examination of government policies and administration, committees may question ministers, senior civil servants and interested bodies and individuals. Through hearings and published reports, they bring before Parliament and the public an extensive body of fact and informed opinion on many issues, and build up considerable expertise in their subjects of inquiry.

In the House of Lords, besides the Appeal and Appellate Committees, in which the bulk of the House's judicial work is transacted, there are two major select committees (with several sub-committees), on the European Communities and on Science and Technology.

Joint Committees

Joint committees, with a membership drawn from both Houses, are appointed in each session to deal with Consolidation Bills and delegated legislation. The two Houses may also agree to set up joint select committees on other subjects.

Party Committees

In addition to the official committees of the two Houses there are several unofficial party organisations or committees. The Conservative and Unionist Members' Committee (the 1922 Committee) consists of the backbench membership of the party in the House of Commons. When the Conservative Party is in office, ministers attend its meetings by invitation and not by right. When the party is in opposition, the whole membership of the party may attend meetings. The leader appoints a consultative committee, which acts as the party's 'shadow cabinet'.

The Parliamentary Labour Party comprises all members of the party in both Houses. When the Labour Party is in office, a parliamentary committee, half of whose members are elected and half of whom are government representatives, acts as a channel of communication between the Government and its backbenchers in both Houses. When the party is in opposition, the Parliamentary Labour Party is organised under the direction of an elected parliamentary committee, which acts as the 'shadow cabinet'.

Other Forms of Parliamentary Control

House of Commons

In addition to the system of scrutiny by select committees, the House of Commons offers a number of opportunities for the examination of government policy by both the Opposition and the Government's own backbenchers. These include:

1. Question time, when for an hour on Monday, Tuesday, Wednesday and Thursday, ministers answer MPs' questions. The Prime Minister's question time is on Tuesday and Thursday. Parliamentary questions are one means of seeking information about the Government's intentions. They are also a way of raising grievances brought to MPs' notice by constituents. MPs may also put questions to ministers for written answer; the questions and answers are published in *Hansard*, the official report. There are some 50,000 questions every year.

2. Adjournment debates, when MPs use motions for the adjournment of the House to raise constituency cases or matters of public concern. There is a half-hour adjournment period at the end of the business of the day, while immediately before the adjournment for each recess (Parliament's Christmas, Easter, spring and summer breaks) a full day is spent discussing issues raised by

private members. There are also adjournment debates following the passage, three times a year, of Consolidated Fund[7] or Appropriation Bills.[8] These take place after the House has voted the necessary supplies (money) for the Government.

In addition, an MP wishing to discuss a 'specific and important matter that should have urgent consideration' may, at the end of question time, seek leave to move the adjournment of the House. If the Speaker accepts the terms of the motion, the MP asks the House for leave for the motion to be put forward. Leave can be given unanimously, or it can be given if 40 or more MPs support the motion or if fewer than 40 but more than ten support it and the House (on a vote) is in favour. If leave is given, the matter is debated for three hours in what is known as an emergency debate, usually on the following day.

3. The 20 Opposition days each session, when the Opposition can choose subjects for debate. Of these days, 17 are at the disposal of the Leader of the Opposition and three at the disposal of the second largest opposition party.

4. Debates on three days in each session on details of proposed government expenditure, chosen by the Liaison Committee.

Procedural opportunities for criticism of the Government also arise during the debate on the Queen's speech at the beginning of each session, during debates on motions of censure for which the Government provides time, and during debates on the Government's legislative and other proposals.

House of Lords

Similar opportunities for criticism and examination of government policy are provided in the House of Lords at daily question time and during debates.

---

[7] At least two Consolidated Fund Acts are passed each session authorising the Treasury to make certain sums of money available for the public service.
[8] The annual Appropriation Act fixes the sums of public money provided for particular items of expenditure.

Control of Finances

The main responsibilities of Parliament, and more particularly of the House of Commons, in overseeing the revenue of the State and payments for the public service, are to authorise the raising of taxes and duties and the various objects of expenditure and the sum to be spent on each. It also has to satisfy itself that the sums granted are spent only for the purposes which Parliament intended. No payment out of the central government's public funds can be made and no taxation or loans authorised, except by Act of Parliament. However, limited interim payments can be made from the Contingencies Fund.

The Finance Act is the most important of the annual statutes, and authorises the raising of revenue. The legislation is based on the Chancellor of the Exchequer's Budget statement. It includes a review of the public finances of the previous year, and proposals for future expenditure. From November 1993 public expenditure and taxation plans have been announced in a single annual statement (see p. 116). Scrutiny of public expenditure is carried out by House of Commons select committees (see p. 55).

European Community Affairs

To keep the two Houses informed of EC developments, and to enable them to scrutinise and debate Community policies and proposals, there is a select committee in each House (see p. 56) and two Commons standing committees debate specific European legislative proposals. Ministers also make regular statements about Community business.

The Commons' Ability to Force the Government to Resign

The final control is the ability of the House of Commons to force the Government to resign by passing a resolution of 'no confidence'. The Government must also resign if the House rejects a proposal which the Government considers so vital to its policy that it has declared it a 'matter of confidence' or if the House refuses to vote the money required for the public service.

Parliamentary Commissioner for Administration

The post of Parliamentary Commissioner for Administration (the 'Parliamentary Ombudsman') was established by the Parliamentary Commissioner Act 1967. He or she investigates, independently, complaints of alleged maladministration when asked to do so by MPs on behalf of members of the public. Powers of investigation extend to administrative actions by staff in central government departments and certain executive non-departmental bodies. They do not include policy decisions (which can be questioned in Parliament) and matters affecting relations with other countries. Complaints by British citizens arising from dealings with British diplomatic posts overseas are open to investigation in some circumstances. The Commissioner has access to departmental papers and reports the findings of his or her investigation to the MP who presented the complaint. The Commissioner is also required to report annually to Parliament. He or she publishes details of selected investigations at quarterly intervals and may submit other reports where necessary. A Commons select committee oversees the Commissioner's work.

Parliamentary Privilege

Each House of Parliament has certain rights and immunities to protect it from obstruction in carrying out its duties. The rights apply collectively to each House and to its staff and individually to each member.

For the Commons the Speaker formally claims from the Queen 'their ancient and undoubted rights and privileges' at the beginning of each Parliament. These include freedom of speech; first call on the attendance of its members, who are therefore free from arrest in civil actions and exempt from serving on juries, or being compelled to attend court as witnesses; and the right of access to the Crown, which is a collective privilege of the House. Further privileges include the rights of the House to control its own proceedings (so that it is able, for

instance, to exclude 'strangers'[9] if it wishes); to decide upon legal disqualifications for membership and to declare a seat vacant on such grounds; and to punish for breach of its privileges and for contempt.

The privileges of the House of Lords are broadly similar to those of the House of Commons.

Her Majesty's Government

Her Majesty's Government is the body of ministers responsible for the administration of national affairs. The Prime Minister is appointed by the Queen, and all other ministers are appointed by the Queen on the recommendation of the Prime Minister. Most ministers are members of the Commons, although the Government is also fully represented by ministers in the Lords. The Lord Chancellor is always a member of the House of Lords.

The composition of governments can vary both in the number of ministers and in the titles of some offices. New ministerial offices may be created, others may be abolished, and functions may be transferred from one minister to another.

Prime Minister

The Prime Minister is also, by tradition, First Lord of the Treasury and Minister for the Civil Service. The head of the Government became known as the Prime Minister during the 18th century. The Prime Minister's unique position of authority derives from majority support in the House of Commons and from the power to appoint and dismiss ministers. By modern convention, the Prime Minister always sits in the House of Commons.

The Prime Minister presides over the Cabinet, is responsible for the allocation of functions among ministers and informs the Queen at regular meetings of the general business of the Government.

The Prime Minister's other responsibilities include recommending a

---

[9] All those who are not members or officials of either House.

number of appointments to the Queen. These include:

- Church of England archbishops, bishops and deans and some 200 other clergy in Crown 'livings';
- senior judges, such as the Lord Chief Justice;
- Privy Counsellors; and
- Lord-Lieutenants.

They also include certain civil appointments, such as Lord High Commissioner to the General Assembly of the Church of Scotland, Poet Laureate, Constable of the Tower, and some university posts; and appointments to various public boards and institutions, such as the BBC (British Broadcasting Corporation), as well as various royal and statutory commissions. Recommendations are likewise made for the award of many civil honours and distinctions and of Civil List pensions (to people who have achieved eminence in science or the arts and are in financial need). The Prime Minister also selects the trustees of certain national museums and institutions.

The Prime Minister's Office at 10 Downing Street (the official residence in central London) has a staff of civil servants who assist the Prime Minister. The Prime Minister may also appoint special advisers to the Office from time to time to assist in the formation of policies.

Departmental Ministers

Ministers in charge of government departments are usually in the Cabinet; they are known as 'Secretary of State' or 'Minister', or may have a special title, as in the case of the Chancellor of the Exchequer.

Non-Departmental Ministers

The holders of various traditional offices, namely the Lord President of the Council, the Chancellor of the Duchy of Lancaster, the Lord Privy Seal, the Paymaster General and, from time to time, Ministers without Portfolio, may have few or no departmental duties. They are thus available to perform any duties the Prime Minister may wish to give them.

Lord Chancellor and Law Officers

The Lord Chancellor holds a special position, as both a minister with departmental functions and the head of the judiciary (see p. 497). The four Law Officers of the Crown are: for England and Wales, the Attorney General and the Solicitor General; and for Scotland, the Lord Advocate and the Solicitor General for Scotland.

Ministers of State

Ministers of State usually work with ministers in charge of departments. They normally have specific responsibilities, and are sometimes given titles which reflect these functions. More than one may work in a department. A Minister of State may be given a seat in the Cabinet and be paid accordingly.

Junior Ministers

Junior ministers (generally Parliamentary Under-Secretaries of State or, where the senior minister is not a Secretary of State, simply Parliamentary Secretaries) share in parliamentary and departmental duties. They may also be given responsibility, directly under the departmental minister, for specific aspects of the department's work. The Parliamentary Secretary to the Treasury and other Lords Commissioners of the Treasury are the formal titles of the Government Whips (see p. 52).

Ministerial Salaries

The salaries of ministers in the House of Commons range from £44,611 a year for junior ministers to £63,047 for Cabinet ministers. In the House of Lords salaries range from £37,689 for junior ministers to £50,558 for Cabinet ministers. The Prime Minister receives £76,234 and the Lord Chancellor £110,940. (The Leader of the Opposition receives £59,736 a year; two Opposition whips in the Commons and the

Opposition Leader and Chief Whip in the Lords also receive salaries.)

The Cabinet

The Cabinet is composed of about 20 ministers (the number can vary) chosen by the Prime Minister and may include departmental and non-departmental ministers.

The functions of the Cabinet are to initiate and decide on policy, the supreme control of government and the co-ordination of government departments. The exercise of these functions is vitally affected by the fact that the Cabinet is a group of party representatives, depending upon majority support in the House of Commons.

Cabinet Meetings

The Cabinet meets in private and its proceedings are confidential. Its members are bound by their oath as Privy Counsellors not to disclose information about its proceedings, although after 30 years Cabinet papers may be made available for inspection in the Public Record Office at Kew, Surrey.

Normally the Cabinet meets for a few hours once a week during parliamentary sittings, and rather less often when Parliament is not sitting. To keep its workload within manageable limits, a great deal of work is carried on through the committee system. This involves referring issues either to a standing Cabinet committee or to an *ad hoc* committee composed of the ministers directly concerned. The committee then considers the matter in detail and either disposes of it or reports upon it to the Cabinet with recommendations for action.

The membership of all ministerial Cabinet committees is published. Where appropriate, the Secretary of the Cabinet and other senior officials of the Cabinet Office attend meetings of the Cabinet and its committees.

Diaries published by several former ministers have given the public insight into Cabinet procedures in recent times.

The Cabinet Office

The Cabinet Office, headed by the Secretary of the Cabinet (who is also Head of the Home Civil Service) under the direction of the Prime Minister, comprises the Cabinet Secretariat and the Office of Public Service and Science (OPSS).

The Cabinet Secretariat serves ministers collectively in the conduct of Cabinet business, and in the co-ordination of policy at the highest level.

> **The Chancellor of the Duchy of Lancaster is in charge of the Office of Public Service and Science and is a member of the Cabinet. The OPSS is responsible for:**
> - **raising the standard of public services across the public sector through the Citizen's Charter (see p. 64);**
> - **improving the effectiveness and efficiency of central government, through, among other things, the establishment of executive agencies and the market testing programme (see p. 66); and**
> - **advice—through its Office of Science and Technology—on science and technology policy, expenditure and the allocation of resources to the research councils.**

It also promotes openness in government.

The Historical and Records Section of the Cabinet Office is responsible for Official Histories and managing Cabinet Office records.

Ministerial Responsibility

'Ministerial responsibility' refers both to the collective responsibility for government policy and actions, which ministers share, and to ministers' individual responsibility for their departments' work.

The doctrine of collective responsibility means that the Cabinet acts unanimously even when Cabinet ministers do not all agree on a subject. The policy of departmental ministers must be consistent with the policy of the Government as a whole. Once the Government's policy on a matter has been decided, each minister is expected to support it or resign. On rare occasions, ministers have been allowed free votes in Parliament on government policies involving important issues of principle.

The individual responsibility of ministers for the work of their departments means that they are answerable to Parliament for all their departments' activities. They bear the consequences of any failure in administration, any injustice to an individual or any aspect of policy which may be criticised in Parliament, whether personally responsible or not. Since most ministers are members of the House of Commons, they must answer questions and defend themselves against criticism in person. Departmental ministers in the House of Lords are represented in the Commons by someone qualified to speak on their behalf, usually a junior minister.

Departmental ministers normally decide all matters within their responsibility. However, on important political matters they usually consult their colleagues collectively, either through the Cabinet or through a Cabinet committee. A decision by a departmental minister binds the Government as a whole.

On assuming office ministers must resign directorships in private and public companies, and must ensure that there is no conflict between their public duties and private interests.

approval of Orders in Council, including those made under prerogative powers, such as Orders approving the grant of royal charters of incorporation and those made under statutory powers. Responsibility for each Order, however, rests with the minister answerable for the policy concerned, regardless of whether he or she is present at the meeting where approval is given.

The Privy Council also advises the Sovereign on the issue of royal proclamations, such as those summoning or dissolving Parliament. The Council's own statutory responsibilities, which are independent of the powers of the Sovereign in Council, include supervising the registration authorities of the medical and allied professions.

Membership of the Council (retained for life, except for very occasional removals) is accorded by the Sovereign, on the recommendation of the Prime Minister (or occasionally, Prime Ministers of Commonwealth countries) to people eminent in public life—mainly politicians and judges—in Britain and the independent monarchies of the Commonwealth. Cabinet Ministers must be Privy Counsellors and, if not already members, are admitted to membership before taking their oath of office at a meeting of the Council. There are about 400 Privy Counsellors. A full Council is summoned only on the accession of a new Sovereign or when the Sovereign announces his or her intention to marry.

The Privy Council

The Privy Council was formerly the chief source of executive power in the State; its origins can be traced back to the Curia Regis (or King's Court), which assisted the Norman monarchs in running the government. As the system of Cabinet government developed in the 18th century, however, much of the role of the Privy Council was assumed by the Cabinet, although the Council retained certain executive functions. Some government departments originated as committees of the Privy Council.

Nowadays the main function of the Privy Council is to advise the Queen on the

Committees of the Privy Council

There are a number of Privy Council committees. These include prerogative committees, such as those dealing with legislation from the Channel Islands and the Isle of Man, and with applications for charters of incorporation. Committees may also be provided for by statute, such as those for the universities of Oxford and Cambridge and the Scottish universities. Membership of such committees is confined to members of the current administration. The only exceptions are the members of the Judicial Committee and the members of any committee for which specific provision authorises a wider membership.

Administrative work is carried out in the Privy Council Office under the Lord President of the Council, a Cabinet minister.

The Judicial Committee of the Privy Council is the final court of appeal for certain independent members of the Commonwealth, the British dependent territories, the Channel Islands and the Isle of Man. It also hears appeals from the disciplinary committees of the medical and allied professions and certain ecclesiastical appeals.

Government Departments

Government departments and their agencies are the main instruments for implementing government policy when Parliament has passed the necessary legislation, and for advising ministers. They often work alongside local authorities, statutory boards, and government-sponsored organisations operating under various degrees of government control.

A change of government does not necessarily affect the number or general functions of government departments, although major changes in policy may be accompanied by organisational changes.

The work of some departments (for instance, the Ministry of Defence) covers Britain as a whole. Other departments, such as the Department of Employment, cover England, Wales and Scotland, but not Northern Ireland. Others, such as the Department of the Environment, are mainly concerned with affairs in England. Some departments, such as the Department of Trade and Industry, maintain a regional organisation, and some which have direct contact with the public throughout the country (for example, the Department of Employment) also have local offices.

Departments are usually headed by ministers. Certain departments in which questions of policy do not normally arise are headed by permanent officials, and ministers with other duties are responsible for them to Parliament. For instance, ministers in the Treasury are responsible for HM Customs and Excise, the Inland Revenue, the National

Investment and Loans Office and a number of other departments as well as executive agencies such as the Royal Mint. Departments generally receive their funds directly out of money provided by Parliament and are staffed by members of the Civil Service.

The functions of the main government departments are set out on pp. 495–502.

Non-Departmental Public Bodies

A number of bodies with a role in the process of government are neither government departments nor part of a department (in April 1992 there were 1,412). Non-departmental public bodies are of three kinds: executive bodies, advisory bodies and tribunals. The last of these are a specialised group of judicial bodies (see p. 98).

Executive Bodies

Executive bodies normally employ their own staff and have their own budget. They are public organisations whose duties include executive, administrative, regulatory or commercial functions. They normally operate within broad policy guidelines set by departmental ministers but are in varying degrees independent of government in carrying out their day-to-day responsibilities. Examples include the British Council, the Commonwealth Development Corporation and the Commission for Racial Equality.

Advisory Bodies

Many government departments are assisted by advisory councils or committees which undertake research and collect information, mainly to give ministers access to informed opinion before they come to a decision involving a legislative or executive act. In some cases a minister must consult a standing committee, but usually advisory bodies are appointed at the discretion of the minister. Examples include the Industrial Injuries Advisory Council and the Committee on Safety of Medicines.

The membership of the advisory councils and committees varies according to the nature of the work involved, but normally includes representatives of the relevant interests and professions.

In addition to the standing advisory bodies, there are committees set up by the Government to examine specific matters and make recommendations. For certain important inquiries, Royal Commissions, whose members are chosen for their wide experience, may be appointed. Royal Commissions examine evidence from government departments, interested organisations and individuals, and submit recommendations; some prepare regular reports. Examples include the standing Royal Commission on Environmental Pollution, set up in 1970, and the Royal Commission on Criminal Justice, which issued its report in July 1993 (see Chapter 8). Inquiries may also be undertaken by departmental committees.

Government Information Services

Each of the main government departments has its own information division, public relations branch or news department. These are normally staffed by professional information officers responsible for communicating their department's activities to the news media and the public (sometimes using publicity services provided by the Central Office of Information—see p. 500). They also advise their departments on the public's reaction.

The Lobby

As press adviser to the Prime Minister, the Prime Minister's Press Secretary and other staff in the Prime Minister's Press Office have direct contact with the parliamentary press through regular meetings with the Lobby correspondents. The Lobby correspondents are a group of political correspondents who have the special privilege of access to the Lobby of the House of Commons where they can talk privately to government ministers and other members of the House. The Prime Minister's Press Office is the accepted channel through which information about parliamentary business is passed to the media.

Administration of Scottish, Welsh and Northern Ireland Affairs

Scotland

Scotland has its own system of law and wide administrative autonomy. The Secretary of State for Scotland, a Cabinet minister, has responsibility in Scotland (with some exceptions) for a wide range of policy matters (see p. 501). Following an examination of Scotland's place in Britain which began after the general election in April 1992 the Government has proposed a number of changes to the responsibilities of The Scottish Office. These would make it responsible for more areas of policy.

The distinctive conditions and needs of Scotland and its people are also reflected in separate Scottish legislation on many domestic matters. Special provisions applying to Scotland alone are also inserted in Acts which otherwise apply to Britain generally.

British government departments with significant Scottish responsibilities have offices in Scotland and work closely with The Scottish Office.

Wales

Since 1964 there has been a separate Secretary of State for Wales, who is a member of the Cabinet and is responsible for many aspects of Welsh affairs. (For further details see p. 502.)

Northern Ireland

Since the British Government's assumption of direct responsibility for Northern Ireland in 1972 (see p. 12), the Secretary of State for Northern Ireland has been the Cabinet minister responsible for Northern Ireland affairs. Through the Northern Ireland Office the Secretary of State has direct responsibility for constitutional developments, law and order, security, and electoral matters. The work of the Northern Ireland departments is also subject to the direction and control of the Secretary of State (see p. 500).

Citizen's Charter

The Citizen's Charter aims to raise the standard of public services and make them more responsive to those who use them. It is closely linked to other reforms, including the Next Steps initiative, efficiency measures and the Government's contracting out and market testing programmes (see p. 66). The Citizen's Charter is a long-term programme which is intended to be at the heart of the Government's policy-making throughout the 1990s.

The Citizen's Charter White Paper was published in July 1991 and contained government proposals to raise standards in the public sector. The proposals cover all public services, at both national and local levels, and the privatised utilities. All major public services are expected to publish separate charters, and so far 37 have been issued. In many cases separate charters have been published for services in Northern Ireland, Scotland and Wales. (Details of many of the charters can be found in the relevant chapters; a full list, together with other information about the charters, appears on pp. 508–9.)

The Principles of Public Service

The Charter sets out a number of key principles which users of public services are entitled to expect:

Standards

Setting, monitoring and publication of explicit standards for the services that individual users can reasonably expect. Publication of actual performance against these standards.

Information and Openness

Full and accurate information should be readily available in plain language about how public services are run, their cost and performance, and who is in charge.

Choice and Consultation

There should be regular and systematic consultation with those who use services.

Users' views about services, and their priorities for improving them, should be taken into account in final decisions about standards.

Courtesy and Helpfulness

Courteous and helpful service from public servants who will normally wear name badges. Services available equally to all who are entitled to them and run to suit their convenience.

Putting Things Right

If things go wrong, an apology, a full explanation and a swift and effective remedy should be given. Well publicised and easy to use complaints procedures with independent review wherever possible should be available.

Value for Money

Efficient and economical delivery of public services within the resources the nation can afford, and independent validation of performance against standards.

Implementing the Charter

In April 1992 the Prime Minister appointed a Cabinet minister, the Chancellor of the Duchy of Lancaster, with responsibility for the Charter programme. The Chancellor of the Duchy is supported by the Citizen's Charter Unit within the OPSS (see p. 495). The Prime Minister also receives advice on the Charter from a Panel drawn from business, consumer affairs and education. The Panel works with the Citizen's Charter Unit and officials in all the departments to implement and develop the Citizen's Charter programme. The Prime Minister holds regular Citizen's Charter seminars with Advisory Panel members and Cabinet ministers to report on progress and plan further action.

Executive agencies (see p. 66) are expected to comply fully with the principles of the Citizen's Charter, and the pay of agency chief executives is normally directly related to their agency's performance.

Performance-related pay is being introduced throughout the public service.

The mechanisms for implementing the Charter cover:

- more privatisation;
- wider competition;
- further contracting-out of service provision to private sector organisations;
- more performance-related pay for public sector staff;
- published performance targets, both local and national;
- comprehensive publication of information on standards achieved;
- more effective complaints procedures;
- tougher and more independent inspectorates; and
- better redress for the citizen if things go wrong.

Charter Mark Awards

A Charter Mark Scheme has been introduced to reward excellence: winners are judged by the Prime Minister's Citizen's Charter Advisory Panel. Applicants have to demonstrate that they have achieved measurable improvements in the quality of services over the previous two years, and that their customers are satisfied with their services. They must also have plans to introduce at least one new improvement to their services which can be implemented without increasing the cost to taxpayers or users.

The first awards were made in September 1992 to 36 of over 300 public service organisations and privatised utilities which had applied. Winners ranged from water companies to schools, local authority services and executive agencies such as the United Kingdom Passport Agency. The Government has increased the potential number of awards from 50 to 100 in 1993. Award winners can use the Charter Mark on their products and equipment, and on stationery, vehicles and promotional material for up to three years.

Progress on the Charter

The Citizen's Charter First Report, published in November 1992, described the programme's achievements in its first year. It showed that over 90 per cent of the commitments in the original White Paper had been met or tackled. The Government has also piloted a telephone information service—Charterline—to enable people to dial one telephone number to obtain information and help about the Charter and public service organisations. In June 1993 a task force was launched to review and recommend improvements to public service complaints systems.

Open Government

The Government has announced proposals for a substantial increase in the amount of information about the working of Government. Its White Paper, published in July 1993, proposes:

- a new code of practice on the provision of government information, to be independently policed by the Parliamentary Ombudsman;
- statutory rights of access to health and safety information, and to personal files; and
- a reduction in the number of public records withheld from release beyond 30 years.

The Civil Service

The Civil Service is concerned with the conduct of the whole range of government activities as they affect the community. These range from policy formulation to carrying out the day-to-day duties of public administration.

Civil servants are servants of the Crown. For all practical purposes the Crown in this context means, and is represented by, the Government of the day. There are special cases in which certain functions are conferred by law upon particular members of the public service. However, in general the executive powers of the Crown are exercised by, and on the advice of, Her Majesty's Ministers, who are in turn answerable to Parliament.

The Civil Service as such has no constitutional responsibility separate from that of the duly constituted Government of the day. The duty of the individual civil servant is first and foremost to the Minister of the Crown who is in charge of the Department concerned. A change of minister, for whatever reason, does not involve a change of staff. Ministers sometimes appoint special advisers from outside the Civil Service. The advisers are normally paid from public funds, but their appointments come to an end when the Government's term of office finishes, or when the Minister concerned leaves the Government or moves to another appointment.

The number of civil servants has fallen from 732,000 in April 1979 to 554,000 in April 1993, reflecting the Government's policy of controlling the cost of the Civil Service and of improving its efficiency.

About half of all civil servants are engaged in the provision of public services. These include paying sickness benefits and pensions, collecting taxes and contributions, running employment services, staffing prisons, and providing services to industry and agriculture. Around a quarter are employed in the Ministry of Defence. The rest are divided between central administrative and policy duties; support services; and largely financially self-supporting services, for instance, those provided by the Department for National Savings and the Royal Mint. The total includes about 51,000 'industrial' civil servants, mainly manual workers in government industrial establishments. Four-fifths of civil servants work outside London.

Equality of Opportunity

The Government is committed to achieving equality of opportunity for all its staff. In support of this commitment, the Civil Service is actively pursuing policies to increase career opportunities for women, ethnic minorities and people with disabilities. The proportion of ethnic minority staff has been in proportion to, or better than, their representation in the

working population since the Civil Service began ethnic monitoring in 1989. Progress is monitored and results published annually by the Cabinet Office (OPSS).

Management Reforms

Civil Service reforms are being implemented to ensure improved management performance, in particular through the increased accountability of individual managers, based on clear objectives and responsibilities. These reforms include performance-related pay schemes and other incentives.

Executive Agencies: Next Steps Initiative

The Next Steps Initiative, launched in 1988, aims to deliver government services more efficiently and effectively within available resources to the benefit of taxpayers, customers and staff. This has involved setting up, as far as is practicable, separate units or agencies to perform the executive functions of government. Agencies remain part of the Civil Service but under the terms of individual framework documents they enjoy greater delegation on financial, pay and personnel matters. Agencies are headed by chief executives who are accountable to ministers but who are personally responsible for the day-to-day operations of the agency. By mid-1993 more than 90 agencies had been set up, together with 30 Executive Units of Customs and Excise and 33 Executive Offices of the Inland Revenue. Almost 348,000 civil servants work in organisations run on Next Steps lines.

Efficiency Measures

In 1991 the Government announced further proposals to extend competition and choice in the provision of public services. Savings in public expenditure are being sought by market testing and competitive tendering of many services carried out by government departments. Services are contracted out to the private sector whenever the evaluation of tenders indicates that better value for money can be achieved.

Central Management and Structure

Responsibility for central co-ordination and management of the Civil Service is divided between the Treasury and the Cabinet Office (OPSS). In addition to its other functions, the Treasury is responsible for the structure of the Civil Service. It is also responsible for recruitment policy and for controlling staffing, pay, pensions and allowances. The OPSS, which is under the control of the Prime Minister, as Minister for the Civil Service, is responsible for the organisation, non-financial aspects of personnel management and overall efficiency of the Service. The function of official Head of the Home Civil Service is combined with that of Secretary to the Cabinet.

At the senior levels, where management forms a major part of most jobs, there are common grades throughout the Civil Service. These unified grades 1 to 7 are known as the Open Structure and cover grades from Permanent Secretary level to Principal level. Within the unified grades each post is filled by the person best qualified, regardless of the occupational group to which he or she previously belonged.

Below this the structure of the non-industrial Civil Service is based on a system of occupational groups. These groups assist the recruitment and matching of skills to posts and offer career paths in which specialist skills can be developed. Departments and agencies are being encouraged to develop their own pay and grading arrangements. These are expected to produce value-for-money benefits which are greater than those available through centrally controlled negotiation.

The Diplomatic Service

The Diplomatic Service, a separate service of some 6,650 or so people, divided between Diplomatic Service and Home Civil Service grades, provides the majority of the staff for the Foreign & Commonwealth Office (see p. 498) and at British diplomatic missions and consular posts abroad.

The Service has its own grade structure, linked for salary purposes with that of the

Home Civil Service. Terms and conditions of service are in many ways comparable, but take into account the special demands of the Service, particularly of postings overseas. Members of the Home Civil Service and the armed forces, and individuals from the private sector, may also serve in the Foreign & Commonwealth Office and at overseas posts on loan or attachment.

Civil Service Recruitment and Training

Recruitment is based on the principle of selection on merit by fair and open competition. Independent Civil Service Commissioners are responsible for approving the selection of people for appointment to the higher levels and to the fast-stream entry to the Home Civil Service and the Diplomatic Service. Recruitment of middle-ranking and junior staff is the responsibility of departments and executive agencies; it is monitored by the Commissioners. Departments and agencies can choose whether to undertake this recruitment work themselves, to employ a private sector recruitment agency or to use the Recruitment and Assessment Services Agency (an executive agency) to recruit on their behalf.

People from outside the Civil Service may be recruited directly to all levels, including the higher levels in the Open Structure, particularly to posts requiring skills and experience more readily found in the private sector. The exchange of staff between the Civil Service and industry is also encouraged.

Training

Individual government departments and agencies are responsible for the performance of their own staff. They provide training and development to meet their business needs, to improve performance, and to help staff respond effectively to changing demands. The majority of training and development takes place within departments and agencies. In addition, the Civil Service College provides high-quality management and professional training, mainly for those who occupy, or hope to occupy, relatively senior positions. Considerable use is made of other providers in the private and public sectors.

Civil servants under the age of 18 may continue their general education by attending courses, usually for one day a week ('day release' schemes). All staff may be entitled to financial support to continue their education, mainly in their own time. There are also opportunities for civil servants to undertake research and study in areas of interest to them and to their department or agency.

Promotion

Departments are responsible for promotion up to and including Grade 4. Promotion or appointment to Grades 1 and 2 and all transfers between departments at these levels are approved by the Prime Minister, who is advised by the Head of the Home Civil Service. Promotions and appointments to Grade 3 are approved by the Cabinet Office.

Political and Private Activities

Civil servants are required to perform loyally the duties assigned to them by the Government of the day, whatever its political persuasion. It is essential that ministers and the public should have confidence that the personal views of civil servants do not influence the performance of their official duties, given the role of the Civil Service in serving successive governments formed by different parties. The aim of the rules which govern political activities by civil servants is to allow them, subject to these fundamental principles, the greatest possible freedom to participate in public affairs consistent with their rights and duties as citizens. The rules are therefore concerned with activities liable to give public expression to political views rather than with privately held beliefs and opinions.

The Civil Service is divided into three groups for the purposes of deciding the extent to which individuals may take part in political activities:

- Those in the 'politically free' group, consisting of industrial staff and non-office grades, are free to engage in any political activity outside official time, including adoption as a candidate for the British or the European Parliament (although they would have to resign from the Service before standing for election).
- Those in the 'politically restricted' group, which comprises staff in Grade 7 and above as well as Administration Trainees and Higher Executive Officers (D), may not take part in national political activities but may apply for permission to take part in local political activities.
- The 'intermediate' group, which comprises all other civil servants, may apply for permission to take part in national or local political activity, apart from candidature for the British or the European Parliament.

Where required, permission is granted to the maximum extent consistent with the Civil Service's reputation for political impartiality and the avoidance of any conflict with official duties. A code of discretion requires moderation and the avoidance of embarrassment to ministers.

Generally, there are no restrictions on the private activities of civil servants, provided that these do not bring discredit on the Civil Service, and that there is no possibility of conflict with official duties. For instance, a civil servant must comply with any departmental instruction on the need to seek authority before taking part in any outside activity which involves official experience.

Security

Each department is responsible for its own internal security. As a general rule the privately-held political views of civil servants are not a matter of official concern. However, no one may be employed in connection with work which is vital to the security of the State who is, or has been involved in, or associated with, activities threatening national security. Certain posts are not open to people who fall into this category, or to anyone whose reliability may be in doubt for any other reason.

The Security Commission may investigate breaches of security in the public service and advise on changes in security procedure if requested to do so by the Prime Minister after consultation with the Leader of the Opposition.

Local Government

Although the origins of local government in England can be traced back to Saxon times, the first comprehensive system of local councils was established in the late 19th century. Over the years the range of services for which local authorities are responsible has grown and this has been one of the factors which has led to reforms in the pattern of local government.

Local Government Reform

A major reform of local government took place in 1974 in England and Wales and in 1975 in Scotland. It was felt at the time that, while for some services it was more efficient for local authorities to cover large areas or serve many people, other services were best organised through smaller units in order to meet the needs of individual communities. In England and Wales functions were therefore allocated to two main tiers of local authority: outside London these were counties and the smaller districts. In Scotland functions were allocated on the mainland to regions and districts; single-tier authorities were introduced for the three Islands areas. In Northern Ireland changes were made in 1973 which left local authorities with fewer functions than in the rest of Britain.

The Local Government Act 1985 abolished the Greater London Council and the six metropolitan county councils in England. In 1986 most of their functions were transferred to the London boroughs and metropolitan district councils respectively (see below).

More recently the Local Government Act 1992 made provision for the establishment of a Local Government Commission to review the structure, boundaries and electoral arrangements of local government in England. The Commission was set up in July 1992. It

will review the structure of local government in all the shire counties of England over the next three to four years. The first changes are likely to be implemented in April 1995. It is expected that, as a result of the reviews, there will be a substantial increase in the number of unitary or single-tier authorities in England. In some areas the existing two-tier structure may remain. The Government is also looking at ways of improving the internal management of local authorities.

Consultation on these subjects is also taking place in Scotland and in Wales. A White Paper published in July 1993 has proposed legislation to introduce a single-tier structure throughout Scotland. In Wales the Government has announced plans to establish 21 new unitary authorities. These would be elected in 1994 and would replace the existing local authorities in 1995.

Local Authorities' Powers

Local authorities' powers and duties are conferred on them by Parliament, or by measures taken under its authority. Administration is the responsibility of the local authority. In the case of certain services, however, ministers have powers to secure some national uniformity in standards in order to safeguard public health or to protect the rights of individual citizens. For some services the minister concerned has wide powers of supervision; in other cases the minister's powers are strictly limited.

Relations with Central Government

The main link between local authorities and central government in England is the Department of the Environment, although other departments such as the Department for Education and the Home Office are concerned with various local government functions. In the rest of Britain the local authorities deal with the Scottish and Welsh Offices and the Department of the Environment for Northern Ireland.

Principal Types of Local Authority

At present England and Wales (outside

Greater London) are divided into 53 counties, sub-divided into 369 districts. All the districts and 47 of the counties—the 'non-metropolitan' counties—have locally elected councils with separate functions. County councils provide large-scale services, while district councils are responsible for the more local ones (see p. 71).

Greater London—with a population of some 6.9 million—is divided into 32 boroughs, each of which has a council responsible for local government in its area; in addition, there is the Corporation of the City of London. In the six metropolitan counties there are 36 district councils; there are no county councils. A number of services, however, require a statutory authority over areas wider than the individual boroughs and districts. These are waste regulation and disposal (in certain areas); the police and fire services, including civil defence, and public transport (in all metropolitan counties); and the fire service, including civil defence (in London). All are run by joint authorities composed of elected councillors nominated by the borough or district councils.

In addition to the two-tier local authority system in England, there are over 8,000 parish councils or meetings. They may provide and manage local facilities such as allotments and village halls and may act as agents for other district council functions. They also provide a forum for discussion of local issues. In Wales community councils have similar functions.

On the mainland of Scotland local government is at present on a two-tier basis: nine regions are divided into 53 districts, each of which has an elected council. There are three virtually all-purpose authorities for Orkney, Shetland and the Western Isles. Provision is also made for local community councils: although these have no statutory functions, they can draw attention to matters of local concern.

The areas and electoral arrangements of local authorities are kept under review by the Local Government Boundary Commissions for Wales and Scotland. In 1992 the responsibilities of the Local Government Boundary Commission for England passed to the Local Government Commission (see p. 69).

In Northern Ireland 26 district councils are responsible for local environmental and certain other services. Statutory bodies, such as the Northern Ireland Housing Executive and area boards, are responsible to central government departments for administering other major services (see below).

Election of Councils

Local authority councils consist of elected unpaid councillors. Councillors may, however, be entitled to a basic flat rate allowance and to certain expenses when attending meetings or taking on special responsibilities. Parish and community councillors cannot claim allowances for duties undertaken within their own council areas.

In England, Wales and Northern Ireland each council elects its presiding officer and his or her deputy annually. Some districts have the ceremonial title of borough, or city, both granted by royal authority. In boroughs and cities the presiding officer is normally known as the Mayor. In the City of London and certain other large cities, he or she is known as the Lord Mayor. In Scotland the presiding officer of the district council of each of the four cities is called the Lord Provost. No specific title is laid down for those of other councils; some are known as conveners, while others continue to use the old title of 'provost'.

Councillors are elected for four years. All county councils in England and Wales, London borough councils, and about two-thirds of non-metropolitan district councils are elected in their entirety every four years. In the remaining districts (including all metropolitan districts) one-third of the councillors are elected in each of the three years between county council elections. In Scotland local elections are held every two years, alternately for districts and for regions and islands authorities. Each election covers the whole council so that councillors are elected for four years at a time.

Voters

Anyone may vote at a local government election in Britain provided he or she is:

70

- aged 18 years or over;
- is a citizen of Britain or another Commonwealth country, or a citizen of the Irish Republic;
- is not subject to any legal incapacity; and
- is on the electoral register.

To qualify for registration a person must be resident in the council area on the qualifying date. In Northern Ireland there are slightly different requirements.

Candidates

Many candidates at local government elections stand as representatives of one of the national political parties, although there are some independent candidates, and some represent local interests. Candidates must be British citizens, other Commonwealth citizens or citizens of the Irish Republic, and aged 21 or over. In addition, they must either:

- be registered as local electors in the area of the local authority to which they seek election; or
- have lived in or occupied (as owner or tenant) land or other premises in that area during the whole of the 12 months preceding the day on which they are nominated as candidates; or,
- have had their main or only place of work in the area throughout this 12-month period.

No one may be elected to a council of which he or she is an employee, and there are some other disqualifications. All candidates for district council elections in Northern Ireland are required to make a declaration against terrorism.

Electoral Divisions

Counties in England and Wales are divided into electoral divisions, each returning one councillor. Districts in England, Wales and Northern Ireland are divided into 'wards', returning one councillor or more. In Scotland the electoral areas in the regions and islands areas are called electoral divisions, each returning a single member; the districts are divided into wards, similarly returning a

single member. Parishes (in England) and communities (in Wales) may be divided into wards. Wards return at least one councillor. The minimum parish/community council size is five councillors.

Voting Procedure

The procedure for local government voting in Great Britain is similar to that for parliamentary elections. In Northern Ireland local government elections are held on the basis of proportional representation, and electoral wards are grouped into district electoral areas.

Council Functions and Services

At present in England county councils are responsible for strategic planning, transport planning, highways, traffic regulation, education (although schools may 'opt out' of local government control—see p. 402), consumer protection, refuse disposal, police, the fire service, libraries and the personal social services. District councils are responsible for local services such as environmental health, housing, decisions on most local planning applications, and refuse collection. Both tiers of local authority have powers to provide facilities like museums, art galleries and parks; arrangements depend on local agreement.

In the metropolitan counties the district councils are responsible for all services apart from the police, the fire service and public transport and, in some areas, waste regulation and disposal (see p. 352).

In Greater London the boroughs and the City Corporation have similar functions, but London's metropolitan police force is directly responsible to the Home Secretary. Responsibility for public transport lies with London Transport (see p. 251).

In Wales the division of functions between county and district councils is much the same as that between county and district councils in non-metropolitan areas of England.

Local authorities in England and Wales may arrange for any of their functions to be carried out on their behalf by another local authority, other than those relating to education, police, the personal social services and National Parks.

In Scotland the functions of regional and district authorities are, at present, divided up in a similar way to the counties and districts in England and Wales. Because of their isolation from the mainland, Orkney, Shetland and the Western Isles have single, virtually all-purpose authorities; they take part in wider-scale administration for their police and fire services, however, and rely on the mainland for assistance in the more specialised aspects of education and social work.

In Northern Ireland local environmental and certain other services, such as leisure and the arts, are administered by the district councils. Responsibility for planning, roads, water supply and sewerage services is exercised in each district through a divisional office of the Department of the Environment for Northern Ireland. Area boards, responsible to central departments, administer education, public libraries and the health and personal services locally. The Northern Ireland Housing Executive, responsible to the Department of the Environment, administers housing.

Internal Organisation of Local Authorities

Local authorities have considerable freedom to make arrangements for carrying out their duties. The main policies are decided by the full council; other matters concerning the various services are the responsibility of committees composed of members of the council. A council may delegate to a committee or officer any function except those concerned with raising loans, levying local taxes or making financial demands on other local authorities liable to contribute. These powers are legally reserved to the council as a whole. Some councils have policy advisory or co-ordinating committees which originate policy for implementation by the full council. The powers and duties of local authority committees are usually laid down in formal standing orders. Parish and community councils in England and Wales are often able to do their work in full

session, although they appoint committees from time to time as necessary.

Committees have to reflect the political composition of the council. In England and Wales people who are not members of the council may be appointed to decision-making committees and are able to speak and take part in debates; they cannot normally vote. The legislation also prevents senior officers and others in politically sensitive posts from being members of another local authority or undertaking public political activity. Some of these provisions have not been introduced in Northern Ireland.

Public Access

The public (including the press) are admitted to council, committee and sub-committee meetings, and have a right of access to agendas, reports and minutes of meetings and certain background papers. Local authorities may exclude the public from meetings and withhold these papers only in limited circumstances.

Employees

Almost 3 million people are employed by local authorities in Great Britain. These include administrative, professional and technical staff, teachers, firefighters, those engaged in law and order services, and manual workers. Nearly half of all local government workers are employed in the education service.

Although a few appointments must be made by all the authorities responsible for the functions concerned, councils are individually responsible within national policy requirements for determining the size and duties of their workforces. In Northern Ireland each council must by law appoint a clerk of the council as its chief officer.

As a general rule, employees are of three kinds: heads of departments or chief officers; administrative, professional, clerical and technical staff; and manual workers. Senior staff appointments are usually made on the recommendation of the committee or committees involved. Most junior appointments are made by heads of

CITIZEN'S CHARTER

The Citizen's Charter commits all sectors of government to provide better services; many departments and agencies have made significant improvements in their standards.

Sister Jeanne Smith, from the Bristol Royal Hospital for Sick Children, receives a Charter Mark award from the Prime Minister, John Major, on behalf of United Bristol Healthcare NHS Trust.

Inland Revenue staff offer personal advice and assistance to members of the public at Tax Enquiry Centres.

Statuary in the garden at Powis Castle,
Powys, Wales. A 13th century castle
that was once the stronghold of Welsh princes,
Powis Castle is now owned by the National
Trust and open to the public.

Restoration of historic houses requires both
traditional craftsmanship and high-tech methods.
Here pulse radar equipment is being used to
detect cracks and crumbling in the walls of
600-year-old Ightham Mote, a medieval
manor house in Kent.

Tynan Cross, in County Armagh, is in the care of Northern Ireland's Department of Environment. It was restored in the 19th century, using sections from two 10th century crosses, and has recently been cleaned.

Eilan Donan Castle, in the western Highlands of Scotland, is still privately owned, by a member of the MacRae clan, but it is open to the public from April to September and often attracts as many as 1,000 visitors a day.

THE NATIONAL HYPERBARIC CENTRE

The National Hyperbaric Centre, in Aberdeen, Scotland, provides onshore facilities simulating conditions for deep-sea divers. Throughout April and May 1993 it was the venue for Aurora '93, a research project funded largely by the European Commission. The research included trials of breathing apparatus and communications equipment, and observations of psychological and physiological performance at depths of up to 470 metres.

Divers in a pressure chamber testing a built-in emergency breathing system. During the project the divers remained in the pressure chamber for 32 days.

Life support technicians in the control room monitor conditions in the pressure chamber continuously, ensuring, for example, that the pressure and temperature are maintained at safe levels.

departments, who are also responsible for engaging manual workers. Pay and conditions of service are usually a matter for each council, although there are scales recommended by national negotiating machinery between authorities and trade unions.

Authorities differ in the degree to which they employ their own permanent staff to carry out certain functions or use private firms under contract. The Government's policy of promoting value for money is encouraging the use of private firms where savings can be made.

Local Authority Finance

Local government expenditure accounts for about 27 per cent of public spending. The Government has sought to influence local government spending as part of a general policy of controlling the growth of public expenditure. Since 1984 the Government has had powers to limit or 'cap' local authority budgets by setting a maximum amount for local authorities which have, in its view, set budgets which are excessive.

In 1992–93 expenditure by local authorities in Britain was about £69,800 million. Current expenditure amounted to £58,095 million, and capital expenditure, net of capital receipts, was £6,370 million and debt interest £5,300 million.

Local authorities in Great Britain raise revenue through the new council tax, which replaced the community charge system in April 1993 (see p. 121).

Expenditure

In 1992–93 education accounted for 44 per cent of local authorities' current expenditure in England, Scotland and Wales. Most of the remainder was spent on roads and transport;

housing and other environmental services; law, order and protective services; and personal social services.

Local government capital expenditure is financed primarily by borrowing and from capital receipts from the disposal of land and buildings. These are supplemented mainly by capital grants from central government.

Control of Finance

Local councils normally have a finance committee to keep their financial policy under constant review. Their annual accounts must be audited by independent auditors appointed by the Audit Commission in England and Wales, or by the Commission for Local Authority Accounts in Scotland. In Northern Ireland this role is exercised by a local government audit section appointed by the Department of the Environment for Northern Ireland.

Local Government Complaints System

Citizens' allegations of injustice resulting from local government maladministration may be investigated by independent statutory Commissions for Local Administration. The English Commission has three local commissioners (or local government ombudsmen). Wales and Scotland each have a single commissioner.

A report is issued on each complaint investigated and, if injustice caused by maladministration is found, the local ombudsman normally suggests a remedy. The council must consider the report and tell the commissioner what action it proposes to take.

In Northern Ireland a Commissioner for Complaints deals with complaints alleging injustices suffered as a result of maladministration by district councils and certain other public bodies.

Further Reading

The British System of Government. Aspects of Britain series, HMSO, 1992.

History and Function of Government Departments. Aspects of Britain series, HMSO, 1993.

Open Government. Cm 2290. HMSO, 1993.

Parliament. Aspects of Britain series, HMSO, 1991.

8   Justice and the Law

Concern about levels of crime and about the administration of the law has been high on the Government's agenda in recent years. As a result, proposals have been put forward for the reform of the police service (see p. 78), and in 1991, following a series of miscarriages of justice, a Royal Commission on Criminal Justice in England and Wales was set up. In July 1993, the Commission reported its findings for consideration by the Government. They included the following recommendations:

- a new independent review authority to consider allegations of miscarriage of justice, with the power to refer a case to the Court of Appeal;

- new rules for disclosure of the prosecution and defence cases before trial;

- preparatory court hearings to clarify and define the issues at stake in a trial before a jury is empanelled;

- a system under which defendants pleading guilty could secure a smaller sentence;

- defendants to lose the right to insist on trial by jury for offences triable in either the magistrates' court or the Crown Court; and

- all public sector forensic science laboratories to be equally available to defence and prosecution.

England and Wales, Scotland, and Northern Ireland all have their own legal systems, with considerable differences in law, organisation and practice. All three have separate prosecution, prison and police services. Crime prevention policy and non-custodial treatment for offenders is very similar throughout Britain. There are different civil court and civil law systems in England and Wales and in Scotland; Northern Ireland's system is in many ways similar to the English and Welsh model.

Common Law and Statute Law

One of the main sources of law in England and Wales and in Northern Ireland is common law, which has evolved over centuries from judges' decisions. It forms the basis of the law except when superseded by legislation. In Scotland, too, the doctrine of legal precedent has been more strictly applied since the end of the 18th century.

Much of the law, particularly that relating to criminal justice, is statute law passed by

Parliament. If a court reaches a decision which is contrary to the intentions of Parliament, then Parliament must either accept the decision or pass amending legislation. Some Acts create new law, while others are passed to draw together existing law on a given topic. Parliament can repeal a statute and replace it with another.

European Community Law

European Community (EC) law, deriving from Britain's EC membership, is confined mainly to economic and social matters; in certain circumstances it takes precedence over domestic law. It is normally applied by the domestic courts, but the most authoritative rulings are given by the EC's Court of Justice (see p. 291).

Certain changes to United Kingdom law have been made to bring it in line with rulings of Strasbourg's European Court of Human Rights.

Branches of the Law

There are two main branches of the law—criminal and civil. Criminal law is concerned with acts punishable by the state. Civil law covers:

- disputes about the rights, duties and obligations of individuals between themselves; and

- dealings between individuals and companies and between one company and another.

Criminal Justice

Crime Statistics

Differences in the legal systems, police recording practices and statistical classifications make it impracticable to analyse in detail trends in crime for the country as a whole. Nevertheless, there has, as in Western Europe generally, been a substantial increase in crime since the early 1950s. Annual official statistics cover crime recorded by the police and can be affected by changes in unreported crime.

Recorded crimes in England and Wales in 1992 are detailed in Table 8.1. In the same year the Scottish police recorded 589,500 crimes, of which 190,600 were cleared up. In Northern Ireland, of the 67,500 recorded crimes about 23,250 were cleared up.

Crime tends to be concentrated in large cities and urban areas. About 94 per cent of crime recorded by the police is directed against property but only 5 per cent involves violence. Rising affluence has provided more opportunities for casual property crime. In 1957, for example, car crime was only one-tenth of total crime but this has risen to about a third. Most crime is committed by young males, is opportunist and is not planned by hardened professional criminals, although these do exist.

Another source of information about crime is the regular crime surveys undertaken in England and Wales, Scotland and in Northern Ireland. The 1992 survey

Table 8.1: Notifiable Crimes Recorded by the Police[a] in England and Wales 1992

Offence Group	Recorded crimes	Crimes cleared up	Per cent
Violence against the person	201,779	153,586	76
Sexual offences	29,528	22,092	75
Burglary	1,355,274	268,355	20
Robbery	52,894	11,703	22
Theft and handling stolen goods	2,844,548	693,578	24
Fraud and forgery	168,600	88,629	53
Criminal damage	691,481	115,298	17
Other	39,383	37,623	96
Total	5,383,487	1,390,864	26

Source: Home Office.

[a]Excludes criminal damage of £20 or under.

in England and Wales asked respondents for information about how crime had affected them in 1991. It estimated a total of 15 million crimes in 1991, the majority of which were against property. Violent crime accounted for only 5 per cent of the total, while 36 per cent involved vehicles, 9 per cent were burglaries and 30 per cent other forms of theft. These surveys indicate that many crimes go unrecorded by the police, mainly because not all victims report them.

Crime Prevention

National publicity campaigns, such as the 'Car Crime Prevention Year' campaign during 1992, are a regular feature of the Government's programmes. The Home Office's Crime Prevention Unit encourages local agencies to implement anti-crime measures and to assess the results.

Local panels assisted by the police try to prevent crime through publicity, marking goods and equipment, and fund-raising to buy security devices. The police have been closely involved in setting up 115,000 neighbourhood watch schemes in England and Wales. There are some 2,000 watch schemes in Scotland. Crime Concern, a national independent organisation, encourages local initiatives and business participation in crime prevention.

The Safer Cities programme tackles crime and the fear of crime in inner city and urban areas through joint action by local government, private businesses, the police and voluntary agencies. By the end of 1992, with projects in 20 local authority areas, the programme had supported over 2,800 crime prevention initiatives with over £17.6 million of grant funds from central government. Each project is led by a committee, drawn from local agencies and supported by a co-ordinator funded by the Home Office. There is a Safer Cities programme in Scotland and similar projects are being funded by the Government in Northern Ireland.

In January 1993 the Government announced new crime prevention measures, including:

- doubling the number of Safer Cities projects;
- a National Board for Crime Prevention to seek new ways of involving all sections of the community, including business, in crime prevention; and
- increased support for local communities' crime prevention initiatives.

Helping the Victim

There are some 400 victim support schemes—with over 8,000 volunteer visitors and covering 98 per cent of the population in England and Wales—providing practical help and emotional support to victims of crime. They are co-ordinated by a national organisation, Victim Support, which receives a government grant (£8.4 million in 1993–94). Most of the grant goes to local schemes to meet either the salaries of co-ordinators or running costs. Similar schemes operate in Scotland and Northern Ireland.

In 1990 the Government published its *Victims' Charter*, setting out the standards of service that victims of crime are entitled to expect from criminal justice agencies.

Blameless victims of violent crime in England, Wales and Scotland, including foreign nationals, may be eligible for compensation assessed on the common law damages awarded in the civil courts.

In Northern Ireland there is statutory provision in certain circumstances for compensation to be paid from public funds for criminal injuries, and for malicious damage to property, including any resulting loss of profits.

In 1990 Britain ratified a European Convention under which mutual arrangements for compensation apply to citizens of those countries in which the Convention is in force.

Strengthening the Law

Measures to strengthen the criminal justice system have been taken in recent years. The courts, for instance, have powers to confiscate the proceeds of drug trafficking. A court can require the offender to pay an amount equal to the full value of the proceeds arising from the trafficking. The laundering of illegal money associated with trafficking is unlawful. Restraint and confiscation orders made by courts can be enforced against assets held overseas, and vice versa, if a mutual enforcement agreement has been made between Britain and another state. A court may also confiscate the proceeds from offences such as robbery, fraud, blackmail and insider dealing in shares. Under new legislation the onus will be placed on the offender to prove that the property is legitimately acquired.

In September 1992 Britain became the first country to ratify the European Convention on the Tracing, Freezing and Confiscation of Assets, which provides for international co-operation in the investigation, search, seizure and confiscation of the proceeds of all crimes.

Legislative controls on firearms have been increased. The private ownership of certain highly dangerous types of weapon, such as high-powered self-loading rifles and burst-fire weapons, is banned. The police license the possession of firearms and have increased powers to regulate their safekeeping and movement. Similar legislation applies in Northern Ireland. The Government has proposed that responsibility for firearms licensing in England, Wales and Scotland should pass from the police to a national civilian control board.

It is unlawful to manufacture, sell or import certain weapons such as knuckledusters or to carry a knife in a public place without good reason.

The Criminal Justice Act 1991 has made a number of reforms to the criminal law in England and Wales. They mainly concern sentencing and the system for early release of prisoners (see p. 91). Similar reforms in Scotland took effect from October 1993.

The Government has announced proposals for reform of the police (see p. 78) and is considering the recommendations made by the 1993 Royal Commission report.

Measures to Combat Terrorism

The Government has certain exceptional powers for dealing with and preventing terrorist activities. These take account of the need to achieve a proper balance between the safety of the public and the rights of the individual.

Northern Ireland

The security forces in Northern Ireland have special powers to search, question and arrest. The police can hold a suspected terrorist on their own authority for up to 48 hours; detention for up to a further five days must be approved by the Northern Ireland Secretary. A person who is detained under emergency provisions is entitled to consult a solicitor privately.

Nobody may be imprisoned for political beliefs. All prisoners, except those awaiting trial, have been found guilty in court of criminal offences. The legislation is reviewed annually by an independent person whose reports are presented to Parliament, which has to renew the legislation each year.

Other Legislation

Other legislation applies throughout Britain and is renewable annually by Parliament. It provides for the exclusion from Great Britain, Northern Ireland or the United Kingdom of people connected with terrorism related to Northern Ireland affairs and for the banning of terrorist organisations in Great Britain. It also gives the police powers to arrest suspects without warrant and hold them for 48 hours and, with ministerial approval, for up to a further five days. This provision also applies to suspected international terrorists.

It is a criminal offence to finance terrorism or receive funds for use in the furtherance of terrorism. Police can apply for a court order to freeze a suspect's assets once he or she has been charged. Funds can be confiscated if a person is convicted. The legislation allows for reciprocal enforcement agreements with other countries.

The Government maintains that there should be no concessions to terrorist demands and that international co-operation is essential in tracking down terrorists and impeding their movement between countries.

THE POLICE SERVICE

Organisation

There are 52 police forces in Britain, mainly organised on a local basis: 43 in England and Wales, eight in Scotland and one (the Royal Ulster Constabulary) in Northern Ireland. The Metropolitan Police Force and the City of London force are responsible for policing London. The police service is financed by central and local government.

At the end of 1992 police strength in Britain was about 140,200, of which the Metropolitan Police numbered over 27,800. The establishment of the Royal Ulster Constabulary was nearly 8,500. Each force has volunteer special constables who perform police duties in their spare time, without pay, acting mainly as auxiliaries to the regular force. In Northern Ireland there is a 5,000-strong part-time and full-time paid reserve.

Police forces are maintained in England and Wales by the local police authority, of which two-thirds of the members are local councillors and one-third magistrates. The Government is proposing to reduce the percentage of local councillors to 50 per cent; each authority would have 16 members—eight local councillors, three local magistrates and five local people. The Home Secretary is responsible for London's Metropolitan Police Force.

The police authorities in Scotland are the regional and islands councils. In Northern Ireland the police force is responsible to a body appointed by the Government.

Chief constables run their police forces and are responsible for the appointment, promotion and discipline of all ranks below assistant chief constable. They are generally answerable to the police authorities, and must submit an annual report. The police authorities appoint the chief constable and other top officers. They also fix the maximum strength of the force, subject to approval by the Government, and provide buildings and equipment.

London's Metropolitan Police Commissioner and his immediate subordinates are appointed on the recommendation of the Home Secretary.

Central Authorities

The Home Secretary and the Scottish and Northern Ireland Secretaries approve the appointment of chief, deputy and assistant chief constables. Where necessary they can:

- approve a police authority's decision to retire a chief constable in the interests of efficiency;
- call for a report from a chief constable on matters relating to local policing; and
- institute a local inquiry.

These ministers can also make regulations covering:

- qualifications for appointment, promotion and retirement;
- discipline;
- hours of duty, leave, pay and allowances; and
- uniform.

Many of these are discussed with the staff associations representing police officers.

Police forces are inspected by inspectors of constabulary whose reports to central government are published. New inspectors are being appointed from outside the police service for the first time.

Police officers are not allowed to join a trade union or to go on strike. All ranks, however, have their own staff associations.

Reforms

A reform programme for the police service in England and Wales has been proposed by the Government. This will require police authorities to:

- ensure that policing meets local and national priorities;
- set their own budgets and develop local policing plans in consultation with the public; and
- inform the public about the performance of the force.

Under the proposals management will be streamlined and responsibility for local policing devolved to local commanders. Police authorities and forces will be free to decide for themselves how many officers are needed without having to seek central government approval.

There will be new procedures to ensure that poor performance by officers is dealt with fairly and effectively. Changes to the police disciplinary system aim to reduce lengthy procedures.

An inquiry, set up by the Government to investigate police responsibilities and rewards throughout Britain, reported in July 1993. Its main recommendations included:

- a reduction in the number of ranks from nine to six;
- a pay system designed to reward individual officers while also reflecting their responsibilities and skills, and the nature of the policing environment;
- additional bonuses for exceptional performance;
- fixed term appointments of ten years initially, followed by periods of five years; and
- the replacement of national statutory regulations on most conditions of service by a limited National Code of Standards and by local arrangements decided by chief police officers in consultation with officers and their representatives.

Co-ordination of Police Operations

Certain police services are provided centrally either by the Government or through co-operation between forces. In England and Wales these include criminal intelligence, telecommunications, and research and development. In Scotland the main common services are centralised police training, the Scottish Crime Squad and the Scottish Criminal Record Office.

The National Criminal Intelligence Service, with five regional offices, provides police forces with information about major criminals and serious crime. Its Drugs Division co-ordinates the police and Customs response to drug trafficking. The Service is also linked with the International Criminal Police Organisation, which promotes international co-operation between police forces.

Britain has taken the lead in developing, with other EC countries, a European police organisation designed to provide Community-wide intelligence about serious crime. (see p. 304)

The services of the Fraud Squad, which is run jointly by the Metropolitan Police and City of London Police to investigate company frauds, are available in England and Wales.

Regional crime squads, co-ordinated at national level in England and Wales, deal with serious crimes, such as drug trafficking, and are used whenever operations cannot be dealt with by individual police forces alone.

The National Identification Bureau, located at Metropolitan Police headquarters but financed by all police forces, maintains records on criminals. The Police National Computer holds a summary of this data and other essential information which is available to police forces. The National Criminal Records System will, from 1994, provide full details of arrests and convictions, thereby replacing paper records at the Bureau. The Police National Network will, from 1994, provide integrated voice and data communications.

Scottish criminal records are held on computer at the Scottish Criminal Record Office, which has an automatic national fingerprint record system; plans for a similar national system in England and Wales are far advanced and the Royal Commission has recommended that it should be set up as soon as possible.

Forensic Science Service

The Forensic Science Service (FSS) provides scientific support primarily for forces in England and Wales. It has 600 staff, of whom about 400 are scientists. There are six operational laboratories and a research establishment.

London's Metropolitan Police Force has its own forensic science laboratory, which is the largest in Europe.

Among the most important FSS customers are the 41 provincial police forces in England and Wales. Others include the Crown Prosecution Service (see p. 83), defence lawyers, coroners and civil litigants.

The Royal Commission has recommended

that all public sector forensic laboratories should be equally available to prosecution and defence. It also proposes that a new Forensic Science Advisory Council should report to the Home Secretary on laboratories' efficiency.

In Scotland forensic science services are also provided by forces' own laboratories.

Police Discipline

A police officer may be prosecuted if suspected of a criminal offence. Officers are also subject to a disciplinary code designed to deal with abuse of police powers and maintain public confidence in police impartiality. If found guilty of breaching the code, an officer can be dismissed from the force.

Members of the public have the right to make complaints against police officers if they feel that they have been treated unfairly or improperly. In England and Wales the investigation and resolution of complaints is scrutinised by the independent Police Complaints Authority. In Scotland complaints against police officers involving allegations of any form of criminal conduct are referred to the procurator fiscal for investigation (see p. 83).

In Northern Ireland the Independent Commission for Police Complaints is required to supervise the investigation of a complaint regarding death or serious injury and has the power to supervise that of any other complaint. In certain circumstances, the Secretary of State may direct the Commission to supervise the investigation of matters that are not the subject of a formal complaint.

Community Relations

Police/community liaison consultative groups operate in every police authority; they consist of representatives from the police, local councillors and community groups.

Particular efforts are made to develop relations with young people through greater contact with schools. Schools governing bodies and head teachers have to describe in their annual reports the steps taken to strengthen their schools' links with the community, including the police.

The Government is committed to improving relations between the police and ethnic minorities. Central guidance recommends that all police officers should receive thorough training in community and race relations issues.

Several Home Office initiatives are designed to tackle racially motivated crime and to ensure that the issue is treated as a police priority. These include the issue of guidance to forces on their response to such crimes and the production of a booklet for victims. In addition, forces' arrangements for responding to racial incidents are monitored by the Inspectorate of Constabulary. Discriminatory behaviour by police officers, either to other officers or to members of the public, is an offence under the Police Discipline Code.

All police forces recognise the need to recruit women and members of the ethnic minorities in order to ensure that the police represent the community. At the end of 1992 there were 1,755 ethnic minority officers and 15,820 women police officers in England and Wales. Scottish police forces had 1,465 women officers. Every force has an equal opportunities policy.

Police Powers

Officers in Great Britain do not normally carry firearms, although in an emergency they can be issued on the authority of a senior officer. In Northern Ireland police officers are issued with firearms for personal protection and other firearms are available for duty purposes.

The Government can authorise interception of postal and telephone services by the police in order to:

- prevent and detect serious crime;
- protect national security; or
- safeguard Britain's economic well-being.

Any interception outside these procedures is a criminal offence.

A police officer in England and Wales has a general power of stop and search if he or she has reasonable grounds for suspicion that a person is carrying stolen goods, offensive weapons or implements that could be used for theft, burglary and other offences. The officer must, however, state and record the grounds for taking this action and what, if anything, was found.

Arrest

In England and Wales the police have wide powers to arrest suspects with or without a warrant issued by a magistrate. For serious offences, known as 'arrestable offences', a suspect can be arrested without a warrant; this covers all offences for which a maximum period of five years' imprisonment can be imposed. For lesser offences, arrest without warrant exists if it is not possible or appropriate to send out a summons to appear in court.

Detention, Treatment and Questioning

A government code of practice regulates detention, treatment and questioning of suspects by the police in England and Wales. A police officer can be disciplined if he or she fails to comply with the code. Evidence obtained in breach of the code may be ruled inadmissible in court.

An arrested person has a statutory right to consult a solicitor and to ask the police to notify a relative or other named person. Where a person has been arrested in connection with a serious arrestable offence, but not yet charged, the police may delay for up to 36 hours the exercise of these rights in the interests of the investigation if certain strict criteria are met.

The police must caution a suspect before any questions are put for the purpose of obtaining evidence. The caution informs the suspect that he or she is entitled to refuse to answer questions—the so-called 'right of silence'. Questions relating to an offence may not normally be put to a person after he or she has been charged or informed that he or she may be prosecuted.

The time a suspect is held in police custody before charge is strictly regulated. For lesser offences this may not exceed 24 hours. A person suspected of committing a serious arrestable offence, such as murder, rape, or kidnapping, can be detained for up to 96 hours without charge but only beyond 36 hours if a warrant is obtained from a magistrates' court. Reviews must be made of a person's detention at regular intervals—six hours after initial detention and thereafter every nine hours as a maximum—to check whether the criteria for detention are still satisfied. If they are not, the person must be released immediately.

Tape recording of interviews with suspected offenders takes place at police stations; a code of practice governing these tape recordings has been approved by Parliament.

> The Royal Commission believes that there should be continuous video recording of activity in police station areas where suspects are being held.

A person who thinks that the grounds for detention are unlawful may apply to the High Court for a writ of habeas corpus, requiring the person who detained them to appear before the court to justify the detention. Habeas corpus proceedings take precedence over others. Similar procedures apply in Northern Ireland and a similar remedy is available to anyone who is unlawfully detained in Scotland.

Charging

Once there is sufficient evidence, the police have to decide whether to charge the person with the offence. As an alternative, they can, for example, decide to defer charging or to take no further action and release the person with or without bail. They may also issue a formal caution, which may be taken into account if the person reoffends.

If charged, a person may be kept in custody if there is a risk that they might fail to appear in court or might interfere with the administration of justice. When no such considerations apply, the person must be released on or without bail. Where someone is detained after charge, they must be brought before a magistrates' court quickly. This is usually no later than the next working day.

Scotland

In Scotland the police have common law

powers of arrest and may search an arrested person. A police officer may also search a person for stolen property if he or she has reasonable grounds for suspicion.

The police may detain and question a suspected person for up to six hours. After this period the person must either be released or charged. Tape recording of interviews with suspects is common practice. A court will only allow as evidence statements fairly obtained by the police. Anyone arrested must be brought before a court as soon as possible (generally on the day after being taken into custody). In less serious cases the police may release a person who gives a written undertaking to attend court.

Where the charges involve serious crime, the accused is brought before the sheriff in private, either to be committed for a period not exceeding 8 days to allow further enquiries to be made or to be committed for trial.

Awaiting Trial

There are time limits on the period a defendant may be remanded in custody awaiting trial in England and Wales. In cases tried before a magistrates' court these are 56 days from first appearance to trial or 70 days between first appearance to committal for trial (see p. 85) in the Crown Court. The limit in Crown Court cases is 112 days from committal to taking of the plea. When a time limit expires, the defendant is entitled to bail unless the court extends the limit; it can only do this if satisfied that there is a good and sufficient reason, and that the prosecution has acted expeditiously.

Bail

Most accused people are released on bail pending trial. They are not remanded in custody except where strictly necessary. In England and Wales, the court decides whether a defendant should be released on bail. Unconditional bail may only be withheld if the court has substantial grounds for believing that the accused would:

- abscond;
- commit an offence;

- interfere with witnesses; or
- otherwise obstruct the course of justice.

A court may also impose conditions before granting bail. If bail is refused, the defendant may apply to a High Court judge or to the Crown Court for bail. An application can also be made to the Crown Court for conditions imposed by a magistrates' court to be varied.

In some cases a court may grant bail to a defendant on condition that he or she lives in an approved bail or probation/bail hostel.

The probation service's bail information schemes provide the Crown Prosecution Service with information about a defendant which assists it to decide whether to oppose bail and enables the courts to take an informed decision on whether to grant bail.

Scotland

Anyone accused of a crime, except murder or treason, is entitled to apply for release on bail. Even in murder cases, bail may exceptionally be granted at the discretion of the Lord Advocate or a quorum of the High Court. There is a right of appeal to the High Court by the accused person against the refusal of bail, or by the prosecutor against the granting of bail, or by either party against the conditions imposed.

If a person charged with a serious crime has been kept in custody pending trial, the trial must begin within 110 days of the date of full committal. Where the person is not in custody, the trial must begin within 12 months of first appearance before the sheriff. The trial of a person charged with a summary offence and held in custody must begin within 40 days of the date of first appearance in court.

Northern Ireland

In Northern Ireland bail may be granted by a resident magistrate except in cases dealt with under emergency provisions (see p. 14), where the decision is made by a judge of the High Court.

CRIMINAL COURTS

Prosecution

England and Wales

Once the police have instituted criminal proceedings against a person, the independent Crown Prosecution Service (CPS) assumes control of the case, reviews the evidence and decides whether the case should be continued.

The Service is divided into regional areas, each of which is run by a locally based Chief Crown Prosecutor. CPS lawyers prosecute in the magistrates' courts while barristers instructed by the Service appear in the Crown Court.

Under the Code for Crown Prosecutors, a prosecution should not be started or continued unless the Prosecutor is satisfied that there is admissible, substantial and reliable evidence that a criminal offence has been committed. Once the Prosecutor is satisfied that there is a realistic prospect of a conviction, he or she must also consider whether the public interest requires proceedings to take place. In nearly all cases the decision to prosecute is delegated to the lawyers in the area offices. However, some especially sensitive or complex cases, including terrorist offences and breaches of the Official Secrets Act, are dealt with by CPS headquarters.

Scotland

The Lord Advocate is responsible for prosecutions in the High Court of Judiciary, sheriff courts and district courts. There is no general right of private prosecution. The permanent adviser to the Lord Advocate on prosecution is the Crown Agent, who is head of the Procurator Fiscal Service and is assisted in the Crown Office by a staff of legally qualified civil servants.

Prosecutions in the High Court of Justiciary are prepared by procurators fiscal and Crown Office officials. They are conducted by the Lord Advocate, the Solicitor General for Scotland (the Lord Advocate's ministerial deputy) and advocates depute, collectively known as Crown Counsel.

Crimes tried before the sheriff and district courts are prepared and prosecuted by procurators fiscal. The police and other law enforcement agencies investigate crimes and offences and report to the fiscal, who decides whether to prosecute, subject to the directions of Crown Counsel.

When dealing with minor crime, the fiscal can use alternatives to prosecution, such as formal warnings, diversion to social work and offers of fixed penalties. In the latter case, the offender does not have to accept such an offer; if he or she chooses to do so, proceedings are not brought and the payment does not count as a criminal conviction. The Royal Commission has recommended that a similar fixed penalty system should be introduced in England and Wales.

Northern Ireland

The Director of Public Prosecutions for Northern Ireland, appointed by the Attorney General, prosecutes all offences tried on indictment and may do so in other (summary) cases. Most summary offences are prosecuted by the police.

Prosecutions for Fraud

The Serious Fraud Office prosecutes the most serious and complex cases of fraud in England, Wales and Northern Ireland. Investigations are conducted by teams of lawyers, accountants, police officers and other specialists. In Scotland the Crown Office Fraud Unit investigates and prepares—in co-operation with the police and other agencies—prosecutions against fraud.

Courts

England and Wales

Very serious offences such as murder, manslaughter, rape and robbery can only be tried on indictment in the Crown Court, where all contested trials are presided over by a judge sitting with a jury. Summary offences—the less serious offences and the vast majority of criminal cases—are tried by unpaid lay magistrates or, in a few areas, by paid stipendiary magistrates; both sit without a jury.

Offences in a third category (such as theft, the less serious cases of burglary and some assaults) are known as 'either way' offences. They can be tried either by magistrates or by jury in the Crown Court. Where magistrates consider an 'either way' case to be too serious for them to deal with, they may commit the offender to the Crown Court for trial. If magistrates are content to deal with the case, the accused has the right to choose trial by jury in the Crown Court; the Royal Commission has proposed that this decision on the trial court should only be taken by magistrates.

All those charged with offences to be tried in the Crown Court must first appear before a magistrates' court, which decides whether to commit them to the Court for trial.

A magistrates' court, which is open to the public and the media, usually consists of three lay magistrates—known as justices of the peace—who are advised by a legally qualified clerk or a qualified assistant.

There are about 29,400 lay magistrates. The 79 full-time, legally qualified stipendiary magistrates may sit alone and usually preside in courts where the workload is heavy.

Most cases involving people under 18 are heard in youth courts. These are specialist magistrates' courts which either sit apart from other courts or are held at a different time. Restrictions are placed on access by ordinary members of the public. Media reports must not identify a young person concerned in the proceedings, whether as defendant, victim or witness.

Where a young person under 18 is charged jointly with someone of 18 or over, the case is heard in an ordinary magistrates' court or the Crown Court. If the young person is found guilty, the court may transfer the case to a youth court for sentence unless satisfied that it is undesirable to do so.

An independent inspectorate has been established to assist in raising performance standards within the magistrates' courts service.

The Crown Court sits at 93 centres and is presided over by High Court judges, full-time Circuit Judges and part-time Recorders.

Courts Charter

A Courts Charter, setting out the standards of service which court users can expect in England and Wales, was published in November 1992 and came into operation in January 1993. A court user is defined in the Charter as a victim of crime, a witness giving evidence, a member of a jury, a defendant in a criminal case, a party in civil or family proceedings, a relative or friend of someone involved in a case or a member of the public wanting to observe justice in the courts.

The Charter outlines arrangements to help court users and ease the strains associated with court attendance. The procedure for dealing with complaints is displayed in all courts.

The Charter also covers the conduct of court business, and sets guideline time limits covering, among other things, the period between the start of proceedings and first appearance in court. It does not cover judicial decisions.

Scotland

The High Court of Justiciary tries the most serious crimes and has exclusive jurisdiction in cases involving murder, treason and rape. The sheriff court is concerned with less serious offences and the district court with minor offences.

Criminal cases in Scotland are heard under solemn or summary procedure. In solemn procedure, the trial takes place before a judge sitting with a jury of 15 people. Details of the alleged offence are set out in a document called an indictment. In summary procedure the judge sits without a jury.

All cases in the High Court and the more serious ones in sheriff courts are tried by a judge and jury. Summary procedure is used in the less serious cases in the sheriff courts, and in all cases in the district courts. District court judges are lay justices of the peace. In Glasgow there are also stipendiary magistrates who are full-time lawyers with the same criminal jurisdiction in summary procedure as the sheriff.

Children under 16 who have committed an offence are normally dealt with by children's hearings (see p. 95).

The levels of service which citizens are entitled to expect from the main criminal justice agencies are set out in the Justice Charter for Scotland, published in 1991.

Northern Ireland

Cases involving minor summary offences are heard by magistrates' courts presided over by a full-time, legally qualified resident magistrate. Young offenders under 17 are dealt with by a juvenile court consisting of the resident magistrate and two specially qualified lay members (at least one of whom must be a woman).

The Crown Court deals with criminal trials on indictment. It is served by High Court and county court judges. Contested cases are heard by a judge and jury, although people charged with terrorist offences are tried by a judge sitting alone, because of the possibility of jurors being intimidated by terrorist organisations.

In non-jury Crown Court trials the onus remains on the prosecution to prove guilt beyond reasonable doubt and defendants have the right to be represented by a lawyer of their choice. The judge must set out in a written statement the reasons for convicting and there is an automatic right of appeal against conviction and sentence on points of fact as well as of law.

Trial

Criminal trials in Britain have two parties: the prosecution and the defence. The law presumes the innocence of an accused person until guilt has been proved by the prosecution. An accused person has the right to employ a legal adviser and may be granted legal aid from public funds (see p. 99). If remanded in custody, he or she may be visited by a legal adviser to ensure a properly prepared defence.

Disclosure to the Defence

The prosecution has a duty to disclose to the defence all information which might have some bearing on the case.

In England and Wales, where cases are to be tried in the Crown Court, the Crown Prosecution Service must also disclose all the statements from the prosecution witnesses upon whom it proposes to rely. This must be done before any committal proceedings begin. This duty does not apply to offences tried in the magistrates' court, except when advance information is requested by the defence in either way cases (see p. 84)—in practice, however, the CPS adopts a more generous approach than is strictly required.

The Royal Commission has recommended that the prosecution in England and Wales should generally supply to the defence all material relevant to the case and that procedures should be governed by codes of practice. The defence would have to disclose the substance of its case in advance of the trial.

The Commission has also suggested that there should be trial preparatory hearings before the jury is selected in order to clarify and define the issues in advance.

In Scottish solemn cases the prosecution must give the defence advance notice of the witnesses it intends to call and of the documents and other items on which it will rely. In summary cases this is usually done as a matter of practice, although there is no obligation on the Crown to do so.

Trial Procedure

Criminal trials normally take place in open court and rules of evidence, which are concerned with the proof of facts, are rigorously applied. If evidence is improperly admitted, a conviction can be quashed on appeal.

During the trial the defendant has the right to hear and cross-examine witnesses for the prosecution. He or she can call his or her own witnesses who, if they will not attend voluntarily, may be legally compelled to do so. The defendant can also address the court in person or through a lawyer, the defence having the right to the last speech before the judge sums up. The defendant cannot be questioned without consenting to be sworn as a witness in his or her own defence. When a defendant does testify, he or she may be cross-examined about character or other conduct only in exceptional circumstances. Generally the prosecution may not introduce such evidence.

In Scotland cross examination about the character or other conduct of the accused may be made in certain circumstances.

In Northern Ireland the judge can draw inferences from a refusal by a defendant to give evidence.

Child Witnesses

In England, Wales and Northern Ireland, child witnesses in cases involving offences of sex, violence or cruelty may now give evidence in Crown Court proceedings from outside the courtroom by means of a live television link. In this way the child need not see his or her alleged attacker in court. In Scotland similar provisions apply. A child's sworn statement no longer has to be corroborated by other evidence for the court to hear it.

The Criminal Justice Act 1991 extended the availability of the live television link to youth court proceedings, and made further reforms to the law of evidence and procedure relating to child witnesses in England and Wales. The presumption that young children are not competent to give evidence in criminal proceedings has effectively been removed, and video-recorded interviews have become admissible as the main evidence of a child witness.

Fraud Proceedings

In England, Wales and Northern Ireland the judge in complex fraud cases may order a preparatory open Crown Court hearing. This provides an opportunity for the judge to determine questions regarding admissibility of evidence and any other questions of law. The judge also has the power to order the prosecution and the defence to serve certain statements on each other and to prepare the case in such a way that it is easier to understand.

Appeals may be made to the Court of Appeal from decisions of the judge in the preparatory hearings. The law on evidence has been changed to enable courts to have before them a wider range of written evidence in the form of business documents. Information technology is increasingly used in complex cases to present the material to the jury in a more comprehensible form.

The Jury

In jury trials the judge decides questions of law, sums up the evidence for the jury, and discharges or sentences the accused. The jury is responsible for deciding questions of fact. In England, Wales and Northern Ireland the verdict may be 'guilty' or 'not guilty', the latter resulting in acquittal. If the jury cannot reach a unanimous decision the judge may allow a majority verdict provided that, in the normal jury of 12 people, there are no more than two dissenters.

In Scotland the jury's verdict may be 'guilty', 'not guilty' or 'not proven'; the accused is acquitted if either of the last two verdicts is given. The jury consists of 15 people and a verdict of 'guilty' can only be reached if at least eight members are in favour. As a general rule no one may be convicted without corroborated evidence from at least two sources.

If the jury acquits the defendant, the prosecution has no right of appeal and the defendant cannot be tried again for the same offence.

A jury is independent of the judiciary. Any attempt to interfere with a jury is a criminal offence. Potential jurors are put on a panel before the start of the trial. In England and Wales the prosecution and the defence may challenge individual jurors on the panel, giving reasons for doing so. In Scotland the prosecution or defence may challenge up to three jurors without reason. In Northern Ireland each defendant has the right to challenge up to 12 potential jurors without giving a reason.

People between the ages of 18 and 70 (65 in Scotland) whose names appear on the electoral register, with certain exceptions, are liable for jury service and their names are chosen at random. Ineligible people include, for example, judges and people who have within the previous ten years been members of the legal profession or the police, prison or probation services. People convicted of certain offences within the previous ten years cannot serve on a jury. Anyone who has received a prison sentence of five years or more is disqualified for life.

Sentencing

If a person is convicted, the magistrate or judge (or their Scottish equivalent) decides on the most appropriate sentence. Account is taken of the facts of the offence, the circumstances of the offender, any previous convictions or sentences and any statutory limits on sentencing. The defence lawyer may make a speech in mitigation.

Courts in England and Wales must obtain a 'pre-sentence' report from the probation service before imposing a custodial sentence or certain community sentences. This applies unless the offence is one which is triable only on indictment and the court considers it unnecessary to obtain such a report.

In Scottish cases where a custodial sentence may be imposed, it is mandatory for a court to obtain a pre-sentence report if the accused is under 21, has never served a custodial sentence or is a first offender. In other cases the judge decides whether to obtain such a report.

Appeals

England and Wales

A person convicted by a magistrates' court may appeal to the Crown Court against the sentence if he or she has pleaded guilty. An appeal may be made against both conviction and sentence if a 'not guilty' plea has been made. The Divisional Court of the Queen's Bench Division of the High Court hears appeals on points of law and procedure—by either prosecution or defence—in cases originally dealt with by magistrates. If convicted by the Crown Court, a defendant can appeal to the Court of Appeal (Criminal Division) against both the conviction and the sentence imposed. The House of Lords is the final appeal court, but it will only consider cases that involve a point of law of general public importance and where leave to appeal is granted.

The Home Secretary may consider representations and intervene in cases tried on indictment where appeal rights have been exhausted. This is normally done only if there is new evidence or some other consideration of substance which was not before the original trial court. In such cases the Home Secretary refers the matter to the Court of Appeal.

The Royal Commission has recommended that a new independent body should be set up to refer cases to the Court of Appeal. Its role would be to consider allegations of miscarriage of justice, launch a new investigation if necessary, supervise the investigation if conducted by the police and refer the case to the Court of Appeal if there were reasons for supposing that a miscarriage of justice had taken place.

The Attorney General may seek the opinion of the Court of Appeal on a point of law in a case where a person tried on indictment is acquitted. The Court has power to refer the point to the House of Lords if necessary. The acquittal in the original case is not affected.

The Attorney General may also refer a case to the Court of Appeal if he considers that a sentence passed by the Crown Court for an offence triable only on indictment is unduly lenient. If the Court of Appeal agrees, it may increase the sentence within the statutory maximum laid down by Parliament for the offence.

Scotland

All appeal cases are dealt with by the High Court of Justiciary and are heard by at least three judges. In both solemn and summary procedure, an appeal may be brought by the accused against conviction, or sentence, or both. The Court may authorise a retrial if it sets aside a conviction. There is no further appeal to the House of Lords. In summary proceedings the prosecutor may appeal on a point of law against acquittal or sentence. The Lord Advocate may seek the opinion of the High Court on a point of law in a case where a person tried on indictment is acquitted. The acquittal in the original case is not affected.

Northern Ireland

In Northern Ireland, appeals from magistrates' courts against conviction or sentence are heard by the county court. An appeal on a point of law alone can be heard by the Northern Ireland Court of Appeal, which also hears appeals from the Crown Court against conviction or sentence. Procedures for a further appeal to the House of Lords are similar to those in England and Wales.

A person convicted of a terrorist offence in a non-jury court has an automatic right of appeal against conviction and sentence.

Coroners' Courts

In England and Wales, the coroner must hold an inquest if the deceased died a violent or unnatural death, a sudden death where the cause is unknown, or in prison or in other specified circumstances. (In Northern Ireland the coroner investigates the matter to decide whether an inquest is necessary.) The coroner's court establishes how, when and where the deceased died. A coroner may sit alone or, in certain circumstances, with a jury.

In Scotland the local procurator fiscal inquires privately into all sudden and suspicious deaths and may report the findings to the Crown Office. In a minority of cases a fatal accident inquiry may be held before the sheriff; this is mandatory in cases of death resulting from industrial accidents and of deaths in custody.

TREATMENT OF OFFENDERS

The Government considers that offenders who commit very serious crimes, particularly crimes of violence, should receive long custodial sentences, but that many other crimes can best be punished within the community through compensation and reparation.

Legislation sets the maximum penalties for offences, the sentence being entirely a matter for the courts, subject to these maxima. The Court of Appeal in England and Wales issues guidance to the lower courts on sentencing issues when points of principle have arisen on individual cases which are the subject of appeal.

The Royal Commission, noting that people pleading guilty in the Crown Court have usually been given a reduction of 25 per cent to 30 per cent in their sentence, recommends that there should be a more open system of sentence discounts, with earlier guilty pleas attracting higher discounts.

In Scotland, where many offences are not created by statute, the penalty for offences at common law range from absolute discharge to life imprisonment.

Custody

England and Wales

The Government maintains that custody should be used for offenders convicted of serious criminal offences. The Court of Appeal requires sentencers in England and Wales to ensure that terms of custody are as short as possible, while remaining consistent with the courts' duty to protect the public and to punish the criminal.

The Criminal Justice Act 1991 requires a court in England and Wales to be satisfied that an offence merits custody. The court also has to give reasons if it considers a custodial sentence to be necessary. Longer custodial sentences—within the statutory maxima—are available for persistent violent and sexual offenders.

A magistrates' court in England and Wales cannot impose a term of more than six months' imprisonment for an individual offence tried summarily. It can impose consecutive sentences for 'either way' offences (see p. 84), subject to an overall maximum of 12 months' imprisonment. If an offence carries a higher maximum penalty, the court may commit the offender for sentence at the Crown Court. The Crown Court may impose a custodial sentence for any term up to life, depending on the gravity of the offence and the maximum penalty available.

If a court decides that an offence warrants an immediate custodial sentence of not more than two years, the sentence may be suspended for a period of at least one year and not more than two years; this occurs if exceptional circumstances justify the suspension. If the offender commits another imprisonable offence during the period of suspension, the court may order the suspended sentence to be served in addition to any punishment imposed for the second offence. When passing a suspended sentence, the court may consider the imposition of a fine or the making of a compensation order at the same time. The court may also order supervision of the offender by a probation officer if the suspended sentence is more than six months.

There is a mandatory sentence of life imprisonment for murder throughout Britain. Life imprisonment is the maximum penalty for a number of serious offences such as robbery, rape, arson and manslaughter.

Scotland and Northern Ireland

In Scottish trials on indictment the High Court of Justiciary may impose a sentence of imprisonment for any term up to life, and the sheriff court any term up to three years. The latter may send any person to the High Court for sentence if the court considers its powers are insufficient. In summary cases, the sheriff or stipendiary magistrate may normally impose up to three months' imprisonment or six months' for some repeated offences. The district court can impose a maximum term of imprisonment of 60 days.

In Northern Ireland the position is generally the same as for England and Wales. A magistrates' court, however, cannot commit an offender for sentencing at the Crown Court if it has tried the case.

Non-custodial Treatment

The Government believes that more offenders, particularly those convicted of property crimes and less serious cases of violence, should be punished in the community by:

- fines levied on the offender and compensation to the victim;
- probation;
- community service;
- a new combined order linking probation and community service; or
- a new curfew order to be used by itself or with other orders.

Fines

About 80 per cent of offenders are punished with a fine. There is no limit to the fine which the Crown Court (and High Court of Justiciary in Scotland) may impose on indictment. The Criminal Justice Act 1991 increased the maximum fine usually available on summary conviction from £2,000 to £5,000 in England and Wales. In fixing the amount of a fine, courts take into account the means of the offender.

Probation

The locally organised probation service in England and Wales supervises offenders in the community under direct court orders and after release from custody. It also provides offenders in custody with help and advice.

A court probation order can last between six months and three years; if the offender fails to comply with the order or commits another offence while on probation, he or she can be brought before the court again. A probation order can be combined with a community service order or a fine.

A probation order requires the offender to maintain regular contact with the probation officer. Special conditions attached to the order may require the offender to attend a day centre for up to 60 days. Although intended as a punishment, the time spent by offenders under supervision in the community offers an opportunity for constructive work to reduce the likelihood of reoffending.

In England and Wales the probation service also administers supervision orders, the community service scheme and supervises those released from prison on parole.

The statutory Probation Inspectorate monitors the work of the voluntary and private sectors with the probation service in addition to its inspection and advisory duties. National objectives for probation work are being introduced.

In Scotland local authority social work departments supervise offenders on probation and supervision orders or on parole.

In Northern Ireland the service is administered by a probation board, whose membership is representative of the community and which is funded by central government.

Community Service

Offenders aged 16 or over convicted of imprisonable offences may, with their consent, be given community service orders. The court may order between 40 and 240 hours' unpaid service to be completed within 12 months. Examples of work done include decorating the houses of elderly or disabled people and building adventure playgrounds.

National standards for community service orders ensure that all orders meet a common set of minimum requirements.

In England and Wales the court may make an order combining community service and probation. The maximum term for the probation element is the same as a probation order and the maximum period of community service is 100 hours.

Curfew Order

Courts in England and Wales can issue a curfew order confining offenders to their homes at certain times to prevent them going to places which may be associated with their offending. It may also be combined with probation, community service or the new combination order.

Compensation

The courts may order an offender to pay compensation for personal injury, loss or damage resulting from an offence. In England and Wales courts are required to give reasons for not awarding compensation to a victim. Compensation takes precedence over fines.

Other Measures

A court in England, Wales and Northern Ireland may discharge a person if it believes that punishment should not be inflicted and a probation order is not appropriate. If he or she is conditionally discharged, the offender remains liable to punishment for the offence if convicted of another offence within a period specified by the court (not more than three years).

The Crown Court may 'bind over' an offender by requiring him or her to keep the peace and/or be of good behaviour. If this requirement is not complied with, the offender may be brought before the court and dealt with for the original offence. Alternatively, a sum of money may be forfeited if conditions stated by the court are not met. Similar powers are available to courts in Northern Ireland.

In Scotland and Northern Ireland there is a system of deferral of sentence until a future date. During this period the accused is required to be of good behaviour and to meet any other conditions stipulated by the court. The court may also warn the offender or grant an absolute discharge.

Police cautions are used particularly for young offenders; the caution is a form of warning and no court action is taken.

Prisons

The Prison Service in England and Wales and the Scottish Prison Service became executive agencies in April 1993. Government ministers remain accountable for policy but the Chief Executives are responsible for the delivery of services.

> **The average prison population in 1992 was 44,718 in England and Wales, 1,810 in Northern Ireland, and 5,257 in Scotland.**

Prisoners may be housed in accommodation ranging from open prisons to high security establishments. In England, Scotland and Wales sentenced prisoners are classified into groups for security purposes. There are separate prisons for women. There are no open prisons in Northern Ireland, where the majority of offenders are serving sentences for terrorist offences. People awaiting trial in custody are entitled to privileges not granted to convicted prisoners. Those under 21 are, where possible, separated from convicted prisoners.

There are about 130 prison establishments in England and Wales and some 20 in Scotland, many of which were built in the 19th century. Improvements are in progress to eliminate cells without access to integral sanitation, while overcrowding is being relieved by a prison building programme.

In Northern Ireland there is no overcrowding in the four prisons and a young offenders' centre. Four of these establishments have been built since 1972.

White Paper on the Prison Service in England and Wales

Building on the recommendations of the Woolf Report on the 1990 prison disturbances, a White Paper published in 1991 set out a programme of reforms for the prison service in England and Wales. The aim is to provide a better prison system, with more effective measures for security and control, more constructive relationships between prisoners and staff, and more stimulating and useful programmes for prisoners.

Private Sector Involvement

Under the Criminal Justice Act 1991 the Home Secretary can contract out to the private sector the management of prisons in England and Wales, as well as escort and guarding functions. A new privately-run remand centre—the Wolds in Humberside—came into use in April 1992. Blakenhurst local prison in Worcestershire, also under private management, opened in May 1993.

A plan for more private sector involvement in the Prison Service was announced by the Government in September 1993. In the initial phase about 10 per cent of prisons in England and Wales (12 in total) will be managed by the private sector.

Early Release of Prisoners

The Criminal Justice Act 1991 has reformed the remission and parole systems in England and Wales, with new arrangements since October 1992 for the early release of prisoners and for their supervision and liabilities after release. The Parole Board continues to advise the Home Secretary on the early release or recall of long-term prisoners.

Prisoners serving terms of less than four years may be released once they have served half of their sentences in custody. Long-term prisoners (those serving more than four years) may be released once they have served two-thirds of their sentence; the Parole Board may release them on licence half-way through their sentence if they are serving between four and seven years. The Home Secretary has to give final consent to such parole if the prisoner is serving more than seven years. All prisoners sentenced to a year or more may be supervised on release until three-quarters of their sentence has passed. Certain sex offenders may be supervised to the end of their sentence.

If convicted of another offence punishable with imprisonment and committed before the end of the original sentence, a released prisoner may be liable to serve all or part of the original sentence outstanding at the time the fresh offence was committed. Similar changes have been adopted in Scotland.

Northern Ireland

In Northern Ireland prisoners serving a sentence of more than five days are eligible for remission of half their sentence. A prisoner serving a sentence of more than 12 months who is given remission is liable to be ordered to serve the remainder of this sentence if convicted of fresh imprisonable offences during this period.

Remission for those convicted of terrorist offences and serving sentences of five years or more is one-third. Any released prisoners convicted of another terrorist offence before the expiry of the original sentence must complete that sentence before serving any term for the second offence.

Life Sentence Prisoners

The Criminal Justice Act 1991 provides for the early release of prisoners serving life sentences for offences other than murder. The Home Secretary is required to release such prisoners after an initial period set by the trial judge if so directed by the Parole Board, which has to be satisfied that the protection of the public does not require their further confinement. These provisions conform with the requirements of the European Convention on Human Rights. Similar procedures have been adopted in Scotland.

People serving life sentences for the murder of police and prison officers, terrorist murders, murder by firearms in the course of robbery and the sexual or sadistic murder of children are normally detained for at least 20 years.

The release on licence of prisoners serving mandatory life sentences for murder may only be authorised by the Home Secretary on the recommendation of the Parole Board. A similar policy applies in Scotland. On release, life sentence prisoners remain on licence for the rest of their lives and are subject to recall if their behaviour suggests that they might again be a danger to the public.

In Northern Ireland the Secretary of State reviews life sentence cases on the recommendation of an internal review body.

At the end of 1991 there were about 3,100 life sentence prisoners in England and Wales, of whom about 376 had been detained for over 15 years.

Repatriation

Sentenced prisoners who are nationals of countries which have ratified the Council of Europe Convention on the Transfer of Sentenced Persons or similar international arrangements may apply to be returned to their own country to serve the rest of their sentence there.

Independent Oversight of the Prison System

Every prison establishment has a Board of Visitors—a Visiting Committee in Scotland— drawn from the local community. In order to see that prisoners are being treated fairly, members may go to any part of the prison and interview any inmate at any time.

The independent Prisons Inspectorates report on the treatment of prisoners and prison conditions. Each establishment is visited about every two years.

Prison Industries

Prison industries aim to give inmates work experience which will assist them when released and to secure a return which will reduce the cost of the prison system. The main industries are clothing and textile manufacture, engineering, woodwork, laundering, farming and horticulture. In England and Wales most production caters for internal needs and for other public services, whereas in Scotland a greater proportion is sold to the private sector. A few prisoners are employed outside prison, some in community service projects.

Prison Education

Full-time education of 15 hours a week is compulsory for young offenders below school leaving age. For older offenders it is voluntary. Some prisoners study for public examinations, including those of the Open University. Competitive tendering for the provision of education services in prisons is taking place and it is hoped that the award of contracts will be completed by January 1994. The Prison Service in England and Wales is placing increasing emphasis on the development and implementation of National Vocational Qualifications (see p. 415) for inmates. Similar moves are underway in Scotland.

All new prisons have purpose-built education units, and schemes to build new education accommodation or enhance existing facilities are also underway or planned at many other establishments.

Physical education is voluntary for adult offenders but compulsory for young offenders. Practically all prisons have physical education facilities, some of which are purpose-built. Opportunities are given for inmates to obtain proficiency awards issued by governing bodies of sport. Inmates also compete against teams in the local community.

Health Care

The Health Care Service for Prisoners in England and Wales is responsible for the physical and mental health of all those in custody. A Health Advisory Committee provides independent medical advice to government ministers, the Prison Service Chief Executive and the Director of Health Care.

In Scotland psychiatric and psychological services are bought in from local Health Boards responsible for the National Health Service. A review of medical services is taking place.

Privileges and Discipline

Prisoners may write and receive letters and be visited by relatives and friends, and those in some establishments may make telephone calls. Privileges include a personal radio, books, periodicals and newspapers, and the opportunity to make purchases from the canteen with money earned in prison. Depending on facilities, prisoners may be granted the further privileges of dining and recreation in association, and watching television.

Breaches of discipline are dealt with by the prison governor. A Prisons' Ombudsman for England and Wales is being appointed as a final appeal stage for prisoners' grievances and a code of standards governing conditions and facilities is being developed.

A new grievance procedure for prisoners in Scotland is under consideration.

Religion

Anglican, Church of Scotland, Roman Catholic and Methodist chaplains provide opportunities for worship and spiritual counselling. They are supported by visiting ministers of other denominations and faiths as required.

Preparation for Release

The Prison Service has a duty to prepare prisoners for release. Sentence planning is being extended progressively to all prisoners serving substantial sentences, in conjunction with extended arrangements for aftercare (see p. 94). Many medium- and long-term prisoners in the later parts of their sentences may be granted home leave for short periods.

The Pre-Release Employment Scheme in England and Wales and the Training for Freedom Scheme in Scotland enable selected long-term prisoners to spend their last six months before release in certain hostels attached to prisons, to help them re-adapt to society. Hostellers work in the outside community and return to the hostel each evening. Frequent weekend leave allows hostellers to renew ties with their families.

In Northern Ireland prisoners serving fixed sentences may have short periods of leave near the end of their sentences and at Christmas. Life-sentence prisoners are given a nine-month pre-release programme which includes employment outside the prison.

Aftercare

Professional support is given to offenders following their release. Most young offenders under the age of 22, adult offenders released early and those released on licence from a life sentence receive a period of compulsory supervision from the probation service or, in Scotland, local authority social work services.

Young Offenders

England and Wales

Criminal proceedings cannot be brought against children below the age of 10 years. Arrangements for dealing with young offenders above that age were amended by the Criminal Justice Act 1991. In addition, proposals to detain persistent 12- to 15-year-old offenders in secure training centres were announced by the Government in March 1993 (see below).

Since October 1992, 17-year-old offenders have fallen within the jurisdiction of youth courts (previously juvenile courts). Treated as a coherent group by the Act, 16- and 17-year-olds may be given the same probation,

93

curfew and community service orders as older offenders. Also available to the court are the same supervision orders or community sentences given to younger offenders.

Under a supervision order—which may remain in force for not more than three years —a child (10-13 years old) or young person (14-17 years old) normally lives at home under the supervision of a social worker or a probation officer. The order can be used to provide for remedial activities through a short residential course or, more usually, attendance at a day or evening centre.

Anyone under 21 years of age found guilty of an offence for which an adult may be imprisoned can be ordered to go to an attendance centre, as can an offender who refuses to comply with another order (for example, default in paying a fine or breach of a probation order). The maximum number of hours of attendance is 36 (or 24 if the offender is aged under 16) spread over a period; the minimum is 12 hours. The order aims to encourage offenders to make more constructive use of their leisure time.

A custodial sentence can be imposed on a young offender if this is necessary to protect the public from harm, or if the offence is so serious that it cannot justify a non-custodial sentence.

In the case of a very serious crime committed by a young person aged 17 or under, detention in a place approved by the Home Secretary may be ordered, and must be ordered in the case of murder. Detention may be in a secure local authority residential unit, a centre managed by the Youth Treatment Service or a young offender institution.

The custodial sentence for those aged 18-20 is also detention in a young offender institution. Alternatives include fines and compensation, attendance centre orders (for up to 36 hours) and community service orders (for between 40 and 240 hours).

The 1991 Act strengthened the courts' duty and powers to involve the parents of young offenders when their cases are heard. If the offender is under 16:

- the parents must attend the hearing unless there are exceptional circumstances;

- the court has to consider whether the parents should be bound over to exercise proper control of the child; and

- the court has to take account of the parents' means when assessing fines imposed on the offender.

Parents may be ordered to pay these fines.

In the case of 16- and 17-year-old offenders, the court's duty to involve parents is replaced by a power. Where local authorities have assumed parental responsibility, the duty to attend court and pay any fines also applies.

The 1991 legislation will allow the courts to send juveniles to secure local authority accommodation instead of adult prisons if they need to be held in secure conditions when awaiting trial or sentence.

Under the proposals announced in March 1993, courts would be able to impose a secure training order on 12- to 15-year-olds convicted of three imprisonable offences and not complying with the requirements of supervision in the community while on remand or under sentence. This proposal is designed to protect the public from persistent reoffending by such juveniles. Before making the order, the court would be required to take account of a pre-sentence report. The order could last for up to two years.

Scotland

Children under 16 who have committed an offence or are considered to be in need of care and protection may be brought before a children's panel, consisting of three lay people, which determines in an informal setting whether compulsory measures of care are required and, if so, the form they should take. An official known as the reporter decides whether a child should come before a hearing. If the grounds for referral are not accepted by the child or parent, the case goes to the sheriff for proof. If he finds the grounds established, the sheriff remits the case to the reporter to arrange a hearing. The sheriff also decides appeals against a hearing's decision.

Young people aged between 16 and 21 serve custodial sentences in a young offender institution. Remission of part of the sentence for good behaviour, release on parole and supervision on release are available.

Northern Ireland

Those aged between 10 and 16 who are charged with a criminal offence are normally brought before a juvenile court. If found guilty of an offence punishable in the case of an adult by imprisonment, the court may order the offender to be placed in care, under supervision or on probation. The offender may also be required to attend a day attendance centre, be sent to a training school or committed to residence in a remand home. Non-custodial options are the same as in England and Wales.

Offenders aged between 16 and 21 who receive custodial sentences of less than three years serve them in a young offenders' centre.

Civil Justice

The Civil Law

The civil law of England, Wales and Northern Ireland covers business related to the family, property, contracts and torts (non-contractual wrongful acts suffered by one person at the hands of another). It also includes constitutional, administrative, industrial, maritime and ecclesiastical law. Scottish civil law has its own, broadly similar, branches.

CIVIL COURTS

England and Wales

In October 1991 the civil jurisdiction of magistrates' courts was reorganised. They now have a concurrent jurisdiction with the county courts and the High Court in cases relating to children. The courts also have jurisdiction regarding public health and the recovery of local taxes.

The jurisdiction of the 270 county courts covers:

- actions founded upon contract and tort;
- trust and mortgage cases;
- actions for the recovery of land;
- cases involving disputes between landlords and tenants;
- complaints about race and sex discrimination;
- admiralty cases (maritime questions and offences) and patent cases; and
- divorce cases and other family matters.

Specialised work is concentrated in certain designated courts. In some types of cases, for example, admiralty cases, a county court is restricted to an upper financial limit. There are special arbitration facilities and simplified procedures for small claims not exceeding £1,000. There are also special care centres and family hearing centres which deal with contested family matters involving children.

The High Court, which is divided into three divisions, deals with the more complicated civil cases. Its jurisdiction covers mainly civil and some criminal cases; it also deals with appeals from tribunals and from magistrates' courts in both civil and criminal matters. The three divisions are:

- the Family Division, which is concerned with law affecting the family, including adoption and uncontested wills;
- the Chancery Division, which deals with corporate and personal insolvency; disputes in the running of companies, between landlords and tenants and in intellectual property matters; and the interpretation of trusts and contested wills; and
- the Queen's Bench Division, which is concerned with contract and tort cases, and deals with applications for judicial review. Maritime law and commercial law are the responsibility of the Division's admiralty and commercial courts.

In the event of overlapping jurisdiction between the High Court, the county courts and the magistrates' courts, cases of exceptional importance, complexity or financial substance are reserved or transferred for trial in the High Court.

Appeals

Appeals in matrimonial, adoption and guardianship proceedings heard by magistrates' courts go to the Family Division of the High Court. Since October 1991 appeals on child care cases have also been dealt with by the High Court. Appeals from the High Court and county courts are heard in the Court of Appeal (Civil Division), and may go on to the House of Lords.

The Law Lords deal with cases submitted to the House of Lords. They are professional judges who are given life peerages. In addition, peers who have held high judicial office are qualified to sit as Lords appeal judges. A group of five judges usually deals with cases. The Lord Chancellor is president of the House in its judicial capacity.

Scotland

The civil courts are the Court of Session and the sheriff court, which have the same jurisdiction over most civil litigation, although cases with a value of less than £1,500 are dealt with only by the sheriff court. Appeals from the sheriff court may be made to the sheriff principal or directly to the Court of Session in ordinary actions.

In summary actions (generally cases where the value of the claim is between £750 and £1,500) the case may be appealed to the sheriff principal on a point of law and to the Court of Session thereafter only if the sheriff principal certifies the case as suitable. In small claims (cases where the value of the claim does not exceed £750) there may be an appeal to the sheriff principal on a point of law.

The Court of Session sits in Edinburgh, and in general has jurisdiction to deal with all kinds of action. It is divided into the Outer House (a court of first instance) and the Inner House (mainly an appeal court). Appeals to the Inner House may be made from the Outer House and from the sheriff court. From the Inner House an appeal may go to the House of Lords.

The Scottish Land Court deals exclusively with matters concerning agriculture. Its chairman has the status and tenure of a judge of the Court of Session and its other members are lay specialists.

Northern Ireland

Civil cases up to the value of £10,000 are dealt with in county courts, although an increase to £15,000 is under consideration. The magistrates' court in Northern Ireland also deals with certain limited classes of civil case. The superior civil law court is the High Court of Justice, from which an appeal may be made to the Court of Appeal. The House of Lords is the final civil appeal court. Appeals from county courts are dealt with by the High Court or the Court of Appeal.

Civil Proceedings

England and Wales

Civil proceedings are started by the aggrieved person. Actions in the High Court are usually begun by a writ served on the defendant by the plaintiff, stating the nature of the claim. Before the case is set down for trial in the High Court, documents (pleadings) setting out the scope of the dispute are filed with the court; the pleadings are also served on the parties. County court proceedings are initiated by a summons, usually served on the defendant by the court. Child care cases are initiated by an application.

In order to encourage parties to confine the issues in dispute, the High Court and the county courts have power to order pre-trial exchange of witness statements. Courts may impose penalties in costs on parties who unreasonably refuse to admit facts or disclose documents before trial.

Civil proceedings, as a private matter, can usually be abandoned or ended by settlement between the parties at any time. Actions brought to court are usually tried without a jury, except in defamation, false imprisonment or malicious prosecution cases or where fraud is alleged, when either party may apply for trial by jury. The jury decides questions of fact and determines damages to be paid to the injured party; majority verdicts may be accepted. The Court of Appeal is able to increase or reduce damages awarded by a jury if it considers them inadequate or excessive.

A decree of divorce must be pronounced

in open court, but a procedure for most undefended cases dispenses with the need to give evidence in court and permits written evidence to be considered by the county court district judge.

In civil cases heard by a magistrates' court, the court issues a summons to the defendant setting out details of the complaint and the date on which it will be heard. Parties and witnesses give their evidence at the court hearing. Domestic proceedings are normally heard by not more than three lay justices, including, where practicable, a woman. Members of the public are not allowed to be present. The court may make orders concerning residence, contact and supervision of children, as well as maintenance payments for spouses and children.

The law has been changed recently to speed up civil proceedings in magistrates' courts by allowing written statements, expert opinions and hearsay evidence to be accepted in court without the presence of the witness, unless the evidence is disputed and the disputing party requests the presence of the witness.

Most judgments are for sums of money and may be enforced, in cases of non-payment, by seizure of the debtor's goods or by a court order requiring an employer to make periodic payments to the court by deduction from the debtor's earnings. Other court remedies may include an injunction restraining someone from performing an unlawful act. Refusal to obey a court order may result in imprisonment for contempt.

Normally the court orders the costs of an action to be paid by the party losing it, but, in the case of family law maintenance proceedings, a magistrates' court can order either party to pay the whole or part of the other's costs.

Scotland

Proceedings in the Court of Session or ordinary actions in the sheriff court are initiated by serving the defender with a summons (an initial writ in the sheriff court). A defender who intends to contest the action must inform the court; if he or she fails to do so, the court normally grants a decree in absence in favour of the pursuer. Where a case is contested, both parties must prepare written pleadings. Time is allowed for either party to adjust their pleadings in the light of what the other has said. At the end of this period a hearing will normally be arranged.

In summary cases (involving sums between £750 and £1,500) in the sheriff court a statement of claim is incorporated in the summons. The procedure is designed to enable most actions to be carried through without the parties involved having to appear in court. Normally they, or their representatives, need appear only when an action is defended.

Northern Ireland

There are differences between proceedings in Northern Ireland and in England and Wales —for example, procedures in the county court start with the issue of a civil bill, which is served by the plaintiff on the defendant.

Tribunals

Tribunals exercise separate judicial functions and tend to be more accessible, less formal and less expensive. They are normally set up under statutory powers, which also govern their constitution, functions and procedure. Tribunals often consist of lay people, but they are generally chaired by a legally qualified person.

Some tribunals decide disputes between private citizens. Industrial tribunals, for example, have a major role in employment disputes. Others, such as those concerned with social security, resolve claims by private citizens against public authorities. A further group (including tax tribunals) decide disputed claims by public authorities against private citizens. Tribunals usually consist of an uneven number of people so that a majority decision can be reached.

In the case of some tribunals a two-tier system operates, with an initial right of appeal to a lower tribunal and a further right of appeal, usually on a point of law, to a higher one and thence to the Court of Appeal. Appeals from single tier tribunals can be made on a point of law only to the High

Court in England and Wales, to the Court of Session in Scotland, and to the Court of Appeal in Northern Ireland.

The independent Council on Tribunals exercises general supervision over many tribunals. A Scottish Committee of the Council exercises the same function in Scotland.

Administration of the Law

GOVERNMENT RESPONSIBILITIES

England and Wales

The Lord Chancellor is the head of the judiciary and is responsible for the administration of all courts other than coroners' courts, and for a number of administrative tribunals. The highest judicial appointments are made by the Queen on the advice of the Prime Minister. The Lord Chancellor recommends all other judicial appointments to the Crown and appoints magistrates. He has general responsibility for the legal aid and advice schemes and for the administration of civil law reform.

The Home Secretary has overall responsibility for:

- criminal law;
- the police service;
- the prison system;
- the probation and after-care service; and
- advising the Queen on the exercise of the royal prerogative of mercy to pardon a person convicted of a crime or to remit all or part of a penalty imposed by a court.

The Attorney General and the Solicitor General are the Government's principal legal advisers and represent the Crown in appropriate domestic and international cases. They are senior barristers, elected members of the House of Commons and hold ministerial posts. The Attorney General is also Attorney General for Northern Ireland. As well as exercising various civil law functions, the Attorney General has final responsibility for enforcing the criminal law.

The Solicitor General is the Attorney's deputy. As head of the Crown Prosecution Service, the Director of Public Prosecutions is subject to superintendence by the Attorney General, as are the Director of the Serious Fraud Office and the Director of Public Prosecutions for Northern Ireland.

Scotland

The Scottish Secretary recommends the appointment of all judges other than the most senior ones, appoints the staff of the High Court of Justiciary and the Court of Session, and is responsible for the administration and staffing of the sheriff courts. (The district and islands local authorities are responsible for the district courts.)

The Scottish Secretary is also responsible for Scottish criminal law, crime prevention, the police, the penal system and legal aid; he or she is advised on parole matters by the Parole Board for Scotland.

The Lord Advocate and the Solicitor General for Scotland are the chief legal advisers to the Government on Scottish questions and the principal representatives of the Crown for the purposes of Scottish litigation. Both are government ministers.

Northern Ireland

Court administration is the responsibility of the Lord Chancellor, while the Northern Ireland Office, under the Secretary of State, deals with policy and legislation concerning criminal law, the police and the penal system. The Lord Chancellor has general responsibility for legal aid, advice and assistance.

THE PERSONNEL OF THE LAW

Judges, who are not subject to ministerial direction or control, are normally appointed from practising barristers, advocates (in Scotland), or solicitors (see below). Lay magistrates in England and Wales and Scottish district court justices are trained to give them sufficient knowledge of the law, including the rules of evidence, and of the nature and purpose of sentencing.

In Northern Ireland members of a lay panel who serve in juvenile courts undertake training courses; resident magistrates are drawn from practising solicitors or barristers.

The Legal Profession

The legal profession has two branches: barristers (advocates in Scotland) and solicitors. Solicitors undertake legal business for individual and corporate clients, while barristers advise on legal problems submitted through solicitors and present cases in the higher courts. Certain functions are common to both, for example, presentation of cases in the lower courts. Although people are free to conduct their own cases, most people prefer to be legally represented, especially in more serious cases.

Legislation in 1990 was designed to stimulate the development of good quality legal services for clients in Great Britain by lifting restrictions on who can provide these services. The Law Society, which represents solicitors in England and Wales, has applied to extend their rights of audience to the higher courts.

In Scotland, solicitor-advocates were introduced to the higher courts in May 1993. Before first appearing there, they have to complete satisfactorily the relevant examination and training requirements.

The 1990 legislation also contains provisions which would allow building societies, banks and other financial organisations to offer conveyancing and probate services under a scheme providing new safeguards to clients. People will also be able to negotiate a form of 'no win, no fee' agreement with their legal advisers in certain types of case in due course. The implementation of these provisions is subject to parliamentary approval.

Complaints systems against solicitors and barristers are backed up by the Legal Services Ombudsman for England and Wales, who conducts investigations into the way the professional bodies handle these complaints. There is a separate Ombudsman for Scotland.

LEGAL AID

A person needing legal advice or legal representation in court may qualify for help with the costs out of public funds, either free or with a contribution according to means.

Green Form Scheme

People whose income and savings are within certain limits are entitled to advice from a solicitor on legal matters.

In England and Wales the scheme provides for up to three hours' work for matrimonial cases where a petition is drafted and two hours' for other work. There are cost limits in Northern Ireland.

Legal Aid in Civil Proceedings

Civil legal aid, which covers representation before the court, may be available for most civil proceedings to those who satisfy the financial eligibility conditions. An applicant for legal aid must also show that he or she has reasonable grounds for taking or defending proceedings or being a party to proceedings. In England and Wales all payments to lawyers are made through the Legal Aid Fund administered by the Legal Aid Board. Legal aid in Northern Ireland is administered by the Law Society for Northern Ireland.

In certain limited circumstances the successful unassisted opponent of a legally aided party may recover his or her costs in the case from the Legal Aid Board. Where the assisted person recovers or preserves money or property in the proceedings, the Legal Aid Fund will usually have a first charge on that money or property to recover money spent on the assisted person's behalf.

Legal Aid in Criminal Proceedings

In criminal proceedings in England, Wales and Northern Ireland legal aid may be granted by the court if it appears to be in the interests of justice and if a defendant is considered to require financial assistance. A legal aid order must be granted (subject to means) when a person is committed for trial on a murder charge or where the prosecutor appeals or applies for leave to appeal from the Court of Appeal to the House of Lords. A financial contribution may be payable.

The Legal Aid Board in England and Wales makes arrangements for duty solicitors to assist unrepresented defendants in the magistrates' courts. Solicitors are available, on a 24-hour basis, to give advice and assistance to suspects at police stations. The services of a solicitor at a police station and of the duty solicitor at court are free.

In Northern Ireland a voluntary duty solicitor scheme has been introduced at the main magistrates' court in Belfast. Legal aid for criminal cases is free.

Scotland

A duty solicitor is available to represent people in custody on their first appearance in the sheriff courts and the district courts without enquiry into the person's means. In other cases, a person seeking legal aid in summary criminal proceedings must apply to the Scottish Legal Aid Board, which must be satisfied that the costs of the case cannot be met by the applicant without undue hardship, and that it is in the interests of justice that legal aid is awarded.

In solemn proceedings the court decides on the availability of legal aid and must be satisfied that the accused cannot meet the costs of the defence without undue financial hardship. Where legal aid is granted in criminal proceedings to the accused, he or she is not required to pay any contribution towards expenses.

Free Representation Units

The Bar Council, the barristers' professional body, runs free representation units in England and Wales for clients at a variety of tribunals for which legal aid is not available. Most of the representation in London is carried out by Bar students supported and advised by full-time case workers. Elsewhere the work is carried out by barristers.

Law Centres

In some urban areas law centres provide free legal advice and representation. Financed from various sources, often including local government authorities, they usually employ full-time salaried lawyers and many have community workers. Much of their time is devoted to housing, employment, social security and immigration problems.

Free advice is also available in Citizens Advice Bureaux, consumer and housing advice centres and in specialist advice centres run by voluntary organisations.

Further Reading

Britain's Legal Systems. Aspects of Britain series, HMSO, 1993.
Criminal Justice. Aspects of Britain series, HMSO, 1992.
Report of the Royal Commission on Criminal Justice. HMSO, 1993.

Economic Affairs

9 National Economy

From 1981 to 1989 the British economy experienced eight years of sustained growth at an annual average rate of over 3 per cent. However, subsequently Britain and other major industrialised nations were severely affected by recession. In Britain growth slowed to 0.6 per cent in 1990, and in 1991 gross domestic product (GDP) fell by 2.3 per cent. GDP fell in 1992 as a whole by 0.4 per cent, but it rose slightly in the second half of the year. The recovery strengthened during the first part of 1993, with GDP in the second quarter being 2 per cent higher than a year earlier; the European Commission expects Britain to be the fastest growing of all the major European economies in 1993 and 1994.

Recent indications that the recovery is under way include:

- an increase in manufacturing output;
- a steady upward trend in retail sales;
- increases in new car registrations;
- record levels of exports (see p. 106);
- increased business and consumer confidence; and
- signs of greater activity in the housing market.

The economy is now benefiting from substantially lower interest rates. In September 1993 base interest rates were at 6 per cent. They had been cut by 9 percentage points since October 1990, and were at their lowest since 1977.

ECONOMIC BACKGROUND

The economy is primarily based on private enterprise, and government policy is aimed at

Table 9.1: Economic Indicators

	1982	1987	1992
Gross domestic product[a]	425,252	511,615	536,260
Exports[a]	94,996	120,607	135,457
Imports[a]	88,146	122,075	148,271
Consumers' expenditure[a]	249,852	311,234	339,941
Gross domestic fixed capital formation[a]	68,404	92,260	95,241
Percentage increase in Retail Prices Index	n.a.	4.2	3.7
Workforce in employment (000s)	n.a.	25,084	25,444
Percentage of workforce unemployed	n.a.	10.0	9.8

Sources: *United Kingdom National Accounts 1993 Edition; Economic Trends; Employment Gazette.*
[a] £ million at 1990 market prices.
n.a. = not available.

encouraging and expanding the private sector, which accounts for about 80 per cent of total output in the whole economy and around three-quarters of total employment.

Values for some of the main economic indicators in selected years since 1982 are shown in Table 9.1. For further information see the Statistical Annex on pp. 505–7.

Inflation

During most of the 1950s and the 1960s the inflation rate in Britain rarely rose above 5 per cent. However, in 1971 inflation reached double figures, climbing to 27 per cent in 1975. Contributory factors included oil price rises in 1973 and increases in the money supply and public spending. Inflation fell in the early 1980s and stayed low for a number of years. However, it picked up towards the end of the decade and the annual rate rose to 10.9 per cent in September and October 1990.

Since this peak, inflation has fallen substantially. In August 1993 the standard Retail Prices Index (RPI)—which measures the change in the price of goods and services purchased by households in Britain—had been below 2 per cent for eight consecutive months, a performance not achieved since 1960. It has been below the European Community average since August 1991.

Inflation, as measured by the RPI, reached 1.2 per cent in June 1993. This was the lowest rate since February 1964.

Excluding mortgage interest payments, the annual rate of inflation was 2.8 per cent in June 1993. This was the lowest annual rate for this series, which began in 1975. Latest figures remain well within the target range of 1 to 4 per cent set by the Government.

Costs have been falling in a number of areas:

- unit wage costs in manufacturing have been falling, and the reduction in the three months to March 1993 was the largest since records began in 1970;

- the underlying increase in average earnings has declined considerably and in the year to July 1993 was 3.5 per cent, the lowest since 1967.

Output

After the oil price rises of 1973–74, manufacturing output dropped sharply. It later increased from this trough, but in the wake of another oil price rise and stagnation in the world economy, it fell back again in the late 1970s and early 1980s. A period of steady growth occurred until 1990, but output fell significantly during the recent recession. Indications are that output is now recovering, both for the economy as a whole and for manufacturing.

Largely as a result of exploitation of North Sea oil and gas, energy output in 1986 was about twice the level of ten years earlier. Oil output has now passed its peak of the mid-1980s and has since fallen back by about 23 per cent. Oil output recovered strongly in the second half of 1992 and rose by 3.3 per cent in 1992.

Only 1 per cent of Britain's workforce is engaged in agriculture, a lower proportion than in any other major industrialised country. However, Britain manages to produce over half of its own food.

Recent decades have generally seen the fastest growth in the services sector. Services account for around two-thirds of GDP and of employment, compared with about half of GDP in 1950. Manufacturing contributes less than a quarter of GDP, compared with over a third in 1950. Table 9.2 compares output and employment in 1991 and 1992.

Productivity

Growth in manufacturing productivity in Britain in the 1980s was faster than in all other leading industrialised countries. Between 1980 and 1990 manufacturing productivity in Britain grew by an average of 4.7 per cent a year. Productivity in the economy as a whole fell very slightly in 1990. However, it has been rising since the start of 1991, reflecting the decline in employment relative to output. In 1992 it rose by 2.3 per cent. Manufacturing productivity has been growing at a higher rate, and in the three

Table 9.2: Output and Employment (Indices: 1990 = 100)

	Output		Employment[a]	
	Index 1991	Index 1992	Index 1991	Index 1992
Agriculture, forestry and fishing	103.9	106.0	96.8	93.9
Production industries	96.0	95.6	92.5	88.2
of which: Electricity, gas and water	105.9	105.4	98.6	93.0
Mining and quarrying	101.0	104.2	95.5	83.4
Manufacturing	94.7	93.9	92.1	88.0
Construction	92.1	87.1	91.0	83.8
Services	98.8	98.7	99.0	98.4
GDP	97.7	97.2		
Employees in employment			97.0	95.2

Sources: *United Kingdom National Accounts 1993 Edition* and *Employment Gazette*.
[a]Employment figures relate to Great Britain and cover employees in employment at June. Figures for construction and services in 1991 and 1992 are not strictly comparable, owing to a change in classification of employees.

months to June 1993 was 8.2 per cent higher than in the same period of 1992.

Investment

From 1983 until 1989 fixed investment increased by about 9 per cent a year on average, with particularly rapid growth of over 10 per cent a year occurring between 1986 and 1988. With the recession, investment declined between 1990 and 1992, but there are now indications of higher investment. Over the decade 1980–90 the private sector's share of fixed investment grew from 70 to 84 per cent, due in part to privatisation (see pp. 143-4). Over the same period there was a rise in the share of investment undertaken by the services sector and a fall in that carried out by manufacturing.

An improvement in the quality of investment contributed to the rise in the late 1980s in the net real rate of return on capital employed in non-North Sea industrial and commercial companies. Profitability declined in 1990 and 1991, but there was a recovery in 1992 when net profitability amounted to 7 per cent. Table 9.3 shows investment by industrial sector.

Employment

Britain's workforce in employment increased by 3.3 million in the seven years to June

Table 9.3: Gross Domestic Fixed Capital Formation (Investment) by Sector 1992

	£ million at market prices	£ million at 1990 prices	Index at 1990 prices (1990 = 100)
Agriculture, hunting, forestry and fishing	1,040	1,057	77.3
Mining and quarrying, including oil and gas extraction	5,751	6,256	133.1
Electricity, gas and water	6,349	6,520	137.5
Manufacturing	12,485	11,907	83.7
Construction and services	46,498	48,518	85.5
Dwellings	17,714	17,405	83.9
Transfer costs	3,055	3,578	84.1
Whole economy	**92,892**	**95,241**	**89.2**

Source: *United Kingdom National Accounts 1993 Edition*.

1990, reaching 26.9 million. It has subsequently declined and in June 1993 amounted to 24.9 million. Nevertheless, Britain has a higher proportion of the population of working age in employment than other EC countries except Denmark. From 1979 to 1990 self-employment rose every year, but between June 1991 and June 1993 it dropped by 320,000 to 3 million.

As in other industrialised countries, there is serious concern about unemployment. Seasonally adjusted unemployment rose to just under 3 million at the start of 1993. However, unemployment is now at a slightly lower level: by August 1993 it was 2.9 million —10.4 per cent of the workforce.

Overseas Trade

Britain has an open economy in which international trade plays a vital part. The proportion of GDP accounted for by exports of goods and services has increased from around one-fifth in the early 1960s to about a quarter. Similar rises have occurred in most other developed countries, reflecting the growing importance of international trade in an increasingly interdependent world economy.

Britain is a major exporter of aerospace products, electrical and electronic equipment, chemicals, oil and many types of machinery. It is also one of the world's largest importers of agricultural products, raw materials and semi-manufactures. For the last ten years Britain has had a deficit on visible trade. This rose to some £13,000 million in 1992, reflecting a higher rise in the volume of imports than of exports and also short-run adverse effects as import prices rose faster than export prices following the depreciation of sterling. However, exports were running at record levels and were rising more strongly than imports towards the end of 1992.

Substantial net earnings on invisible transactions kept the current account of the balance of payments[1] in surplus in most years up to 1986, but it has been in deficit since then. The contribution made by invisibles to the current account partly reflects Britain's position as a major financial centre. The surplus on invisibles was nearly £4,800 million in 1992, although this is still at a lower level than in the mid-1980s. Britain's invisibles account has been affected by the abolition of exchange controls in 1979 and the growth in world markets for insurance, banking, tourism, consultancy and other services. In 1992 exports of services were valued at around 30 per cent of exports of goods.

Membership of the EC has had a major impact on Britain's pattern of trade, increasing the proportion of trade with other member countries. Between 1972 and 1992 the share of Britain's exports of goods going to other members of the Community rose from 33 to 56 per cent. Imports followed a similar trend, growing from 36 to 53 per cent. Trade with Japan and with the newly industrialised countries, including Singapore, Korea, Taiwan and Malaysia, has also risen significantly.

Inward Investment

Britain is recognised as an attractive location for inward direct investment and some 13,000 overseas companies are currently operating in Britain. This reflects its membership of the EC and proximity to other European markets, its stable labour relations and comparatively low personal and corporate taxation. Overseas-owned firms are offered the same incentives as British-owned ones.

Britain attracts about a third of all inward investment in the European Community. At the end of 1992 total United States direct investment in Britain was valued at US$77,800 million, representing about two-fifths of US investment in the EC. Britain has for many years been the leading destination for US manufacturing investment in Europe. It also has around two-fifths of Japanese manufacturing investment in the EC.

Energy

With the exploitation of oil and natural gas from the Continental Shelf under the North

---

[1] For further information on trade and the balance of payments see Chapter 15, Overseas Trade.

Sea, Britain is self-sufficient in energy in net terms and expects to remain so for some years. In 1992 it was the world's ninth largest oil producer and the extraction of oil and gas accounted for some 4 per cent of GDP, while crude oil and petroleum products accounted for 6.4 per cent of visible exports.

The benefits to the balance of payments began to appear in the second half of the 1970s and in 1980 Britain had its first surplus on oil trade. The oil surplus reached its peak in 1985, at £8,100 million. With the reduction in oil prices the surplus has fallen and amounted to some £1,500 million in 1992. Exports, mainly to other EC countries, are equivalent to well over half of domestic oil production. They are partly offset in balance-of-payments terms by imports of other grades of crude oil from the Middle East and elsewhere.

ECONOMIC STRATEGY

The Government's policy is to ensure sustainable economic growth through low inflation and sound public finances. Following the suspension in September 1992 of sterling's membership of the exchange rate mechanism (ERM) of the European Monetary System, the Government set out a new policy framework for its counter-inflation strategy. This includes a target of keeping underlying inflation—as measured by the RPI excluding mortgage interest payments—between 1 and 4 per cent, and of bringing it down to the lower part of this range by the end of the present Parliament.

The Government's economic policy is set in the context of a medium-term financial strategy, which is reviewed each year. Within this strategy, monetary and fiscal policies are designed to defeat inflation. Short-term interest rates remain the essential instrument of monetary policy. Fiscal policy is set over a medium-term horizon to support monetary policy.

Macroeconomic policy is directed towards keeping down the rate of inflation as the basis for sustainable growth, while microeconomic policies seek to improve the working of markets and encourage enterprise, efficiency and flexibility through measures such as

privatisation, deregulation and tax reforms (see below).

Monetary Policy

Monetary policy is aimed at achieving the Government's objectives for inflation. The main instrument of monetary policy is the use of market operations to raise or lower interest rates as appropriate to the Government's assessment of inflationary trends in the economy.

In assessing the overall stance of monetary conditions, the Government has set monitoring ranges for the monetary aggregates M0 and M4.[2] For example, narrow money, as measured by M0, has a monitoring range of 0 to 4 per cent in 1993–94 and in the medium term broad money (M4) has a monitoring range of 3 to 9 per cent. The Government also pays attention to a range of indicators including the exchange rate index and changes in asset prices (especially house prices).

The Government's view is that re-entry into the ERM cannot be considered until there has been greater convergence between the monetary policy requirements of all EC economies and the Government is satisfied that the system will be operated to the benefit of all its members. It believes that these conditions are unlikely to apply for some years.

Fiscal Policy

The objectives of the Government's fiscal policy are to ensure sound public finances, return the budget towards balance over the medium term, and reduce the share of public expenditure in national income. The deficit is expected to fall as the economy recovers, and the tax measures in the March 1993 Budget and tight control of public expenditure will reinforce this trend.

Within the overall policy of moving towards a balanced budget over the medium

---

[2] M0 is notes and cash in circulation with the public and banks' holdings of cash and their operational balances at the Bank of England. M4 is notes and cash in circulation with the public, together with all sterling deposits held with banks and building societies by the rest of the private sector.

term, the Government aims to reduce taxes when possible so as to leave people with more of their own money. The basic rate of income tax has been cut from 33 to 25 per cent, and in the 1992 Budget the Government introduced a new lower rate of income tax of 20 per cent on the first £2,000 of taxable income (£2,500 from 1993–94).

In line with the Government's policy, the ratio of general government expenditure, excluding privatisation proceeds, to GDP fell from 47.5 per cent in 1982–83 to 42 per cent in 1991–92. However, recently the ratio has risen, due mainly to the impact of the recession. The Public Sector Borrowing Requirement (PSBR) has also grown since 1989–90 largely as a result of the recession, and in 1993–94 is expected to peak at about 8 per cent of GDP. However, the PSBR is expected to fall as the economy recovers and as revenue-raising measures announced in the March 1993 Budget begin to take effect.

Supply-side Policies

While macroeconomic policy is directed towards ensuring sustainable growth through low inflation and sound public finances, the Government has sought to improve the supply response, and thus the efficiency, of the economy through microeconomic policies. Action has been taken to expose more of the economy to market forces. Direct controls—for example, on pay, prices, foreign exchange, dividend payments and commercial credit—have been abolished and competition in domestic markets strengthened.

Steps have been taken to reduce regulatory burdens on business and to reduce the number of administrative obstacles facing small firms and the self-employed. Government support to industry has become more selective. Where there is evidence of market failure, particular efforts have been made to improve the flow of investment funds to small firms, assist innovation in industry and attract industry to the inner cities. Measures have been implemented to encourage saving and share ownership.

A substantial amount of activity has been transferred from the public sector to the private sector by privatisation and contracting out. In addition, the Government is seeking greater efficiency in the public sector through market testing; it aims to have tested about £1,500 million of public sector activities by September 1993. Efforts have also been made to improve value for money in the public sector by, for example, transferring many of the executive functions of government to new executive agencies.

Labour Market

The Government has sought to improve work incentives by reducing personal income tax rates, raising tax thresholds and reforming the benefits system. It has also, through the tax system, encouraged the extension of share ownership among employees. A scheme of income tax relief has been introduced to encourage the spread of profit-related pay. The Government has taken steps to achieve a more balanced legal framework for industrial relations. It has expanded training opportunities and put in place a new training framework, with a greater role for employers, so that training better reflects local needs.[3]

Obstacles to the mobility of labour have been reduced. For example, the rights of those leaving occupational pension schemes early have been improved and new arrangements for personal pensions introduced; both of these changes will reduce the pension disadvantage of changing jobs. Reforms in the housing market have been introduced to make it easier for people to move house.

Economic Management

HM Treasury has prime responsibility for the formulation and conduct of economic policy, which it carries out in conjunction with the Bank of England (the central bank) and the Departments of Trade and Industry, Employment, the Environment, Transport, and the Ministry of Agriculture, Fisheries and Food.

---

[3] For further information see Chapter 11, Employment.

Table 9.4: Gross Domestic Product, Gross National Product and National Income

	£ million 1982	£ million 1992
Total final expenditure	347,343	745,801
less imports of goods and services	−67,762	−149,164
GDP at market prices	279,041	596,165
plus net property income from abroad	1,460	5,777
Gross national product at market prices	280,501	601,942
less factor cost adjustment (taxes less subsidies)	−40,656	−81,571
GDP at factor cost	238,385	514,594
Net property income from abroad	1,460	5,777
Gross national product at factor cost	239,845	520,371
less capital consumption	−33,653	−63,984
National income (net national product at factor cost)	206,192	456,387

Source: *United Kingdom National Accounts 1993 Edition.*
Note: Differences between totals and the sums of their component parts are due to rounding.

A number of other bodies deal with specific aspects of economic policy and the regulation of certain sectors of the economy. These include bodies such as the Office of Fair Trading and the Monopolies and Mergers Commission.

On major matters of public policy, such as the broad economic strategy, and on the economic problems it faces, the Government makes known its policies and keeps in touch with developments throughout the economy by means of informal and continuous links with the chief industrial, financial and other interests. Final responsibility for the broad lines of economic policy rests with the Cabinet.

To assist in the process of economic forecasting, the Government announced in October 1992 the establishment of a Panel of Independent Forecasters. The Panel publishes a full range of forecasts on the main economic indicators.

NATIONAL INCOME AND EXPENDITURE

The value of all goods and services produced in the economy is measured by gross domestic product. This may be expressed either in terms of market prices (the prices people pay for the goods and services they buy) or at factor cost (the cost of the goods and services before adding taxes and subtracting subsidies). It can also be expressed in current prices or in constant prices (that is, removing the effects of inflation to measure the volume of growth in the economy). In 1992 GDP at current factor

Table 9.5: Total Final Expenditure in 1992 at Market Prices

	£ million	per cent
Consumers' expenditure	382,696	51.3
General government final consumption	132,378	17.7
Gross domestic fixed capital formation	92,892	12.5
Value of physical increase in stocks and work in progress	−1,992	−0.3
Total domestic expenditure	605,974	81.3
Exports of goods and services	139,827	18.7
Total final expenditure	**745,801**	**100.0**

Source: *United Kingdom National Accounts 1993 Edition.*
Note: Differences between totals and the sums of their component parts are due to rounding.

cost totalled £514,594 million. Between 1982 and 1992 the index of GDP at constant factor cost increased by some 26 per cent.

Table 9.4 gives figures for GDP, at both current market prices and current factor cost. It also shows the components of two other main aggregates, gross national product and national income.

Table 9.5 shows the categories of total final expenditure in 1992. Consumers' expenditure accounted for one-half of total final expenditure, and exports of goods and services for nearly one-fifth.

Personal Incomes and Expenditure

Personal disposable income consists of personal incomes after deductions—mainly taxation and social security contributions. This rose fairly steadily from £190,976 million in 1982 to £437,463 million in 1992. Personal disposable income in 1992 was 2.7 per cent higher in real terms than in 1991. Consumers' expenditure amounted to 69.5 per cent of pre-tax personal income in 1992, compared with 70.7 per cent in 1991.

Table 9.6 shows the changing pattern of consumers' expenditure. Housing, food, alcoholic drink, clothing and footwear, and fuel and power together accounted for 43 per cent of the total in 1992. The changes in the pattern between 1982 and 1992 in Britain were paralleled in other industrialised countries, with declining proportions being spent on food, tobacco, clothing and footwear, and fuel and power. Over the longer term, as incomes rise, people tend to spend increasing proportions on services. Spending on leisure pursuits and tourism, health and financial services have all shown significant growth in recent years. Consumers' expenditure fell by 2 per cent in real terms between 1990 and 1991, following a long upward trend, and was virtually unchanged in 1992.

The ratio of savings to personal disposable income declined substantially during the 1980s, from a peak of 13.4 per cent in 1980 to 5.7 per cent in 1988. However, the savings ratio has more than doubled since 1988, reaching 12.5 per cent in 1992, reflecting a number of factors such as the recession, and government measures to encourage saving.

Sources of Income

The proportion of total personal pre-tax income accounted for by income from employment was 62 per cent in 1992; average gross weekly earnings in April 1993 in Great

Table 9.6: Consumers' Expenditure in 1982 and 1992 at Market Prices

	1982	1992	
	per cent	per cent	£ million
Food (household expenditure)	15.6	11.8	45,264
Alcoholic drink	7.1	6.4	24,612
Tobacco	3.5	2.6	10,104
Clothing and footwear	6.5	5.6	21,246
Housing	15.4	15.1	57,598
Fuel and power	5.1	3.8	14,404
Household goods and services	6.6	6.3	24,266
Transport and communications	17.0	16.8	64,358
Recreation, entertainment and education	9.2	9.8	37,674
Other goods	3.1	3.7	14,215
Other services	9.7	15.5	59,327
Other items[a]	1.3	2.5	9,628
Total	100.0	100.0	382,696

Source: *United Kingdom National Accounts 1993 Edition.*
[a] Household expenditure overseas plus final expenditure by private non-profit-making bodies, minus expenditure by foreign tourists in Britain.
Note: Differences between totals and the sums of their component parts are due to rounding.

Britain were £354 for full-time male workers and £253 for full-time female workers. The three other main sources of personal income were self-employment (11 per cent), rent, dividends and interest (13 per cent), and social security benefits and other current grants from government (14 per cent).

Current Government Expenditure

Final consumption by central government and local authorities amounted to £132,378 million in 1992; it rose by 14 per cent in real terms over the period 1982 to 1992. The main cause of this was the growth over the period in spending on the social services, health, and law and order.

In addition to their expenditure on goods and services, public authorities transfer large sums to other sectors, mainly the personal sector, in National Insurance and other social security benefits, grants, and interest and subsidies. Central government also makes grants to local authorities to finance a proportion of their current expenditure (about 85 per cent in 1992–93).

Further Reading

Financial Statement and Budget Report 1993–94. HMSO.
United Kingdom National Accounts 1993 Edition. HMSO.

10 Public Finance

The Government's policy is to maintain tight control on public expenditure. Its programme of tax reform has sought to create a climate in which business can thrive and individual initiative is rewarded. Plans for taxation and public expenditure will in future be announced together. The first unified Budget will be in November 1993.

INTRODUCTION

Public finance is concerned with taxation, expenditure and borrowing or debt repayment by central and local government; management of the public sector's assets and liabilities; and the financing of public corporations.

Central government raises money from individuals and companies by direct and indirect taxation and from National Insurance contributions. It spends money on goods and services, such as health and defence, and in payments to people, for instance, social security and pensions.

Local government raises revenue mainly through the new council tax, introduced in April 1993, and other taxes levied on domestic and business properties. The council tax has not been introduced in Northern Ireland, where domestic rates remain in operation. Local government provides services such as education, police and fire services, and refuse collection.

The diagram on p. 119 shows the relative importance of the various items of receipts, including borrowing, and expenditure for general government.

The government department responsible for broad control of public finance and expenditure is HM Treasury. The Bank of England—the central bank—advises the Government on financial matters, executes monetary policy and acts as banker to the Government.

PUBLIC EXPENDITURE

The three main definitions of public expenditure are general government expenditure, the 'new control total' and Supply expenditure.

General Government Expenditure

General government expenditure is the spending of central and local government, excluding transfers between them such as central government grants to local authorities. It is the key public spending aggregate and is used in the medium-term financial strategy (see p. 113), where public spending is set in the context of broader economic policy. As it is usually less affected by institutional differences, it is the most appropriate measure for making international comparisons.

New Control Total

The new control total is used by the Government for the purposes of planning and control. The Government seeks to achieve its wider medium-term objective—expressed in terms of general government expenditure—by controlling spending within this total. The new control total covers:

- expenditure for which central government is itself responsible;
- the support it provides or approves for local authority expenditure;
- local authority self-financed expenditure;
- the external financing requirements of public corporations, including nationalised industries; and
- a reserve to cover unanticipated expenditure.

It excludes the items of expenditure most affected by the economic cycle—debt interest and cyclical social security. By excluding these items, the Government is able to set firm limits on the growth of the new control total.

Supply Expenditure

Supply expenditure is financed out of money voted by Parliament in the Supply Estimates (see p. 115). More than four-fifths of all Supply expenditure counts in the new control total. The main element of the new control total not funded through Supply Estimates is expenditure financed from the National Insurance Fund.

Medium-term Financial Strategy

The background to the Government's planning of public expenditure is the medium-term financial strategy, which provides a framework for monetary and fiscal policy. The central objective of the strategy is to achieve sustainable economic growth based on permanently low inflation. Public expenditure (measured by general government expenditure, excluding privatisation proceeds) is expected to grow by less than the economy as a whole over time, and to provide constantly improving value for money.

General government expenditure (excluding privatisation proceeds), as a proportion of gross domestic product (GDP), fell from over 47 per cent in 1982–83 to under 40 per cent in 1989–90. Since then, recession has pushed up the ratio, which is projected to peak at 45.5 per cent in 1993–94 before resuming a downward path. For 1993–94 taxes and social security contributions are forecast to amount to 34.5 per cent of GDP.

Between 1987–88 and 1990–91 the public sector was in surplus so that the Government repaid debt. Following a Public Sector Borrowing Requirement (PSBR) of £13,800 million—2.4 per cent of GDP—in 1991–92, the PSBR for 1992–93 rose to £36,700 million—5.75 per cent of GDP—largely reflecting the impact of the recession. Even with economic recovery, the Government expects that the recession will continue to affect public finances for a while and it forecasts a PSBR of £50,000 million—8 per cent of GDP—for 1993–94.

The Government's objective is to bring the PSBR back towards balance over the medium term. Tight control over public expenditure and fiscal measures announced in the March 1993 Budget are intended to reinforce the tendency of the PSBR to fall as the economy recovers.

Public Expenditure Control

In 1992 the Government announced a new system of public expenditure control to ensure that the share of national income taken by public spending will fall over time. Annual ceilings are set for the growth of the new control total, in line with the Government's medium-term objectives. By restricting real growth in the new control total to below 1.5 per cent, the Government will ensure that the ratio of general government expenditure to national income falls over time.

This 'top-down' approach separates decisions on overall public expenditure levels from the allocation between programmes. Departmental spending decisions are based on allocating available resources within agreed ceilings for aggregate spending; resources are devoted to priority areas, with an emphasis on obtaining maximum value for money. Together with the move to a unified budget (see below), the new framework represents an important reform of fiscal planning procedures. In addition, a more fundamental examination of spending programmes has been started, which is intended to ensure better targeting of public expenditure and to identify areas where expenditure may no longer be appropriate. This process started in 1993–94 with four of the larger programmes: education, health, Home Office and social security.

Table 10.1 gives projections for government expenditure and receipts and the borrowing requirement for 1993–94 and 1994–95.

Planning Cycle

Each year the Government conducts a review of its spending plans for the forthcoming three years, known as the 'Public Expenditure Survey'. The plans agreed in the Survey have in recent years been announced by the Chancellor of the Exchequer in the Autumn Statement, usually in November. More detailed analyses are published in the following January or February in a Statistical Supplement and in individual departmental reports. In March or April the Chancellor has presented his taxation proposals and forecast for the economy in the Budget (see p. 116). Revenue and expenditure have been brought together in the Financial Statement and Budget Report issued on the day of the Budget.

The Chancellor announced that from November 1993 the Government would present taxation and spending proposals to Parliament at the same time to allow comparison. The Budget would, therefore, cover both the Government's taxation plans for the coming financial year and its spending plans for the next three years. It would also give a review of recent developments in the economy, an economic forecast and a statement of the Government's medium-term financial strategy (see p. 113). The Government would publish a second short-term economic forecast in the summer. The Finance Bill, with details of the taxation changes, would be published in January for parliamentary consideration.

Public Expenditure Totals

Public expenditure is analysed in Table 10.2. The largest departmental programmes are:

- the Department of Social Security (35.5 per cent of central government expenditure in 1992–93);
- the Department of Health (17.6 per cent); and
- the Ministry of Defence (15 per cent).

About 85 per cent of local authority spending is financed by grants from central government. The rest is met from the council tax, domestic rates and business rates, surpluses on trading, rents and borrowing. Education accounts for about two-fifths of local authority spending; law and order, housing and other environmental services, personal social services, social security, and roads and transport take up most of the remainder.

Table 10.1: Projected Public Expenditure, Receipts and Borrowing Requirement

£ thousand million

	1993–94	1994–95
General government expenditure	280	296
of which: public expenditure control total	*244*	*254*
General government receipts	229	251
of which: taxes	*176*	*192*
social security contributions	*39*	*44*
Public sector borrowing requirement (PSBR)	50	44
PSBR as percentage of GDP	8	6.5

Source: *Financial Statement and Budget Report 1993–94.*

Reserve

Planned expenditure includes an unallocated reserve to cover additions to departmental spending, whether arising from policy changes, new initiatives or revisions to the estimated costs of demand-led programmes.

Estimates

The annual Public Expenditure Survey conducted by HM Treasury provides the basis for the Estimates which each government department submits to the Treasury, giving details of its cash requirements for the coming financial year. After Treasury approval, these Supply Estimates are presented to Parliament. Parliamentary authorisation is required for the major part of the new spending plans for the year ahead announced in the unified Budget. Parliament approves them as part of the annual Appropriation Act. Supplementary Estimates may also be presented to Parliament during the course of the year.

If any Supply Estimate is overspent, the Committee of Public Accounts (see p. 116) may investigate before Parliament is asked to approve any Excess Vote to balance the account. In each parliamentary session, up to three 'Estimates days' are available for debates on the Supply Estimates, following scrutiny by select committees of the House of Commons.

Cash Limits

The Government sets cash limits on 60 per cent of Supply expenditure. The imposition of cash limits indicates that the Government intends to avoid extra provision for programmes even in the event of unexpected increases in costs. It is government policy to extend the coverage of cash limits whenever possible. They cover the major part of grants to local authorities, which are financed out of Supply expenditure. Cash limits also apply to some expenditure not voted in the Estimates.

Running cost limits are imposed on the administrative costs of central government, which are identified separately in the Estimates.

There is a facility for carrying forward underspending on the capital components of cash limits and on running cost limits. Any overspending of cash or running cost limits leads to an investigation into the causes and, where appropriate, a reduction in the limits in the following year.

Those Estimates not subject to cash limits mainly finance demand-led services like income support from the Department of

Table 10.2: Public Expenditure

	£ thousand million	
	1993–94	1994–95
Central government expenditure	166.4	172.2
Central government support for local authorities	58.4	61.5
Local authority self-financed expenditure	11.1	11.0
Financing requirements of nationalised industries	3.9	1.9
Reserve	4.0	7.0
New control total	243.8	253.6
Cyclical social security	15.1	16.0
Central government debt interest	19.4	23.5
Other adjustments	7.5	8.5
General government expenditure, excluding privatisation proceeds	285.8	302.0
Privatisation proceeds	-5.5	-5.5

Source: *Financial Statement and Budget Report 1993–94.*

Note: Differences between totals and the sums of their component parts are due to rounding.

Social Security. In such cases, once policy and rates of payment are determined, expenditure depends on factors beyond the direct control of government, such as the number of eligible recipients.

Examination and Audit of Public Expenditure

Examination of public expenditure is carried out by select committees of the House of Commons. These study in detail the activities of particular government departments and require the attendance of ministers and officials for cross-examination. Audit of the Government's spending, which follows up the control inherent in parliamentary approval of the Estimates, is exercised through the functions of the Comptroller and Auditor General.

Comptroller and Auditor General

The Comptroller and Auditor General, an officer of the House of Commons appointed by the Crown, has two distinct functions. As Comptroller General he or she is responsible for ensuring that all revenue and other public money payable to the Consolidated Fund and the National Loans Fund (see below) is duly paid and that all payments from these funds are authorised by statute. As Auditor General he or she must certify the accounts of all government departments and executive agencies and those of a wide range of other public sector bodies; scrutinise the economy, efficiency and effectiveness of their operations; examine revenue accounts and inventories; and report the results of these examinations to Parliament.

Committee of Public Accounts

The Committee of Public Accounts considers the accounts of government departments and other public sector bodies; the Comptroller and Auditor General's reports on them; and on departments' use of their resources. The Committee takes evidence from the heads of departments and relevant public sector bodies and submits reports to Parliament. The Government's formal replies to the reports are presented to Parliament by the Treasury in the form of Treasury minutes, and the reports and minutes are usually debated annually in the Commons.

Central Government Funds

The Government's sterling expenditure is largely met out of the Consolidated Fund, an account at the Bank of England into which tax receipts and other revenues are paid. Any excess of expenditure over receipts is met by the National Loans Fund, which is another official sterling account at the Bank of England and is the repository for funds borrowed by the Government. The National Insurance Fund, into which contributions are paid by employers and employed people, is used mainly to pay for social security benefits.

BUDGET

The Budget in November 1993 will set out the Government's proposals for changes in taxation and spending and will be the main annual review of economic policy. The proposals are announced to the House of Commons by the Chancellor of the Exchequer in the Budget statement and are published in the Financial Statement and Budget Report. This report also contains a review of recent developments in the economy, together with an economic forecast, and sets out the fiscal and monetary framework within which economic policy operates. This is the medium-term financial strategy (see p. 113).

The Budget statement is followed by the moving of a set of Budget resolutions in which the proposals are embodied. These resolutions are the foundation of the Finance Bill, in which the proposals are set out for detailed consideration by Parliament. The Provisional Collection of Taxes Act 1968 allows the tax authorities to collect taxes provisionally, at the levels provided by the Budget proposals, pending enactment of the Finance Bill.

For two taxes—income tax and corporation tax—annual Ways and Means resolutions followed by Finance Bill clauses are required to maintain their existence, since they are annual rather than permanent taxes. Tax changes can be made at other times, either by specific legislation or by the use of the regulator, which permits limited changes between Budgets in the rates of VAT (value added tax—by up to 25 per cent) and of the main excise duties (by up to 10 per cent).

MAIN SOURCES OF REVENUE

The main sources of revenue are:

- taxes on income (including profits), which include personal income tax, corporation tax and petroleum revenue tax; and

- taxes on expenditure, which include VAT and customs and excise duties.

Other sources of revenue are stamp duties; inheritance tax; capital gains tax; National Insurance contributions, which give entitlement to a range of benefits; and the council tax and business rates.

> The personal income tax allowances, basic rate limit, capital gains tax annual exempt amount and inheritance tax threshold are statutorily linked to the increase in the Retail Prices Index (RPI), unless Parliament decides otherwise. In the March 1993 Budget the Chancellor announced that in 1993–94 these allowances and limits would be the same as in 1992–93.

The Inland Revenue assesses and collects the taxes on income, profits and capital, and also stamp duty (see p. 120). Taxes on individual incomes are generally progressive in that larger incomes bear a proportionately greater amount of tax. HM Customs and Excise collects the most important taxes on expenditure (VAT and most duties). Vehicle excise duty is the responsibility of the Department of Transport and National Insurance contributions that of the Department of Social Security (although the latter are generally collected by the Inland Revenue). The council tax and business rates are collected by local authorities.

Taxes on Income

Income Tax

Income tax is imposed for the year of assessment beginning on 6 April. In the March 1993 Budget the new lower rate of 20 per cent was widened to the first £2,500 of taxable income. The basic rate of 25 per cent applies to the next £21,200 of taxable income. A rate of 40 per cent is levied on income above £23,700. These rates apply to total income, including both earned and investment income.

A number of allowances and reliefs reduce the amount of a person's taxable income compared with gross income. All taxpayers, irrespective of sex or marital status, are entitled to a personal allowance against income from all sources. Married women pay their own tax on the basis of their own income. In addition, there is a married couple's allowance, which may be allocated to either partner or they may receive half each. Wives are entitled to claim half of the allowance as of right. For 1993–94, the values of the main allowances are £3,445 for the personal allowance and £1,720 for the married couple's allowance. From April 1994 tax relief for some allowances, including the married couple's allowance, will be restricted to 20 per cent.

Among the most important of the reliefs is that for mortgage interest payments on borrowing for house purchase up to the statutory limit of £30,000. Relief is restricted to the basic rate of 25 per cent (and will be further restricted to the lower rate of 20 per cent from April 1994). It is usually given 'at source', that is, repayments which the borrower makes to the lender are reduced to take account of tax at the basic rate and the tax refund is then passed directly by the tax authorities to the building society or bank making the loan rather than to the individual taxpayer.

Employees' contributions to their pension schemes also qualify for tax relief within limits laid down by Parliament.

Most wage and salary earners pay their income tax under a Pay-As-You-Earn (PAYE) system whereby tax is deducted and accounted for to the Inland Revenue by the employer, in a way which enables employees to keep as up to date as possible with their tax payments.

In general, income tax is charged on all income which originates in Britain—although some forms of income are exempt, such as certain social security benefits—and on all income arising abroad of people resident in Britain. Interest on certain British government securities belonging to people not ordinarily resident in Britain is exempt. Britain has entered into agreements with many countries to provide relief from double taxation; where such agreements are not in force unilateral relief is often allowed. British residents working abroad for the whole year benefit from 100 per cent tax relief.

The option of self-assessment will be extended to all who fill in tax returns (some 8 million people) from 1996–97, and the assessment of tax for the self-employed will be simplified.

Corporation Tax

The rates of company tax in Britain are lower than in most other industrialised countries. Companies pay corporation tax on their income and capital gains after deduction of certain allowances. A company which distributes profits to its shareholders is required to pay advance corporation tax (ACT) to the Inland Revenue. This ACT can be set against the company's liability to corporation tax, subject to a limit. If resident in Britain, a shareholder receiving dividends from companies resident in Britain is entitled to a tax credit, which satisfies some or all of the shareholder's liability to income tax on his or her dividend income.

The main rate of corporation tax is 33 per cent for 1993–94, with a reduced rate of 25 per cent for small companies (those with profits below £250,000 in a year). Marginal relief between the main rate and the small companies' rate is allowed for companies with profits between £250,000 and £1.25 million. Expenditure on plant and machinery, on scientific research and on industrial and agricultural buildings qualifies for annual allowances.

Petroleum Revenue Tax

Petroleum revenue tax, deductible in computing profits for corporation tax, is charged on profits from the production, as opposed, for example, to the refining, of oil and gas under licence in Britain and on its Continental Shelf. The rate of tax was reduced from 75 to 50 per cent from 1 July 1993. New fields given consent for development on or after 16 March 1993 are not liable to this tax.

Each licensee of an oilfield is charged on the profits from that field after deduction of certain allowances and reliefs. There is no distinction between capital and revenue expenditure: both receive 100 per cent relief.

Inheritance Tax

Inheritance tax is charged on the value of estates after death and is also immediately chargeable on certain lifetime transfers. The majority of business assets are now exempt from inheritance tax, so that most family businesses can be passed on without a tax charge. Tax is charged at a single rate of 40 per cent above the threshold for inheritance tax of £150,000.

There are several important exemptions. Generally, transfers between spouses are exempt, and gifts and bequests to British charities, major political parties and heritage bodies are also normally exempt.

Capital Gains Tax

Capital gains realised on the disposal of assets are liable to capital gains tax or, in the case of companies, to corporation tax. For 1993–94, individuals are exempt from tax in respect of total net gains of up to £5,800 in any one year and most trusts on gains of up to £2,900. Gains are treated as the taxpayer's top slice of income, and are therefore charged at the individual's highest income tax rate or the company's higher corporation tax rate.

Only gains arising since March 1982 are subject to tax and the effects of inflation are allowed for when measuring gains. Some assets, including the principal private residence, are normally exempt. Gains on government securities and certain corporate bonds are exempt from the tax, as are gains on shares owned under personal equity plans. This last exemption is designed to encourage wider share ownership.

Taxpayers aged 55 or over, or retiring earlier owing to ill-health, can get relief when disposing of business assets. The March 1993 Budget extended this relief to include some employees and full-time working directors who have a minimum 5 per cent shareholding in a company. The Budget also proposed a new relief for entrepreneurs where gains from the sale of shares in a person's business are reinvested in new unquoted trading companies.

Taxes on Expenditure

Value Added Tax

VAT is a broadly based expenditure tax, chargeable at 17.5 per cent. It is collected at each stage in the production and distribution of goods and services by taxable persons— generally those whose business has a turnover of more than £37,600 a year. The final tax is borne by the consumer. When a taxable person purchases taxable goods or services, the supplier charges VAT—the taxable person's input tax. When the taxable person supplies goods or services, the customers are then in turn charged VAT, which is the taxable person's output tax. The difference between the output tax and the input tax is paid to, or repaid by, Customs and Excise.

Certain goods and services are relieved from VAT, either by being charged at a zero rate, in which case a taxable person does not charge tax to a customer but reclaims any input tax paid to suppliers, or by exemption, in which case a taxable person does not charge any output tax but is not entitled to reclaim the input tax. Among the main categories where zero-rating applies are goods exported to other countries, and goods shipped as stores on ships and aircraft; most food; water and sewerage; domestic and international passenger transport; books, newspapers and periodicals; fuel and power for domestic consumption (until April 1994); construction of new residential buildings;

Government Receipts and Expenditure 1992–93

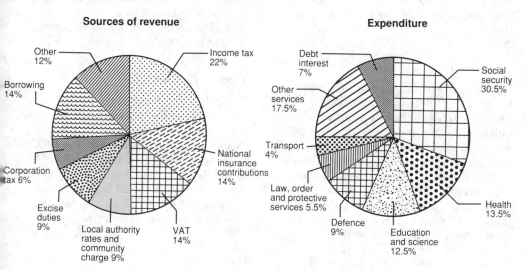

Sources of revenue

Other 12%
Borrowing 14%
Corporation tax 6%
Excise duties 9%
Local authority rates and community charge 9%
VAT 14%
National insurance contributions 14%
Income tax 22%

Expenditure

Debt interest 7%
Other services 17.5%
Transport 4%
Law, order and protective services 5.5%
Defence 9%
Education and science 12.5%
Health 13.5%
Social security 30.5%

Note: As a result of rounding and omission of minor items, percentages do not add up to 100.

Source: HM Treasury.

young children's clothing and footwear; drugs and medicines supplied on prescription; specified aids for handicapped people; and certain supplies by or to charities. VAT will be charged on domestic fuel and power at 8 per cent from April 1994 and at the full standard rate from April 1995. The main categories where exemption applies are many supplies of land and buildings; insurance; postal services; betting; gaming (subject to certain important exceptions); lotteries; finance; much education and training; and health and welfare.

A European Community agreement established a Community-wide minimum standard rate of VAT of 15 per cent for four years from January 1993.

Customs Duties

Customs duties are chargeable on goods from outside the EC in accordance with the EC's Common Customs Tariff. The introduction of the single European market from 1 January 1993 means that goods can move freely across internal frontiers between different member states, without making customs entries at importation or stopping for routine fiscal checks. For commercial consignments, excise duty and VAT are charged in the member state of destination, at the rate in force in that state.

Excise Duties

Hydrocarbon oils used as road fuel bear higher rates of duty than those used for other purposes, although the rate of duty on unleaded petrol is lower than that on leaded. Kerosene, most lubricating oils and other oils used for certain industrial processes are free of duty. There are duties on spirits, beer, wine, made-wine (wine with added constituents, such as fruit juice), cider and perry, based on alcoholic strength and volume. Spirits used for scientific, medical, research and industrial processes are generally free of duty. Cigarette duty is charged partly as a cash amount per cigarette and partly as a percentage of retail price. Duty on other tobacco products is based on weight. Duties are charged on off-course betting, pool

betting, gaming in casinos, bingo and gaming machines. Rates vary with the particular form of gambling. Duty is charged either as a percentage of gross or net stakes or, in the case of gaming machines, as a fixed amount per machine according to the cost of playing it and its prize level. A 12 per cent duty on gross stakes will be levied on the new National Lottery due to start in 1994 (see p. 481); there will be no tax on winnings.

Vehicle excise duty (VED) on a privately owned motor car, light van or taxi with less than nine seats is £125 a year; for motor cycles it is £15, £35 or £55 a year according to engine capacity. The duty on goods vehicles is levied on the basis of gross weight and, if over 12 tonnes, according to the number of axles; the duty is designed to ensure that such vehicles at least cover their share of road expenditure through the tax paid (VED and fuel duty). Duty on taxis and buses varies according to seating capacity.

Stamp Duty

Certain kinds of transfer are subject to stamp duty. These include purchases of houses, at 1 per cent on the total price if this exceeds £60,000, and instruments such as declarations of trust. The Government has plans to abolish stamp duty on shares. Transfers by gift and transfers to charities are exempt.

Taxpayer's Charter

The Taxpayer's Charter, relaunched in 1991, was one of the first separate charters issued following the publication of the Citizen's Charter (see p. 64). It sets out the standard of service that people can expect from the Inland Revenue and Customs and Excise. Both departments should be fair, helpful, courteous, efficient and accountable, and keep taxpayers' financial affairs private.

OTHER REVENUE

National Insurance Contributions

There are four classes of National Insurance contribution:

- Class 1—paid by employees and their employers;
- Class 2—paid by the self-employed;
- Class 3—paid voluntarily for pension purposes; and
- Class 4—paid by the self-employed on their taxable profits over a set lower limit, currently £6,340 a year, and up to a set upper limit, currently £21,840 a year (in addition to their Class 2 contribution).

Details of the rates of contribution are given in Chapter 26, Social Security, on pp. 390–8.

Local Authority Revenue

Local authority revenue in Great Britain (but not Northern Ireland) is obtained from three main sources: central government grants, non-domestic rates and the council tax. In England, for example, these will provide 56, 28 and 16 per cent respectively of the revenue of local authorities in 1993–94.

Non-domestic rates are a tax on the occupiers of non-domestic property. The rateable value of property is assessed by reference to annual rents and reviewed every five years. In England and Wales the non-domestic rate is set nationally by central government and collected by local authorities. It is paid into a national pool and redistributed to local authorities in proportion to their population. In Scotland non-domestic rates are levied by local authorities. In Northern Ireland rates are not payable on industrial premises or on commercial premises in enterprise zones. Certain other properties in Northern Ireland, such as freight transport and recreational premises, are partially derated.

Domestic property is subject to the council tax, which replaced the community charge in April 1993. Each dwelling is allocated to one of eight valuation bands, depending on its estimated open market value in April 1991. Tax levels are set by local authorities, but the relationship between the tax for each band is fixed. Discounts are available for dwellings with fewer than two resident adults. A council tax payer on a low income may receive a rebate of up to 100 per cent of his or her tax bill. There is a transitional relief scheme to ensure that no household faces an unreasonable increase in its local tax bill as a result of the replacement of the community charge by the council tax. The average council tax per dwelling is £456 in England, £425 in Scotland and £276 in Wales.

In Northern Ireland, rates—local domestic property taxes—are payable; they are collected by local authorities.

PUBLIC SECTOR FINANCE

The major government debt instrument is known as gilt-edged stock as there is no risk of default. Gilt-edged stock is marketable and is widely traded. Individuals may also make transactions through post offices in stocks included on the National Savings Stock Register. Pension funds and life insurance companies have the largest holdings. On behalf of the Government, the Bank of England issues both conventional and indexed stock (on which principal and interest are linked to the movement in the Retail Prices Index). Issues are mostly by auction or fixed price 'tap' sales.

An important additional source of government finance is the range of National Savings products, which are non-marketable and are designed to attract personal savings. The chief products (see p. 184) are Income Bonds, National Savings Certificates (which may be index-linked), the Investment Account, Capital Bonds, a Children's Bonus Bond and the First Option Bond.

Other central government debt instruments are Treasury bills and certificates of tax deposit. Sterling Treasury bills are sold at a weekly tender; the majority have a maturity of three months. The Government has also issued bills denominated and payable in European Currency Units (ECUs) since 1988 and longer-dated ECU notes since 1992. The proceeds have been added to the official foreign exchange reserves as opposed to being used to finance public expenditure.

The bulk of public corporations' borrowing is funded by central government, although their temporary borrowing needs are met largely from the market, usually under Treasury guarantee. That part of local authority borrowing met by central government is supplied by authorisation of Parliament through the Public Works Loan Board from the National Loans Fund. The Board remains an independent body even though it is merged for administrative purposes with the former National Debt Office, forming the National Investment and Loans Office. Local authorities may also borrow directly from the market, both short-term and long-term, through a range of instruments. Some public corporations and local authorities borrow on occasion, under special statutory power and with Treasury consent, in foreign currencies.

Public Sector Debt

Public sector borrowing, or debt repayment, each year represents an addition to, or subtraction from, the net debt of the public sector. This debt is the consolidated debt of the public sector less its holdings of liquid assets. Public sector debt held outside the public sector amounted to £207,600 million at the end of March 1992. Net public sector debt in 1993–94 is expected to be 39 per cent of GDP, compared with 50 per cent in 1979.

Further Reading

Financial Statement and Budget Report 1993–94. HMSO.

11 Employment

Employment in Britain grew substantially during the 1980s, although during the early 1990s it has declined as a result of the recession. There have, though, been significant shifts in the pattern of work in recent years. One of the most noticeable has been the continuing move towards employment in services. Now nearly three-quarters of employees are engaged in the service sector, compared with around one-fifth in manufacturing.

The Government has taken a number of steps to improve the labour market, with the aim of creating an economic climate in which business can flourish and create more jobs. These include:

- increasing the flexibility of the labour market;

- removing burdens on employers and workers, including regulatory barriers which hinder recruitment; and

- encouraging better training, especially by setting up employer-led Training and Enterprise Councils and, in Scotland, Local Enterprise Companies (see p. 126).

In February 1992 the Government set out its proposals for action to widen the opportunities and choices for people at work in a White Paper *People, Jobs and Opportunity*.

The Government supports a social dimension to the European Community (see p. 297) which gives priority to the creation and development of jobs and takes into account the different employment patterns and practices in the 12 member states.

PATTERNS OF EMPLOYMENT

The total workforce in June 1992 was 28.2 million. The workforce in employment totalled 25.5 million (see Table 11.1), of whom 21.8 million (11.2 million men and 10.6 million women) were classed as employees in employment.

Recent labour market trends have included:

- a substantial growth in self-employment which occurred in the 1980s;

- increasing participation by women, especially married women, in the labour market;

- a continuing increase in the proportion of jobs in the service sector; and

- higher productivity arising out of the growing use of information technology and advanced manufacturing systems.

Between 1983 and 1990 employment growth in Britain was nearly twice that in the rest of the European Community (EC). Much of the growth in jobs arose in small firms or among the self-employed. In spring 1993,

Table 11.1: Workforce in Employment in Britain

Thousands, seasonally adjusted, June

	1982	1987	1990	1991	1992
Employees in employment	21,395	21,586	22,913	22,251	21,835
Self-employed	2,169	2,869	3,298	3,143	2,989
HM Forces	324	319	303	297	290
Work-related government training programmes	–	311	423	353	338
Workforce in employment	23,889	25,084	26,937	26,044	25,452

Source: *Employment Gazette.*

according to the Labour Force Survey, 12.4 per cent of those in employment in Britain were self-employed, compared with 11.2 per cent in 1984.

Women account for a growing proportion of the workforce in employment and in June 1992 they represented nearly 49 per cent of employees in employment. The proportion of women in work in Britain is well above the EC average, being exceeded only by Denmark. Many employers have developed policies to help women to return to the labour market. The Government is encouraging voluntary action by employers to increase the employment opportunities for women, and in 1991 it joined the 'Opportunity 2000' campaign (see p. 35).

Part-time employment accounted for much of the increase in employment during the 1980s. Some 5.8 million people were engaged in part-time employment in their main jobs in Great Britain in spring 1993. This represented 24 per cent of those in employment, compared with just under 21 per cent in 1984. The proportion in part-time employment is much higher for women than for men. About 50 per cent of married women work part-time, compared with just over 30 per cent of non-married women.

Employment by Sector

As in other industrialised countries, there has been a marked shift in jobs from manufacturing to service industries (see Table 11.2). Between 1955 and 1992 the proportion of employees in employment engaged in service industries doubled from 36 per cent to 72 per cent as higher living standards and technological developments stimulated the growth of many service industries.

During the period 1982 to 1992 the number of employees in service industries in Great Britain rose by 2.2 million (17 per

Table 11.2: Employees by Main Sector in Britain (at June)

	1982	1987	1990	1991	1992
Thousands					
Service industries	13,408	14,568	15,951	15,803	15,718
Manufacturing industries	5,873	5,171	5,125	4,728	4,521
Energy and water supply	680	508	450	439	404
Other industries	1,434	1,338	1,387	1,280	1,192
Per cent of employees					
Service industries	62.7	67.5	69.6	71.0	72.0
Manufacturing industries	27.5	24.0	22.4	21.3	20.7
Energy and water supply	3.2	2.4	2.0	2.0	1.8
Other industries	6.7	6.2	6.1	5.8	5.5

Source: Department of Employment.

Note: From September 1991 certain local authority employees were reclassified from services to other industries. Accordingly, the figures for 1992 are not strictly comparable with those for earlier years.

cent) to 15.4 million (see Table 11.3). The largest rise was in the banking, finance and insurance sector, where employment grew by 46 per cent to 2.6 million. A substantial increase, of 26 per cent, also occurred in hotels and catering, mostly in part-time jobs.

Manufacturing industry accounted for 42 per cent of employees in employment in 1955, but by 1992 the proportion had halved to 21 per cent. Nearly all manufacturing industries have experienced a decline in employment as productivity has increased and as markets for manufactured goods have changed. Some of Britain's traditional manufacturing industries, such as steel and shipbuilding, have experienced particularly large falls in employment. In June 1992 employment in the main sectors of manufacturing industry in Great Britain included:

- 649,000 in mechanical engineering;
- 627,000 in office machinery, electrical engineering and instruments;
- 489,000 in food, drink and tobacco;
- 456,000 in timber, wooden furniture, rubber and plastics;
- 453,000 in paper products, printing and publishing; and

- 407,000 in textiles, leather, footwear and clothing.

Occupational Changes

There has been a gradual move away from manual occupations towards non-manual occupations, which now account for nearly three-fifths of jobs. The main growth areas have been in managerial and professional occupations, and in the personal and protective service occupations.

Unemployment

So far during the 1990s unemployment has generally risen. By January 1993 it had reached just under 3 million on a seasonally adjusted basis, which is below the previous peak reached in 1986. However, subsequently unemployment has been at a slightly lower level, and in August 1993 it totalled 2.9 million, 10.4 per cent of the workforce. Unemployment varies considerably by region, ranging in August 1993 from 8.4 per cent in East Anglia to 14.1 per cent in Northern Ireland.

The Government has introduced a wide range of measures to help combat

Table 11.3: Employees in Employment in Services in Great Britain

Thousands, not seasonally adjusted, June

	1982	1987	1990	1991	1992
Wholesale distribution and repair	1,115	1,138	1,198	1,131	1,087
Retail distribution	1,984	2,057	2,301	2,294	2,287
Hotels and catering[a]	959	1,028	1,257	1,232	1,205
Transport	932	852	924	899	893
Postal services and telecommunications	428	413	437	429	405
Banking, finance, insurance, business services and leasing[a]	1,771	2,250	2,701	2,633	2,583
Public administration[a]	1,825	1,910	1,942	1,960	1,811
Education[a]	1,541	1,641	1,735	1,710	1,836
Medical and other health services, veterinary services	1,258	1,337	1,450	1,491	1,552
Other services[a]	1,305	1,620	1,664	1,677	1,710
All services	13,117	14,247	15,609	15,457	15,367

Source: *Employment Gazette.*
[a]Industries affected by the reclassification of some local authority employees in September 1991. Accordingly, the figures for June 1992 for these services are not strictly comparable with those for earlier years.

unemployment. A new series of measures was announced in the Budget in March 1993, of particular relevance to the needs of the long-term unemployed. The measures, intended to provide over 100,000 extra opportunities for individuals, include:

- Community Action, providing 60,000 opportunities for people to do voluntary work of benefit to the community on a part-time basis while they actively look for work; and

- Learning for Work, offering 30,000 opportunities for unemployed people to pursue vocationally relevant full-time education.

TRAINING, EDUCATION AND ENTERPRISE

Employers in Britain spend over £20,000 million a year on employee training and development. The Labour Force Survey in spring 1993 found that the number of employees who had received recent training was almost 70 per cent higher than it had been in 1984. Individuals are being encouraged to train by means of tax reliefs and loan schemes.

The Government funds a number of training, enterprise and vocational education programmes. Expenditure by the Department of Employment Group, The Scottish Office and the Welsh Office in Great Britain on training, enterprise and vocational education programmes will be some £2,800 million in 1993–94.

Government Policy

Responsibility for training policy in Great Britain rests with the Secretary of State for Employment, who draws up national training guidelines in consultation with the Secretaries of State for Scotland and Wales, and in Northern Ireland with the Secretary of State for Northern Ireland. The Secretaries of State for Scotland and Wales will assume responsibility for training policy in Scotland and Wales respectively in April 1994.

The Government's strategic priorities for training, vocational education and enterprise are that:

- employers, the self-employed and individual people in the workforce should invest effectively in the skills needed for business creation and growth, and for individual success;

- people who are out of work or at a disadvantage in the market should acquire and maintain relevant skills and obtain appropriate support to enable them to compete better for employment, and to contribute more effectively to the economy;

- young people should be encouraged and enabled to gain the skills and enterprising attitudes needed for entry to the workforce and to prepare them to realise their full potential throughout working life; and

- the market for vocational education and training should be more responsive to the changing needs of employers and individuals.

Training and Enterprise Councils

A network of 82 employer-led Training and Enterprise Councils (TECs) has been set up throughout England and Wales. Their main functions are:

- to promote more effective training by employers and individuals;

- to develop innovative solutions to local problems;

- to provide readily accessible, high quality business and enterprise support;

- to deliver and develop Youth Training and Training for Work (see below);

- to stimulate enterprise and economic growth by providing support to new and existing small firms; and

- to build relationships with the education sector through Department of Employment programmes and other initiatives.

TECs are playing an increasingly important role in the delivery of training programmes and in influencing local education provision. Each TEC has a local initiative fund to allow it to develop new ideas in support of the Department of Employment's objectives to improve skills and promote individual choice and enterprise.

Local Enterprise Companies

A separate network of 22 Local Enterprise Companies (LECs) exists in Scotland. These have wider-ranging responsibilities than the TECs, covering economic development and environmental improvement. LECs operate the same major training programmes as TECs, but, unlike them, have no responsibility for work-related further education. They run under the supervision of the two enterprise bodies: Scottish Enterprise and Highlands and Islands Enterprise (see p. 147).

Industry Training Organisations

Industry Training Organisations (ITOs) act as the focal point for training matters in their particular sector of industry, commerce or public service. Their role is to ensure that the skills needs of their sectors are being met and that occupational standards are being established and maintained for key occupations. There are over 120 independent ITOs, covering sectors employing about 85 per cent of the civilian workforce. The National Council of Industry Training Organisations, a voluntary body set up to represent the interests of ITOs, aims to improve the effectiveness of these bodies, for example, by encouraging good practice.

National Education and Training Targets

National Education and Training Targets were launched by the Confederation of British Industry in 1991 and were agreed by over 100 national and local organisations, including all TECs, LECs and ITOs, and other major education, training and employer bodies. The Government confirmed its support for the targets, since they underpin its aims and are a measure of action needed to raise skill levels.

The targets cover both young people and the workforce as a whole. Among the 'foundation targets' are:

- immediate moves to ensure that by 1997 at least 80 per cent of all young people attain NVQ/SVQ Level 2 (see p. 415) or its academic equivalent in their foundation education and training; and

- that by 2000, 50 per cent of young people should attain NVQ/SVQ level 3 or its academic equivalent, as a basis for further progression.

A new National Advisory Council for Education and Training Targets was launched in March 1993. It is employer-led and includes members from education and trade unions. It is operating in parallel with a separate advisory body for Scotland.

Training for Work

Training for Work is a new programme introduced in April 1993 to replace the Employment Training and Employment Action programmes. It has the objective of helping long-term unemployed people to find jobs and to improve their work-related skills through the provision of relevant training and structured work activity based on a careful assessment of individual needs. Training is carried out by training providers under contract with the local TEC or LEC. Each new participant receives an individually adapted package of training and/or structured work activities. The new programme focuses more closely on the long-term unemployed than did the previous Employment Training programme. Over 150,000 places for Training for Work will be available in Great Britain in 1993–94, when the programme is expected to help up to 320,000 people.

Training for Young People

An estimated 71 per cent of 16- and 17-year-olds in England leaving school to enter the labour market go into Youth Training. Youth Training gives young people who choose not to stay on in full-time education and who are not already employed the opportunity to acquire a broad-based vocational education and to achieve a vocational qualification or a credit towards one. It is designed to:

- provide help for young people to acquire the broadly based skills necessary for a flexible and self-reliant workforce;
- meet skill needs, especially for technician and craft-level training; and
- provide participants with training leading to NVQs or equivalent qualifications (see p. 415) at or above Level 2.

Youth Credits, which operate within the broad framework of Youth Training, give young people who have left full-time education to join the labour market an entitlement to train to approved standards. They carry a monetary face value and can be presented to an employer or training provider in exchange for high-quality training. Pilot projects started in 1991, and Youth Credits are now available in 20 areas in Britain. Over 51,000 young people have benefited from the scheme. The Government aims to offer Youth Credits to all school-leavers aged 16 and 17 by 1996. The intention is that Youth Credits will eventually replace Youth Training.

Investors in People

In 1990 the Government launched the Investors in People initiative, developed by employers. As its focus, it has a national standard for effective investment in people, and aims to encourage employers to develop the potential of all employees in line with business goals. Investors in People is delivered locally by TECs and LECs, which provide advice and information to help organisations to work towards the standard. By September 1993, nearly 380 employers had achieved the Investors in People standard, and nearly 4,000 had made a formal commitment to work towards the standard.

Improving the Training Market

The Improving the Training Market programme is aimed at bringing about change and improvements in the operation of the vocational education and training systems. It includes projects to strengthen the institutional framework within which training is delivered; helps to ensure the successful establishment of NVQs; and develops effective information, advice, assessment and accreditation systems.

National Training Awards

The National Training Awards aim to complement TEC/LEC activities and the competition is designed to promote good training practice by example, rewarding companies which have carried out exceptionally effective training. Around 80 corporate awards and approximately 20 individual awards are presented to national winners, who are selected from 200 regional commendations.

Skill Choice

A new Skill Choice initiative was introduced in April 1993 and is intended to improve the commitment of individuals, primarily those already in employment, to training. Under the initiative, people are offered credits which they can use to buy guidance and assessment services; part of the cost is being met by the Government. In the initial stage, 15 TECs and LECs are involved, providing credits to 250,000 people in the two years 1993–94 and 1994–95. If credits prove successful, the Government intends to make them available throughout Great Britain.

Career Development Loans

People who live in or intend to undertake vocational training in Great Britain can apply to one of three major banks for a Career Development Loan. Loans of £200 to £5,000 can help to pay for vocational courses lasting up to a year, or a year of a longer course. Some 39,000 people have borrowed over £100 million through the programme to pay for training. A substantial expansion of the programme is planned over the three years from April 1993, with loan capacity increasing from 30,000 in 1993–94 to 52,000 by 1995–96.

Education Initiatives

A major government objective is to raise the motivation and attainment of young people to achieve their full potential and develop the skills needed by the economy. This requires close working relationships between industry and education. A number of education initiatives are being implemented, including the Technical and Vocational Education Initiative, Education Business Partnerships, the Teacher Placement Service, Compacts and the National Record of Achievement. Details are given in Chapter 27.

Vocational Qualifications

The proportion of the workforce with qualifications, gained either in school or further education, is growing. Between 1984 and 1992 it rose from 63 per cent to 76 per cent.

The National Council for Vocational Qualifications (NCVQ), established in 1986, has been charged with reforming and rationalising vocational qualifications. New National Vocational Qualifications (NVQs) have been established in England, Wales and Northern Ireland (see p. 415). In Scotland the Scottish Vocational Education Council (SCOTVEC) has established parallel Scottish Vocational Qualifications (SVQs).

NVQs and SVQs are designed mainly for people in employment, although they can also be studied full-time. They are job-specific, based on national standards of competence set by industry and are assessed in the workplace. There are five levels within the NVQ and SVQ framework (see p. 415). NVQs and SVQs at levels 1 to 5 to cover 90 per cent of the employed workforce are expected to be in place by the end of 1995.

Open Learning

Britain is acknowledged as an innovative world leader in open and flexible learning, for example, through the Open University and the Open College (see p. 415). Open Learning Credits are being tested during 1993–94, aimed primarily at the adult unemployed. TECs and LECs are running 14 pilot schemes.

Northern Ireland

The Training and Employment Agency, an executive agency within the Department of Economic Development for Northern Ireland, has primary responsibility for training and employment services. Its overall aim is to assist economic growth by ensuring the provision and operation of training and employment services that contribute to Northern Ireland companies becoming more competitive and individuals obtaining the skills and competences needed to secure worthwhile employment. The Agency works closely with employers and is encouraging each of the key sectors of industry to form a sectoral representative body to represent the opinions of employers and others on individual sectoral training needs. It has also established sectoral working groups to develop training strategies for individual sectors.

Several new initiatives have been implemented. For example, in 1992 the Manpower Training Scheme, under which assistance on training is given to businesses, was changed to make it more relevant to modern business needs—it became the Company Development Programme. The Agency's Client Advisory Staff promote the benefits of training and offer advice suited to the needs of individual companies and industrial sectors.

Northern Ireland has its own range of training and employment programmes. These include:

- the Action for Community Employment programme, which provides temporary jobs with a training input for long-term unemployed people;
- the Job Training programme; and
- the Youth Training programme.

RECRUITMENT AND JOB-FINDING

There are a variety of ways in which people can find jobs. In autumn 1992 the main methods, according to the Labour Force Survey, were:
- visiting a jobcentre (30 per cent);
- studying situations vacant columns (30 per cent);

- answering other adverts (12 per cent);
- personal contacts (11 per cent); and
- direct approaches to employers (10 per cent).

Government Employment Services

The Government provides a range of services to jobseekers through the Employment Service, an executive agency within the Department of Employment. These include:

- a network of local offices, at which people can find details of job opportunities;
- advice and guidance so that people can find the best route back into employment, for example, by training; and
- a range of special programmes.

The Employment Service has over 1,300 jobcentres and unemployment benefit offices, and employs about 48,000 staff. Jobcentres are now being integrated with benefit offices to provide a comprehensive service to unemployed people. By April 1993 nearly 800 integrated offices had been established. In 1992–93 the Employment Service placed some 1.42 million unemployed people into jobs and conducted over 4 million advisory interviews to help people find appropriate work or places on employment and training programmes.

The Jobseeker's Charter contains a number of provisions governing the standard of service for users of the Service. Local offices have introduced a number of innovations under the charter to meet the needs of users, for example, electronic noticeboards and appointment control systems.

Advisory Services

Help for unemployed people is provided through the mainstream jobcentre services which provide access to vacancies, employment advice and training opportunities. Advisers provide unemployed people with information on employment and training opportunities available locally. New client advisers interview newly unemployed people to check their eligibility for benefit. Together with the unemployed person, they agree a 'Back to Work Plan' which shows them the best course of action to follow to get back to work. These plans are reviewed at every advisory interview.

Under the Restart programme, everyone who has been unemployed for six months or longer is asked to attend a Restart interview with a claimant adviser. The adviser and unemployed person discuss that person's circumstances, with the aim of helping him or her back into work as soon as possible.

The Service has a number of programmes, some of which are designed to help the long-term unemployed. These include:

- Jobclubs, where participants are given training and advice in job-hunting skills and have access to facilities to help an intensive job search;
- Restart courses, designed to rebuild self-confidence and motivation, and including help with job-hunting skills; and
- Jobplan workshops, introduced in 1993–94, which are designed to enable those unemployed for a year to assess their skills, qualities and training needs, and to act as an introduction to future job and training options.

Help for People with Disabilities

The Employment Service also aims to help people with disabilities find work. All Employment Service programmes make provision for people with disabilities. Services for people with disabilities are now being delivered through local integrated specialist teams—Placing Assessment and Counselling Teams. They are supported by nine regional Ability Development Centres, which carry out training and development work, and provide special advice for employers who may be considering employing people with disabilities. A wide range of programmes, such as one offering sheltered employment opportunities, is available for people with disabilities who need specialist help.

Employment Agencies

There are many private employment agencies, including several large firms with many branches. The total value of the market has been estimated at about £7,000 million a year.

The main trade body for the employment agency industry is the Federation of Recruitment and Employment Services, which regulates the activities of its members by means of a Code of Good Recruitment Practice and by specialist section codes of practice. Agencies are less restricted by state regulation in Britain than in most other EC countries.

By law, employment agencies are allowed to charge only the employer, not the employee (except for specialist theatrical and model agencies). They also have to register with the Government for each branch they operate. Their number increased from 7,800 in 1984–85 to 15,600 in 1991–92, although recently there has been a fall in the number of offices as a result of the recession.

TERMS AND CONDITIONS OF EMPLOYMENT

Employment Rights

Employment protection legislation provides a number of safeguards for employees. For example, most employees are entitled to receive from their employers written information on their main terms and conditions of employment, while minimum periods of notice when employment is to be terminated are laid down for both employers and employees. The Trade Union Reform and Employment Rights Act 1993 (see p. 136) includes provisions giving employees who work eight hours or more a week a right to a written statement setting out details of the main conditions including pay, hours of work and holidays.

Employees with the necessary period of continuous employment with their employer (currently two years for those working 16 hours a week or more, or five years for those working at least eight but less than 16 hours a week) are entitled to lump-sum redundancy payments if their jobs cease to exist (for example, because of technological improvements or a fall in demand) and their employers cannot offer suitable alternative work. Where employers are insolvent, redundancy payments are met directly from the National Insurance fund.

Most employees who believe they have been unfairly dismissed have the right to complain to an industrial tribunal, provided they have the necessary qualifying period of employment. If the complaint is upheld, the tribunal may make an order for re-employment or award compensation.

Most pregnant women who have the necessary qualifying period of continuous employment have the right to return to their former job, or a suitable alternative, after maternity absence. New rights for women in employment are contained in the Trade Union Reform and Employment Rights Act 1993: the right of a pregnant employee to have 14 weeks' statutory maternity leave, regardless of length of service or the number of hours worked in a week, and to be protected against dismissal because of her pregnancy. Existing rights are preserved.

Legislation forbids any employment of children under 13 years of age, and employment in any industrial undertaking of children who have not reached the statutory minimum school-leaving age, with some exceptions for family undertakings.

Equal Opportunities

The Race Relations Act 1976 makes it generally unlawful to discriminate on grounds of colour, race, nationality (including citizenship) or ethnic or national origin, in employment, training and related matters. The Department of Employment operates a nationwide Race Relations Employment Advisory Service. Its objective is to promote the Government's policies aimed at eliminating racial discrimination in employment and promoting fair treatment and equality of opportunity in employment. Advisers provide employers with advice and practical help in developing and implementing effective equal opportunity strategies.

The Sex Discrimination Act 1975, as amended, makes it generally unlawful in Great Britain to discriminate on grounds of sex or marital status when it comes to recruiting, training, promoting, dismissing or retiring staff. It also provides redress against victimisation and may also do so against sexual harassment. The Equal Pay Act 1970 makes it generally unlawful to discriminate between men and women in pay and other terms and conditions of employment. The Act was significantly extended in 1984 to meet EC requirements by providing for equal pay for work of equal value. There is equivalent legislation in Northern Ireland.

Practical advice to employers and others on the best arrangements for implementing equal opportunities policies in Great Britain is given in codes of practice from the Commission for Racial Equality and from the Equal Opportunities Commission (see p. 36).

Northern Ireland

Similar legislation to that in Great Britain on equal pay and sex discrimination applies in Northern Ireland; there is at present no legislation on race relations, but this is under review. Discrimination, both direct and indirect, in employment on grounds of religious belief or political opinion is unlawful. The Fair Employment Commission has the task of promoting equality of opportunity and investigating employment practices, with powers to issue legally enforceable directions. The Fair Employment Tribunal adjudicates on individual complaints of religious or political discrimination and enforces the Commission's directions. All but the smallest employers are required to monitor the religious composition of their workforce and periodically to review their employment practices. Where fair participation is not being enjoyed by both Protestants and Roman Catholics, the introduction of 'affirmative action' measures must be considered.

Earnings

According to the Department of Employment's New Earnings Survey, the average weekly earnings, unaffected by absence and including overtime payments, in April 1993 of full-time employees on adult rates were £317. Earnings were higher for non-manual employees (£350) than for manual employees (£257). Managerial and professional groups are the highest paid. The industries with the highest average weekly earnings were energy and water supply (£403) and banking, finance, insurance and business services (£372).

Overtime and other additional payments are particularly important for manual employees, for whom such additional payments represented over one-fifth of earnings. Some 48 per cent of manual employees and 18 per cent of non-manual employees received overtime payments.

There has been a considerable fall in the rate of increase in earnings in recent years. In the year to July 1993 the underlying average increase was about 3.5 per cent.

Fringe Benefits

A variety of fringe benefits are used by employers in Britain to provide additional rewards to their employees, including schemes to encourage employee financial participation in their companies, pension schemes, private medical insurance, subsidised meals, company cars and childcare schemes.

The Government has introduced tax reliefs to encourage employers to set up financial participation schemes, and give employees a direct financial stake in the business they work for.

Profit-related pay (PRP) schemes link part of pay to changes in a business's profits. By the end of March 1993 nearly 1.2 million employees were covered by over 4,600 registered PRP schemes. Employee share schemes allow employees to receive low-cost or free shares from their employer without paying income tax. By the end of 1992 some 2.9 million employees had benefited from all-employee profit sharing and Save-As-You-Earn (SAYE) share option schemes.

Many employees are covered by pension schemes provided by their employers. Such benefits are more usual among clerical and professional employees than among manual workers. Over 11 million people in Britain are members of occupational schemes.

Company cars are provided for directors and employees in a wide variety of circumstances. It is estimated that 1.9 million people had a company car in 1991–92, and half of these received fuel for private motoring in their cars.

Hours of Work

The basic working week (excluding overtime and main meal breaks) in Great Britain is in the range 37.5 to 40 hours for manual work and 35 to 38 for non-manual work; a five-day week is usually worked. While the basic working week has been gradually shortening, the general trend in total hours worked has been rising since 1981. In April 1993 total hours a week actually worked (including overtime) for full-time adult employees were 41.3 for men, compared with 37.4 for women. Men and women in non-manual occupations generally work less overtime than manual employees.

In general, there are no limits on hours worked by adults except in a few occupations (such as for drivers of goods vehicles and public service vehicles).

The Government has opposed proposals in a draft EC directive on working time for a maximum of 48 hours for the working week.

Holidays with Pay

There are no general statutory entitlements to holidays, and holiday entitlements are frequently determined by collective agreements. Recent decades have seen a considerable increase in holiday entitlements. In 1961, 97 per cent of full-time manual employees were entitled to two weeks a year. Nowadays, holiday entitlements (excluding public holidays) generally provide for at least four weeks' paid holiday a year. Nearly all manual employees covered by national collective agreements have entitlements of four weeks or more, with about 30 per cent

having five weeks or more. Non-manual workers tend to have longer holidays than manual workers. Holiday entitlements may also be dependent upon length of service.

INDUSTRIAL RELATIONS

The structure of industrial relations in Britain has been established mainly on a voluntary basis. The system is based chiefly on the organisation of employees and employers into trade unions and employers' associations, and on freely conducted negotiations at all levels.

Trends in Collective Bargaining and Pay

There has been a considerable reduction in the proportion of employees and workplaces where pay is determined by collective bargaining. The proportion of the workforce covered by multi-employer national agreements declined from 60 per cent in 1978 to 34 per cent in 1991. Private sector employees are much less likely to be covered by collective bargaining than are public sector employees. National agreements covering over 1.2 million employees have ended since 1986 in sectors such as engineering, banking, the multiple food trade, electricity supply and water supply.

Where agreements in the private sector are industry-wide, they are often supplemented by local agreements in companies or factories (plant bargaining). These company or plant agreements frequently produce pay rates which are higher than the minima set by national agreements, as well as other detailed terms and conditions of employment. Where there is no collective bargaining, pay is usually determined by management at local level.

Another trend has been the growth in systems linking pay to performance. A substantial majority of medium to large employers make some use of performance-related pay systems such as merit pay, financial participation (see p. 132) and individual payment by results. Private sector organisations are much more likely to use performance-related pay than public sector bodies.

The Government is committed to the further development of performance-related pay in the public sector as part of its wider objectives for improving the quality of the public services as set out in the Citizen's Charter (see p. 64). Performance-related pay is being extended in areas such as the Civil Service and education. Greater pay flexibility is also being encouraged in other ways, such as the facility for delegating pay determination to individual departments and agencies within central government, to self-governing trusts in the National Health Service and to grant-maintained schools.

A relatively recent feature has been the development of 'new style' agreements, often associated with overseas-owned companies, although they are also found in British-owned firms. These agreements often involve:

- the recognition of a single union for all of a company's employees (particularly for companies recognising unions for the first time);

- 'single status', involving the elimination of the traditional distinction between managers, supervisors and other employees;

- a greater emphasis on employee participation; and

- flexibility in working practices.

Employee Involvement

Employers practise a wide variety of methods of informing and consulting their employees, not only through committees but also through direct communication between management and employees. These methods include:

- employee bulletins and reports;

- briefing systems;

- quality circles;

- financial participation schemes; and

- attitude surveys.

The Government is, however, opposed to the proposals put forward by the EC, which would impose statutory requirements on some multinational employers to inform and consult their employees, and provide for worker participation in decision-making through works councils. It believes that companies should be free to develop employee involvement arrangements which are appropriate to their own circumstances and the needs of their employees.

Trade Unions

Trade unions have members in nearly all occupations. They are widely recognised by employers in the public sector and in large firms and establishments. As well as negotiating pay and other terms and conditions of employment with employers, they provide benefits and services such as educational facilities, financial services, legal advice and aid in work-related cases. In recent years several unions have extended considerably the range of services for members. Trade unions vary widely in the composition of their membership, and may be organised either by occupation (for example, they may recruit clerical staff or managers wherever employed) or by industry, while some are based on a combination of both.

There has been a decline in trade union membership, and by the end of 1991 total union membership was about 9.5 million, of whom 81 per cent were in the 23 largest unions. The decline reflects the moves away from manufacturing and public services, both of which have a relatively high level of membership. The number of unions has also fallen, reflecting a number of mergers and the absorption by larger unions of small unions and of long-established craft unions. Several unions are discussing possible mergers.

A merger of the Confederation of Health Service Employees, the National Union of Public Employees and the National and Local Government Officers Association to form a new union, Unison, took effect in July 1993. With some 1.5 million members, it has become the biggest union in Britain.

The other unions with over 500,000 members are:

- the Transport and General Workers Union (with 1 million members);
- the Amalgamated Engineering and Electrical Union (884,000);
- GMB (799,000); and
- Manufacturing Science Finance (552,000).

At the end of 1992 there were 302 trade unions on the list maintained by the Certification Officer, who, among other duties, is responsible for certifying the independence of trade unions. To be eligible for entry on the list a trade union must show that it consists wholly or mainly of workers and that its principal purposes include the regulation of relations between workers and employers or between workers and employers' associations.

Trade union organisation varies widely, but the central governing body usually consists of a national executive council or committee, elected by a secret ballot of the individual members and responsible to the conference of delegates from local branches, normally held annually. Many unions also have regional and district organisations. At the level of the individual member there are local branches, covering one or more workplaces. The organising of members in individual places of work and the negotiation of local pay agreements with management at the workplace may be done by full-time district officials of the union or, in many cases, by elected workplace representatives, often called 'shop stewards'. Where two or more unions have members in the same workplace, shop stewards' committees may be formed to discuss matters of common concern.

Trades Union Congress

In Britain the national centre of the trade union movement is the Trades Union Congress (TUC), founded in 1868. Its affiliated membership comprises 69 trade unions, which together represent some 7.6 million people, or about 80 per cent of all trade unionists in Britain.

The TUC's objectives are to promote the interests of its affiliated organisations and to improve the economic and social conditions of working people. The TUC deals with all general questions which concern trade unions, both nationally and internationally, and provides a forum in which affiliated unions can collectively determine policy. There are eight TUC regional councils for England and a Wales Trades Union Council.

The annual Congress meets in September to discuss matters of concern to trade unionists. A General Council represents the TUC between annual meetings by:

- carrying out Congress decisions;
- watching economic and social developments;
- providing educational and advisory services to unions; and
- presenting in national debate the trade union viewpoint on economic, social and industrial issues.

The TUC plays an active part in international trade union activity, through its affiliation to the International Confederation of Free Trade Unions and the European Trade Union Confederation. It also nominates the British workers' delegation to the annual International Labour Conference.

Scotland and Northern Ireland

Trade unions in Scotland also have their own national central body, the Scottish Trades Union Congress, which in many respects is similar in constitution and function to the TUC. Trade unions in Northern Ireland are represented by the Northern Ireland Committee of the Irish Congress of Trade Unions (ICTU). Most trade unionists in Northern Ireland are members of organisations affiliated to the ICTU, while the majority also belong to unions based in Great Britain which are also affiliated to the TUC. The Northern Ireland Committee of the ICTU enjoys a high degree of autonomy.

Legal Framework

The Government's reforms of industrial relations and trade union law have helped to change the balance of power between trade unions and employers, and between trade unions and their own members. Legislation is consolidated in the Trade Union and Labour

Relations (Consolidation) Act 1992, as amended by the most recent Act, the Trade Union Reform and Employment Rights Act 1993. These reforms have played a key role in transforming Britain's industrial relations.

> The Trade Union Reform and Employment Rights Act 1993 contains several provisions, including:
>
> ● giving individuals greater freedom to join the union of their choice;
>
> ● protecting against abuse of any arrangements for deducting union subscriptions directly from pay;
>
> ● giving union members the right to a fully postal ballot before a strike and before a union merger; and
>
> ● creating a right for anyone to seek the protection of the law if he or she were the victim of unlawful industrial action.

The 1993 Act also strengthens and extends the rights of individual employees, including stronger rights on maternity leave (see p. 131). Under the Act the 26 wages councils in Great Britain were abolished on 30 August 1993, while the nine wages councils in Northern Ireland are also to be abolished.

There were 528,000 working days lost in 253 stoppages of work as a result of industrial action in 1992 (see Table 11.4), the lowest calendar year totals since records began in 1891.

Trade Union Recognition

The previous statutory recognition procedure

was repealed in 1980. Employers are now free to decide whether or not they wish to recognise, or continue to recognise, a particular union, or unions, for collective bargaining purposes.

Industrial Action

Under common law, it is unlawful to induce workers to break a contract or to threaten to do it. Thus, without special protection, trade unions (or any other person or organisation) would face the possibility of legal action for inducing breaches of contract every time they called a strike or other form of industrial action. To prevent this, 'statutory immunities' were introduced, which provide that trade unions and others can, in certain circumstances, organise industrial action without fear of being sued in the courts. These immunities only protect those who call for or organise industrial action. They do not protect individuals who choose to take industrial action from being dismissed, or from legal action by their employer.

Prior to the 1980s, the circumstances in which these immunities applied were very wide, so that the organisation of almost any industrial action was protected. The legislative reforms of the past decade have restricted the scope of these immunities in a number of ways. To have the benefit of statutory immunity (that is, to be 'lawful'), the organisation of industrial action must now be wholly or mainly in contemplation or furtherance of a trade dispute between workers and their own employer, and must not:

Table 11.4: Industrial Disputes 1982–1992

	Working days lost (thousands)	Working days lost per 1,000 employees[a]	Workers involved (thousands)	Number of stoppages
1982	5,313	248	2,103	1,538
1987	3,546	164	887	1,016
1990	1,903	83	298	630
1991	761	34	176	369
1992	528	24	148	253

Source: Department of Employment.
[a]Based on the mid-year (June) estimates of employees in employment.

POLLUTION CONTROL

Herbicides, pesticides and liquid
industrial wastes are among the
substances that can pollute
ground and surface water.
Researchers at the University of
Kent's Biological Laboratory are
investigating the effectiveness of
naturally-occurring bacteria in
breaking down certain herbicides.

Lloyd's Register operates a
mobile laboratory for assessing
air quality and identifying
pollution sources. The
laboratory can respond quickly
to air pollution incidents, and
the sensors on the taller mast
enable it to monitor weather
conditions.

WATERWAYS

Canoeing on the River Llugwy, near Capel Curig, in north Wales.

Game angling on the River Blackwater, County Tyrone, in Northern Ireland.

A tanker on the
Firth of Forth, Scotland.

A narrow-boat breaks the
ice on the Grand Union
Canal, on the western
outskirts of London.

Constructed from highly advanced composite materials, these rotor blades are in use on the world's fastest helicopter, the Lynx, built by Westland Helicopters.

Final assembly of the Rolls-Royce Pegasus 11-61 engine, which is in use in the Harrier 'jump jet'. This latest version is capable of a 15 per cent increase in vertical lift and has a longer engine life.

5

- involve workers who have no dispute with their own employer (so-called 'secondary' action);
- involve unlawful picketing;
- be done to establish or maintain a union-only labour agreement (the 'closed shop'); or
- be done in support of any employee dismissed while taking unofficial industrial action.

Before calling for industrial action, a trade union must first obtain the support of its members in a fully postal secret ballot and must notify employers of its intention to conduct such a ballot. The union must also provide employers, in writing, with at least seven days' notice of official industrial action following a ballot, and with details of the ballot result.

A trade union is responsible in law if industrial action is called for or organised by any of its officials. This means that if a trade union acts unlawfully, for example, by calling for industrial action without a proper secret ballot, legal proceedings can be taken against the union itself.

Any trade union member has the right to restrain his union from calling on him, and other members, to take action unless a properly conducted secret ballot has supported the action. Anyone deprived of goods or services because of unlawful organisation of industrial action has the right to obtain a court order to stop this happening.

Trade Union Elections

The law requires a trade union to elect every member of its governing body, its general secretary and its president. Elections must be held every five years and be carried out by secret postal ballot of the union's members. The election must be held under independent scrutiny. Any union member who believes that the union has not complied with the statutory requirements may complain to the courts or to the Certification Officer.

Members' Rights

All individuals have the right under the law not to be dismissed or refused employment because they are, are not or will not become, trade union members. They also have the right not to be refused any of the services of an employment agency because they are, or are not, members of a union. Individuals who believe that they have been dismissed or refused employment on grounds related to their union membership or non-membership may complain to an industrial tribunal. Other members' rights include:

- a statutory remedy if unjustifiably disciplined by their union; and
- the right to inspect their union's accounting records and obtain an annual statement from the union about its financial affairs.

Political Funds

A trade union may establish a political fund if it wishes to use its money for what the law defines as 'political objects'. If a union wishes to set up a political fund, its members must first agree in a secret ballot a resolution adopting those political objectives as an aim of the union. The union must also ballot its members every ten years to maintain the fund. Union members have a statutory right to opt out of contributing to a political fund.

Employers' Organisations

Many employers in Britain are members of employers' organisations, some of which are wholly concerned with labour matters, although others are also concerned with commercial matters or trade associations. With the move away from national pay bargaining, many employers' associations have looked at their functions and have moved towards concentrating on areas such as supplying information for bargaining purposes and dealing with specialist questions.

Employers' organisations are usually established on an industry basis rather than a product basis, for example, the Engineering Employers' Federation. A few are purely local in character or deal with a section of an industry or, for example, with small businesses; most are national and are concerned with the whole of an industry. In some of the main industries there are local or regional organisations combined into national federations. In others, within which different firms are engaged in making different principal products, there is a complex structure with national and regional federations for parts of an industry as well as for the industry as a whole. At the end of 1992, 128 listed and 134 unlisted employers' associations were known to the Certification Officer.

Most national organisations belong to the Confederation of British Industry (see p. 142), which represents directly or indirectly some 250,000 businesses.

Advisory, Conciliation and Arbitration Service

The Advisory, Conciliation and Arbitration Service (ACAS) is an independent statutory body providing industrial relations services to employers, employees and trade unions. ACAS seeks to discharge its responsibilities through the voluntary co-operation of employers, employees and their representatives. Its main functions are collective conciliation, provision of arbitration and mediation facilities, advisory services for promoting the improvement of industrial relations through the joint involvement of employers and employees, and providing an information service. ACAS also conciliates in disputes on individual rights.

In 1992 ACAS:

- received some 1,200 requests for collective conciliation, with a further 162 requests referred to arbitration, mediation or investigation;

- dealt with over 72,000 individual conciliation cases;

- made nearly 5,000 advisory visits;

- assisted with 225 joint working exercises; and

- dealt with 488,000 enquiries through its public enquiry points.

In Northern Ireland the Labour Relations Agency, an independent statutory body, provides services similar to those provided by ACAS in Great Britain.

HEALTH AND SAFETY AT WORK

Recent statistics indicate a reduction in the rate of major and other reported injuries to employees. About 23 million working days a year are lost as a result of work-related injuries. Employers have a duty in law to take reasonable care of their staff, as well as others affected by their work activities. Employees have a duty to take care of their own safety and that of their fellow workers.

The principal legislation is the Health and Safety at Work etc. Act 1974. It places general duties on everyone concerned with work activities, including employers, the self-employed, employees, and manufacturers and suppliers of materials for use at work. Associated Acts and regulations deal with particular hazards and types of work. Employers with five or more staff must prepare a written statement of their health and safety policy and bring it to the attention of their staff.

The 1974 Act provides for the Health and Safety Commission (see p. 139) to develop proposals to update earlier legislation, much of which was not adaptable to technical innovation. Reforms have since been completed in many areas. Much of the old law has been replaced by modern provisions, supported as necessary by codes of practice and other guidance material.

The Control of Substances Hazardous to Health Regulations 1988 are one of the most important sets of regulations made under the 1974 Act. They replaced a range of outdated legislation by a comprehensive and systematic approach to the control of exposure to virtually all substances hazardous to health. These include chemicals, fumes, dust and micro-organisms.

Six new sets of health and safety regulations came into force at the beginning of 1993, giving effect in Britain to various EC directives. They cover:

- the management of health and safety;

- the provision and use of work equipment;

- personal protective equipment;

- manual handling equipment;
- display screen equipment; and
- general health, safety and welfare in the workplace.

These also replaced a number of old laws. The regulations cover a wide range of basic health, safety and welfare issues.

The Health and Safety Commission is conducting a review, expected to be substantially completed by April 1994, of all health and safety legislation to assess whether it is still relevant and necessary. The review will look at the impact on business, and assess whether repeal or simplification is possible without endangering health and safety standards.

Health and Safety Commission

The Health and Safety Commission (HSC), which is accountable to Parliament through the Secretary of State for Employment, has responsibility for developing policy on health and safety at work, including guidance, codes of practice, or proposals for regulations. In the case of proposals for changes in legislation, the HSC has an obligation to consult those who would be affected and makes recommendations to the Secretary of State concerned.

The HSC has seven advisory committees covering subjects such as toxic substances, genetic manipulation and the safety of nuclear installations. There are also several industry advisory committees, each of which deals with a specific industry.

Health and Safety Executive

The Health and Safety Executive (HSE) is the primary instrument for carrying out the HSC's policies and has day-to-day responsibility for enforcing health and safety law, except where other bodies, such as local

authorities, are responsible. Its field services and inspections over the country as a whole are carried out by the Field Operations Division. This incorporates the Factory, Agricultural and Quarries inspectorates, together with the regional staff of the Employment Medical Advisory Service (which provides advice on medical aspects of employment problems), and the Field Consulting Groups, which provide technical support to the inspectorates. The HSE also includes:

- the policy divisions covering health, safety and strategic considerations;
- the Technology and Health Services Division, which provides technical advice on industrial health and safety matters; and
- the Research and Laboratory Services Division, which provides scientific and medical support and testing services, and carries out research.

In premises such as offices, shops, warehouses, restaurants and hotels, health and safety legislation is enforced by inspectors appointed by local authorities, working under guidance from the HSE. Some other official bodies work under agency agreement with the HSE.

Northern Ireland

In Northern Ireland the Health and Safety Agency, roughly corresponding to the HSC but without its policy-making powers, and an Employment Medical Advisory Service were set up by the Health and Safety at Work (NI) Order 1978. The general requirements of the Northern Ireland health and safety legislation are broadly similar to those for Great Britain. They are enforced mainly by the Department of Economic Development through its Health and Safety Inspectorate.

Further Reading

People, Jobs and Opportunity. White Paper. Cm 1810. HMSO, 1992.

Employment Gazette. Department of Employment. Monthly. Harrington Kilbride plc.

Labour Force Survey Quarterly Bulletin. Department of Employment.

12 Industry and Commerce

Private enterprises generate over three-quarters of total domestic income. Since 1979 the Government has privatised 46 major businesses and reduced the state-owned sector of industry by about two-thirds. The Government is taking measures to cut unnecessary regulations imposed on business, and runs a number of schemes which provide direct assistance or advice to small and medium-sized businesses.

STRUCTURE AND ORGANISATION

In some sectors a small number of large companies and their subsidiaries are responsible for a substantial proportion of total production, notably in the vehicle, aerospace and transport equipment industries. Private enterprises account for the greater part of activity in the agricultural, manufacturing, construction, distributive, financial and miscellaneous service sectors. The private sector contributed 75 per cent of total domestic final expenditure in 1992, general government 24 per cent and public corporations 1 per cent.

About 250 British industrial companies in the latest reporting period each had an annual turnover of more than £500 million. The annual turnover of the biggest company, British Petroleum (BP), makes it the 11th largest industrial grouping in the world and the second largest in Europe. Five British firms are among the top 25 European Community (EC) companies.

Industrial Financing

Over half of companies' funds for investment and other purposes are internally generated. Banks are the chief external source of finance, but companies have increasingly turned to equity finance. The main forms of short-term finance in the private sector are bank overdrafts, trade credit and factoring (making cash available to a company in exchange for debts owing to it).

Types of medium- and long-term finance include bank loans, mortgaging of property and the issue of shares and other securities to the public through the London Stock Exchange. The leasing of equipment may also be regarded as a form of finance. Other sources of finance for industry include the Government, the European Community and specialist financial institutions.

Venture Capital

Equity capital, known as venture capital, is a major source of funding for the start-up,

Table 12.1: Gross Domestic Product by Industry[a]

	1982		1992	
	£ million	per cent	£ million	per cent
Agriculture, hunting, forestry and fishing	5,601	2.3	9,309	1.8
Electricity, gas and water supply	7,780	3.3	13,717	2.7
Mining and quarrying, including oil and gas extraction	17,581	7.4	9,842	1.9
Manufacturing	61,468	25.8	114,698	22.3
Construction	14,244	6.0	32,002	6.2
Wholesale and retail trade, repairs, hotels and restaurants	30,817	12.9	72,549	14.1
Transport, storage and communications	17,811	7.5	41,613	8.1
Financial and business activities, real estate and renting	42,373	17.8	121,704	23.7
Public administration, defence and social security	16,870	7.1	36,605	7.1
Education, health and social work	21,255	8.9	52,509	10.2
Other services	13,069	5.5	32,892	6.4
Total	248,869	104.4	537,440	104.4
Adjustment for financial services	− 11,147	−4.7	− 23,058	−4.5
Statistical discrepancy	663	0.3	212	–
GDP at factor cost	238,385	100.0	514,594	100.0

Source: *United Kingdom National Accounts 1993 Edition.*
[a]Before provision for depreciation but after deducting stock appreciation.
Note: Differences between totals and the sums of their component parts are due to rounding.

expansion or the management buy-out or buy-in (see below) of a company. Equity capital is provided by major institutions and is managed by both independent fund managers and wholly owned subsidiaries or divisions of large financial institutions such as banks. Since 1985, members of the British Venture Capital Association (BVCA) have invested about £8,800 million and currently command an investment pool of some £2,000 million. The venture capital industry has been growing substantially.

Buy-ins and Buy-outs

In the late 1980s there was a rise in the number of buy-outs, in which the staff or management of a company raise the finance to purchase it, and buy-ins, whereby the staff or management of one firm purchase another. Since 1983 there have been over 4,300 buy-outs and buy-ins, with a total value of

£28,611 million. The amount invested in management buy-outs and buy-ins in 1992 was £3,262 million. Buy-outs and buy-ins accounted for 65 per cent of venture capital investments by BVCA members in Britain in 1991.

Taxation

Rates of corporate taxation have been progressively reduced. In the case of business plant and machinery, an annual allowance is available against profits for tax purposes of 25 per cent (on a reducing balance basis), beginning in the year in which expenditure occurs. For investment in industrial building, there is an allowance of 4 per cent a year. Special arrangements exist for short-life, often high-technology, assets. There are 100 per cent allowances for capital expenditure on scientific research, and, in designated enterprise zones, for construction expenditure.

INDUSTRIAL ASSOCIATIONS

Confederation of British Industry

The Confederation of British Industry (CBI) is the largest employers' organisation in Britain, representing about 250,000 companies from all sectors, which together employ over 60 per cent of Britain's workforce. Membership ranges from the smallest to the largest companies, private sector and nationalised, and includes companies in manufacturing, agriculture, construction, distribution, mining, finance, retailing and insurance. Most national employers' organisations, trade associations, and some chambers of commerce are members.

The CBI aims primarily to ensure that the Government, national and international institutions and the public understand the needs, intentions and problems of business, so as to create a climate of opinion in which business can operate efficiently and profitably. It campaigns to lessen the burdens on business, tackle handicaps on competition, and help improve the performance of companies. It offers members a forum, a lobby and a range of advisory services. The CBI also conducts surveys which provide a useful barometer of activity in manufacturing, distribution, financial services, the regions, innovation, and pay and productivity. It has 12 regional offices and an office in Brussels. The CBI is the British member of the Union of Industrial and Employers' Confederations of Europe.

British Chambers of Commerce

The British Chambers of Commerce (BCC) represents business views and interests to the Government at national and local levels. It promotes local economic development—for example, through regeneration projects, tourism, inward investment promotion in certain areas of Britain and business services, including overseas trade missions, exhibitions and training conferences. It also provides member firms with information about overseas buyers and product sourcing. The BCC represents over 214,000 businesses in over 240 chambers of commerce and trade throughout Britain.

Institute of Directors

The Institute of Directors (IOD) has more than 49,000 members worldwide, including 33,600 members in Britain, many of whom are in the small business sector. The IOD provides business advisory services on a range of matters affecting company directors, such as corporate management, insolvency and career counselling, and represents the interests of members to authorities in Britain and the EC. It also offers a full training programme of courses and lectures.

Trade and Employers' Organisations

Trade associations consist of companies producing or selling a particular product or group of products. They exist to supply common services, regulate trading practices and represent their members to government departments.

Employers' organisations are usually concerned with the negotiation of wages and conditions of work in a particular industry, although sometimes one institution may combine this function with that of a trade association.

GOVERNMENT AND INDUSTRY

The Government believes that economic decisions are best taken by those competing in the market place, and that government should encourage enterprise and create the right climate for markets to work better.

The Department of Trade and Industry (DTI) is the department mainly responsible for the Government's relations with industry and commerce. Specific responsibilities include technology and innovation, overseas trade and export promotion, competition policy and consumer affairs, regional industrial development, small firms, company legislation and patents. Through the Invest in Britain Bureau, it gives advice and assistance to overseas companies on locating in Britain (see p. 150). The Scottish, Welsh and Northern Ireland Offices are responsible for industrial policies in their areas.

The Government has reorganised the DTI so that it relates more closely to individual sectors of business. In October 1992 the DTI specified its objectives as:

- identifying the needs of business through close contact with individual sectors of industry;
- ensuring these needs are taken into account by Government and within the European Community;
- identifying influences on competitiveness at home and abroad;
- working for trade liberalisation worldwide;
- widening choice and stimulating enterprise by promoting competition and privatisation;
- maintaining confidence in markets and protecting consumers by fair regulation;
- reducing burdens on business;
- stimulating innovation and encouraging best practice in quality, design and management;
- helping to create small and medium-sized businesses;
- responding to regional needs; and
- stimulating an effective business response to environmental developments.

Education and Training

A well-educated and well-trained workforce is considered essential for economic growth, particularly at a time of intense international competition and rapid technological advance. The Government takes measures to see that education and training are broadly based and that people of all ages can acquire relevant knowledge and skills. Education–business links are being improved (see Chapter 27).

Training and Enterprise Councils and Local Enterprise Companies

The Government has set up a network of 82 business-led Training and Enterprise Councils in England and Wales and 22 Local Enterprise Companies in Scotland. TECs and LECs are independent companies run by boards of directors, the majority of whom are drawn from private sector business. From April 1993, grants are being provided to TECs to enable them to provide a range of training, education and enterprise programmes on behalf of the Government. The LECs encourage investment in the development of skills throughout the workforce and invest directly in training, particularly for school-leavers and the long-term unemployed. In addition, they offer a range of advisory and training services to businesses, including schemes to enhance the expertise of managers. TECs are expected to play a strategic role and are not engaged in the direct delivery of services, particularly where this may compete with existing provision.

Single European Market

The Government believes that the completion of the single European market, which was achieved by the end of 1992 (see p. 296), will benefit the economy of each member state, and that the removal of trade barriers should lead to a reduction in business costs as well as increasing competition, stimulating efficiency, benefiting consumers and encouraging the creation of jobs and wealth. In the years leading up to the completion of the single market legislative framework, the DTI's Single Market Campaign informed business organisations on specific issues and opportunities that would arise. In 1993 the Government launched Business in Europe, an initiative to strengthen export advisory services to help British companies compete effectively.

Privatisation

The Government believes that the best way to improve the performance of public sector companies and nationalised industries is to expose them to market forces, through privatisation and the promotion of competition. Privatisation has also provided an opportunity for the Government to widen and deepen share ownership by encouraging both employees and the general public to take a direct stake in industry. In major flotations, employees in privatised companies are normally given a preferential right to buy shares in the new privatised companies.

Table 12.2: Major Government Sales

	Year of sale	Net equity proceeds (£ million)
BAA	1987	1,182
BT	1984–93	13,900[a]
British Aerospace	1981–85	390
British Airways	1987	853
British Gas	1986–90	5,293
British Petroleum	1979-87	6,084
British Steel	1988	2,425
Britoil	1982-85	962
Cable and Wireless	1981-85	1,021
Rolls-Royce	1987	1,031
Water companies (England and Wales)	1989	3,454
Regional electricity companies (England and Wales)	1990 }	7,100[a]
Electricity generating companies (England and Wales)	1991	
Scottish electricity companies	1991	2,800[a]

Source: HM Treasury.
[a] Includes value of future instalment payments.

Since 1979 the Government has privatised 46 major businesses, with forecast net proceeds to the end of 1993–94 of some £55,500 million. Recent privatisations include the electricity industry in Northern Ireland and the Government's residual shareholding in BT (British Telecom). British Coal is to be privatised and legislation is being introduced to enable the private sector to operate rail services. The future of the Post Office is under review and the ten companies operating London's buses are to be sold from late 1993. Privatisation is also being extended to non-core government activities and other public sector areas.

Benefits

The economy has benefited through higher returns on capital in the privatised industries, which can no longer pre-empt or command resources from elsewhere in the economy but must compete for funds in the open capital markets. Privatised companies have welcomed the freedom to raise finance in private sector capital markets.

The consumer has benefited from downward pressure on prices and from rising standards of service. The Government established a system of independent regulation for the privatised utilities (see p. 153). For each of the privatised utility sectors, such as gas or telecommunications, there is a regulatory body which has a wide range of powers and duties to promote competition and the interests of consumers. These include considering all complaints and representations about the company's services. Each privatised utility has a pricing policy which usually limits annual price increases to no more than the rate of inflation.

Nationalised Industries

The remaining major nationalised industries are British Coal, British Rail, the Post Office, London Transport and Nuclear Electric. Their managing boards are appointed by ministers who have the power to give general directions but are not involved in day-to-day management. The managing boards and staffs of the nationalised industries are not civil servants.

The Government considers that nationalised industries should act as commercial enterprises and has set policies with which they are expected to conform. These involve:

● clear government objectives for the industries;

- regular corporate plans and performance reviews;
- agreed principles relating to investment appraisal and pricing;
- financial targets and performance aims;
- external financing limits; and
- systematic monitoring.

Deregulation

The Government's objective is to reduce or simplify administrative and legislative burdens imposed on business, particularly small businesses, where the burden of compliance is most demanding.

Under a Deregulation Initiative, the Government is working to reduce burdens on business by:

- achieving better regulation, cutting unnecessary regulation and minimising the cost of compliance with essential regulation;
- ensuring that the views of business, and potential costs of compliance, are taken into account in framing new regulations and in negotiating EC proposals;
- improving official awareness of the needs of business through training and better consultation and communication; and
- improving the quality of service to business generally, whether provided by central or local government.

Proposed regulations, including EC directives, are to be accompanied by an assessment of the costs they would impose on business. The existing 3,500 regulations affecting companies are being reviewed by task forces of business people working with government departments.

It is intended that deregulation should complement the Citizen's Charter, which aims to ensure public services are efficient and responsive to their users. Measures are being taken to ensure business forms are simplified and that contracting out does not impose additional burdens on business.

Small Firms

Small businesses make a major contribution to the economy. Firms with fewer than 100 employees account for 50 per cent of the private sector workforce and produce 27 per cent of British turnover. Some 400,000 new businesses were started in 1992, slightly fewer than the 460,000 in 1991, but higher than the average for the 1980s. Industries with the fastest growth rates between 1980 and 1991 were in the services sector, particularly finance, property and professional services.

The Government runs schemes giving either direct assistance or advice and guidance on a range of business problems affecting small firms. In addition to DTI schemes such as those available under the Enterprise Initiative, TECs offer small and medium-sized enterprises a comprehensive package of business and training support. The range of support is varied. A TEC portfolio of business support would typically include business information and advice services, business counselling for new and existing companies, and business skills training programmes.

One-stop Shops

The DTI has set up a pilot network of 23 business advice centres—'One-stop Shops'—to bring together organisations supporting enterprise, such as local companies, TECs and chambers of commerce, to offer a full range of business advisory services to established medium-sized and small firms. It is envisaged not as a government scheme but as a network of local partnerships, in which larger firms can make contacts and expertise available to small firms. The Government intends contracting out all consultancy services at present run by DTI to the One-stop Shops.

The first One-stop Shops are being set up in six areas at a cost of £5.6 million. Additional government funds will be provided to set up a London-wide network of One-stop Shops. If successful, it is intended to establish a national network of such centres.

In Scotland the arrangements for the provision of integrated business advice are slightly different. The LECs play a significant role, both individually and in their partnerships with other agencies, and a number of local Business Information Centres have been opened.

Enterprise Initiative

The Enterprise Initiative brings together a wide range of the services that the DTI provides for industry and commerce. The consultancy scheme encourages small and medium-sized businesses to use outside consultancy services as a regular part of their management strategy and offers short-term consultancy support in design, marketing, manufacturing and services systems, quality, business planning, and financial and management information systems. Some 12,000 consultancy projects were completed in 1992–93.

In Scotland and Wales the consultancy scheme is delivered by Enterprise Services Scotland (a subsidiary of Scottish Enterprise—see p. 147) and the Welsh Development Agency (see p. 147). Assistance is available to most manufacturing and service businesses with fewer than 500 employees. In the Assisted Areas (see below) and Urban Programme Areas, half of the costs of a project are met; elsewhere the rate is one-third. Some £50 million is being provided in 1993–94 to support the consultancy scheme. The target in 1993–94, the last year for applications, is to assist 10,000 firms. Thereafter consultancy support will be channelled through One-stop Shops and TECs.

Small Firms Schemes

The Support for Products Under Research scheme (SPUR) offers grants to businesses with up to 500 employees for new product and process development requiring a significant technological advance. The Small Firms Merit Award for Research and Technology (SMART) is an annual competition which provides grants to individuals and businesses with fewer than 50 employees in support of highly innovative technological projects with commercial potential. The DTI has allocated over £70 million to the SPUR and SMART programmes.

Other government help to small firms includes:

- the Small Firms Loan Guarantee Scheme, which helps businesses with viable proposals to obtain finance where conventional loans are unavailable as a result of a lack of financial security or previous performance—the scheme provides banks and other financial institutions with a government guarantee on a certain percentage of the loan in return for a premium payment;
- an initiative to encourage the growth of informal investment for small firms from a wider range of sources. The Government is providing support to a number of TECs and other organisations to bring together investors and small firms; and
- the Business Start-Up scheme, enabling unemployed people to claim an allowance while establishing a new business.

REGIONAL INDUSTRIAL DEVELOPMENT

Industrial policy is designed to encourage enterprise and economic growth in all areas of Britain. In some areas, however, where additional help is needed, it is provided under the Enterprise Initiative. Help is focused on the Assisted Areas (Development Areas and Intermediate Areas), which cover around 34 per cent of Britain's working population.

Following a review of the Assisted Areas, in July 1993 the Government announced a number of changes. The new map (see p. 148) represents the Government's assessment of those areas now facing problems of structural unemployment. The review took into account a wide range of factors, including levels of unemployment and the nature of the problems faced in each area. Some regions, such as Wales, which have experienced a relative improvement in unemployment levels, now have less of their area covered by Assisted Areas. Areas which have become eligible for regional aid include parts of the South East, such as inner areas of London and some coastal towns affected by high unemployment; and areas in the East Midlands and Yorkshire affected by coal mine closures.

The principal regional policy instruments are:

- regional selective assistance, available throughout the Assisted Areas, for investment projects undertaken by firms meeting certain criteria;
- Regional Enterprise Grants, which are available to support investment and innovation in small firms. Investment grants are available to firms with fewer than 25 employees in Development Areas and certain Intermediate Areas;
- Regional Innovation Grants, which are made to firms employing fewer than 50 employees in all Development, Intermediate, Task Force and City Challenge areas (see pp. 321–6), as well as some other areas covered by EC schemes; they are also available in certain Scottish urban areas. The promotion of inward investment is a key element in the Government's regional policy.

England

The English Industrial Estates Corporation makes available industrial and commercial premises in certain parts of the Assisted Areas in England where private sector provision is insufficient.

The Rural Development Commission is responsible for advising the Government on issues affecting rural England and for promoting its economic and social development. The Commission's resources are concentrated in areas of greatest need, known as Priority Areas. It provides:

- small factories and workshops built and managed by English Estates or in partnership with local authorities or the private sector;
- a grant scheme for the conversion of redundant buildings to industrial or commercial premises;
- technical, management and financial advice, as well as training facilities and loans to small businesses;
- support for local enterprise agencies, which in turn offer help to small firms;

- support for voluntary bodies in rural areas to encourage community activity and self-help; and
- support for the provision of small-scale rural housing and local rural transport schemes.

Scotland

Scottish Enterprise and Highlands and Islands Enterprise provide support to industry and commerce, in lowland and highland Scotland respectively, operating mainly through the network of LECs (see p. 143).

Scottish Enterprise and Highlands and Islands Enterprise seek to ensure that economic development in Scotland is not artificially constrained by inadequate provision of sites and factories, and that there is sufficient investment funding for businesses in the private sector. Where necessary they contribute financially to such provision. They also remove obstacles to economic development through the treatment of derelict land and by contributing to tackling deficiencies in the physical environment and infrastructure of towns and cities. In addition, The Scottish Office Industry Department provides support to exporters and small firms through the SPUR and SMART programmes and Regional Enterprise Grants.

Wales

The Welsh Development Agency (WDA) promotes industrial efficiency and international competitiveness and aims to improve the environment in Wales. Through Welsh Development International, it seeks to attract high-quality investment into Wales and co-ordinates the approach for responding to the needs of investors. The WDA provides a range of support services, particularly for small and medium-sized enterprises.

The Business Services programme helps companies plan strategically for long-term competitiveness, growth and improved profitability, and for meeting customer requirements, and understanding and implementing best practice. The programme also includes technology exploitation, skills

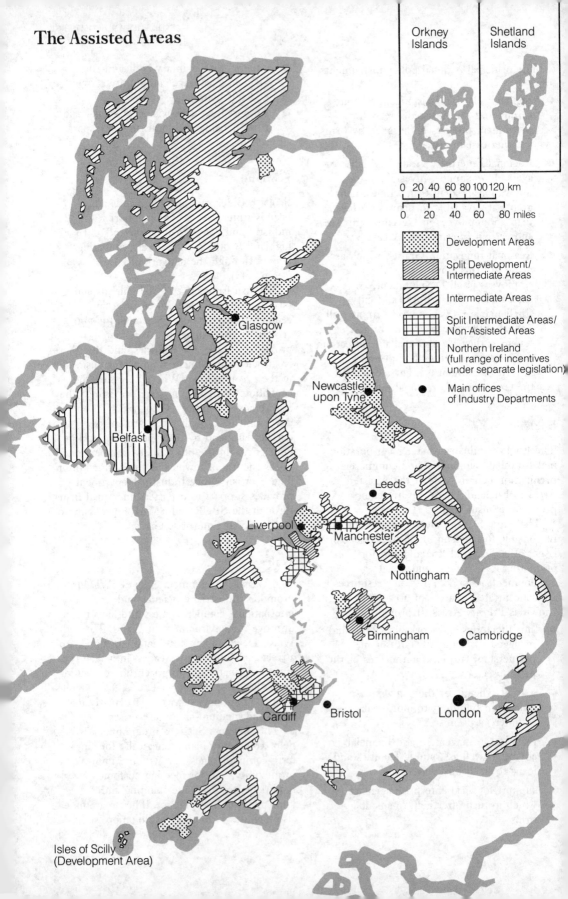

The Assisted Areas

Orkney Islands

Shetland Islands

0 20 40 60 80 100 120 km	
0 20 40 60 80 miles	

Development Areas

Split Development/
Intermediate Areas

Intermediate Areas

Split Intermediate Areas/
Non-Assisted Areas

Northern Ireland
(full range of incentives
under separate legislation)

● Main offices
of Industry Departments

Glasgow

Belfast

Newcastle
upon Tyne

Leeds

Liverpool

Manchester

Nottingham

Birmingham

Cambridge

Cardiff

Bristol

London

Isles of Scilly
(Development Area)

development, financial advice and help, and a comprehensive European programme.

The WDA aims to ensure that an adequate supply of industrial and commercial property is available in Wales. Its direct building programme focuses on areas where private sector provision is not adequate; increasingly the Agency operates through land assembly and servicing of sites, and by encouraging participation from the private sector, for example, through joint ventures. Development projects, such as a major programme of land reclamation and environmental improvement and an urban development programme, aim to regenerate selected areas by opening up development opportunities for private enterprise.

The Rural Prosperity Programme includes comprehensive action plans to develop specific rural areas. There are also initiatives and schemes designed to stimulate new rural enterprise and business growth. The Development Board for Rural Wales supplies factories, key worker housing and advice for small businesses.

Northern Ireland

Development policy in Northern Ireland is the responsibility of the Department of Economic Development and is delivered through various agencies, including:

- the Industrial Development Board, which deals with overseas companies considering Northern Ireland as an investment location, as well as the development of local companies with more than 50 employees;
- the Local Enterprise Development Unit, responsible for the promotion of enterprise and the development of small businesses;
- the Industrial Research and Technology Unit, providing advice and assistance on research and development, innovation and technology transfer; and
- the Training and Employment Agency, which helps with in-company training and management development.

A variety of schemes are available to help

companies with marketing, exporting, product development and design, improved productivity and quality, training, and research and development. The full range of assistance is made available to those companies which are able to demonstrate development potential and prospect of long-term competitive growth. Where appropriate, this assistance includes capital grants, loans and share capital investment. The Industrial Development Board also offers stocks of land and industrial premises for purchase or lease. There is exemption from local taxes for manufacturing premises.

European Community Regional Policy and Aid

The European Community seeks to reduce disparities between regions. The principal responsibility for helping less prosperous areas remains with national authorities, but the Community may complement schemes through aid from a number of sources.

The European Regional Development Fund is intended to stimulate economic development in the EC's least prosperous regions and those where economic development is at a relatively low level. For 1993, £571 million has been allocated to Britain. The Fund is used to co-finance a variety of measures, including industrial facilities, transport infrastructure, environmental improvement schemes, tourism developments, and support for research and development (R & D) and vocational training.

The European Investment Bank (see p. 297) also helps to finance projects of common interest to several member states. The Channel Tunnel (see Chapter 18) is one such project currently being assisted in Britain.

INWARD INVESTMENT

Britain is considered a favourable location for inward direct investment, attracting more than any other EC country. This reflects its membership of the European Community and proximity to other European markets, stable labour relations, a flexible and productive workforce, and comparatively low corporate and personal taxation. In 1992–93 the DTI's Invest in Britain Bureau reported over 300 investment decisions taken by overseas companies, with associated employment estimated at more than 56,000.

Benefits

Inward investment brings many benefits to Britain's economy, such as new jobs, management practices, products and processes. Overseas companies are estimated to provide 16 per cent of manufacturing jobs in Britain, 22 per cent of net output and 27 per cent of net capital expenditure. Over the past three years they have bought over a half of their capital equipment from companies within Britain and have built long-term contacts with suppliers.

The regions benefiting most from inward investment by multinational companies are Scotland, Wales, Northern Ireland, north-east England, Yorkshire and Humberside, and the Midlands. Many projects are expansions by companies already established in Britain.

Promotion

Overseas-owned firms are offered the same incentives by the Government as British-owned ones. The Invest in Britain Bureau gives overseas companies advice and assistance on locating and relocating businesses in Britain, and on expanding existing facilities. It operates overseas through British Embassies, High Commissions and Consulates-General, and within Britain through the DTI's network of regional offices in England, which provide local information about available sites, wages and skills, markets and housing. They operate with the aid of the six English Regional Development Organisations (RDOs), which also promote their own areas to potential investors overseas and elsewhere in Britain.

Similar advice and assistance to that provided by the RDOs is available through:

- Locate in Scotland, operated jointly by The Scottish Office Industry Department and Scottish Enterprise;
- Welsh Development International, the investment arm of the Welsh Development Agency; and
- the Industrial Development Board in Northern Ireland.

REGULATION OF MARKETS

While preferring to let markets operate as freely as possible, the Government recognises that intervention may sometimes be needed to ensure that markets are open and fair. The Government therefore seeks to control restrictive or anti-competitive practices.

Within the public sector it has taken a number of steps to increase competition, notably through privatisation (see p. 143). Deregulation measures seek to reduce regulations which inhibit competition, innovation or consumer choice (see p. 145).

Government policy provides for the regulation of monopolies, mergers, anti-competitive practices and restrictive trade practices. The Office of Fair Trading, headed by its Director General, administers the legislation on competition, consumer credit, fair trading and resale price maintenance. Among other things, it takes action against cartels and anti-competitive practices; examines company mergers for adverse effects on competition; and scrutinises rules and practices of regulatory bodies in sectors such as financial services.

The Government has taken measures to increase competition in professional services by tackling restrictive practices. The opticians' monopoly on the dispensing of spectacles and the solicitors' monopoly on conveyancing have been ended. Certain professional groups (for example, accountants, solicitors, veterinary surgeons, stockbrokers, doctors, dentists and surveyors) have eased the restrictions on advertising by their members, and rules on fee scales have been made more liberal in a number of areas. Building societies are now allowed to offer a greater range of services. Legislation has also provided for greater competition in the provision of legal services. Legislation exists to offer greater protection to investors. The Securities and Investments Board (see p. 179) is empowered to set out general principles governing the conduct of investment business.

European Community rules provide for free and fair competition in trade between member states. Enforcement of these rules is primarily the responsibility of the European Commission, which has powers to investigate and terminate alleged infringements and to impose fines, and the competition authorities in Britain liaise closely with the Commission.

Following a Green Paper in 1992 on the abuse of market power, the Government announced in April 1993 that it proposed to strengthen the law against anti-competitive practices, including increasing the investigative powers of the Director General of Fair Trading.

Monopolies

The Director General of Fair Trading and the President of the Board of Trade can refer monopolies for investigation by the Monopolies and Mergers Commission, an independent body. Its members are drawn from a variety of backgrounds and include industrialists, lawyers, economists and trade unionists. The governing legislation defines a monopoly situation as one in which at least a quarter of the market for a particular product or service is supplied or consumed by a single person or a group of connected companies or by two or more people acting in a way which prevents, restricts, or distorts competition. The market definition of a monopoly can relate to all of Britain or part of it.

If the Commission finds that a monopoly situation operates against the public interest, the President of the Board of Trade has powers to take action to remedy this. Alternatively the Director General may be asked to negotiate undertakings to remedy the adverse effects identified by the Commission. In 1992 the Commission reported on four monopoly situations, three of which were found to operate against the public interest. Eight further monopoly references were under investigation at the end of 1992.

The President of the Board of Trade has powers to refer to the Commission any questions concerning the efficiency and costs of the service provided by, or the possible abuse of a monopoly situation by, certain bodies in the public sector.

Mergers

The Government believes that the market is, in most cases, the best judge of the advantages and disadvantages of mergers. The great majority of mergers which do not pose a threat to competition are, therefore, allowed to take place. However, under the Fair Trading Act 1973, the President of the Board of Trade can refer mergers for investigation by the Monopolies and Mergers Commission if they could lead to a significant reduction in competition or otherwise raise matters of public concern.

A merger is defined as occurring when two or more enterprises are brought under common ownership or control. A merger qualifies for investigation by the Commission where:

- an existing market share of 25 per cent or more is increased; or

- the total value of gross assets to be taken over exceeds £30 million.

After considering advice from the Director General of Fair Trading, the President of the Board of Trade may refer a merger or proposed merger to the Commission. The primary criterion of the Government's referral policy is the possible effects on competition. If the Commission finds that a merger or proposed merger may be expected to operate against the public interest, the President of the Board of Trade can prohibit it. Alternatively, the Director General may be asked to obtain suitable undertakings from the companies involved to remedy the adverse effects identified. If the merger has already taken place, the President of the Board of Trade can take similar action to reverse it. There are special provisions for newspaper and water company mergers.

The Companies Act 1989 made changes to improve merger control procedure. This provided for:

- a voluntary procedure for pre-notification of proposed mergers which, for the majority of cases, permits prompt clearance;
- the acceptance of statutory undertakings by the parties concerned in order to obviate the need for a full investigation by the Commission in certain cases; and
- the temporary prohibition on reciprocal share dealing by the parties to a merger referred to the Commission.

During 1992, 16 acquisitions valued at more than £500 million were completed, eight of which exceeded £1,000 million. The number of mergers qualifying for investigation in 1992 was 125, compared with 185 in 1991.

Large mergers with an EC dimension, which are assessed by reference to turnover, normally come under the exclusive jurisdiction of the European Commission. The Commission can ban them if it considers that they create or strengthen a dominant position which would significantly impede effective competition within the Community.

Anti-competitive Practices

The Director General of Fair Trading can, with limited exceptions, investigate any course of conduct by a business which appears to be anti-competitive. If the Director General concludes in the report following his investigation that a practice is anti-competitive, undertakings may be offered by the business responsible for the conduct. If a suitable undertaking is not given, the matter may be referred to the Monopolies and Mergers Commission to establish whether the course of conduct is an anti-competitive practice and if so whether it operates against the public interest. In the case of an adverse finding by the Commission, the President of the Board of Trade has powers to take remedial action.

Restrictive Trade Practices

Certain kinds of commercial agreements containing restrictions on, for example,

matters such as prices or conditions of sale have to be notified to the Director General of Fair Trading for registration. Failure to register an agreement within the required period means that the restrictions are void and unenforceable and the parties may be liable to legal proceedings.

Once an agreement has been registered, the Director General is under a general duty to refer it to the Restrictive Practices Court. In practice, however, the great majority of agreements never reach the Court because the parties elect to give up the restrictions rather than go to court. Alternatively, the President of the Board of Trade accepts the Director General's advice that the restrictions are not significant enough to warrant referral to the Court.

If an agreement goes to the Court, the Court must declare the restrictions contrary to the public interest unless the parties can satisfy it that the agreement is in the public interest, using set criteria ('gateways'). Restrictions declared contrary to the public interest by the Court are void, and the Court has the power to order the parties not to implement them.

Resale Price Maintenance

With two exceptions, it is unlawful for suppliers to notify dealers of a minimum resale price for their goods or to make it a condition of supply that their goods must not be sold below a specified price. Similarly, it is also unlawful for suppliers to seek to impose minimum resale prices by withholding supplies of goods or discriminating in other ways. The Director General of Fair Trading, or anyone affected, can take proceedings in the civil courts.

Consumer Protection

The Government believes that consumers' interests are best served by open and competitive markets offering the widest range of choice in goods and services. There are, however, laws to ensure that consumers are adequately protected.

Legislation covers the sale of goods, the supply of goods and services, and the way that goods and services are described. The marking and accuracy of quantities are regulated by weights and measures legislation. The Food Safety Act 1990 and, for Northern Ireland, the Food Safety (NI) Order 1991 contain measures to improve food safety and to protect consumers. Another law provides for the control of medical products, and certain other substances and articles, through a system of licences and certificates. Under EC legislation, it is a criminal offence to supply unsafe consumer products. A range of public safety information for consumers has been made available by the DTI.

The Director General of Fair Trading promotes good trading practices and acts against malpractices. Under the Fair Trading Act 1973, the Director General makes recommendations for legislative or other changes to stop practices adversely affecting consumers' economic welfare, encourages trade associations to adopt codes of practice promoting consumers' interests, takes action against those breaching the law to the detriment of consumers, and disseminates guidance to consumers on their rights. The Director General is also responsible for administering legislation regulating consumer credit and estate agency work, and has responsibilities for controlling misleading advertisements.

The European Community's consumer programme covers a number of important activities, such as health and safety, protection of the consumer's economic interests, promotion of consumer education and strengthening the representation of consumers. The views of British consumer organisations on Community matters are represented by the Consumers in the European Community Group (UK). British consumer bodies are also represented on the European consumer 'watchdog' body, the Bureau Européen des Unions de Consommateurs.

Consumer Advice and Information

Advice and information on consumer matters are given by Citizens Advice Bureaux, trading standards or consumer protection departments of local authorities (in Northern Ireland the Department of Economic Development), and,

in some areas, by specialist consumer advice centres.

The independent, non-statutory National Consumer Council (and the associated councils for Scotland and Wales), which receives government finance, presents the consumer's view to government, industry and others. The General Consumer Council for Northern Ireland has wide-ranging duties in consumer protection and consumer affairs in general.

Consumer bodies for the rail industry and for some privatised utilities investigate questions of concern to the consumer. Some trade associations in industry and commerce have established codes of practice. In addition, several private organisations work to further consumer interests. The largest is the Consumers' Association, funded by the subscriptions of its 800,000 members.

Company Law

All British companies are registered with the Registrar of Companies in Cardiff, Edinburgh or Belfast, depending on whether a company's registered office is in England or Wales, Scotland or Northern Ireland. Legislation deals with capital structure, the rights and duties of directors and members, and the preparation and filing of accounts. Most corporate businesses are 'limited liability' companies. The liability of members of a limited company is restricted to contributing an amount related to their shareholding. In the case of unincorporated businesses, such as sole proprietorships or partnerships, individuals are personally liable for any business debts, except where a member of a partnership is a limited liability company.

Companies may be either public or private. A company must satisfy three conditions before it can become a public limited company (plc). It must:

- be limited by shares and have a share capital;
- state in its memorandum of association that it is to be a public limited company; and
- meet specified minimum capital requirements.

153

All other British companies are private companies and are generally prohibited from offering their shares to the public. Companies with a place of business in Britain, but which are incorporated overseas, are also required to register.

Laws relating to companies are designed to meet the need for proper regulation of business, secure open markets and create greater safeguards for those wishing to invest in companies or do business with them. They implement EC directives dealing with company law, and company and group accounts and their auditing. The 1992 Cadbury Committee Report on the management of companies has proposed a Code of Best Practice for company boards. It is based on the need for open management and for checks and balances to prevent abuses of power.

Insider dealing in shares is a criminal offence. Inspectors may be appointed to investigate possible insider dealing. Throughout Britain there is a licensing procedure to ensure the professional competence, integrity and independence of people acting as trustees of bankrupt individuals, or as liquidators, receivers or administrators of insolvent companies.

MANAGEMENT INITIATIVES

The DTI is working with other government departments and with industry to improve management education, and to spread awareness about best management practices through schemes such as the Enterprise Initiative (see p. 146).

Another programme, 'Managing in the 90s', offers advice to managers in small and medium-sized businesses on design, quality, production and purchasing, and materials management. Having been extended until 1995, the programme will focus on innovation and management practices in the manufacturing sector.

Management Development and Industrial Training

Management education is on offer at many universities and colleges of higher and further education. Some regional management centres have been established in England and Wales by associations of these colleges, and there are several similar organisations in Scotland. Universities run full-time postgraduate programmes at business schools such as those of London, Manchester, Durham, Warwick and Strathclyde universities.

The British Institute of Management encourages excellence in management. Other professional bodies are concerned with standards and training in specialised branches of management. The employer-led Management Charter Initiative (MCI) is the operating arm of the National Forum for Management Education and Development and the leading industrial body for management standards. Some 1,700 employers, representing a quarter of the total workforce, are members of the MCI, which has 86 local networks working with local employers.

Teaching Company Scheme

The Teaching Company Scheme (TCS) provides industrially relevant training for young graduates over a two-year period while they undertake key technology transfer projects in companies under the joint supervision of academic and company staff. There are over 450 TCS partnerships in progress at any one time. A similar programme, the Senior Academics in Industry Scheme, supports the placement of senior academic staff into firms for six months, where they work directly on projects which will benefit from their research experience.

QUALITY AND STANDARDS

The Government is urging industry and commerce to consider quality at all stages of design, production, marketing and delivery to customers.

Through its support for consultancy projects, the Government helps small and medium-sized firms to learn about and apply quality management techniques based on a national standard meeting international requirements. In order to increase customer confidence, companies are encouraged to obtain assessment and registration to this standard. The competence and performance of organisations undertaking such certification are officially accredited by the President of the Board of Trade through the National Accreditation Council for Certification Bodies. Companies certified by accredited bodies are permitted to use the national 'crown and tick' accreditation mark. The DTI's Register of Quality Assessed Companies lists accredited certification bodies and companies assessed by them.

British Standards Institution

The British Standards Institution (BSI), incorporated by Royal Charter, is the British member of the European and international standards organisations. It works with industry and government to produce standards of the required quality, relevant to the needs of the market, internationally respected, and suitable for public purchasing and regulatory purposes.

Government support for the BSI is directed particularly towards European and international standards work. Common standards are contributing to the aim of removing technical barriers to trade in the European Community. About 5,000 of the 12,500 British Standards are now identical with European or international standards; of all standards published in 1992–93, over three-quarters are identical. The Kitemark is the BSI's registered certification trade mark.

Measurement Standards

The DTI is responsible for policy relating to the National Measurement System. Through its contractors, it provides many of the physical measurement standards and associated calibration facilities necessary so that measurements in Britain are made on a common basis and to the required accuracy. Contractors include three DTI executive agencies: the National Physical Laboratory, the Laboratory of the Government Chemist, and the National Weights and Measures Laboratory. Links with laboratories in other countries are maintained to ensure international compatibility in standards and measurement, which is essential for overseas trade and technological co-operation. The National Measurement Accreditation Service (NAMAS) is the national accreditation service for calibration and testing laboratories. For example, NAMAS-accredited calibration laboratories offer calibration of scientific instruments and supply official certificates in, primarily, the physical, chemical and engineering fields.

Design

The Design Council promotes effective design in industry and commerce. It works with manufacturing industry to promote the importance of design, and to encourage manufacturers to make better use of it, and supports training and education in design at all levels.

As the DTI's main agent for design promotion, the Design Council has responsibility for linking design to innovation and technology so as to ensure that British products compete effectively. It is also responsible for the design elements of the Enterprise Initiative consultancy scheme and the 'Managing in the 90s' programme.

The Design Council, in operating the DTI's consultancy initiative on design, offers firms employing up to 500 people five to 15 days of subsidised consultancy. The Council runs the British Design Awards in four categories: consumer and contract goods, transport industry products, computer software, and industrial products.

In September 1993 the Government announced that the Council would be reorganised into a smaller body acting primarily as a provider of analysis and advice on all aspects of design policy.

Awards to Industry and Commerce

The Queen's Awards for Export and Technological Achievement recognise outstanding performance in their respective fields. Awarded annually, they are valid for five years and are granted by the Queen on the advice of the Prime Minister, who is assisted by an Advisory Committee consisting of senior representatives from industry, commerce, the trade unions and government departments. Any self-contained 'industrial unit' in Britain is eligible to apply, regardless of size, provided it meets the scheme's criteria. The Queen's Award for Environmental Achievement was launched in 1993.

Other awards include the Export Award for Smaller Businesses (for firms employing fewer than 200 people) and the MacRobert Award, the major award for engineering in Britain made by the Fellowship of Engineering for successful technological innovation.

INNOVATION

Innovation—the successful exploitation of new ideas—is vital in maintaining an economy based on competitive wealth creation. Through its Innovation Unit, which includes five seconded industrialists, the DTI seeks to influence the thinking of business, education, the media and Government, as well as the general public, by:

● improving commercial exploitation of Britain's science and technology base;

● improving management of innovation in business by spreading best practice;

● improving communications between investors and business regarding innovation;

● increasing appreciation of the importance of innovation within education at all levels;

● encouraging a more positive attitude to innovation, as well as to science and technology;

● informing the public of the importance of innovation in wealth creation; and

● ensuring consistency and co-operation in the delivery of innovation schemes and services provided by the DTI and other government departments.

There has been an increase in the DTI's budget for industrial innovation (see p. 277).

In Northern Ireland the basic aim of the Industrial Research and Technology Unit is to improve the competitiveness of industry by encouraging innovation, industrially relevant R & D and technology transfer. It does this through the provision of scientific services and the delivery of R & D support programmes, such as its Product and Process Development Programme and its Science and Technology Programme.

Industrial and Intellectual Property

The Government supports innovation by protecting the rights of the originators of inventions, industrial designs, trade marks and copyright in literary, artistic and musical works. These matters are the responsibility of the Patent Office, which includes the Design Registry and the Trade Marks Registry. The Patent Office is an executive agency of the DTI. Patent protection is also available under the European Patent Convention and the Patent Co-operation Treaty. Benefits may be claimed in other countries by virtue of separate conventions on industrial property, literary and artistic works, and music and broadcasting. Recent measures include:

● the adoption of EC directives on copyright which harmonise rental and lending rights, the rights of performers, record producers and broadcasters, and legal protection of computer programs. The directive on computer programs has been implemented into British law.

● a regulation on patents to create a supplementary protection certificate for medicinal products.

Proposals have been made for a Community Design Right and some harmonisation of national design legislation. Negotiations continue on the Community's regulation on trade marks, and the proposed EC directive for the legal protection of biotechnological inventions is also being discussed.

13 Manufacturing and Construction Industries

Britain became the world's first industrialised country in the mid 19th century. Wealth was based on manufacturing iron and steel, heavy machinery and cotton textiles, and on coal mining, shipbuilding and trade. As in other industrialised nations, service industries have become much more important. However, manufacturing still plays an important role and many high-technology industries have been developed. Major export industries with a high proportion of research and development (R & D) spending are chemicals, aerospace, electronics and offshore equipment, where Britain is a world leader in technological expertise.

Introduction

Manufacturing accounted for 22 per cent of gross domestic product (GDP) in 1992 and for about the same percentage of employment. Over 80 per cent of visible exports consisted of manufactured or semi-manufactured goods. Almost all manufacturing is carried out by private sector businesses.

In 1992 manufacturing output was 11 per cent higher than in 1985, but 6 per cent lower than in 1990 (see Table 13.2). The recent recession led to a decline in manufacturing output of 1 per cent in 1992.

Table 13.1: Manufacturing—Size of Businesses by Turnover and Employment

Annual turnover (£'000)	Number of businesses[a] 1992	Employment size	Number of businesses[a] 1992	Employment 1990
1–25	21,002	1–9	94,991	303,982
26–49	24,217	10–19	16,758	229,667
50–99	23,727	20–49	14,899	458,568
100–249	32,537	50–99	5,926	411,040
250–499	20,346	100–199	3,360	468,314
500–999	14,531	200–499	2,251	690,124
1,000–1,999	9,774	500–999	752	517,815
2,000–4,999	7,393	1,000 and over	570	1,538,733
5,000–9,999	3,093			
10,000 and over	3,796			
Total	160,416	Total	139,507	4,618,243

Source: *Size Analysis of United Kingdom Businesses 1992. Business Monitor PA 1003.*
[a]Defined as legal units, which includes companies, partnerships, sole proprietors, general government and non-profit-making bodies.

Employment in manufacturing in Britain fell from 5.9 million in 1982 to 4.5 million in 1992. Total capital investment in manufacturing was £12,485 million in 1992, comprising £10,384 million in plant and machinery, £1,377 million in new building work and £724 million in vehicles (investment by sector is shown in Table 13.3).

The ten largest manufacturing concerns, by £ million of turnover, are:

BAT Industries	13,817
Imperial Chemical Industries (ICI)[1]	12,488
British Aerospace	10,562
Grand Metropolitan	8,748
Hanson	7,691
Unilever	7,596
Ford Motor Company	7,509
BTR	6,742
General Electric Company (GEC)	6,042
Allied-Lyons	5,360

The construction industry contributed 7 per cent of GDP and employed about 1.3 million people in 1992, over 4 per cent of the total number of employees.

---

[1] Now split into ICI and Zeneca (see p. 160).

Total domestic fixed capital spending was £618 million in 1992.

Sectors of Manufacturing

Relative sizes of the main sectors are shown in Tables 13.1 and 13.2. Table 13.3 indicates output and investment. A more detailed description of the main sectors is given below.

Mineral and Metal Products

Steel Products

British producers delivered 14.9 million tonnes of finished steel in 1992, of which 51 per cent was exported. Over the past ten years annual exports of the steel industry have more than doubled, from around 3.5 million tonnes to nearly 8 million tonnes, creating a favourable balance of trade in steel products. The major areas of steel production are in Wales and northern England, with substantial further processing in the Midlands. Major restructuring in the steel industry took place during the 1980s and

Table 13.2: Indices of Manufacturing Output (1990 = 100)

1992 Standard Industrial Classification Category	Share of output 1990 (weight per 1,000)	1988	1991	1992
Food and beverages	29	98.3	99.5	100.5
Tobacco products	2	98.7	101.8	107.5
Textiles and leather products	14	106.1	89.8	89.4
Wood and wood products	7	102.1	86.9	86.0
Pulp, paper products, printing and publishing	25	93.0	95.1	95.7
Solid and nuclear fuels, oil refining	6	99.3	106.8	110.6
Chemicals and synthetic fibres	24	95.6	102.5	104.5
Rubber and plastics products	10	92.5	94.6	96.6
Other non-metallic mineral products	11	102.6	90.5	86.7
Basic metal and metal products	21	100.8	90.1	86.3
Machinery and equipment	27	93.9	89.8	85.0
Electrical and optical equipment	30	93.1	95.7	95.2
Transport equipment	28	89.0	93.1	91.1
Other manufacturing	3	93.3	87.1	84.4
Total	237	95.9	94.7	93.9

Source: *United Kingdom National Accounts 1993 Edition.*

Table 13.3: Output and Investment in Manufacturing

1992 Standard Industrial Classification category	Gross output (£ million) 1991	Gross domestic fixed capital formation (£ million) 1992
Solid and nuclear fuels, oil refining	2,908	768
Chemicals and synthetic fibres	12,906	
Other non-metallic mineral products	4,696	3,148
Basic metals and metal products	9,082	
Machinery and equipment	12,718	
Electrical and optical equipment	14,337	3,894
Transport equipment	11,291	
Food and beverages	14,514	
Tobacco products	1,365	
Textiles and leather products	6,260	
Wood and wood products	3,237	
Pulp, paper products, printing and publishing	12,767	4,675
Rubber and plastics products	5,295	
Other manufacturing	1,367	
Total	112,743	12,485

Source: *United Kingdom National Accounts 1993 Edition.*

early 1990s. Productivity and efficiency have improved and the industry is now one of the lowest cost producers in Europe. The number of people employed in 1992 was 50,000, compared with 90,000 in 1985.

British Steel is the fourth largest steel company in the world, producing about three-quarters of Britain's crude steel. The company's output is based on flat steel products, plate, heavy sections and tubes. These are used principally in the construction, automotive, engineering, transport, metal goods, packaging and energy industries.

Other important steel producers in Britain include United Engineering Steels, Allied Steels and Wires, Co-Steel Sheerness, the Glynwed Group and the specialist stainless steel producer Avesta Sheffield. Products manufactured by these companies include wire rod, hot rolled bars, reinforcing bars for the construction industry, engineering steels and other special steels.

Non-ferrous Metals

Output of non-ferrous metals and their alloys in 1992 included primary aluminium, of which nearly 244,000 tonnes were delivered, and secondary aluminium, of which over 252,000

tonnes were delivered. Britain produced over 42,000 tonnes of refined copper and nearly 436,000 tonnes of copper and copper alloy semi-manufactures. Primary metal production relies mainly on imported ores, concentrates and partially refined metal. Recycled metal plays an important part in raw material supply. Nearly half of the industry is situated in the Midlands and Wales.

Specialised Alloys

Britain is a major producer of specialised alloys for high-technology requirements in the aerospace, electronic, petrochemical, and nuclear and other fuel industries. Titanium and titanium alloys are used in aircraft production, power generation and North Sea oil production, and nickel alloys for aero-engines operating in high-temperature environments.

In recent years considerable progress has been made in the development of 'superplastic' alloys, which are more ductile and elastic than conventional alloys. Aluminium lithium, developed by British Alcan Aluminium, is ideal for use in aircraft, being lighter, stronger and more rigid than normal aluminium.

Table 13.4: Minerals and Metal Products

	Sales (£ million) 1991	Exports (£ million) 1992	Imports (£ million) 1992
Iron products	1,098	300	80
Non-ferrous metals	4,455	1,752	2,590
Non-metallic mineral products	7,734	1,217	1,271
of which: glass and glassware	2,206	422	661
ceramic and heat-resistant goods	1,691	566	355

Ceramics

The ceramics industry manufactures clay products, such as domestic pottery, sanitaryware and tiles, and clay pipes for the building trade. Domestic pottery production includes the manufacture of china, earthenware and stoneware. Tableware is produced in Stoke-on-Trent, and Britain is the world's leading manufacturer and major exporter of fine bone china.

Research is being conducted into ceramics for use in housebuilding and diesel and jet engines. Important industrial ceramics invented in Britain include silicon carbides and sialons.

Glass Products

Glass-reinforced cement composites for the construction industry were invented in Britain in the early 1970s and are made under licence in over 40 countries.

Flat glass is manufactured through the float glass process, which was developed by Pilkington Brothers and licensed to glassmakers throughout the world. Pilkington has also produced an energy-saving window glass which reflects room heat without impairing visibility. Export sales of flat glass principal products amounted to £106 million in 1992. United Glass is a leading manufacturer of bottles and other glass containers.

China Clay

Britain is the world's biggest exporter of china clay (kaolin), four-fifths of which is used in paper-making. In 1992, 2.8 million tonnes, valued at more than £195 million, were sold overseas. The main company involved is ECC International, part of the English China Clays Group.

Chemicals and Related Products

Britain's chemicals industry is at the forefront of modern technology, spending the equivalent of 6 per cent of total sales on R & D. It is the third largest chemicals industry in Western Europe, and the fifth largest in the Western world. The nation's fourth biggest manufacturing industry, it provides direct employment for more than 290,000 people. Around a half of its production of principal products is exported, making it Britain's greatest single export earner. Exports in 1992 were worth £14,974 million, while imports were valued at £11,618 million.

Traditionally Britain has been a major producer of basic industrial chemicals, such as inorganic and basic organic chemicals, plastics and fertilisers, which together comprise around two-fifths of output. The most rapid growth in recent years has been in speciality chemicals, particularly pharmaceuticals, pesticides and cosmetics.

Many major chemical companies in Britain are multinationals; several are subsidiaries of overseas companies and others are specialist manufacturers of pharmaceuticals, such as Glaxo and Wellcome. In 1992 Imperial Chemical Industries (ICI) was the fourth largest chemicals company in the world, with a range of 15,000 products. In a major restructuring programme, ICI was demerged into two companies in June 1993 to form 'new' ICI, built around industrial chemicals, paints, materials and explosives, and a separate company, Zeneca, comprising ICI's pharmaceuticals, agrochemicals and seeds, and specialities businesses.

Organic Chemicals

Sales of the principal products of organic chemicals amounted to £3,644 million in 1992 and those of miscellaneous chemicals for industrial use to £3,114 million. The most important products sold in the organic chemicals range are ethylene (1.9 million tonnes produced in 1992), propylene (832,000 tonnes) and benzene (778,000 tonnes).

Inorganic Chemicals

Much of inorganic chemicals production consists of relatively simple bulk chemicals, such as sulphuric acid and metallic and non-metallic oxides, serving as basic materials for industry. Other speciality chemicals include industrial gases, essential oils and flavourings, adhesives and sealants, and explosives, including those used for car safety airbags. Investment in environmentally safe products and processes, such as substitutes for chlorofluorocarbons (CFCs), is increasing.

Plastics

Total annual turnover of the plastics industry is estimated at £13,000 million. In 1991 Britain consumed over 3.3 million tonnes of plastics materials, with British producers exporting over 1.2 million tonnes.

Around 200,000 people are employed in the plastics industry, three-quarters working in the processing or conversion sector. Some 4,000 firms are engaged in plastics processing—the conversion of plastics

materials into finished, semi-finished or sub-assemblies of final products. Production includes housewares and semi-finished products for the automotive, domestic appliance, mechanical goods and business equipment industries.

Paints

Sales of paint, varnishes and painters' fillings were worth £1,718 million in 1992. ICI is the world's largest paint manufacturer. Among specialised products are new ranges of synthetic resins and pigments, powder coatings, non-drip and quick-drying paints and paints needing only one top coat. Its best-known consumer product is the Dulux paint range. Two recent innovations have been solid emulsion paint and a temporary water-based finish which can be removed easily by chemical treatment, for vehicle bodies and road markings.

Pharmaceuticals

Britain is the world's fourth biggest exporter of medicines. This sector has some of the world's largest multinational research-intensive manufacturers, as well as medium-sized and smaller specialist companies. Total sales in 1992 were around £7,300 million. Pharmaceuticals exports, which include some of the world's best-selling medicines, were valued at £2,993 million. The main markets are Western Europe and North America, with Japan an expanding market. The pharmaceuticals industry's trade surplus of over £1,300 million in 1992 was the second largest of all manufacturing sectors, and represented an increase of 12 per cent on 1991.

Table 13.5: Chemicals and Related Products

	Sales (£ million) 1991	Exports (£ million) 1992	Imports (£ million) 1992
Chemicals and related products	31,563	14,974	11,618
of which: basic chemicals	13,147	6,401	6,343
specialised industrial products	5,875	2,328	1,533
pharmaceuticals	7,283	2,993	1,663
soap and toilet preparations	4,173	1,015	629

Employing over 85,000 people directly, pharmaceuticals support employment for 250,000 people in related activities. The industry invested more than £1,450 million in R & D in 1992. This sum amounts to more than 14 per cent of British manufacturing industry's R & D and represents about 8 per cent of total world expenditure on medicines research. Progress in pharmaceuticals research has helped to reduce dramatically the impact of diseases such as polio, diphtheria and measles.

Britain has two of the world's top seven pharmaceuticals groups, Glaxo and SmithKline Beecham. In 1992 British firms made six of the world's 20 best-selling medicines, including Glaxo's ulcer treatment Zantac, the world's best-selling medicine, and ICI's (now Zeneca's) beta-blocker Tenormin, for treating high blood pressure. Among Zeneca's newer products are Zestril (for combating high blood pressure), Zoladex (a prostate cancer therapy) and Deprivan (an anaesthetic).

Other recent major developments pioneered in Britain are semi-synthetic penicillins and cephalosporins, both powerful antibiotics, and new treatments for asthma, arthritis, migraine and coronary heart disease. SmithKline Beecham, which manufactures four of the world's top-selling antibiotics, has developed Augmentin, which is used to treat a range of infections that have become resistant to antibiotics. Glaxo's Zofran, an anti-nausea drug used to counter the unpleasant side-effects of cancer treatments, is one of the company's most successful new medicines.

A growing trend is the production of cheaper, unbranded (generic) drugs. The biggest British company making these, Medeva, is also the world's fifth largest vaccine maker. It develops generic medicines by improving existing drugs or buying the companies which make them.

Agrochemicals

A large proportion of world R & D in agrochemicals is conducted in Britain. Notable British discoveries include pyrethroid insecticides, ICI's diquat and paraquat herbicides, systemic fungicides and aphicides, genetically engineered microbial pesticides and methods of encouraging natural parasites against common pests in horticulture.

Soap and Toilet Preparations

Exports of soap and toilet preparations in 1992 were valued at £1,015 million, compared with imports of £629 million. Total sales amounted to £4,173 million. This sector includes soap and synthetic detergents, dominated by Lever Brothers (part of Unilever) and by the US-owned Proctor and Gamble. Boots and SmithKline Beecham are significant producers of perfumes, cosmetics and toilet preparations.

Biotechnology

Biotechnology includes the manufacture of products using genetic modification. Britain has made major advances in the development of drugs such as human insulin and interferons, genetically-engineered vaccines, and in the production of antibiotics by fermentation; alternative bacteriocidal drugs based on Nisin, a food preservative made in Britain; agricultural products such as infection-resistant crops; and medical diagnostic materials like biosensors.

Major companies, such as ICI, Wellcome, Glaxo and SmithKline Beecham, undertake extensive research in biotechnology. A second generation of vaccines based on recombinant DNA technology includes SmithKline Beecham's Engerix-B vaccine against hepatitis, which more than doubled its sales in 1992. Drugs are being developed that act on defective genes either in the human host or in the infecting organism.

Specialist products of Britain's 50 small independent biotechnology firms comprise, among other items, medical diagnostics and microbial pesticides. The British company Celltech was the first licensed by the United States Government for the large-scale production of monoclonal antibodies, proteins which can seek out a particular substance in the body. They are used to diagnose diseases, identify different blood types and can be employed in the treatment of a range of conditions, including cancer.

Britain leads in the development of molecular graphics, which contribute to the rational design of new and improved medicines through a computer-aided technique for analysing the structures of complicated organic molecules on a visual display unit.

Fibres

The main types of synthetic fibre are still those first developed: regenerated cellulosic fibres such as viscose, and the major synthetic fibres like nylon polyamide, polyester and acrylics. Extensive research continues to produce a wide variety of innovative products with characteristics designed to meet market needs; antistatic and flame-retardant fibres are examples. More specialist products include the aramids (with very high thermal stability and strength), elastanes (giving very high stretch and recovery) and melded fabrics (produced without the need for knitting or weaving).

Britain's second biggest chemicals company, Courtaulds, has developed a new, solvent-spun, biodegradable fibre, Tencel, which is twice as strong as cotton while being soft enough to be used by designers of luxury garments. ICI's Tactel, a fine nylon micro-fibre originally used to make sportswear, is now being used by the fashion industry and accounts for around 35 per cent of the company's fibre output by value.

Mechanical Engineering and Metal Goods

Exports of mechanical machinery represented 13 per cent of total visible exports in 1992. Output includes pressure vessels, heat exchangers and storage tanks for chemical and oil-refining (process) plant, steam-raising boilers (including those for power stations), nuclear reactors, water and sewage treatment plant, and fabricated steelwork for bridges, buildings and industrial installations.

Agricultural Machinery

Britain is among the Western world's major producers of tractors, which make up over three-quarters of the country's total output of agricultural equipment. Sales of the principal products of the tractor industry were £1,041 million in 1992, of which about two-thirds were accounted for by overseas sales. Widely used technical innovations include computer-controlled tractors, a highly efficient pesticide sprayer and combined mower/conditioners that significantly reduce the drying time for grass. Much of the new machinery is designed for use in a variety of conditions to meet the needs of overseas farmers. The Royal International Agricultural Exhibition, held annually near Coventry, has a specialised tropical machinery centre, where demonstrations of such machinery are given.

Machine Tools

Britain is the world's seventh largest producer of machine tools. Almost all are

Table 13.6: Mechanical Engineering and Metal Goods

	Sales (£ million) 1991	Exports (£ million) 1992	Imports (£ million) 1992
Mechanical engineering	17,012	6,632	5,455
of which: industrial plant and steelwork	4,950	682	516
agricultural machinery and tractors	1,295	860	626
machine tools	2,228	776	926
machinery for process industries and non-metallic materials working	3,503	2,241	2,101
mining, construction and mechanical handling equipment	5,036	2,073	1,286
Other metal goods	13,143	1,805	2,292

purchased by the engineering, vehicles and metal goods industries. Total sales reached £2,228 million in 1991, of which over a third were exports. British manufacturers have made technological advances in probes, sensors, co-ordinate measuring devices, laser melting and the installation of flexible manufacturing systems. Computer numerical-controlled machines account for an increasing proportion of output.

Textile Machinery

Most sales of textile machinery are to export markets. British innovations include computerised colour matching and weave simulation, friction spinning, high-speed computer-controlled knitting machines and electronic jacquard attachments for weaving looms.

Mining and Tunnelling Equipment

Sales of mining machinery and tunnelling equipment are substantial. Britain's mining equipment industry leads in the production of coal-cutting and road-heading (shearing) equipment, hydraulic roof supports, conveying equipment, flameproof transformers, switchgear, and subsurface transport equipment and control systems. J.C. Bamford is the world's leading manufacturer of backhoe loaders and telescopic handlers.

Other Equipment

The mechanical handling equipment industry produces cranes and transporters, lifting devices, escalators, conveyors, powered industrial trucks and air bridges, as well as electronically controlled and automatic handling systems. Britain is also a major producer of industrial engines, pumps, valves and compressors, and of pneumatic and hydraulic equipment. Companies like Babcock manufacture steam generators and other heavy equipment for power plants. Despite an overall decline in the castings industry, some foundries have been investing in new melting, moulding and quality control equipment.

Electrical, Electronic and Instrument Engineering

Britain has the fourth largest electronics industry in the world, accounting for around 10 per cent of visible exports.

Electrical Engineering and Electrical and Electronic Appliances

Making extensive use of the most advanced technologies, the electrical engineering industry manufactures products for the electricity supply sector, including power plant, cable transformers and switchgear, and lighting, plugs and sockets. The domestic electrical appliance sector is dominated by a few large firms.

The major electronic consumer goods produced are radio and television sets, and high-fidelity audio and video equipment. Several Japanese companies have established manufacturing bases in Wales, making television sets, video recorders and compact disc players. In the audio field British manufacturers have a reputation for high-quality goods, but are less strong in the mass market.

Computers

This sector produces an extensive range of systems, central processors and peripheral equipment, from large computers for large-scale data-processing and scientific work to mini- and microcomputers for control and automation systems and for home, educational and office use.

Britain makes 40 per cent of Europe's desktop computers. Nearly half of Britain's computers and peripheral equipment intended for export are made in Scotland. Several leading overseas manufacturers of data-processing equipment—for example, IBM, Unisys and Compaq—have established manufacturing plants in Britain. Britain's biggest computer manufacturer is the largely Japanese-owned ICL. Other companies, such as Psion, have concentrated on developing new products for specialised markets. These include hand-held, pocket-sized computers, increasingly used by company sales forces, and notebook and pen computers.

British firms make communications software for portable and mainframe computers. The world's first modem (computer telephone link) for portable computers was designed in Britain. Psion is a pioneer of the 'palmtop' computer, which has the equivalent power of a desktop machine. A Scottish firm, Calluna, has designed an extremely small disc drive for use in notebook-sized computers.

British firms and research organisations, with government support, have been involved in the development and application of the family of 'three-five' semiconductor materials, such as gallium arsenide; these are used in a number of microwave devices and in the production of much faster-working computers. The Trax, a novel design of supercomputer processor with a wide range of applications, including high-definition television and defence systems, was originally developed at Brunel University, near London. Advances are being made by British firms in 'virtual reality' (VR) technology, an advanced simulation technique. It is being used to design buildings and a range of products, including cars, pharmaceuticals and machine tools.

Communications Equipment

Britain's main communications products are switching and transmission equipment, telephones and terminals. Mercury Communications is licensed to compete with BT in the provision of network services, while the market for terminals and telephones has been fully liberalised. This has led to increased demand from BT and Mercury for new equipment and services.

Innovative work is being stimulated by the expansion of cable television and the growth in value added network services. There has been rapid expansion in the market for cellular telephones since the second half of the 1980s.

Transmission equipment and cables for telecommunications and information networks include submarine and high-specification data-carrying cables. Supported by a technically advanced cable industry, BT has led in the development of optical fibre communications systems and has paved the way for simpler and cheaper optical cables by laying the first non-repeatered cable over 100 km (62 miles) long, and by developing the first all-optical repeater.

More than half of the world's undersea communications cables have been made and laid by STC Submarine Systems, which, with its United States and French partners, completed the laying of the first transatlantic optical fibre cable in 1988. Now part of Canada's Northern Telecom, STC is building the first fibre-optic cable linking Canada and Europe. The cable, which will be made in Britain and the United States, will carry up to 30,000 telephone calls simultaneously down each of two pairs of optical fibres.

Britain also has a world lead in the transmission of computerised data along telephone lines for reproduction on television screens.

Another sector of the industry manufactures radio communications equipment, radar, radio and sonar navigational aids for ships and aircraft, thermal imaging systems, alarms and signalling equipment, public broadcasting equipment and other capital goods. Radar was invented in Britain and British firms are still

Table 13.7: Electrical and Electronic Engineering

	Sales (£ million) 1991	Exports (£ million) 1992	Imports (£ million) 1992
Data-processing equipment	7,778	5,764	7,519
Basic electrical equipment	4,411	1,982	2,051
Radio and electronic capital goods	1,940	1,037	897
Electronic components	3,881	3,431	4,127
Consumer electrical and electronic goods	3,884	1,607	2,781

in the forefront of technical advances. Racal Avionics' X-band radar for aircraft ground movement control is in use at airports in several countries. Solid-state secondary surveillance radar, manufactured by Cossor Electronics, is being supplied to 50 overseas civil aviation operators. Cable and Wireless's submarine cable-laying robot 'CIRRUS', which can work at depths of up to 1 km (3,280 ft), is controlled entirely by a computer on its mother ship.

Medical and Other Electronic Equipment

A range of electronic measurement and test equipment is made in Britain, as well as analytical instruments, process control equipment, and numerical control and indication equipment for use in machine tools. Companies such as GEC and Oxford Instruments produce advanced electronic medical equipment, like ultrasound scanners, electromyography systems and patient monitoring systems for intensive and coronary care and other uses. Britain pioneered the development of magnetic resonance imaging.

The indigenous electronics components industry is supplemented by subsidiaries of several leading overseas companies. An area of very rapid change in which Britain is particularly strong is the manufacture of advanced components, such as integrated circuits.

Instrument Engineering

The instrument engineering industry makes measuring, photographic, cinematographic and reprographic equipment; watches, clocks and other timing devices; and medical and surgical instruments.

Motor Vehicles and Other Transport Equipment (excluding Aerospace)

Some 1.8 million new cars and commercial vehicles were sold in 1992. Production has recently recovered following the recession, although sales of new cars were 31 per cent below the 1989 peak of 2.3 million. Car output is dominated by seven groups, accounting for 99 per cent of the total: Rover, Ford (including Jaguar), Vauxhall, Peugeot-Talbot, Honda, Nissan and Toyota. The remainder is in the hands of smaller, specialist producers such as Rolls-Royce, whose cars are renowned for their quality and durability. Rover's production includes the successful Land Rover four-wheel drive vehicle and the new 600 range of family cars, launched in April 1993. Some 584,000 passenger cars valued at £4,060 million were exported in 1992.

A period of major change has accompanied the arrival of the three major Japanese manufacturers—Nissan, Toyota and Honda—which have invested in projects worth some £2,100 million. The established motor vehicle manufacturers are restructuring as a result. Japanese inward investment has introduced new management and production methods into the sector.

The motor components industry consists of over 2,000 companies, such as GKN, Lucas and Bosch, and is ranked as one of the most important industries in Britain.

Demand for pedal cycles at home and abroad continues to rise significantly. Raleigh is the leading bicycle manufacturer.

Shipbuilding and Marine Engineering

Britain has a long tradition of shipbuilding and remains active in the construction,

Table 13.8: Motor Vehicles and Other Transport Equipment

	Sales (£ million) 1991	Exports (£ million) 1992	Imports (£ million) 1992
Motor vehicles (including bodies, trailers, caravans and engines)	17,674	6,390	8,038
Motor vehicle parts	4,682	3,460	4,654
Other transport equipment	3,248	196	482

conversion and repair of merchant vessels, warships and offshore structures. The largest sector is the building of warships. In addition to meeting all the needs of the Royal Navy, the warship yards build and convert ships for overseas governments.

The Shipbuilders and Ship Repairers' Association estimates that orders taken by British merchant shipbuilders for the construction of vessels were worth around £250 million in 1992. The marine equipment industry is a major contributor to the shipbuilding sector, as equipment installed in a ship's hull accounts for some 70 per cent of its cost. It offers a complete range of products, from engines to sophisticated navigational systems, around 70 per cent of which is exported to shipbuilders and ship-repairers overseas.

More than two decades of oil and gas exploitation in the North Sea have generated a major offshore industry (see p. 209). Shipbuilders and fabricators build fixed platforms and semi-submersible units for drilling, production and emergency/maintenance support, drill ships, jack-up rigs, modules and offshore loading systems. Several thousand manufacturing and service industry firms supply goods and services, including consultancy, design, project management, and R & D to the offshore industry. Their experience of North Sea projects has enabled them to establish themselves in oil and gas markets throughout the world.

Aerospace

Britain's aerospace industry is the third largest in the world, after the United States and France. With some 200 member companies of the Society of British Aerospace Companies (SBAC) employing around 148,000 people, it had a turnover in 1992 of about £11,000 million. Exports totalled £7,700 million and contributed £2,500 million in net terms to the balance of payments. Aircraft and parts account for around three-fifths of overseas sales, with engines and parts, and aerospace equipment making up the rest. The impact of recession on the civil aerospace market and reductions

in defence orders have led to further rationalisation and consolidation of the aerospace industry.

The industry's activities cover designing and constructing airframes, aero-engines, guided weapons, simulators and space satellites, together with a full range of flight systems, particularly avionics and complex components, and associated services. To improve fuel economy, engine and airframe manufacturers use lighter materials such as titanium and carbon-fibre composites, combined with improved aerodynamic techniques.

Civil Aircraft

As the leading British exporter of manufactured goods, British Aerospace (BAe) produces both civil and military aircraft, as well as satellites, space systems, guided weapons and components. Civil aircraft include the 146 family of regional quiet-jet airliners; the 64-seat Jetstream ATP (advanced turboprop) airliner, being developed as the 70-seat Jetstream 61; the 19-seat Jetstream 31 and 29-seat Jetstream 41 regional airliners; and the 125—the world's best-selling medium-sized business jet.

Collaborative development of civil and military aircraft is increasing to save on costs of new production programmes. BAe has a 20 per cent share of the European consortium Airbus Industrie, which had sold over 1,800 aircraft by the end of 1992. BAe designs and supplies the wings for all Airbus airliners. Four types are in production: the A310 and A300 medium to long-range airliners, the long-range, four-engine A340 and the short-to medium-haul A320, the first civil airliner to be fitted with 'fly-by-wire' controls. Two further aircraft—the A321 and A330—are under development; both are undergoing flight test programmes. Together with other international aerospace organisations, BAe is studying the feasibility of developing a successor to the Concorde supersonic airliner, and an ultra high-capacity aircraft.

Short Brothers of Belfast is engaged in the production of civil aircraft, advanced nacelle (engine casings) systems and components for aerospace manufacturers. It designs and builds the wings for the Fokker 100 jetliner and is a partner in manufacturing the 50-seat Canadair Regional Jet airliner, and the recently launched Lear Jet 45, a medium-sized business jet aircraft.

Military Aircraft and Missiles

British Aerospace is among the world's top three defence companies. More than three-quarters of its military production was exported in 1992. It includes the Harrier, a unique vertical/short take-off and landing (V/STOL) military combat aircraft. Sea Harriers are supplied to the Royal Navy and, in association with McDonnell Douglas in the United States, BAe has developed the improved Harrier II. BAe also produces the Hawk fast-jet trainer and, with McDonnell Douglas, the Goshawk T45 carrier jet trainer. It has a 33 per cent share in the development of the next-generation European Fighter Aircraft (EFA), now known as Eurofighter 2000, with adapted design—a co-operative venture between Britain, Germany, Italy and Spain.

The Tornado combat aircraft is built by a company set up jointly by BAe, Alenia of Italy and Deutsche Aerospace. A £5,000 million order for 48 Tornado bombers was placed in 1992 by Saudi Arabia, making it one of Britain's biggest ever export deals. A small Yorkshire company, Slingsby Aviation, makes the T67 Firefly trainer aircraft. It has been chosen by the United States Air Force as its new basic trainer for pilots and is in service in ten other countries. Slingsby also designs and makes aerospace components and parts for airships.

BAe and Shorts are major suppliers of tactical guided weapon systems for use on land, at sea and in the air.

Helicopters

In addition to producing aerospace equipment, Westland manufactures the Sea King and Lynx military helicopters. In collaboration with Agusta of Italy, it is developing the multi-role EH101 three-engine helicopter, which will be delivered to the Royal Navy and the Italian Navy by the mid-1990s. The company is a leading manufacturer of composite helicopter blades.

Aero-engines

Rolls-Royce is one of the world's three major manufacturers of aero-engines, with a turnover in 1992 of £3,562 million and an order book worth £6,700 million. The company's civil engine group produces engines for airliners and executive and corporate jets. Rolls-Royce RB211-535 engines have been selected by 80 per cent of airlines using Boeing 757 airliners. The RB211-524G and RB211-524H engines, which power Boeing 747-400 airliners, give improved thrust and fuel efficiency. The company's Tay engines are in service on the Gulfstream IV and Fokker 100 airliners, and are available as replacement engines for older aircraft.

The Trent engine, currently under development, will be Rolls-Royce's largest to date, providing improved fuel efficiency and lower maintenance costs. It will power the new generation of large airliners, such as the Airbus A330 and Boeing 777, entering service in 1995.

Rolls-Royce is a partner in the five-nation International Aero Engine consortium, which produces the low-pollution V2500 aero-engine, now in service on some versions of the Airbus A320.

The military engine group of Rolls-Royce produces engines for both aircraft and helicopters, and is a partner in the EJ200 engine project for the Eurofighter 2000. The company also produces gas turbines for power generation and for oil and gas pumping, gas turbines for 25 of the world's navies, and propulsion systems for the Royal Navy's nuclear-powered submarines.

Aviation Equipment

Around one-third of the aerospace industry is devoted to designing and manufacturing aviation equipment. British firms have made significant technological advances.

Manufacturers provide essential systems for engines and aircraft, including navigation and landing systems, engine and flight controls, electrical generation, mechanical and hydraulic power systems, cabin furnishings, flight-deck control and information displays, including head-up display (HUD), of which GEC Avionics is the world's largest manufacturer. Numerous other companies supply components, sub-assemblies and spare parts. Consortia are being formed with other European companies to reduce costs on long-term projects.

British firms have made important advances in developing ejection seats, firefighting equipment and flight simulators, as well as fly-by-wire and fly-by-light technology, where control surfaces are moved by means of automatic electronic signalling and fibre optics respectively, rather than by mechanical means. Fly-by-wire is being used on the Airbus A320 and A330/A340. Britain's aerospace companies provide radar and air traffic control equipment and ground power supplies to airports and airlines worldwide. A consortium including Siemens Plessey Radar and Logica has won a £130 million contract to equip a new air traffic control centre at Farnham, Hampshire.

Hovercraft

Britain pioneered the development of hovercraft and is a world leader in their technology and production. Westland Aerospace hovercraft range from large commercial craft to smaller, 10-passenger craft. Slingsby Aviation builds amphibious hovercraft for passenger transport, cargo, ambulance and rescue, and surveying.

Satellite Equipment

Over 400 companies in Britain are involved in space activities. The industry is strong in the manufacture of satellites, in manufacturing ground infrastructure for satellite systems and in the analysis and exploitation of data from satellites. British Aerospace Space Systems is one of Europe's leading producers of communications satellites. It was the prime contractor for all

such satellites built for the European Space Agency (ESA), and for the Marecs and Inmarsat-2 series of maritime communications satellites. It built payload pallets for the United States Space Shuttle and supplies SPELDA, a structure that enables the ESA's Ariane 4 launcher to carry two spacecraft on the same mission. It was also involved in developing and producing the Intelsat III, IV and V series of satellites, and is a subcontractor for the Intelsat VI satellites launched from the Space Shuttle. It supplied equipment for the ESA Ulysses satellite mission to Jupiter and the Sun, and for the Hubble Space Telescope. Work is now in progress on ESA's latest Cluster and SOHO scientific spacecraft and BAe is acting as prime contractor for the European Polar Platform, the first of ESA's new generation of environmental monitoring missions due for launching in 1998.

Matra-Marconi Space (UK) has acted as principal contractor on many telecommunications payloads, for example, for ESA. In addition, it was prime contractor for the principal radar instrument on the ESA's European Remote Sensing Satellites ERS-1 and ERS-2, and is prime contractor for an advanced synthetic aperture radar for ESA's ENVISAT-1 mission.

A new Earth Observation Data Centre was built by a consortium led by BAe to process data from ERS-1 and other satellites, and to develop the market for earth observation data. GEC Ferranti Defence Systems produces the inertial guidance system for the European Ariane launcher and Pilkington Space Technology is the world's leading producer of solar cell coverglasses for satellites. Several companies, such as Logica, Data Sciences, EOS and Cray Electronics, are involved in processing earth observation data, and a wide range of smaller companies specialise in its interpretation.

Food, Drink and Tobacco

Britain has a large food and drink manufacturing industry, which has accounted for a growing proportion of total domestic food supply in recent decades. The industry's interests are represented by the Food and

Drink Federation (FDF) and several sector associations. In recent years, major British food manufacturers have increased their productivity and are planning further restructuring, in particular to take advantage of the single European market.

Convenience foods (particularly frozen foods and ready-cooked meals, annual sales of which now stand at approximately £4,400 million and £600 million respectively), yoghurts, other dairy desserts and instant snacks have formed the fastest-growing sector of the food market in recent years. The market in health and slimming foods also continues to expand. Companies have introduced new low-fat and fat-free spreads and ice creams to meet consumer demand.

Dairy Products

Nearly 60 per cent of households in Britain receive milk through a doorstep delivery system employing about 32,000 people. Domestic milk consumption per head—2.23 litres (3.93 pints) per week in 1992—is among the highest in the world. Consumption of skimmed and semi-skimmed milk continues to rise as people seek to reduce the fat content in their diet.

The main milk products are butter, cheese, condensed milk and dried whole and skimmed milk. The British dairy industry accounted for 67 per cent of butter supplies to the domestic market in 1991 and 73 per cent of cheese supplies. Butter exports in 1992 were worth £96 million. The other main exports are skimmed milk powder and whole milk powder, worth £187 million in total.

Bread

About 75 per cent of bread is manufactured in large bakeries; the total bread market is worth some £3,000 million a year. A dramatic increase in the number of varieties available and greater demand for 'wholemeal' bread have stabilised consumption. Biscuit exports were valued at £216 million in 1992.

Drink

Of major significance among the alcoholic drinks produced in Britain is Scotch whisky, which is one of Britain's top five export earners. There are 110 distilleries in Scotland, where the best known brands of blended Scotch whisky, such as J & B, Johnnie Walker, Famous Grouse and Teachers, are made from the products of single malt and single grain whisky distilleries. Some 85 per cent of Scotch whisky is exported, to 190 countries. The value of whisky exports was over £1,958 million in 1992, Europe taking 40 per cent and the United States about 17 per cent by volume.

In 1992 purchases of beer in Britain were valued at £13,539 million, about 3.5 per cent of consumers' expenditure and a rise of 5 per cent compared with 1991.

The brewing industry has six major national brewery groups, and 160 regional and local brewers. British malt, which is made almost entirely from home-grown barley, is used by brewers throughout the world. Demand for traditional cask-conditioned ales ('real ale'), which fell in the

Table 13.9: Food, Drink and Tobacco

	Sales (£ million) 1991	Exports (£ million) 1992	Imports (£ million) 1992
Food	33,199	5,291	11,401
of which: meat and meat preparations	n.a.	827	2,033
dairy products and eggs	n.a.	534	1,111
cereals and animal feedstuffs	n.a.	1,541	1,721
fruit and vegetables	1,292	331	3,118
Beverages	8,291	2,448	1,565
Tobacco	7,891	970	460

n.a. = not available.

1970s, is rising, while lager now accounts for just over half of all beer sales. Cider is made primarily in south-west England. Wine is mainly produced in parts of southern England.

The soft drinks industry—comprising still and carbonated drinks, concentrates, squashes, cordials, frozen drinks, fruit juices, natural mineral and bottled waters—is the fastest growing sector of the grocery business, with an annual turnover of about £5,500 million.

Tobacco

The British tobacco industry manufactures 99 per cent of cigarettes and tobacco goods sold in Britain. Almost all domestic output is provided by three major manufacturers (Imperial Tobacco, Gallaher and Carreras Rothmans). The industry specialises in the production of high-quality cigarettes made from flue-cured tobacco and achieves significant exports. Europe, the Middle East and Africa are important markets.

Textiles and Clothing

These products make a substantial contribution to the British economy in terms of employment, exports and turnover. Together with the footwear and leather industries, they employ around 400,000 people, equal to nearly 9 per cent of manufacturing employment. For textiles, there is a high degree of regional concentration. Particularly important areas are the North West, West Yorkshire (mainly wool), the East Midlands (knitwear), Scotland and Northern Ireland.

Most of the clothing industry is widely scattered throughout the country, although there are significant concentrations in cities such as Manchester, Leicester and London. The industries' main products are yarn, woven and knitted fabrics, apparel, industrial and household textiles, and carpets based mainly on wool, cotton and synthetic fibres.

The textile and clothing industry has around 15,000 firms, comprising a few large multi-process companies and two of the world's largest firms—Coats Viyella and Courtaulds Textiles—as well as a large number of small and medium-sized firms.

Increased investment in new machinery and greater attention to design, training and marketing have helped the industry to raise competitiveness. New technologies, largely designed to improve response times and give greater flexibility in production, are being used throughout the industry.

The Multi-Fibre Arrangement (MFA) of the General Agreement on Tariffs and Trade (GATT—see p. 201) allows a measure of restraint on imports into the European Community of textiles and clothing from low-cost countries.

Wool

Britain's wool textile industry is one of the largest in the world, with two main branches making woollen and worsted. In the past few years the industry's export earnings have been significant, wool worsted export values totalling more than £500 million in 1992. Synthetic fibre is sometimes blended with wool. West Yorkshire is the main producing

Table 13.10: Textiles, Footwear, Clothing and Leather

	Sales (£ million) 1991	Exports (£ million) 1992	Imports (£ million) 1992
Wool textiles	1,289	544	373
Cotton and silk	1,166	724	1,977
Hosiery and other knitwear	1,921	760	1,563
Carpets, rugs and matting	1,105	211	471
Footwear	1,269	331	1,141
Clothing, hats and gloves	4,802	1,391	2,988
Household and other made-up textiles	1,097	171	291
Leather and leather goods	709	360	517

area, but Scotland is also famous as a specialised producer of high-quality yarns, tweeds and cloth. Substantial quantities of raw wool are scoured and cleaned in Britain in preparation for spinning. British mills also process the bulk of rare fibres such as cashmere. Sales of the woollen and worsted industry amounted to almost £1,300 million in 1992.

Cotton

Low-cost competition has cut progressively into British markets for cotton and allied products. Production includes yarn and fabrics of cotton, synthetic fibres and cotton-synthetic mixes, with large-scale dyeing and printing of cotton and synthetic fibre fabric. The linen industry is centred in Northern Ireland.

Carpets

Over half the value of carpet and rug output is made up of tufted carpets. Woven carpets, mainly Axminster, account for most of the remaining sales. There is a higher wool content in woven types, although in these, too, considerable use is being made of synthetic fibres. The high quality and variety of design make Britain one of the world's leading producers of woven carpets.

Industrial textiles account for an increasing proportion of the industry's output, covering products such as conveyor belting and geotextiles used in civil engineering projects. Many of these are non-woven, made of fibres assembled using advanced techniques. Synthetic polypropylene yarn is used in the manufacture of carpet backing and ropes, and woven into fabrics for a wide range of applications in the packaging, upholstery, building and motor vehicle industries.

Clothing and Footwear

The clothing industry is labour intensive, involving about 5,000 companies. While a broad range of clothing is imported from the rest of Europe and Asia, British industry supplies over half of domestic demand.

Exports have risen since the British fashion designer industry regained prominence during the 1980s and traditional British tailoring enables clothing companies such as Burberry's to compete overseas. The hosiery and knitwear industry comprises about 1,500 companies, mainly in the East Midlands and Scotland.

The footwear manufacturing industry is made up predominantly of small companies, increasingly under pressure from cheap imports.

Other Manufacturing

Wood and Paper

Over 14,000 companies in the wooden and upholstered furniture industry supply domestic, contract and institutional markets. Domestic production of wood for industrial use has been steadily increasing.

There were 106 paper and board mills employing 28,000 people in 1992. Among the largest British groups are Arjo Wiggins Appleton, St Regis and BPB Paper and Packaging. Over the past decade, inward investment has transformed the paper and board industry. Production has been concentrated in large-scale units to compete more effectively within the single European market. Between 1984 and 1992 output increased by 43 per cent. Over half the industry is made up of forestry product companies from Scandinavia, North America, Australia and elsewhere. There has been a significant trend towards waste-based packaging grades in order to reduce the industry's reliance on imported woodpulp supplies. Usage of recycled waste paper is increasing and research is helping to extend it. In 1992 the total amount of waste paper used in British newspapers accounted for nearly 27 per cent of the total newsprint consumed. Waste paper provides over half of the industry's fibre needs. In 1992 domestically produced wood pulp represented 11 per cent of fibrous raw material input.

Publishing

Total employment in the paper, printing and publishing industries in June 1993 was

440,000. Most of the printing and publishing industry's employment and output is concentrated in firms based in south-east England. Mergers have led to the formation of large groups in newspaper, magazine and book publishing. Reed Elsevier, one of the world's biggest publishing businesses, resulted from a merger between Reed International and the Dutch company Elsevier in 1993.

Printing, engraving, bookbinding and specialist publishing activities still involve many small firms, now often using new technology such as desktop publishing. The book-publishing industry is a major exporter, selling one-third of production in overseas markets. Security printers (of, for example, banknotes and postage stamps) are important exporters, the major company being De La Rue.

Rubber

Rubber tyres and inner tubes sold by British manufacturers in 1991 were valued at £1,315 million, about half of which went overseas. Other important rubber goods are vehicle components and accessories, conveyor belting, cables, hoses, latex foam products, and footwear, gloves and clothing. Tyre manufacturers include subsidiaries of United States and other overseas companies. The industry's consumption of rubber comprises natural, synthetic and recycled rubber.

Toys, games and sports equipment are established in export markets, while jewellery, gold and silverware and the refining of precious metals are industries maintaining a strong craft tradition.

Construction

Construction work is carried out mainly by private contractors but also by public authorities employing their own labour. From 1990 the industry was in recession, with employment falling from 1.7 million to 1.3 million in 1992. However, in 1993 there were signs of recovery in the construction industry.

Most work is done by private firms, 98 per cent of which employ fewer than 25 people. While only 95 out of a total of 206,000 firms employ more than 600 people directly, these companies undertake about one-fifth of all construction in Britain. Some of the larger firms own quarries and factories for materials manufacture, and sophisticated plant. Some firms undertake responsibility for all stages of projects from initial design to finished building. Efficiency and productivity in construction have benefited from greater off-site fabrication of standardised components and from computerised techniques such as electronic load safety measures for cranes, distance measuring equipment, computerised stock ordering and job costing, and computer-aided design.

Building Materials and Products

A vast range of products is used in the construction process, from glass and bricks to tiles and bathroom fittings. These materials are estimated to make up around 40 per cent of the value of construction output. In 1992 sales of construction materials were around £18,000 million, with exports amounting to £2,300 million.

Table 13.11: Other Manufacturing

	Sales (£ million) 1991	Exports (£ million) 1992	Imports (£ million) 1992
Timber and wooden furniture	9,556	595	2,693
Paper and paper products	10,510	1,785	4,412
Printing and publishing	17,792	1,310	1,016
Processing of rubber and plastics	12,828	2,922	3,558
Toys and sports goods	748	362	947

Aggregates, Bricks and Cement

The aggregates industry quarried around 255 million tonnes of crushed rock, sand and gravel in 1991, of which 235 million tonnes were used in construction. The brick industry, one of Britain's oldest, is regarded as the world's most technically advanced. In the late 1980s over £300 million was invested in improving production of bricks, which now stands at a capacity of 4,000 million a year. Portland cement, a 19th-century British innovation, is the most widely used chemical compound in the world.

Glass and Windows

Britain is a world leader in the manufacture of glass used in windows, doors and cladding. Pilkington developed the float process for manufacturing distortion-free flat glass (see p. 160), which is licensed throughout the world. Substantially more energy efficient, flat glass is increasingly used to allow more light into buildings and to provide insulation against heat loss in winter. The manufacture and supply of windows and doors is carried out by a large number of companies operating in one of three distinct product sectors—timber, metal (aluminium and steel) and UPVC.

Project Procurement, Management and Financing

The common basis of procurement is a lump-sum contract with provision for variation. The largest projects are often carried out under the direction of construction managers or management contractors. Clients generally employ architects, project managers or civil engineers to advise on the feasibility of projects, draw up plans and inspect and supervise the construction work.

Private and public sector projects are managed in a variety of ways. Most clients invite construction firms to bid for work by competitive tender, having used the design services of a consultant. The successful contractor will then undertake on-site work with a number of specialist sub-contractors. However, alternative methods of contracting are becoming more common. For example, contracts might include subsequent provision of building maintenance or a comprehensive 'design-and-build' service, where a single company accepts responsibility for every stage of a project.

The Government provides substantial work for the construction industry. Recently, a number of schemes have been built and paid for by private consortia, which then charge the public for their use for a fixed period of time before transferring ownership back to the public sector; these are known as 'BOOT' ('Build, Own, Operate and Transfer') schemes. One example is the toll bridge over the River Thames at Dartford, Kent (see p. 248).

Major Construction Projects in Britain

The most important recent construction project is the Channel Tunnel, the largest single civil engineering project ever undertaken in Europe (see p. 255). Nearing completion, its estimated cost is over £8,000 million. Building work was carried out by a consortium of ten French and British contractors working together as Transmanche Link (TML). The Tunnel is nearly 50 km (31 miles) long and is 70 m (230ft) below sea level at its deepest. Associated projects include a new international station at Waterloo in London and an international terminal at Folkestone.

Other major building projects in hand or recently completed are the M25 motorway widening scheme; the A55 Conwy Tunnel in Wales; the extensive development in London's Docklands (including the Limehouse link road); and the Sizewell B nuclear power station in Suffolk. Expansion of Britain's road network covers over 270 km (170 miles) of new motorway. Both Stansted and Manchester airports have been substantially redeveloped. There has also been large-scale redevelopment of sports stadiums, including Twickenham and Murrayfield (in Edinburgh) rugby grounds, and Manchester United and Arsenal football grounds. A £15 million stadium for the ground at Millwall in south-east London, completed in 1993, was the first major new stadium to be built in Britain since the end of the Second World War.

Housing

During 1992 a total of around 155,900 dwellings were started in Great Britain, slightly fewer than in 1991. Starts by private enterprise were 120,200, by housing associations 33,200 and in the public sector 2,600. Some 169,500 dwellings were completed: 140,000 by the private sector, 25,000 by housing associations and 4,600 by the public sector. The total value of new housing orders was £5,262 million.

Building Regulations

The Department of the Environment's building regulations prescribe minimum standards of construction in England and Wales. Administered and enforced by local government, the regulations apply to new building, the installation or replacement of fittings, and alterations and extensions to existing buildings. New regulations came into force in 1992. There are similar controls in Scotland and Northern Ireland. An alternative to local authority building control was introduced in 1984; under this there is a system of private certification of compliance with building regulations. The British Standards Institution is making Britain's contribution to the drafting of European standards, which are increasingly replacing national construction standards.

Research and Advisory Services

The Government's research and advisory body on construction is the Building Research Establishment. It has four laboratories, including a fire research station, and is the site of a building energy management systems centre. It has links with most major overseas research and technical organisations in the field and has a key role in developing European codes and standards. Major construction and materials firms, universities, colleges and research associations, as well as the British Board of Agrément, carry out research and provide advisory services. The Building Centre provides exhibition and information services on materials, products, techniques and building services.

Overseas Contracting and Consultancy

British companies are involved in many major projects throughout the world and have been in the forefront of innovative methods of management contracting and construction management. Contractors undertake the supervision and all or part of the construction of a project. Consultants are involved in the planning and design of construction projects. British contractors and consultants have long enjoyed a worldwide reputation for their integrity and independence.

Contracting

British contractors are currently undertaking, or have recently completed, work in 112 overseas countries and have a permanent presence in 74. Important international contracts won in 1992–93 included:

- management contracts for the EuroDisney Theme Park, near Paris (£1,000 million) and the 1996 Olympics in Atlanta, United States (£250 million);

- Tsing Ma Bridge in Hong Kong (£583 million);

- a hydro-electric project in Malaysia (£400 million);

- a light railway transit system in Kuala Lumpur (£300 million); and

- site preparation for the new Hong Kong airport (£100 million).

Consultancy

In 1992 members of the Association of Consulting Engineers were involved in new work overseas valued at almost £28,000 million. The capital value of projects under way at the end of 1992 or completed during the year was almost £60,000 million. British consulting engineers had estimated gross earnings in 1992 of £625 million from overseas commissions. The three largest categories of work covered roads, bridges and tunnels; airports; and water supply. The largest markets were the Far East, Africa, India and the Middle East. Major international projects include:

- Bangkok Elevated Transport System (£10,000 million);
- Hong Kong International Airport (£4,000 million); and
- thermal power stations in China (£2,500 million).

Further Reading

The Aerospace Industry. Aspects of Britain series, HMSO, 1993.

14 Finance and Other Service Industries

The service industries, which include finance, retailing, tourism and business services, contribute about 65 per cent of gross domestic product and over 70 per cent of employment. Britain is responsible for some 10 per cent of the world's exports of services: overseas earnings from services amounted to 30 per cent of the value of exports of manufactures in 1992. The number of employees in services rose from over 13 million in 1982 to 15.5 million by the end of 1992, much of the rise being accounted for by growth in part-time (principally female) employment.

INTRODUCTION

Average real disposable income per head increased by nearly three-quarters between 1971 and 1990 and this was reflected in a rise in consumer spending on financial, personal and leisure services and on the maintenance and repair of consumer durables. Demand for British travel, hotel and catering services rose as real incomes in Britain and other countries increased. The spread of home ownership, particularly during the 1980s, increased demand for legal and estate agency services.

Britain is a major financial centre, housing some of the world's leading banking, insurance, securities, shipping, commodities, futures, and other financial services and markets. Financial services are an important source of employment and overseas earnings. Business services include advertising, market research, management consultancy, exhibition and conference facilities, computing services and auction houses.

By the year 2000, tourism is expected to be the world's biggest industry, and Britain is one of the world's leading tourist destinations. The industry is Britain's second largest, employing nearly 7 per cent of the workforce. Retailing is also a major employer and Britain has an advanced distribution network. An important trend in retailing is the growth of out-of-town shopping centres.

The computing services industry continues to be one of the fastest-growing sectors of the economy, and information technology is widely used in retailing and financial services.

A notable trend in the services sector is the growth of franchising, an operation in which a company owning the rights to a particular form of trading licenses them to franchisees, usually by means of an initial payment with continuing royalties. The main areas include cleaning services, film processing, print shops, hairdressing and cosmetics, fitness centres, courier delivery, car rental, engine tuning and servicing, and fast food retailing. It is estimated that franchising's share of total retail sales is over 3 per cent, a figure which is likely to increase.

FINANCIAL SERVICES

Historically the financial services industry in Britain has been located in the famous 'Square Mile' in the City of London. This remains broadly the case, even though the markets for financial and related services have grown and diversified greatly. Manchester, Cardiff and Liverpool are also financial centres and Edinburgh is a world-leader in fund management. 'The City'—the collection of markets and institutions in and around the Square Mile—is noted for having:

- the greatest concentration of foreign banks in the world;
- a banking sector that accounts for about a fifth of total international bank lending;
- one of the world's largest international insurance markets;
- the largest centre in the world for trading overseas equities;
- the world's largest foreign exchange market;
- one of the world's largest financial derivatives markets;
- the greatest concentration of international bond dealers; and
- a full range of ancillary and support services—legal, accountancy and management consultancy—which contribute to London's strength as a financial centre.

Banking, finance, insurance, business services and leasing accounted for around one-fifth of Britain's total output in 1992, a share which has risen sharply over the past decade.

Banking, finance and insurance accounted for 12 per cent of all employment in Great Britain at the end of 1992. British financial institutions' overseas earnings amounted to £18,800 million in 1992.

Development of Financial Services

The growth in international movements of capital in the 1960s and 1970s mainly took the form of increased bank lending and foreign exchange trading. London became the international centre of this activity, particularly in the eurocurrency markets (see p. 189), and the number of overseas banks represented in London is larger than in any

other financial centre. During the 1980s, with increasing international competition in financial services and developments in technology, London's securities markets grew rapidly. Edinburgh also developed as a centre for fund management.

Some traditional distinctions between financial institutions have been eroded, so that single firms supply a broader range of services, both in domestic and international markets. Landmarks in the deregulation of Britain's financial services in recent years include:

- the abolition of exchange controls in 1979;
- the ending in 1980 of the supplementary special deposits scheme, which was designed to curb bank lending;
- the abolition in 1981 of the Reserve Asset Ratio requirement, under which banks had to hold 12.5 per cent of their deposits as liquid assets with the Bank of England;
- the abolition of hire purchase restrictions in 1982;
- the Building Societies Act 1986 (see p. 183); and
- 'Big Bang', also in 1986 (see p. 187).

Supervision

HM Treasury is the government department with responsibility for financial services. In particular, it is responsible for legislation covering the supervision of banks, building societies, friendly societies and investment businesses which are subject to the new regulatory system established under the Banking Act 1987 (see p. 181), the Building Societies Act 1986 (see p. 183) and the Financial Services Act 1986 (see p. 180). The Treasury also oversees the Securities and Investments Board (SIB—see p. 179).

The Department of Trade and Industry (DTI) is responsible for company law and insolvency matters, and for investigations and prosecutions under the Financial Services, Insolvency and Companies Acts. Investigations are carried out with the Serious Fraud Office. DTI's responsibilities also include prudential supervision of insurance undertakings, European Community (EC) insurance directives, insurance interests in the Organisation for Economic Co-operation and Development (OECD) and the General Agreement on Tariffs and Trade (GATT), and general questions affecting the insurance industry. It also has powers to investigate 'insider dealing'—securities trading carried out on the basis of privileged access to relevant information.

The Treasury negotiates and implements EC directives relating to financial services and is responsible for arrangements with overseas regulators for exchanging information. It is also charged with encouraging international liberalisation in financial services both bilaterally and through GATT and the OECD. International supervisory forums include the Basle Committee on Banking Supervision and the International Organisation of Securities Commissions (IOSCO). IOSCO is the primary international meeting place for regulatory authorities. Its 1992 conference, held in London, approved a set of principles for the supervision of financial conglomerates and released guidelines for clearing and settlement systems in energy markets.

The main provisions of the Financial Services Act came into force in 1988; and most of the Act's powers are delegated to the SIB. Under the Act, investment businesses (those dealing in, arranging, managing or giving advice on investments or operating collective investment schemes) require authorisation and are subject to rules on the conduct of business and other rules made under the legislation. The SIB has recognised a number of self-regulating organisations (SROs) and recognised professional bodies (RPBs). It has a duty to assist SROs and RPBs to fulfil their regulatory functions. Most investment businesses are authorised under the Act by virtue of membership of one of these. The SROs are:

- the Financial Intermediaries, Managers and Brokers Regulatory Association (FIMBRA), which covers firms such as independent financial advisers and insurance brokers;

- the Investment Management Regulatory Organisation (IMRO), whose members include merchant banks and pension fund managers with mainly corporate clients;
- the Life Assurance and Unit Trust Regulatory Organisation (LAUTRO), which has responsibility for the way in which its members, mainly the large life assurance companies, market life insurance and unit trusts; and
- the Securities and Futures Authority (SFA), whose members include member firms of the London Stock Exchange, as well as futures brokers and dealers, and eurobond dealers.

The SIB proposes to merge FIMBRA and LAUTRO in April 1994.

Other information relating to supervision and regulation is contained in the following section and in the sections dealing with the various types of financial institutions and markets.

Bank of England

The Bank of England was established in 1694 by Act of Parliament and Royal Charter as a corporate body. Its entire capital stock was acquired by the Government in 1946. The Bank acts as banker to the Government, holding its main accounts, managing Britain's reserves of gold and foreign exchange, arranging new government borrowing and managing the stock of its existing debt. The Bank's main objectives are to:

- ensure the soundness of the financial system through the direct supervision of banks and specialised City institutions;

- promote the efficiency and competitiveness of the financial system, especially in domestic and international payment and settlement systems; and

- maintain the value of the nation's money, mainly through policies and market operations agreed with government.

The Banking Act 1987 assigns the Bank of England the overriding objective of protecting depositors. To this end institutions intending to take deposits from the public must gain authorisation from the Bank and submit to its continued supervision. Under the Financial Services Act 1986, the Bank is also responsible for overseeing money-market institutions (see p. 188). The Bank's supervision is 'prudential'—it sets minimum standards for authorised institutions but offers no guarantee that those institutions will not fail or that investors or depositors will be compensated in full. The Banking Act established the Deposit Protection Fund, financed by contributions levied on the banking system; this entitles depositors to limited compensation if an authorised bank fails. In order to be and remain authorised, an institution has to satisfy the Bank that it has:

● adequate capital and liquidity;

● a realistic business plan;

● adequate systems and controls;

● adequate provision for bad and doubtful debts; and

● that its business is carried out with integrity and skill, and in a prudent manner.

As agent for the Government, the Bank is responsible for managing the National Debt, which involves arranging government borrowing and repayment of debt. It also maintains the register of holdings of government securities on behalf of the Treasury, and manages the Exchange Equalisation Account (EEA) holding Britain's official reserves of gold, foreign exchange, Special Drawing Rights (SDRs—claims on the International Monetary Fund) and European Currency Units (ECUs). The Bank may intervene in the foreign exchange markets on the Government's behalf, using the resources of the EEA, to check undue fluctuations in the exchange value of sterling.

The Bank is able to influence money-market conditions through its dealings with the discount houses (see p. 183), which developed in the 19th century as bill brokers for industrialists. Discount houses hold mainly Treasury, local authority and commercial bills, and negotiable certificates of deposit financed by short-term loans from the banks. If on a particular day there is a shortage of cash in the banking system as a result, for example, of large tax payments, the Bank relieves the shortage either by buying

bills from the discount houses or by lending directly to them. This permits banks to replenish their cash balances at the Bank by recalling some of their short-term loans to the discount houses. The Bank's dealings with the discount houses give it powerful influence over short-term interest rates.

The Bank of England has the sole right in England and Wales to issue banknotes. The note issue is no longer backed by gold but by government and other securities. Three Scottish and four Northern Ireland banks also issue notes. These issues, apart from a small amount specified by legislation for each bank, must be fully covered by holdings of Bank of England notes and coinage. Responsibility for the provision of coin lies with the Royal Mint, a government trading fund which became an executive agency in 1990.

The Bank of England seeks to ensure that Britain's financial markets are efficient and competitive. To this end it runs two securities settlement systems with in-built payment arrangements—the Central Gilts Office and the Central Moneymarket Office. A permanent body of market and legal practitioners—the Financial Law Panel—has been established by the Bank to help find practical solutions to problems of legal uncertainty in the wholesale financial markets.

Banks and Building Societies

In addition to banks, the chief institutions offering banking services are the building societies and the National Savings Bank. The 'single passport' system created by the European Community Second Banking Directive allows 'credit institutions' (banks and building societies) to operate throughout the EC on the basis of their home-state authorisation.

A useful distinction can be made between 'retail' and 'wholesale' banking. Retail banking is primarily for personal customers and small businesses. Its main services are cash deposit and withdrawal facilities, and money transmission systems. Competition between the banks and the building societies in providing money transmission services to individuals has increased during the last two decades and is expected to intensify further (see p. 182). Building societies can also offer money transmission services to companies.

Wholesale business involves taking large deposits at higher rates of interest, deploying funds in money-market instruments (see p. 188) and making large loans and investments. Nearly all banks in Britain engage in some wholesale activities and some, such as the merchant and overseas banks, centre their business on them. Many such wholesale dealings are conducted on the inter-bank market, that is, between banks themselves.

In 1993 there were 508 institutions authorised under the Banking Act 1987, or EC legislation, including retail banks, merchant banks, branches of overseas banks, discount houses and banking subsidiaries of both banking and non-banking institutions from Britain and overseas. Of these, around 320 were members of the British Bankers' Association, the main representative body for British banks.

Retail Banks

The major retail banks have a significant branch network, offering a full range of financial services to both individuals and companies. Among services generally available are interest-bearing current accounts; deposit accounts; and various kinds of loan arrangements. In addition, there is a full range of money transmission facilities that increasingly feature plastic card technology.

The major banks in England and Wales are Barclays, Lloyds, Midland, National Westminster, the TSB Group and Abbey National; and in Scotland the Bank of Scotland and the Royal Bank of Scotland. Other important retail banks are the Clydesdale Bank, the Co-operative Bank, the Yorkshire Bank and Girobank. Girobank, previously a subsidiary of the Post Office, was privatised in 1990 and became a subsidiary of the Alliance and Leicester Building Society. Northern Ireland is served by branch networks of four major banking groups.

With the growth of financial services and a relaxation of restrictions on competition among financial institutions, the major banks have diversified their services. They are lending more money for house purchases, and most now own finance houses, leasing and factoring companies, merchant banks, securities dealers, insurance companies and unit trust companies.

The banks offer loan facilities to companies; since the 1970s they have provided more medium- and long-term loans than they did formerly. They have become important suppliers of finance for small firms. A loan guarantee scheme is supported by the banks, under which 70 per cent of the value of loans to small companies is guaranteed by the Government. Some banks have set up special subsidiaries to provide venture capital for companies (see p. 187). Most retail banks maintain overseas subsidiaries which may account for a substantial proportion of their business, and are active in eurocurrency markets (see p. 189).

The total liabilities/assets of the retail banks amounted to over £500,000 million in 1993. Of the liabilities, 63 per cent were sterling deposits, 22 per cent foreign currency deposits, and the remainder items in suspense or transmission, and capital and other funds. Of the £324,000 million of sterling deposits, sight deposits withdrawable on demand constituted 50 per cent; time deposits requiring notice of withdrawal and certificates of deposit and other short-term instruments accounted for the remainder. The banks' main liquid assets consist of money at call (mainly short-term loans to discount houses), their holdings of Treasury and other bills, short-dated British government securities and balances at the Bank of England. They also hold a proportion of their assets as portfolio investments (mainly longer-dated British government securities) or trade investments.

The main retail banks operate through some 12,450 branches and sub-branches in Britain. National Westminster has the largest number, with some 2,700 branches, followed by Barclays (2,200), Lloyds (1,850), Midland (1,740), TSB (1,400), the Royal Bank of Scotland (750), Abbey National (680), Clydesdale Bank (600), Bank of Scotland (350), Yorkshire Bank (270) and the Co-operative Bank (88). Around three-quarters of adults in Britain have a current account and over one-third a deposit account.

Payment Systems

Apart from credit and debit card arrangements, the main payment systems are run by three separate companies operating under an umbrella organisation, the Association for Payment Clearing Services (APACS), of which 21 banks and building societies are members. One covers bulk paper clearings—cheques and credit transfers. A second deals with high-value clearings for same-day settlement, namely the nationwide electronic transfer service Clearing House Automated Payment System (CHAPS) and the cheque-based Town Clearing (which operates only in the City of London). A third covers bulk electronic clearing for standing orders and direct debits. Membership of each of these clearing companies is open to any bank, building society or other financial institution meeting the criteria for appropriate supervision and volume of transactions.

Plastic Card Technology

All the major retail banks and building societies have substantial networks of automated teller machines, which give customers access to cash and other services for up to 24 hours a day. Almost 18,500 machines were in operation at the end of 1992.

The banks and major building societies also offer their customers cheque guarantee cards—typically for amounts up to £50 or sometimes £100. The cards entitle holders to cheque-cashing facilities in participating institutions and guarantee retailers that transactions up to the specified guarantee limit will be honoured. Uniform eurocheques supported by a eurocheque card are available from all major banks. These standard-format cheques may be used to obtain cash or make payments in Britain, elsewhere in Europe and in a few other overseas countries. The cheques are made out in the currency of the country in which they are being used, with a guarantee limit of the equivalent of £100 per cheque.

Credit cards issued by major retail banks and building societies are a popular means of payment and are widely accepted throughout Britain and overseas. Most cards are affiliated to one of the two major international credit card organisations, Visa and MasterCard. Some of the major retail stores issue their own cards, which operate like credit cards. A charge card, like a credit card, enables the holder to make retail payments, but there is either no credit limit or a very high limit, and the balance must be settled in full on receipt of a monthly statement.

As well as the traditional paper-based systems for making retail payments by credit or charge cards, an increasing number of stores and garages now provide EFTPOS (see p. 193) facilities. Using debit cards, payments can be deducted directly from the purchaser's bank account. Most cards are affiliated either to Visa or to the Switch organisation, which is based in Britain.

Home Banking

Many banks and building societies offer home banking services whereby customers use a telephone or personal computer to obtain account information, make transfers and pay bills. Midland's First Direct is one such service.

Building Societies

Building societies are mutual institutions, owned by their savers and borrowers. They raise short-term deposits from savers, who are generally able to withdraw their money on demand or at short notice. The societies make long-term loans, mostly at variable rates of interest, against the security of property—usually private dwellings purchased for owner-occupation.

Competition between the building societies and other financial institutions has increased in the last decade. A variety of savings schemes have been established, and a growing number of societies provide current account facilities such as cheque books and automated teller machines. In 1992 there were some 3,500 building society automated teller machines, about one-sixth of the total. Three building societies issue credit cards.

> Building societies are the major lenders for house purchase in Britain and are the principal repository for the personal sector's liquid assets, although banks' shares have increased in both areas since 1985. Some 60 per cent of adults have building society savings accounts.

In 1993 there were 90 registered societies, of which 87 were members of the Building Societies' Association. Building societies' assets totalled £263,000 million at the end of 1992; about £33,000 million was advanced in new mortgages in the course of 1992. The three largest—the Halifax, Nationwide and Woolwich—account for about one-half of the total assets of all societies. Societies may operate throughout the EC.

The Building Societies Act 1986 enabled societies to diversify into banking and other services. Up to 25 per cent of a society's commercial assets may be used for purposes other than loans on first mortgage of owner-occupied houses, including as much as 15 per cent in other types of asset such as unsecured loans. Directly or through subsidiaries, societies may offer services within the general areas of banking, investment, insurance, trusteeship, executorship and estate agency. However, their main business will continue to be financial and housing-related services.

The 1986 Act established the Building Societies Commission to carry out the prudential supervision of building societies. It also made provision for a society to seek the approval of its members to convert into a public limited company. In this event the society becomes an authorised institution under the Banking Act 1987 (see p. 181) and is then supervised by the Bank of England. Abbey National pursued this course and no longer contributes to building society statistics.

The Council of Mortgage Lenders is a trade body established in 1989 for all mortgage lending institutions, including building societies, insurance companies, finance houses and banks.

Merchant Banks

Merchant banks have traditionally been concerned primarily with accepting, or guaranteeing, commercial bills and with sponsoring capital issues on behalf of their customers. Today they undertake a diversified and complex range of activities. They have important roles in equity and debt markets and the provision of advice and financial services to industrial companies, especially where mergers, takeovers and other forms of corporate reorganisation are involved. Management of investment holdings, including trusts, pensions and other funds, is also an important function of merchant banks. The sector is split between independent houses and those which are part of larger banking groups.

Overseas Banks

A total of 255 banks incorporated overseas were represented in Britain in 1993. Of these, 26 were from the United States and 27 from Japan. Some 78 institutions incorporated in Britain were subsidiaries of overseas companies. They offer a comprehensive banking service in many parts of the world and engage in the financing of trade not only between Britain and other countries but also between third-party countries.

British-based Overseas Banks

A small number of banks have their head offices in Britain, but operate mainly abroad, often specialising in particular regions. Standard Chartered, which is represented in Asia, Africa and the Middle East, is the major example of this type of bank.

Discount Houses

There are seven discount houses authorised under the Banking Act 1987. These are specialised institutions unique in their function and central position in the British monetary system. They act as financial intermediaries between the Bank of England and the rest of the banking sector, promoting an orderly flow of short-term funds. They guarantee to tender for the whole of the weekly offer of the Government's Treasury bills, which are instruments to raise funds over a period of up to six months. In return for acting as intermediaries, the discount houses have secured borrowing facilities at the Bank of England, acting as 'lender of last resort'. Assets of the discount houses consist mainly of Treasury and commercial bills, negotiable certificates of deposit and short-term loans. Their liabilities are for the most part short-term deposits.

National Savings Bank

The National Savings Bank is run by the Department for National Savings, a government department. It contributes to government borrowing and aims to encourage saving by offering personal savers a range of investments, designed to meet various requirements. Important products include:

- Savings Certificates, which either pay a fixed rate of interest alone or a lower fixed rate of interest combined with index-linking;
- Premium Bonds, where interest is paid in the form of prizes chosen by lottery;
- Income and Capital Bonds;
- Children's Bonus Bonds, which are designed to accumulate capital sums for those under 21;
- Ordinary and Investment Accounts, where deposits and withdrawals can be made at over 19,000 post offices throughout Britain; and
- FIRST Option Bonds, launched in 1992, which are 'tax-paid' and offer a guaranteed rate of interest that is fixed for one year.

With the exception of FIRST Option Bonds, interest on National Savings products is paid without deduction of tax at source. Certain National Savings products offer tax exempt returns. In some cases the best returns are paid to those who leave their savings untouched for several years. In August 1993 the total amount of money invested in National Savings was over £45,000 million.

Insurance

London is the world's leading centre for insurance and for placing international reinsurance; it handles an estimated 20 per cent of the general insurance business placed on the international market. There are two broad categories of insurance: long-term life insurance, where contracts may be for periods of many years; and general insurance, including accident and short-term life insurance, where contracts are for a year or less. Authorised insurance companies are supervised by the Department of Trade and Industry under the Insurance Companies Act 1982.

In addition to the British companies and Lloyd's (see p. 185), a large number of overseas companies are represented, with which many British companies have formed close relationships. Some British companies confine their activities to domestic business but most large companies undertaking general business transact a substantial amount overseas through branches and agencies or affiliated local companies.

Over 820 companies are authorised to carry on one or more classes of insurance business in Britain. About 450 companies belong to the Association of British Insurers (ABI). Some companies are mutual institutions, owned by their policy holders. Insurance is also available from certain friendly societies (see p. 186).

EC directives introducing the 'single-licence' system in insurance are due to be in force by July 1994. Life and non-life insurers will be able to operate throughout the EC on the basis of authorisation in their home state. Restrictions on carrying both life and non-life insurance business within the same firm (a 'composite' insurer) will be lifted. Separate directives cover reinsurance, motor insurance and co-insurance.

Long-term Insurance

As well as providing life cover, life insurance is a vehicle for saving and investment because premiums are invested in securities and other assets. Some 31 per cent of adults have life assurance policies. The net long-term insurance premium income of companies representing about 99 per cent of the British market in 1992 was almost £52,000 million from their worldwide operations, £43,000 million of which was earned in Britain. Long-term insurance is handled by 196 companies.

General Insurance

General insurance business is undertaken by insurance companies and by Lloyd's. It covers fire, accident, general liability, short-term life, motor, marine, aviation and transport. Total ABI member company premiums worldwide in 1992 were £31,000 million, of which £19,000 million was earned in Britain. Over £5,700 million was for motor insurance in Britain and £1,700 million for marine, aviation and transport insurance. Fire and accident insurance was worth around £10,600 million. The bulk of business by ABI companies in the latter categories was written through the Institute of London Underwriters (see below).

Lloyd's

Lloyd's, the origins of which go back to the 17th century, is an incorporated society of private insurers in London. Although its activities were originally confined to the conduct of marine insurance, a considerable worldwide market for the transaction of other classes of insurance business, such as aviation and motor insurance, has been built up.

Lloyd's is not a company but a market for insurance administered by the Council of Lloyd's, the Lloyd's Market Board and Lloyd's Regulatory Board. Business is carried out for individual elected underwriting members, or 'names', who must show sufficient available wealth and lodge a deposit. Insurance is transacted for them with unlimited liability, in competition with each other and with insurance companies. In 1993 there were 19,500 members, grouped into 228 syndicates. Each syndicate is managed by an underwriting agent responsible for appointing a professional underwriter to accept insurance risks and settle claims on the syndicate members' behalf. Insurance may only be placed through accredited Lloyd's brokers,

who negotiate with Lloyd's syndicates on behalf of the insured.

Lloyd's net premium income in 1990, the most recent year for which figures are available, was £5,280 million, which can be broken down as follows:

- £634 million for motor insurance;
- £1,703 million for marine insurance;
- £324 million for aviation insurance; and
- £2,619 million for non-marine insurance.

Lloyd's has suffered severe losses in recent years, partly as a result of a series of natural disasters, including the storms in Britain in October 1987, the *Exxon Valdez* oil tanker disaster off the coast of Alaska in 1989, and Hurricane Andrew, which struck Florida and Louisiana in 1992.

A business plan published in April 1993 set out a series of reforms for Lloyd's, the most radical of which is the introduction of incorporated capital. From 1 January 1994 corporate members with limited liability will operate alongside individual unlimited liability members, to give the market the additional capacity needed to take advantage of improved trading conditions.

Institute of London Underwriters

The Institute of London Underwriters was formed in 1884, originally as a trade association for marine underwriters. It now provides a market where insurance companies transact marine, commercial transport and aviation business. The Institute issues combined policies in its own name which are underwritten by member companies. The premium income processed by the Institute's member companies in 1992 was some £2,600 million. About half of the 80 member companies are branches or subsidiaries of overseas companies.

Insurance Brokers

Insurance brokers, acting on behalf of the insured, are a valuable part of the company market and play an essential role in the Lloyd's market. Many brokers specialise in reinsurance business, serving as intermediaries in the exchange of contracts between companies, both British and overseas, and often acting as London representatives of the latter. The Insurance Brokers (Registration) Act 1977 makes provision for the voluntary registration and regulation of insurance brokers by the Insurance Brokers Registration Council. Only those registered with the Council can use the title 'insurance broker'. In 1993 some 13,400 individuals were registered with the Council, through 2,115 partnerships or sole traderships and 2,650 limited companies.

Friendly Societies

Friendly societies have traditionally been unincorporated societies of individuals, offering their members a limited range of financial services, particularly provision for retirement and against loss of income through sickness or unemployment. The Friendly Societies Act 1992 enabled friendly societies to incorporate, take on new powers and offer a broad range of financial services through subsidiaries.

Investment Funds

Britain has a great deal of expertise in fund management, which involves managing funds on the investor's behalf, or advising investors on how to invest their funds. The main types of investment fund include pension schemes, life assurance, investment trusts and unit trusts.

Pension Funds

Virtually all occupational pension schemes are established under trust law to protect the interests of members and most pay benefits related to final salary. Benefits are funded in advance by employer (and wholly employee) contributions, which are held and invested by trustees on behalf of beneficiaries. Pension funds are major investors in securities markets. Total British pension fund assets were worth in the region of £400,000 million in 1993 and pension funds hold around 40 per cent of securities listed on the London Stock Exchange. Since 1986, members of occupational pension schemes have been able

to opt out and set up a personal pension scheme. Over 11 million people belong to occupational pension schemes and more than 4 million to personal pension schemes.

The Pensions Law Review Committee submitted a report to the Government in autumn 1993 outlining a legal and regulatory framework for occupational pension schemes. The report has reviewed the framework within which these pension schemes operate, and has recommended a range of measures for improving the security of pension entitlements under the schemes.

Investment and Unit Trusts

Investment trust companies, which offer the opportunity to diversify risk even on a relatively small investment, are listed on the London Stock Exchange and their shares are traded in the usual way. They must invest mostly in securities, and the trusts themselves are exempt from capital gains tax. Assets are purchased mainly out of shareholders' funds, although investment trusts are also allowed to borrow money for investment. There were 235 members of the Association of Investment Trust Companies in April 1993, with some £31,250 million worth of assets under management.

Authorised unit trusts are open-ended mutual or pooled investment vehicles which place funds in a wide range of securities markets all over the world. As with investment trusts, investors with relatively small amounts to invest are able to benefit from diversified and expertly managed portfolios. The industry has grown rapidly during the last decade, and in 1993 there were over 1,500 authorised unit trusts with total assets exceeding £70,000 million. Unit trust management groups are represented by the Association of Unit Trusts and Investment Funds and regulated by IMRO. The trusts themselves are authorised by the SIB.

Special Financing Institutions

There are many specialised institutions offering finance to personal and corporate sector borrowers. These borrowers are found in both the public and the private sectors.

Among public sector agencies are Scottish Enterprise, Highlands and Islands Enterprise, the Welsh Development Agency, the Industrial Development Board for Northern Ireland and ECGD (Export Credits Guarantee Department—Britain's official export credit insurer). The part of ECGD that handled the export of capital goods sold on short-term credit was privatised in 1991 and is now dealt with by NCM Credit Insurance.

Some private sector institutions were set up with government support and with financing from banks and other financial institutions. They may offer loan finance or equity capital. The main private sector institutions are described below.

Finance and Leasing Companies

At the beginning of 1992 the Finance Houses Association and the Equipment Leasing Association together formed a single new representative body, the Finance and Leasing Association (FLA). This represents the interests of companies offering motor finance, consumer credit, and business finance and leasing. The FLA's 108 members undertook new business worth £22,172 million in 1992.

Factoring Companies

Factoring comprises a range of financial services which provide growing companies with a flexible source of finance in exchange for the outstanding invoices due to them. Factoring has developed as a major financial service since the early 1960s, covering international activities as well as domestic trade. Member companies of the Association of British Factors and Discounters handled business worth £16,000 million in 1992, 47 per cent of which was undertaken for clients in manufacturing industry, 29 per cent for clients in distribution and 17 per cent for clients in the services sector.

Venture Capital Companies

Venture capital companies offer medium- and long-term equity financing for new and developing businesses when such funds are not easily or directly available from traditional sources, such as the stock market or banks. The British Venture Capital Association has 115 full members and makes up virtually all the industry. Many venture capital companies are subsidiaries of other financial institutions, including banks, insurance companies and pension funds.

> Britain's venture capital industry invested £1,400 million worldwide in 1992; management buy-outs and buy-ins accounted for 64 per cent of the capital invested. The South East of England remains the dominant region for investment, accounting for 44 per cent of the total.

The largest of Britain's venture capital companies is *3i*, shares in which are owned by the Bank of England (15 per cent) and six of the major retail banks.

Financial Markets

The City of London has a variety of financial markets. They include the London Stock Exchange, the foreign exchange market, the financial futures and options market, eurobond and eurocurrency markets, Lloyd's insurance market (see p. 185), and bullion and commodity markets. The securities markets are supervised jointly by the Treasury, the Bank of England, SIB and the London Stock Exchange among others.

London Stock Exchange

The London Stock Exchange has its main administrative centre in London, as well as centres in Belfast, Birmingham, Leeds, Glasgow and Manchester. As a result of a set of reforms implemented in 1986 and known popularly as 'Big Bang', the Exchange has changed radically in recent years. The main reforms were as follows:
- the Exchange's rules on membership were altered to allow corporate ownership of member firms;
- the system under which dealers charged fixed minimum scales of commission to investors was abolished in favour of negotiated commissions;

- dealers were permitted to trade in securities both on their own behalf, as principals, and on behalf of clients, as agents, these two roles formerly having been kept distinct; and
- a screen-based price quotation system was introduced and led to the closing of the trading floor.

The London Stock Exchange is one of the largest in the world in terms of the number and variety of securities listed. It accounts for some 10 per cent of equity trading worldwide. Some 7,500 securities are listed; in 1993 these had a market value of almost £3,000,000 million. About 4,400 company securities are listed, including those of a growing number of leading overseas companies, with a value of around £2,500,000 million. The remainder is made up of British and overseas government and corporate stocks as well as eurobonds (see p. 189).

Throughout the 1980s a trend towards the 'securitisation of debt' developed, with major borrowers increasingly raising funds by issuing securities rather than by seeking out bank loans. In recent years the largest market for new issues has been that for companies' securities, including issues of shares resulting from the Government's privatisation programme.

> More than 9 million people, over 22 per cent of the adult population, own shares, according to a survey carried out by Mori and ProShare (which promotes share ownership) in December 1992.

The gilt-edged market allows the Government to borrow money by issuing loan stock through the Bank of England. The Stock Exchange offers a secondary market where investors can buy and sell gilts. Average daily turnover in the market reached £6,000 million in 1993.

European Community Directives

The London Stock Exchange altered its rules in 1990 to conform to EC directives on listing particulars, prospectuses and mutual recognition. The major effect of the EC directive on Mutual Recognition of Listing Particulars is that, subject to certain limitations, each member state is required to recognise listing particulars accepted in another member state. In order to put British companies on an equal footing with those in other EC countries, the Exchange reduced the minimum trading record requirement for full listing from five years to three.

Money Markets

The London money markets comprise the interbank deposit markets plus a range of other instruments, usually short-term in maturity. They are wholesale in the sense that the participants are professional operators dealing in substantial amounts of money.

Banks are the major participants in these markets, and are supervised by the Bank of England. The Bank also supervises other institutions which operate in the foreign exchange and other wholesale money markets. In close consultation with market participants, the Bank has issued the *London Code of Conduct*, which defines the instruments that comprise the wholesale money markets and the standards and dealing procedures which participants should follow.

Since 1986, large companies have been permitted to issue sterling commercial paper (SCP): this consists of debt denominated in sterling with a maturity of up to one year. The range of qualifying issuers of SCP has broadened since 1986 to include, for example, banks, building societies and overseas public authorities.

Euromarkets

These are markets in currencies lent or invested outside their domestic marketplace, particularly as a means of financing international trade and investment. Transactions can thus be carried out in eurodollars, eurodeutschmarks, euroyen and so on. London is at the heart of the euromarkets and houses most of the major international banks and securities firms.

The euromarkets developed in the late 1950s following the restoration of convertibility between the major currencies, partly to avoid incurring the costs of exchange control and other regulations. In recent years distinctions between markets have been breaking down and the euromarkets form a major part of the wider international money and capital markets. Participants in the markets include multinational trading corporations, financial companies and governments.

The euro-securities markets have grown considerably in recent years because the instruments traded on them, including euro-commercial paper, euro-medium-term notes and eurobonds, are seen as flexible alternatives to bank loans. Euro-medium-term note (EMTN) programmes were introduced in 1986, and EMTN issues rose threefold between 1990 and 1992. British building societies are prominent among EMTN issuers. There is a growing private sector market in ECU-denominated deposits, securities and eurobonds.

Foreign Exchange Market

London is the world's biggest centre for foreign exchange trading, with an average daily turnover of about US $300,000 million. Along with Singapore, it has the most diversified exchange market in the world.

The foreign exchange market consists of telephone and electronic links between the participants, which include banks, other financial institutions and several foreign exchange broking firms acting as intermediaries between the banks. It provides those engaged in international trade and investment with foreign currencies for their transactions. The banks are in close contact with financial centres abroad and are able to quote buying and selling rates for both immediate ('spot') and forward transactions in a range of currencies and maturities. The forward market enables traders and dealers who, at a given date in the future, wish to receive or make a specific foreign currency payment, to contract in advance to sell or buy the foreign currency involved for sterling at a fixed exchange rate.

Derivatives

Financial derivatives are contracts to buy or sell, at a future date, financial instruments such as equities, bonds or money-market instruments. They offer a means of hedging against changes in prices, exchange rates and interest rates. Derivatives include futures (agreements to buy or sell financial instruments or physical commodities at a future date), options (the right to buy or sell financial instruments or physical commodities for a stated period at a predetermined price) and 'over-the-counter' products, including swaps. A foreign exchange swap can convert a money-market instrument in one currency into a money-market instrument in another—a dollar deposit into a sterling deposit, for example.

The use of derivatives has grown rapidly and instruments have become more complex, especially as advances have been made in information technology and links between markets and institutions strengthened. Between 1991 and 1992 the turnover on London's futures and options exchanges grew by almost 50 per cent to reach 112 million contracts. LIFFE (see below) accounted for almost two-thirds of the contracts traded in 1992 and the London Metal Exchange (see p. 190) accounted for about a fifth.

Financial Futures and Options

Over 200 banks, other financial institutions, brokers and individual traders are members of the London International Financial Futures and Options Exchange (LIFFE), which trades at the Cannon Bridge development. Futures contracts cover the purchase or sale of a fixed amount of a commodity at a given date in the future at a price agreed at the time of trade. There is also dealing in options on the equity of prominent British companies and in stock index options. LIFFE has the most internationally diverse range of financial futures and options products of any exchange in the world. In September 1992, trading on LIFFE for the first time exceeded that on the Chicago exchanges, which pioneered the development of financial futures and options.

London Bullion Market

Some 60 banks and other financial trading companies comprise the London gold and silver markets, which, like the foreign exchange market, trade by telephone or other electronic means. Five of the members of the London Bullion Market Association meet twice daily to establish a London fixing price for gold—a reference point for worldwide dealings. The silver fixing is held once a day. Although much interest centres upon the fixings, active dealing takes place throughout the day. London and Zurich are the main world centres for gold dealings.

Commodity, Shipping and Freight Markets

Britain is a major international centre for commodities trading and the home of many of the related international trade organisations. At London FOX (the London Futures and Options Exchange), futures in grains, meat, potatoes, and soya bean meal are traded, as are futures and options on 'soft' commodities (cocoa and coffee). White sugar and dry freight index futures contracts are also traded. The London Metal Exchange is the primary base metals market in the world, trading both spot and forward contracts in aluminium, aluminium alloy, copper, lead, nickel, tin and zinc. The International Petroleum Exchange is Europe's only energy futures exchange. The Baltic Exchange, which finds ships for cargoes and cargoes for ships throughout the world, is the world's leading shipping market.

OTHER SERVICES

Distribution

Distributing goods to their point of sale by road, rail, air and sea is a significant economic activity, accounting for about a sixth of national income. In 1992 there were some 3.4 million employees in the distributive and allied trades in Great Britain. The large retailers and wholesalers of food, drink and clothing operate, either directly or through contractors, extensive distribution networks using fleets of trailers, vans and lorries. There is also a highly competitive specialist express delivery sector.

Wholesaling

There were 120,600 businesses, with a turnover valued at almost £225,500 million (see Table 14.1), engaged in wholesaling and dealing in Great Britain in 1990. Total turnover increased by 9 per cent between 1988 and 1990.

In the food and drink trade almost all large retailers have their own buying and central distribution operations. Elsewhere in the trade, voluntary groups have been formed by wholesalers and small independent retailers; the retailers are encouraged by discounts and other incentives to buy as much as possible from the wholesaler. This has helped to preserve many smaller retail outlets, including the traditional 'corner shops' and village stores. It has also given small retailers the advantages of bulk buying and co-ordinated distribution.

London's wholesale markets play a significant part in the distribution of foodstuffs. New Covent Garden is the main market for fruit and vegetables, Smithfield for meat and Billingsgate for fish.

The co-operative movement has its own distribution organisation, the Co-operative Wholesale Society (CWS). Retail co-operative societies are encouraged to buy from the CWS, which is their main supplier. The CWS is also a major retailer in Scotland, Northern Ireland, the Midlands and south-east and northern England.

Retailing

Of the 25 largest retailers in Western Europe (by sales in the period 1988–90), ten were British firms. In 1990 there were 242,000 retail businesses, with 349,000 outlets, in Great Britain (see Table 14.2). In recent years the large multiple retailers have grown in size, reducing numbers of stores but increasing outlet size and diversifying their product ranges. Decline has been particularly . evident among small independent businesses and retail co-operative societies. The largest multiple retailers in the grocery market are

Table 14.1: Wholesale Trade in Great Britain 1990

	Number of businesses	Turnover[a] (£ million)
Food and drink	16,435	47,286
Petroleum products	969	21,660
Clothing, furs, textiles and footwear	10,217	9,587
Coal and oil merchants	3,210	2,340
Builders' merchants	4,381	8,540
Agricultural supplies and livestock dealing	3,083	8,351
Industrial materials	6,016	26,967
Scrap and waste products	3,946	2,922
Industrial and agricultural machinery	8,778	15,218
Operational leasing	2,860	3,095
Other goods	60,685	79,495
Total wholesaling and dealing	120,580	225,461

Source: *Business Monitor SDA26. Wholesaling, 1990.*
[a]Excludes value added tax.

Sainsbury, Tesco, Safeway, Asda and Gateway. These five groups are responsible for around £25,000 million of grocery sales a year. Other important groups are Waitrose and Morrisons.

About 20 million people regularly purchase all kinds of goods and services through mail order catalogues. In 1992 sales by general mail order totalled some £3,900 million, representing about 3 per cent of all retail sales. The largest selling items sold by the mail order companies are clothing, footwear, furniture, household textiles, televisions, radios and electrical goods.

Retail co-operative societies are voluntary organisations controlled by their members, membership being open to anyone paying a small deposit on a minimum share. There are 4,750 retail co-operative outlets, 48 per cent of which sell food and groceries.

The leading mixed retail businesses include Marks and Spencer, Boots, Kingfisher, Storehouse, W. H. Smith, Argos, Littlewoods, Savacentre, John Menzies, Sears, Burton Group and House of Fraser.

Large Shopping Centres

Britain has a wide range of complementary shopping facilities inside and outside town and city centres. One of the most significant trends in retailing is towards the development of large and medium-sized supermarkets and superstores in order to increase efficiency and the range of goods available. However, the five largest multiple retailers have only 19 per cent of retail turnover, partly because there continues to be a demand for the services provided by small, specialised shops.

The main multiple grocery companies have been steadily increasing the size of their stores both in towns and cities and on suburban and out-of-town sites. Also, retailers of goods such as do-it-yourself (DIY) products, furniture and electrical appliances have built retail warehouses outside town and city centres, particularly to attract shoppers with cars. More recently, there has been a trend towards the grouping of retail warehouses into retail warehouse parks. Many towns and cities have purpose-built shopping centres.

A number of regional out-of-town shopping centres have been established on sites offering good access to large numbers of customers with cars. One of the first centres was the Metro Centre at Gateshead, Tyne and Wear, which has 209,000 sq m (2.25 million sq ft) of floorspace and is the largest of its kind in Europe. Other centres include the Meadowhall shopping centre in

Sheffield and the Lakeside centre at Thurrock in Essex, both opened in 1990.

All new retail development requires planning permission from the local government planning authority. These authorities must consult the appropriate central government department before granting permission for developments of 23,325 sq m (250,000 sq ft) or more. The Government's policy is to encourage the provision of a broad range of shopping facilities to the public, while ensuring that the effects of major new retail development do not undermine the viability and vitality of existing town centres.

Diversification

Many of the large multiple groups sell a much greater number of goods and services than previously. However, in some cases extensive diversification has proved unprofitable and large food retailers are increasing their range of foods instead. More emphasis is also being placed on selling own-label goods and environmentally friendly products, including organic produce. Many superstores and large supermarkets offer fresh food, such as meat, fish, vegetables and bread baked on the premises, as well as selling packaged foods. Some large retailers have in recent years begun to provide financial services.

Promotions

Retailers are placing greater emphasis on price competition and quality as a means of promoting sales. Some large retailers have issued their own credit cards for regular customers in an attempt to encourage sales, particularly of high-value goods.

Information Technology

Information technology has become increasingly central to distribution and retailing. Computers are used to monitor stock levels and record sales figures through developments such as electronic point-of-sale (EPOS) systems. EPOS systems read a bar-code, printed on the retail product, that holds price and product information and can be used to generate orders for stock replenishment.

Techniques such as 'just-in-time' ordering, in which produce arrives at the store at the last possible moment before sale, have become widespread as a result. Most

Table 14.2: Retail Trade in Great Britain 1990

	Number of businesses	Number of outlets	Number of people engaged ('000s)	Turnover[a] (£ million)
Single-outlet retailers	215,456	215,346	825	35,736
Small multiple retailers	25,346	65,445	324	15,515
Large multiple retailers	901	68,019	1,319	81,454
Food retailers	65,169	85,085	852	48,171
Drink, confectionery and tobacco retailers	48,376	60,584	289	12,834
Clothing, footwear and leather goods retailers	30,688	60,236	312	12,716
Household goods retailers	51,379	68,880	318	20,619
Other non-food retailers	41,707	56,993	273	12,749
Mixed retail businesses	2,877	11,451	391	24,286
Hire and repair businesses	1,508	5,691	33	1,330
Total retail trade	241,704	348,920	2,468	132,704

Source: *Business Monitor SDA25. Retailing, 1990.*
[a] Includes value added tax.
Note: Differences between totals and the sums of their component parts are due to rounding.

large retailers have set up electronic data interchange (EDI) systems; these enable their computers to communicate with those of their suppliers, and transmit orders and invoices electronically, so reducing errors and saving time. A legal change permitting tax invoices in forms other than paper has made it easier for retailers to use EDI when dealing with their suppliers.

EFTPOS (electronic funds transfer at point of sale) systems enable customers to pay for purchases using debit cards which automatically transfer funds from their bank account. Several major EFTPOS schemes are well established and the number of terminals, which currently stands at about 200,000, is growing rapidly.

Vehicle and Petrol Retailing

In 1992 there were 260,000 people employed in the retail distribution of motor vehicles and parts, in petrol stations and in the repair and recovery of vehicles. Many businesses selling new vehicles are franchised by the motor manufacturers. Over one-third of the 19,000 petrol stations are owned by oil companies. The three companies with the largest number of outlets are Shell, Esso and BP. Unleaded petrol accounts for over half of petrol sold. The majority of petrol stations are self-service. About 16,000 outlets sell diesel fuel.

Hotels and Catering

The hotel and catering trades employed some 1.1 million people in Great Britain at the end of 1992:

- 329,100 in public houses and bars;
- 294,800 in restaurants, cafés and snack bars;
- 251,000 in hotels and other residential establishments;
- 117,700 in canteens; and
- 137,300 in clubs.

A large number of self-employed people also work in hotels and catering.

There were about 60,200 hotels in Great Britain in 1992, with a turnover of £12,900

million. The largest hotel business is Forte, with 338 hotels in Britain, as well as catering and leisure interests. At the other end of the scale, numerous guest houses and hotels each have fewer than 20 rooms. Holiday centres—including holiday camps with full board, self-catering centres and caravan parks—are run by Butlins, Holiday Club, Center Parcs, Warner Holidays and Pontin's.

Britain has a very wide range of restaurants, offering cuisine from virtually every country in the world. The Food Safety Act 1990 has contributed to a raising of food safety standards, as has the application of the relevant British standard on quality. In 1992 there were about 58,000 public houses (pubs), which mainly sell beer, wines, soft drinks and spirits for consumption on the premises. Many pubs are owned by the large brewing companies, which either provide managers to run them or offer tenancy agreements; others, called free houses, are independently owned and managed. The Government has acted to strengthen competition in the sale of beer and other drinks in pubs.

Permitted opening hours for some 100,000 licensed premises in England and Wales were extended in 1986. The introduction of liquor licences for 'café-style' premises has been proposed, which would allow children under 14 to accompany their parents to places where alcoholic drinks are available. In Scotland a similar type of licence called a 'refreshment licence' has been available since 1976, and licensed premises can apply for a 'children's certificate' permitting children to accompany an adult on the premises within certain hours.

Advertising

Spending on advertising in 1992 amounted to £8,769 million. The press accounted for 55 per cent of the total, television for 28 per cent, direct mail for 11 per cent, posters for 3 per cent, and commercial radio and cinema for the rest. The largest advertising expenditure is on food, retail and mail order services, cars, financial services, household goods, toiletries and cosmetics, drink, and holidays and travel. Campaigns are planned by several hundred advertising agencies which, in some cases, offer marketing, consumer research and other services.

Computing Services

The computing services industry comprises software houses; production of packaged software; consultancy; facilities management; processing services; and the provision of complete computer systems. It also includes companies providing information technology education and training, independent maintenance, contingency planning and recruitment, and contract staff.

The turnover of companies in the Computing Services Association, which represents some 75 per cent of the industry in Britain, totalled almost £5,000 million in 1992. Important areas for software development include data and word processing, telecommunications, computer-aided design and manufacturing, defence and consumer electronics. The financial services sector is a major user of computer services.

Management Consultancy

Management consultants provide business solutions by giving advice and technical assistance to business and government clients. Typically, consultants identify and investigate problems and opportunities, recommend appropriate action and help to implement recommendations. Many British-based consultancies operate internationally—the most recent trend has been for the largest firms to set up offices in Eastern Europe. The 34 member firms of the Management Consultancies Association are among the largest in the industry. In 1992 they earned £696 million in Britain and £114 million overseas.

Market Research

A wide range of clients and industries use market research, and Britain accounts for about 10 per cent of worldwide research spending. The Association of Market Survey Organisations is the main trade organisation and in 1992 its member companies earned total research revenues of £293 million.

Exhibition and Conference Centres

Britain is one of the world's three leading countries for international conferences—the others being the United States and France. London and Paris are the two most popular conference cities. Some 95 towns and cities in Britain now have facilities for conferences and exhibitions.

Among the most modern purpose-built conference and exhibition centres are the International Conference Centre in Birmingham and the Queen Elizabeth II and Olympia Conference Centres, both in London. Others are situated in Brighton (East Sussex), Harrogate (North Yorkshire), Bournemouth (Dorset), Cardiff, Birmingham, Manchester, Nottingham and Torquay. In Scotland both Glasgow and Aberdeen have exhibition and conference centres, and an International Conference Centre is being built in Edinburgh. Other large exhibition facilities are situated in London at the Barbican, Earls Court/Olympia, Alexandra Palace and Wembley Arena.

Many of the larger sites belong to a marketing group, the British Conference and Exhibition Centres Export Council. A new 4,000-seat Arena and World Trade Centre is being developed in Cardiff.

Auction Houses

Britain's chief auction houses are active in the international auction markets for works of art, trading on their acknowledged expertise. The two largest houses, Sotheby's and Christie's, are established worldwide. In 1994 Sotheby's celebrates its 250th anniversary. Sotheby's handled sales valued at £674 million in 1992, while Christie's sales were valued at £636 million.

Tourism and Travel

More than 1.4 million people are employed in tourism, and the industry contributes some £25,000 million annually to the economy— about 4 per cent of gross domestic product. There were a record 18.1 million visitors to Britain in 1992, 9 per cent more than in 1991, when the number was unusually low as a result of recession in key markets and the Gulf War. Overseas visitors' total spending in Britain exceeded £7,600 million in 1992. An estimated 64 per cent of visitors came from Europe and 18 per cent from North America. Business travel accounts for about one-fifth of all tourism overseas revenue. Britain's tourist attractions include theatres, museums, art galleries, historic houses, as well as shopping, sports and business facilities.

Some 98 per cent of travel agencies belong to the Association of British Travel Agents (ABTA). Although most travel agents are small businesses, there are a few large firms—such as Lunn Poly and Thomas Cook—which have hundreds of branches. Computerised information and booking systems are used extensively in travel agencies. There are also 656 tour operator members of ABTA; about half are both retail agents and tour operators. ABTA operates financial protection schemes to safeguard its members' customers and maintains codes of conduct drawn up with the Government's Office of Fair Trading. It also offers a free consumer affairs service to help resolve complaints against members and an independent arbitration scheme for tour operators' customers.

Tourist Authorities

The Department of National Heritage is responsible for tourism in England, and the Scottish, Welsh, and Northern Ireland Offices have responsibility for tourism in their respective countries. The government-supported British Tourist Authority (BTA) promotes Britain overseas as a tourist destination and encourages the development of tourist facilities in Britain to meet the needs of overseas visitors. The tourist boards for England, Scotland, Wales and Northern Ireland encourage the development and promotion of domestic tourism and work with the BTA to promote Britain overseas.

The BTA and the national tourist boards inform and advise the Government on issues of concern to the industry. They also help businesses and public sector bodies to plan by researching and publicising trends affecting the industry. The national tourist boards work closely with regional tourist boards, on which local government and business interests are represented. The national tourist boards offer financial assistance to the industry. There are 800 or so Tourist Information Centres in Britain, operating an information service for visitors.

Three accommodation classification and grading schemes are operated by the national tourist boards:

- the Crown scheme for hotels, guest houses, inns, bed and breakfast and farmhouse holiday accommodation. A new Lodge category has been introduced for purpose-built accommodation alongside motorways and major roads;

- the Key (Dragons used in Wales) scheme for self-catering holiday homes; and

- the Quality 'Q' scheme for holiday caravan, chalet and camping parks.

Common standards are applied throughout Britain. All participating establishments are inspected every year, involving more than 25,000 inspections in 1991–92.

Further Reading

Financial Services. Aspects of Britain series, HMSO, 1994.

15 Overseas Trade

Overseas trade has been of vital importance to the British economy for hundreds of years, and especially since the mid-19th century, when the rapid growth of industry, commerce and shipping was accompanied by Britain's development as an international trading centre. Although small in area and accounting for only about 1 per cent of the world's population, Britain is the fifth largest trading nation in the world, and, as a member of the European Community, part of the world's largest established trading bloc, accounting for about a third of all trade.

Exports of goods and services in 1992 were equivalent to about a quarter of gross domestic product (GDP). Britain exports a higher proportion of its output than many other industrial nations. It is a leading supplier of machinery, aerospace products, pharmaceuticals and other chemicals, and electrical and electronic equipment, and a significant oil exporter. It relies upon imports for about a third of total consumption of

Table 15.1: Visible Trade 1989–92

	1989	1990	1991	1992
Value (£ million)[a]				
Exports f.o.b.[b]	92,154	101,718	103,413	106,775
Imports f.o.b.[b]	116,837	120,527	113,703	120,546
Volume index (1985 = 100)[c]				
Exports	116.6	124.2	126.3	129.8
Imports	140.8	142.7	138.6	147.4
Unit value index (1985 = 100)[c]				
Exports	101.6	107.0	107.3	108.7
Imports	104.0	107.9	108.4	108.5
Terms of trade (1985 = 100)[c][d]	97.7	99.2	99.0	100.2

Source: *Monthly Review of External Trade Statistics.*
[a] Balance-of-payments basis.
[b] f.o.b. = free on board, that is, all costs accruing up to the time of placing the goods on board the exporting vessel having been paid by the seller.
[c] Overseas trade statistics basis. This differs from a balance-of-payments basis because, for imports, it includes the cost of insurance and freight and, for both exports and imports, includes returned goods.
[d] Export unit value index as a percentage of import unit value index.

foodstuffs, and for many of the basic materials and semi-manufactures needed for its industries.

VISIBLE TRADE

In 1992 Britain's exports of goods were valued at about £107,000 million and its imports of goods at £121,000 million on a balance-of-payments basis (see Table 15.1). Between 1991 and 1992 the volume of exports rose by almost 3 per cent and the value of exports by more than 3 per cent. Over the same period imports grew by 6 per cent in terms of volume and total value.

Commodity Composition

Britain has traditionally been an exporter of manufactured goods and an importer of food and basic materials. In 1970 manufactures accounted for 85 per cent of Britain's exports. The proportion fell in the early 1980s—to around 67 per cent by the middle of the decade—as North Sea oil exports increased their share. The proportion of manufactures in exports has since risen, to 82 per cent in 1992. The share of finished manufactures in total imports rose from 25 per cent in 1970 to 53 per cent in 1992. Britain has not had a surplus on manufactures since 1982. Machinery and transport equipment account for two-fifths of exports and a similar proportion of imports. Aerospace, chemicals and electronics have become more significant export sectors, while textiles and vehicles have declined in relative importance.

Since the mid-1970s North Sea oil has made a significant contribution to Britain's overseas trade both in terms of exports and

Table 15.2: Commodity Composition of Visible Trade 1992[a]

	Exports (f.o.b.)		Imports (c.i.f.)[b]	
	£ million	per cent	£ million	per cent
Non-manufactures	17,561	16.2	25,503	20.3
Food, beverages and tobacco	8,713	8.0	13,426	10.7
Basic materials	1,965	1.8	5,092	4.0
Fuels	6,881	6.4	6,985	5.5
Manufactures	88,672	81.9	98,729	78.4
Semi-manufactures	30,484	28.1	32,339	25.7
of which: Chemicals	14,996	13.8	11,615	9.2
Textiles	2,456	2.3	3,944	3.1
Iron and steel	3,007	2.8	2,524	2.0
Non-ferrous metals	1,753	1.6	2,591	2.1
Metal manufactures	2,211	2.0	2,571	2.0
Other	6,061	5.6	9,095	7.2
Finished manufactures	58,188	53.7	66,389	52.7
of which: Machinery	30,690	28.3	31,801	25.3
Road vehicles	8,895	8.2	12,121	9.6
Clothing and footwear	2,427	2.2	5,633	4.5
Scientific instruments and photographic apparatus	4,455	4.1	4,255	3.4
Other	11,721	10.8	12,579	10.0
Miscellaneous	2,065	1.9	1,661	1.3
Total	108,298	100·0	125,896	100·0

Source: *Monthly Review of External Trade Statistics.*
[a] On an overseas trade statistics basis.
[b] c.i.f. = cost, insurance and freight, that is, including shipping, insurance and other expenses incurred in the delivery of goods as far as their place of importation in Britain.
Note: Differences between totals and the sums of their component parts are due to rounding.

import substitution. In 1992 exports of fuels in volume terms were about four times their 1975 level; imports were around three-quarters of their 1975 level. During this period the share of fuels in exports changed from 4 to 6 per cent and in imports from 18 to 5.5 per cent. North Sea oil production has now passed its peak of the mid-1980s, when exports of fuels accounted for over 20 per cent of total exports. In 1992 the surplus on trade in oil amounted to about £1,500 million.

Since the early 1960s Britain's imports of semi-manufactures have exceeded those of basic materials; they are now more than six times as high. This reflects the increasing tendency for producing countries to carry out the processing of primary products up to the semi-finished or finished stage. Imported manufactures have also taken a greater share of the domestic market. The share of basic materials in total imports has fallen from 15 per cent in 1970 to 4 per cent in 1992. The share of food, beverages and tobacco in total

imports has been falling since the 1950s, reaching almost 11 per cent in 1992, as a result both of the increasing extent to which food demand has been met from domestic agriculture and the decline in the proportion of total expenditure on food.

Geographical Distribution

Britain's overseas trade is mainly—and increasingly—with other developed countries. In 1970 these accounted for 73 per cent of exports and a similar proportion of imports; by 1992 the shares were 81 and 83 per cent respectively. In 1970 non-oil developing countries accounted for 17 per cent of Britain's exports and 15 per cent of its imports; by 1992 they accounted for 13 per cent of Britain's exports and 14 per cent of its imports.

In 1972, the year before Britain joined the European Community, around a third of Britain's trade was with the other 11

Table 15.3: Britain's Main Markets and Suppliers 1992[a]

	Value (£ million)	Share (per cent)
Main markets		
Germany	15,052	13.9
United States	12,238	11.3
France	11,490	10.6
Netherlands	8,452	7.8
Italy	6,153	5.9
Irish Republic	5,740	5.3
Belgium/Luxembourg	5,720	5.3
Spain	4,409	4.1
Sweden	2,431	2.2
Japan	2,233	2.1
Main suppliers		
Germany	19,038	15.1
United States	13,713	10.9
France	12,221	9.7
Netherlands	9,910	7.9
Japan	7,453	5.9
Italy	6,773	5.4
Belgium/Luxembourg	5,744	4.6
Irish Republic	5,067	4.0
Switzerland	3,919	3.1
Norway	3,835	3.0

Source: *Monthly Review of External Trade Statistics.*
[a]On an overseas trade statistics basis. Exports are f.o.b.; imports c.i.f.

Geographical Distribution of Trade 1992

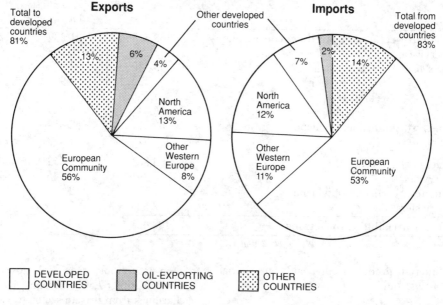

Differences between totals and the sums of their component parts are due to rounding.
Source: *United Kingdom Balance of Payments 1993 Edition.*

countries which today make up the Community. The proportion rose to more than one-half in 1992 and is expected to rise further as a result of the completion of the single European market (see p. 296). Western Europe as a whole took nearly two-thirds of Britain's exports in 1992. Trade with other Commonwealth countries has declined in importance.

EC countries accounted for seven of Britain's top ten export markets and for six of the ten leading suppliers of goods to Britain in 1992 (see Table 15.3). From 1981 to 1989 the United States was Britain's largest single market but it was overtaken in 1990 by Germany. Germany is also Britain's largest single supplier. In 1992 Germany took almost 14 per cent of Britain's exports and supplied 15 per cent of Britain's imports.

There have been a number of other changes in the pattern of Britain's overseas trade in recent years. The growth in wealth

of the oil-exporting countries during the 1970s led to a sharp increase in their imports from all sources, and by the early 1980s they were taking some 12 per cent of Britain's exports. However, by 1992, their share of Britain's exports had fallen to 6 per cent, partly because of a reduction in the price of oil. In 1973 the oil-exporting countries supplied 10 per cent of Britain's imports but, with Britain achieving self-sufficiency in oil, the proportion had fallen to 2 per cent by 1992.

There were large increases in Britain's exports to Hong Kong, Indonesia, Malaysia and Singapore in 1992. Japan has steadily increased its share of Britain's imports and now accounts for around 6 per cent. Since 1980 the percentage of Britain's total exports to Japan has doubled, and Japan is Britain's tenth largest market.

INVISIBLE TRANSACTIONS

Transactions on invisible trade fall into three main groups:

- internationally tradeable services;

199

Table 15.4: Britain's Invisible Transactions 1992

£ million

	Credits	Debits	Balance
Private sector and public corporations	**103,575**	**91,289**	**12,286**
Services	32,389	26,165	6,224
of which: Sea transport	3,440	3,837	-397
Civil aviation	4,422	4,969	-547
Travel	7,686	11,090	-3,404
Financial and other services	16,841	6,269	10,572
Interest, profits and dividends	69,211	62,874	6,337
Transfers	1,975	2,250	-275
General government	**4,863**	**12,363**	**-7,500**
Services	391	2,546	-2,155
Interest, profits and dividends	1,584	2,144	-560
Transfers	2,888	7,673	-4,785
Total invisible transactions	**108,438**	**103,652**	**4,786**

Source: *United Kingdom Balance of Payments 1993 Edition.*

- interest, profits and dividends on external assets; and

- transfers between governments.

Britain's earnings from invisible trade in 1992 were £108,000 million, exceeded only by those of the United States and Japan. Earnings from services alone in 1992 were £33,000 million. Britain accounts for 6 per cent of the world's exports of services and 16 per cent of its credits on interest, profits and dividends.

Services range from banking, insurance and stockbroking, tourism, and shipping and aviation to specialist services such as consultancy, computer programming and training. Britain's trade in services has been in surplus for about 200 years, excluding war periods.

Interest, profits and dividends on external assets have rarely been in deficit; transfers, however, have almost always been in deficit. For invisible trade as a whole, the deficit of general government is more than offset by the substantial surplus of the private sector (including public corporations), resulting in an overall surplus. General government transactions are relatively unimportant in either the services or the interest, profits and dividends accounts but they form the greater part of the transfers account. In 1992 the private sector had a surplus of £12,300

million on invisible trade while government had a deficit of £7,500 million.

Earnings from private sector services rose in value by 7 per cent in 1992 to £32,400 million; debits, at £26,200 million, were 8 per cent higher than a year previously. The surplus on private sector interest, profits and dividends was a record £6,300 million in 1992.

The deficit on private sector transfers in 1992 was £275 million, while that on government transfers was £4,800 million.

COMMERCIAL POLICY

Britain remains committed to the open multilateral trading system and to the further liberalisation of world trade. To this end it has taken a leading part in the activities of such organisations as the General Agreement on Tariffs and Trade (GATT), the International Monetary Fund (IMF) and the Organisation for Economic Co-operation and Development (OECD). It has given full support to the current round of multilateral trade negotiations. Since 1973, when Britain joined, the European Community has acted for Britain in international trade negotiations. The Community's common customs tariff is, at a trade-weighted average of 2.5 per cent, similar to the tariffs of most major industrialised countries.

Single European Market

The single European market programme, launched in 1985, was completed on 1 January 1993, ensuring the free movement of goods, services, people and capital within the Community. It is providing substantial opportunities for exporters. Member states are trying to ensure that the market operates efficiently, with even application and enforcement of Community measures throughout member countries.

General Agreement on Tariffs and Trade

Tariffs and non-tariff barriers to trade have been considerably reduced in the seven rounds of multilateral trade negotiations completed since 1947 under the auspices of GATT, the most recent one completed being the Tokyo Round (1973–79). Britain participates in these negotiations as a member of the European Community.

The eighth round of GATT multilateral trade negotiations (the Uruguay Round) was launched in 1986. It is the most ambitious and wide-ranging round of trade negotiations ever. The most recent stage of negotiations started in February 1991. The Uruguay Round's main concerns are to:

- bring trade in agriculture and textiles fully within the GATT system;

- achieve further reductions in tariff and non-tariff barriers;

- extend GATT disciplines to the new areas of intellectual property, investment and services; and

- strengthen the GATT system, so that it can deal more effectively with trade distortions and disputes.

The extension of the deadline for the completion of the talks under the 'fast track' procedure proposed by the United States allows more time to reach agreement while maintaining the discipline of a deadline. The British Government continues to urge on all parties the importance of a successful conclusion to the Uruguay Round.

European Community Agreements

In October 1992 EC finance ministers agreed on a package of measures that enabled fiscal frontiers within the EC to be abolished from January 1993. The agreement was a vital step towards the completion of the single market because it enabled businesses to transport goods throughout the EC without stopping at borders to deal with time-consuming paperwork.

The EC signed an agreement in May 1992 with the members of the European Free Trade Association (EFTA—Austria, Finland, Iceland, Liechtenstein, Norway, Sweden and Switzerland) on the creation of the European Economic Area (EEA). The EEA would have been created on 1 January 1993 if all the signatories had ratified the agreement by then. However, following a referendum in December 1992, Switzerland decided not to participate, and will not be covered by the agreement. The Community and the rest of EFTA remain committed to the EEA and are aiming for it to come into force as soon as possible.

> The European Economic Area would form the world's largest single market area, with some 370 million consumers and the free movement of goods, services, capital and people based on Community legislation.

At the European Council meeting in December 1992, agreements were reached on the promotion of economic recovery, subsidiarity, openness, the future financing of the Community and on arrangements for enlarging its membership. Austria, Finland, Norway and Sweden are currently negotiating to join the EC and a target date of 1 January 1995 has been set for their accession. Switzerland, Turkey, Malta and Cyprus have also applied for membership.

The EC has reciprocal preferential trading agreements with Cyprus, Israel, Malta and Turkey and non-reciprocal agreements with Algeria, Morocco, Tunisia, Egypt, Jordan, the occupied territories, Lebanon, Syria and former Yugoslavia and, under the Lomé Convention, with a group of 69 African,

Caribbean and Pacific developing countries. The Lomé Convention gives these countries tariff-free access, subject to certain safeguards, to the EC for industrial goods and most agricultural products. Tariff preference is given to developing countries under the Generalised System of Preferences, and also to the Faroe Islands and the overseas dependencies and territories of member states.

Economic co-operation agreements exist between the EC and several Latin American countries, the People's Republic of China, the Association of South East Asian Nations and the six members of the Gulf Co-operation Council. Negotiations are in progress which may lead to the establishment of a free trade area embracing the Community and the Council.

Association agreements are in place between the EC and Poland, Hungary, the Czech Republic, Slovakia, Bulgaria and Romania. They are designed to facilitate closer political and economic ties and the eventual creation of a free trade zone with a view to those countries becoming full members of the EC. Trade and economic co-operation agreements are also in place with Albania, Slovenia and the Baltic states. Negotiations for partnership and co-operation agreements with the former Soviet Union republics are also in progress.

CONTROLS ON TRADE

Britain maintains few restrictions on its international trade. Most goods may be imported freely and only a narrow range of goods is subject to any sort of export control.

Import Controls

In accordance with its international obligations under GATT and to the European Community, Britain has progressively removed almost all quantitative import restrictions imposed on economic grounds. The few remaining quantitative restrictions mainly affect textile goods (in view of the rapid contraction of the domestic textile industry). They stem primarily from the Multi-Fibre Arrangement (MFA), under

which a series of bilateral agreements cover international trade in textiles, designed to balance the interests of both exporting and importing countries. The present MFA expired in 1991 but has been extended pending its phasing out as part of the Uruguay Round of GATT. A small number of quantitative restrictions are also maintained against non-GATT countries. Quantitative restrictions have been removed from imports of goods of EC origin.

Britain continues to apply internationally recognised restrictions on non-economic grounds to imports from all countries of products such as firearms, ammunition and nuclear materials. Non-economic restrictions are also applied to goods such as meat and poultry; animals, birds, bees, fish and plants and some of their derivatives; unlicensed controlled drugs; explosives; fireworks; certain offensive weapons; certain citizens' band radios; indecent or obscene articles; and products derived from endangered species.

Export Controls

The great majority of British exports are not subject to any government control or direction except for presentation and declaration to HM Customs and Excise to enable them to exercise any necessary controls and collect overseas trade statistics. Controls govern the export of goods associated with biological, chemical and nuclear weapons and missiles. There are also controls on the export of firearms, military equipment and of dual-use industrial goods—those that can be used for both civil and military purposes.

Other controls include those for health certification purposes on certain animals, meat and fish exported to another member of the EC; on endangered animal and plant species; and on antiques and works of art, including photographic material, documents, manuscripts and archaeological items.

The Co-ordinating Committee for Multilateral Export Controls (COCOM), of which Britain is a member, has already agreed on extensive relaxation in East/West controls because of the political changes in

Eastern Europe. The break-up of the former Soviet Union is expected to reduce these controls still further.

Britain is a member of the Australia Group and of the Missile Technology Control Regime, international bodies which aim to prevent the spread of weapons of mass destruction. Britain has issued a list of countries of concern, along with lists of controlled goods and technologies used in the production, handling or storage of nuclear, chemical and biological weapons and missile technology. Also listed are controlled dual-use items. When new controls are introduced, an attempt is made to minimise the regulatory burden on business.

GOVERNMENT SERVICES

The Government assists exporters by creating conditions favourable to the export trade and by providing practical help, advice and financial support. This includes a wide range of services and assistance to meet the requirements of exporters.

Export Promotion Services

Overseas Trade Services comprises the leading government departments involved in export promotion, including the Department of Trade and Industry (DTI), the Foreign & Commonwealth Office, the Industry Department of the Welsh Office, Scottish Trade International and the Industrial Development Board of Northern Ireland. There are around 2,000 staff worldwide, based at the DTI in London, in 11 regional offices around Britain and at 196 diplomatic posts overseas.

The range of services available includes the dissemination of export intelligence, assistance in researching potential markets, help at trade fairs and support for firms participating in trade missions. In 1992–93 some £177 million was spent on support for exporters. The proposed network of One-stop Shops (see p. 145) will make the export services operation more accessible.

Overseas Trade Services is advised by the British Overseas Trade Board (BOTB), which aims to:

- help improve the export performance of British industry and commerce;

- guide the Government's export promotion efforts, including the provision of export services; and

- provide advice on policy issues affecting international trade and exports.

The BOTB's Area Advisory Groups, which are made up of business people with expert knowledge of trade with particular world markets, provide advice on the world's main trading areas. The Overseas Projects Board advises on major project business overseas and the Small Firms Committee on matters relating to small businesses. Nearly 200 businessmen and women are involved in the Board's work.

Overseas Trade Services pays special attention to the promotion of exports to its top priority areas in Western Europe, North America, and Japan and the Asia Pacific Rim. These three areas contain the world's largest and richest markets, and account for more than three-quarters of Britain's exports. Other targets include the many emergent markets in South America, Africa, South Asia and Australasia, where there is great potential for growth and the markets are becoming more open.

British Invisibles promotes Britain's financial and other services overseas. It seeks to increase awareness of London as an international financial centre and of the role of the service sector in the British economy.

ECGD

ECGD (Export Credits Guarantee Department) is a government department, responsible to the President of the Board of Trade. It provides medium- and long-term support for projects and capital goods exports sold on credit terms of two years or more. By guaranteeing credit, ECGD helps British exporters overcome many of the risks in selling overseas. In order to encourage investment in less developed countries, ECGD also insures against the main political risks of such investment.

The cover available to exporters was extended in the 1992 Autumn Statement and spring 1993 Budget. Particular attention is being paid to increasing cover for exports to countries like Hong Kong, China, Indonesia, South Africa and Malaysia. ECGD's Insurance Services Group, dealing with exports sold on credit terms of less than two years, was sold to the private sector in 1991.

BALANCE OF PAYMENTS

The balance-of-payments statistics record transactions between residents of Britain and non-residents. The transactions are classified into two groups: current account (visibles and invisibles) and transactions in assets and liabilities. The balance on current account shows whether Britain has had a surplus of income over expenditure.

Since 1983 Britain has had a deficit on visible trade. It has traditionally run a surplus on trade in invisibles. Between 1991 and 1992 the deficit on visible trade grew from £10,300 million to £13,400 million. The surplus on invisibles rose from £2,600 million to £4,800 million. The surplus on services increased by £412 million; that on interest, profits and dividends by £5,500 million; and the deficit on transfers grew by £3,700 million.

Capital Flows

Britain has no exchange controls; residents are free to acquire foreign currency for any purpose, including direct and portfolio investment overseas. There are also no controls on the lending of sterling abroad and non-residents may freely acquire sterling for any purpose. Gold may be freely bought and sold. Exchange controls were abolished in 1979, and Britain meets in full its obligations on capital movements under the OECD code on capital movements and under EC directives.

The Government welcomes both outward and inward investment. Outward investment helps to develop markets for British exports while providing earnings in the form of interest, profits and dividends. Inward investment is promoted by DTI's Invest in Britain Bureau as a means of introducing new technology, products, management styles and attitudes; creating employment; and increasing exports or substituting imports.

Inward direct investment in 1992 was £10,300 million, compared with £9,000 million in 1991. In 1992 direct investment overseas by British residents was £9,400 million, £600 million more than a year previously. Outward portfolio investment was £32,800 million. The inflow of portfolio investment into Britain amounted to £21,400 million. An analysis of transactions in Britain's external assets and liabilities is given in Table 15.6.

External Assets and Liabilities

At the end of 1992 Britain's identified external assets exceeded identified external liabilities by £27,000 million, compared with

Table 15.5: Britain's Balance of Payments 1988–92					£ million
	1988	1989	1990	1991	1992
Current account					
Visible trade balance	−21,480	−24,683	−18,809	−10,284	−13,406
Invisible transactions balance	4,863	2,171	541	2,632	4,786
Current balance	−16,617	−22,512	−18,268	−7,652	−8,620
Financial account					
Transactions in assets and liabilities					
British external assets	−58,458	−90,089	−82,187	−18,925	−84,976
British external liabilities	68,812	109,503	93,148	25,652	93,295
Balancing item	6,265	3,097	7,308	924	301

Source: *United Kingdom Balance of Payments 1993 Edition.*
Note: Differences between totals and the sums of their component parts are due to rounding.

Table 15.6: Summary of Transactions in External Assets[a] and Liabilities[b] 1990–92

£ million

	1990	1991	1992
Overseas direct investment in Britain	18,520	9,032	10,343
Overseas portfolio investment in Britain	7,724	19,230	21,390
British direct investment overseas	-10,544	-8,841	-9,424
British portfolio investment overseas	-16,470	-29,240	-32,818
Borrowing from overseas	66,207	-281	63,131
Deposits and lending overseas	-54,074	22,731	-43,457
Official reserves[a]	-76	-2,679	1,406
Other external liabilities of general government	699	-2,329	-1,569
Other external assets of central government	-1,025	-894	-682
Total	10,961	6,728	8,319

Source: *United Kingdom Balance of Payments 1993 Edition.*
[a]Increase –/decrease +
[b]Increase +/decrease –
Note: Differences between totals and the sums of their component parts are due to rounding.

£6,300 million a year earlier. Net assets of the private sector and public corporations amounted to £24,000 million and those of general government to £3,300 million.

The significance of any inventory of Britain's aggregate external assets and liabilities is limited because a variety of claims and obligations are included that are very dissimilar in kind, in degree of liquidity and in method of valuation. For example, while portfolio investment is valued at market prices, direct investment is given at book value, which is likely to understate its current market value.

Direct investment assets overseas of British residents (investment in branches, subsidiaries and associated companies) totalled £163,000 million at the end of 1992 and portfolio investment £304,000 million. At the end of 1991 (the latest year for which data are available) over 83 per cent of direct investment was in developed countries, with over 38 per cent in the United States and nearly 27 per cent in the EC. In terms of industries, manufacturing accounted for 36 per cent of direct investment holdings. By type of company, oil companies were responsible for 18 per cent, insurance companies for 8 per cent and banks for 2 per cent.

Direct investment in Britain by overseas residents amounted to £131,500 million at the end of 1992 and portfolio investment to £181,000 million. At the end of 1991, investment from developed countries accounted for 97 per cent of overseas direct investment in Britain: 40 per cent originated in the United States and 31 per cent in the EC. A total of 34 per cent was in manufacturing. Oil companies were responsible for 23 per cent, banks for 8 per cent and insurance companies for 4 per cent.

Further Reading

Monthly Review of External Trade Statistics. Central Statistical Office.

United Kingdom Balance of Payments 1993 Edition. Central Statistical Office, HMSO.

16 Energy and Natural Resources

Britain is a major producer of fuels. Energy efficiency measures are a key part of its national programme to reduce carbon dioxide emissions and to conserve energy. More competition in the gas and electricity supply industries is being encouraged. For the 12th year running the increase in known oil and gas reserves has exceeded production.

The value of minerals produced in Britain in 1991 was £16,967 million (just over 4 per cent of gross domestic product—GDP). Crude oil accounted for 44 per cent, coal 24 per cent and natural gas 21 per cent.

With the exception of gold, silver, oil and natural gas (owned by the Crown), and coal and some minerals associated with coal, minerals in Great Britain are mainly privately owned. In Northern Ireland gold and silver are owned by the Crown, while rights to exploit petroleum and other minerals are vested in the Department of Economic Development.

On the United Kingdom Continental Shelf (UKCS) the right to exploit all minerals except coal is vested in the Crown.

The exclusive right to extract coal, or license others to do so, both on land in Great Britain and under the sea, is vested in the British Coal Corporation. Normally, ownership of minerals belongs to the owner of the land surface, but in some areas, particularly those with a long history of mining, these rights have become separated.

Mining and quarrying, apart from deep coal mining, are usually carried out by privately owned companies.

Energy Resources

Britain has the largest energy resources of any country in the European Community and is a major world producer of oil, natural gas and coal—called primary sources. The other main primary sources are nuclear power and some water power; secondary sources (derived from primary sources) are electricity, coke and smokeless fuels, and petroleum products. In 1992 Britain was a small net importer of energy, amounting to 11.3 million tonnes of oil equivalent. In financial terms, however, the higher value of its exports meant that it was a net exporter of fuels, to the value of £104 million. Coal is expected to continue to supply a significant proportion of the country's energy needs. Nuclear power provided about 24 per cent of electricity supplied by the British electricity companies in 1992.

ENERGY POLICY

The President of the Board of Trade and the Secretary of State for the Environment are responsible for energy matters in Great Britain, except for electricity in Scotland, which is under the Secretary of State for Scotland. The Secretary of State for Northern Ireland is responsible for all energy matters there.

Energy policy stresses the importance of energy to a prosperous and successful economy. Its aim is to ensure secure, diverse and sustainable supplies of energy in the forms that people and businesses want, and at competitive prices. When pursuing this aim, the Government has to consider Britain's health, safety and environmental policies, as well as its EC and other international commitments.

Key elements are to:

- encourage competition among producers and choice for consumers, and to establish a legal and regulatory framework to enable markets to work well;

- ensure service in a commercial environment, with consumers paying the full cost of the energy resources they consume;

- privatise state-owned industries where possible, thus exposing them to the discipline of the capital markets;

- promote energy efficiency; and

- promote wider share ownership.

Independent regulators have been established by legislation. Their main role is to encourage the development of competition and to protect the interests of consumers by administering price controls and enforcing standards of service.

Privatisation

British Gas, Britoil, Enterprise Oil, and the non-nuclear electricity supply industry in Britain are in the private sector. The Government intends to privatise the coal industry as soon as possible, to give it the freedom and flexibility it will need to compete in the future. The Citizen's Charter

commitment has been fulfilled by the Competition and Service (Utilities) Act 1992. This aims to give customers of privatised utilities fair treatment and strengthens the powers of regulators. Customers are to be compensated when standards are not met and greater competition introduced into the gas industry.

International Commitments

Britain is actively engaged in international collaboration on energy questions, notably through its membership of the Community and of the International Energy Agency (IEA; an autonomous sub-body of the Organisation for Economic Co-operation and Development, with 23 member countries).

Britain supports the continuing development of the single market in energy, in particular through the removal of obstacles to trade in the Community's gas and electricity markets.

European Energy Charter

In 1991 Britain (along with other member states of the Community and European Free Trade Association, Eastern European countries, the republics of the former Soviet Union, the Baltic states, the United States, Japan, Australia and Canada) signed the European Energy Charter. Associated legally binding agreements are currently under negotiation. The main objectives are an open competitive market for trade in energy, including a framework for investment promotion and protection; improving the energy economies of Eastern Europe, the former Soviet Union and the Baltic states; and the security of supply of all participating countries.

Energy Report

The Government intends to publish an annual energy report to provide information for business and investment. This will deal with trends in energy supply and demand, licensing activity, and regulatory developments in the energy field.

Table 16.1: Inland Energy Consumption (in terms of primary sources)

million tonnes oil equivalent

	1982	1987	1990	1991	1992
Oil	65.4	64.3	71.3	71.1	71.6
Coal	65.1	68.3	64.2	63.8	59.8
Natural gas	42.2	50.5	49.2	53.0	52.5
Nuclear energy	9.4	11.7	14.2	15.2	17.0
Hydro-electric power	1.4	1.2	1.6	1.4	1.7
Net imports of electricity	–	2.8	2.9	3.9	4.0
Total	183.5	199.0	203.4	208.4	206.6

Source: Department of Trade and Industry.
Note: Differences between totals and the sums of their component parts are due to rounding.

An independent energy advisory panel will advise on the preparation of the report. Energy suppliers and energy users will serve on the panel.

ENERGY CONSUMPTION

During 1981–93, when Britain's GDP rose by 26.7 per cent, final energy consumption on a 'heat supplied' basis increased by only 9.5 per cent. Energy consumption by final users in 1992 amounted to 60,153 million therms[1] on a 'heat supplied' basis, of which transport consumed 32 per cent, industrial users 25 per cent, domestic users 29 per cent, and commerce, agriculture and public services 14 per cent.

ENERGY EFFICIENCY

Britain's consumers spend about £50,000 million a year on energy. The Energy Efficiency Office (EEO), part of the Department of the Environment, estimates that 20 per cent—or £10,000 million—could be saved. Energy efficiency improvements are recognised as offering one of the fastest and most cost-effective means of reducing carbon dioxide (CO_2) emissions. The EEO aims to tackle barriers to investment in energy efficiency improvements through special programmes. It provides consumers with the necessary information to make energy efficiency improvements, supplemented by

[1] 1 therm = 105,506 kilojoules.

grant schemes where the need is greatest. The EEO budget for 1993–94 has been increased to nearly £70 million.

Technical information and advice on the best energy efficient practice in industry and buildings are researched and disseminated under the EEO's Best Practice programme. Its target is to achieve savings of £800 million a year, along with increasing the capacity of Combined Heat and Power (CHP) to 5,000 megawatts (MW), by 2000. CHP produces usable heat as well as electricity, is significantly more efficient than conventional energy, generates substantial energy cost savings and is an environmentally friendly technology.

The EEO operates two grant schemes. The Home Energy Efficiency Scheme gives advice and grants for low-income households to carry out basic energy efficiency measures, such as insulation of lofts, tanks and pipes, and draughtproofing. The Energy Management Assistance Scheme provides companies employing fewer than 500 people with financial help towards the cost of consultancy advice on energy efficiency investments, covering energy surveys, feasibility studies and project management costs.

Among the EEO's publicity initiatives, the 'Making a Corporate Commitment' campaign aims to encourage heads of companies and public sector organisations to make a corporate commitment to responsible energy management. Over 1,500 companies have made the commitment. 'Helping the Earth Begins at Home' includes television and press advertising, and other publicity initiatives. It stresses to householders the fact that they can help combat global warming by improving the energy efficiency of their homes.

Other work includes the promotion of home energy labelling and energy labelling of domestic appliances. In addition, the Department of the Environment's Green House Demonstration Programme has established a network of demonstration projects throughout England. Revisions to the Building Regulations, including double glazing, improved insulation, heating controls, and home energy labelling, are also under consideration.

The Government has established an independent Energy Saving Trust, in partnership with British Gas and the electricity companies, to develop and propose new programmes to promote the efficient use of energy.

OIL AND GAS

Britain has substantial oil and gas reserves offshore on the United Kingdom Continental Shelf. The trend in offshore oil and gas developments is towards the exploitation of smaller reservoirs, and advances in science and technology have made this a more economic proposition. A 20-year project to map the geology of the UKCS offshore was completed in 1992.

The Government must approve all plans for the development of oil and gas fields. It has granted exploration and production licences as a result of 14 offshore licensing rounds since 1964. The 13th (frontier) round was aimed at promoting exploration of deep water areas north and west of Scotland. By the end of 1992, 5,144 wells had been or were being drilled in the UKCS: 2,365 development wells, 1,734 exploration wells and 1,045 appraisal wells.

Oil and Gas Licensing

In the 14th round, announced in June 1993 and the biggest in terms of blocks available and applications received since 1971–72, 484 blocks were offered. Applications were received for 128 blocks and 110 were awarded. Thirty-three of the latter had not previously been licensed or were relatively lightly explored. These include blocks in the English Channel, Cardigan Bay, Solway Firth and the North Channel. There is interest in the more mature areas of the UKCS. Blocks were also licensed in frontier acreage in the south-west approaches.

Licensing rounds have been held approximately every two years, but companies may now compete for licences outside the formal round system where significant prospects have been identified. Licences for five blocks in the West of Shetland Basin and seven blocks in the Cardigan Bay area were granted ahead of the other 14th round awards.

Offshore Supplies

The Offshore Supplies Office (OSO) of the Department of Trade and Industry aims to promote fair commercial opportunity in all oil and gas markets, to support development of the latest technologies and to foster British exports.

UKCS activity in the engineering, design and project management sectors was down on the peak of 1991. British-based companies maintained a good proportion of the work available both at home and in export markets.

Research

The Offshore Energy Technology Board advises the OSO on its offshore technology programme. The Petroleum Science and Technology Institute, set up in Edinburgh in 1989, is funded by oil companies and the OSO. It supports oil-related research in British universities. The Offshore Technology Park in Aberdeen comprises several projects and is part-funded by Scottish Enterprise.

Economic and Industrial Aspects

In 1992 UKCS oil and gas production accounted for about 1.3 per cent of Britain's gross national product at factor cost. Total revenue from the sale of oil and gas produced from the UKCS in 1992 is estimated to have been £7,700 million and £3,000 million respectively. Taxes and royalty receipts attributable to UKCS oil and gas are estimated to have been £1,350 million in 1992–93.

Expenditure on offshore and onshore development amounted to some £5,400 million in 1992. This was about 22 per cent of British industrial investment and 7 per cent of gross domestic fixed capital formation. Total investment between 1965 and 1992 came to about £52,000 million (£94,000 million at 1992 prices). Some 29,500 people were employed offshore in September 1992.

Offshore Safety

The Offshore Safety Act 1992 assists in enabling the major recommendations of the Cullen report of 1990 to be implemented. It raises the maximum penalties for offences which show a failure to manage health and safety adequately and to comply with an improvement or prohibition notice. The Act will also allow the recommendations to be implemented by regulations rather than primary legislation. It completes the statutory transfer of offshore safety responsibilities to the Health and Safety Executive (HSE). Government funding for the HSE's Offshore Safety Division will reach £35 million in 1994–95.

OIL

Before the 1970s Britain was almost wholly dependent for its oil supplies on imports, the only indigenous supplies coming from a few land-based oilfields. However, the first notable offshore discovery of oil in the UKCS was made in 1969 and the first oil brought ashore in 1975. Output of crude oil in Britain in 1992 averaged over 1.93 million barrels (about 257,300 tonnes) a day, making Britain the world's ninth largest producer.

North Sea Fields

There were 53 offshore fields producing crude oil at the end of February 1993, and nine new offshore development projects were approved during the year.

> Output is likely to increase until the mid-1990s, and Britain should remain self-sufficient in oil well into the 1990s and a significant producer into the 21st century.

The fields with the largest cumulative production totals are Forties and Brent. Ninian, Piper, Beryl, Fulmar, Thistle and Claymore are other high-producing fields. Production from most large fields is controlled from production platforms of either steel or concrete which have been built to withstand severe weather, including gusts of wind of up to 260 km/h (160 mph) and waves of 30 m (100 ft). The Petroleum Act 1987 lays down measures to be taken in connection with the abandonment of offshore installations and pipelines.

The Government's oil policy encourages exploration, development and investment—to maximise economic oil production for the foreseeable future. Remaining recoverable reserves of UKCS oil in the proven plus probable categories amount to 1,365 million tonnes, while the total remaining potential of the UKCS could be as high as 5,946 million tonnes.

Structure of the Oil Industry

About 250 private sector companies, including many large oil firms, operate in Britain or engage in work in the UKCS. Exploration and development of the UKCS are carried out by the private sector. The Government receives royalties from UKCS oil.

The two leading British oil companies are British Petroleum (BP) and Shell Transport and Trading, which has a 40 per cent interest in the Royal Dutch/Shell Group of Companies. BP and Shell are the two largest industrial companies in Britain in terms of turnover.

Oil

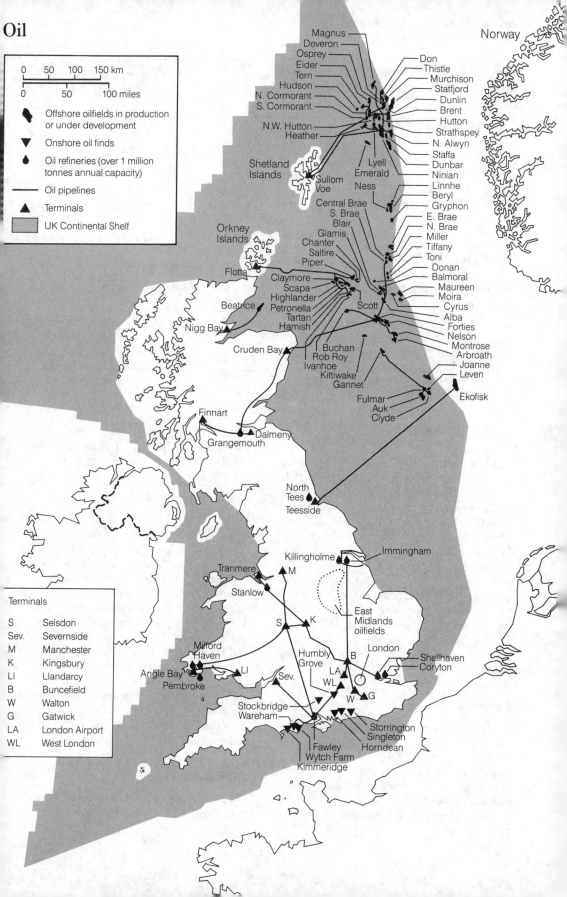

Norway

0 50 100 150 km	
0 50 100 miles	

◆ Offshore oilfields in production or under development

▼ Onshore oil finds

⬤ Oil refineries (over 1 million tonnes annual capacity)

— Oil pipelines

▲ Terminals

▨ UK Continental Shelf

Terminals

S	Seisdon
Sev.	Severnside
M	Manchester
K	Kingsbury
Ll	Llandarcy
B	Buncefield
W	Walton
G	Gatwick
LA	London Airport
WL	West London

Magnus
Deveron
Osprey
Eider
Tern
Hudson
N. Cormorant
S. Cormorant
N.W. Hutton
Heather

Don
Thistle
Murchison
Statfjord
Dunlin
Brent
Hutton
Strathspey
N. Alwyn
Staffa
Dunbar
Ninian

Lyell
Emerald
Ness

Shetland
Islands

Sullom
Voe

Central Brae
S. Brae
Blair
Glamis
Chanter
Saltire
Piper

Linnhe
Beryl
Gryphon
E. Brae
N. Brae
Miller
Tiffany
Toni
Donan
Balmoral
Maureen
Moira
Cyrus
Alba
Forties
Nelson
Montrose
Arbroath
Joanne
Leven

Orkney
Islands

Flotta

Claymore
Scapa
Highlander
Petronella
Tartan
Hamish

Scott

Beatrice

Nigg Bay

Cruden Bay

Buchan
Rob Roy
Ivanhoe
Kittiwake
Gannet

Fulmar
Auk
Clyde

Ekofisk

Finnart

Dalmeny
Grangemouth

North
Tees
Teesside

Killingholme

Immingham

East
Midlands
oilfields

Tranmere
Stanlow

M

K

S

Milford
Haven
Angle Bay
Pembroke

Ll

Sev.

Humbly
Grove

B

London

Shellhaven
Coryton

LA
WL

W

G

Stockbridge
Wareham

Fawley
Wytch Farm
Kimmeridge

Storrington
Singleton
Horndean

Table 16.2: Oil Statistics

million tonnes

	1982	1987	1990	1991	1992
Oil production:[a]					
land	0.3	0.6	1.8	3.7	4.0
offshore	102.9	122.8	89.8	87.6	90.3
Refinery output	70.7	74.7	82.3	85.5	85.8
Deliveries of petroleum:					
products for inland					
consumption	67.2	67.7	73.9	74.5	74.5
Exports (including re-exports):					
crude petroleum, natural					
gas liquids (NGLs)					
and feedstocks	61.7	83.2	57.0	55.1	57.6
refined petroleum products	12.6	15.0	16.9	19.4	20.2
Imports:					
crude petroleum, NGLs					
and feedstocks	33.8	41.5	52.7	57.1	57.7
refined petroleum					
products	12.5	8.6	11.0	10.1	9.6

Source: Department of Trade and Industry.

[a] Crude oil plus condensates.

Land-based Fields

Onshore production of crude oil is much less significant than offshore production. In 1992, however, it increased by 7 per cent to 3.96 million tonnes, 86 per cent of which came from Britain's largest onshore field at Wytch Farm (Dorset), which started production in 1979. In addition to minor production from various mining licensees, other onshore fields include Welton (Lincolnshire) and Wareham (Dorset). Small, independent companies play an increasingly prominent role in onshore exploration. At the end of 1992, 183 landward petroleum licences were in force, covering an area of 26,629 sq km (10,281 sq miles).

Refineries

At the beginning of 1993 the distillation capacity of Britain's 11 major oil refineries stood at 91.7 million tonnes a year. Excess crude distillation capacity has largely been eliminated, while existing refineries have been adapted to the changing pattern of demand by the construction of upgrading facilities (for example, 'catalytic crackers'), which are leading to a higher output of lighter products, mainly petrol, at the expense of fuel oil.

Consumption and Trade

Deliveries of petroleum products for inland consumption (excluding refinery consumption) in 1992 included 23.9 million tonnes of motor spirit, 9.1 million tonnes of kerosene, 18.9 million tonnes of gas and diesel oil (including derv fuel used in road vehicles), and 11.2 million tonnes of fuel oil. Virtually all exports went to Britain's partners in the European Community and the IEA, the largest markets being the Netherlands, France, Germany, Canada and the United States. Though self-sufficient, Britain continues to import other crude oils, to enable the full range of petroleum products to be made efficiently and economically.

Oil Pipelines

Oil pipelines brought ashore about 78 per cent of offshore oil in 1992. Some 2,024 km

(1,265 miles) of major submarine pipeline brings oil ashore from the North Sea oilfields. Major crude oil onshore pipelines in operation from harbours, land terminals or offshore moorings to refineries include those connecting Grangemouth to Finnart, Cruden Bay to Grangemouth, and Purbeck to Southampton. Onshore pipelines also carry refined products to major marketing areas; for example, a 423-km (263-mile) pipeline runs from Milford Haven to the Midlands and Manchester, while similar pipelines also run from Fawley to Wolverhampton and from Lindsey to north London. Chemical pipelines include one from Mossmorran to Grangemouth and another (405 km—252 miles) from Grangemouth to Stanlow.

GAS

Public supply of manufactured gas in Britain began in the early 19th century in central London. For many years gas was produced from coal, but during the 1960s growing imports of oil brought about production of town gas from oil-based feedstocks. Following the first commercial natural gas discovery in the UKCS in 1965 and the start of offshore gas production in 1967, supplies of offshore natural gas grew rapidly and by 1977 natural gas had replaced town gas in the public supply system in Great Britain. Some £13,530 million has been spent on developing natural gas resources on the UKCS and 896,284 million cubic metres have been produced. Britain is the world's fifth largest gas producer.

Structure

The gas industry in Great Britain, in state ownership since 1949, was privatised in 1986. British Gas plc supplies gas to consumers in accordance with its authorisation as a public gas supplier under the Gas Act 1986. It is currently the only public gas supplier. It has, however, an obligation to act as a common carrier for other companies. In early 1993 there were about 30 independent companies supplying gas in competition with British Gas, using

the company's transport network. The regulatory regime for the private gas sector was established by the Gas Act 1986 and places responsibility on the Office of Gas Supply (Ofgas) for ensuring that British Gas is operating within the terms of its authorisation as a public gas supplier. The Act also established the Gas Consumers' Council, independent of both British Gas and Ofgas, and responsible for investigating consumer complaints.

> British Gas has about 2 million private and institutional shareholders. In 1992 the turnover of British Gas and its subsidiary companies amounted to £10,254 million, of which gas supply in Britain accounted for £8,129 million. Current cost operating profit was £1,429 million. British Gas has about 76,000 employees in Britain.

Production

In 1992 indigenous production of natural gas amounted to 55,179 million cubic metres. This included 3,810 million cubic metres of gas used for drilling, production and pumping operations on North Sea production platforms and at terminals. Total availability of UKCS gas amounted to 51,369 million cubic metres—1 per cent lower than in 1991. In addition, 6,000 million cubic metres of gas were imported from Norway. British production of gas accounts for some 20 per cent of total primary fuel consumption in Britain. Natural gas from the seven largest of the 37 gasfields—Leman, Indefatigable, Ravenspurn North, Hewett and Della, Audrey, Amethyst and Viking—accounted for over one-third of the total gas produced in the UKCS. In addition to supplies from gasfields, associated gas delivered to land via the Far North Liquids and Associated Gas System (FLAGS) and from Alwyn North made further significant contributions. Gas from the South Morecambe field in the Irish Sea and from the twin North Sean and South Sean fields is used to augment supplies to meet peak demand in winter.

Gas

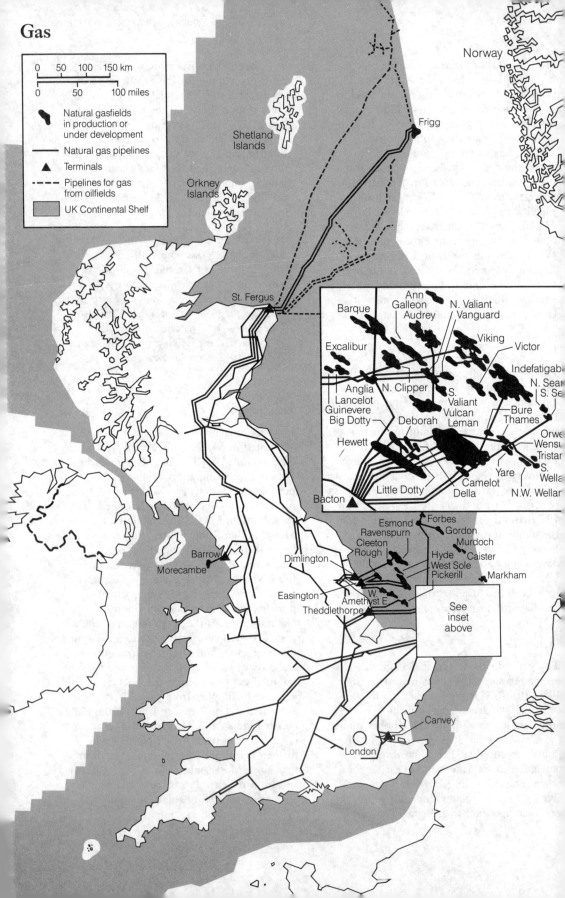

Scale:
0 50 100 150 km
0 50 100 miles

Legend:
- Natural gasfields in production or under development
- Natural gas pipelines
- ▲ Terminals
- Pipelines for gas from oilfields
- UK Continental Shelf

Norway

Shetland Islands

Orkney Islands

Frigg

St. Fergus

Inset labels:
Barque
Ann
Galleon
Audrey
N. Valiant
Vanguard
Viking
Victor
Excalibur
Indefatigab[le]
N. Clipper
N. Sea[r]
S. Se[a]
Anglia
Lancelot
Guinevere
Big Dotty
S. Valiant
Vulcan
Leman
Bure
Thames
Deborah
Orwe[ll]
Wens[um]
Tristar
S. Wella[r]
Hewett
Yare
Little Dotty
Camelot
Della
N.W. Wellar
Bacton

Barrow
Morecambe

Dimlington
Esmond
Ravenspurn
Cleeton
Rough
Forbes
Gordon
Murdoch
Caister
Hyde
West Sole
Pickerill
Markham

Easington
W.
Amethyst E
Theddlethorpe

See inset above

Canvey

London

Reserves

Remaining recoverable gas reserves are estimated at between 610,000 million and 1.02 million million cubic metres. If possible gas from existing discoveries and potential future discoveries are added, total reserves are estimated to be in the range of 1.88 million million to 4.32 million million cubic metres. Indigenous offshore natural gas reserves are likely to meet most of the British demand well into the next century.

Transmission and Storage

The British Gas national and regional high-pressure pipeline system of some 17,900 km (11,125 miles) transports natural gas around Great Britain. It is supplied from four North Sea shore terminals, and from a terminal in Barrow-in-Furness (Cumbria). The high-pressure transmission system is inspected regularly, using a British Gas invention, the 'intelligent pig'.

Newly built natural gas pipelines, not operated by British Gas, run from Horndean to Barking and from Theddlethorpe to Killingholme.

Various methods of storage of natural gas to meet peak load conditions are used, including salt cavities and storage facilities for liquefied natural gas. British Gas has also developed the partially depleted Rough field as a major gas store. This, the first such use of an offshore field, involves the injection into the Rough reservoir in summer of gas drawn from the national transmission system for recovery at high rates during periods of peak winter demand.

Consumption

Sales of natural gas in Britain totalled 593 terawatt hours (TWh) in 1992. About 44 per cent of this is for industrial and commercial purposes, the remainder being for domestic use by 17.8 million consumers. Gas is used extensively in industries requiring the control of temperatures to a fine degree of accuracy, such as the pottery and glass industries, and in certain processes for making iron and steel products.

Some 160 TWh of this gas were sold to industry in Britain, and 100 TWh to commercial (including other non-domestic) users. Industrial gas prices have fallen by about 36 per cent in real terms since privatisation, and domestic prices by 16 per cent. An increasingly large part of domestic demand is for gas for central heating. In 1992, 330 TWh were sold to domestic users.

Research

British Gas has a worldwide reputation for gas technology, with a research and development programme costing £89 million in 1992. It is involved in joint research with overseas gas companies. The company is assisting utilities in over 20 countries in transmission, distribution and other areas. British Gas is today exploring for and producing gas and oil in some 20 countries.

Competition in Gas Marketing

An inquiry into the gas market by the Monopolies and Mergers Commission was completed in 1993. It followed two references by the Government into the supply, conveyance and storage of gas, and two references by the Director General of Gas Supply into conveyance and storage, and fixing of tariffs for gas supply.

Two key issues for the Government arise from the inquiry's two reports: the future structure of British Gas and the possible relaxing of its statutory monopoly in supplying gas to domestic customers.

COAL

Coal mining in Britain can be traced back to Roman times. It played a crucial part in the industrial revolution of the 18th and 19th centuries. In its peak year, 1913, the industry produced 292 million tonnes of coal, exported 74 million tonnes and employed over 1 million workers. In 1947 (when 200 million tonnes were produced) the coal mines passed into public ownership, and the National Coal Board (now the British Coal Corporation) was set up. The Government

Coal

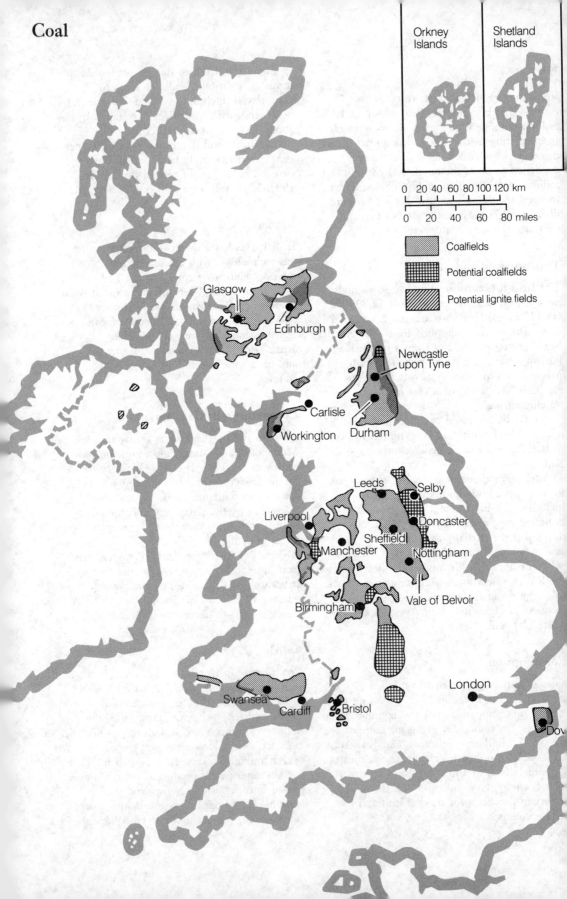

Orkney Islands

Shetland Islands

0 20 40 60 80 100 120 km

0   20   40   60   80 miles

Coalfields

Potential coalfields

Potential lignite fields

Glasgow

Edinburgh

Newcastle upon Tyne

Carlisle

Workington

Durham

Leeds

Selby

Liverpool

Doncaster

Sheffield

Manchester

Nottingham

Vale of Belvoir

Birmingham

London

Swansea

Cardiff

Bristol

Dov

has reduced the debt under which the industry was operating and eliminated accumulated liabilities incurred by British Coal.

British Coal licenses private operators to work mines with an employee limit of 150 and opencast sites.

Its deep and opencast mines are to be offered for sale in five businesses—based on Scotland, Wales, the North East and the Central Coalfield (in two parts).

Market for Coal

Some 80 per cent of the 101 million tonnes (British and imported) consumed in 1992 were used for electricity generation. Increasing competition in this market has put greater pressure on the coal industry to reduce costs. In 1990 British Coal signed three-year contracts with the electricity generators in England and Wales, giving it a guaranteed market for much of its output— 65 million tonnes in 1992–93. Five-year contracts were signed with the Scottish electricity supply industry.

In 1993 agreement was reached for British Coal to supply 160 million tonnes of coal to the generators in England and Wales over five years.

However, long-term contracts for the supply of gas for electricity generation, improvement in nuclear output, and cheaper coal from overseas, have helped to squeeze British Coal markets.

Production

In 1992–93 total output of 80.8 million tonnes comprised 61.8 million tonnes of British Coal deep-mined coal, 15 million tonnes from its opencast mines and 4 million tonnes from licensed mines (deep and opencast). In March 1992 there were 50 British Coal collieries in operation and 44,000 miners (compared with 850 and 695,000 in 1955).

In October 1992 British Coal announced that it would close 31 deep mines: ten as loss-making with no prospect of viability and 21 as without a market for their coal. The Government accepted these proposals, but subsequently established a review of the

prospects for the 21 pits (see above), as well as a range of related issues. Its conclusions were published in a White Paper in March 1993: the October assessment of the prospects for coal had been realistic, but temporary support should be given to the coal industry to give it a better chance of a competitive future. The Government would therefore make a subsidy available to allow the deep-mine industry a chance of additional sales for electricity generation at world-related prices.

Of the 21 pits covered by the review, 12 are to continue to produce while British Coal seeks additional sales; six are to be put on a care and maintenance basis; one (Maltby in South Yorkshire) is to be developed as a low-cost mine; and two are to be closed. British Coal is to offer to the private sector any pit which it does not intend to continue in production.

British Coal Opencast also had 45 sites in operation at the end of March 1993. Since 1984, British Coal, through its job creation activity, British Coal Enterprise, has helped create job opportunities for 87,500 people in areas where mining was previously the main source of employment.

Development

Britain has the largest hard-coal industry in Western Europe, and one of the world's most technologically advanced. British Coal's investment programme amounted to £186 million in 1992–93. A new colliery, Asfordby (Leicestershire), is expected to begin production by April 1994. It is being designed as a single longwall operation, employing approximately 450 people and producing about 1.75 million tonnes a year.

Companies under government licence are prospecting in Northern Ireland to determine the extent of significant reserves, possibly over 1,000 million tonnes, of lignite (brown coal) in the clay basins around Lough Neagh and at Ballymoney.

Consumption

In 1992–93 inland consumption of coal was 97.6 million tonnes, of which 78 per cent was by power stations, 9 per cent by coke ovens and 4 per cent by domestic users. British Coal sales of coal to power stations totalled 66.5 million tonnes in 1992–93. Exports of coal in 1992–93 were 0.6 million tonnes, while imports amounted to 19.8 million tonnes.

Research

Over £500 million has been spent by the public sector in Britain on coal utilisation research and development since the early 1980s. Some £1,000 million has been spent, if all coal research and development work were to be included. The Government has increased its support for coal research and development from £3 million to £7 million a year during 1993–94. Most of this additional funding will be used to secure the future of the Coal Research Establishment before its transition to the private sector is completed.

Among clean coal technologies being exploited in Britain, about 100 fluidised bed boilers are used in industry, and two advanced systems, Integrated Gasification Combined Cycle and Pressurised Fluidised Bed Combustion, are being demonstrated on a commercial scale in Europe. The British Coal topping cycle programme, in which some of the coal is converted to hot gas for use in a gas turbine and the remaining char is burnt in a fluidised bed to raise steam for a conventional steam turbine, is to be taken forward by an industry-led consortium. The Government and the EC are to contribute to the development phase.

The coal liquefaction plant at Point of Ayr (Clwyd) opened in 1990 at a cost of £40 million. It converts 2.5 tonnes of coal a day into petrol, diesel and other transport fuels.

ELECTRICITY

England and Wales

The privatised electricity supply industry in England and Wales consists of three main generating companies, the National Grid Company (NGC) and 12 regional electricity companies (RECs). The two main non-nuclear generators, National Power and PowerGen, the publicly owned nuclear generator, Nuclear Electric plc, and other generators and importers sell electricity to suppliers through a market known as the pool. The NGC operates the transmission system—the bulk transfer of electricity across the national grid—and owns the pumped storage stations at Dinorwig and Ffestiniog. It is owned by the RECs through a holding company.

Distribution and supply of electricity are the business of the RECs. Distribution involves transfer of electricity from the national grid and its delivery, across local systems, to consumers. Supply is the sale of electricity to customers. Each REC is authorised to supply any premises within its area. Other companies may obtain a second-tier licence to supply, although initially competition is limited to premises with a maximum consumption of 1 MW. This limit will be reduced to 100 kW in April 1994.

The Government retains approximately 40 per cent of the issued ordinary share capital of each of National Power and PowerGen.

Scotland

Industry restructuring in Scotland created three companies. Scottish Power plc and Scottish Hydro-Electric plc generate, transmit, distribute and supply electricity. They are also contracted to buy all the output from Scottish Nuclear Ltd, a government-owned company which operates the nuclear power stations at Hunterston (Strathclyde) and Torness (Lothian), and have contracts to share the output from each other's generation capacity. Opportunities exist to export and import electricity to and from the pool (see above).

Associated Functions

Certain service and co-ordinating functions for the industry are undertaken by the Electricity Association, jointly owned by the electricity companies of Great Britain. Regulation of the industry is the responsibility of the Office of Electricity Regulation, headed by the Director General

Electricity

Orkney Islands

Shetland Islands

| 0 | 20 | 40 | 60 | 80 | 100 | 120 km |

| 0 | 20 | 40 | 60 | 80 miles |

■ Conventional power stations (1,000 MW and over)

● Nuclear power stations

○ Under construction

◆ Power-producing reactors of the UKAEA or BNFL

★ Hydro-electric power stations (over 45-MW capacity)

▲ Pumped storage schemes

Dounreay
Fasnakyle
Foyers
Peterhead
Errochty
Rannoch
Cruachan
Clunie
Lochay
Sloy
Longannet
Torness
Inverkip
Cockenzie
Hunterston B
Chapelcross
Blyth A and B
Galloway
Hartlepool
Calder Hall
Wilton
Heysham II
Heysham I
Ferrybridge B and C
Drax
Thorpe Marsh
Eggborough
Fiddler's Ferry
Killingholme
Wylfa
Cottam
West Burton
Ince
High Marnham
Dinorwig
Staythorpe
Castle Donington
Ffestiniog
Ratcliffe-on-Soar
Rugeley A and B
Willington A and B
Rheidol
Drakelow B and C
Ironbridge
Barking
Sizewell A
Sizewell B
Tilbury
W. Thurrock
Bradwell
Pembroke
Aberthaw B
Grain
Oldbury
Didcot
Littlebrook
Kingsnorth
Hinkley Pt. A
Hinkley Pt. B
Dungeness B
Fawley
Dungeness A

Table 16.3: Generation by and Capacity of Power Stations owned by the Major Generating Companies in Britain

	Electricity generated (GWh)			Per cent	Output capacity (MW)
	1982	1987	1992[a]	1992	
Nuclear plant	40,001	50,282	74,930	25	10,733
Other steam plant	209,957	226,382	222,773	73	48,309
Gas turbines and oil engines	517	512	363	–	2,968
Pumped storage plant	1,080	2,207	1,703	1	2,787
Natural flow hydro-electric plant	3,884	3,312	4,721	2	1,308
Renewables other than hydro	–	–	7[b]	–	5
Total	255,439	282,695	304,496	100	66,110
Electricity supplied (net)[c]	237,787	261,884	283,478		

Source: Department of Trade and Industry.

[a] 53-week year.

[b] Mainly wind.

[c] Electricity generated less electricity used at power stations (both electricity used on works and that used for pumping at pumped-storage stations).

Note: Differences between totals and the sums of their component parts are due to rounding.

of Electricity Supply, whose duties include the promotion of competition and the protection of consumer interests.

Northern Ireland

After the restructuring of its electricity supply industry Northern Ireland's four power stations were transferred to the private sector by means of a trade sale in 1992. The flotation of Northern Ireland Electricity (NIE) plc in 1993 completed the privatisation of the industry. Regulation is shared between the Department of Economic Development and the Director General of Electricity Supply (NI).

Consumption

In 1991 sales of electricity through the distribution system in Britain amounted to 280,143 gigawatt[2] hours (GWh). Domestic users took 36 per cent of the total, industry 33 per cent, and commercial and other users the remainder. About 24 per cent of domestic

[2] 1 GW = 1,000 MW.

sales is for space heating, 13 per cent for water heating and 8 per cent for cooking. Electricity is used in industry mainly for motive power, melting, heating and lighting.

Generation

National Power owns 35 operational fossil-fuelled power stations which generate about 46 per cent of the electricity supplied to the transmission and distribution networks in England and Wales. PowerGen owns 19 fossil-fuelled power stations which generate about 30 per cent of this electricity. The 11 nuclear stations of Nuclear Electric generate almost 22 per cent.

In 1992–93, 47 per cent of electricity supplied in Scotland was produced by Scottish Nuclear's two stations. In addition to nuclear generation, Scotland's electricity needs are met from hydro generation, coal generation and, from 1992, from gas generation, using gas from the Miller field at Peterhead power station. All of Scottish Nuclear's production is sold to Scottish Power and Hydro-Electric in the proportions 74.9 per cent and 25.1 per cent respectively.

Non-nuclear power stations owned by Britain's major generating companies consumed 69.7 million tonnes of oil equivalent in 1992, of which coal accounted for 66 per cent and oil 7 per cent.

Independent generators are allowed to compete on equal terms with the major generators and have equal access to the grid transmission and local distribution systems.

To control acid emissions the Government expects National Power and PowerGen each to fit flue gas desulphurisation (FGD) equipment to 4 GW of their existing coal-fired power stations. Work is in progress towards fitting FGD equipment to National Power's Drax station (North Yorkshire). PowerGen is retrofitting 2 GW of FGD to its Ratcliffe on Soar power station (Leicestershire). Scottish Power expects to fit FGD as necessary at its main coal station, Longannet. In addition, a ten-year programme to control nitrogen oxide (NOx) emissions through the installation of low-NOx burners at the 12 major power stations in England and Wales is in progress. Scottish Power is fitting low-NOx burners at Longannet.

The pumped storage station at Dinorwig (Gwynedd), the largest of its type in Europe, has an average generated output of 1,728 MW. In pumped storage schemes electricity generated in off-peak periods is used to pump water to high-level reservoirs, from which it descends to drive turbines, rapidly providing a large supply of electricity at peak periods or to meet sudden increases in demand.

For new stations the trend is towards the construction of combined cycle gas turbines (CCGTs). They are less costly to build than other types of station, and have shorter construction times and lower capital costs. Their use of natural gas, low in sulphur, also helps to reduce acid and CO_2 emissions. In England and Wales, 18 such stations over 50 MW are commissioned or under construction. Britain's first independent CCGT station, in Cumbria, was opened in 1991. Some 1.3 per cent of electricity in Britain was derived from gas in 1992.

The NGC, together with Electricité de France, runs a 2,000-MW cross-Channel cable link, providing the capacity for the transmission of electricity between the two countries. An eight-year export contract agreed in 1993 represents potential sales of over £100 million from Britain to France.

Transmission lines linking the Scottish and English grid systems enable cross-border trading. This interconnector is run jointly by the NGC and Scottish Power. Work is in progress to increase its capacity from 850 MW to 1,600 MW by 1994–95. NIE plc and Scottish Power have plans to construct a 250-MW interconnector between Scotland and Northern Ireland, to come into use in 1997.

Nuclear Power

In 1956 the world's first industrial-scale nuclear power station, at Calder Hall (Cumbria), began to supply electricity to the national grid. There are in Britain 13 commercial nuclear power stations operated by Nuclear Electric and Scottish Nuclear. The former has six Magnox stations (with capacities ranging from 245 to 840 MW) and five Advanced Gas-cooled Reactor stations (AGRs; ranging from 1,020 MW to 1,320 MW). Scottish Nuclear operates two 1,320 MW AGR stations. Completion of a pressurised water reactor (PWR) of 1,175 MW at Sizewell (Suffolk) is expected in 1994. There are also three Magnox stations which have been shut down and are in the process of being decommissioned.

Two main advantages are recognised in continued nuclear power generation: first, it increases diversity of energy supply and helps maintain its security; and secondly, nuclear stations produce no sulphur dioxide (SO_2), NOx or CO_2. The Government wishes to maintain the nuclear option, but only if nuclear power can demonstrate that it is more competitive with other sources. Work on the Government's full-scale review of nuclear power is set to begin in late 1993.

In England and Wales a 'fossil fuel levy' has been introduced, currently set at 10 per cent, on electricity sales. Most of the revenue raised is to pay a premium to nuclear generators, as the cost of producing energy from nuclear sources is greater than that of producing it from fossil fuel sources. The levy is expected to raise £9,100 million to help cover the unavoidable costs associated with the closure of existing stations and the reprocessing and disposal of spent fuel. It is, however, set to be phased out by 1998, when it is hoped that nuclear power generation will be economically competitive.

British Nuclear Fuels

British Nuclear Fuels plc (BNFL) provides services covering the whole nuclear fuel cycle. All of its shares are held by the Government.

BNFL's major project is the thermal oxide reprocessing plant (THORP), construction of which has been completed at a cost of some £2,800 million, including its share of associated facilities. Further consultation before opening is in progress. THORP has been built to reprocess spent fuel from British and overseas oxide reactors. At the same time, BNFL plans to bring into operation the latest of its waste management and effluent treatment facilities. The enhanced actinide removal plant (EARP) will use a revolutionary ultrafiltration process to provide further treatment facilities for low-level liquid radioactive streams.

Nuclear Research

Almost all the nuclear research and development funded by the Department of Trade and Industry is carried out by the United Kingdom Atomic Energy Authority (UKAEA). The UKAEA, which operates commercially as AEA Technology, offers a wide range of science and engineering services and has four nuclear businesses involved in research and development, the provision of reactor fuel services, and decommissioning and radioactive waste management. Work is carried out at six sites: Harwell and Culham (Oxfordshire), Risley (Cheshire), Winfrith (Dorset), Windscale (Cumbria) and Dounreay (Highland).

Co-operation on nuclear energy between Britain and other countries takes place within a framework of intergovernmental agreements and through membership of bodies such as the International Atomic Energy Agency based in Vienna and the Nuclear Energy Agency in Paris. There are also direct links between AEA Technology and corresponding establishments overseas.

Britain is also a partner in the co-operative research programmes of the European Atomic Energy Community (Euratom). A major component of this programme is the Joint European Torus (JET) nuclear project at Culham, a world leader in this branch of research.

Nuclear Safety

Britain has a rigorous system of nuclear safety regulation, enforced by the HSE's Nuclear Installations Inspectorate, which ensures that high standards of safety are incorporated into the design, construction, operation, maintenance and decommissioning of all nuclear plant, and eventual disposal of resulting wastes. While the safety of such plant in Britain is the ultimate responsibility of the nuclear operator, the Inspectorate has the power to shut down a plant if it is believed to be unsafe and may also require improvements to an installation if it thinks the appropriate standards of safety are not being met.

Discharges have to be kept within the limits and conditions set by authorisations granted under the Radioactive Substances Act 1960. In England and Wales separate authorisations are required from the Secretaries of State for the Environment and for Wales, and from the Minister of Agriculture, Fisheries and Food, and in Scotland from the Secretary of State for Scotland. Within maximum dose limits, operators of nuclear facilities are required to keep discharges as low as is reasonably achievable and failure to do so makes them liable to prosecution.

Emergency Plans

The precautions taken in the design and construction of nuclear installations in Britain, and the high safety standards in their operation and maintenance, reduce the chance of accidents which might affect the public to an extremely low level. However, all operators are required, as a condition of their site licences, to prepare emergency plans, including those for dealing with an accidental release of radioactivity; these are regularly tested in exercises under the supervision of the Nuclear Installations Inspectorate.

International conventions have been established on the early notification of a nuclear accident which may have possible transboundary effects, and on the mutual provision of assistance in the event of a nuclear accident or radiological emergency.

NEW AND RENEWABLE SOURCES OF ENERGY

The Government encourages development of new and renewable technologies which promise to be economically attractive and environmentally acceptable—to contribute to:

- diverse, secure and sustainable energy supplies;

- a reduction in the emission of pollutants; and

- encouragement of internationally competitive renewables industries.

The Government aims to work towards a figure of 1,500 MW of new electricity generating capacity from renewable energy sources, for Britain as a whole, by 2000. Under the non-fossil fuel obligation (NFFO), by mid-1993 two renewables orders had resulted in contracts for 197 renewables projects, with a total capacity of over 600 MW. In 1993 the third NFFO renewables order for England and Wales, and the first for Scotland and Northern Ireland, were announced.

Research and development policy concentrates resources on key technologies— biofuels, wind, hydro, solar and fuel cells— and aims to remove inappropriate market barriers. Emphasis on technology transfer continues. Expenditure on the Government's renewables programme for 1992–93 was about £24 million.

International collaboration is undertaken through multilateral and bilateral arrangements within the IEA and the European Community. These include JOULE, THERMIE and ALTENER.

Wind

Wind energy is one of the most promising renewable energy sources, with the potential to contribute perhaps 10 per cent of Britain's electricity needs. The Government's research and development expenditure was £8.7 million in 1992–93. Its programme has provided a strong technical base and a reliable assessment of the size and cost of Britain's resource. Through the NFFO wind energy has the opportunity to prove itself commercially.

Tidal

The programme, on which the Government spent £1.7 million in 1992–93, aims to reduce the technical, economic and environmental uncertainties associated with tidal barrages through a number of site and generic studies.

Wave

A review of wave power, published in 1992 after consultation with members of Britain's wave energy community, covers all the leading British wave devices from shoreline to offshore. Britain is collaborating in a European programme which is assessing the prospects for wave power. Government research and development expenditure was some £300,000 in 1992–93.

Biofuels

The programme, which received £3.2 million for research and development in 1992–93, includes work on further understanding of, and increasing the energy available from, landfill gas, and on the preparation and combustion of refuse and dry wastes, including straw and forestry residues. The latter are closely connected to the exploitation of short-rotation arable coppice, an energy crop which could exploit land not required for growing food.

Solar

A major element of the programme is the Energy Design Advice Scheme, which aims to improve the energy and environmental performance of building stock. The Government provided £2.3 million on solar energy research and development expenditure in 1992–93.

The photovoltaic industry has considerable potential, particularly in the export market. The Government is assessing the potential of buildings-integrated photovoltaic systems, the most promising application in Britain.

Geothermal Hot Dry Rocks

The aim of the current programme (costing £1.1 million in 1992–93), in collaboration with the European programme, is to exploit the expertise developed in Britain and to pursue opportunities for transferring the technology to industry.

Technology Dissemination

Marketing and promoting renewables has seen a shift of emphasis from technology towards promotion to likely users and developers. Established in 1991, the commercialisation part of the programme aims to remove a number of barriers to investment in renewables. Resource studies with potential developers, planning policy studies with local authorities and contacts with possible financiers are key activities.

Non-fuel Minerals

Although much of Britain's requirements for industrial raw materials is met by imports, the non-fuel minerals it produces make an important contribution to the economy. Output of non-fuel minerals in 1991 totalled over 335 million tonnes, valued at £1,814 million. Construction raw materials, in particular aggregates, form the bulk of the value of non-fuel minerals production. The total number of employees in the extractive industry was some 43,500 in 1991.

Exploration

The British Geological Survey is carrying out a long-term programme for the Department of Trade and Industry aimed at identifying

Table 16.4: Production of Some of the Main Non-fuel Minerals

million tonnes

	1981	1986	1991
Sand and gravel	97.0	112.0	106.4
Silica sand	4.5	4.1	4.2
Igneous rock	30.8	41.0	54.0
Limestone and dolomite	79.1	100.5	114.3
Chalk[a]	11.8	12.5	10.3
Sandstone	12.2	14.0	16.6
Gypsum	2.9	3.4	2.5
Salt, including salt in brine	6.7	6.9	6.9
Common clay and shale[a]	18.8	17.6	13.0
China clay	2.6	2.9	2.9
Ball clay	0.7	0.6	0.7
Fireclay	1.0[a]	0.9	0.9
Iron ore	0.7	0.3	0.1
Potash	0.5	0.7	0.9
Fluorspar	0.2	0.1	0.1
Fuller's earth	0.2	0.2	0.2

Source: *British Geological Survey, United Kingdom Minerals Yearbook 1992.*
[a] Great Britain only.

Some Minerals Produced in Britain

Orkney Islands

Shetland Islands

talc

talc

0 20 40 60 80 100 120 km

0 20 40 60 80 miles

● Major metallic and industrial mineral workings

▲ Major mineral deposits (unworked)

marble

silica sand

barytes
gold
barytes
gold

silica sand

silica sand

fluorspar, lead
NORTHERN PENNINE OREFIELD
gypsum
barytes
salt
potash

gold
salt
diatomite

silica sand

zinc, copper, lead, silver
silica sand
SOUTHERN PENNINE OREFIELD
salt
fluorspar, barytes, lead
gypsum
salt
gold
CHESHIRE SALTFIELD
gypsum
gypsum
silica sand
silica sand

fuller's earth
fuller's earth
silica sand

fuller's earth

celestite
fuller's earth
silica sand
fuller's earth
gypsum

ball clay
china clay
ball clay
ball clay
china clay
china clay
tungsten, tin
tin

areas with mineral potential. Gold exploration by the private sector has decreased, but continues, especially in Scotland, Northern Ireland and south-west England. In Wales small-scale production of gold takes place at the Gwynfynydd and Clogau mines.

Production

In terms of value, production of limestone and dolomite was estimated at £529 million in 1991, sand and gravel £459 million, clays £266 million, igneous rock £224 million, sandstone £67 million, potash £64 million, salt £48 million, silica sands £46 million, chalk £43 million, gypsum and anhydrite £22 million, fuller's earth £14 million, fluorspar £10 million and tin £7 million. In 1992 the production of metals in non-ferrous ores totalled 2,500 tonnes, mainly tin from Cornwall. South Crofty, the one remaining Cornish mine and one of the very few sources of tin in the Community, produced some 2,040 tonnes of tin-in-concentrate in 1992, equivalent to about 20 per cent of Britain's demand. Some lead and a little zinc are produced as by-products of fluorspar.

Water

Britain's water supplies are obtained partly from surface sources such as mountain lakes, streams dammed in hills and lowland river intakes, and partly from underground sources. About 99 per cent of the population in Great Britain and 97 per cent in Northern Ireland are served by the public water supply system. Water put into the public supply system in England and Wales amounted to about 16,500 megalitres (Ml) a day in 1992 and average daily consumption per head was 0.324 Ml. An average of 2,239 Ml a day was supplied in Scotland in 1991–92.

Some 33,463 Ml a day were abstracted in England and Wales in 1991, of which public water supplies accounted for 17,563 Ml a day. The electricity generating companies and other industry took some 16,400 Ml a day. Agriculture took 500 Ml a day.

England and Wales

The Secretaries of State for the Environment and for Wales, the Director General of Water Services and the National Rivers Authority (NRA) are the principal regulators of the privatised (since 1989) water industry. The Minister of Agriculture, Fisheries and Food and the Secretary of State for Wales are responsible for policy relating to land drainage, flood protection, sea defence, and the protection and development of fisheries. The Drinking Water Inspectorate regulates drinking water quality.

Water Companies

The ten water service companies are the principal operating subsidiaries of the ten water holding companies. They have statutory responsibilities for water supply, quality and adequacy, and for sewerage and sewage treatment. The supply-only companies, of which there were 29 in the private sector in 1989, now number 22. They supply water to about a quarter of the population.

The Water Industry Act 1991 allows the water companies to determine their own methods of charging. An alternative to the charging system based on rateable values, however, must be found by the year 2000. Water metering is one of the choices being considered. Customers may choose to pay to have a water meter installed. In general, companies require new properties to have metered supplies.

A system of economic regulation and guaranteed standards of service is overseen by the Director General of Water Services. The Water Supply (Water Quality) Regulations 1989 define wholesomeness and incorporate the requirements of the EC's drinking water directive. They impose physical, chemical and microbiological standards for water intended for domestic and food production purposes. The task of the Drinking Water Inspectorate is to ensure that drinking water is wholesome and that companies comply with the Regulations. Of 3.75 million tests carried out in 1992, 98.7 per cent came within the legal limits.

National Rivers Authority

The NRA, the environmental regulator, is a non-departmental public body with statutory duties and powers in relation to water resources, pollution control, flood defence, fisheries, recreation, conservation and navigation in England and Wales. The water environment for which it has responsibility includes all rivers, lakes, reservoirs, estuaries, coastal waters and water stored naturally underground. The NRA's consent is needed for the abstraction of water and for discharges to water.

Development Projects

The water industry in England and Wales is committed to a ten-year investment programme costing over £30,000 million at 1989–90 prices. Thames Water's 80-km (50-mile) distribution system to meet the growing demand for water in London is due for completion in 1996. North West Water has a major 25-year programme of investment to clean up the polluted rivers of the Mersey Basin.

Water is an increasingly scarce resource. The industry, through contingency planning and publicity campaigns, encourages the wise use of water, especially when supplies run low because of prolonged warm, dry weather. A national review of water consumption and conservation, partly prompted by four years of drought in south-east and eastern England which ended in 1992, has been put in hand by the Government. The NRA is investigating the strategic development of water resources, including major new transfer schemes, and is reviewing the possibilities of a national grid and desalination.

Scotland

In Scotland responsibility for public water supply, sewerage and sewage disposal rests with the nine regional and three islands councils ('the water authorities'). In addition, the Central Scotland Water Development Board is responsible for providing water in bulk to five regional councils in central

Scotland. In 1991–92 the Board supplied authorities with an average 294 Ml a day. After public consultation the Government has announced that three public water authorities will take over provision of these services from the local authorities. An independent representative body for consumers will also be established.

The Secretary of State for Scotland is responsible for promoting conservation of water resources and provision by water authorities and water development boards of adequate water supplies. He has a duty to promote the cleanliness of rivers and other inland waters, and the tidal waters of Scotland. River purification authorities have a statutory responsibility for water pollution control. Water is charged for according to type of consumer: domestic consumers pay council water charges or through metered charges; non-domestic consumers pay by means of non-domestic water rates, or through metered charges. For sewerage services, domestic consumers pay through the council tax, and non-domestic consumers pay non-domestic sewerage rates and, where appropriate, trade effluent charges. Charges and rates are decided by each authority.

Scotland has a relative abundance of unpolluted water from upland sources.

Northern Ireland

The Department of the Environment for Northern Ireland is responsible for public water supply and sewerage throughout Northern Ireland. It is also responsible for the conservation and cleanliness of water resources and, with the Department of Agriculture for Northern Ireland, may prepare a water management programme with respect to water resources in any area. There is a domestic water charge which is contained in the regional rate, while agriculture, commerce and industry pay metered charges. There are abundant potential supplies of water for both domestic and industrial use. An average of 667 Ml of water a day was supplied in 1992–93.

Research

Several organisations and centres of expertise provide water research services to government, the NRA, water companies and the Scottish river purification boards.

The Water Research Centre, a private company, has a large programme of research into, for example, environmental issues and drinking water safety.

Research carried out by institutes of the Natural Environment Research Council embraces river modelling, water quality, climate change, effects on resources and the impact of pollution on freshwater.

Among its various roles the Institute of Hydrology studies the statistics of floods and droughts.

Further Reading

Development of the Oil and Gas Resources of the United Kingdom 1993. Department of Trade and Industry. HMSO.

Digest of the United Kingdom Energy Statistics 1993. Department of Trade and Industry. HMSO.

Energy and Natural Resources. Aspects of Britain series, HMSO, 1992.

United Kingdom Minerals Yearbook, annual report. HMSO.

17 Agriculture, the Fishing Industry and Forestry

The agricultural industry's productivity rose by some 3 per cent in 1992. Total income from farming rose by about 15 per cent and farming income (covering only farmers and their spouses) by about 24 per cent. Among a series of environmental initiatives announced by the Government have been the development and extension of the Environmentally Sensitive Areas scheme and an improved Farm Woodland Premium Scheme.

Agriculture

British agriculture is noted for its high level of efficiency and productivity. In 1992 it employed 2.1 per cent of the total workforce and Britain was self-sufficient in 56 per cent of all types of food and animal feed. It was self-sufficient in 72 per cent of indigenous-type food and feed. Food, feed and beverages accounted for 10.7 per cent of Britain's imports by value in 1992, compared with about a quarter in the 1960s. The agricultural contribution to gross domestic product was £6,790 million in 1992, 1.3 per cent of the total. Britain is also a major exporter of agricultural produce and food products, agrochemicals and agricultural machinery.

The Government aims to foster an efficient and competitive agriculture industry through the provision and sponsorship of research, development and advisory services; the provision of financial support where appropriate; measures to control disease, pests and pollution; and improved marketing arrangements for food and food products. It also insists on high standards of animal welfare. The needs of an efficient agricultural industry must be balanced with other interests in the countryside. These include conservation of its natural beauty and promotion of its enjoyment by the public.

In accordance with the Citizen's Charter, the agencies of the Ministry of Agriculture, Fisheries and Food are set annual targets which emphasise quality of service. Its regional organisation has published details of the levels of service that it will provide to customers. A similar initiative operates in Scotland.

Land Use

The area of agricultural land has been declining, although there has been a reduction in the net rate of loss in recent years. In 1992 there were 11.8 million hectares (29.2 million acres) under crops and grass. A further 5.9 million hectares (14.6 million acres) were used for rough grazing, most of it in hilly areas. Soils vary from the thin poor ones of highland Britain to the rich fertile soils of low-lying areas such as the fenlands of eastern England. The temperate climate and the relatively even distribution of rainfall over the year ensure a long growing season; streams rarely dry up and grassland normally remains green throughout the year.

Land Use in Britain

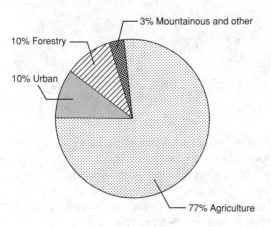

- 3% Mountainous and other
- 10% Forestry
- 10% Urban
- 77% Agriculture

Farming

In 1992 there were some 242,300 farm holdings in Britain (excluding minor holdings), with an average size of 70.8 hectares (175 acres)—again excluding minor holdings. About two-thirds of all agricultural land is owner-occupied. Some 43 per cent of holdings are of 4 British Standard Units (BSUs)[1] or less.

The number of people (excluding spouses) engaged in agriculture in 1992 was about 546,000, compared with an average of 630,000 in 1981–83. The total for whole-time farmers, partners and directors in 1992—about 177,000—had declined from an average of 204,000 in 1981–83. The number of farmers, partners and directors working part time (104,000 in 1992) has continued to increase (from an average of 88,000 in 1981–83). Regular whole-time workers (family and hired) have continued to decline, to 114,500 in 1992, compared with an average of 171,000 in 1981-83. The number of regular part-time workers (family and hired) showed a

[1] BSUs measure the gross income potential of the holding and 4 BSUs is judged to be the minimum size for full-time holdings.

decline—to 57,000, compared with an average of 62,000 in 1981–83.

Labour productivity has increased by 3.8 per cent over the past ten years. Total income from farming (that of farmers, partners, directors and their spouses and family workers) was estimated at £2,831 million in 1992, over 15 per cent more than in 1991.

Agricultural Land Use 1992

TOTAL AREA ON AGRICULTURAL HOLDINGS

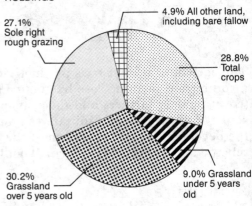

- 27.1% Sole right rough grazing
- 4.9% All other land, including bare fallow
- 28.8% Total crops
- 9.0% Grassland under 5 years old
- 30.2% Grassland over 5 years old

CROPS

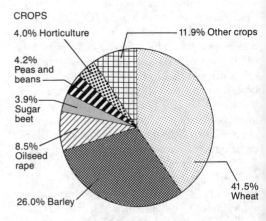

- 4.0% Horticulture
- 11.9% Other crops
- 4.2% Peas and beans
- 3.9% Sugar beet
- 8.5% Oilseed rape
- 41.5% Wheat
- 26.0% Barley

At the end of 1991 the industry's capital stock amounted to some £23,320 million, of which buildings and works made up nearly two-thirds. The overall stock of fixed capital is estimated to be about 2.5 per cent down on 1981–83.

Table 17.1: British Production as a Percentage of Total New Supplies

Food Product	1990–91 average	1992–93 (provisional)
Beef and veal	95	95
Eggs	100	96
Milk for human consumption (as liquid)	100	99
Cheese	70	64
Butter	62	56
Sugar (as refined)	53	57
Wheat	103	124
Potatoes	91	90

Source: Ministry of Agriculture, Fisheries and Food.

PRODUCTION

Home production of the principal foods is shown in Table 17.1 as a percentage by weight of total supplies (that is, production plus imports minus exports).

Livestock

Over half of full-time farms are devoted mainly to dairying or beef cattle and sheep. The majority of sheep and cattle are reared in the hill and moorland areas of Scotland, Wales, Northern Ireland and northern and south-western England. Beef fattening occurs partly in better grassland areas, as does dairying, and partly on arable farms. British livestock breeders have developed many of the cattle, sheep and pig breeds with worldwide reputations, for example, the Hereford and Aberdeen Angus beef breeds, the Jersey, Guernsey and Ayrshire dairy breeds, Large White pigs and a number of sheep breeds. Developments in artificial insemination and embryo transfer have enabled Britain to export semen and embryos from high-quality donor animals. Livestock totals are given in Table 17.2.

Cattle and Sheep

Most dairy cattle in Britain are bred by artificial insemination. In 1992 the average size of dairy herds in Britain was 63 (excluding minor holdings), while the average yield of milk per dairy cow was 5,256 litres (1,157 gallons). Average household consumption of liquid (including low-fat)

milk per head in 1992 was 1.96 litres (3.45 pints) a week.

About two-thirds of home-fed beef production originates from the national dairy herd, in which the Friesian breed is predominant. The remainder is derived from suckler herds producing high-quality beef calves in the hills and uplands, where the traditional British beef breeds, such as Hereford and Aberdeen Angus, continue to be important. Imported breeds which have been established include the Charolais, Limousin, Simmental and Belgian Blue. In 1992 the size of the beef-breeding herd continued to expand and reached its highest level for 17 years. The increase to December 1992 more than offset the further decrease in the dairy herd.

Britain has a long tradition of sheep production, with more than 40 breeds and many cross-bred varieties. Research has provided vaccine and serum protection against nearly all the epidemic diseases. Lamb production is the main source of income for sheep farmers, but wool is a significant by-product.

Grass (including silage) supplies 60 to 80 per cent of the feed for cattle and sheep. Grass production has been enhanced by the increased use of fertilisers, methods of grazing control, and improved herbage conservation for winter feed. Rough grazings are used for extensively grazed sheep and cattle, producing young animals for fattening elsewhere.

A harmonised identification system throughout the European Community aims to enable animals to be traced back to their farm

Table 17.2: Livestock and Livestock Products

	1981–83 average	1990	1991	1992 (provisional)
Cattle and calves ('000 head)	13,224	12,059	11,866	11,788
Sheep and lambs ('000 head)	33,078	43,799	43,621	43,973
Pigs ('000 head)	8,008	7,449	7,596	7,608
Poultry ('000 head)[a]	80,297	92,341	94,664	91,963
Milk (million litres)	15,973	14,535	14,075	13,995
Eggs (million dozen)[b]	1,023	811	822	812
Beef and veal ('000 tonnes)	1,021	997	1,023	970
Mutton and lamb ('000 tonnes)	282	393	418	392
Pork ('000 tonnes)	744	749	797	805
Bacon and ham ('000 tonnes)	203	180	176	167
Poultry meat ('000 tonnes)	788	1,027	1,074	1,069

Source: Ministry of Agriculture, Fisheries and Food.
[a]Includes ducks, geese and turkeys. Figures for the latter are for England and Wales only.
[b]Hen and duck eggs.

of origin, for disease control purposes and for checking payments made under the Common Agricultural Policy.

Pigs and Poultry

Pig production occurs in most areas but is particularly important in eastern and northern England. There is an increasing concentration into specialist units and larger herds. Of the pig herd 72 per cent are on 13 per cent of the holdings with pigs.

Output of poultry meat benefits from better husbandry and genetic improvements. The number of broilers from the 7 per cent of holdings of over 100,000 table birds accounts for over a half of the total population. Output of hen and duck eggs fell from 822 million dozen in 1991 to 812 million dozen in 1992. Some 73 per cent of laying birds are on the 1 per cent of holdings with 20,000 or more birds. Britain remains broadly self-sufficient in poultry meat and eggs.

Animal Welfare

The welfare of farm animals is protected by legislation and it is an offence to cause unnecessary pain or distress to commercially reared livestock. Detailed regulations require owners of intensive units to arrange for the daily inspection of their stock and the equipment on which it depends. The law

bans close confinement crates for keeping veal calves, and is phasing out close confinement systems for keeping pigs. There are further controls to safeguard the welfare of animals in markets, during transport and at slaughter. The Farm Animal Welfare Council, an independent body set up by the Government, advises on legislative or other changes it considers necessary. Britain continues to take the lead in pressing for higher standards of animal welfare throughout Europe.

Crops

The farms devoted primarily to arable crops are found mainly in eastern and central-southern England and eastern Scotland. The main crops are shown in Table 17.3. In Britain in 1992 cereals were grown on 3.5 million hectares (8.6 million acres), an area similar to that planted in 1991. Production of cereals, at 22.1 million tonnes, was 0.6 million down on 1991. A reduction of 7 per cent in the planted area of barley was partially offset by a 4 per cent increase in yield.

A little over 50 per cent of available domestic wheat supplies (allowing for imports and exports) are normally used for flour milling, and just under half for animal feed. About a third of barley supplies are used for brewing, malting and distilling, and virtually all the remainder for animal feed.

SMALL BUSINESSES

Blacksmith Frances Plowden runs a metalwork business, producing furniture and decorative ironwork to her own designs and to her clients' specifications.

New communications technology has made running a business from home an increasingly attractive option: electronic mail, voice messaging and paperless invoicing offer the user instant access to customers and suppliers.

EXPORTS

In 1993, 68 companies won the Queen's Award for Export Achievement,
with products ranging from pet food to sports cars,
and financial and other services.

The Academy of St Martin in
the Fields orchestra, which
receives no subsidy, gains over
two-thirds of its earnings from
overseas concert performances
and from royalties on export
sales of its recordings.

The Financial Times Group Limited,
whose flagship newspaper the
Financial Times is read by over
one million people worldwide, has joined
forces with the Russian newspaper *Izvestia*
to produce a business publication,
Financial Izvestia, in Russian.

Based in Wales, B.C.B. International has only been trading for 14 years, but has now won two Export Awards. The company specialises in equipment for outdoor pursuits, such as the Raven meals and camping gas supplied for an expedition to Iceland by members of Ardingly College.

Churchill was established in 1795 and now exports to 37 countries worldwide. It offers a wide range of tableware manufactured from fine quality clay, and a reliable packing and delivery service. The 'Tamarind' tableware seen here is a new design based on the Jacobean decorative style.

NEW TECHNOLOGY

The International Wool Secretariat Development Centre, based in a traditional wool-processing area of Yorkshire, uses state-of-the-art knitting machines to develop increasingly lightweight and adaptable woollen fabrics.

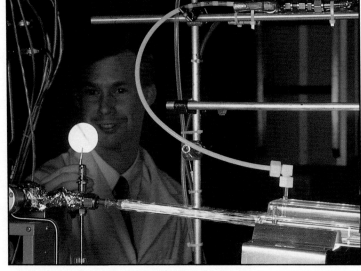

The Optical Research Division of BT (British Telecom) won a Queen's Award for Technological Achievement for the development of metal organic vapour phase epitaxy, a technique for the precision manufacture of devices used in optical telecommunications.

Table 17.3: Main Crops

	1981–83 average	1990	1991	1992 (provisional)
Wheat				
Area ('000 hectares)	1,616	2,013	1,981	2,066
Production ('000 tonnes)	9,942	14,033	14,363	14,092
Yield (tonnes per hectare)	6.16	6.97	7.25	6.82
Barley				
Area ('000 hectares)	2,232	1,517	1,393	1,297
Production ('000 tonnes)	10,388	7,911	7,627	7,366
Yield (tonnes per hectare)	4.65	5.22	5.47	5.68
Oats				
Area ('000 hectares)	127	107	104	101
Production ('000 tonnes)	553	530	523	504
Yield (tonnes per hectare)	4.35	4.96	5.04	5.01
Potatoes				
Area ('000 hectares)	194	178	177	180
Production ('000 tonnes)	6,317	6,488	6,279	7,882
Yield (tonnes per hectare)	32.60	36.40	35.50	43.80
Oilseed rape				
Area ('000 hectares)	175	390	440	421
Production ('000 tonnes)	494	1,258	1,294	1,152
Yield (tonnes per hectare)	2.82	3.23	2.94	2.74
Sugar beet				
Area ('000 hectares)	204	194	196	196
Production ('000 tonnes)	8,299	7,902	7,673	9,298
Yield (tonnes per hectare)	41.27	40.66	41.15	47.44

Sources: *Agriculture in the United Kingdom 1992*, and *Agricultural Census, June 1992*.

The area planted to oilseed rape fell from 440,000 hectares (1.1 million acres) in 1991 to an estimated 421,000 hectares (1.04 million acres) in 1992. Production was about 1.15 million tonnes, compared with 1.29 million tonnes in 1991.

Large-scale potato and vegetable cultivation is undertaken in the fens (in Cambridgeshire and south Lincolnshire), the alluvial areas around the rivers Thames and Humber, and the peaty lands in south Lancashire. Early potatoes are an important crop in Pembrokeshire (Dyfed), Kent and Cornwall. High-grade seed potatoes are grown in Scotland and Northern Ireland.

Sugar from home-grown sugar beet provides just under 60 per cent of home needs, most of the remainder being refined from raw cane sugar imported levy-free from developing countries under the Lomé Convention (see p. 201).

Horticulture

In 1992 the land utilised for horticulture (excluding potatoes, peas for harvesting dry and mushrooms) was about 197,000 hectares (486,806 acres). Vegetables grown in the open accounted for 68 per cent of this, orchards for 18 per cent, and soft fruit and ornamentals (including hardy nursery stock, bulbs and flowers grown in the open) each for 7 per cent. More than one vegetable crop is, in some cases, taken from the same area of land in a year, so that the estimated area actually cropped in 1992 was 263,500 hectares (651,100 acres).

Mushrooms are the single most valuable horticultural crop, with a farm gate value of £171 million in 1991. Britain's mushroom production has increased from some 70,000 tonnes to just over 122,000 tonnes between 1982 and 1991. Apples are also a significant crop. Output (of dessert and cooking apples) increased from 292,000 tonnes in 1991 to 326,000 in 1992.

Field vegetables account for about one-third of the value of horticultural output and are widely grown throughout the country. Most horticultural enterprises are increasing productivity with the help of improved planting material, new techniques and the widespread use of machinery. Some field vegetables, for example, are raised in blocks of compressed peat or loose-filled cells, a technique which reduces root damage and allows plants to establish themselves more reliably and evenly.

Glasshouses are used for growing tomatoes, cucumbers, sweet peppers, lettuces, flowers, pot plants and nursery stock. Widespread use is made of automatic control of heating and ventilation, and semi-automatic control of watering. Energy-efficient glasshouses use thermal screens, while low-cost plastic tunnels extend the season for certain crops previously grown in the open.

Under the EC's Common Agricultural Policy (see below), a wide range of horticultural produce is subject to common quality standards.

Under Community rules, Britain has a production limit of 2.5 million litres of wine a year. It is produced mainly in southern England and south Wales. A pilot Quality Wine Scheme was launched by the Government for the 1991 vintage.

Organic Farming

The Government aims to establish a framework in which organic farming in Britain can respond to consumer demand. The organic sector is eligible for the support given to all farmers under a number of general schemes. Other support includes a significant commitment to research and development.

The United Kingdom Register of Organic Food Standards (UKROFS) is an independent body set up in 1987 with government support. It has established national voluntary standards for organic food production tied to a certification and inspection scheme. It also enforces the Organic Products Regulations 1992, which require producers or preparers of organic

food, or importers from outside the EC, to be registered and to operate to Community regulation standards.

FOOD SAFETY

Government spending on programmes to promote food safety and against diseases affecting food supply is some £116 million in 1993–94. Its expenditure on food safety research was about £20 million in 1992–93. Among significant findings in 1992 was that any risk to health from dioxins was likely to be remote.

The Food Safety Directorate within the Ministry of Agriculture, Fisheries and Food focuses ministry resources on ensuring adequate supplies of the right kinds of food, and its safety, wholesomeness and proper labelling, through regulations and guidelines. The Food Safety Act 1990 ensures food safety and consumer protection throughout the food chain. It combines basic provisions with wide enabling powers, so that detailed regulations made under the Act can adapt to technological change and innovation. It also combines enforcement powers and increased penalties for offenders.

The Food Advisory Committee advises ministers on the exercise of powers in the Food Safety Act 1990 relating to the labelling, composition and chemical safety of food. The Advisory Committee on Novel Foods and Processes advises on any matter relating to the irradiation of food or to the manufacture of novel foods or foods produced by novel processes.

The Steering Group on Chemical Aspects of Food Surveillance directs the extensive programme of checks, tests and analyses which monitor the chemical safety, nutritional adequacy and authenticity of Britain's food supply. There is an Advisory Committee and a Steering Group on the Microbiological Safety of Food.

In accordance with the principles of the Citizen's Charter, a consumer panel—ten consumer members nominated by the main consumer organisations, but appointed to serve as individuals—enables consumers directly to convey their views on food safety and consumer protection issues to the Government.

EXPORTS

Today Britain imports about 42 per cent of its food. The volume of exports related to agriculture rose by 3 per cent in 1992, when their value amounted to £7,522 million, the main markets being Western Europe, North America and the Middle East. Exports include speciality products such as fresh salmon, Scotch whisky (of which exports to the EC alone were worth over £720 million in 1992), biscuits, jams and conserves, as well as beef and lamb carcasses and cheese.

Food From Britain is an organisation funded by the Government and industry, to assist the food and drink industry in Britain to improve its marketing at home and overseas. Through its export association, the British Food Export Council, and its network of seven overseas offices, Food From Britain identifies market opportunities and arranges promotions. It also co-ordinates the British presence at major international food and drink trade exhibitions.

> The British Agricultural Export Committee of the London Chamber of Commerce represents exporters of technology, expertise and equipment. In 1992 Britain exported £764 million of farm machinery and spares.

One of the world's largest agricultural events, the annual Royal International Agricultural Exhibition, held at Stoneleigh in Warwickshire, enables visitors to see the latest techniques and improvements in British agriculture. Some 177,500 visitors attended in 1993, of whom 25,000 were from overseas. Other major agricultural displays include the annual Royal Smithfield Show, held in London, which exhibits agricultural machinery, livestock and carcasses; the Royal Highland Show; the Royal Welsh Show; and the Royal Ulster Agricultural Show. There are also important regional shows.

MARKETING

A government food marketing initiative began in 1991 to encourage collaboration and improved marketing throughout the agriculture and food industries. A Group Marketing Grant, introduced in 1992, encourages the development of professionally managed and market-oriented producer groups.

Agricultural products are marketed by private traders, producers' co-operatives and some marketing boards. The Agriculture Act 1993 ends the milk marketing schemes in Great Britain and the wool and potato guarantees. It provides enabling powers for terminating the Potato Marketing Scheme, but no decision has been taken to invoke this provision. Marketing arrangements for wool continue to be administered by the British Wool Marketing Board. The legislation also provides new powers for making marketing grants. For home-grown cereals, meat and livestock, and apples and pears there are marketing organisations representing producer, distributor and independent interests.

Co-operatives

Much agricultural and horticultural produce, such as grain, fruit and vegetables, is handled by marketing co-operatives; these had a turnover of some £2,000 million in 1992. Their aim is to meet the demand for a continuous supply of fresh, quality produce.

ROLE OF THE GOVERNMENT

Four government departments have joint responsibility for agriculture and fisheries matters—the Ministry of Agriculture, Fisheries and Food; The Scottish Office Agriculture and Fisheries Department; the Welsh Office; and the Department of Agriculture for Northern Ireland.

Common Agricultural Policy

The EC's Common Agricultural Policy (CAP) accounts for over 50 per cent of the Community's budget. It aims to ensure stable markets, a fair standard of living for agricultural producers and regular supplies of food at reasonable prices. For many commodities support prices are set annually; there are also levies on imports to maintain internal market prices. Surpluses are bought by intervention boards (the Intervention Board executive agency in Britain) to be stored and sold when appropriate. Intervention stocks can be disposed of within the Community where this can be done without disrupting internal markets.

Exports, from the market and intervention stocks, are facilitated by the provision of export refunds to bridge any gap between Community prices and world prices. In some cases there are also direct payments to producers—for example, the arable area scheme (see below), the suckler cow premium, the beef special premium and the annual premium on ewes. The support prices, as well as rates of levy, export refunds and other aids, are set in European Currency Units and are converted into the currencies of the member states at fixed rates of exchange—'green rates'. These green rates are to be kept broadly in line with market rates in accordance with agreed criteria.

Nearly all the EC's agricultural expenditure (£28,000 million in 1993) is channelled through the European Agricultural Guidance and Guarantee Fund. The Fund's guarantee section finances market support arrangements, while the guidance section provides funds for structural reform—for example, farm modernisation and investment —and payments to assist certain farmers to change to alternative enterprises.

Agricultural production under the CAP has increased considerably in recent years, reflecting rapid technical progress and farming efficiency as well as the high level of price support. As consumption has remained relatively stable, this has resulted in the emergence of surpluses.

Britain has consistently pressed for CAP reform, to bring supply and demand into better balance, to increase the role of market forces in agriculture and to make environmental considerations an integral part of the CAP. Since 1988 there has been a legally binding limit on CAP market support expenditure (the agricultural guideline).

Public Expenditure under the CAP by the Intervention Board and the Agricultural Departments

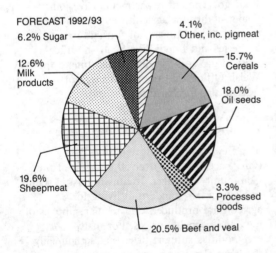

FORECAST 1992/93
6.2% Sugar
4.1% Other, inc. pigmeat
12.6% Milk products
15.7% Cereals
18.0% Oil seeds
19.6% Sheepmeat
3.3% Processed goods
20.5% Beef and veal

Reform

Agreement was reached in 1992 on measures to reform the CAP in the arable, milk, beef and sheepmeat sectors. The agreement cut prices for major commodities and introduced measures aiming to curb over-production and to reduce the role of intervention.

Arable Crops. From the start of the 1993–94 marketing year a new price support structure for cereals came into effect. Support prices will be reduced from the present level by about 30 per cent over three years. Under the arable area scheme producers can claim a direct subsidy on an area basis provided that they agree to take 15 per cent of their arable land out of production.

Beef. Intervention prices are being reduced by 15 per cent over three years, starting in July 1993. The ceiling on intervention purchases introduced in 1993 will continue to be reduced each year until 1997. To compensate for this, in 1993 there were significant increases in both the beef special premium and the suckler cow premium. There will be further increases in both premiums in 1994 and 1995.

Milk. The butter support price is to be cut by 5 per cent over two years.

Environment. All member states are to run

programmes to encourage environmentally sensitive farming, including extensification,[2] organic farming, and environmentally friendly management or upkeep of land.

An integrated administration and control system has been introduced. By using a computerised database, an identification system for fields and animals, and an integrated system for checking and inspection, it is designed to ensure uniform enforcement of the reformed CAP and to reduce the scope for fraud.

GATT Uruguay Round

Agriculture was identified as a major issue for the GATT round of multinational trade negotiations (see p. 201) launched in 1986. These have aimed to achieve a liberalisation of world trade in agricultural products and to reduce the distorting effects which agricultural support policies have on world trade.

Participants have been trying to reach binding agreements, including:

● reductions in internal support to agriculture;

● improvements in market access for agricultural products (by converting all import market access restrictions to tariffs, to be subsequently reduced);

● reductions in subsidising agricultural exports; and

● greater harmonisation of rules relating to animal and plant health as they affect trade.

Price Guarantees, Grants and Subsidies

Expenditure in Britain in 1992–93 on price guarantees, grants and subsidies and on CAP market regulation was estimated to be £326 million and £1,740 million respectively.

Farmers are eligible for grants aimed at environmental enhancement of their farms and pollution control. Hill and upland farmers can also benefit from headage payments on cattle and sheep, known as compensatory allowances. The Group Marketing Grant

---

[2] Reduction of surpluses through the offer of financial payments to farmers to lessen production.

(see p. 235) is helping farmers and growers to develop effective marketing.

In Less Favoured Areas (LFAs), where land quality is poor, farmers benefit from enhanced rates of grant and special payments on livestock—nearly £500 million a year. Their purpose is to support the continuation of livestock farming in the hill and upland areas, thereby conserving the countryside and maintaining a viable population in the LFAs.

Smallholdings and Crofts

In England and Wales county councils let smallholdings to experienced people who want to farm on their own account. Councils may lend working capital to them. At 31 March 1992 there were about 5,370 smallholdings in England and 900 in Wales. Land settlement in Scotland has been carried out by the Government, which, while now seeking to dispose of holdings to its sitting tenants, still owns and maintains 118,957 hectares (293,823 acres) of land settlement estates, comprising 1,446 crofts and holdings.

In the crofting areas of Scotland (the former counties of Argyll, Inverness, Ross and Cromarty, Sutherland, Caithness, Orkney and Shetland) much of the land is tenanted by crofters (smallholders). They enjoy the statutory protection provided by crofting legislation and can benefit from government schemes which exist to support and help crofting communities. Most crofters are part-time or spare-time agriculturalists using croft income to supplement income from activities such as weaving, fishing, tourism and other occupations. The Crofters Commission has a statutory duty to promote the interests of crofters and to keep all crofting matters under review.

Agricultural Landlords and Tenants

Approximately 37 per cent of agricultural land in England and Wales is rented. In Scotland, where approximately 50 per cent of farms are rented, the proportion of land is somewhat higher because of the relatively large areas of common grazings tenanted by crofters. The relationship between agricultural landlords and tenants is governed by specific legislation and the terms of individual tenancy agreements. The legislation covers matters such as variations of rent; liability for maintenance, repairs and insurance; security of tenure; and compensation on termination of tenancy.

The majority of farms in Northern Ireland are owner-occupied, but, under a practice known as 'conacre', occupiers not wishing to farm all their land let it annually to others. About one-fifth of agricultural land is let under this practice and is used mainly for grazing.

Agriculture and Protection of the Countryside

Agriculture ministers have a general duty, under the Agriculture Act 1986, to seek to achieve a reasonable balance between the needs of an efficient and stable agriculture industry and other interests in the countryside, including the conservation of its natural beauty and amenity and the promotion of its enjoyment by the public. In addition, they are required, as far as it is consistent with these schemes, to further conservation of the countryside in the administration of farm capital grant schemes, both in National Parks and in Sites of Special Scientific Interest designated by the nature conservation agencies (see p. 343).

Environmentally Sensitive Areas

Under the Environmentally Sensitive Areas (ESA) scheme, a British scheme which other EC members are following, 30 areas in Britain—16 in England, seven in Scotland, four in Wales and three in Northern Ireland—have been designated up to mid-1993 (see Table 17.4). Six further areas in England, three in Scotland, two in Wales and two in Northern Ireland, have also been proposed for designation. The scheme is designed to help protect some of the most beautiful parts of the country from the damage and loss that can come from agricultural practice. ESAs are notable for their landscape, wildlife or historic importance. Significant changes and improvements have been made to the scheme since it began in 1987, including opportunities for farmers to restore key environmental features of their land.

ESAs are unique and diverse in character, and include, for example, the Lake District and South Wessex Downs in England; Radnor in Wales; part of the coastal areas of the North and South Uists, Benbecula, Barra and Vatersay in the Outer Hebrides off north-west Scotland; and the steep-sided glens and unique farming patterns of Antrim in Northern Ireland.

Participation in the ESA scheme is voluntary, and farmers enter into agreements with the relevant agriculture department; initially they lasted for five years. In the reviewed areas ten-year agreements are offered—with a five-year break clause. An agreement specifies the agricultural management practices to be carried out by the farmer. Each ESA has varying tiers of management practices, from basic care and maintenance to more extensive forms of management. Details vary from one ESA to another, but all participants are prohibited from converting grassland to arable and are subject to restrictions on fertiliser and chemical usage.

Table 17.4: Environmentally Sensitive Areas at the end of 1992

	Number of ESAs	Farmers with agreements	Land designated	Areas covered by agreements
			'000 hectares	
England	16	3,329	387	125
Wales	4	895	193	69
Scotland	7	884	287	123
Northern Ireland	3	1,059	40	19

Source: Ministry of Agriculture, Fisheries and Food.

Most ESAs also restrict the numbers of stock that can be carried on the land as well as other operations—including the timing of cultivation. The annual payments are designed to compensate the farmers for reduced profitability, through the adoption of these less intensive production methods, and for the further work some management practices require. Additional payments are made for distinct items of conservation work set out in conservation plans. Annual government expenditure on payments to farmers within ESAs throughout Britain is expected to rise to £60 million in 1994–95.

Other Schemes

The Farm Woodland Premium Scheme offers incentives to farmers to encourage planting of woodlands on agricultural land. Trees planted on arable or improved grassland qualify for annual payments of up to £250 a hectare for either ten or 15 years, depending on the type of woodland created. For trees planted on unimproved grassland in the LFAs, the annual payment is £60 a hectare. Planting must not, in total, exceed more than 50 per cent of any individual agricultural unit.

The EC's system of arable support offers area payments to growers of cereals, oilseeds, linseed and protein crops. To receive these payments all but the smallest producers must set land aside. The land set aside may either be on a rotational basis (in which case farmers must set aside 15 per cent of the land they are claiming on) or on a non-rotational basis (in which case farmers must set aside 18 per cent of the land they are claiming on). The Farm and Conservation Grant Scheme, part-funded by the Community, provides grants for farmers to undertake environmental improvements and a limited range of farm investments. In addition to the expansion of the ESA programme, the Government proposes to introduce a wide ranging package of new voluntary incentive schemes to encourage environmentally beneficial farming practices. In England these include:

- a Moorland Scheme to protect and improve the condition of heather and other shrubby moorland;

- 30 new nitrate sensitive areas (bringing the total in England to 40) which will help to protect groundwater sources used to supply drinking water;
- a Habitat Scheme to create or improve a range of wildlife habitats over a 20-year period;
- an Organic Aid Scheme to help farmers convert to organic production methods;
- new payments to increase opportunities for public access in ESAs; and
- a Countryside Access Scheme to promote public access to set aside land.

The proposals for Scotland, Wales and Northern Ireland are along broadly similar lines. By the time they are fully operational, expenditure on these new measures throughout Britain is expected to rise to £31.5 million a year.

Farm Diversification

Farm-based enterprises other than food production have become increasingly important. A University of Exeter survey published in 1991 calculated that diversified enterprises generated an average trading profit of over £5,000 a year, with 80 per cent of farmers considering their ventures to be successful. The survey showed that diversification is estimated to provide over 30,000 full-time jobs. The most common diversification enterprises provide leisure amenities such as golf courses, tourist accommodation, or riding. Often such enterprises are small-scale, with low financial returns. In contrast, many farmers run large-scale farm shops which make a substantial contribution to farm business income.

In the Highlands and Islands of Scotland the Rural Enterprise Programme offers special funding, with EC support, to encourage farmers and crofters to develop new businesses.

Agricultural Training

From 1994 an independent non-statutory body, ATB-Landbase, is to act as the industry training organisation for the agricultural and horticultural industries. The

Government is to finance it through a contract and will also fund the resources necessary to ensure support is provided for local training initiatives. ATB-Landbase is to be responsible for the co-ordination of training provision, involving the agricultural colleges and many independent instructors.

Professional, Scientific and Technical Services

In England and Wales the Agricultural Development and Advisory Service (ADAS), an executive agency, provides professional, scientific and technical services for agriculture and its ancillary industries. Most types of advice and servicing are on a fee-paying basis, although initial advice to farmers on conservation, rural diversification (including use of land for woodlands) and animal welfare is available free. Similar services are provided in Scotland by The Scottish Office Agriculture and Fisheries Department through the Scottish Agricultural College. In Northern Ireland these services are available from the Department of Agriculture's agriculture and science services.

ADAS carries out research and development work under commission from the Ministry of Agriculture, Fisheries and Food, and works under contract directly for others and for levy-funded bodies. These undertakings are carried out at experimental husbandry farms across England and Wales, and through regional centres or on clients' premises. The Central Science Laboratory also carries out research and development work commissioned by the Ministry.

CONTROL OF DISEASES AND PESTS

Farm Animals

Britain is free from many serious animal illnesses. If they were to occur, diseases such as foot-and-mouth disease and classical swine fever would be combated by a slaughter policy applied to all animals infected or exposed to infection, and by control over animal movements during the outbreaks.

The Government has taken comprehensive measures to control bovine spongiform

encephalopathy and to ensure that consumers are protected from any remote risk. It has also established an expert committee to advise on all matters relating to spongiform encephalopathies.

Trade in animals, birds, meat and meat products is covered by harmonised rules within the EC. Under implementing legislation control measures permit action to be taken to prevent the introduction or spread of diseases. Special measures apply to prevent the introduction of rabies, and dogs, cats and certain other mammals are subject to import licence and six months' quarantine. Commercially traded dogs and cats, which comply with strict conditions, will be allowed entry without quarantine from other Community member states after 1 July 1994. There are severe penalties for breaking the law. There have been no cases of rabies outside quarantine in Britain since 1970.

Professional advice and action on the control of animal disease and the welfare of farm livestock are the responsibility of the government State Veterinary Service, whose veterinary investigation centres also advise private practitioners responsible for treating animals on the farm. Government laboratories perform specialist research work.

Fish

The fisheries departments operate statutory controls to prevent the introduction and spread of serious diseases of fish and shellfish. These controls include the licensing of live fish imports, the licensing of deposits of shellfish on the seabed, and movement restrictions on sites where outbreaks of notifiable diseases have been confirmed.

Plants

The agriculture departments are responsible for limiting the spread of plant pests and diseases and for preventing the introduction of new ones. They issue the health certificates required by other countries to accompany plant material exported from Britain; and authorise growers who wish to sell on the EC's single internal market.

Certification schemes encourage the
development of healthy and true-to-type
planting stocks.

Pesticides

All pesticides must be approved for their
safety and efficacy. There are strict controls
on the supply, storage and use of pesticides,
and their maximum residue levels in food.
Controls on pesticides are the joint
responsibility of six government departments
on the basis of advice from the independent
Advisory Committee on Pesticides.
Arrangements for the approval of pesticides
in Britain are being integrated into a
Community-wide system under the terms of a
directive on pesticides authorisations which
came into effect in 1992.

Veterinary Medicinal Products

The manufacture, sale and supply of
veterinary medicinal products are controlled
by legislation. Licences are issued by the
Veterinary Medicines Directorate on behalf of
the agriculture and health ministers. Advice
on the safety, quality and efficacy of
veterinary medicines and on suspected
adverse reactions is given by the Veterinary
Products Committee, which comprises
independent experts.

The Fishing Industry

Britain, one of the EC's leading fishing
nations, plays an active role in the
implementation and development of the
Community's Common Fisheries Policy
(CFP) agreed in 1983 (see p. 242).

The fishing industry provides 55 per cent
by quantity of British fish supplies, and is an
important source of employment and income
in a number of ports. Cod, haddock, whiting,
herring, plaice and sole are found in the
North Sea off the east coasts of Scotland and
England; mackerel, together with cod and
other demersal fish, off the west coast of
Scotland; sole, plaice, cod, herring
and whiting in the Irish Sea; and mackerel,
sole and plaice off the south-west coast of

England. Nephrops, crabs, lobsters and other
shellfish are found in the inshore waters all
around the coast.

The Government aims to conserve the fish
stocks and to encourage the development of a
viable, efficient and market-oriented fisheries
industry within the CFP framework.

Fish Caught

In 1992 demersal fish (caught on or near the
bottom of the sea) accounted for 40 per cent
by weight of total British landings, pelagic
fish (caught near the surface) for 42.5 per
cent and shellfish for 17.5 per cent. Landings
of all types of fish (excluding salmon and
trout) by British fishing vessels totalled
613,297 tonnes. Cod and haddock represented
24 and 13 per cent respectively of the total
value of demersal and pelagic fish landed,
while anglerfish (11 per cent), whiting
(8 per cent), plaice (8 per cent), mackerel
(6 per cent), and sole (4 per cent) were the
other most important sources of earnings to
the industry. The quayside value of the
British catch of wetfish and shellfish in 1992
was £401.1 million.

Imports of fresh, frozen, cured and
canned salt-water fish and shellfish in 1992
totalled 420,377 tonnes, those of freshwater
fish 52,973 tonnes, those of fish meal 237,350
tonnes and those of fish oils 6,729 tonnes.
Exports and re-exports of salt-water fish
and fish products amounted to 398,860
tonnes and those of freshwater fish to
22,665 tonnes.

The Fishing Fleet

At the end of 1992 the British fleet consisted
of 11,050 registered vessels, including 440
deep-sea vessels longer than 24.4 m (80 ft).

Among the main ports from which the
fishing fleet operates are Aberdeen,
Peterhead, Fraserburgh (Grampian), Lerwick
(Shetland), Kinlochbervie, Ullapool
(Highland), North Shields (Tyne and Wear),
Hull, Grimsby (Humberside), Lowestoft
(Suffolk), Brixham (Devon), Newlyn
(Cornwall), and Kilkeel, Ardglass and
Portavogie (Northern Ireland).

A package of measures, including

new licensing rules, a £25 million decommissioning scheme and restrictions on the time vessels may spend at sea, is being introduced in January 1994.

Fish Farming

Fish farming production is centred on Atlantic salmon and rainbow trout, which are particularly suited to Britain's climate and waters. Production of salmon and trout has grown from less than 1,000 tonnes in the early 1970s to some 36,000 tonnes of salmon and 15,000 tonnes of trout in 1992. Scotland produces the largest amount of farmed salmon (36,000 tonnes in 1992—with a first-sale value of £120 million) in the Community. Shellfish farming concentrates on molluscs such as oysters, mussels, clams and scallops, producing an estimated 5,000 tonnes a year.

The fish and shellfish farming industries make an important contribution to rural infrastructure, especially in remote areas such as the Highlands and Islands of Scotland. In 1992 the industries were estimated to have a combined wholesale turnover of some £150 million. Production is based on almost 1,400 businesses operating from some 2,100 sites and employing more than 5,000 people.

Administration

The fisheries departments are responsible for the administration of legislation concerning the fishing industry and for fisheries research. The safety and welfare of crews of fishing vessels and other matters common to shipping generally are provided for under legislation administered by the Department of Transport.

The Sea Fish Industry Authority is concerned with all aspects of the industry, including consumer interests. It undertakes research and development, provides training, and encourages quality awareness. It also administers a government grant scheme for fishing vessels, to promote a safe, efficient and modern fleet.

Fishery Limits

British fishery limits extend to 200 miles or the median line (broadly halfway between the British coast and the opposing coastline of another coastal state), measured from baselines on or near the coast of Britain. Only British vessels may fish within 6 miles of the coast. Certain other EC member states have fishing rights between 6 and 12 miles in certain areas and for named species, as British vessels have in other member states' coastal waters. Outside 12 miles Community vessels may fish against agreed EC quotas in named areas, while the only non-Community countries whose vessels may fish in EC waters are those with which the EC has reciprocal fisheries agreements (Norway, Sweden and the Faroes) which define areas and quantities of species of permitted catch.

Common Fisheries Policy

The CFP's system for the conservation and management of the EC's fishing resources means that total allowable catches—with these decisions based on independent scientific advice—are set each year in order to conserve stocks. These catch levels are then allocated between member states on a fixed percentage basis, taking account of traditional fishing patterns. Activity is also regulated by a number of technical conservation measures, including minimum mesh sizes for towed nets and net configuration restrictions, minimum landing sizes and closed areas designated mainly to protect young fish. Each member state is responsible for ensuring that its own fishermen and those of other member states in its own waters abide by Community fisheries regulations and are monitored by EC inspectors.

The CFP also covers the common organisation of the market in fishery and aquaculture products and policies on the size and structure of the Community fleet.

The provisions of the CFP are supplemented by a number of fisheries agreements between the EC and third countries, the most important for Britain being the agreements with Norway, Greenland and the Faroe Islands. Community catch quotas have also been established in the international waters in the north-west Atlantic and around Spitzbergen (Svalbard).

Fish and Shellfish Hygiene

Community legislation sets minimum hygiene standards for the production and marketing of fish and shellfish. Live bivalve molluscs (oysters, mussels and scallops) can be marketed only if they come from areas classified by the Government according to strict microbiological standards. Minimum standards cover the handling, marketing and processing of all forms of fish from the vessel to wholesale vending.

Salmon and Freshwater Fisheries

Salmon and sea-trout are fished commercially in inshore waters around the British coast. Eels and elvers are also taken commercially in both estuaries and freshwater. Angling for salmon and sea-trout (game fishing) and for other freshwater species (coarse fishing) is popular throughout Britain. There is no public right to fish in freshwater lakes and rivers in England and Wales. Those wishing to fish such waters must first obtain permission from the owner of the fishing rights and a licence from the National Rivers Authority. In Scotland salmon fishing is administered by district salmon fishery boards. In Northern Ireland fishing is licensed by the Fisheries Conservancy Board for Northern Ireland and the Foyle Fisheries Commission in their respective areas, and 65 public angling waters, including salmon, trout and coarse fisheries, are accessible to Department of Agriculture permit holders.

Research

The total government-funded programme of research and development in agriculture, fisheries and food in 1993–94 amounts to some £319 million, including funding by the Ministry of Agriculture, Fisheries and Food, The Scottish Office Agriculture and Fisheries Department, the Department of Agriculture for Northern Ireland and the Office of Science and Technology. The Government funds research essential for the public good—for example, into food safety, human health,

animal welfare and flood protection. It also funds research which seeks to encourage an efficient and competitive industry consistent with high standards of consumer protection and care for the environment. It looks to industry, however, to fund those areas of research where the benefits can be captured by individual firms or ventures. Research is carried out in a network of research organisations, including research institutes, specialist laboratories and higher education institutions.

Agriculture and Food Research

The work of the Agricultural and Food Research Council (AFRC) and the agriculture departments is co-ordinated into national programmes of research, based primarily on the recommendations of the Priorities Board for Research and Development in Agriculture and Food. The Board advises on the research needs and on the allocation of available resources between and within areas of research.

The AFRC (see p. 276) is to be absorbed into the Biotechnology and Biological Sciences Research Council from 1994. It receives funds from the science budget through the Office of Science and Technology, and income from work commissioned by the Ministry of Agriculture, Fisheries and Food, by industry and by other bodies. The Council is responsible for research carried out in its eight institutes and in British higher education institutions through its research grants scheme.

In addition to commissioning research with the AFRC and other organisations, the Ministry commissions research and development at its agencies—the Central Veterinary Laboratory, the Central Science Laboratory (which is to incorporate the Food Science Laboratory from 1994), and ADAS. The five Scottish Agricultural Research Institutes, funded by The Scottish Office Agriculture and Fisheries Department, cover areas of research complementary to those of the AFRC institutes, while including work relevant to the soils, crops and livestock of northern Britain. Development work in Scotland is carried out by the Scottish

Agricultural College, which operates from three centres.

In Northern Ireland basic, strategic and applied research is carried out by the Department of Agriculture in its specialist research divisions and at its three agricultural colleges. It also has links with the Queen's University of Belfast and the Agricultural Research Institute of Northern Ireland.

Fisheries and Aquatic Environment Research

The Ministry of Agriculture, Fisheries and Food laboratories deal with marine and freshwater fisheries, shellfish, marine pollution, fish farming and disease. Research work is also commissioned by the Ministry with the Natural Environment Research Council, with the Sea Fish Industry Authority and with a number of universities. The Ministry has two seagoing research vessels. In Scotland, The Scottish Office Agriculture and Fisheries Department undertakes a similar, and complementary, range of research and also has two seagoing vessels. The Department of Agriculture laboratories in Northern Ireland undertake research on marine and freshwater fisheries, and also have a seagoing research vessel.

Forestry

Woodland covers an estimated 2.44 million hectares (6 million acres) in Britain: about 7 per cent of England, 15 per cent of Scotland, 12 per cent of Wales and 6 per cent of Northern Ireland—about 10 per cent of the total land area and well below the 25 per cent average for the whole of Europe. The Government supports the continued expansion of forestry, which makes an increasing contribution to meeting the national demand for timber; brings employment in forestry and related industries; creates opportunities for recreation and public access to the countryside; is a component of landscapes and a habitat for wildlife; and provides an effective means by which carbon dioxide can be absorbed from the atmosphere and stored over long periods. Over 215,000

hectares (530,000 acres) of new forest have been created during the last decade, mainly on the initiative and enterprise of private owners.

The area of productive forest in Great Britain is 2.17 million hectares (5.4 million acres), 39 per cent of which is managed by the Forestry Commission. The rate of new planting in 1992–93 was 2,356 hectares (5,822 acres) by the Commission and 15,295 hectares (37,795 acres) by other woodland owners, with the help of grants from the Commission, mainly in Scotland. In 1992–93, 8,625 hectares (21,312 acres) of broadleaved trees were planted, a practice encouraged on suitable sites. An increasing proportion of new planting is by private owners.

Wood production has nearly doubled since 1970. British woodlands meet 15 per cent of the nation's consumption of wood and wood products. The volume of timber harvested on Commission lands in 1992–93 totalled 4.1 million cubic metres (145 million cubic feet).

The Commission's expanded Woodland Grant Scheme pays establishment grants to help in the creation of new woodlands and forests and for the regeneration of existing ones. Management grants under the scheme contribute to the cost of managing woodlands to provide silvicultural, environmental and social benefits. Supplements are available for planting community woodlands and for planting on better land.

Total employment in state and private forests in Great Britain was estimated at some 42,000 in 1991–92, including about 10,000 people engaged in the haulage and processing of home-grown timber.

The Forestry Commission and Forestry Policy

The Forestry Commission, established in 1919, is the national forestry authority in Great Britain. The Commissioners give advice on forestry matters and are responsible to the Secretary of State for Scotland, the Minister of Agriculture, Fisheries and Food, and the Secretary of State for Wales.

Within the Commission, reorganised in 1992, the Forestry Authority administers felling licence procedures, provides advice to private woodland owners, administers payment of grants for approved planting and restocking schemes, and liaises with local authorities and woodland and countryside groups. Forest Enterprise develops and manages the Commission's forests and forestry estate as a multiple-use resource, provides timber for the wood-using industries and opportunities for recreation, and is responsible for nature conservation and the forest environment. A Policy and Resources Group is responsible for parliamentary business, policy development, and European and international liaison.

The Commission has sold 82,000 hectares (200,000 acres) of plantation and plantable land since 1981 and has been asked by the Government to dispose of 100,000 hectares (247,000 acres) during the 1990s. The Commission is financed partly by the Government and partly by receipts from sales of timber and other produce, and from rents.

Forestry Initiatives

The Forestry Commission and the Countryside Commission are creating 12 community forests (covering between 10,000 and 25,000 hectares each—40 to 100 sq miles) on the outskirts of major cities in England. They are in Tyneside, Cleveland, South Yorkshire, Merseyside, Greater Manchester, south Staffordshire, Nottingham, north Bedfordshire, south Hertfordshire, east of London, Swindon and Bristol. The Countryside Commission plans a large new forest, the National Forest, principally in Leicestershire, but extending into Derbyshire and Staffordshire. As part of its rural initiative for Wales, the Government encourages local communities to participate in the continuing development of 35,000 hectares (135 sq miles) of existing forest in the coalfield valleys of south Wales—about 20 per cent of the land area—which is owned by the Forestry Commission. The Central Scotland Woodlands Company, a Countryside Trust, has planted over 6 million trees.

Forestry Research

The Forestry Authority maintains two principal research stations, at Alice Holt Lodge, near Farnham (Surrey), and at Bush Estate, near Edinburgh, for basic and applied research into all aspects of forestry. Aid is also given for research work in universities and other institutions. A database on forestry and tree-related research in Great Britain has been compiled by the Forestry Research Co-ordination Committee and is updated annually.

The Forestry Authority conducts an annual forest health survey which monitors the effects of air pollution and other stress factors on a range of broadleaves and conifers. Research continues into the genetic improvement of broadleaves for farm forestry as well as into the afforestation of land reclaimed from industrial use.

Forestry in Northern Ireland

The Department of Agriculture may acquire land for afforestation and give financial and technical assistance for private planting. The state forest area has grown steadily since 1945. By 1992, 61,800 hectares (153,000 acres) of plantable land had been acquired, of which 60,800 hectares (150,000 acres) were planted. There were 16,000 hectares (39,500 acres) of privately owned forest. Some 435 professional and industrial staff work in state forests.

Further Reading

Agriculture, Fisheries and Forestry, Aspects of Britain series, HMSO, 1993.
Agriculture in the United Kingdom 1992. HMSO.

18 Transport and Communications

Britain's transport and communications infrastructure is developing rapidly. With the opening of the Channel Tunnel (see p. 255), the rail transport system of Great Britain becomes linked to that of the European mainland. Britain's road network is developing, with the emphasis now on upgrading existing routes rather than building new motorways. Investment at seaports and airports and in air traffic control equipment continues to expand capacity and facilitate the international movement of people and goods. In telecommunications, more operators are seeking to enter the market following a review of government policy (see p. 265) and existing operators are maintaining a high level of investment to create a thoroughly modern infrastructure.

Transport

There has been a considerable increase in passenger travel in recent years. Travel in Great Britain rose by 35 per cent between 1982 and 1992. Travel by car and van rose by 44 per cent and air travel expanded rapidly. However, travel by motor cycle and by bus and coach has been declining. In all, car and van travel accounts for 86 per cent of passenger mileage within Great Britain, buses and coaches for about 6 per cent, rail for 6 per cent and air less than 1 per cent.

Car ownership has also risen substantially. Some 67 per cent of households in Britain have the regular use of one or more cars, with 23 per cent having the use of two or more cars in 1991. At the end of 1992 there were 24.8 million vehicles licensed for use on the roads of Great Britain, of which 20.7 million were cars (including 2.3 million cars registered in the name of a company); 2.2 million light goods vehicles (that is, vehicles other than cars in the passenger and light goods category of vehicle); 437,000 other goods vehicles; 688,000 motor cycles, scooters and mopeds; and 108,000 public transport vehicles (including taxis).

ROADS

Total motor traffic for 1992 is estimated at 408,800 million vehicle-km. The total road network in Great Britain in 1992 was 362,400 km (225,200 miles). Trunk motorways accounted for 3,160 km (1,960 miles) of this length, less than 1 per cent, and other trunk roads for 12,330 km (7,660 miles), or about 3.5 per cent. However, motorways carry nearly 15 per cent of all traffic and trunk roads about 17 per cent. Combined, they carry over half of all goods vehicle traffic in Great Britain.

The Citizen's Charter commits the Government to improving service to motorists. The Department of Transport has speeded up repairs and deregulated the provision of motorway service areas. Legislation has also been passed to improve the standard of street repairs and minimise the frequency and duration of roadworks.

Administration

Responsibility for trunk roads in Great Britain, including most motorways, rests in England with the Secretary of State for Transport, in Scotland with the Secretary of State for Scotland and in Wales with the Secretary of State for Wales. The costs of construction and maintenance are paid for by central government.

The highway authorities for non-trunk roads are:

● in England, the county councils, the metropolitan district councils and the London borough councils;

● in Wales, the county councils; and

● in Scotland, the regional or islands councils.

In Northern Ireland the Department of the Environment for Northern Ireland is responsible for the construction, improvement and maintenance of all public roads.

Research on transport provides information necessary for the Department of Transport to set standards for highway and vehicle design;

to obtain better value for money in highway construction and repair; and to formulate transport, environmental and safety policies and legislation. Research is carried out by the Transport Research Laboratory (TRL). This is presently an executive agency of the Department of Transport, but the Government announced in May 1993 that it intends to transfer the TRL to the private sector. Research is also carried out by universities and other higher education institutions, consultants and industry, while some is done collaboratively within EC programmes.

Road Programme

The Government is implementing a major programme to improve the motorway and trunk road network (see map on page facing inside back cover). This programme is aimed at increasing the traffic capacity of major through routes and removing traffic from unsuitable roads in towns and villages. Over one-third of schemes in the programme are bypasses or relief roads. In spring 1993 some 50 motorway and trunk road schemes were under construction in England and over 400 further schemes were in preparation. Expenditure of about £1,380 million on new trunk road construction is planned for 1993–94, with 41 new schemes due to start. These include the upgrading of 21 km (13 miles) of the A1 to motorway status. A major package of improvements to ease congestion on the M25 was announced in July 1993. The trunk road maintenance programme is a record £550 million. Some 316 major local

Table 17.1: Road Length (as at April 1992)

	Public roads	All-purpose trunk roads and trunk motorways	Trunk motorways[a]
England	276,851	10,582	2,712
Scotland	52,049	3,197	325
Wales	33,513	1,710	120
Northern Ireland	24,218	2,325	113
Britain	**386,631**	**17,814**	**3,270**

Sources: Department of Transport, Northern Ireland Department of the Environment, Scottish Office and Welsh Office.
[a] In addition, there were 68 km (42 miles) of local authority motorway in England and 24 km (15 miles) in Scotland.

authority road schemes are being supported by the Department of Transport, including 41 new schemes. Some £1,047 million is available to support local authority road schemes in England in 1993–94.

> A new deregulated regime for the provision of motorway service areas was announced by the Government in August 1992. It passes responsibility for development to the private sector while ensuring that all sites continue to meet a specified range of minimum standards.

Road communications in Wales will benefit from the second Severn crossing, the completion of the M4 motorway and improvements in the A55 coast road in north Wales. Improvements to the A55 include the construction under the Conwy estuary of the first immersed tube road tunnel to be built in Britain, opened in 1991. Work on upgrading the final section of the A55 to dual carriageway began in February 1993. The Welsh Office's roads and transport programme for 1993–94 totals £201 million. Some £73 million is also being made available to support major local authority road schemes in Wales.

The Government has committed almost £290 million over three years to new road construction in Scotland. The main priorities within the trunk road programme in Scotland are the upgrading of the A74 to motorway standard, which is now well advanced, and completion of the central Scotland motorway network. These routes provide important links for commerce and industry to the south and to mainland Europe. The Government's future strategy also includes a series of 'route action plans' designed significantly to improve safety and journey times on specific major routes. The possibility of a privately funded second road bridge across the Firth of Forth is also being considered.

In Northern Ireland the emphasis is on improving arterial routes, constructing more bypasses, and improving roads in the Belfast area, including the construction of a new cross-harbour link planned for the mid-1990s.

Private Finance

The Government encourages greater private sector involvement in the design, construction, operation and funding of roads. A framework for encouraging privately funded schemes is provided for in recent legislation. Privately funded schemes recently completed or being undertaken include:

- a crossing of the River Thames at Dartford, which opened to traffic in late 1991 and links into the M25 London orbital motorway;

- a second crossing of the River Severn, which should be completed by 1996;

- a relief road north of Birmingham, which will be the first overland toll route in Britain; and

- a bridge between the mainland of Scotland and Skye, the construction of which is now under way.

In 1993 the Government issued a consultation paper on the wider application of tolls on routes between cities and on ways of involving private finance.

Licensing and Standards

Official records of drivers and vehicles are maintained by the Driver and Vehicle Licensing Agency (DVLA). At the end of 1992 it held records on 34.5 million drivers and 24.8 million licensed vehicles in Great Britain. New drivers of motor vehicles are required to pass a driving test before being granted a full licence to drive.

The Driving Standards Agency is the national driver testing authority. It also supervises professional driving instructors and the compulsory basic training scheme for new motor cyclists. Minimum ages are:

- 16 for riders of mopeds and disabled drivers of specially adapted vehicles;

- 17 for drivers of cars and other passenger vehicles with nine or fewer seats (including that of the driver), motor cycles and goods vehicles not over 3.5 tonnes permissible maximum weight;

- 18 for goods vehicles over 3.5 but not over 7.5 tonnes; and

- 21 for passenger vehicles with over nine seats and goods vehicles over 7.5 tonnes.

Before most new cars and goods vehicles are allowed on the roads, they are required to meet a number of safety and environmental requirements, based primarily on standards drawn up by the European Community. This form of control, known as type approval, is operated by the Vehicle Certification Agency.

The Secretary of State for Transport has a statutory responsibility for ensuring the roadworthiness of vehicles in use on the roads. The Vehicle Inspectorate is the national testing and enforcement authority. It meets this responsibility mainly through:

- annual testing and certification of heavy and light goods vehicles, buses and coaches;

- administration of the 'MOT' testing scheme, under which cars and motor cycles are tested at private garages authorised as test stations and light goods vehicles may be tested there rather than at a government test centre;

- roadside enforcement checks of roadworthiness, overloading and drivers' hours;

- carrying out, on behalf of the Traffic Commissioners, investigations and assessments of operators' vehicle maintenance arrangements; and

- the investigation of serious accidents and vehicle defects, and overseeing vehicle recall campaigns.

In Northern Ireland the Driver and Vehicle Testing Agency (DVTA) is responsible for testing drivers and vehicles under statutory schemes broadly similar to those in Great Britain. Private cars five or more years old are tested at DVTA centres.

Road Safety

Although Great Britain has one of the highest densities of road traffic in the world, it has a good record on road safety, with the lowest road accident death rate in the European Community. Figures for 1992 show that some 4,230 people were killed on the roads, 49,200

seriously injured and 257,200 slightly injured. The figure for deaths was the lowest since records began in 1926, and compares with nearly 8,000 deaths a year in the mid-1960s. A number of factors, such as developments in vehicle safety standards, improvements in roads, the introduction of legislation on seat-belt wearing and drinking and driving, and developments in road safety training, education and publicity, have contributed to the long-term decline in serious casualties.

A new edition of the *Highway Code*, launched in January 1993, notched up sales of 2 million copies in less than three months.

The Government's aim is to reduce road casualties by one-third by the end of the century, compared with the 1981–85 average. To achieve this, resources are being concentrated on measures which are demonstrably cost-effective in reducing casualties. Priority is given to reducing casualties among vulnerable road-users (children, pedestrians, cyclists, motor cyclists and older road users), particularly in urban areas, where some 75 per cent of road accidents occur. For example, the child road safety campaign is directed at encouraging drivers to slow down when children are likely to be about, particularly in urban areas. Other areas for achieving lower casualties are improvements in highway design, better protection for vehicle occupants, encouraging the use of cycle helmets and measures to combat drinking and driving.

The Road Traffic Act 1991 introduced several additional measures to improve road safety, including the use of new technology, such as remote-operated cameras, to improve the detection of speeding and traffic-light offences.

Traffic in Towns

Traffic management schemes are used in many urban areas to reduce congestion, create a better environment and improve road safety. Such schemes include, for example, one-way streets, bus lanes, facilities for pedestrians and cyclists, and traffic-calming measures such as road humps and chicanes to constrain traffic speeds in residential areas. Many towns have shopping precincts designed for the convenience of pedestrians, from which motor vehicles are excluded for all or part of the day. Controls over on-street parking are enforced through excess charges and fixed penalties, supported where appropriate by powers to remove vehicles. In parts of London wheel clamping to immobilise illegally parked vehicles is also used.

> The fiftieth 20 mph (32 km/h) zone in England was opened in March 1993 in Poole, Dorset, little more than two years after the 20 mph zone concept was approved by the Government. Early evidence from the TRL suggests that the zones are reducing casualties by well in excess of 50 per cent.

In June 1992 the Government announced the designation of a network of priority 'red routes' in London some 480 km (300 miles) long. It is expected that the first of these routes will be in operation during 1994. Red routes, to be marked by red lining and special signs, will be subject to special stopping controls and other traffic management measures, strictly enforced with higher penalties. The Traffic Director for London has been appointed to co-ordinate the introduction and operation of the priority routes throughout London. A pilot scheme in north and east London, introduced in 1991, has brought about significant falls in journey times and greater reliability for buses, with a consequent rise in passenger numbers. Accident casualties along the route have dropped significantly.

The Government has also set up a wide-ranging study into urban traffic congestion, including the lessons to be learnt from improvements to traffic management in other countries, and the question of 'congestion charging' in London and other cities.

ROAD HAULAGE

Road haulage traffic by heavy goods vehicles amounted to 121,250 million tonne-km in 1992, 3 per cent less than in 1991. There has been a move towards larger and more efficient vehicles carrying heavier loads— about 78 per cent of the traffic, measured in tonne-km, is carried by vehicles of over 25 tonnes laden weight. Much of the traffic is moved over short distances, with 74 per cent of the tonnage being carried on hauls of 100 km (62 miles) or less. Public haulage (private road hauliers carrying other firms' goods) accounts for 71 per cent of freight carried in Great Britain in terms of tonne-km. In 1992 the main commodities handled by heavy goods vehicles were:

- crude minerals (327 million tonnes);
- food, drink and tobacco (290 million tonnes); and
- building materials (136 million tonnes).

Road haulage is predominantly an industry of small, privately owned businesses. There were some 133,600 holders of an operator's licence in 1991. About half the heavy goods vehicles are in fleets of ten or fewer vehicles. The biggest operators in Great Britain are NFC plc, Transport Development Group plc, TNT Express (UK) Ltd and United Carriers International Ltd.

Licensing and Other Controls

In general, those operating goods vehicles or trailer combinations over 3.5 tonnes gross weight require a goods vehicle operator's licence. Licences are divided into restricted licences for own-account operators carrying goods connected with their own business, and standard licences for hauliers operating for hire or reward. Proof of professional competence, financial standing and good repute is needed to obtain a standard licence. Responsibility for granting licences rests with seven independent Traffic Commissioners. In Northern Ireland own-account operators do not require a licence, although this matter is under consideration.

Regulations lay down limits on the hours worked by drivers of goods vehicles, and minimum rest periods. Tachographs, which automatically record speed, distance covered, driving time and stopping periods, must be fitted and used in most goods vehicles over 3.5 tonnes gross weight in Great Britain.

Speed limiters must also be fitted to heavy lorries. Originally these had to be set to limit speed to 60 mph (97 km/h), but from January 1994 a programme is beginning to reduce this gradually to 56 mph (90 km/h).

International Road Haulage

International road haulage has grown rapidly and in 1992 about 1.4 million road goods vehicles were ferried to mainland Europe or the Irish Republic. Of these, 374,000 were powered vehicles registered in Britain. In 1992 British vehicles carried almost 10 million tonnes internationally either inwards or outwards, double the amount carried in 1984. About 95 per cent of this traffic was with the European Community.

International road haulage within the EC was fully liberalised from January 1993. Pending the liberalisation of 'cabotage' (the operation of domestic road haulage services within a member state by a non-resident), quotas of permits are available which allow cabotage anywhere within the EC. Haulage with other countries takes place under bilateral agreements, most of which allow unrestricted numbers of British lorries into the country concerned, while some specify an annual quota of permits. The European Conference of Transport Ministers issues a limited number of permits which allow free access to, and transit across, a number of countries in Central and Eastern Europe and in Scandinavia.

PASSENGER SERVICES

Major changes in the structure of the passenger transport industry have occurred in recent years. Privatisation of the National Bus Company (which was the largest single bus and coach operator in Britain, operating through 72 subsidiaries in England and Wales) was completed in 1988. Each subsidiary was sold separately, and encouragement was given for a buy-out by the local management or employees. London Transport (LT) is a statutory corporation, with its board members appointed by the Secretary of State for Transport. Within LT

the main wholly-owned operating subsidiaries are London Underground Ltd (LUL) and London Buses Ltd; the Government intends to offer the latter's operating companies for sale from late 1993 (see p. 252). The privatisation as ten separate companies of the Scottish Bus Group, formerly the largest operator of bus services in Scotland, with some 3,000 vehicles, was completed in 1991. The Government is committed to the privatisation of the remaining local authority-owned bus companies, but these sales are on a voluntary basis at present.

> LT is testing a new bus passenger information system. Called Countdown, the system gives information via dot-matrix displays installed at 50 stops along the number 18 route in north London.

In Northern Ireland almost all road passenger services are provided by subsidiaries of the publicly owned Northern Ireland Transport Holding Company. Citybus Ltd operates services in Belfast, and Ulsterbus Ltd operates most of the services in the rest of Northern Ireland. These companies have some 300 and 1,000 vehicles respectively. As part of the Northern Ireland Citizen's Charter initiative, the bus companies published a bus passengers' charter in February 1993. This sets out the companies' commitment to customer care and higher standards of service through targets for punctuality, reliability and cleanliness. Reports on the quality of service are published twice a year in conjunction with the General Consumer Council for Northern Ireland.

As well as major bus operators, there are also many small, privately owned undertakings, often operating fewer than five vehicles. Double-deck buses are the main type of vehicle used for urban road passenger transport in Britain, with some 21,000 in operation. However, there has been a substantial increase in the number of minibuses and midibuses in recent years, with some 20,000 now in use. In addition, there are some 30,000 other single-deck buses and coaches. Some 3,500 million local bus journeys were made in 1991–92.

Some £15.5 million has been allocated by the Government in 1993–94 to local authorities in England alone for measures to promote bus use, such as bus lanes, bus priority signalling and park-and-ride schemes.

International Travel

British coaches regularly travel across the continent of Europe, carrying passengers as far afield as Greece and increasingly to Eastern European countries. Regular coach services still require authorisation or permission from the authorities of the countries to or through which they travel. However, most tourist bus services within the EC have now been liberalised. Operators no longer need prior permission to run either holiday shuttle services, where accommodation is included as part of the package, or occasional coach tours to, from or within another member state.

Deregulation

Local bus services in Great Britain (except in London) were deregulated in 1986, so that bus operators are now able to run routes without needing a special licence. Deregulation led to an increase of 20 per cent in local bus mileage outside London between 1985–86 and 1991–92, with some 84 per cent of services operated without subsidy in 1991–92. Over the same period the number of passengers has fallen by 22 per cent outside London, in line with long-term trends. Long-distance express coach services have also been deregulated, bringing about reductions in fares, the provision of more services and an increase in passengers. Local authorities can subsidise the provision of socially necessary local bus services after competitive tendering.

The Government is proposing the deregulation of bus services in London and the privatisation of London Buses Ltd. LT is already required to involve the private sector in the provision of services where this is more efficient, and many London bus routes are now run by private firms operating under

contract to LT. It is proposed to begin the sale of the London Buses Ltd subsidiaries in late 1993, once all the services have been put on a contractual basis. Deregulation is unlikely before 1995. On deregulation, provision would be made for the operation of socially necessary but uneconomic services and for the continuation of a London-wide concessionary travel scheme.

Taxis

There are about 56,000 licensed taxis in Great Britain, mainly in urban areas; London has about 17,000. In London and a number of other cities taxis must be purpose-built to conform to very strict requirements and new ones have to provide for people in wheelchairs. In most cases, drivers must have passed a test of their knowledge of the area. Private hire vehicles with drivers may be booked only through the operator and not hired on the street; in most areas outside London private hire vehicles are licensed.

A local authority can only limit the number of licensed taxis if it is satisfied that there is no unfulfilled demand for taxis in its area. Taxi operators are able to run regular local services and can tender in competition with bus operators for services subsidised by local authorities. To do this, they may apply for a special 'restricted' bus operator's licence, allowing them to run local services without having to obtain a full bus operator's licence. Taxis and licensed private hire vehicles may also offer shared rides to passengers paying separate fares.

There are some 4,000 licensed taxis in Northern Ireland. Licences are issued by the Department of the Environment for Northern Ireland on a basis broadly similar to that in Great Britain.

RAILWAYS

Railways were pioneered in Britain: the Stockton and Darlington Railway, opened in 1825, was the first public passenger railway in the world to be worked by steam power. The main railway companies in Great Britain were nationalised in 1948.

Organisation

The British Railways Board, set up in 1962, controls most of the railway network in Great Britain. Of its six business sectors, InterCity, Network SouthEast and Regional Railways services are responsible for the passenger services. The other three sectors are Railfreight Distribution, Trainload Freight and Parcels. A subsidiary company, European Passenger Services Ltd, has been set up to operate international passenger rail services through the Channel Tunnel. Other subsidiary businesses include Union Railways, which is responsible for taking forward proposals for a high-speed rail link between London and the Channel Tunnel.

Proposed Privatisation

The Government wishes to improve services as rapidly as possible and considers that privatisation—giving the private sector the opportunity to operate existing services and introduce new ones—is the best way to bring this about for both passengers and freight customers. Its proposals, published in July 1992, include:

- the franchising of all British Rail's existing passenger services to the private sector;

- the transfer of British Rail's existing freight and parcels operations to the private sector;

- the creation of a new right of access to the rail network for private operators of both passenger and freight services;

- the separation of track from train operations, expected in April 1994, under which British Rail will be divided into track management—Railtrack—and a unit to operate passenger services until they are franchised to the private sector;

- the creation of two independent authorities responsible to the Government—a Rail Regulator to oversee the fair application of arrangements for track access and charging, and a Franchising Director responsible for negotiating, awarding and monitoring franchises;

- opportunities for the private sector to lease stations; and

- improved grant arrangements for individual rail services or groups of services.

Legislation has been introduced in Parliament to secure these objectives. The Government has set British Rail the aim of privatising Red Star, its parcels service, during 1993.

Table 17.2: Railway Operations

	1988–89	1989–90	1990–91	1991–92	1992–93
Passenger journeys (million)	764	758	763	740	745
Passenger-km (million)	34,322	33,648	33,191	32,057	31,693
Freight traffic (million tonnes)	150	143	138	136	122
Trainload and wagonload traffic (million net-tonne km)	18,103	16,742	15,986	15,347	15,509
Assets at end of period:					
Locomotives	2,180	2,095	2,030	1,896	1,794
High Speed Train power units	197	197	197	197	197
Other coaching units	14,258	13,833	13,631	12,925	12,309
Freight vehicles[a]	24,922	21,970	20,763	19,877	15,912
Stations (including freight and parcels)	2,596	2,598	2,615	2,556	2,543
Route open for traffic (km)	16,598	16,588	16,584	16,558	16,527

Source: British Railways Board.

[a] In addition, a number of privately owned wagons and locomotives are operated on the railway network for customers of British Rail.

Operations

In 1992–93 British Rail's turnover, including financial support and income from other activities but excluding internal transactions, was £3,863 million, of which £2,153 million was derived from rail passenger services and £635 million from freight services. It received grants of £1,150 million as compensation for the public service obligation to operate sections of the passenger network in the Regional sector and Network SouthEast that would not otherwise cover their cost.

As part of the Citizen's Charter initiative, British Rail has agreed detailed service standards with the Government for the InterCity, Network SouthEast and Regional Railways sectors and published its Passenger's Charter. Compensation is payable to passengers when service falls by more than a small margin below these standards. Several standards have since been raised as part of a 1993 review. Service is also being improved through better information, staff training and extra assistance for disabled passengers. British Rail launched its TrackRecord initiative in May 1992, keeping passengers informed of reliability and punctuality at main stations throughout the country. Quality of service is one of the key objectives that the Government has set for British Rail.

British Rail has a substantial investment programme, which totalled £1,354 million in 1992–93. Major areas of expenditure in British Rail's investment programme include rolling stock and facilities for Channel Tunnel traffic from the opening of the tunnel (see p. 255) and new rolling stock and infrastructure improvements in Network SouthEast.

Safety continues to be a priority for British Rail. Railways remain one of the safest means of transport, with the number of significant train accidents per million miles in 1991–92 the lowest on record. British Rail's safety plan, first published in 1991, shows a commitment to achieving even higher standards of railway safety.

Passenger Services

The passenger network (see map facing inside back cover) comprises a fast inter-city network, linking the main centres of Great Britain; local stopping services; and commuter services in and around the large conurbations, especially London and south-east England. British Rail runs some 750 InterCity trains a day, serving about 90 business and leisure centres. InterCity 125 trains, travelling at maximum sustained speeds of 125 mph (201 km/h) are the world's fastest diesel trains. With the introduction of the new electric InterCity 225 trains, British Rail now has more trains running at over 100 mph (160 km/h) than any other country in Europe.

About 30 per cent of route-mileage is electrified, including British Rail's busiest InterCity route, linking London, the West Midlands, the North West and Glasgow. The most recent major electrification scheme was that for the east coast main line between London and Edinburgh (including the line from Doncaster to Leeds). This scheme, covering some 644 km (400 miles) and costing £531 million at 1991 prices, commenced full passenger services between London King's Cross and Edinburgh in July 1991, using InterCity 225 electric trains.

A new generation of diesel multiple-unit trains has been introduced on regional services, while many of the older electric multiple units used for commuting services in London and south-east England are being replaced by more efficient rolling stock. The first of a new generation of 'Networker' trains entered service in Kent in November 1992, and some 674 coaches will be in service by mid-1994. Investment in the trains and associated track improvements will total £800 million. A diesel version is being brought into service on lines to the west of London, with some 240 vehicles due to be delivered between 1992 and 1994.

Three major new rail links to airports have recently been built or are planned:

- a new link between Stansted airport and London Liverpool Street, which opened in 1991;

- a link to connect Manchester airport to the Manchester to Wilmslow (Cheshire) line, which opened in May 1993; and

- a £235 million project for a line between London Paddington and Heathrow airport, to be built as a joint venture with BAA plc, the airport's owner.

Freight

Over 90 per cent of rail freight traffic is of bulk commodities, mainly coal, coke, iron and steel, building materials and petroleum. The opening of the Channel Tunnel will present an important opportunity for non-bulk freight movement. The Government makes grants to encourage companies to move goods by rail rather than road; some 200 schemes have been assisted since 1975 at a cost of £78 million. It is intended that freight users will enjoy rights of open access to the rail network from April 1994. This will allow the introduction of services by new rail freight operators and companies operating on their own account.

One of the largest ever grants to help companies move freight by rail rather than road was announced in June 1992. A total of £4.25 million will assist in the construction of facilities to move 500,000 tonnes of coal a year from the Neath Valley to Cardiff docks. This will remove some 25,000 lorry movements a year from the south Wales road network.

Northern Ireland

In Northern Ireland the Northern Ireland Railways Company Ltd, a subsidiary of the Northern Ireland Transport Holding Company, operates the railway service on some 320 km (200 miles) of track. It published a revised passenger charter in November 1992. This includes a compensation scheme that operates if targets for punctuality and reliability are not met. Reports on the quality of service are published in conjunction with the General Consumer Council for Northern Ireland.

Channel Tunnel

Work is almost complete on the Channel Tunnel, the largest civil engineering project in Europe to be financed by the private sector. Services through the tunnel are estimated to start in early 1994, with the full range of services operating by mid-1994. The project,

which is estimated to have cost £8,400 million up to the opening, is being undertaken by Eurotunnel, a British–French group which has a 55-year concession agreement from the British and French governments. This gives Eurotunnel the right to build the tunnel and operate it for 55 years. Construction is being carried out for Eurotunnel by Transmanche Link, a consortium of ten British and French construction companies. The first link-up under the Channel, that of the central service tunnel, took place in December 1990, and break-through of the two rail tunnels was achieved by mid-1991.

Eurotunnel Services

Eurotunnel will operate shuttle trains through the tunnel between the terminals near Folkestone and Calais, with the journey taking about 35 minutes from platform to platform. Eurotunnel trains will provide a drive-on, drive-off service, with separate shuttle trains for passenger and freight vehicles. Car and coach passengers will stay with their vehicles during the journey. Lorry drivers will travel separately from their vehicles, in a carriage at the front of the shuttle. When full services are established, Eurotunnel plans to run passenger shuttle services every 15 minutes and freight shuttle services every 20 minutes at peak periods. As traffic grows, it should be possible for the frequency of services to be increased.

British Rail Services

British Rail plans to invest some £1,400 million in new passenger and freight rolling stock and infrastructure improvements for Channel Tunnel services; over £1,000 million has already been approved. Some 30 high-speed through passenger services are planned to run each day between the London terminal at Waterloo and Paris or Brussels, starting in summer 1994 and using specially-designed international rolling stock. Further rolling stock, incorporating additional modifications, is on order to provide through passenger day-services from the Midlands, northern England and Scotland to the mainland of

Europe. Rolling stock is on order to provide overnight passenger services from Scotland, the North West, south Wales and the South West, as well as from London, to continental destinations.

Nine regional intermodal freight terminals will be established for Channel Tunnel services. With the infrastructure improvements that British Rail has under way, and the design of wagons that British Rail intends to use, well over 90 per cent of standard continental swap-bodies and containers will be able to travel over the lines between the tunnel and the British terminal network, even though the British loading gauge is smaller than the continental loading gauge. The terminal facilities will allow the easy transfer of freight between road and rail. British Rail forecasts that it will transport some 6 million tonnes of freight a year through the tunnel.

To meet the forecast growth in demand for through rail services, additional capacity will eventually be required between London and the Channel Tunnel. In March 1993 the Government announced detailed proposals for the route of a new high-speed rail link crossing the River Thames and running through east London to a second London terminal, for which the preferred location is St Pancras. It is intended that the £2,500 million project is taken forward as a joint venture between the private and public sectors. The Government has said that it is willing to provide substantial public sector support. The route is being designed so that it can also carry freight if necessary.

Railways in London

London Underground Ltd operates services on 392 km (244 miles) of railway, of which about 167 km (105 miles) are underground. The system has 248 stations, with 459 trains operating in the peak period. Some 728 million passenger journeys were made on London Underground trains in 1992–93. Major investment in the Underground is planned, including an extension of the Jubilee Line to Stratford (east London) via Docklands and the north Greenwich peninsula, dependent upon negotiations over a substantial private

sector contribution. A proposed CrossRail scheme would link Paddington with Liverpool Street via a tunnel which would be used by British Rail as well as Underground trains. Much work is also under way updating the existing system, including a £750 million modernisation of the Central Line and the refurbishment of over 200 trains at a cost of £195 million. Total LUL investment will be about £500 million in 1993–94, rising to over £600 million in 1995–96.

LUL now has a charter that sets out standards of service to passengers and the compensation arrangements that apply if these standards are not met.

The Docklands Light Railway (DLR), a 12-km (7.5-mile) route with 17 stations, provides a service between the City of London and Docklands. An extension eastward to Beckton in the Royal Docks is expected to open in autumn 1993 and, subject to private finance being available, the line may be extended under the River Thames to Lewisham (south-east London). The ownership of the DLR was transferred from LT to the London Docklands Development Corporation in April 1992. The Government is currently considering the best way of privatising the DLR.

A light rail network, which would link Wimbledon, Beckenham and New Addington to the centre of Croydon, is being promoted by LT and the London borough of Croydon. The 28-km (18-mile) network could be open by 1997.

Other Urban Railways

Other urban railways in Great Britain are the Glasgow Underground and the Tyne and Wear Metro, a 59-km (37-mile) light rapid transit system. In Greater Manchester the first phase of the 31-km (19-mile) Metrolink light rail system was officially opened in July 1992. Owned by the Greater Manchester Passenger Transport Executive and operated and maintained by GMML, a private sector consortium, it links Manchester's main railway termini with Bury and Altrincham. Midland Metro, a major light rail project in the West Midlands, has been approved by Parliament. Light rail schemes are being considered in a number of other areas, including Bristol, Cardiff, Chester, Cleveland, Edinburgh, Glasgow, Leeds, Nottingham, and Portsmouth.

> The Government has allocated nearly £120 million in 1993–94 to local authorities in England in support of local passenger transport schemes. Of this, some £50 million is allocated towards the construction of the 29-km (18-mile) South Yorkshire Supertram system in Sheffield. The system is scheduled to be completed by the end of 1995.

Private Railways

There are over 100 small, privately owned passenger-carrying railways in Great Britain, mostly operated on a voluntary basis and providing limited services for tourists and railway enthusiasts. The main aim of most of these railways is the preservation and operation of steam locomotives. They are generally run on old British Rail branch lines, but there are also several narrow-gauge lines, mainly in north Wales.

INLAND WATERWAYS

Inland waterways are popular for recreation, make a valuable contribution to the quality of Britain's environment, play an important part in land drainage and water supply, and are used to a limited extent for freight-carrying. The most significant amounts of freight are carried on the Rivers Thames, Forth, Humber and Mersey and the Manchester Ship Canal.

A government working group was established in December 1992 to study the use of the River Thames for transport. It aims to identify the scope for private sector development which would assist in fulfilling the river's potential for freight and passenger traffic.

The publicly owned British Waterways Board (BWB) is responsible for some 3,200 km (2,000 miles) of waterways in Great Britain. The majority of waterways are primarily for leisure use, but about 620 km (385 miles) are maintained as commercial waterways. The BWB is developing its historical heritage for recreational and commercial use, often in conjunction with the private sector. In 1992–93 the BWB's turnover amounted to £84.6 million, including a government grant of £51.1 million to maintain its waterways to statutory standards.

SHIPPING AND PORTS

In March 1993 British companies owned 704 trading vessels of 13.6 million deadweight tonnes. Among the ships owned by British companies were 169 vessels totalling 8.1 million deadweight tonnes used as oil, chemical or gas carriers and 507 vessels totalling 5.5 million deadweight tonnes employed as dry-bulk carriers, container ships or other types of cargo ship. Some 73 per cent of British-owned vessels are registered in Britain or British dependent territories such as Bermuda.

The tonnage of the British-registered trading fleet has been declining in recent years. In recognition of this and in response to the 1990 report of a joint government and shipping industry working party, the Government has simplified technical procedures and regulations for the purpose of ship registration. The Government also makes funds available for Merchant Navy officer training, the repatriation of crews in the deep-sea trades and to support a Reserve of ex-seafarers willing to serve in the Merchant Navy in an emergency.

Cargo Services

About 94 per cent by weight (76 per cent by value) of Britain's overseas trade is carried by sea. In 1992 British seaborne trade amounted to 311 million tonnes (valued at £178,000 million) or 1,240,000 million tonne-km (770,000 million tonne-miles). British-registered ships carried 19 per cent by weight and 36 per cent by value. Tanker cargo accounted for 44 per cent of this trade by weight, but only 7 per cent by value; dry cargoes including foodstuffs and manufactured goods accounted for 93 per cent by value.

Virtually all the scheduled cargo-liner services from Britain are containerised. The British tonnage serving these trades is dominated by a relatively small number of private sector companies and, in deep-sea trades, they usually operate in conjunction with other companies on the same routes in organisations known as 'conferences'. The object of these groupings is to ensure regular and efficient services with stable freight rates, to the benefit of both shipper and shipowner. In addition to the carriage of freight by liner and bulk services between Britain and the rest of Europe, there are many roll-on, roll-off services to carry cars, passengers and commercial vehicles.

Passenger Services

In 1992 there were 33 million international sea passenger movements between Britain and the rest of the world, compared with some 82 million international air movements. Almost all the passengers who arrived at or departed from British ports travelled to or from the continent of Europe or the Irish Republic. In 1992 some 72,000 people embarked on pleasure cruises from British ports. Traffic from the southern and south-eastern ports accounts for a substantial proportion of traffic to the continent of Europe. The main British operators are Sealink Stena Line, P & O and Hoverspeed, although not all their vessels are under the British flag. Services are provided by roll-on, roll-off ferries, hovercraft, hydrofoils and high-speed catamarans. There has been a trend towards larger vessels in recent years as the ferry companies prepare for competition from the Channel Tunnel. For example, P & O has recently introduced the *Pride of Burgundy*, which can carry 600 cars, on the Dover–Calais route, and the *Pride of Bilbao*, at 37,500 tonnes the largest ferry plying out of a British port, on the Portsmouth–Bilbao route.

Domestic passenger and freight ferry services also run to many of the offshore islands, such as the Isle of Wight, the Orkney and Shetland islands, and the islands off the west coast of Scotland. It is estimated that in

1991 there were some 36 million passengers on such internal services.

Merchant Shipping Legislation and Policy

The Government's policy is one of minimum intervention and the encouragement of free and fair competition. However, regulations administered by the Department of Transport provide for marine safety and welfare, the investigation of accidents and the prevention and cleaning up of pollution from ships.

Britain also plays an important role in the formulation of shipping policy within the EC. The first stage of a Common Shipping Policy involved agreement in 1986 on regulations designed to:

- liberalise the Community's international trade;
- establish a competitive regime for shipping; and
- enable the Community to take action to combat protectionism from other countries and to counter unfair pricing practices.

For the second stage, now under consideration, a range of measures has been proposed to harmonise operating conditions and strengthen the competitiveness of Community members' merchant fleets. Some measures, such as facilitating the transfer of ships between member states' registers and liberalising shipping within member states, have already been agreed. The Government has welcomed a European Commission document, *A Common Policy on Safe Seas*, which sets out an action programme for maritime safety and pollution prevention within the Community.

Ports

There are about 80 ports of commercial significance in Great Britain, and in addition there are several hundred small harbours that cater for local cargo, fishing vessels, island ferries or recreation. Port authorities are of three broad types—trusts, local authorities and companies—and most operate with statutory powers under private Acts of

Parliament. Major ports controlled by trusts include Aberdeen, Dover, Ipswich, Milford Haven and Tyne. Local authorities own many small ports and a few much larger ports, including Portsmouth and the oil ports in Orkney and Shetland. The Ports Act 1991 facilitates the transfer of trust ports fully to the private sector; Clyde, Forth, Medway, Tees and Hartlepool and the Port of London Authority dock undertaking at Tilbury have already moved to the private sector.

Associated British Ports Holdings plc (a private sector company) operates 22 ports, including Cardiff, Grimsby and Immingham, Hull, Newport, Southampton and Swansea. Together its ports handled 105 million tonnes of cargo in 1992. Other major ports owned by companies include Felixstowe, Liverpool, Manchester and a group of ferry ports, including Harwich (Parkeston Quay) and Stranraer.

Port Traffic

In 1992 traffic through the ports of Britain amounted to 495 million tonnes, comprising 150 million tonnes of exports, 182 million tonnes of imports and 163 million tonnes of domestic traffic (which included offshore traffic and landings of sea-dredged aggregates). About 54 per cent of the traffic was in fuels, mainly petroleum and petroleum products.

Britain's main ports, in terms of total tonnage handled, are given in Table 17.3.

Sullom Voe (Shetland), Milford Haven and Forth mostly handle oil, while the main ports for non-fuel traffic are Dover, Felixstowe, Grimsby and Immingham, Liverpool, London, and Tees and Hartlepool.

Container and roll-on, roll-off traffic in Britain has more than trebled since 1975 to 93 million tonnes in 1992 and now accounts for about 77 per cent of non-bulk traffic. The leading ports for container traffic are Felixstowe, London and Southampton. Those for roll-on, roll-off traffic are Dover (Britain's leading seaport in terms of the value of trade handled), Felixstowe, Portsmouth and Ramsgate.

Development

Most recent major port developments have been at east- and south-coast ports. For example, at Felixstowe a £50 million extension to the terminal was completed in 1990, and a new £100 million terminal on the River Medway caters for deep-sea container traffic. Recent investment by Associated British Ports includes:

- a £14 million extension of the oil terminal at Immingham;

- an £11 million roll-on, roll-off terminal at Hull; and

- a new riverside quay at King's Lynn, costing £3 million.

Purpose-built terminals for oil from the British sector of the North Sea have been

Table 17.3: Traffic Through the Principal Ports of Great Britain

million tonnes

	1982	1987	1988	1989	1990	1991	1992
London	46.9	48.9	53.7	54.0	54.5	52.8	48.9
Tees and Hartlepool	35.7	33.9	37.4	39.3	40.2	42.9	43.4
Sullom Voe	46.3	50.0	50.6	40.7	30.6	35.9	41.4
Grimsby and Immingham	27.6	32.2	35.0	38.1	38.9	40.2	40.8
Milford Haven	36.0	32.7	33.3	33.0	32.2	35.7	35.6
Southampton	21.6	27.2	31.4	26.1	28.8	31.5	29.6
Liverpool	9.8	10.2	19.6	20.2	23.2	24.8	27.8
Forth	27.5	30.0	29.0	22.9	25.4	22.9	23.3
Felixstowe	7.6	13.3	15.6	16.5	16.4	16.1	17.0
Medway	12.6	11.6	12.7	14.0	15.9	16.1	14.3
Dover	7.7	10.6	10.4	13.5	13.0	12.0	13.1

Source: Department of Transport.

built at Hound Point on the Forth, on the Tees, at Flotta and at Sullom Voe (one of the largest oil terminals in the world). Supply bases for offshore oil and gas installations have been built at a number of ports, notably Aberdeen, Great Yarmouth and Heysham.

Safety at Sea

HM Coastguard Service, part of the Department of Transport, is responsible for co-ordinating civil maritime search and rescue operations around the coastline of Britain. In a maritime emergency the coastguard calls on and co-ordinates facilities such as:

- coastguard helicopters and cliff rescue companies;

- lifeboats of the Royal National Lifeboat Institution (a voluntary body);

- Ministry of Defence aeroplanes, helicopters and ships; and

- merchant shipping and commercial aircraft.

In 1992 the Coastguard Service co-ordinated action in some 8,530 incidents (including cliff rescues), in which 14,530 people were assisted. The establishment of new coastal search and rescue consultative committees was announced in 1992. These aim to improve liaison between the coastguards, potential users of the rescue services and interested authorities.

Compliance with rules of behaviour when navigating in traffic separation schemes around the shores of Britain is mandatory for all vessels of countries party to the Convention on the International Regulations for Preventing Collisions at Sea 1972. The most important scheme affecting British waters is in the Dover Strait, the world's busiest seaway. Britain and France jointly operate the Channel Navigation Information System, which provides navigational information and also monitors the movement of vessels in the strait. A new radar system was officially opened in October 1993, providing increased coverage of the area.

Following the loss of the tanker MV *Braer* off Sumburgh in the Shetland Islands in January 1993, the British Chamber of Shipping agreed a voluntary code for the routeing and operation of tankers around Britain's coast. A government inquiry has also been set up to examine whether further measures are appropriate to protect the coastline from pollution from merchant shipping.

The lighthouse authorities, which between them control about 370 lighthouses and other lights and buoys, are:

- the Corporation of Trinity House, which covers England, Wales and the Channel Islands;

- the Northern Lighthouse Board, for Scotland and the Isle of Man; and

- the Commissioners of Irish Lights for Northern Ireland and the Irish Republic.

They are funded mainly by light dues levied on shipping in Britain and Ireland. The Ports Act 1991 provided for the transfer of certain lights and buoys to harbour authorities where these are used mainly for local rather than general navigation. Responsibility for pilotage within harbours rests with harbour authorities under the Pilotage Act 1987.

CIVIL AVIATION

An innovative British air transport industry responds to the demands of both international and domestic passengers. Airlines are seeking opportunities for modernisation, and this is complemented by the work of the aviation authorities in negotiating new international rights and improving facilities such as air traffic control. British airlines are entirely in the private sector, as are a number of the major airports.

Role of the Government

The Secretary of State for Transport is responsible for aviation matters, including:

- negotiation of air service agreements with more than 100 other countries;

- control of air services into Britain by overseas airlines;

- British participation in the activities of international aviation bodies;

- aviation security policy;

- environmental matters, such as aircraft noise and emissions;
- investigation of accidents; and
- airports policy.

The Government's civil aviation policy aims to maintain high standards of safety and security and to achieve environmental improvements through reduced noise and other emissions from aircraft. It is concerned to promote the interests of travellers by encouraging a competitive British industry, and is committed to encouraging more international services to and from regional airports. The Government has taken the lead in the EC and with bilateral partners in negotiating freer arrangements within which airline competition can flourish; agreement was reached within the EC in 1992 on a further package of liberalisation measures. New arrangements with an increasing number of countries are resulting in better provision of services at more competitive fares.

Civil Aviation Authority

The Civil Aviation Authority (CAA) is an independent statutory body, responsible for the economic and safety regulation of the industry and, jointly with the Ministry of Defence, for the provision of air navigation services. Its board members are appointed by the Secretary of State for Transport. The CAA's primary objectives are to ensure that British airlines provide air services to satisfy all substantial categories of public demand at the lowest charges consistent with a high standard of safety and to further the reasonable interests of air transport users.

Air Traffic

Total capacity offered on all services by British airlines amounted to 23,200 million available tonne-km in 1992: 17,100 million tonne-km on scheduled services and 6,100 million tonne-km on non-scheduled services. The airlines carried 38.2 million passengers on scheduled services and 24.5 million on charter flights; some 83 million passengers travelled by air (international terminal passengers) to or from Britain, a 14 per cent increase on 1991.

The value of Britain's overseas trade carried by air in 1992 was some £44,140 million—20 per cent of exports by value and 18 per cent of imports. Air freight is important for the carriage of goods with a high value-to-weight ratio, especially where speed is essential.

British Airways

British Airways plc is one of the world's leading airlines. In terms of international scheduled services it is the largest in the world. During 1992–93 British Airways' turnover was £5,566 million (including £5,519 million from airline operations), and the British Airways group carried 28.1 million passengers on scheduled and charter flights both domestically and internationally.

The British Airways scheduled route network serves 155 destinations in 72 countries. Its main operating base is London's Heathrow airport, but services from Gatwick and regional centres such as Manchester and Birmingham have been expanding. Scheduled Concorde supersonic services are operated from London Heathrow to New York, Washington and, in the summer, Toronto, crossing the Atlantic in about half the time taken by subsonic aircraft. In March 1993 British Airways had a fleet of 241 aircraft, the largest fleet in Western Europe, comprising 7 Concordes, 56 Boeing 747s, 7 McDonnell-Douglas DC-10s, 5 Lockheed TriStars, 42 Boeing 757s, 10 Airbus A320s, 74 Boeing 737s, 20 Boeing 767s, 6 BAC One-Elevens and 14 BAe Advanced Turboprops. A total of 68 aircraft were on firm order.

Other Airlines

Other major British airlines include:
- Air UK, which has 28 aircraft and is the only British airline to operate from all three main airports in the London area (Heathrow, Gatwick and Stansted);
- Britannia Airways, the world's largest charter airline, which carried over 6.9 million passengers in 1992 and has 33 aircraft;

- British Midland, which operates a large network of scheduled services, and has 31 aircraft; and
- Virgin Atlantic, which operates scheduled services between Britain, five North American destinations and Tokyo, using eight Boeing 747 aircraft, with four more 747s and four Airbus A340s on order.

Helicopters and Other Aerial Work

Helicopters are engaged on a variety of work, especially operations connected with Britain's offshore oil and gas industry. The main operators in Britain are Bond Helicopters, Brintel Helicopters and Bristow Helicopters, with 47, 22 and 64 helicopters respectively. Light aircraft and helicopters are also involved in other activities, such as charters, search and rescue services, crop-spraying, aerial surveying and photography, and police and air ambulance operations.

Air Safety

The CAA is responsible, through its Safety Regulation Group, for all aspects of civil aviation safety. It licenses flight crew, ground engineers, air traffic control officers, aerodromes and fire and rescue services, and it certifies the airworthiness of aircraft.

Every company operating aircraft used for commercial purposes must possess an Air Operator's Certificate, which is granted by the CAA when it is satisfied that the operator is competent to secure the safe operation of its aircraft. The CAA's flight operations inspectors, all of whom are experienced airline pilots, and airworthiness surveyors check that satisfactory standards are maintained. All aircraft registered in Britain must be granted a certificate of airworthiness by the CAA before being flown. In this and many other aspects of its work, the CAA is increasingly working to standards developed with its European partners in the Joint Airworthiness Authorities.

Each member of the flight crew of a British-registered aircraft, every ground engineer who certifies an aircraft fit to fly,

and every air traffic controller must hold the appropriate official licence issued by the CAA. Except for those with acceptable military or other qualifying experience, all applicants for a first professional licence must have undertaken a full-time course of instruction which has been approved by the CAA.

Air Traffic Control and Navigation Services

Civil and military air traffic control over Britain and the surrounding seas, including a large part of the North Atlantic, is carried out by the National Air Traffic Services (NATS), jointly responsible to the CAA and the Ministry of Defence. NATS also provides air traffic control at most of the major British airports.

Britain plays a major role in European air traffic control developments through participation in a number of international forums. Britain has put forward several European initiatives, including the centralised management of traffic flows throughout Europe, which is being progressively implemented over the period 1991–95. Within Britain, NATS has an investment programme currently running at around £80 million a year, which includes the construction of a new air traffic control centre for England and Wales, due to be completed in 1996. A scheme for a new centre for Scotland is under consideration by NATS.

Airports

Of the 148 licensed civil aerodromes in Britain, about one-fifth handle more than 100,000 passengers a year each. Of these, 13 handle over 1 million passengers a year each (see Table 17.4). In 1992 Britain's civil airports handled a total of 107.8 million passengers (106.1 million terminal passengers and 1.7 million in transit), and 1.2 million tonnes of freight. Heathrow airport is the world's busiest airport for international travel and is Britain's most important airport for passengers and air freight, handling 45 million passengers (including transit passengers) and 758,000 tonnes of freight in 1991. Proposals have been put forward for a fifth terminal, which will be the subject of a public inquiry and could eventually handle 30 million passengers a year. Gatwick is also one of the world's busiest international airports.

Ownership and Control

Seven airports—Heathrow, Gatwick, Stansted and Southampton in south-east England, and Glasgow, Edinburgh and Aberdeen in Scotland—are owned and operated by BAA plc. Together they handle about 73 per cent of air passengers and 84 per cent of air cargo traffic in Britain.

Many of the other airports are controlled by local authorities. A total of 15 major local authority airports now operate as Companies Act companies. The Government is encouraging the introduction of private capital into these new companies. It is intended that Belfast International Airport will be privatised in the second half of 1994.

The CAA has responsibility for the economic regulation of the larger airports. It has powers to take action to remedy practices considered to be unreasonable or unfair, in particular any abuse of an airport's monopoly position, and also to limit increases in charges to airlines at certain airports. All airports used for public transport and training flights must also be licensed by the CAA for reasons of safety. Stringent requirements, such as the provision of adequate fire-fighting, medical and rescue services, must be satisfied before a

licence is granted. Strict security measures are in force, and the Aviation and Maritime Security Act 1990 provides for greater powers to enforce security requirements.

Tighter requirements for aviation security were announced by the Government in February 1993. In particular, airlines will have to account for all baggage and subject any unaccompanied or unaccounted item to security controls before carrying it. It is provisionally envisaged that all baggage at British airports will be screened by April 1996.

Development

Major expansion has been undertaken at several airports, including:

- Birmingham, where a second terminal was opened in 1991, increasing capacity to 6 million passengers a year;

- Manchester, where the first phase of a second terminal opened in spring 1993, increasing capacity by one-half to 18 million passengers a year; and

- Stansted, in Essex, where a new terminal was opened in March 1991, with an initial capacity of 8 million passengers a year.

Table 17.4: Passenger Traffic at Britain's Main Airports

million passengers

	1988	1989	1990	1991	1992
London Heathrow	37.8	39.6	42.6	40.2	45.0
London Gatwick	20.8	21.1	21.0	18.7	19.8
Manchester	9.7	10.1	10.1	10.1	11.7
Glasgow	3.7	3.9	4.3	4.2	4.7
Birmingham	2.9	3.3	3.5	3.2	3.7
Edinburgh	2.1	2.4	2.5	2.3	2.5
London Stansted	1.0	1.3	1.2	1.7	2.3
Belfast International	2.2	2.2	2.3	2.2	2.2
Aberdeen	1.6	1.7	1.9	2.0	2.2
Luton	2.8	2.8	2.7	2.0	2.0
Newcastle	1.4	1.5	1.6	1.5	2.0
East Midlands	1.3	1.5	1.3	1.1	1.3
Bristol	0.7	0.8	0.8	0.8	1.0

Source: Civil Aviation Authority.

Communications

The telecommunications industry is one of the most rapidly growing sectors of the British economy. Postal services also continue to be important, with the volume of mail in Britain growing rather than declining despite the growth in electronic means of communication in recent years.

TELECOMMUNICATIONS

Major changes have occurred since 1981, with the progressive introduction of competition into the markets for telecommunications equipment and services. In 1984 British Telecommunications (BT) was privatised, and it faces increasing competition in the provision of services over fixed links. The main feature of the regulatory regime is an independent industry regulator, the Director General of Telecommunications.

Duopoly Review

In 1991 a major review of government telecommunications policy resulted in the publication of a White Paper, *Competition and Choice: Telecommunications Policy for the 1990s*. This stated that the Government would end the 'duopoly policy', under which only two companies, BT and Mercury Communications, were permitted to run fixed-link telecommunications systems. Other important points of the review were:

● greater freedom for existing mobile telecommunications operators and the ability of cable television operators to provide telephone services in their own right;

● more effective and streamlined procedures for the interconnection of systems;

● guidelines for the introduction of 'equal access', by which customers can exercise choice over the trunk operator that carries their calls; and

● the establishment of a new regime for national numbering, and the modification of operators' licences to allow for the introduction of number portability.

Office of Telecommunications

The Office of Telecommunications (OFTEL), a non-ministerial government department, is the independent regulatory body for the telecommunications industry. It is headed by the Director General of Telecommunications, among whose functions are to:

● ensure that licensees comply with the conditions of their licences;

● initiate the modification of licence conditions by agreement or a reference to the Monopolies and Mergers Commission;

● promote effective competition in the telecommunications industry;

● provide advice to the President of the Board of Trade on telecommunications matters; and

● investigate complaints.

The Director General also has a duty to promote the interests of consumers in respect of prices, quality and variety in telecommunications services.

Under the White Paper proposals, OFTEL will be taking over responsibility for administering the new national telephone numbering scheme. It will also oversee the introduction of a limited 'number portability' scheme, enabling someone who wishes to change service provider at the same address to retain their existing number, rather than change it, as at present.

OFTEL's 1992 quality of service report, published in December 1992, showed that written complaints and enquiries to OFTEL ranged between 2,000 and 3,000 a quarter. The largest category was disputes over bills, but the number of cases was decreasing, possibly because the introduction of itemised billing and premium-rate call barring was giving customers more control over bills.

BT

In 1984 BT was reconstituted as a public limited company, and a majority of the ordinary voting shares were sold to private investors. In December 1991 the Government sold a further tranche of shares in a public offer, reducing its holding in BT to about 22 per cent. The sale of the remaining holding took place in July 1993.

BT runs one of the world's largest public telecommunications networks, including:

- 20.1 million residential lines;
- 6 million business lines;
- about 58,000 telex connections;
- more than 104,000 public payphones; and
- a wide range of specialised voice, data, text and visual services.

The inland telephone and telex networks are fully automatic. International direct dialling is available from Britain to 200 countries, representing 99 per cent of the world's telephones.

Network Modernisation

BT has invested more than £17,000 million in the modernisation and expansion of its network to meet the increasing demand for basic telephone services and for more specialised services. The company has more than 2 million km (1.2 million miles) of optical fibre laid in its network in Britain, a higher proportion than any other world operator. There are more than 3,650 digital and modern electronic exchanges serving some 80 per cent of telephone lines. The combination of digital exchange switching and digital transmission techniques, using optical fibre cable and microwave radio links, is substantially improving the quality of telephone services. It also makes possible a wider range of services through the company's main network.

General Services

BT's services include:

- a free facility for emergency calls to the police, fire, ambulance, coastguard, lifeboat and air-sea rescue services;
- directory enquiries;
- various chargeable operator-connected services, such as reversed-charge calls and alarm calls;
- an operator-handled Freefone service and automatic 'LinkLine' facilities that enable callers to contact organisations anywhere in Britain, either free or at local-call rates;

- Callstream, a premium-rate service which allows callers to obtain information from independent providers; and
- network services such as three-way calling, call waiting and call diversion, which are available to customers on digital exchanges.

Under a public payphone service modernisation programme, a total of £165 million has been spent on modernisation and additional provision on sites convenient for travellers, such as railway stations and motorway service areas. A number of cashless call services are available, including the Phonecard service using prepaid cards and phones that accept credit cards. Phonecard payphones account for more than 19,000 of the total of 113,000 payphones. There are about 280,000 private rented payphones on premises to which the public has access and these are also being upgraded with push-button equipment.

BT Electronic Information Services (an electronic mail and information service) forms part of the company's portfolio of global network services. Through links with other databases, a wide range of other services, such as company accounting and market research information, banking services, holiday booking and reservation facilities, insurance and financial markets information, and BT's telephone directories, are available.

International Services

BT is the second largest shareholder in the International Telecommunications Satellite Organisation (of which 125 countries are members) and in the European Telecommunications Satellite Organisation. It is also a leading shareholder in the International Maritime Satellite Organisation, with interests in a number of other consortia.

A substantial proportion of the intercontinental telephone traffic to or from Britain is carried by satellite. BT operates satellite earth stations in the London Docklands and at Goonhilly Downs (Cornwall), Madley (near Hereford) and Aberdeen. Its range of digital transmission services includes a number available overseas, including 'Satstream' private-circuit digital links covering North America and Western Europe using small-dish aerials, and an 'International Kilostream' private-circuit service available to the United States, Australia and most major business centres in Asia and the rest of Europe. Extensive direct-dial maritime satellite services are available for vessels worldwide. In-flight operator-controlled telephone call facilities are available via Portishead radio station near Bristol. Digital transmission techniques have been introduced for services to the United States, Japan, Hong Kong and Australia via the Madley and Goonhilly stations.

Recent advances in submarine cable design, with the use of optical fibre technology, have significantly increased capacity. A high-capacity transatlantic optical fibre cable (TAT 9), which cost about £250 million and can carry about 75,000 telephone calls simultaneously, came into operation in 1992 to supplement an earlier link.

BT's overseas consultancy service, Telconsult, has so far completed 270 projects in more than 60 countries.

Mercury Communications

Mercury Communications Ltd, a subsidiary of Cable and Wireless plc and BCE, is licensed as a public telecommunications operator in Britain. Mercury has constructed its own long-distance all-digital network comprising over 5,690 km (3,560 miles) of optical fibre cables and 2,700 km (1,685 miles) of digital microwave links. The network runs from the north of Scotland to the south coast, serving over 100 cities and towns across Britain. Coverage is enhanced through Mercury's own city cable networks and through partnerships with local cable television operators. Service is also provided over microwave connections.

Mercury offers a full range of long-distance and international telecommunications services for both business and residential customers. In addition to voice and data transmission, the company supplies sophisticated messaging systems, mobile telecommunications and a range of equipment for customers' premises. Major customers can have a direct digital link between their

premises and the Mercury network. A number of routeing devices have also been developed to enable customers to use Mercury indirectly via their existing exchange lines. Residential customers can buy a Mercury-compatible phone and gain access to the company's network at the push of a button. In addition, customers will soon be able to use the Mercury network by dialling an access code.

International services are provided by satellite communications centres in London's Docklands and in Oxfordshire, as well as by submarine cable links to Europe and the United States.

Other Operators

Other operators include Kingston Communications, which is the long-established network operator for the Kingston upon Hull area of Britain.

The duopoly review (see p. 264) allowed other would-be operators to apply for licences to provide telecommunications services over fixed links. By June 1993, the Government had received 59 applications, and 21 licences had been granted. Major licences have been granted to Ionica, COLT, Energis (a subsidiary of National Grid) and Scottish Hydro-Electric. Ionica is installing a new national network using radio to provide the final connection to customers. COLT is focusing on business customers in the Greater London area. Energis and Scottish Hydro-Electric are the first two electricity companies to expand their interests into telecommunications, using their infrastructure as a platform for installing new optical fibre networks.

Mobile Communications

The Government has encouraged the expansion of mobile telecommunications services. It has licensed Vodafone Ltd and Telecom Securicor Cellular Radio Ltd to run competing national cellular radio systems. Considerable investment has been made in establishing their networks to provide increased capacity for the growing numbers of cellular radio telephone users (over 1.3

million by the end of 1992). The two companies will also run the new pan-European mobile system, known as GSM, in Britain.

Britain was the first country to offer personal communications network (PCN) services, which are intended to allow the same telephone to be used at home, at work and as a portable wherever there is network capacity. In 1991 the Government issued licences to three operators—Mercury Personal Communications Ltd, Microtel Communications Ltd and Unitel Ltd (which has since merged with Mercury Personal Communications to form Mercury One-2-One) to run PCNs in the frequency range around 1.8 gigahertz. The Mercury One-2-One service was launched in September 1993.

Hutchison launched its 'Rabbit' telepoint service in 1992. It allows calls to be made within range of a base station situated in a public place, and the handset can be used within the home as a cordless telephone.

National Band Three Ltd is licensed to offer a nationwide trunked radio service, while 15 licences have now been awarded for London and regional services. Four licences to operate mobile data networks have also been granted, and another eight to run nationwide paging networks.

Cable Television

The Government has licensed 121 companies that were awarded local cable television franchises to run broadband cable telecommunications systems. All 62 systems due to be in operation by the end of 1993 will provide television programmes, but many also offer voice telephony services. The Government concluded in the duopoly review that cable operators should be able to offer voice telephony in their own right, which they could previously provide only in conjunction with BT or Mercury. By May 1993 the cable operators had installed 156,000 telephone lines in Britain, compared with 2,200 lines in January 1991.

Cable & Wireless

Cable and Wireless plc provides a wide range of telecommunications in some 50 countries worldwide. Its main business is the provision and operation of public telecommunications services in over 30 countries and territories, including Hong Kong, the United States and Japan, under franchises and licences granted by the governments concerned. It also provides and manages telecommunications services and facilities for public and private sector customers, and undertakes consultancy work. It operates a fleet of 11 ships and three submersible vehicle systems for laying and maintaining submarine telecommunications cables. In recent years the company has been constructing and bringing into service a broadband digital network linking major world economic and financial centres in Europe, north America and the Pacific rim. Cable & Wireless is pursuing a strategy of providing premium services for business customers, expanding basic telecommunications services and building up mobile communications businesses around the world.

POSTAL SERVICES

The Post Office, founded in 1635, pioneered postal services and was the first to issue adhesive postage stamps as proof of advance payment for mail.

The Royal Mail provides deliveries to 24.5 million addresses and handles over 61 million letters and parcels each working day, which comes to over 15,400 million items a year. Some 180 million parcels were handled in 1991–92. Mail is collected from over 100,000 posting boxes, as well as from post offices and large postal users.

Mail sorting is increasingly done through mechanised letter offices; some 80 are now in operation. The British postcode system is one of the most sophisticated in the world, allowing mechanised sorting down to part of a street on a postman's round and, in some cases, to an individual address.

Britain has good international postal services, with prices among the cheapest. Royal Mail International dispatches 659 million items a year, including some 600 million by air. It has its own mail handling centre at Heathrow, opened in 1989, which handles some four-fifths of outward airmail.

It uses 1,400 flights a week to send mail direct to over 300 destinations worldwide.

Post Office Counters Ltd handles a wide range of transactions; it acts as an agent for the letters and parcels businesses, government departments, local authorities and Girobank, which was transferred to the private sector in 1990. There are over 19,000 post offices, of which some 900 are operated directly by the Post Office. The remainder are franchise offices or are operated on an agency basis by sub-postmasters.

Post Office Specialist Services

The Post Office offers a range of specialist services. Parcelforce 'Datapost', a door-to-door delivery service, provides overnight delivery throughout Britain and an international service to over 160 countries. 'Datapost Sameday' provides a rapid delivery within or between more than 100 cities and towns in Britain. The Philatelic Bureau in Edinburgh is an important outlet for the Post Office's philatelic business, including sales to overseas collectors or dealers. The British Postal Consultancy Service offers advice and assistance on all aspects of postal business to overseas postal administrations, and over 50 countries have used its services since 1965.

Competition in Postal Services

The Post Office has a monopoly on the conveyance of letters within Britain, but the President of the Board of Trade has the power to suspend the monopoly in certain areas or for certain categories of mail and to license others to provide competing services. He has suspended the monopoly on letters subject to a minimum fee of £1, and has issued general licences enabling mail to be transferred between document exchanges and allowing charitable organisations to carry

Christmas cards. As set out in the Citizen's Charter, the Government intends to introduce wider competition in postal services by:

- the reduction of the present £1 letter monopoly to a level much closer to the price of a first-class stamp;
- an extended discount system, so that the Post Office could offer further discounts to users who carry their mail in bulk as far as the final delivery office; and
- the licensing of 'niche' services under the monopoly limit.

Under these proposals, the President of the Board of Trade would be advised by a new regulator on ways of preventing the Post Office from cross-subsidising its services in ways which may be unfair to its competitors or to specific groups of customers. The Government has subsequently announced its intention to privatise Parcelforce, the Post Office's parcels operation, in due course. An essential requirement would be the continuation of a universal parcels service at a uniform and affordable price. The Government is also conducting a review of the Post Office's organisation and structure, which builds upon the proposals set out in the Citizen's Charter. Both public and private sector options are being considered.

Private Courier and Express Service Operators

Private-sector couriers and express operators are able to handle time-sensitive door-to-door deliveries, subject to a minimum fee of £1. The courier/express service industry has grown rapidly and the revenue created by the carriage of these items is estimated at over £3,000 million a year. Britain is one of the main providers of monitored express deliveries in Europe, with London an important centre for air courier/express traffic.

Further Reading

Competition and Choice: Telecommunications Policy for the 1990s. Cm 1461. HMSO, 1991.
New Opportunities for the Railways. Cm 2012. Department of Transport, HMSO, 1992.
Telecommunications. Aspects of Britain series, HMSO, 1993.
Transport and Communications. Aspects of Britain series, HMSO, 1992.
Transport Statistics Great Britain 1993. HMSO, 1993.

19 Science and Technology

Britain has a long tradition of research and innovation in science, technology and engineering in universities, research institutes and industry. Its record of achievement is in many ways unsurpassed, from the contributions of Isaac Newton to physics and astronomy in the 16th and 17th centuries (theory of gravitation and three laws of motion) and the inventions of Michael Faraday in the 19th century (the first electric motor, generator and transformer) to more recent breakthroughs in the 20th century.

INTRODUCTION

British achievements in science and technology in the 20th century include fundamental contributions to modern molecular genetics through the discovery of the three-dimensional molecular structure of DNA (deoxyribonucleic acid) by Francis Crick, Maurice Wilkins, James Watson and Rosalind Franklin in 1953.

Further notable contributions over the past 20 years have been made by Stephen Hawking in improving the understanding of the nature and origin of the universe; Brian Josephson in superconductivity (abnormally high electrical conductivity at low temperatures); Martin Ryle and Anthony Hewish in radio-astrophysics; and Godfrey Hounsfield in computer-assisted tomography (a form of radiography) for medical diagnosis.

Much pioneering work was done during the 1980s. For example, in 1985 British Antarctic Survey scientists discovered the hole in the ozone layer over the Antarctic. Also in 1985 Alec Jeffreys invented DNA fingerprinting, a forensic technique which can identify an individual from a small tissue sample. More recently there have been several breakthroughs in genetics research, including the identification of the gene in the Y chromosome responsible for determining sex, and the identification of other genes linked to diseases, including cystic fibrosis and a type of inherited heart disease. Gene therapy has begun on the treatment of cystic fibrosis. The world's first pig with a genetically modified heart has been bred by scientists at Cambridge University, an important milestone in breeding animals as organ donors for people.

Nobel prizes for science have been won by 70 British citizens, more than any other country except the United States. The two most recent prize-winners were Richard Roberts (medicine) and Michael Smith (chemistry).

Research and Development Expenditure

Total expenditure in Britain on scientific research and development (R & D) in 1991 was £11,906 million, 2.1 per cent of gross domestic product. Some 50 per cent was provided by industry and 35 per cent by government. Significant contributions were also made by private endowments, trusts and charities. In many cases private-sector and state industries finance their own research and run their own laboratories. Industry also funds university research and finances contract research at government establishments. Some charities have their own laboratories and offer grants for outside research. Contract research organisations carry out similar R & D for companies and are playing an increasingly important role in the transfer of technology to British industry.

Total spending on R & D in industry amounted to £7,768 million in 1991–92. Of this total, industry's own contribution was 69 per cent, with 15 per cent from government and the rest from overseas. The main areas of expenditure were electronics (£2,180 million, amounting to 28 per cent of the total); chemicals (£1,886 million); and aerospace (£1,121 million). Some examples of recent notable R & D projects in these sectors are given below.

Electronics

British firms and research organisations, with government support, are involved in the development and application of the family of 'three-five' semiconductor materials (such as gallium arsenide). These materials are used mainly in microwave devices in satellite communications and radar equipment, and are leading to the development of much faster computers.

BT (British Telecom) has led in the development of optical fibre communications systems and has paved the way for simpler and cheaper optical cables by laying the first non-repeatered cable over 100 km (62 miles) long, and by developing the first all-optical repeater. Britain also has a world lead in the transmission of computerised data along telephone lines for reproduction on television screens. Up to 800 R & D projects are carried out by BT at any one time; a recent example is the development of a video handset with an optical telephone link. Around two-thirds of its research is in software engineering.

The transputer, a powerful 'computer on a chip', was designed and built in Britain.

Several companies have developed powerful machines based on the transputer.

Chemicals

Research performed by the chemicals industry over the past few years has led to significant technological and commercial breakthroughs. ICI has pioneered the microbial production of a biodegradable plastic, Biopol, and is at the forefront of global efforts to develop substitutes for chlorofluorocarbons (CFCs).

Pharmaceuticals is the most research-intensive sector of the chemicals industry (see p. 162). Research conducted by Zeneca, Glaxo, SmithKline Beecham and Fisons has led to the development of the first successful beta-blockers, drugs used in the treatment of cardiovascular conditions; semi-synthetic penicillins; vaccines; and treatments for cancer, asthma, migraine and arthritis. Glaxo is Britain's biggest pharmaceutical company. Its new £500 million research centre at Stevenage (Hertfordshire) is to be opened in 1994. It manufactures the world's best-selling pharmaceutical, Zantac, which is used in the treatment of gastric ulcers.

Among a host of other research interests are the application of biotechnology to pharmaceuticals, disease-resistant crops, new forms of food, plant science, and the development of advanced materials such as engineering plastics. The biotechnology sector consists of some 70 companies whose activities include the development and manufacture of products using genetic engineering techniques.

Aerospace

Britain has led the world in many aspects of aerospace R & D over the past 80 years. Pioneering achievements include radar, jet engines, Concorde, automatic landing, vertical take-off and landing, flight simulators and ejector seats. British Aerospace, with Marconi and Dowty Boulton Paul, developed a system known as 'fly-by-wire', in which flying control surfaces are moved by electronic rather than mechanical means. GEC Avionics has also developed the world's first optically signalled ('fly-by-light') system. The concept of head-up display (HUD) was pioneered and developed in Britain. This system electronically projects symbols into the pilot's view, avoiding the need to look down at instruments. GEC Avionics has developed a holographic HUD, which enables pilots to fly at high speeds at very low altitude in darkness.

Government Policy and Organisation

Organisation to 1 April 1994

Science and technology issues are the responsibility of a Cabinet Minister, the Chancellor of the Duchy of Lancaster, acting on behalf of the Prime Minister. The Minister is supported by the Office of Science and Technology (OST)—part of the Office of Public Service and Science within the Cabinet Office—headed by the Government's Chief Scientific Adviser. The OST receives independent advice from eminent scientists, technologists, engineers and industrialists.

In addition to its role in overall science policy and co-ordination, the OST is responsible for the science budget and the five government-financed research councils: the Science and Engineering Research Council (SERC), the Medical Research Council (MRC), the Natural Environment Research Council (NERC), the Agricultural and Food Research Council (AFRC) and the Economic and Social Research Council (ESRC). (Organisational changes to these councils, taking effect from April 1994, are described on p. 272.) OST funding provides assistance for research, through the research councils, in the following ways:

- grants and contracts to universities and other higher education establishments and to research units;

- funding of research council establishments;

- support for postgraduate study; and

- subscriptions to international scientific organisations.

The OST also provides support to universities through programmes administered through the Royal Society and the Royal Academy of Engineering (see p. 282).

Finance

Government finance for R & D goes to research establishments, institutions of higher education and private industry, as well as to collaborative research programmes.

Total net government R & D expenditure (both civil and defence) in 1992–93 was £5,404 million, of which £2,954 million was devoted to civil science. The science budget (net of receipts) totalled £994 million in 1992–93. The planned net expenditure of £1,142 million for the research councils in 1994–95 represents a 23 per cent increase in real terms compared with 1991–92.

Among other government departments, the Ministry of Defence (MoD—see p. 278) has the largest research budget. The main civil departments involved are the Department of Trade and Industry (DTI—see p. 276), the Ministry of Agriculture, Fisheries and Food (MAFF—see p. 279) and the Department for Education (DFE—see p. 279).

Future Plans

A White Paper *Realising Our Potential: A Strategy for Science, Engineering and Technology* was published in May 1993, containing the first major policy review on science for over 20 years. The Government's strategy is to improve Britain's competitiveness and quality of life by maintaining the excellence of science, engineering and technology in Britain. This will be done by:

- developing stronger partnerships with and between the science and engineering communities, industry and the research councils;

- supporting the science and engineering base to advance knowledge, increase understanding and produce highly educated and trained people;

- contributing to international research efforts, particularly European research;

271

- promoting the public understanding of science, technology and engineering; and
- ensuring the efficiency and effectiveness of government-funded research.

A number of changes are planned to the organisation and direction of government-funded science and technology:

- A new Council for Science and Technology will be set up by the end of October 1993. It will be chaired by the Chancellor of the Duchy of Lancaster and will involve research customers, industrialists, academics, business people and departmental chief scientists. It will provide advice to assist in the setting of research priorities, and will draw on the findings of a new Technology Foresight Programme which will be produced by the end of 1994.
- A new 'Forward Look' will be published by the Government each year. This will give industrialists and researchers a regular statement of the Government's strategy.
- The research council system will be restructured. SERC and AFRC will cease to exist in their present form. Two new councils, the Engineering and Physical Sciences Research Council and the Particle Physics and Astronomy Research Council, will divide between them most of SERC's portfolio. A third, the Biotechnology and Biological Sciences Research Council, will take over responsibility for the AFRC programme and SERC's work in biology and biotechnology. All councils will have 'mission statements' with commitments to enhancing industrial competitiveness and quality of life. Management structures will be modified, and councils will have part-time chairmen and women selected to bring in industrial and commercial experience. These changes will take effect on 1 April 1994. A Director General of Research Councils within OST will advise ministers on the performance and needs of the science and engineering base.
- The customer-contractor principle will be maintained and strengthened.

- The OST will play the major role in co-ordinating science and technology issues involving more than one department.
- Improved co-ordination of European and other international negotiations is planned.

RESEARCH COUNCILS

Each research council is an autonomous body established under Royal Charter, with members of its governing council drawn from the universities, professions, industry and the Government. Councils conduct research through their own establishments and by supporting selected research, study and training in universities and other higher education institutions. In addition to funding from the OST, they also receive income for research commissioned by government departments and from the private sector. Income from commissioned research is particularly important for the AFRC and NERC.

LINK is an important scheme for the research councils' collaboration with industry. It is designed to bridge the gap between scientific research and the resulting commercial applications. It encourages collaboration on high-quality, industrially relevant research between industry and higher education institutions and research bodies. Under the scheme, government funds 50 per cent of costs and industry the other half. Formerly a joint DTI–OST project, in 1993 the OST was given the leading responsibility for LINK in line with its responsibilities for cross-governmental projects.

By May 1993 government funding worth £200 million had been committed to 32 LINK programmes, mainly in the areas of biotechnology, advanced materials, advanced manufacturing and electronics, and oil exploration. A new LINK programme plans to use micro-organisms to clean contaminated soil and water.

Institutions undertaking research with the support of research council grants have the rights and responsibility for the commercial exploitation of that research, subject to prior agreement with the sponsoring research council. Universities and research institutes may make use of the expertise of the British Technology Group (BTG—see p. 281) to patent and license their inventions.

Science and Engineering Research Council

On 1 April 1994 SERC is to be split into two research councils and its responsibilities reallocated. Until then SERC is responsible for supporting research and postgraduate training in pure and applied science and engineering outside the areas of agriculture, medicine and the environment covered by the other research councils. With the largest share of research council funding, expenditure in 1992–93 totalled £524 million, including:

- research grants, chiefly to higher education institutions (£198.8 million);

- contributions to international organisations (£103.2 million—see p. 284); and

- funding of postgraduate training (£85.2 million).

The Council has funded interdisciplinary research centres in fields such as high-temperature superconductivity, engineering design, molecular sciences, high performance materials, and optical- and laser-related science and technology. It has developed stronger links with industry to improve the transfer of knowledge from the science and engineering base. Collaboration between higher education and industry has been encouraged, partly by sponsoring co-ordinated research programmes in areas of special industrial concern. SERC's allocation for 1993–94 is £582 million. The increase in funding is benefiting the development of new materials, clean technologies, earth observation and atmospheric chemistry. SERC is the largest single national source of support for postgraduate students.

SERC maintains six research establishments: the Rutherford Appleton Laboratory at Chilton (Oxfordshire), which is the largest; Daresbury Laboratory in Warrington (Cheshire); Royal Greenwich Observatory in Cambridge; the Royal Observatory in Edinburgh; and two overseas observatories on La Palma in the Canary Islands, and Hawaii. These centres of specialised research have experimental facilities beyond the resources of individual academic institutions; they also undertake contract research.

Until 1 April 1994 SERC's research support is organised under three boards, covering science and materials; engineering and technology; and particles, space and astronomy.

Science and Materials

The Science and Materials Board's main objective is to ensure the vitality of the core sciences—chemistry, physics, biology and mathematics—and of materials science. The Board supports academic and interdisciplinary research, and promotes collaboration between the academic sector, industry and the international scientific community. Research is supported through grants and by providing access to major world-class facilities. It may be either on a national basis, such as the ISIS pulsed neutron source at the Rutherford Appleton Laboratory, or through international collaboration, such as projects at the Institut Laue-Langevin and the European Synchrotron Radiation Facility in Grenoble (see p. 284).

Engineering and Technology

The Engineering and Technology Board supports fundamental and strategic research into the development of advanced technology. It initiates and sustains co-ordinated programmes of research which may be developed by others to give direct benefit to industry, particularly the aerospace, electrical engineering, power generation, mechanical engineering, and motor vehicle sectors. With the DTI, the Board supports the improved use of information technology for all categories of user.

The Clean Technology programme, launched in 1992 with the AFRC, aims to stimulate research leading to new technologies to prevent pollution caused by industry and agriculture. In collaboration with the MAFF, the Coastal Engineering Research Programme is investigating beach erosion and estuary pollution. SERC has contributed about £2 million towards a new coastal research facility at Wallingford (Oxfordshire), where advanced computer and modelling techniques are being developed to investigate problems in coastal protection.

Particles, Space and Astronomy

Particle physics funding is provided to allow researchers in higher education institutions access to leading facilities such as those at CERN (the European Organisation for Nuclear Research—see p. 284) and DESY (Deutsches Electronen Synchrotron).

The Particles, Space and Astronomy Board supports a number of eminent researchers in theoretical particle physics who have gained an international reputation for their work on the unification of the fundamental forces of nature.

The Board's support for space science includes contributions to international programmes (see pp. 284–5), ground-based astronomy and geophysics. In optical astronomy SERC is a principal partner in the international observatory on La Palma in the Canary Islands. The observatory's four telescopes include the 4.2-m William Herschel. Opened in 1987, it is the third largest single-mirror optical telescope in the world. On Mauna Kea, Hawaii, SERC has a 3.8-m infra-red telescope, the largest telescope in the world designed specifically for infra-red observations, and the 15-m James Clerk Maxwell radio telescope (built in collaboration with the Netherlands and Canada). Such telescopes have proved invaluable to scientists researching the creation of the universe. A centre is planned to co-ordinate data from four satellite-borne instruments in the Solar Heliospheric Observatory (SOHO) cluster satellite missions, due to be launched in 1995 (see p. 285). This programme has been set up to investigate the sun and its impact on the Earth's environment.

Medical Research Council

The MRC is the main government agency supporting medical research. Its budget amounted to £253 million in 1992–93, of which £228 million came from the science budget. The Council supports research in its own establishments and through its grant systems to research workers at higher education institutions and hospitals. The MRC's major research establishments are the National Institute for Medical Research at Mill Hill, London; the Clinical Research Centre at Northwick Park Hospital, London; and the Laboratory of Molecular Biology at Cambridge. Interdisciplinary research centres have been established in molecular medicine, protein engineering, cell biology, brain activity and human behaviour, brain repair, and toxicology.

The Council's scientists and doctors have pioneered developments in molecular biology, therapeutic clinical trials, applied psychology, and methods of imaging the body such as magnetic resonance and ultrasound. Larger research programmes include psychiatric and neurological (like Alzheimer's) disease, heart and respiratory ailments, cancer, tropical medicine, intra-uterine and infant origin of adult disease, and infection and immunity.

Recent important medical developments include: the discovery of gene defects linked to a form of Alzheimer's disease and to the commonest form of inherited heart disease; the construction of a silicon neuron which acts like a human brain cell; the development of artificial blood; the development of a treatment for rheumatoid arthritis using humanised antibodies; and the discovery that folic acid prevents spina bifida and other birth defects.

Major projects currently being undertaken are:
- specially funded work on AIDS;
- research on vaccines against meningitis and whooping cough;

- the Human Genome Mapping project, involving mapping of the complete sequence of 100,000 genes in a human cell;
- the genetic and neurosciences approach to human health;
- the Clinical Research Initiative, which aims to carry forward major advances in the laboratory for the benefit of patients; and
- physiological mechanisms and public health, which covers research in nutrition, the environment, diabetes and imaging techniques.

Technology Transfer

The MRC encourages collaboration between its establishments and industry in order to promote the transfer of skills and technologies, the exploitation of its discoveries, and the development of new health care products. The MRC Collaborative Centre at Mill Hill, London, and the Clinical Research Centre provide an important technology transfer function for the MRC. The Council has set up a company, Therexsys, to harness commercially the gene therapy technologies developed by its researchers.

Natural Environment Research Council

NERC seeks to advance understanding of the biological, physical and chemical processes of the planet, and how the natural environment is changing, either by natural causes or through human activities. Its objectives include contributions to exploration and exploitation of natural resources, land-use planning, environmental protection and conservation, energy supply and aid to overseas countries. High priority is given to the successful transfer of technology from the science base to government and the private sector.

In 1991–92 about £129 million (74 per cent) of NERC's funds came from the science budget, with the remainder coming from commissioned work for public authorities and industry in Britain and overseas.

The Council supports research and training in 15 NERC institutes, units and research centres and also in universities. It also provides and operates a range of facilities for use by the environmental science community. NERC institutes include the British Geological Survey (BGS), the Institute of Terrestrial Ecology, the Institute of Oceanographic Sciences Deacon Laboratory, and the British Antarctic Survey.

NERC conducts local and regional research in Britain and in other countries, while also participating in major international environmental projects, such as the World Climate Research Programme. Examples of NERC research include:

- the Land Ocean Interaction Study (LOIS), a major new project to study the dynamics of coastal environments and the flow of various materials into and across the coastal zone from the air, from the land and rivers and from the sea. The study will provide the basis for predictions of the impact of future natural and man-made changes on the coasts;
- the Terrestrial Initiative in Global Environment Research (TIGER), a programme involving research institutes and universities which focuses on the causes and consequences of climate change at sites in Britain and in selected tropical sites; and
- the British Institutions Reflection Profiling Syndicate (BIRPS) which, using seismic techniques to study geology at great depth, is helping to explain the structure and processes in the Earth's continental crust and how it has been formed. Results are of scientific importance and of commercial relevance to the mineral resources industry.

Among applied projects in progress overseas are initiatives in biological pest control; regeneration of tropical hardwoods; drip irrigation techniques for tropical crops; and surveys of potential resources, such as freshwater and underground water supply and geothermal energy.

Several environmental data centres have been established at NERC sites. The UK

Environmental Change Network, launched in 1992, provides an early warning system to detect the impact of environmental change on the ecology of Britain.

> **Recent major achievements in environmental research include:**
> - production of the BGS map series—1:250,000 scale—of Britain's offshore areas;
> - evidence of a link between hydrogen peroxide production and thinning of the ozone layer in the southern hemisphere; and
> - improved understanding of complex interactions in the middle atmosphere affecting changes in the global ozone layer.

Agricultural and Food Research Council

The AFRC supports research underpinning agriculture, food and the biologically based industries, including the pharmaceutical, chemical and health care industries. Research is carried out at eight AFRC institutes, at Horticulture Research International and in higher education institutions. The Council also provides scientific advice to The Scottish Office Agriculture and Fisheries Department on research in the Scottish Agricultural Research Institutes.

The Council's funding in 1992–93 totalled £168 million, primarily drawn from the science budget and from MAFF for commissioned research. In addition, it receives funding from other government departments, the European Community and commercial companies.

Significant advances have been made in the study of modified and novel oilseed crops for industry; genome mapping in cattle and chickens; strategies to combat plant virus replication; and preserving diversity in the countryside.

Economic and Social Research Council

The ESRC is Britain's leading research agency for the social sciences. Its main aim is to enable government, business and the public to find out more about social and economic change and the reasons behind it. It does this by supporting social science research in British higher education institutions and independent research institutes; by investing in the training of social scientists; and by developing and improving research methods and data sources.

Subject areas supported by the Council include economics, education, environment and planning, industry, information technology, management, politics, psychology and sociology. In 1992–93 it received nearly £46 million (95 per cent of its funding) from the science budget, and has been allocated over £53 million in 1993–94.

Recent Council initiatives include the Innovation Agenda campaign, a series of seminars and research reports aimed at highlighting the contribution that social science is making towards improving the competitiveness of the British economy. The Council has also commissioned major new research programmes into contracts and competition in the public and private sectors; local government; the nation's diet; transport and environment; and law and order.

GOVERNMENT DEPARTMENTS

Department of Trade and Industry

Direct government support for research in industry is led by the Department of Trade and Industry. Although most industrial research and development is financed by industry itself, the DTI provides assistance where there is a sound case for doing so.

In 1991–92 the DTI spent £365 million on R & D, covering general industrial innovation, aeronautics, space (see p. 284), nuclear and non-nuclear energy and support for statutory, regulatory and policy responsibilities. A further £113 million was allocated to technology transfer and related activities.

The largest part of the DTI's R & D expenditure on energy is on nuclear energy (£83 million in 1992–93), most of which is carried out by the former United Kingdom Atomic Energy Authority, now AEA Technology. The DTI also funds research in support of offshore oil and gas technology, coal technology and renewable energy.

DTI Industrial Innovation Programmes

The DTI's policy on science and technology builds on the commitment contained in the White Paper to improve the partnership between government, industry and the science base. The balance of DTI's industrial innovation programmes has shifted away from supporting technology generation towards concentrating on the exploitation and transfer of technology and the promotion of innovation. In particular, the DTI is:

- encouraging industry to collaborate with the science base in R & D projects under the LINK initiative (see p. 272);

- putting more effort into helping firms of all sizes work together to undertake R & D projects, including those under the EUREKA initiative (see p. 284);

- facilitating companies' access to technology from overseas and helping small and medium-sized establishments to identify technological opportunities and potential partners, both in Britain and overseas;

- designing its innovation services for local delivery through the 'One-stop Shops' (see p. 145);

- continuing direct single-company support to smaller firms under the SMART competition and the SPUR scheme (see p. 146) for the development of new products and processes; and

- concentrating support from the DTI's innovation budget for industry R & D collaboration on those projects which will result in exceptional economic benefits.

To carry out these measures, the provision for DTI's budget for industrial innovation increased from some £110 million in 1991–92 to about £125 million in 1992–93.

A number of schemes support the development and demonstration of new environmental technology. Projects receiving funding include recycling, treatment of industrial effluent, and monitoring atmospheric emissions.

Aeronautics

The DTI's Civil Aircraft Research and Demonstration Programme (CARAD) supports research and technology demonstration in the aircraft and aeroengine industry, helping it to compete effectively in world markets. The programme is part of a national aeronautics research effort, with over half of the research work supported being conducted in industry and the universities, and the remainder at the Defence Research Agency (see p. 278). Priority areas are aircraft exhaust emissions, advanced materials, and safety problems such as explosion hazards. In 1992–93 CARAD funding amounted to £26.4 million. Around 28 per cent was used to finance the DTI's contribution to the construction of the European Transonic Windtunnel test facility in Cologne. This proportion will fall in future years, with the facility becoming fully operational in mid-1997.

Launch Aid is a scheme providing government assistance—£31 million in 1992–93—for specific development projects in the aerospace industry. Westland is currently receiving aid for its participation in the commercial EH 101 helicopter.

Industrial Research Establishments

The DTI has three research establishments. Their primary role is to provide the Government with an effective source of scientific and technological expertise. They supply technological services to industry and also undertake research commissioned by industry. The laboratories are also involved in a variety of international activities.

- The Laboratory of the Government Chemist is the focus for chemical measurement within government. It provides both public and private sectors with a comprehensive service based on analytical chemistry and promotes sound chemical measurement in Britain in support of the National Measurement System.

- The National Engineering Laboratory (NEL) carries out a range of technical services, including R & D, testing and consultancies in engineering and related disciplines. It also maintains British Standards of flow measurement, which are of special importance in the oil and gas industries. The NEL manages technology transfer programmes for the DTI in open systems, as well as operating the National Wind Turbine Centre.

- The National Physical Laboratory (NPL) is Britain's national standards laboratory, with responsibility for maintaining national measurement standards for physical quantities. It supplies essential calibration and technology transfer services for industry, and undertakes research on standards for engineering materials and information technology. The NPL is also the base for the National Measurement Accreditation Service, which provides accreditation of calibration and testing laboratories in both the public and private sectors.

The three laboratories are now executive agencies. Consultants are examining options on the DTI's laboratories, including the possibilities of privatisation or rationalisation. The DTI's former Warren Spring Laboratory has been merged with AEA Technology to create a new National Environmental Technology Centre.

Technology Transfer

The DTI concentrates support on helping firms gain access to, and assimilate, technology; building up partnerships among firms; working with higher education; learning from overseas; and ensuring firms have the facilities to enable them to innovate and to do business better. The DTI is significantly improving companies' access to science and technology by making innovation services available locally—for example, through Business Link. Business Link will help sustained partnerships to be formed; it will bring together those in the public and private sectors offering business support services (including the DTI's technology and innovation services) for the benefit of the local company customer. Many local innovation networks already exist which bring together expertise in higher education institutions, technical colleges, industrial research organisations and other bodies. The DTI intends to build on these networks and improve access to them for small and medium-sized establishments.

DTI initiatives to enhance companies' awareness of management best practice will continue through the Managing in the 90s programme (see p. 154), which will be extended to include the management of innovation. The DTI Innovation Unit works nationally and regionally, predominantly through the use of secondees from industry, to promote innovation best practice. The DTI is also developing a more comprehensive information service about technology overseas.

Ministry of Defence

Expenditure by the Ministry of Defence on research and development in 1992–93 amounted to more than £2,800 million. Some £474 million of this was medium- and long-term applied research relevant to military needs, much of it carried out in the MoD's Defence Research Agency (DRA) and other smaller establishments. The Government is committed to achieving a gradual reduction in real terms in spending on defence R & D.

Several research establishments merged to form the Defence Research Agency in 1991. With an annual turnover of just under £800 million, it is the largest single scientific employer in Britain. Its role is to provide scientific and technical services primarily to the MoD and also to other government departments.

The DRA subcontracts some £200 million of research to industry and universities, ensuring that their know-how is harnessed to meeting military requirements. The DRA also works closely with industry in order to ensure that scientific and technological advances are taken forward at an early stage into development and production. This technology transfer is not just confined to the defence industry but has also led to important 'spin-offs' from defence into civil markets, in fields ranging from new materials and electronic devices to advanced aerodynamics. The latter in particular has been instrumental in giving Britain a leading role in civil aircraft design.

The DRA's work for other government departments in 1992–93 amounted to £46 million. A further £23 million of work was carried out for non-government customers.

Recent technological innovations by the DRA include the invention of a technique for detecting low concentrations of gas at great distances at sea, which has potential civil applications for the identification of hazardous gases.

Other Government Departments

Ministry of Agriculture, Fisheries and Food

MAFF co-ordinates its research programme with The Scottish Office Agriculture and Fisheries Department, the Department of Agriculture for Northern Ireland and the AFRC (see p 276). It also covers the research interests of the Welsh Office Agriculture Department.

Its research programme reflects the Ministry's wide-ranging responsibilities for protection and enhancement of the rural and marine environment, food safety and quality, improving animal health and welfare, the prevention of flooding and coastal erosion, and improving the economic performance of the agriculture, fisheries and food industries.

Research expenditure deployed with contractors in 1992–93 was £124 million, including the AFRC (£35 million); ADAS (see p. 239—£17 million); Horticulture Research International (£14.5 million); Central Science Laboratory (£10.8 million); and the Central Veterinary Laboratory (£9.2 million).

Department for Education

The DFE remains the main source of public funding for the universities. Together with the Scottish and Welsh education departments, the DTI and the Department of Employment, the DFE funds a number of schemes for training full-time students and those working in industry in the latest technology.

Department of the Environment

The Department of the Environment funds research in several policy areas: environmental protection, including radioactive substances; water; the countryside; planning and inner cities; local government; housing; building and construction; and energy efficiency. The three largest sub-programmes are those on pollution-related climate change, regional and urban air quality, and the safe disposal of radioactive waste. Total research expenditure in 1992–93 was £94 million.

Department of Health

The Department of Health has introduced the first comprehensive R & D strategy for the National Health Service in England and Wales. This focuses on improving methods of health care and achieving a cost-effective use of resources. The Department also manages a Health and Personal Social Services research programme concerned with the needs of ministers and policy-makers, with emphasis on improving efficiency.

Overseas Development Administration

The Overseas Development Administration (ODA) conducts research programmes which are directly targeted on the main needs of developing countries. Some of these may be addressed by adapting suitable existing Western technology, while others are unique to the developing world and therefore require special treatment.

The ODA supports research worth over £34 million a year on renewable natural resources and the environment, with the objective of developing basic technologies with a regional or global application (see p. 307).

It also supports the work of the Consultative Group on International Agricultural Research and the EC's Science and Technology for Development programme.

Using the expertise of agencies such as the Transport Research Laboratory, the British Geological Survey, Hydraulics Research Ltd and the Institute of Hydrology, the ODA supports a research programme worth around £10 million a year to tackle infrastructure problems. It also commissions research from universities and industry. Current programmes include reduced cost sewerage systems; water disinfection and waste treatment techniques; simple pump technology; and heat storage technology for cooking.

The Scottish Office

The Scottish Office both contracts and undertakes itself a wide range of R & D commissions. Total R & D expenditure in 1992–93 was £72 million.

RESEARCH IN UNIVERSITIES

The new higher education funding councils in England, Scotland and Wales (see p. 401) are the largest single source of finance for universities in Great Britain. About 40 per cent of research carried out in universities is financed from resources allocated by these bodies. These funds contribute to the cost of academic staff—who usually teach as well as carry out research—and pay for support staff, administration, equipment and accommodation. In Northern Ireland the universities are funded by the Department of Education for Northern Ireland.

The research councils also support scientific research in the universities and other institutions of higher education in two main ways. First, they provide postgraduate awards to over a quarter of postgraduate students in science and technology. Secondly, they give grants and contracts to universities and other institutions for specified projects, particularly in new or developing areas of research. The research councils have become responsible for meeting all the costs of the research projects they support in universities and other higher education institutions, except for costs associated with the salaries of permanent academic staff and computing costs. These are met by the higher education institutions. Research performance of departments is a key element in the selective allocation of funding to universities.

The other main channels of support for scientific research in universities are government departments, charities and industry. The European Community also provides substantial funding. Universities are expected to recover the full cost of short-term commissioned research from the Government and industry.

The high quality of research in universities, and their marketing skills, have enabled them to attract more funding from a larger range of external sources, the main growth in funding having been in contract income from industry. Co-operation continues between the universities, industry and the Government in joint projects. The research income of universities from industry and other outside sources is rising rapidly and amounted to £110 million in 1992.

Recent Research Developments

Universities in Britain have achieved a number of recent technological breakthroughs and enjoy a world-class reputation:

- A team of British and Japanese researchers at Cambridge University has made a breakthrough in semiconductor technology, which will enable microchips to store 500,000 times more memory data and consume far less power than those currently available. The development is expected to have far-reaching implications for portable computers, including the storage of sound and moving video images.

- Researchers at Imperial College, London, have developed extra-thin computer wires using thin film layers of crystals. These will be vital in linking increasingly tiny components, such as miniature electronic switches, used in ultra-fast computers.

- Scientists from Cambridge and Sheffield universities and a Cambridge biotechnology company have created a genetically disabled version of the herpes virus that could induce protective immunity against infection more efficiently than vaccination.

Science Parks

Science parks are partnerships between higher education institutions and industry to promote commercially focused research, often involving advanced technology. By mid-1993 there were 40 such parks in operation, at or near universities, with accommodation for over 1,000 companies. Most are involved in computing, electronics, instrumentation, robotics, electrical engineering, chemicals and biotechnology. Research, development and training activities are prevalent, rather than large-scale manufacturing. The biggest science park is at Cambridge, with some 85 companies on site. The most recently opened parks are at Oxford, Cranfield, Westlakes (Cumbria) and York.

A growing number of universities now offer industry interdisciplinary research centres with exploitable resources. These include access to analytical equipment, library facilities and worldwide databases as well as academic expertise.

OTHER ORGANISATIONS

Charitable Foundations

The combined contribution of charitable foundations to medical research in Britain in 1992–93 was about £320 million. The Wellcome Trust made the greatest contribution to this overall total, at over £77 million. The next largest spender was the Imperial Cancer Research Fund at £50 million.

British Technology Group

British Technology Group (BTG) is among the world's leading technology transfer companies. It promotes the profitable commercialisation of technology by:

- developing and protecting technology arising from research carried out by individuals, universities and other research organisations which BTG considers will be commercially viable;
- licensing the resulting intellectual property rights to companies throughout the world; and

- assessing the commercial potential of companies' proprietary technology and licensing this technology to other companies worldwide.

BTG administers over 9,000 patents covering more than 1,500 technologies. In 1992–93 the Group's total revenue exceeded £26 million. Annual sales value of products currently licensed by BTG amounts to more than £1,500 million. The company is owned by a consortium consisting of BTG management, employees and financial institutions.

Professional Institutions and Learned Societies

There are numerous technical institutions and professional associations in Britain, many of which promote their own disciplines or the education and professional well-being of their members.

The Council of Science and Technology Institutes has seven member institutes representing biology, chemical engineering, chemistry, food science and technology, geology, hospital physics and physics. The Engineering Council promotes the study of all types of engineering in schools and other organisations, in co-operation with its 240 industry affiliates. These include large private sector companies and government departments. Together with 42 professional engineering institutions, the Council accredits courses in higher education institutions. It also advises the Government on a range of academic, industrial and professional issues.

More than 300 learned societies play an important part in the promotion of science and technology through meetings, publications and sponsorship.

The Royal Society

The most prestigious learned society is the Royal Society, founded in 1660. It has over 1,100 Fellows and over 100 Foreign Members, many of whom serve on governmental advisory councils and committees concerned with research. The Society's expenditure in 1992–93 was nearly

£22 million. Nearly 80 per cent of funding is derived from the Government, the remainder coming from private sources.

The Society encourages scientific research and its application through a programme of meetings and lectures, publications, and by awarding grants, fellowships and other funding. It recognises scientific and technological achievements through election to the Fellowship and the award of medals and endowed lectureships. As the national academy of sciences, it represents Britain in international non-governmental organisations and is involved in a variety of international scientific programmes. It also facilitates collaborative projects and the exchange of scientists through bilateral agreements with academies and research councils throughout the world. It gives independent advice on scientific matters, notably to government, and represents and supports the scientific community as a whole.

The Society is increasingly active in promoting science understanding and awareness among the general public, as well as science education. It also supports research into the history of scientific endeavour.

Royal Academy of Engineering

The national academy of engineering in Britain is the Royal Academy of Engineering, which was founded in 1976 and received its Royal Charter in 1982. The Academy, which has some 900 Fellows and 43 Foreign Members, promotes the advancement of engineering for the benefit of the public. It administers a grant from the OST amounting to £1.7 million in 1993–94, which accounts for nearly 30 per cent of its total budget.

Other Societies

In Scotland the Royal Society of Edinburgh, established in 1783, promotes science by awarding scholarships, organising meetings and symposia, publishing journals and awarding prizes. It also administers fellowship schemes for post-doctoral research workers.

Three other major institutions publicise scientific developments through lectures and publications for specialists and for schoolchildren. Of these, the British Association for the Advancement of Science (BAAS), founded in 1831, is mainly concerned with science, while the Royal Society of Arts, dating from 1754, deals with the arts and commerce as well as science. The Royal Institution, founded in 1799, also performs these functions and runs its own research laboratories.

The Committee on the Public Understanding of Science (COPUS), set up in 1986 by the Royal Society, the BAAS, and the Royal Institution, acts as a focus for a broad-ranging programme in Britain to improve public awareness of science and technology. It recommends initiatives to its sponsoring bodies and promotes activities of other organisations and institutions.

Zoological Gardens

The Zoological Society of London, an independent scientific body, runs London Zoo, which occupies some 15 hectares (36 acres) of Regent's Park, London. The zoo has successfully operated a captive breeding programme to conserve some of the world's most endangered animals, such as Brazilian golden lion tamarins. The Society is responsible for the Institute of Zoology, which carries out research in conservation and comparative medicine. It also organises scientific meetings and symposia, and publishes scientific journals.

Whipsnade Wild Animal Park near Dunstable (Bedfordshire) is also managed by the Society. Other well-known zoos include those at Edinburgh, Bristol, Chester, Dudley and Marwell (near Winchester).

Botanic Gardens

The Royal Botanic Gardens, founded in 1759, cover 121 hectares (300 acres) at Kew in west London and a 187-hectare (462-acre) estate at Wakehurst Place, Ardingly, in West Sussex. They contain the largest collections of living and dried plants in the world. Research is conducted into all aspects of plant life, including physiology, biochemistry, genetics, economic botany and the conservation of habitats and species. Kew has the world's largest seed bank for wild origin species and is active in programmes to return endangered plant species to the wild. It participates in joint research programmes in 52 countries.

The Royal Botanic Garden in Edinburgh, founded in 1670, is a centre for research into taxonomy (classification of species), for the conservation and study of living plants and for horticultural education.

Scientific Museums

The Natural History Museum, which includes the Geological Museum, has 60 million specimens ranging in size from a blue whale skeleton to minute insects. It is one of the world's principal centres for research into natural history, offering an advisory service to institutions all over the world. The museum is keen to promote public appreciation of nature conservation and in 1991 opened a major exhibition on ecology, illustrating the diversity of living species.

The Science Museum promotes understanding of the history of science, technology, industry and medicine. Its extensive collection of scientific instruments and machinery is complemented by interactive computer games and audio-visual equipment for visitors to use. In this way the museum explains scientific principles to the public and documents the history of science, from early discoveries to space age technology. These two museums are in South Kensington, London. Other important collections include those of the Museum of Science and Industry in Birmingham, the Museum of Science and Industry in Manchester, the Museum of the History of Science in Oxford, and the Royal Scottish Museum, Edinburgh.

INTERNATIONAL SCIENTIFIC RELATIONS

European Community

Since 1984 the European Community has run a series of R & D framework programmes in a number of strategic sectors, with the aim of strengthening the scientific and technological basis of European industry and improving its international competitiveness. The Third Framework Programme lasts from 1990 to 1994, with an EC budget of 6,600 million ECUs (£5,079 million). It covers the following broad categories:

- information and communication technologies;
- industrial and material technologies;
- the environment;
- life sciences and technologies;
- energy; and
- human capital and mobility.

Negotiations on the Fourth Framework Programme are well under way.

Britain hosts the Joint European Torus nuclear fusion project (JET), based at Culham, Oxfordshire. In an experiment conducted in December 1991, JET produced a power release of 1 megawatt for a period of two seconds. This is regarded as a potentially significant step towards demonstrating the feasibility of fusion as an energy source.

Other International Activities

EUREKA is an industry-led scheme to encourage co-operation in the development and production of high-technology products with the aim of improving Europe's competitiveness in world markets. The members of EUREKA are the 12 countries of the EC, six European Free Trade Association members, Hungary, Turkey and the European Commission.

In June 1993, 193 new projects were announced by EUREKA members, the total number of agreed projects reaching 816. The 49 new British projects involve a total of 76 British organisations.

The European Co-operation in the Field of Scientific and Technical Research (COST) programme encourages the co-ordination of national research activities. There are currently 25 member states, including the 12 EC countries. Of 77 current COST actions, Britain participates in 65.

Britain is a member of CERN (European Organisation for Nuclear Research) in Geneva. Its contributions to CERN, to the high-flux neutron source at the Institut Laue-Langevin and to the European Synchrotron Radiation Facility, both in Grenoble, are currently paid through SERC.

The European Synchrotron Radiation Facility, due for completion in 1998, has received 12 per cent of its total costs from Britain. British scientists and engineers had a role in designing and constructing detectors for three of the four major experimental stations of the Large Electron Positron collider at CERN. SERC is also a partner in the European Incoherent Scatter Radar facilities in northern Scandinavia, which conduct research on the middle and upper atmosphere.

Through the MRC, Britain participates in the Human Frontier Science Program, which supports international collaborative research in neuroscience and molecular biology. Britain is to host the European Bioinformatics Institute at Cambridge, which will be fully operational by 1995. As an outstation of the European Molecular Biology Laboratory, the Institute will provide up-to-date information on molecular biology and genome sequencing. Britain is also a member of the science and technology committees of international organisations such as the Organisation for Economic Co-operation and Developmen, NATO (North Atlantic Treaty Organisation) and various specialised agencies of the United Nations.

A number of intergovernmental and inter-agency agreements have been concluded with other countries for co-operation in science and technology. Among non-governmental organisations, the research councils, the Royal Society and the British Academy were founder members of the European Science Foundation in 1974. The research councils also maintain a joint office in Brussels to further European co-operation in research. Staff in British Embassies and High Commissions promote contacts in science and technology between Britain and overseas countries: there are science and technology sections at British Embassies in Paris, Bonn, Washington, Tokyo and Moscow.

The British Council (see p. 290) promotes better understanding and knowledge of Britain and its scientific and technological achievements. It encourages exchanges of specialists, supplies specialised information, and fosters co-operation in research, training and education. The Council also identifies and manages technological, scientific and educational projects in developing countries.

Space Activities

Britain's support for civil space research is co-ordinated by the British National Space Centre (BNSC), a partnership between various government departments and research councils. BNSC encourages industry to exploit opportunities in space, based on appraisal of project costs and potential technological and commercial benefits. Through BNSC, Britain spent some £170 million on space activities in 1992–93, financed mainly by the DTI and SERC. Around 62 per cent—£106 million—was devoted to programmes shared with the European Space Agency (ESA). The remainder supported a programme of R & D in government establishments, universities and industry.

The major part of Britain's space programme is concerned with satellite-based Earth observation (remote sensing) for commercial and environmental applications. Britain has committed around £60 million to the ESA's satellite ERS-1, which was launched in 1991 and provides all-weather, 24-hour coverage of the Earth. Britain provided the main active microwave instrument for ERS-1, along with a precision instrument to measure thermal infra-red emissions from the sea surface. British remote sensing instruments are also being flown on the Upper Atmosphere Research satellite launched and operated by the United States National Aeronautics and Space Administration (NASA).

The Earth Observation Data Centre at Farnborough (Hampshire), operated by the National Remote Sensing Centre, processes the data output from ERS-1 and successor missions. It is also one of the ESA's four processing and archiving facilities which store and distribute remotely-sensed data for both scientific and commercial purposes.

Britain is also contributing £284 million to the Columbus Polar Platform and ENVISAT-1 programmes. The Columbus programme is Europe's contribution to the International Space Station project, led by the United States. ENVISAT will be the first of a new generation of ESA environmental satellite missions to utilise the Polar Platform.

In space science, Britain participates in all of the ESA's missions. These range from the investigation of Halley's Comet (1986) and the comet Grigg Skjellerup (1992) by the British-built Giotto spacecraft to the Ulysses solar polar probe, which will become the first spacecraft to overfly the poles of the sun. Britain is contributing substantially to the Cluster and SOHO missions to be launched in 1995 to study the sun, the Earth's magnetosphere and the solar wind. It is also expected that Britain will participate in the ESA's X-ray spectroscopy mission due for launching in 1999.

There are bilateral arrangements for space research between Britain and other countries, notably the United States through NASA, the Commonwealth of Independent States and Japan. British groups have participated in several NASA space science missions, developing, for example, the wide-field camera for Germany's X-ray satellite ROSAT and a spectrometer for the Japanese-built Yohkoh satellite.

In Europe, Britain is both a leading producer and main user of satellite communications technology, exploiting commercially the expertise developed within the ESA's satellite communications programmes.

Further Reading

Realising Our Potential: A Strategy for Science, Engineering and Technology. Cm 2250. HMSO, 1993.

Review of Allocation Management and Use of Government Expenditure on Science and Technology. HMSO, 1993.

External Affairs

20 Overseas Relations

Britain is a member of some 120 international organisations, including the United Nations (UN), NATO (North Atlantic Treaty Organisation) and the European Community (EC). Closer co-operation between member states of the EC is the central aim of the Maastricht Treaty on European Union, which was ratified by Britain in August 1993. Britain plays an active part in maintaining international peace and security and is fully involved, for example, in efforts to bring about peace in former Yugoslavia. Britain also protects the interests of its dependent territories, which include Hong Kong, the Falkland Islands and Gibraltar.

ADMINISTRATION

The Foreign & Commonwealth Office (FCO) is in charge of overall foreign policy. The Foreign and Commonwealth Secretary is responsible for the work of the FCO and the Diplomatic Service. He is assisted by five ministers without Cabinet rank, one of whom is the Minister for Overseas Development responsible for the Overseas Development Administration (ODA). The FCO's Permanent Under-Secretary of State is head of the Diplomatic Service and provides advice to the Foreign and Commonwealth Secretary on all aspects of foreign policy.

Work overseas is carried out by Diplomatic Service staff, staff from other government departments and locally engaged personnel. About 26 per cent of frontline diplomatic staff are engaged on political/economic work, 17 per cent on commercial work, 20 per cent on entry clearance to Britain, 8 per cent on consular work, 6 per cent on aid administration, 4 per cent on information and 3 per cent on other activities, such as culture, and science and technology. Heads of post account for the remaining 16 per cent.

Britain remains committed to maintaining a worldwide diplomatic presence. There are British embassies and high commissions in 140 countries and missions at nine international organisations.

Other Departments

Other government departments, too, are concerned with overseas relations and foreign policy. The Ministry of Defence is responsible for British defence policy and for liaison with Britain's allies and NATO; it also

controls and administers the armed forces.
The Department of Trade and Industry
(DTI) has an important say on international
trade policy and commercial relations with
other countries, including other EC member
states. The FCO and the DTI have a joint
export promotion organisation—Overseas
Trade Services (see p. 203). The Treasury is
involved in British international economic
policy and is responsible for Britain's
relations with the World Bank and other
international financial institutions.

When other departments are involved the
FCO decides policy in consultation with
them. The department with the main interest
usually takes the lead, particularly in EC
matters and international economic policy.
The FCO co-ordinates EC policy through the
Cabinet Office European Secretariat.

The British Council

The British Council is the main agency for
British cultural relations overseas and is
represented in 100 countries. Its activities are:

- helping people to study, train or make
professional contacts in Britain;
- enabling British specialists to teach,
advise or establish joint projects
abroad;
- teaching English and promoting its use;
- providing library and information
services;
- promoting British education, science and
technology; and
- making British arts and literature more
widely known.

The Council is financed partly by a grant
from the FCO. The training and education
programmes organised by the Council on
behalf of the ODA and the FCO are another
important source of revenue. About a quarter
of the Council's income comes from its own
earnings.

The Council runs 143 libraries and
information centres and 72 English language
teaching centres. In 1991–92 nearly
8.5 million loans of books and other materials
were made to 500,000 library members. Up to
80,000 students at any one time were taking
part in the Council's English courses.

INTERNATIONAL ORGANISATIONS

The United Nations

Britain is a member of the United Nations
and one of the five permanent members of
the Security Council along with France, the
People's Republic of China, Russia and the
United States. It is the sixth largest
contributor to the UN budget. Britain is fully
committed to the principles of the UN
Charter and believes that all member states
should ensure that the organisation maintains
peace, assists developing countries effectively
and protects human rights and fundamental
freedoms. Under the UN Charter, member
states are committed to:

- refrain from the threat or use of force
against the territory or political
independence of any state; and
- seek solutions to their disputes by
peaceful means.

The Charter recognises and permits the
right of individual or collective defence
against armed attack and the existence of
regional arrangements designed to maintain
security.

The European Community

Britain is an active and committed member of
the European Community, which was set up
by the 1957 Treaty of Rome (see p. 294). As
one of the larger countries, it provides two of
the 17 members of the European
Commission, which puts forward policy
proposals, executes decisions taken by the
Council of Ministers and ensures that
Community rules are correctly observed.
Britain is represented at each meeting of the
EC Council of Ministers, which is the
Community's main decision-taking body.
Each Council consists of government
ministers from the 12 member states,
representing national interests in the subjects
under discussion—for example, trade,
agriculture or transport. Each member state
has a permanent representative at Community
headquarters in Brussels.

The membership of the European
Parliament will increase from 518 to 567 in

1994 and Britain's allocation of seats will rise to 87. Of its current 81 representatives, 66 were elected in England, eight in Scotland, four in Wales and three in Northern Ireland.

The Parliament, which is consulted about major Community decisions, has substantial shared power with the Council of Ministers over the setting of the Community budget.

The European Court of Justice interprets and adjudicates on Community law; there are 13 judges, one from each member state and an extra one to prevent a deadlock. Six advocates-general advise the Court. The Court is assisted by a Court of First Instance, which handles certain cases brought by individuals and companies.

Britain is also represented on the Court of Auditors, which examines Community revenue and expenditure to see that it is legally received and spent.

Community policies are implemented by:

- regulations, which are legally binding on all member states;
- directives, which are binding on the member states to which they are addressed, but which allow national authorities to decide on methods of implementation;
- decisions, which are binding on member states, firms or individuals; and
- recommendations, which have no binding force.

NATO

Membership of NATO is the keystone of British defence policy (see pp. 309–14). NATO is based on the principle of collective security and its core security functions are to:

- provide a foundation for security in Europe;
- deter aggression and defend member states against it; and
- provide a forum for allied transatlantic consultation.

Each of the 16 member states has a permanent representative at NATO headquarters in Brussels. The main decision-taking body is the North Atlantic Council, at which foreign ministers meet at least twice a year. Permanent representatives meet on a weekly basis at other meetings of the Council. Defence ministers attend meetings of the Defence Planning Committee and the Nuclear Planning Group.

Western European Union

Britain is one of the nine members of the Western European Union, which is the main forum for co-operation and consultation on defence issues for NATO's European members. The current membership is Belgium, Britain, France, Germany, Italy, Luxembourg, the Netherlands, Portugal and Spain. It is being widened to include Greece as the tenth full member. Iceland, Norway and Turkey are becoming associate members, and Denmark and the Irish Republic observer members. For further information, see p. 311.

Council of Europe

Britain is a founding member of the Council of Europe, which is open to any European parliamentary democracy accepting the rule of law and the protection of fundamental human rights and freedoms. The member states co-operate on culture, education, sport, health, crime and drug prevention, youth affairs and the improvement of the environment. In 1950 the Council adopted its European Convention on Human Rights (see p. 302).

The Commonwealth

There are 50 members of the Commonwealth, including Britain. It is a voluntary association of states, nearly all of which were British territories to which independence was granted. The members are Antigua and Barbuda, Australia, Bahamas, Bangladesh, Barbados, Belize, Botswana, Britain, Brunei, Canada, Cyprus, Dominica, The Gambia, Ghana, Grenada, Guyana, India, Jamaica, Kenya, Kiribati, Lesotho, Malawi, Malaysia, Maldives, Malta, Mauritius, Namibia, Nauru, New Zealand, Nigeria, Pakistan, Papua New Guinea, Saint Christopher and Nevis, Saint Lucia, Saint

Vincent and the Grenadines, Seychelles, Sierra Leone, Singapore, Solomon Islands, Sri Lanka, Swaziland, Tanzania, Tonga, Trinidad and Tobago, Tuvalu, Uganda, Vanuatu, Western Samoa, Zambia and Zimbabwe. Nauru and Tuvalu are special members, entitled to take part in all Commonwealth meetings and activities, with the exception of Commonwealth Heads of Government meetings.

Consultation between member states takes place through:

- meetings of heads of government;
- specialised conferences of other ministers and officials;
- diplomatic representatives known as high commissioners; and
- non-governmental organisations.

The Queen is recognised as head of the Commonwealth and is head of state in some member countries.

The Commonwealth Secretariat promotes consultation, disseminates information, and organises heads of government meetings, ministerial meetings and other conferences. It administers co-operative programmes agreed at these meetings, including the Commonwealth Fund for Technical Co-operation, which provides expertise to Commonwealth developing countries.

Membership of the Commonwealth enables Britain to play a responsible part alongside other nations in aiding the development and stability of the Third World. Some two-thirds of British aid (see p. 304) goes to Commonwealth countries. The British Government participates fully in all Commonwealth activities and welcomes it as a means of consulting and co-operating with peoples of widely differing cultures.

Other International Bodies

Britain is a member of many other international bodies, including the International Monetary Fund, which regulates the international financial system and provides a source of credit for member countries facing balance of payments difficulties.

In addition, Britain, along with 23 other industrialised countries, belongs to the Organisation for Economic Co-operation and Development (OECD), which promotes economic growth, helps less developed countries and encourages worldwide trade expansion.

Other organisations to which Britain belongs or extends support include the regional development banks in Africa, the Caribbean, Latin America and Asia.

BRITAIN'S DEPENDENT TERRITORIES

Britain's dependent territories have a combined population of about 6 million, of whom 5.8 million live in Hong Kong. Most territories have considerable self-government, with their own legislature. Britain is generally responsible for defence, security, external affairs, the civil service and the judiciary. The territories are:

- Anguilla;
- Bermuda;
- British Antarctic Territory;
- British Indian Ocean Territory;
- British Virgin Islands;
- Cayman Islands;
- Falkland Islands;
- Gibraltar;
- Hong Kong;
- Montserrat;
- Pitcairn, Ducie, Henderson and Oeno;
- St Helena and St Helena Dependencies (Ascension and Tristan da Cunha);
- South Georgia and the South Sandwich Islands; and
- Turks and Caicos Islands.

Few are rich in natural resources, and some are scattered groups of islands. There are no permanent inhabitants in the British Antarctic Territory, British Indian Ocean Territory or South Georgia and the South Sandwich Islands.

Britain's policy is to help the inhabitants of the dependent territories to take independence if they want it and where it is practicable to do so. The reasonable needs of the dependent territories are a first call on the British aid programme.

Hong Kong

In 1984 an agreement was signed between Britain and the People's Republic of China on the future of Hong Kong, 92 per cent of which is leased from China until 1997. Under the Sino-British Joint Declaration, which was ratified by the two governments in 1985, Britain is responsible for the administration of Hong Kong until 30 June 1997. Hong Kong will then become a Special Administrative Region (SAR) of China, but its capitalist system and lifestyle will remain unchanged for at least 50 years. With the exception of foreign affairs and defence, the Hong Kong SAR will enjoy a high degree of autonomy and its government and legislature will be composed of Hong Kong people.

In September 1991 direct elections took place for the first time for 18 seats in the Legislative Council. Another 21 of the 60 seats were elected indirectly. In October 1992 the Governor announced a package of constitutional proposals designed to extend the franchise for the 1995 Council elections.

In April 1993 the British and Chinese governments started talks with the intention of reaching an understanding on the 1995 election arrangements. Britain wants these elections to be open, fair and acceptable to the people of Hong Kong. Another important objective is that the Council elected in 1995 should be able to serve for its full four-year term, during which Hong Kong will revert to Chinese sovereignty in 1997.

Falkland Islands

The Falkland Islands are the subject of a territorial claim by Argentina but the inhabitants wish to remain under British sovereignty. The Government does not accept the Argentine claim to sovereignty and is committed to defend the Islanders' right to live under a government of their own choosing. The Islanders' right of self-determination is set out in the 1985 Falkland Islands Constitution.

In 1982 Argentina invaded and occupied the Islands but its forces were expelled as a result of British military action following Argentina's failure to abide by United Nations resolutions requesting its forces to withdraw. In recent years Britain and Argentina, while maintaining their respective positions on sovereignty, have restored diplomatic relations and continue to discuss their common interests in the South Atlantic, such as fisheries conservation.

Gibraltar

Gibraltar is the subject of a territorial claim by Spain. Britain is committed to honouring the wishes of the people of Gibraltar on their future, as set out in the 1969 Gibraltar Constitution. Britain and Spain, while maintaining their respective positions on sovereignty, are pledged to increase practical co-operation between Gibraltar and Spain to the benefit of both peoples.

THE EUROPEAN COMMUNITY

As a European power, Britain is concerned first of all with the prosperity and security of this area of the world.

The main instrument for achieving European prosperity is the European Community, which is an association of 12 democratic nations—Belgium, Britain, Denmark, France, Germany, Greece, the Irish Republic, Italy, Luxembourg, the Netherlands, Portugal and Spain.

The British Government is strongly in favour of enlarging the Community to include other democratic nations in Europe. In early 1993 accession negotiations were launched with Austria, Finland, Norway and Sweden. A target date of 1 January 1995 has been set for accession.

Britain regards the Community as a means of strengthening democracy and reinforcing political stability in Europe, and of increasing the collective strength of member states in international negotiations. The Government wants Britain to be at the heart of a Community in which member states work effectively together by pooling their ideas and resources for shared purposes, provided that

The European Community

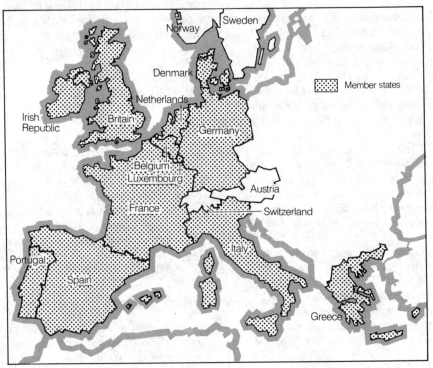

such objectives cannot be achieved by member states acting on their own.

The Community had its origins in the resolve by Western European nations, particularly France and Germany, not to allow wars to break out again between themselves. The Rome Treaty defined Community aims as the harmonious development of economic activities, a continuous and balanced economic expansion and an accelerated rise in the standard of living. These objectives were to be achieved by the creation of a common internal market and progressive harmonisation of economic policies involving:

- the elimination of customs duties between member states;

- free movement of goods, people, services and capital;

- a common commercial policy towards other countries;

- the elimination of distortions in competition within the common market;

- the creation of a Social Fund to improve job opportunities for workers and raise their standard of living;

- the adoption of common agricultural and transport policies; and

- the association of overseas developing countries with the Community in order to increase trade and promote economic and social development.

These objectives have been confirmed and augmented by the Single European Act of 1986 and the 1991 Maastricht Treaty on European Union.

European Union

The Rome Treaty's signatories declared themselves 'determined to establish the foundations of an ever closer union between the peoples of Europe'. This aim was restated in the Maastricht Treaty.

The nature of European union has never been formally defined. Successive British governments have opposed the creation of a unitary state or federal structure in which national sovereignty would be submerged. In practice, European union has been a step-by-step process of greater co-operation, building on existing policies and elaborating new ones within the framework of the Treaties.

Maastricht Treaty

The Maastricht Treaty amends the Rome Treaty and makes other new commitments. It:
- introduces the concept of Union citizenship as a supplement to national citizenship, provides some measure of institutional reform and strengthens control of the Community's finances;
- provides on an intergovernmental basis for a common foreign and security policy and for greater co-operation on issues concerned with justice and home affairs;
- clarifies and codifies Community competences in areas such as regional strategy, consumer protection, education and vocational training, the environment and public health;
- provides for moves towards economic and monetary union; and
- embodies the principle of subsidiarity under which action is taken at Community level only if its objectives cannot be achieved by member states acting alone.

The 1992 Edinburgh summit agreed to apply a subsidiarity test to all future proposals for Community action. A review of existing EC legislation is under way to ensure that it conforms to the subsidiarity principle.

Following approval by Parliament, the Treaty was ratified by Britain in August 1993. All the other member states have also ratified the Treaty.

Economic and Monetary Union

During the negotiations on economic and monetary union (EMU), the Government sought to ensure that:
- there would be no commitment by Britain to move to a single monetary policy or single currency;

- monetary matters would remain a national responsibility until the Community moved to a single currency and monetary policy;
- member states would retain primary responsibility for their economic policies; and
- there were clear and quantifiable convergence conditions which member states would have to satisfy before moving to a single currency.

The Treaty provides for progress towards EMU in three stages: the first—completion of the single market—has been achieved (see p. 296). Under stage 2, a European Monetary Institute will be established with a largely advisory and consultative role. Although the Institute will prepare for stage 3, monetary policy will still be a national responsibility. Member states will co-ordinate economic policies in the context of agreed non-binding policy guidelines. The British Government supports the first and second stages of EMU.

Under the Treaty a single currency is envisaged by 1 January 1999, although member states will have to satisfy certain criteria on inflation rates, government deficit levels, currency fluctuation margins and interest rates. A special protocol recognises that Britain is not obliged or committed to move to this final stage of EMU without a separate decision to do so by the Government and Parliament at the appropriate time.

The Community Budget

The Community's revenue consists of:
- levies on agricultural imports;
- customs duties;
- the proceeds of a notional rate of value added tax (VAT) of up to 1.4 per cent on a standard 'basket' of goods and services; and
- contributions from member states based on gross national product (GNP).

Overall Community revenue is limited by a ceiling of 1.2 per cent of Community GNP.

When it first joined the Community, Britain made a net contribution to the budget far in excess of that justified by its share of

GNP. Following a series of negotiations to put this right, Britain has received since 1984 a rebate which is worth some £2,000 million a year.

An agreement on future Community finance was reached at the 1992 Edinburgh summit. Under this there is no increase in the revenue ceiling until 1995, when it will rise in steps, reaching 1.27 per cent of Community GNP in 1999. The revenue system will be reformed to ensure that member states' contributions reflect more accurately their relative prosperity. Agricultural spending will be less than half the Community budget by the end of the century, compared with 80 per cent in 1973 and 50 per cent at present. More resources will be allocated to the poorer regions of the Community.

Single Market

The Single European Act set the deadline of 31 December 1992 for the completion of the single market. The Edinburgh summit agreed that this programme had been successfully completed in all essential respects. The Government believes that the single market will reduce business costs, stimulate efficiency and encourage the creation of jobs and wealth. The single market programme covers, among other things, the liberalisation of capital movements, the opening up of public procurement markets and the mutual recognition of professional qualifications.

Transport

Britain fully supports the liberalisation of transport in the Community. Measures so far taken include the removal of permits and quotas on road haulage and the establishment of a single market in civil aviation. Airlines meeting established safety and common financial fitness criteria are entitled to an operating licence allowing virtually unrestricted access to routes within the Community. They are free to set fares and rates according to their commercial judgment.

In 1992 a regulation was agreed on slot allocation at airports designed to back up the single market in aviation; it aims to protect the legitimate interests of established carriers while promoting competition by assisting new entrants.

The opening of the Channel Tunnel in 1994 (see p. 255) will improve Britain's links with other member states.

European Economic Area

In 1992 the Community reached an agreement with the seven members of the European Free Trade Association (EFTA) to extend free movement of goods, services and capital to the EFTA countries in a new European Economic Area (EEA, see p. 201). Implementation of this agreement was delayed by the result of a referendum in Switzerland which narrowly turned down Swiss membership of the EEA. The EEA is expected to be the world's largest single market when it comes into operation.

Trade

Britain is the world's fifth largest trading nation and the Community is the world's largest trading bloc, accounting for about a third of all trade.

The British Government fully supports a world open trading system on which EC member states depend for future economic growth and jobs.

Under the Rome Treaty, the European Commission speaks on behalf of Britain and the other EC member states in international trade negotiations, such as the various rounds of the General Agreement on Tariffs and Trade (GATT). The Commission negotiates on a mandate agreed by the Council of Ministers.

For further information on trade, see Chapter 15.

The Environment

The Community is at the forefront of many international measures on environmental issues, such as car exhaust pollution and the depletion of the ozone layer. For further information, see pp. 349–50.

AGRICULTURE .

Domestic pigs can now 'root' for food in the way they would in the wild, thanks to a food ball designed at the Scottish Agricultural College. The ball dispenses food pellets as the pig pushes it around. 'Playing' with the food ball also keeps pigs fitter.

A field of oilseed rape at Cookham Dean, Berkshire: the amount of land planted to oilseed rape has increased significantly in recent years.

TOURISM

The Military Tattoo, held in the dramatic setting of Edinburgh Castle every year, is one of Scotland's biggest tourist attractions.

Reconstruction of an emigrant ship at the Ulster-American Folk Park, which specialises in the history of Irish emigration to America.

Visitors at Madame Tussauds view wax figures of Henry VIII and his wives. Madame Tussauds is London's top tourist attraction, with over 2 million visitors a year.

Snowdonia National Park, in north Wales, is a popular holiday destination for those who want to participate in outdoor pursuits such as walking, climbing, canoeing and pony-trekking.

HEALTH

Researchers at the Institute of Ophthalmology have devised a test to detect glaucoma two years earlier than conventional tests. Early diagnosis and treatment can slow down, or even stop, the progress of the disease.

Dr Janet Rennie, part of a team working on behalf of the charity Action Research, scans the brain of a premature baby girl. The aim of this research project, at Addenbrooke's Hospital, Cambridge, is to reduce the risk of brain damage in premature babies.

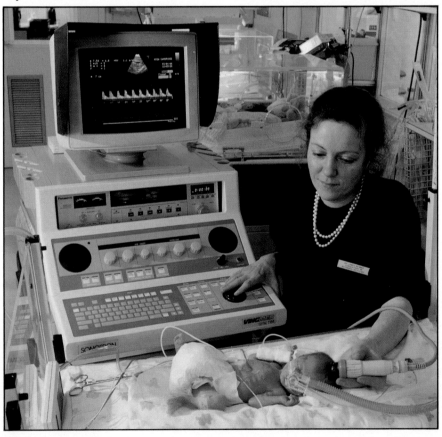

Agriculture and Fisheries

The Common Agricultural Policy (CAP) is designed to secure food supplies and to stabilise markets. It has also, however, created overproduction and unwanted food surpluses, placing a burden on the Community budget.

The Common Fisheries Policy is concerned with the rational conservation and management of fishery resources. The operation of these policies, and Britain's advocacy of CAP reform, are described in Chapter 17.

Structural Funds

The EC Structural Funds are designed to:

- promote economic development in poorer regions;

- improve regions seriously affected by industrial decline;

- combat long-term unemployment;

- train young people to find jobs; and

- promote development in rural areas.

Infrastructure projects and productive investments are financed by the European Regional Development Fund. The European Social Fund supports training and employment measures for the long-term unemployed and young people. The Guidance Section of the European Agricultural Guidance and Guarantee Fund supports agricultural restructuring and some rural development measures. A new fund to support restructuring in the fishing industry was created in 1993.

Other Community programmes aim to assist the development of new economic activities in regions affected by the restructuring of traditional industries such as steel, coal and shipbuilding.

The European Investment Bank, a non-profit-making institution, lends at competitive interest rates to public and private capital projects. Lending is directed towards:

- less-favoured regions;

- transport infrastructure;

- protection of the environment;

- improving industrial competitiveness; and

- supporting loans to small and medium-sized enterprises.

The Bank also provides loans in support of the Community's policy of co-operation with the countries of the Mediterranean basin, Central and Eastern Europe and the African, Caribbean and Pacific (ACP) states (see pp. 201–2).

The Maastricht Treaty provides for the setting up of a Cohesion Fund in order to reduce the gaps between the prosperity of the poorest member states of the Community and the others. The Fund will finance projects on environmental protection and transport infrastructure in Spain, Portugal, Greece and the Irish Republic.

Employment and Social Affairs

In Britain's view, Community social policy should be primarily concerned with job creation and with maintaining a well-educated and trained workforce to ensure competitiveness in world markets. The Government supports:

- measures to safeguard health and safety at work, freedom of movement for workers, Community-wide recognition of professional and vocational qualifications and equal opportunities at work; and

- practical measures to increase jobs and cut unemployment.

The Government is opposed to measures which, in its view, would impose further regulations and costs on employers and damage Community competitiveness. For this reason, the Government negotiated a clause in the Maastricht Treaty, under which new and far-reaching Community powers in the social area apply only to the other 11 member states and not to Britain.

Research and Development

Community research collaboration is promoted primarily through a series of framework programmes defining priorities and setting out the overall level of funding. The British Government actively encourages British companies and organisations to participate in collaborative research and development (R & D) with European partners.

Under the current programme, which ends in 1994 (see p. 284), priority is given to information technology (ESPRIT), telecommunications (RACE) and industrial materials and technologies; however, there are other important programmes covering the environment, biotechnology, agriculture, health and energy. There is also a scheme for the exchange of researchers.

INTERNATIONAL PEACE AND SECURITY

Britain believes that states should not use, or threaten, force against other sovereign states and that they should resolve their disputes by peaceful means.

The United Nations has the authority to seek to resolve disputes which threaten international peace and stability. In January 1992 a special meeting of the UN Security Council was convened by Britain at the level of heads of state or government. The meeting:

- reaffirmed that all disputes should be settled peacefully in accordance with the UN Charter;

- requested the Secretary General to make recommendations on a more effective role for the UN in preventive diplomacy and as peacemaker and peacekeeper; and

- committed Council members to arms control and the conclusion of a convention on chemical weapons.

Peacekeeping

Britain is playing a full role in the expansion of UN peacekeeping and is one of the largest contributors of troops to UN operations. In addition, it pays its assessed share of 6.4 per cent of the costs of UN peacekeeping.

By the end of 1993 there are likely to be nearly 100,000 troops taking part in 15 UN operations. British troops are serving on peacekeeping missions in Cyprus and Kuwait, as well as in former Yugoslavia and Cambodia. Their tasks include mine clearance, logistic support, relief convoy

escort, naval monitoring and acting as unarmed military observers.

Former Yugoslavia

Britain is committed to supporting efforts to establish a lasting and equitable peace in former Yugoslavia and is deeply involved in efforts to relieve suffering caused by the fighting in Bosnia-Herzegovina and to prevent it spreading.

Since the outbreak of inter-ethnic hostilities in mid-1991 the European Community and the UN have led the search for peace. In September 1991 the EC established a peace conference to try and obtain a ceasefire between Serbian and Croatian forces. It also set up a mission based in Zagreb to monitor tension and to resolve conflict at local level. In February 1992 the UN Protection Force (UNPROFOR) was set up to monitor a ceasefire between Serbia and Croatia.

On the basis of recommendations made by an arbitration commission attached to the EC Conference, the EC recognised Slovenia and Croatia in January 1992 and Bosnia-Herzegovina in April 1992. Serbia and Montenegro proclaimed themselves the Federal Republic of Yugoslavia, which has not achieved international recognition and is excluded from nearly all international forums. Britain and some of its EC partners recognised the former Yugoslav republic of Macedonia by voting for its admission to the UN in April 1993.

In April 1992 the conflict in Bosnia between Serbs, Croats and Muslims escalated. The UN imposed sanctions in May on Serbia and Montenegro because of their failure to take measures to cease military intervention in Bosnia. In August 1992 Britain, as President of the EC, convened the London Conference, co-chaired by the British Prime Minister and the UN Secretary General. The Conference brought together all the main parties to the conflict, who agreed to documents setting out clear principles for a negotiated settlement. Efforts to resolve the conflict on the basis of these principles have continued in the International Conference on the former Yugoslavia under the co-chairmanship of EC and UN mediators.

Fighting in Bosnia has displaced many people from their homes, some 2 million people becoming dependent on humanitarian relief. The airlift of humanitarian supplies to Sarajevo began in June 1992. UNPROFOR's mandate was enlarged in September 1992 to provide for military escorts for the aid convoys. Britain subsequently deployed 2,400 troops to the UN for this purpose. Since the beginning of the crisis, the EC and its member states have contributed some £400 million to the aid effort. Britain's total EC and bilateral contributions are over £140 million.

Cambodia

Between 1991 and 1993 the United Nations was involved in the implementation of an international peace agreement designed to end 13 years of civil war in Cambodia. Britain and the other permanent members of the UN Security Council agreed on the main principles for a settlement, which were endorsed by the UN General Assembly in 1990. These formed the basis of the 1991 Paris agreements creating the UN Transitional Authority in Cambodia (UNTAC). In May 1993 UNTAC organised free and fair elections to a constituent assembly and its mandate ended when the assembly formed a new government in September 1993. Britain contributed over 6 per cent of UNTAC's costs and provided over 120 personnel to UNTAC's military component, including the commander of a mine clearance training unit. Some 40 British polling station officers helped to run the 1993 election. Britain has pledged $30 million of aid since October 1991 to assist the reconstruction of Cambodia.

EASTERN EUROPE AND THE FORMER SOVIET UNION

With the formation of democratically elected governments in Eastern and Central Europe, the European security situation has been transformed. Remaining Russian forces in the eastern part of Germany will be withdrawn by 1994.

In November 1990 NATO member states and former Warsaw Pact states signed a joint declaration in Paris saying that:

- they were no longer adversaries and would build new partnerships; and

- they would only maintain enough military forces to prevent war and provide for effective defence.

In 1991 the North Atlantic Co-operation Council was established, in which consultations between NATO members and former Communist countries take place on issues such as defence planning, civilian–military relations and arms control. The Eastern and Central European countries are implementing policies designed to achieve a pluralist democracy, the rule of law, respect for human rights and a market economy.

Former Soviet Republics

The three Baltic states—Estonia, Latvia and Lithuania—which were annexed by the Soviet Union in 1940—regained independence following the failure of a military coup in Moscow in August 1991. At the end of 1991 the Soviet Union was replaced by 12 separate states. The threat of a simultaneous full-scale attack on NATO's European fronts has been effectively removed.

Britain and its EC partners welcomed the fact that Russia had taken over responsibility for the former Soviet Union's international obligations. They agreed to recognise the independence of the former Soviet republics, subject to certain assurances, namely:

- respect for the provisions of the UN Charter and commitments on the rule of law, democracy and human rights;

- guarantees for the rights of minorities and ethnic and national groups;

- respect for the inviolability of frontiers;

- acceptance of commitments on arms control and nuclear non-proliferation; and

- a commitment to settle by agreement all regional disputes.

Having obtained the necessary assurances, the Community recognised all the former Soviet republics as independent countries.

Economic Help

Because of the vast economic problems created by the fall of Communism, Britain and other Western countries took action to help deal with these and promote the development of market economies. Britain and other OECD countries set up the European Bank for Reconstruction and Development to channel investment to the region. The European Community's PHARE scheme, worth some £700 million in 1992, is designed to assist the process of reform and development of infrastructure; Britain contributes about 18 per cent of the budget. Independent states of the former Soviet Union receive help through a separate Community programme (TACIS), which concentrates on financial services, transport, food distribution, energy (including nuclear safety) and human resource development.

Know How Fund and Other Schemes

The British Government decided that more needed to be done to finance the transfer of skills to assist the economic transformation. In June 1989 it therefore launched its Know How Fund, which now covers Albania, Bulgaria, the Czech Republic, Hungary, Poland, Romania, Slovakia, Slovenia, the Baltic States and the countries of the former Soviet Union. Since 1989 over £113 million has been spent by the Fund. By 1993 over 700 projects were either under way or completed.In 1993–94 the Know How Fund budget is £53 million.

The Fund concentrates on limited areas of key importance to economic reform and the functioning of a democratic society. Priority sectors include energy, financial services, management training, food production and distribution, small business and public sector reform.

Britain is giving full support to the Russian Government's economic reform programmes. Under the Know How Fund, a total of £120 million in technical assistance has been pledged for Russia alone. In November 1992 a British–Russian co–operation treaty was signed in London in which both countries emphasised their willingness to promote more business links between the two countries. British export credits will support several projects, including the construction of a polyethylene complex for a Russian gas company and the building of a new terminal at Moscow airport. Under a separate defence agreement, British and Russian chiefs of staff exchange views on defence policy and arms control.

Another British scheme is designed to contribute to the development of a modern and efficient financial services industry in the former Soviet Union. Financed by the Treasury, salaried secondments are made to British firms operating in banking, accountancy, law, insurance, stockbroking and financial and actuarial services. Total British investment in the scheme will be about £20 million over three years.

EC Association Agreements

The European Community is strengthening its relations with the former Communist countries by concluding association agreements with Bulgaria, the Czech Republic, Hungary, Poland, Romania and Slovakia. In 1992 the Community agreed to negotiate partnership and co-operation agreements with all the states of the former Soviet Union. Negotiations with Russia, Belarus, Kazakhstan and Ukraine are under way. The purpose of all these agreements is to open up trade, develop co-operation and hold regular consultations on key international issues.

Trade and co-operation agreements have been concluded with Albania, Slovenia and the three Baltic states.

OTHER REGIONS

The Middle East

Arab–Israeli Dispute

British policy towards the Arab–Israeli dispute is in line with the European Council's 1980 and 1989 declarations setting out two basic principles—the right of all countries in the area, including Israel, to live within recognised and guaranteed frontiers, and the right of the Palestinian people to self-determination. Britain and the other EC member states are playing a constructive and active role in the multilateral aspects of the Middle East peace negotiations based on UN Security Council Resolutions 242 and 338. These were inaugurated at the 1991 Madrid Conference co-sponsored by the United States and the former Soviet Union.

In September 1993 a major breakthrough occurred in negotiations between Israel and the Palestine Liberation Organisation, when both sides agreed to recognise each other and signed a declaration of principles.

The Gulf Conflict

As a permanent member of the UN Security Council, Britain strongly condemned Iraq's invasion of Kuwait in August 1990 and supported all the Council's resolutions designed to force Iraqi withdrawal and restore international legality. Because of Iraq's failure to withdraw, its forces were expelled in February 1991 by an international coalition led by the United States, Britain, France and Saudi Arabia acting under the UN mandate.

As part of the agreement ending hostilities, the Security Council authorised the creation of a Special Commission to supervise the elimination of Iraq's weapons of mass destruction and set out a number of other ceasefire conditions. UN economic sanctions against Iraq, introduced in August 1990, still apply because of the Iraqi Government's failure to comply fully with these conditions.

Britain takes an active part in helping to apply UN-approved 'no-fly zones' over Iraq designed to monitor the actions of the Iraqi regime and deter military attacks against civilians in southern and northern areas of the country.

Southern Africa

For many years Britain has been concerned with the affairs of Southern Africa. Positive developments in the region since 1989 have included:

- a trend towards more accountable government and liberal economic policies with countries committed to a greater degree of democracy; and
- steady progress towards non-racial democracy in South Africa.

British policy towards South Africa is to:

- encourage multi-party negotiations on the building of a new constitution; and
- help end political violence and intimidation.

A successful political settlement must be underpinned by a return to economic growth. Britain therefore supports the lifting of all remaining sanctions against South Africa. Britain contributes to EC and Commonwealth Observer Missions in South Africa. Through its aid programme, the British Government is helping to prepare black South Africans to play their full part in the government and economy of their country. Some £10 million was contributed in 1992 and a similar amount was given to EC programmes.

Asia–Pacific Region

Britain has long-standing political interests in the Asia–Pacific region. These stem originally from Commonwealth links, particularly in the South–Asian sub-continent, and from its responsibility for Hong Kong (see p. 292). There are also large-scale economic and commercial interests. Because economic growth rates in East and South-East Asia continue to outstrip those elsewhere, important export and investment opportunities are being created for British companies, as well as investment into Britain which increases jobs and benefits from technology transfer.

This shift of economic power is being accompanied by greater political liberalisation in countries like South Korea, Taiwan, Thailand and Vietnam. Moreover, Japan, China, India and the Association of South-East Asian Nations (Malaysia, Singapore, Indonesia, the Philippines, Thailand and Brunei) are becoming much more influential in world politics.

Assistance to British exporters forms a vital part of the activities of all British diplomatic posts in the region. Britain is also stepping up political dialogue with the main countries there and is working to make the most of opportunities offered in areas such as educational exchanges, technical co-operation, science and technology and English teaching.

North and South America

Britain has long-established political and cultural links with the United States. In particular, as founding members of NATO, both countries are closely involved in Western defence arrangements (see p. 311) and work together as permanent members of the UN Security Council.

Britain has welcomed the replacement of authoritarian regimes in Latin America by constitutionally elected governments and believes that these changes, together with the trend towards free market economies, present many opportunities for Britain to strengthen its relations with countries in the region.

There is a British post in every Latin American country and the programme of ministerial visits to the region has increased in recent years, notable examples being the Prime Minister's visit to Columbia and Brazil in 1992 and the Foreign and Commonwealth Secretary's visit to Argentina and Chile in early 1993.

HUMAN RIGHTS

In formulating its foreign policy, Britain attaches great importance to promoting universal respect for human rights. This is an obligation under the UN Charter, reinforced by human rights law in the form of UN and regional human rights treaties. Human rights violations can now no longer be insulated from external criticism on the grounds that they are a domestic matter. The British Government believes that the expression of concern about violations of human rights does not mean interference in a state's internal affairs.

The Universal Declaration of Human Rights was adopted by the UN General Assembly in 1948. Since this is not a legally binding document, the General Assembly adopted two international covenants in 1966, placing legal obligations on those states ratifying or acceding to them. The covenants came into force in 1976, Britain ratifying both in the same year. One covenant deals with economic, social and cultural rights and the other with civil and political rights. States which are parties to the covenants undertake to submit periodic reports detailing compliance with their terms. Each covenant has a UN treaty monitoring committee which examines these reports. Britain recognises the competence of these committees to receive and consider state-to-state complaints.

Other international conventions to which Britain is a party include those on:

- the elimination of racial discrimination;
- the elimination of all forms of discrimination against women;
- prevention of genocide;
- the abolition of slavery;
- the status of refugees;
- the status of stateless people;
- the political rights of women;
- consent to marriage;
- the rights of the child; and
- the ending of torture and other cruel, inhuman or degrading treatment or punishment.

The Council of Europe

Britain is bound by the Council of Europe's Convention for the Protection of Human Rights and Fundamental Freedoms, which covers:

- the right to life, liberty, security and a fair trial;
- respect for private and family life, home and correspondence;
- freedom of thought, conscience and religion;
- freedom of expression;
- freedom of peaceful assembly and association;
- the right to have a sentence reviewed by a higher tribunal; and

- the prohibition of torture and other inhuman or degrading treatment.

Complaints about violations of the Convention are made to the European Commission of Human Rights in Strasbourg. Although one state may lodge a complaint against another, most complaints are brought against states by individuals or groups. The Commission decides whether cases are admissible and, if so, examines the matter with the parties with a view to achieving a friendly settlement. If this fails, the Commission or the state concerned can refer the case to the European Court of Human Rights, which rules on whether the Convention has been breached. Britain accepts the Court's compulsory jurisdiction and the right of individual petition.

Conference on Security and Co-operation in Europe

In 1975 Britain was among the states which signed the Helsinki Final Act containing, among other things, commitments to respect human rights and fundamental freedoms.

In 1989 Final Act signatories recognised the need to improve implementation of these commitments. In 1991 it was agreed that states could invite experts to examine human rights cases or situations in their own territories or that of another participating state. States have also agreed to provide written responses and meet requests for bilateral meetings on human rights issues.

In order to improve monitoring there is a High Commissioner on National Minorities, as well as fact-finding missions and seminars run by the Office for Democratic Institutions and Human Rights.

Westminster Foundation for Democracy

Following consultations between the British Government and the British political parties, the Westminster Foundation for Democracy was set up in 1992 to assist in building and strengthening pluralistic democratic institutions overseas.

The three main political parties (see p. 50) are represented on the Board of Governors, who are appointed by the Foreign and Commonwealth Secretary. There is also a representative of the smaller political parties, plus non-party figures drawn from business, trade unions, the academic world and other non-governmental organisations. The Foreign & Commonwealth Office has a non-voting advisory member. The Foundation is independent and the British Government cannot veto projects the Board chooses to support.

Projects supported by the Foundation may include the development of:

- election systems, administration or monitoring;
- parliaments or other representative institutions;
- political parties;
- free media;
- trade unions; and
- human rights groups.

The aim is to build up organisations which can be self-sustaining and to assist projects designed to achieve concrete results. The Foundation is concentrating its efforts initially on Central and South-Eastern Europe, the former Soviet Union and on anglophone Africa. It does, however, consider sympathetically applications for projects elsewhere in the world.

INTERNATIONAL CRIME

The British Government attaches importance to action against international terrorism and to international co-operation against drug traffickers and organised crime. Britain and the other members of the European Community have agreed not to export arms or other military equipment to countries clearly implicated in supporting terrorist activity, and to take steps to prevent such material being diverted for terrorist purposes.

It is EC policy that:

- no concessions should be made to terrorists or their sponsors; and
- there should be solidarity between member states in the prevention of terrorism.

Britain stations drug liaison officers in a number of countries in order to help the host authorities in the fight against drug trafficking. In December 1991 Community member states agreed to set up a central European Police Office (EUROPOL) to provide Community-wide intelligence about serious crime. As a first step in this process, a EUROPOL Drugs Unit will be established. All EC member states belong to the International Criminal Police Organisation (INTERPOL).

British liaison with INTERPOL is provided by the National Criminal Intelligence Service (see p. 79).

Under the Maastricht Treaty, work in these areas will be intensified through increased inter-governmental co-operation.

DEVELOPMENT CO-OPERATION

The aim of Britain's overseas aid effort to developing countries is the promotion of sustainable economic growth and social development in order to improve the quality of life and reduce poverty, suffering and deprivation in developing countries.

In 1991–92 British aid to developing countries was over £1,800 million. Of this, £983 million was allocated bilaterally and £831 million through international organisations such as the European Community (£431 million), the World Bank Group (£228 million), the United Nations agencies (£137 million) and the regional development banks (£33 million). Assistance to former Communist countries in Europe totalled £36 million; bilateral technical assistance to these countries is given through the Know How Fund (see p. 300).

From 1994–95 there will be a unified aid budget covering assistance to developing countries and to Eastern and Central Europe and the former Soviet Union.

The British aid programme seeks to:

- promote economic liberalisation;
- enhance productive capacity;
- promote good government;
- help developing countries to define and carry out poverty reduction programmes;
- promote improved education and health;
- improve the social, economic, legal and political status of women in developing countries; and

- assist developing countries to tackle national environmental problems.

Economic Liberalisation

Sustainable development requires sound economic policies designed to encourage investment, give incentives to producers and improve public sector efficiency. Britain provides:

- balance of payments support;
- technical co-operation for countries undertaking policy and institutional reforms; and
- support for the private sector, including small enterprises, and assistance with the reform of the public sector and the management of public expenditure.

British multilateral aid supports the financing of reforms through contributions to the World Bank Group and the European Development Fund.

Most British support for reforms has gone to eight low-income countries in the Special Programme of Assistance for Africa led by the World Bank. Bilateral balance of payments support is conditional on recipients sticking to reform programmes agreed with the International Monetary Fund and the World Bank.

Assistance with economic liberalisation has been significant in Eastern Europe and the former Soviet Union.

Britain encourages more efficient and effective public expenditure programmes to ensure priority for basic social and economic services and provides aid to improve public infrastructure and utilities.

Good Government

Good government, including respect for human rights, popular participation in decision-taking and the rule of law, remains a central concern of the British aid programme. In 1991, £50 million was committed to public sector and civil service reform, police training, improved accounting and audit procedures, legal sector assistance and assistance in democratic procedures. The Know How

Fund finances similar activities in Eastern Europe and the former Soviet Union.

In some circumstances good government concerns override other factors and result in a cessation or reduction in all but emergency aid.

Reducing Poverty

About 80 per cent of bilateral aid allocable by income group is directed towards low-income countries with gross national product of less than $750 per head in 1990. In India, Pakistan and Bangladesh—the major grant recipients in Asia—projects include rural development, urban slum upgrading and the provision of health, population and educational services for poor people. Some of these are carried out in conjunction with non-governmental organisations.

Britain encourages recipient countries to focus social expenditure on the needs of the poor. It also helps these countries to establish affordable social safety nets designed to assist the poor and the vulnerable. In addition, the Government encourages multilateral initiatives, such as those of the European Community and the World Bank, to strengthen poverty reduction programmes.

Education

Britain places a high priority on assistance for education and training. About £112 million of the British bilateral aid programme goes to education; projects supported emphasise literacy and numeracy and skills which build on these. The aid is concentrated so that it benefits the community as a whole and develops skills needed to achieve sustainable economic development. British aid also helps education ministries plan and manage their systems more efficiently and equitably.

One of the most ambitious education projects supported by British aid is the provision of teacher training to 150,000 primary school teachers in 50,000 schools in Andhra Pradesh, India. Another is the provision of over 1 million books to 170 secondary schools in Jamaica; there is also a teacher training programme for 4,000 secondary teachers annually and a textbook development programme for less able pupils.

Training for project personnel and scholarship awards for overseas students from developing countries are an essential part of the aid programme. In 1992–93 some 13,000 training awards were granted, most of which were taken up in British universities and further education colleges. Some training is provided in the trainee's own country or in other countries.

Assistance is given for the provision of books and journals. The Education Low-Priced Books Scheme provides textbooks for purchase by students at subsidised prices in about 86 developing countries. The Ranfurley Library Service is a registered charity which supplies books free of charge to education institutions and libraries in developing countries.

Support is also given for distance learning activities through the Commonwealth of Learning in Vancouver. The ODA is helping to finance a database at the British Open University's International Centre for Distance Learning. The database provides information about distance learning courses available to students throughout the Commonwealth and elsewhere.

Health

The ODA invests over £100 million a year on health care, water and sanitation, and population projects. The main aim is to help bring affordable health care services to the poorest and most vulnerable sections of the community. To ensure effective use of these resources, assistance is targeted on a number of countries and special attention is given to:

- strengthening primary health care services, particularly for women and children;
- improving control of communicable diseases;
- helping to establish management systems to ensure the provision of good-quality care at an affordable cost; and
- improving access to reproductive health services.

Britain assists countries to develop family planning programmes designed to help women in particular to exercise choice over their own fertility. ODA spending totalled £29 million in 1992, which represents an increase of over 60 per cent compared with 1988. This concentrates on improving the availability, accessibility and quality of family planning services, as well as information about them. No support is given for any programme in which there is an element of coercion of individuals to practise family planning. In 1992 the ODA agreed new contraceptive supply projects in Kenya, Ghana and Zimbabwe and a large new health and population programme in Bangladesh which is co-funded with the World Bank and other donors.

New population projects have been approved during the last two years in Bangladesh, Pakistan, Malawi, Nigeria, Ghana, Namibia, Zimbabwe and South Africa.

The ODA provides finance to the United Nations Population Fund (£9 million in 1992) and the International Planned Parenthood Federation (£7.5 million in 1992) for population initiatives undertaken by these organisations. Support is also given to the World Health Organisation's (WHO) Special Programme of Research and Training in Human Reproduction (£2.75 million in 1992).

In addition, the ODA supports a number of other WHO programmes dealing with tropical diseases, acute respiratory infection and diarrhoeal diseases. Britain funds the International Centre for Diarrhoeal Diseases Research in Bangladesh and provides funds to the London and Liverpool Schools of Tropical Medicine and for individuals and institutions to undertake research on health-related subjects.

Britain gives high priority to international efforts to reduce the spread of HIV and AIDS. The Government fully supports the work of the WHO in co-ordinating international action. It has committed £30 million to the WHO's Global Programme on AIDS, which provides technical support and policy guidance to developing countries for the establishment and implementation of national AIDS control programmes.

Other assistance includes a grant of £1.5 million over three years to the International Planned Parenthood Federation for the development of its Sexual Health Programme and some £4.5 million for research into the demographic, behavioural, social and economic aspects of AIDS in the developing world. Assistance amounting to £2.3 million has also been provided under a joint funding scheme to British-based non-governmental organisations for small AIDS-related projects in developing countries. Britain's share of the European Community's AIDS Programme is about £2.7 million.

Women in Development

The successful implementation of British aid objectives requires the active involvement of women in economic and political decision-taking.

To this end, Britain supports the promotion of female literacy and recognises the need to remove barriers to economic participation by women. The ODA funds projects aimed at providing women with additional skills, giving them access to credit and enabling them to develop small-scale business initiatives. Support is also given to training courses to help women overcome the barriers to advancement in public administration.

The Environment

Britain helps developing countries tackle national and local environmental concerns such as forestry conservation, biodiversity, energy efficiency and sustainable agriculture.

Forestry

There are over 200 British aid projects under way or in preparation at a cost of £161 million. These are designed to:
● enable developing countries to maximise the economic and social benefits they enjoy from their forests in a sustainable way;

- limit deforestation by tackling its causes and supporting projects concerned with conservation; and
- promote the reforestation of degraded land.

In addition, the ODA helps finance 46 other forestry projects run by non-governmental organisations, and 50 research projects to improve the productivity of forests.

Climate Change

Some £40 million is being given to the Global Environment Facility, which helps developing countries meet the cost of measures to control climate change. In addition, nearly $14 million is being contributed to the Montreal Protocol Fund, which assists these countries to comply with the Montreal Protocol on the ozone layer (see p. 356).

The British aid programme is supporting:
- increased efficiency of fuel use in countries such as Pakistan, Ghana and Uganda;
- economic reform programmes addressing the question of energy pricing; and
- projects in India to make more effective use of power generating capacity.

Biodiversity

Britain supports 78 projects concerned with biodiversity. In Kenya, for example, the ODA is helping the National Museum to conserve the country's native flora; a British botanist is working with museum staff on a system to identify plant species at risk and to conserve them.

The ODA also assists conservation of the world's genetic material in gene banks, botanic gardens and zoos. One of the most important priorities for a secure future is the safeguarding of the unique genetic material in food and fodder crops and wild plants. British support is given to the International Board for Plant Genetic Resources, the International Rice Research Institute and the International Crops Research Institute for the Semi-Arid Tropics.

Industry and Urban Pollution

Examples of British aid projects dealing with environmental problems in cities include:
- a £68 million project to improve the living conditions of people in five Indian cities—Calcutta, Vijayawada, Hyderabad, Indore and Vishakhapatnam. This includes investment in roads and other essential services, health facilities and nursery schools; and
- a study of air pollution problems in Mexico City caused by industrial activities in and around Tula. A similar study is being funded in northern Chile.

Water Resources

In 1992 British aid provided £39.7 million for water-related projects, including £16.8 million devoted to the provision of clean drinking water and/or sanitation in over 30 developing countries.

New projects committed in 1993 include:
- training in water resources management in Bangladesh, China and Chile:
- groundwater assessment studies in China and Mexico;
- provision of rural drinking water supply and sanitation in Zimbabwe; and
- assistance with fish farming in Cambodia, India and Mozambique.

Renewable Natural Resources

Britain funds some £34 million of research each year in renewable natural resources. This covers programmes in agriculture, fisheries, forestry, livestock, land resources assessment, pest control and post-harvest technology.

The Natural Resources Institute is the ODA's scientific arm and runs three programmes focused on environmental concerns. These are:
- the Resource Assessment and Farming Systems Programme, in which environmental monitoring and identification of areas for conservation play an important part;

- the Integrated Pest Management Programme, which aims to improve pest control by minimising disturbance of wildlife habitats and relying less heavily on chemical pesticides; and
- the Food Science and Crop Utilisation Programme.

Desertification

Britain is taking an active part in United Nations negotiations on a desertification convention. It has commissioned expert papers on the issues to be addressed by such a convention and on institutional arrangements arising from it. The ODA has also funded participation by developing countries in the negotiations.

Emergency Relief

The ODA's Disaster Unit co-ordinates the British Government's response to natural and man-made disasters worldwide; it also provides relief to refugees and displaced people. To do so, it funds operations carried out by agencies such as the United Nations, the Red Cross, Oxfam and Save the Children.

As part of co-ordinated international responses, the ODA provides funds, supplies and personnel. Direct relief operations are mounted to address specific needs, which are assessed by trained personnel sent out to direct the British effort on the ground.

Britain strongly supports UN actions in complex emergencies. In 1992 a joint British–German proposal led to the establishment of the UN's Department of Humanitarian Affairs, responsible for co-ordinating prompt responses to emergencies.

In 1992–93 British humanitarian relief aid amounted to over £160 million. In addition, the British public sends substantial sums for emergency relief overseas through non-governmental organisations.

The Private Sector

Increasing emphasis is being placed on capital market development and case-by-case technical assistance to private sector organisations. A Small Enterprise Development Fund was set up in 1990 to investigate and promote new projects and activities. Britain is supporting the establishment of a Business Extension and Advisory Service in Zimbabwe and a training programme at the Entrepreneur Development Institute in India.

The Commonwealth Development Corporation (CDC) promotes economic development by providing loans, equity funds and management services for financially viable investments in agriculture, fisheries, minerals, industry, public utilities, transport, communications and housing. In 1992 the CDC invested just over £175 million in 98 projects in 32 countries. By the end of 1992 it had investments and commitments worth £1,448 million in 316 projects:

- £547 million in Africa;
- £491 million in Asia;
- £270 million in the Caribbean and Latin America;
- £134 million in Pacific Islands; and
- £7 million in other areas.

Further Reading

Britain and the Arab–Israeli Conflict. Aspects of Britain series, HMSO, 1993.
Britain and the Commonwealth. Aspects of Britain series, HMSO, 1992.
Britain and the Gulf Crisis. Aspects of Britain series, HMSO, 1993.
Britain in the European Community. Aspects of Britain series, HMSO, 1992.

Annual Reports

British Overseas Aid. Overseas Development Administration.
Foreign & Commonwealth Office Departmental Report 1993. Cm 2202. Foreign & Commonwealth Office, HMSO.

21 Defence and Arms Control

The strength of the regular armed forces, all volunteers, was nearly 271,000 in mid-1993—133,000 in the Army, 79,300 in the Royal Air Force (RAF), and 58,500 in the Royal Navy and Royal Marines. There were 18,800 women personnel—7,500 in the Army, 6,800 in the RAF, and 4,400 in the Royal Navy.

INTRODUCTION

British forces' main military roles are to:

- ensure the protection and security of Britain and its dependent territories;
- ensure against any major external threat to Britain and its allies; and
- contribute towards promoting Britain's wider security interests through the maintenance of international peace and security.

Most of Britain's nuclear and conventional forces are committed to NATO (North Atlantic Treaty Organisation) and about 95 per cent of defence expenditure to meeting its NATO responsibilities. In recognition of the changed European security situation (see p. 310), Britain's armed forces are being restructured in consultation with other NATO allies.[1]

Under these plans, the strength of the armed forces is being cut by 22 per cent, leaving by the mid-1990s some 119,000 in the Army, 70,000 in the RAF and 52,500 in the Royal Navy and the Royal Marines. This involves reductions in main equipment of:

---

[1]NATO's 16 member countries are Belgium, Britain, Canada, Denmark, France, Germany, Greece, Iceland, Italy, Luxembourg, the Netherlands, Norway, Portugal, Spain, Turkey and the United States.

- three Tornado GR1 squadrons, four Phantom squadrons, two Buccaneer squadrons and part of a squadron of Nimrod maritime patrol aircraft;
- 12 submarines, nine destroyers and frigates and 13 mine countermeasures ships; and
- 327 main battle tanks.

Civilian staff employed by the Ministry of Defence will be reduced from 169,100 in 1991 to 135,000 by the mid-1990s.

NATO STRATEGY

As a member of NATO, Britain fully supports the Alliance's current strategic concept, under which its tasks are to:

- help provide a stable security environment, in which no country is able to intimidate or dominate any European country through the threat or use of force;
- serve as a transatlantic forum for Allied consultations affecting member states' vital interests;
- deter aggression and defend member states against military attack; and
- preserve the strategic balance within Europe.

NATO has always sought to achieve its objectives through political as well as military means. The new NATO strategy therefore seeks to:
- reduce the risk of conflict;
- increase confidence and understanding between all European states; and
- expand the possibilities of partnership among all European countries.

Military Strategy

NATO military policies reflect the following fundamental precepts:
- none of the Alliance's weapons will ever be used except in self-defence and it does not consider itself to be anyone's adversary;
- it will retain enough military strength to convince potential aggressors that the use of force against one member state will be met with collective and effective action by all the allies;
- the European members will assume a greater degree of responsibility for the defence of Europe; and
- the transatlantic link will be enhanced in parallel with the emergence of a European security identity and defence role.

An integrated military structure will be retained, including common force and operational planning, multinational military formations, joint exercises, common standards for equipment, co-operation on infrastructure and armaments, and, where appropriate, the stationing of forces outside home territory on a mutual basis. Britain takes part in the integrated military structure.

The size, readiness, availability and deployment of NATO forces will continue to reflect the Alliance's defensive nature. NATO strategy involves:
- the deployment in Europe of smaller, highly mobile forces;
- a move away from the concept of forward defence towards a reduced forward presence; and
- the scaling back of the state of readiness of Allied armed forces and a reduction in training requirements and exercises.

New Force Structure

In future there will be greater emphasis on multinational forces, as part of collective defence. In 1991 NATO defence ministers agreed the basis of the new force structure, to be achieved by 1995, involving:
- immediate and rapid reaction forces, available at short notice, capable of providing an early military response to a crisis;
- main defence forces to deter attack and defend against aggression; and
- reinforcements providing operational and strategic reserves in times of crisis or war.

NATO maritime reaction forces will be based on two multinational Standing Naval Forces for the Atlantic and the Mediterranean, supplemented as necessary by other maritime forces able to respond to a range of contingencies. Britain will contribute Harrier, Tornado and Jaguar aircraft to multinational air reaction forces.

Britain has been invited to lead the major element of the land reaction forces: the Allied Command Europe Rapid Reaction Corps, which was established in October 1992 in order to provide an early military response to a crisis.

The radical changes in the European security situation mean that NATO can have a reduced reliance on non-strategic nuclear weapons. All of NATO's ground-launched and naval tactical nuclear weapons were removed by July 1992 and the number of air delivered nuclear weapons has been reduced by over a half. Since October 1991 the size of the NATO stockpile of non-strategic nuclear weapons has been reduced by over 80 per cent.

Western European Union

Although European countries supply most of NATO's forces, as well as military facilities for US forces stationed in Western Europe, all Allies are agreed that Europe needs to take on a larger share of the burden of providing international security. It has, therefore, been agreed that the Western European Union (WEU—see p. 291) should be the best vehicle for this.

Britain, in common with other Allies, believes that the WEU should be built up as an effective bridge between NATO defence structures and the developing political and security policies of the 12 EC member states.

NUCLEAR FORCES

The Royal Navy's independent nuclear deterrent remains the ultimate guarantee of Britain's security. The Polaris strategic nuclear force, assigned to NATO but remaining at all times under the control of the British Government, enables Britain to provide a second and independent centre of decision-making within the Alliance, thereby adding to deterrence.

The Polaris force now comprises three nuclear submarines, each one equipped with 16 Polaris missiles armed with improved British nuclear warheads. The Polaris force is being replaced by four British-built submarines, each of which will be capable of accommodating Trident D5 missiles bought from the United States. This force will ensure that one boat is always at sea, invulnerable to pre-emptive attack. Trident's nuclear warheads are British-designed and built.

The Government has no intention of increasing Britain's nuclear capability beyond the minimum level necessary to ensure adequate deterrence, and plans for Trident do not involve using the system's full capacity. The number of warheads deployed will be decided nearer completion and will be reviewed in the light of changes in the strategic environment and any improvements in defensive capabilities.

The armed forces also possess non-strategic nuclear weapons, providing a link between strategic and conventional forces. Because of the end of the Cold War, Britain has made substantial reductions in these weapons, including the elimination of maritime non-strategic nuclear weapons and a reduction of over a half in the stockpile of WE177 free-fall nuclear bombs. The remainder of these bombs will be deployed on eight squadrons of dual-capable Tornado aircraft, all of which are available to NATO.

DEFENCE OF BRITAIN

The armed forces continue to have day-to-day responsibilities for safeguarding Britain's territory, airspace, territorial waters and those of the dependent territories.

Air Defence

The air defence of Britain and the surrounding seas is maintained by a sophisticated system of layered defences. Continuous radar cover is provided by an improved United Kingdom Air Defence Ground Environment, supplemented by the RAF's six Boeing Sentry airborne early warning (AEW) aircraft. The RAF also provides six squadrons of all-weather Tornado F3 interceptor aircraft, supported by tanker aircraft and, in wartime, 50 armed Hawk trainer aircraft. In addition, the Royal Navy's air defence destroyers are also linked to the improved air defence system, providing radar and electronic warfare coverage and surface-to-air missiles. Ground-launched Rapier missiles will continue to defend the main RAF bases. From the end of the century Eurofighter 2000, a collaborative project involving Britain, Germany, Italy and Spain, is planned to be the cornerstone of the RAF's capability, including air defence.

Role of the Navy

In addition to contributing to Britain's air defence, the Royal Navy plays a key part in keeping open the country's sea lanes, ports and anchorages. The Navy's flotilla of patrol craft and mine countermeasures vessels, which makes an important contribution to this task, is being modernised, with the Sandown class single-role minehunters replacing the ageing Ton class.

The Army

By the mid-1990s there will be 17 regular infantry battalions—compared with 21 at

311

present—earmarked for home defence, rising to 18 after 1997, when British forces will be withdrawn from Hong Kong. These will be augmented by regular engineer, signals and aviation units and armoured reconnaissance regiments, infantry battalions and supporting units of the Territorial Army (TA). The diminution of the land threat to Britain will in future allow the TA to take on a greater part of the home defence task, as well as becoming increasingly a flexible general reserve. The Home Service Force, formed in 1985 to guard key points, is being absorbed within the TA.

Dependent Territories

Britain continues to maintain garrisons in Hong Kong, the Falkland Islands and Gibraltar. In Hong Kong, Britain is to reduce the garrison in stages until 1997, when the territory will become part of China. Gibraltar provides headquarters and communications facilities for NATO in the Western Mediterranean.

British forces are stationed on the Falkland Islands to deter possible aggression from Argentina, which maintains its claim to the Islands. These forces include air defence aircraft, Hercules tankers, helicopters and Rapier surface-to-air missiles. There is an infantry company group and the Royal Navy is present in adjacent waters.

Northern Ireland

The armed forces continue to support the Royal Ulster Constabulary (RUC) in the fight against terrorism in Northern Ireland. There are 18 infantry units, six of which comprise the home service element of the Royal Irish Regiment. The Royal Navy carries out patrols to prevent arms smuggling, while the Royal Marines provide troops to meet Navy and Army commitments.

The armed forces help deter and combat terrorist activity through foot patrols, vehicle check points, patrols to combat cross-border attacks by terrorists and specialist assistance, including helicopter support, bomb disposal and search teams.

Other Functions

Other functions performed by the armed forces in Britain include military assistance to civil ministries where it is necessary to maintain the essentials of life in the community or undertake urgent work of national importance. Other duties include fishery protection, operations against drug smugglers and search and rescue operations.

INTERNATIONAL COMMITMENTS

Defence of Europe

The defence of the European mainland is essential not merely for the defence of Britain and other NATO members but for Western security and stability as a whole. It is, therefore, important for NATO that British and North American forces remain there in peacetime.

Britain's Contribution

Britain's main contribution to the defence of mainland Europe is provided by the British Army and the RAF. The number of regular Army personnel based in mainland Europe in peacetime is being reduced from some 56,000 in April 1991 to about 23,000 in the mid-1990s.

Some 55,000 regular British soldiers will be assigned to NATO's new Allied Command Europe Rapid Reaction Corps (see p. 314). This will comprise:

- an armoured division made up of three armoured brigades, each of which will have two armoured regiments and two infantry regiments based in Germany; and

- a more lightly-equipped division, based in Britain, of two mechanised brigades.

In addition, Britain will provide the permanent commander for the Corps and contribute to the headquarters infrastructure and combat support. An airborne brigade will also join one of the two multinational divisions in the Corps. Britain will continue to base part of an infantry brigade in Berlin until Russian forces leave the eastern part of Germany in 1994.

On mobilisation the British force would be increased by a substantial number of TA troops in formed units and individual reservists.

The armoured division, to be deployed in Germany from the mid-1990s, will be equipped with the new Challenger 2 tank, which will serve in two regiments and replace the remaining Chieftain tanks in the Royal Armoured Corps. The Challenger 2 will significantly improve armoured forces, particularly in NATO's Rapid Reaction Corps. There are plans to replace the Lynx anti-tank helicopter with an attack helicopter designed to increase the effectiveness of the Army's airmobile forces.

The Royal Artillery will gain more new anti-armour capability with the procurement of Phase 2 ammunition for the Multiple Launch Rocket System. These rockets are designed to scatter anti-tank mines at long range. The AS90 self-propelled howitzer, which is replacing the Abbot and M-109 guns, began entering service in 1992.

The RAF is making a major contribution to NATO's air reaction force. Up to 80 aircraft from squadrons based in Britain and Germany will be made available, including Tornado F3s, offensive support Harriers, offensive support and reconnaissance Jaguars, and strike/attack Tornado GR1As. Rapier surface-to-air missiles will also be assigned to this task. Logistical and tactical support is provided by the tanker, transport and helicopter forces.

Major improvements to the Army's air defence are being planned, including the Starstreak high velocity missile, the next generation of Rapier missiles and a new air defence command and control system.

Since 1991 RAF forces in Germany have undergone significant restructuring. The number of squadrons has been reduced to four Tornado GR1 strike/attack squadrons, two Harrier offensive support squadrons and a mixed Puma/Chinook support helicopter squadron. Two bases in Germany have been closed, leaving RAF Bruggen and RAF Laarbruch as the main operating bases.

Maritime Defence

NATO is dependent on the free use of the sea, since all supply and reinforcement from North America has to go through the Atlantic and the Channel. Britain and the other European members of NATO rely on trade and raw materials from overseas.

Most Royal Navy ships are committed to NATO. Permanent contributions are made to NATO's standing naval forces in the Atlantic and the Mediterranean, and a mine countermeasures vessel is allocated to the standing naval force in the Channel. These forces would form part of the immediate reaction forces available to NATO in the event of a crisis.

The Royal Navy will also make a considerable contribution to NATO's reaction, main and augmentation forces. This will include:

- three anti-submarine warfare (ASW) aircraft carriers, operating Sea Harrier FRS1 fighters and ASW Sea King helicopters, to be replaced later with the modernised Sea Harrier, FRS2 and the EH101 Merlin helicopters respectively;

- about 35 destroyers and frigates, mainly multi-role Type 22 and Type 23 frigates; and

- 12 nuclear-powered attack submarines.

The amphibious forces—including two assault ships, a newly ordered carrier deploying helicopters and the Royal Marines—will be retained for deployment throughout the NATO area. From 1995 the RAF's Buccaneer maritime attack aircraft will be replaced by specially modified Tornado GR1s, equipped with the Sea Eagle missile. The RAF will also continue to provide Nimrod maritime patrol aircraft, and search and rescue helicopters.

Specialist Reinforcement Forces

Combat units based in Britain form an important part of NATO's mobile reinforcement forces. There is an infantry battalion group, including artillery, engineer, and communications elements and support helicopters for the Allied Mobile Force available for deployment at short notice. A Royal Marines brigade forms part of a joint British–Netherlands amphibious force and is assigned to the Supreme Allied Commander Atlantic as part of NATO's rapid reaction forces.

Assisting these reinforcement forces are RAF fighters and a strengthened air transport force. In addition, a Harrier squadron could be deployed as part of NATO's strategic air reserve. There are various other individual reinforcement forces, including units of the Special Air Forces.

Wider Security Interests

In addition to their commitment to collective defence against direct attack on an ally, Britain and the other NATO members believe that Alliance security can be affected by other events.

An example of rapid response to such an event occurred in 1991, when Britain, the United States and other NATO members contributed forces which helped to expel Iraqi forces from Kuwait (see p. 301).

Britain continues to deploy the Armilla naval patrol, designed to provide reassurance and assistance to merchant shipping in and around the Gulf area.

Since mid-1992 NATO has been closely involved in operations in support of UN efforts to resolve the crisis in former Yugoslavia (see p. 298). In July 1992 a NATO maritime operation was mounted in the Adriatic in co-ordination with operations undertaken by the WEU (see p. 311) to monitor and enforce compliance with UN Security Council resolutions imposing economic sanctions on Serbia and Montenegro. NATO's early-warning aircraft are monitoring the no-fly zone established over Bosnia-Herzegovina, established by the UN Security Council in November 1992. NATO has also provided elements of its Northern Army group, Central Europe, command for the operational headquarters of the UN Protection Force in Bosnia.

In addition to its contribution to NATO maritime and air operation, Britain has 2,500 personnel in the UN Protection Force in Bosnia (see p. 299).

British Garrisons

A British garrison is maintained in Brunei at the request of the Brunei Government. Britain is committed to keeping a Gurkha battalion there until 1998.

There is also a British garrison in Belize, originally maintained to deter and, if necessary, defend against possible Guatemalan aggression. As Guatemala now recognises Belize's sovereignty and independence, Britain will transfer responsibility for the defence of Belize to the Belize Government in January 1994. Jungle warfare training will continue in Belize.

Military Assistance

Britain provides military assistance to other countries in order to contribute to regional stability. In 1991–92 some 4,200 students from 72 countries attended military training courses in Britain. In early 1993, some 370 British servicemen were on loan in 30 countries.

In the Middle East Britain is helping a number of Gulf states to reorganise, train and equip their armed forces and has undertaken a programme of air and land exercises in the area.

Naval deployments take place outside Europe to develop military links with other countries and to support Britain's security interests. In 1992, for instance, a Royal Navy task group went to South East Asia and the Far East, visiting some 24 countries in the Asia Pacific Rim and the Indian Ocean, the Gulf and the Mediterranean.

THE ARMED FORCES

Commissioned Ranks

Commissions, either by promotion from the ranks or by direct entry based on educational and other qualifications, are granted for short, medium and long terms. All three Services have schemes for school, university and college sponsorships.

Commissioned ranks receive initial training at the Britannia Royal Naval College, Dartmouth; the Royal Military Academy,

Sandhurst; or in the Royal Air Force College, Cranwell. This is followed by specialist training, often including degree courses at Service establishments or universities.

Higher training for officers is provided by the Royal Naval College, Greenwich; the Army Staff College, at Camberley; and the Royal Air Force Staff College, at Bracknell. Selected senior officers and civilian officials attend the Joint Services Defence College, Greenwich, and the Royal College of Defence Studies, London, which is also attended by officers and officials from other countries. These provide the wider background necessary for those destined to fill higher appointments.

Non-commissioned Ranks

Engagements for non-commissioned ranks range from 3 to 23 years, with a wide choice of length and terms of service. Subject to a minimum period of service, entrants may leave at any time, at 18 months' notice (12 months for certain engagements). Discharge may also be granted on compassionate grounds, by purchase or on grounds of conscience.

Throughout their Service careers non-commissioned personnel receive basic training supplemented by specialist training. Study for educational qualifications is encouraged and Service trade and technical training lead to nationally recognised qualifications.

Reserve Forces

Trained reserve and auxiliary forces supplement the regular forces on mobilisation and are able immediately to take their places either as formed units or as individual reinforcements. They are also a link between the Services and the civil community. Some members of these forces become reservists following a period of regular service (regular reserve); others are volunteers who train in their spare time. Volunteer reserve forces include the TA, which is responsible for the direct defence of Britain as well as providing a flexible general reserve.

Other volunteer forces include the Royal Naval and Royal Marines Reserves, the Royal Naval Auxiliary Service, the Royal Auxiliary Air Force and the Royal Air Force Volunteer Reserve.

In the summer of 1993 regular reserves totalled 261,700 and volunteer reserves and auxiliary forces 81,700. Cadet forces, which make a significant contribution to recruitment in the regular forces, numbered 137,000.

ADMINISTRATION

Defence Budget

The estimated defence budget for 1993–94 is £23,520 million, with expenditure plans for 1994–95 and 1995–96 of £23,750 million and £23,220 million respectively. The Government anticipates a reduction in the budget of 12 per cent in real terms between 1990–91 and 1995–96, excluding costs of redundancies and the Gulf War (see p. 301).

Britain spent 4.1 per cent of Gross Domestic Product (GDP) on defence in 1992; this is expected to reduce to 3.2 per cent by 1995–96.

Defence Management

Within the Ministry of Defence a military-civilian Defence Staff is responsible for defence policy and strategy, operational requirements and commitments. An Office of Management and Budget handles budgets and resources. Each Service Chief of Staff reports through the Chief of Defence Staff to the Defence Secretary on matters related to the fighting effectiveness, management, efficiency and morale of his Service. The management of the three services is exercised through executive committees of their Service Boards, which are chaired by their respective Chiefs of Staff and act in accordance with centrally determined policy objectives and budgets. The Procurement Executive deals with the purchase of equipment, including equipment collaboration with allies and friendly nations.

Military and civilian managers have greater discretion in the most efficient use of their allocated resources. This approach aims to promote better value for money and to provide clear direction for local managers.

Defence Procurement

About 39 per cent of the defence budget is spent on defence equipment, making the Ministry of Defence one of British industry's largest customers. Contracts are awarded by open international competition where possible. Strict guidelines ensure companies are given the maximum incentive to perform efficiently.

Research is undertaken by the Ministry's Defence Research Agency and other smaller establishments (see p. 278).

Alliance Co-operation

Britain favours international co-operation on defence equipment wherever it makes economic and military sense by reducing costs and improving standardisation. It therefore plays an active role in NATO's Conference of National Armaments Directors, which promotes equipment collaboration between NATO members.

Britain is also a member of the WEU's Western European Armaments Group (WEAG), which is the main European forum for consultations about armaments.

Current collaborative projects involving Britain include:

- Eurofighter 2000 (with Germany, Italy and Spain);

- anti-tank guided weapons (with Belgium, France, Germany and the Netherlands); and

- the EH101 helicopter (with Italy).

Britain is also discussing with France and Italy arrangements for the development of a new air defence frigate, planned to enter service early in the next decade.

Many weapons systems in production or in service with British forces are the result of equipment collaboration with NATO members. These include:

- the Harrier GR5 aircraft (with the United States);

- Tornado aircraft (with Germany and Italy); and

- Jaguar aircraft (with France).

The Scorpion reconnaissance vehicle range is a British–Belgian project. Britain has produced with Germany and Italy a 155-mm towed howitzer, the FH70. The multiple launch rocket system programme, in which Britain participates, is another NATO project.

A further example of NATO co-operation is an air defence system, funded by 14 nations, which comprises radar and computer centres providing NATO with early warning of attack over an area stretching from northern Norway to eastern Turkey.

Civil Defence

Civil defence is based on the peacetime arrangements of government departments, local government authorities and emergency services, supplemented by the efforts of voluntary organisations.

Following the end of the Cold War, civil defence arrangements have been reviewed and changes made. New regulations, which came into force in August 1993, removed obsolete civil defence duties previously placed on local authorities. At the same time local authorities are being encouraged to develop arrangements capable of responding to any crisis, whether in peace or war.

Civil defence spending is being reduced to reflect the new situation. In 1992–93 spending was about £60 million and is forecast to be reduced to just under £38 million in 1994–95.

ARMS CONTROL

Britain and the other members of NATO are pledged to pursue further progress in arms control and confidence-building measures. Far reaching and historic treaties limiting nuclear weapons and conventional forces in Europe have recently been signed.

Nuclear Arms Control

In July 1991 the United States and the former Soviet Union signed the first Strategic Arms Reduction Treaty, under which an equal limit of 6,000 nuclear warheads on each side was agreed, with an equal sub-limit of 4,900 ballistic missile warheads. The Treaty required the parties to reduce their strategic missiles and warheads by about 35 per cent over 15 years, including a reduction of up to 50 per cent in the most destabilising systems.

In January 1993 the United States and Russia signed a new treaty agreeing to reduce their strategic nuclear weapons by two-thirds within ten years.

The United States and Russia eliminated their intermediate-range nuclear weapons under a separate treaty signed in 1987.

Conventional Weapons

The most potent conventional weapons held within Europe by NATO allies and the former Warsaw Pact states are regulated by the Conventional Armed Forces in Europe (CFE) Treaty, signed in Paris in November 1990. It entered into force in November 1992. The objectives of the Treaty are to eliminate disparities of forces and the capacity for launching surprise and large-scale offensive action.

Under the Treaty the NATO countries and the members of the former Warsaw Pact are restricted to common ceilings in five categories of equipment. The ceilings for both groups of states are 20,000 tanks, 30,000 armoured combat vehicles, 6,000 pieces of artillery, 2,000 attack helicopters and 6,800 combat aircraft.

Conventional weapons above the agreed ceilings must be destroyed or rendered permanently unfit for further military use by November 1995. 'Intrusive' arrangements to verify compliance are included in the Treaty.

In July 1992 an agreement was concluded containing measures to limit, and where necessary reduce, the personnel strength of national armed forces within Europe.

Chemical Weapons

Britain took a leading part in the recent negotiations on a chemical weapons ban. These were completed in June 1992 and the text of a convention was adopted by the UN General Assembly in November 1992. Britain has signed the convention, which is expected to enter into force in 1995. It bans the production, stockpiling and use of chemical weapons. There is a system of 'challenge' inspection to verify compliance and, once ratified, the convention will provide for the monitoring of chemicals which could be used to make weapons.

Britain abandoned its chemical weapons in the late 1950s.

Non-Proliferation

Britain aims:

- to prevent the proliferation of nuclear weapons;
- to ban the manufacture and possession of chemical and biological weapons;
- to control the transfer of ballistic missiles and their components and technology; and
- to prevent accumulations of conventional armaments which create regional instability.

To this end, the Government is a signatory to a number of international agreements for the control of proliferation of weapons of mass destuction, including the 1968 Non-Proliferation Treaty (NPT) on nuclear weapons and the 1993 Chemical Weapons Convention. A review conference is to be held in 1995 to consider the length of the NPT's extension. The British Government will be seeking an indefinite extension.

Nuclear Testing

In July 1993 the United States President announced an extension of a US moratorium on nuclear testing till the end of September 1994, as a possible precursor to a comprehensive test ban treaty. Negotiations on this treaty are due to start in the Conference on Disarmament early in 1994.

The British Government's policy has been to carry out only the minimal testing necessary to maintain the safety and credibility of its nuclear deterrent. In supporting the goal of a test ban treaty, the Government will wish to ensure that it has the means to maintain the highest standards of nuclear safety in the long term while also wishing to see the proposed treaty promote efforts to prevent the proliferation of nuclear weapons.

UN Register of Arms Transfers

Following a British initiative, the UN General Assembly voted to establish a universal and non-discriminatory register of conventional arms transfers. The register is designed to introduce greater openness and make it easier for the international community to monitor an excessive arms build-up in any one country. The register came into effect in January 1992, requiring participating states to provide details of their import and export of seven major categories of weapons.

Confidence-building Measures

Steps have been taken in recent years to implement important confidence-building measures regarding military exercises and other activities in Europe.

The Conference on Security and Co-operation in Europe (CSCE) provides a forum for dialogue on such measures as arms control. Participants include the republics of the former Soviet Union, the other European states and the United States and Canada. All are committed to working for improvements in European security, including promotion of human rights, democracy and the rule of law.

Under the Stockholm agreement concluded in 1986, CSCE member states agreed on a number of measures, including:
- prior notification of military activities above a certain size;
- invitation of military observers to notifiable activities;
- an exchange of annual forecasts of notifiable activities planned for up to two years ahead, according to the size of the activity; and
- 'challenge' inspections.

In 1990 the Paris CSCE summit agreed further measures, including:
- annual exchanges of military information on forces, equipment and budgets;
- further prior notification of military manoeuvres;
- provisions for the exchange and evaluation of information on military forces; and
- the establishment of a common communications network linking all CSCE capitals.

In May 1992 these measures entered into force; new commitments were added, including a risk reduction mechanism and arrangements for military contacts.

Open Skies Treaty

Britain played an important role in the negotiations leading to the signing in March 1992 of the Open Skies Treaty by all NATO member states, Russia, Belarus, Georgia, Ukraine and the six Central European states of Bulgaria, the Czech Republic, Hungary, Poland, Romania and Slovakia. The Treaty will allow flights over the entire territories of its participants by aircraft equipped with sensors, cameras and radar with the ability to detect military activity and equipment in all weathers, day and night.

The Treaty, which is of unlimited duration, will be phased in over three years; when fully in force, it will play a valuable stabilising role by allowing the major CSCE countries to check on military deployments.

Further Reading

Britain, NATO and European Security, Aspects of Britain series, HMSO, 1994.
Statement on the Defence Estimates 1993. HMSO, 1993.

The
Environment

22 Urban Regeneration and Housing

Job creation, training, rents-to-mortgages schemes, and improving security and lighting on estates are just some of the many strategies employed in Britain with the aim of enhancing both the urban and rural environments, and ensuring the availability and diversity of tenure of suitable housing.

Urban Regeneration

Despite much progress in urban regeneration, areas of deprivation still exist. These relatively small areas can have a blighting effect on a city's image. The Government is therefore continuing to tackle urban deprivation with a range of programmes, bringing together a comprehensive package for revival in England, involving government departments in a co-ordinated effort. Increased private sector involvement is being sought. Urban problems in Scotland, Wales and Northern Ireland are being tackled by Partnerships, the Programme for the Valleys and Belfast Action Teams respectively, as well as by many other government programmes.

Leasehold Reform, Housing and Urban Development Act

The Leasehold Reform, Housing and Urban Development Act 1993 will establish a new Urban Regeneration Agency for England. It will take over responsibility for the Government's Derelict Land Grant programme (see p. 325), the payment of City Grant (see p. 321) and the work of English Estates (see p. 147).

Urban Initiatives

City Action Teams

Eight City Action Teams (CATs) co-ordinate government efforts in inner city areas (see map, pp. 324–5) and encourage partnerships between business, local and central government, the voluntary sector and local people. They bring together senior officials of three government departments—Employment, Environment, and Trade and Industry—to ensure that the main programmes for which each is responsible are working together effectively. CATs are primary points of contact with local authorities on City Challenge (see p. 322).

Each CAT has a small budget to assist co-ordination of government action in the inner city. CAT grants are available to local authorities, expanding businesses, local community groups and voluntary organisations working in or moving to an inner city area.

Task Forces

Task Forces were first set up in 1986 and are small teams which operate in the most deprived urban areas. They consist primarily of civil servants, but include secondees from local authorities and the private and voluntary sectors. Task Forces concentrate on the economic regeneration of designated inner city areas, by improving local people's employment prospects, by supporting training and education initiatives, and by identifying and removing barriers to their employment. They also aim to stimulate enterprise development and strengthen the capacity of communities to meet local needs. Once a Task Force area has improved prospects for continued regeneration and local organisations have been strengthened, the Task Force is closed. As part of a rolling programme of openings and closures, a total of 16 Task Forces has been maintained. Since their inception they have committed some £127 million in support of 5,000 projects.

Urban Programme

The Urban Programme is a special allocation to local authorities in addition to their normal resources. In England, it is concentrated on 57 target areas where the problems are greatest and the levels of deprivation most severe, so as to achieve a greater impact with available funds. The local authorities concerned receive 75 per cent grant from central government to cover spending on approved projects, with a further 25 per cent in supplementary credit approvals for capital projects.

In 1992–93 the Urban Programme in England was estimated to have supported 788 new firms, helped to create or preserve 40,000 jobs and supported 74,100 training places. It improved 1,000 buildings and about 2,100 hectares (5,100 acres) of unsightly land. It also supported environmental improvement schemes for 52,600 dwellings. From 1993–94, no new projects will be supported through the Urban Programme, although projects approved in previous years will continue to be funded.

Capital Partnerships

The Government announced its £600 million Capital Partnership programme, several elements of which related to urban regeneration, in November 1992. The various components of Capital Partnership provided incentives to top up the estimated £1,750 million of local authority capital receipts released by the Government from spending controls[1] between November 1992 and December 1993, to be spent on projects best placed to stimulate growth. Components of the programme included:

● Housing Partnership, which made use of Estate Action funding and a new Housing Partnership Fund; and

● Urban Partnership, using a new Urban Partnership Fund within the Urban Programme.

Under the scheme, local authorities eligible for Urban Partnership Fund resources could bid for assistance with new 1993–94 projects. Money from this source would supplement funds denied from their own capital receipts—money coming from the sale of capital assets such as land. The Fund will help to support 82 new projects in 46 inner city areas. Local authorities will contribute about £33 million in capital receipts, and the projects are estimated to be attracting over £130 million in private sector resources.

City Challenge

Under the City Challenge initiative, launched in 1991, local authorities are invited, in partnership with the private and voluntary sectors, local communities and government agencies, to submit imaginative and comprehensive plans for regenerating key neighbourhoods by tackling the problems of physical decay, lack of opportunity and poor quality of life. The best of these proposals receive government

---

[1] In general, some 50 per cent of most local government capital receipts (and 75 per cent of housing receipts) had to be retained for debt redemption; in November 1992 the Government announced that for a one-year period local authorities would be free to spend all their capital receipts on new capital projects.

funding of £7.5 million a year over five years, subject to satisfactory progress being made towards achieving agreed targets and objectives. Public sector investment of over £1,000 million in City Challenge is expected to attract considerable additional private sector investment.

There have been two rounds of the City Challenge competition. In the first pilot round, 11 of the 15 local authorities in England invited to submit bids were selected to draw up detailed plans for action which commenced in April 1992. The 20 successful authorities in the second round competition, which was open to all 57 Urban Programme authorities, began work on their five-year programmes in April 1993.

Urban Development Corporations

A total of 13 urban development corporations (UDCs) have been set up by the Government to reverse large-scale urban decline. London Docklands and Merseyside were established in 1981. By the end of March 1992 the London Docklands Development Corporation had received over £1,347 million in government grant and secured private investment commitments of over £9,000 million, with £5,700 million having been spent. It has reclaimed about 600 hectares (1,500 acres) of derelict land for housing, commercial and recreational use. Over 17,000 homes have been completed and, up to March 1992, 49,000 jobs had been attracted to the area. The Merseyside Development Corporation has reclaimed 337 hectares (832 acres) of derelict land, and 342,000 sq m (3.7 million sq ft) of commercial or industrial floorspace have been built or refurbished in its area.

Eleven further UDCs have been set up: Birmingham Heartlands, Black Country (West Midlands), Bristol, Leeds, Central Manchester, Plymouth, Sheffield, Trafford Park (Greater Manchester), Teesside, and Tyne and Wear in England; and Cardiff Bay in Wales. UDCs cover about 16,000 hectares (about 40,000 acres), and public expenditure on the programme will be £316 million in 1993–94.

City Grant

City Grant is available to encourage private sector developments in inner cities in England. It is paid direct to the private sector for projects which contribute to the economic and environmental regeneration of Urban Programme areas. By May 1993, 330 schemes had been approved, with £292 million of public money bringing in £1,230 million of private investment. Under these schemes, some 40,000 jobs and 9,700 homes were being provided and 700 hectares (1,720 acres) were being reclaimed. Under the provisions of the Leasehold Reform, Housing and Urban Development Act, responsibility for this programme will be undertaken by the new Urban Regeneration Agency.

Education, Training and Employment

The first of a network of City Technology Colleges was opened near Birmingham in 1988; 15 are currently in operation. Intended to raise educational standards, the colleges are established jointly by the Government and industry.

A number of schools/industry 'Compacts' have been introduced since August 1988 in nearly all English Urban Programme areas. Employers work with schools to guarantee a job with training for all school-leavers aged 16 to 18 who meet agreed targets for motivation and achievement. By July 1993 there were 62 Compacts in operation in inner city areas, with some 180,000 young people, 10,000 employers and training organisations and about 800 schools involved, creating over 9,000 jobs and training places.

Training programmes such as Youth Training for young people and Training for Work, the new adult programme (see p. 127), are helping many people in the inner cities. About one-third of the young people participating in Youth Training are from inner cities. There are some 110 Employment Service 'outreach' staff based in or visiting inner city areas, helping unemployed people look for jobs and encouraging them to participate in employment and training programmes. In 1992–93, there were about 500 inner city Jobclubs, many catering for

Urban Policy Initiatives

Scale: 0 20 40 60 80 100 120 km / 0 20 40 60 80 miles

○ City Challenge areas
□ Partnership areas
● Target areas
◉ Enterprise zones
★ Urban Development Corporations
△ City Action Teams
∗ Areas with task forces
■ Valleys Programme towns
━ Boundaries of economic planning regions

Scotland

Fraserburgh
Peterhead
Inverness
Aberdeen
Arbroath
Dundee
Tayside
Perth

Inset A

Ayr
Hawick
North
Dumfries
Newcastle
Stranraer
Northern Ireland
Workington
Belfast
Teesside

Tyne and Wear
North Tyneside
South Tyneside
Sunderland
Hartlepool
Middlesbrough
Cleveland
Stockton-on-Tees

Yorkshire and Humberside

Inset B
North West
East Midlands

West Midlands   Derby ∗△ ○△ ∗ Nottingham
Black Country
Leicester
East Anglia

Telford
Wolverhampton
Dudley
Sandwell
Birmingham
Walsall

Wales

Milford Haven

Inset C

Bristol

Inset D
London
North-west Kent

South East

South West

Plymouth

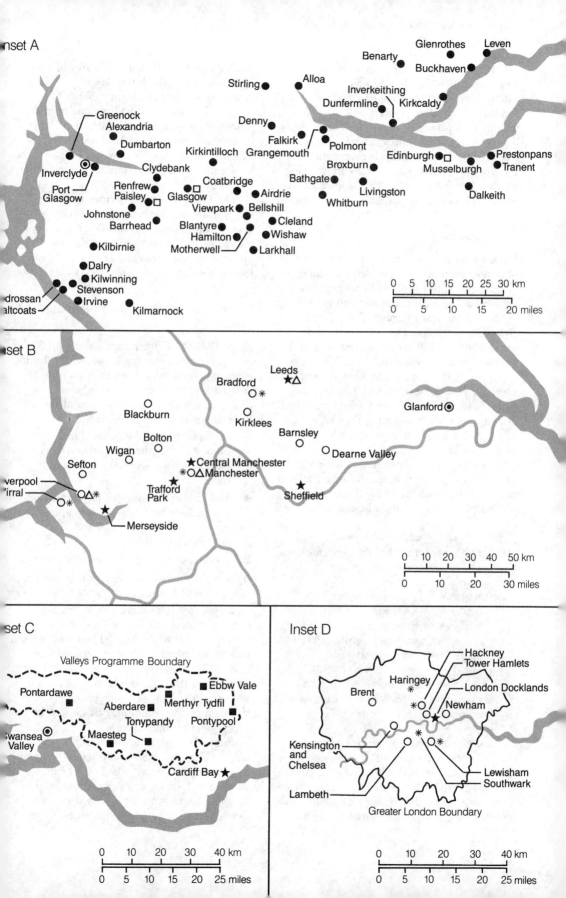

Inset A

Glenrothes
Leven
Benarty
Buckhaven
Stirling
Alloa
Inverkeithing
Kirkcaldy
Dunfermline
Denny
Falkirk
Polmont
Edinburgh
Prestonpans
Grangemouth
Musselburgh
Tranent
Greenock
Alexandria
Broxburn
Dumbarton
Kirkintilloch
Bathgate
Clydebank
Inverclyde
Coatbridge
Livingston
Dalkeith
Port
Renfrew
Glasgow
Whitburn
Glasgow
Paisley
Airdrie
Johnstone
Viewpark
Bellshill
Barrhead
Blantyre
Cleland
Hamilton
Wishaw
Motherwell
Larkhall
Kilbirnie
Dalry
Kilwinning
Stevenson
drossan
Irvine
altcoats
Kilmarnock

0 5 10 15 20 25 30 km
0 5 10 15 20 miles

Inset B

Leeds
Bradford
Blackburn
Kirklees
Glanford
Bolton
Barnsley
Wigan
Dearne Valley
Sefton
Central Manchester
verpool
Manchester
irral
Trafford
Park
Sheffield
Merseyside

0 10 20 30 40 50 km
0 10 20 30 miles

Inset C

Valleys Programme Boundary
Pontardawe
Ebbw Vale
Aberdare
Merthyr Tydfil
Tonypandy
Pontypool
Swansea
Maesteg
Valley
Cardiff Bay

0 10 20 30 40 km
0 5 10 15 20 25 miles

Inset D

Hackney
Tower Hamlets
Haringey
Brent
London Docklands
Newham
Kensington
and
Chelsea
Lewisham
Southwark
Lambeth
Greater London Boundary

0 10 20 30 40 km
0 5 10 15 20 25 miles

people with literacy and numeracy or language difficulties. In addition, Employment Service regional directors have funds for innovative projects to help unemployed people in inner cities and other deprived areas back into work or training. Many of the independent Training and Enterprise Councils (see p. 126) are working in Task Force areas, City Challenge areas or other pockets of deprivation.

Other Measures

Higher than average crime rates, and the fear of crime, are particular problems in the inner cities. Safer Cities projects bring together all sections of the local community to tackle crime and the fear of crime. A total of 20 Safer Cities projects are under way, and have initiated over 3,150 crime prevention and community safety measures with funding of more than £19 million. The Government's objective is to achieve up to 40 Safer Cities projects within the present Parliament. The starting point for a project is the preparation of a detailed local crime profile, which the local team can then use to draw up an action plan. Examples of help include providing activities for young people otherwise likely to commit crime and fitting good quality locks to houses on estates with a high burglary rate.

Safer Cities successes include:
- a scheme in East London which has reduced repeat racial incidents by 50 per cent;
- a motor education project in Bradford which has reduced the number of new car crime offenders by 74 per cent; and
- an 80 per cent reduction in burglaries on an estate in Salford as a result of improved security measures undertaken as part of a community regeneration scheme.

The Government encourages tourism as a force for the improvement of inner city areas. Several major projects which create a cultural and artistic focus for inner city regeneration have been undertaken. Examples include the development of the Museum of Science and Technology in the Castlefields area of Manchester and the International Convention Centre in Birmingham. The English Tourist Board and regional tourist boards encourage promotional activities in inner city areas through local initiatives which bring together the tourist boards, local authorities, the private sector and other agencies.

The Government's priorities for inner city housing are to secure a wide range of good quality housing available for rent or purchase, and to improve conditions and opportunities for residents, particularly on local authority estates (see p. 334).

Enterprise and Simplified Planning Zones

Since 1981 the Government has set up 33 enterprise zones (see map, pp. 324–5). Each zone runs for a period of ten years from designation; many of the zones have therefore already reached the end of their lives. Benefits in the zones include:

- exemption from the national non-domestic rate (the local property tax payable by non-domestic property owners);
- 100 per cent allowances for corporation and income tax purposes for capital expenditure on industrial and commercial buildings;
- a much simplified planning system; and
- a reduction in government requests for statistical information.

In January 1994 there will be ten zones operating, although five of these will expire before the end of the year. Three new zones will be designated during the year in areas affected by job losses in the mining industry. At present, there is no intention to extend the enterprise zone scheme generally, although further zones may be created in exceptional circumstances.

Simplified planning zones (SPZs) can help local authorities to secure development in parts of their areas. An SPZ scheme, which also lasts for ten years, provides full planning permission for specified types of development. Like enterprise zones, from which the concept was derived, SPZs are useful as part of an overall package to generate private sector interest in an area. The procedures for establishing an SPZ were recently streamlined to encourage their use. By March 1993, there were six zones in operation.

Land Reclamation and Use

The new Urban Regeneration Agency will co-ordinate efforts to bring derelict land back into effective use and provide new opportunities for local people. Its role will be to promote the reclamation of derelict land throughout England and develop it in partnership with the private, public and voluntary sectors.

In England government grants are available to local authorities and to other public bodies, to the private sector and to nationalised industries for the reclamation of such land to bring it into beneficial use or to improve its appearance. Since 1979 some 18,600 hectares (46,000 acres) of derelict land in England have been reclaimed with the help of Derelict Land Grant. The 1993–94 programme of £103 million should allow an additional 1,800 hectares (some 4,500 acres) to be reclaimed. The total amount of derelict land in England fell by 11 per cent between 1982 and 1988.

In Scotland responsibility for derelict land reclamation rests with the enterprise bodies Scottish Enterprise, Highlands and Islands Enterprise and the Local Enterprise Companies. They may acquire and reclaim land either by agreement or compulsorily; increasingly they seek to work with the private sector to bring land back into use. In Wales the Welsh Development Agency may acquire and reclaim land or make grants to local authorities for that purpose. Land use is also encouraged by the Land Authority for Wales, a statutory body with powers to make land available for development in circumstances where the private sector would find this difficult or impossible. In Northern Ireland grants may be paid to landowners who restore or improve derelict sites.

Registers of Unused and Under-used Land

The Department of the Environment is currently increasing its efforts to promote the sale and development of vacant and under-used public sector land. Information is being assembled on key sites with development potential, and where there are no firm plans to market or develop land, action will be taken to encourage and promote the sale of sites. Until 1989, the Secretary of State for the Environment maintained a central register of unused or under-used land in the ownership of public bodies. Since then, the owners have had the responsibility for maintaining their own registers. Under the 'Public Request to Order Disposal' scheme, members of the public are encouraged to request the Secretary of State to order public bodies to dispose of such land on the open market. This process has been simplified by the Leasehold Reform, Housing and Urban Development Act 1993, which removed the need for a site to be entered on the Secretary of State's register before a direction to dispose could be issued. Registers are also published for certain areas of Wales.

Wales, Scotland and Northern Ireland

Wales

Spending on the Urban Programme in Wales is some £28.4 million in 1993–94. All local authorities are eligible to apply. Spending has been targeted at wards rather than at whole districts, so that small pockets of deprivation in otherwise prosperous areas can benefit. Over a quarter of the total has been targeted at the ten most deprived districts in Wales. The Government aims to remove much of the remaining major industrial dereliction in Wales by the end of the 1990s.

The Programme for the Valleys, launched in 1988, was an extensive programme of economic and urban regeneration, covering an area of some 2,200 sq km (860 sq miles) in the south Wales valleys (see map, p. 325). The Programme ended in March 1993. In April 1993 the Secretary of State for Wales launched a new five-year Programme for the Valleys. It involves increased levels of factory building, land clearance and Urban Programme support, and action, among other things, to:

- create long-term access to employment through education, training and transport;

- strengthen local communities;

- improve the environment; and

- improve the quality of housing.

Some £17 million of Urban Programme support will benefit the Valleys in 1993–94.

The Cardiff Bay Development Corporation was set up in 1987 to bring forward redevelopment in an area of south Cardiff, once its commercial centre. By April 1993 the Corporation had received £191 million in government grant. Government support for the Corporation in 1993–94 will be £45 million. The Corporation's regeneration strategy includes proposals for the construction of a barrage across Cardiff harbour mouth, which would create a large freshwater lake and 12 km (7 miles) of waterside frontage. It is expected that more than 23,000 new jobs will be created and that over £1,200 million of private investment will be attracted.

Scotland

In 1988 the Government set out in the White Paper *New Life for Urban Scotland* its strategy for improving the quality of life for people living on peripheral estates in Scotland. Building on the experience gained from inner city regeneration schemes such as the Glasgow Eastern Area Renewal, the main aim of the strategy was to encourage residents to take more responsibility for the improvement of their own communities.

The focus of this effort was the establishment of four Partnerships in areas of Dundee, Edinburgh, Glasgow and Paisley. These are led by The Scottish Office and involve other bodies and groups, including Scottish Enterprise (see p. 147), Scottish Homes (see p. 332), the local authorities, the private sector and the local communities. Their objectives include plans to:

- improve the type and tenure mix of housing available to local people;

- improve employment prospects by providing increased avenues for training and further education; and

- tackle social and environmental problems on the estates.

Other peripheral estates and inner city areas continue to receive substantial support through such sources as the Urban Programme, Scottish Homes and Scottish Enterprise. The Government is committed to seeking ways to improve the Partnerships and to strengthening the Urban Programme in Scotland by emphasising those projects which form part of a concerted effort to assist a deprived area.

The Urban Programme in Scotland has grown from £44 million in 1988–89 to over £81 million in 1993–94. In addition to any new projects approved, these resources already support about 1,200 existing projects. Five Safer Cities programmes have been launched in Scotland, including projects in Edinburgh, Glasgow and Dundee. Another is being established in Aberdeen. Central funding for the programme in 1993–94 is £900,000.

The Local Enterprise Companies (see p. 143), working under contract to Scottish Enterprise, have substantial budgets and a flexible range of powers and functions to improve the environment and encourage business and employment in their areas. In particular, Scottish Enterprise operates a Local Enterprise Grants for Urban Projects scheme, which aims to encourage private sector investment for projects in deprived areas. The areas of need in which the scheme operates include the four Partnership areas, and other areas showing similar characteristics of deprivation. Local Enterprise Companies can also support projects in their areas.

The Compact scheme (see p. 323) has been introduced in Scotland, with ten Compacts in operation and four under consideration. Some 9,000 young people and 1,000 employers and training organisations are involved with the operational Compacts. The Training and

Enterprise Grants scheme is designed to increase access to employment opportunities for young and long-term unemployed people.

Northern Ireland

A comprehensive development programme aims to revitalise the commercial areas of Belfast. In 1993–94 regeneration programmes had a combined allocation of over £34 million. Nine Action Teams have been established to tackle the problems of particularly deprived areas of the city. The 'Making Belfast Work' initiative, launched in 1988, is designed to reinforce the efforts to alleviate the economic, educational, social and environmental problems in the most disadvantaged areas of Belfast. In addition to extensive funding already allocated to mainstream departmental programmes, Making Belfast Work has provided a further £124 million for the period 1988–89 to 1993–94. The Laganside Corporation was established in 1989 to regenerate Belfast's riverside area. Its government grant in 1993–94 is £5.3 million.

Housing

The pattern of housing tenure has changed considerably in recent years, with a substantial increase in owner-occupation and a decline in private renting.

Administration

The Secretary of State for the Environment in England and the Secretaries of State for Wales, Scotland and Northern Ireland are responsible for formulating housing policy and supervising the housing programme. Although the policies are broadly similar throughout Britain, provisions in Northern Ireland and Scotland differ somewhat from those in England and Wales.

The construction or structural alteration of housing is subject to building regulations laid down by the Government. In addition, most new houses are covered by warranty arrangements provided either by the National House-Building Council or the Housing Standards Company Ltd. Both organisations set standards and enforce them by inspection, and provide cover against major structural defects for not less than ten years.

In November 1992 the Government announced a £750 million housing market package to take houses off the market. In England £580 million was used to enable housing associations to buy 18,000 new, empty or refurbished properties for letting to homeless families. A further £50 million was used to provide cash incentives to housing association and local authority tenants to enable them to buy houses on the open market and release their existing accommodation for housing homeless families.

The promotion of home ownership and more choice in the rented sector are central to government housing policy. New house construction is undertaken by both public and private sectors, but most dwellings are now built by the private sector for sale to owner-occupiers. Housing associations are becoming the main providers of new housing in the subsidised rented sector. Local authorities are being encouraged to see their housing role as more of an enabling one, working with housing associations and the private sector to increase the supply of low-cost housing for rent without necessarily providing it themselves. This allows them to concentrate their resources on improving the management of their own stock. In order to stimulate the private rented sector, which has declined to less than 8 per cent of the total stock, rents on new private sector lettings in Great Britain have been deregulated.

Leasehold Reform, Housing and Urban Development Act 1993

The provisions of this Act will introduce:

- a collective right for residential leaseholders in blocks of flats in England

and Wales[2] to acquire the freehold of their block at market prices;

● a right for leaseholders who live in blocks that do not qualify for freehold purchase to buy an extended lease;

● a nationwide rents-to-mortgages scheme, which will enable council tenants to buy their homes on payment of an initial sum requiring mortgage payments no greater than the rent, the remainder not needing to be paid off until resale;

● a right to improve, under which council tenants will receive compensation for certain home improvements which they undertake;

● a right for tenants' organisations to manage estates where they want to take on that role; and

● compulsory competitive tendering for local authority housing management.

Home Ownership

Over the last 40 years the proportion of people owning their own homes has risen from 29 per cent to 67 per cent, and the number of owner-occupied dwellings in Great Britain amounted to over 15.8 million at the end of 1992, compared with some 4.1 million in 1950. Most public sector tenants

---

[2] Leasehold is not a common form of residential tenure in Scotland; consequently the provisions with regard to leasehold will not apply there.

have the right to buy the homes they occupy. Local authorities have been asked to encourage low-cost home ownership in a variety of ways. Scottish Homes has a scheme to encourage private developers to build for owner-occupation or market rents in areas they would not normally consider. In 1992–93 the funding available was about £26 million. In Northern Ireland shared ownership has been developed by the Northern Ireland Co-ownership Housing Association.

The Government also funds cash schemes. Under these, local authority and housing association tenants are given grants to help them purchase housing in the private sector. The council homes released by these tenants moving out are then available to be re-let to homeless families.

Mortgage Loans

Most people buy their homes with a mortgage loan, with the property as security. Building societies are the largest source of such loans, although banks and other financial institutions also take a significant share of the mortgage market, while some companies make loans for house purchase available to their own employees. The amount that lenders are prepared to advance to a would-be house purchaser is generally calculated as a multiple of his or her annual income, typically up to two-and-a-

Table 22.1: Number of Dwellings Constructed in Britain 1981–91

	Private sector	Housing associations	Local authorities	Other public sector	Total
1981	115,022	19,291	54,867	10,618	199,798
1982	125,398	13,137	33,244	4,033	175,812
1983	148,050	16,136	32,833	2,292	199,311
1984	159,416	16,613	31,699	2,354	210,082
1985	156,507	13,123	26,115	1,102	196,847
1986	170,427	12,521	21,587	1,289	205,824
1987	183,731	12,545	18,823	1,280	216,379
1988	199,331	12,760	19,030	739	231,860
1989	179,536	13,866	16,465	1,164	211,031
1990	156,388	17,077	15,780	931	190,176
1991	148,248	19,498	9,457	625	177,828

Source: Housing and Construction Statistics.

half times earnings, and the term of the loan is commonly 25 years. The two main forms of mortgage are 'repayment' and 'endowment' mortgages. In the former, the borrower repays principal and interest on the sum outstanding. In the latter, he or she pays only interest to the lender but also puts money into an endowment policy, which on maturity provides a lump sum to repay the principal. Owner-occupiers get tax relief on interest payments on mortgages of up to £30,000 on their main home; from April 1994 this will be assessed at 20 per cent rather than the basic rate of 25 per cent.

A package of measures to protect homeowners from unnecessary repossession owing to arrears was announced by the Government in December 1991. These include provision for benefits covering mortgage interest to be paid directly to lenders, and agreement with the mortgage lenders on the introduction of schemes to help borrowers in difficulty remain in their homes. Government figures show that mortgage possession orders in 1992 were 11 per cent down on the 1991 total, and a higher proportion of the orders that were made were suspended. Figures from the Council of Mortgage Lenders show that the number of properties actually repossessed in the second half of 1992 was 16 per cent lower than in the second half of 1991.

Social Housing

Public Sector Housing

Most of the public housing in Great Britain is provided by 460 local housing authorities. These are:

- the district councils in England and Wales, apart from in London;

- the London borough councils and the Common Council of the City of London; and

- in Scotland, the district and islands councils.

Public housing is also provided by the new town authorities, Scottish Homes (which has a stock of about 60,000 houses) and the Development Board for Rural Wales,

although the latter aims to transfer all its 1,200 houses to other social landlords in the short term. The Northern Ireland Housing Executive is responsible for the provision and management of public housing in Northern Ireland. Public housing authorities in Great Britain own some 5 million houses and flats; the Northern Ireland Housing Executive owns 160,000 homes. A few local authorities have transferred all their housing stock to housing associations, and others are considering doing so.

Local authorities meet the capital costs of new house construction and of modernisation of their existing stock by:

- raising loans on the open market;

- borrowing from the Public Works Loan Board (an independent statutory body set up to make loans to local authorities);

- using part of the proceeds from the sale of local authority houses and other assets; or

- drawing on their revenue accounts.

Councils must maintain housing revenue accounts on a 'ring-fenced' basis to keep them separate from other council funds. The Government provides local authorities in England and Wales with Housing Revenue Account Subsidy, worth more than £3,900 million in England alone in 1993–94. Local authority housing investment programmes in England will total some £1,920 million in 1993–94. In Scotland, Housing Support Grant of almost £36 million is available for 1993–94; local authorities have been given £393 million in capital allocations to build new homes or improve existing ones. In Northern Ireland, the Housing Executive's capital programme is financed mainly by borrowing from government and receipts from house sales. In 1993–94 borrowing will total £81 million. Revenue expenditure is financed by rental income and by a government grant, which in 1993–94 is some £159 million.

Housing Associations

Housing associations, which are non-profit-making, are now the main providers of additional low-cost housing for rent and for sale to those on low incomes and in the greatest housing need. Many associations specialise in providing accommodation to meet the special needs of the elderly, disabled people and the mentally ill. The housing association sector is expanding rapidly; associations own, manage and maintain over 600,000 homes and some 55,000 hostel bed-spaces in England alone, providing homes for well over 1 million people; over 60,000 new homes for rent or shared ownership were provided in 1992–93.

People in housing need with insufficient income to obtain a mortgage for outright purchase may be able to buy a share in a house which a housing association has developed, or which they themselves have chosen on the open market. They pay rent on the share retained by the association and may purchase it later if they wish.

In Great Britain housing schemes carried out by associations qualify for Housing Association Grant if the association concerned is one of about 2,800 registered with the Housing Corporation (in England), Scottish Homes or Housing for Wales. These three organisations are statutory bodies which supervise and pay grant to housing associations in their respective parts of Great Britain. Broadly similar assistance is available to associations in Northern Ireland.

The Government has increased the resources distributed to housing associations through the Housing Corporation's capital programme from £1,062 million in 1990–91 to £1,280 million in 1993–94. The Government also aims to increase the amount of private finance being used by housing associations, allowing more homes to be built with the available public resources than would otherwise be the case. It is anticipated that around 170,000 homes will be provided over the three years 1992–93 to 1994–95.

In 1993–94 Scottish Homes' total programme expenditure is expected to be about £372 million, of which about £260 million will go to housing associations. Housing for Wales is managing a programme of £197 million in 1993–94, with a target of providing 4,000 new homes. On current plans, government provision to the housing association movement in Wales will be over £500 million between 1991–92 and 1994–95. Northern Ireland's registered housing associations started 1,000 units of accommodation in 1992–93, and now have a stock of 12,300 units for rent. They have a 1993–94 budget of £36 million, with a target to start 850 new units of rented accommodation. Government plans provide for total funding of some £195 million over the period 1992–93 to 1995–96.

In England and Wales the rights of housing association tenants are protected under Tenants' Guarantees, which are issued by the Housing Corporation and Housing for Wales. They cover matters such as tenancy terms, principles for determining rent levels and the allocation of tenancies. Under these guarantees, tenants receive contractual rights in addition to their basic statutory rights, and associations are required to set and maintain rents at levels affordable by those in low-paid employment. In Scotland, similar non-statutory guidance, in the form of a model tenancy agreement, has been implemented as proposed jointly by Scottish Homes and the Scottish Federation of Housing Associations.

Tenants' Rights

Legislation gives public sector tenants in England and Wales statutory rights, including security of tenure. Under the Tenants' Choice provisions, public sector tenants have the right to change their landlord where they are not satisfied with the service provided by their local authority. With a few exceptions, secure tenants with at least two years' public sector standing are entitled to buy their house or flat at a discount which depends on the length of tenancy (the 'right to buy'). Similar provisions are made for Scotland and Northern Ireland. Some 1.8 million council, housing association and new town homes were sold in Great Britain between April 1979 and the end of 1991.

Government support is focused on tenants rather than on property through the housing benefit system. Depending on their personal circumstances, occupiers may qualify for housing benefit to help them pay their rent (see p. 396).

> The Government launched a new Tenant's Charter in England in January 1992 as part of its Citizen's Charter initiative. Many of the new rights for council tenants which it promised are being introduced in the Leasehold Reform, Housing and Urban Development Act, such as the right to receive recompense for improvements that the tenant makes to the property. New Tenant's Charters for Scotland, Wales and Northern Ireland have also been launched.

Housing for the Elderly

Sheltered housing, which comprises accommodation with an alarm system and the services of a resident warden, may be provided for elderly people who need support. Increasing emphasis is being placed on schemes to help elderly people to continue to live in their own homes, such as adaptations to existing housing to meet their needs. Home improvement agencies help the elderly, people with disabilities and those on low incomes to carry out repairs and improvements to their properties; a permanent government grant regime was introduced in 1991 to support this work. Over £4 million of government help will go to home improvement agencies in 1993–94 in England alone, which will enable the number of agencies supported to be increased to 122, seven more than in the previous year.

Rural Housing

Social changes have put pressure on rural housing in many areas. Where there is a need for low-cost housing in rural areas, therefore, the Government has announced that sites which would not normally be released for housing development can exceptionally be used, provided arrangements are made to reserve the housing for local needs. The Housing Corporation has also funded a special rural programme to build houses in small villages: between 1989–90 and 1992–93 it approved the building of around 5,500 such homes.

Similar arrangements were introduced in Wales in 1991. Housing for Wales has a major role, alongside local authorities, in rural housing provision in Wales. In Scotland, considerable progress is being made through the range of initiatives launched in 1990 as part of the Scottish Homes Rural Strategy. In Northern Ireland, the Housing Executive operates a rural strategy which directs special action both in its primary responsibility for public housing and also on the house renovation grant scheme for private housing, which it administers. A new housing association was registered there in 1992 to tackle housing need in rural areas.

Privately Rented Housing

There has been a steady decline in the number of rented dwellings available from private landlords, from over 50 per cent of the housing stock in 1950 to 7 per cent in Great Britain in 1990.

The Government's policy is to increase the availability of privately rented accommodation by removing disincentives to letting. To accomplish this, from January 1989, new private sector lettings were deregulated, and two new forms of tenancy were introduced:

- the assured tenancy, which gives the tenant long-term security in return for a freely negotiated market rent; and

- the assured shorthold tenancy (short assured tenancy in Scotland), which is for a fixed term, again at a free market rent.

Existing lettings are unaffected; they continue on the old basis. Also, the law concerning harassment of tenants was strengthened. Tenants and most other residential occupiers may not be evicted without a court order. A 'Rent a Room' scheme encourages homeowners to let rooms to lodgers without having to pay tax on the rent they receive; rents of up to about £62 a week are now tax-free.

In Northern Ireland only certain pre-1956 properties subject to rent restriction come under statutory control. Rent levels are linked to those of the Northern Ireland Housing Executive, and both landlords and tenants may apply to a rent assessment committee for rent determination in cases where the current rent is considered to be inappropriate. Rent increases are allowed only for properties which meet a prescribed standard. The only assured tenancies in Northern Ireland are those on properties made available under a business expansion scheme; shorthold tenancies are available.

Homelessness

Under the homelessness legislation, local authorities have a duty to secure permanent accommodation for households which they accept as unintentionally homeless and in priority need. The latter category includes pregnant women, people with dependent children, and those who are vulnerable because of old age, mental or physical handicap or other special reasons.

A three-year government programme of measures to tackle the problem of people sleeping rough in central London has provided about 950 new places in short-term hostels and about 2,200 permanent and 700 leased places in accommodation for hostel dwellers to move on into. Some £86 million is being made available to continue the initiative until 1996. A further £20 million is being spent in the period to 1994–95 specifically to help mentally–ill people who are sleeping rough.

An audit of the main sites in London where people sleep rough, carried out by voluntary organisations in November 1992, found some 420 people sleeping rough, down from 1,000 or more at the beginning of the Rough Sleepers Initiative in 1990.

Improving Existing Housing

In urban areas of Britain slum clearance and redevelopment used to be major features of housing policy, but there has been a trend in recent years towards the retention of existing communities, accompanied by the modernisation and conversion of sub-standard homes. Housing conditions have improved considerably, but problems remain in some areas where there are concentrations of dwellings lacking basic amenities or requiring substantial repairs, and there are still some pockets of unfit housing for which demolition is the best solution. The emphasis now is on area renewal, with an integrated approach to renewal and renovation.

In Scotland, Scottish Homes has been given a major role in tackling housing-related urban dereliction and providing rural housing opportunities, in co-operation with local communities, the private sector, local authorities and other statutory agencies. Some groups of tenants are joining together to form community-based housing associations and tenant ownership co-operatives.

The Government is committed to introducing a pilot homesteading scheme under which local authorities would be encouraged to offer those in housing need the chance to restore suitable council properties in exchange for a reduced rent or the opportunity to buy at a reduced price.

Estate Action Programme

The Estate Action programme provides local authorities in England with additional resources to regenerate their run-down housing estates. Funds are provided to enable authorities to carry out an agreed package of measures on an estate, including physical refurbishment and improved management. Since the Estate Action programme began in 1985, more than £1,250 million has been allocated to or earmarked for over 1,000 schemes. In 1993–94 some £356 million is available for 225 continuing schemes and up to 167 new schemes. As a result of the Housing Partnership initiative (see p. 322), it has been possible to increase the number of new schemes in the 1993–94 programme by almost 20 per cent.

In Wales, local authorities can bid for Estate Partnership funding to tackle the problems of selected estates; some £13.3 million of central and local government money and private sector funding has been allocated for 1993–94. This programme, which is distinct from the English scheme of the same name, parallels Estate Action in England but is designed to address the different problems typical of Welsh council estates.

Housing Action Trusts

Housing Action Trusts (HATs) can be established in England to focus resources on some of the most run-down areas of predominantly local authority housing. The Government can designate a HAT for a particular area or estate, subject to a tenants' vote. If the majority of tenants who vote support the proposal, the HAT would be established by parliamentary order. It takes over responsibility for the housing in its designated area in order to renovate it, improve the housing management, the environment and living and social conditions, and stimulate local enterprise. The tenants participate fully in the work of a HAT. On completion of its work, the Trust is wound up and its property transferred to other owners and managers, such as housing associations or tenants' co-operatives, or back to the local authority. Tenants are consulted on their future landlords. Tenants as well as local authorities may apply for the establishment of a HAT. By April 1993 three HATs had been established, with two more expected to be established, having secured ballot approval, and other proposals were under consideration.

House Renovation Grants

Nearly 1.3 million home improvement grants, worth almost £4,487 million, were paid in respect of privately owned dwellings in England alone between 1983 and 1992. In England and Wales, local authorities give mandatory renovation grants to enable unfit dwellings to be brought up to a revised fitness standard, with discretionary grants available for a wider range of works. Grants of up to 100 per cent may be available,

subject to a test of the applicant's resources. Grants are also available in certain circumstances for the provision of facilities for disabled people and for the repair of houses in multiple occupation and of the common parts of blocks of flats. Minor works assistance is also available to help people in receipt of income-related benefits, particularly the elderly, with small-scale works.

In Scotland, local authorities give grants for improvement and repair. Scottish Homes also has the power to provide grants to complement the role of local authorities in private house renewal.

In Northern Ireland, grants are provided on a similar basis to that in England and Wales through the House Renovation Grants scheme, administered by the Northern Ireland Housing Executive. In isolated rural areas, a grant to replace dwellings which cannot be restored is also available through this scheme.

Renewal Areas

Renewal areas in England and Wales are intended to provide a sharper focus to area action, covering both renovation and selective redevelopment and taking account of a range of issues wider than just housing. Authorities are free to declare renewal areas without the specific consent of the Secretaries of State for the Environment and for Wales, provided they fulfil certain criteria. Authorities have additional powers to buy land in renewal areas and to carry out improvement works for which additional government support is available.

In Scotland housing action area powers are available for the improvement of areas in which at least half the houses fail to meet a statutory tolerable standard. Since 1975, 1,844 housing action areas have been declared. Outside such areas in Scotland local authorities have powers to apply improvement orders to houses below the statutory tolerable standard or lacking certain basic amenities. Local authorities may also give grants towards improving the environment of mainly residential areas.

Considerable progress has been made in

improving housing conditions in Northern Ireland. Some 97 per cent of its dwellings have all amenities, 91 per cent are classified as fit and 89 per cent are in a good state of repair. Urban renewal has been promoted through redevelopment and housing action area activity. Since 1977, 53 housing action areas have been declared.

Further Reading

Housing, Aspects of Britain series. HMSO, 1993.
New Life for Urban Scotland. HMSO, 1988.

Annual Reports

Building Societies Commission. HMSO.
Housing and Construction Statistics. HMSO.
The Housing Corporation. Housing Corporation.

23 Planning and Conservation

Britain seeks to balance the demands for land from business, housing, transport, farming and leisure, and to protect the environment by means of a statutory system of land-use planning and development control. Government agencies and voluntary bodies work to conserve Britain's natural heritage and historic monuments. Britain is committed to a number of international treaties and obligations on conservation.

Planning

Direct responsibility for land-use planning[1] in Great Britain lies with local authorities. The Secretaries of State for the Environment, Wales and Scotland have overall responsibility for the operation of the system. The Department of the Environment brings together the major responsibilities in England for land-use planning, housing and construction, countryside policy and environmental protection. The Welsh Office and The Scottish Office have broadly equivalent responsibilities. In Northern Ireland the Department of the Environment for Northern Ireland is responsible for planning matters through six divisional planning offices, which work closely with the district councils.

In Great Britain these departments provide national and regional guidance on planning matters, while strategic planning at the county level is the responsibility of the county councils. District councils are responsible for local plans and development control. In the metropolitan areas and London, the borough and district councils are preparing new unitary development plans for each administrative area. In Scotland the planning context is set by The Scottish Office and planning functions are undertaken by regional and district councils, whose responsibilities are divided on a basis broadly similar to that in England and Wales. In the more rural regions and the islands, the regional and islands councils respectively have responsibility for planning.

Development Plans

The present development plan system in England and Wales involves structure, local and unitary development plans:

● structure plans, setting out broad policies for the development and use of land, are adopted by county councils, which also adopt minerals and wastes local plans;

---

[1] For further details see *Planning* (Aspects of Britain: HMSO, 1992).

- local plans, prepared in general conformity with the adopted structure plan, and providing detailed guidance for development expected to start within about ten years, are adopted by district councils; and
- unitary development plans, setting out both strategic and detailed land use and development policies, are adopted by metropolitan districts or London boroughs.

Members of the public have an opportunity to express their views on the planning of their area during the early stages of plan preparation.

In Scotland structure plans are prepared by regional or islands authorities, and local plans by those districts with planning responsibilities, and by general planning and islands authorities. Under Northern Ireland's single-tier system, plans are prepared by the Department of the Environment for Northern Ireland.

The Planning and Compensation Act 1991 introduced improvements in the efficiency and effectiveness of the planning system. Decisions on planning applications and appeals are to be made in accordance with the relevant development plan unless material considerations indicate otherwise. The majority of local planning authorities are aiming to complete and adopt plans covering the whole of their areas by the end of 1996. When formulating their plans, planning authorities must take account of any strategic or regional guidance issued by the Secretary of State as planning policy guidance notes and regional policy guidance notes. The Government's aim is for full use to be made of urban land for new development, having regard to the need to retain green spaces within the urban environment and the need to ensure that the cumulative effects of development do not harm the character of established residential areas.

Green Belts

'Green Belts' are areas intended to be left open and free from inappropriate development. Their purposes are to:

- restrict the sprawl of large built-up areas;

- safeguard the surrounding countryside;
- prevent neighbouring towns merging;
- preserve the special character of historic towns; and
- assist in urban regeneration.

They also have a recreational role. Green Belts have been established around major cities, including London, Edinburgh, Glasgow, Merseyside, Greater Manchester and the West Midlands, as well as several smaller towns. Some 1.5 million hectares (3.8 million acres) are designated as Green Belt in England and 200,000 hectares (500,000 acres) in Scotland. The Government attaches great importance to the protection of Green Belts and expects local planning authorities to do likewise when considering planning applications.

Development Control

Certain minor developments do not need specific planning permission. However, most development does require this. Applications are dealt with in the light of development plans and other material planning considerations, including national and regional guidance. In 1992 some 473,000 applications for planning permission were received in England alone; in total, 369,000 applications were granted in this period.

Local planning authorities in England and Wales are required to publicise planning applications locally. Methods commonly used include site notices, newspaper advertising and neighbour notification. In Scotland a neighbour notification system requires the applicant to notify the owners and occupiers of land and buildings adjoining the site of a proposed development when the application is submitted to the local planning authority.

The applicant has a right of appeal to the Secretary of State if the local authority refuses planning permission, grants it with conditions attached, or fails to decide an application within an agreed period (usually eight weeks). The great majority of appeals are decided on the basis of written submissions. However, either party has the right to be heard by an inspector at a public local inquiry or, where a less formal arrangement is appropriate, at a hearing. A local inquiry is usually held for more complicated or controversial applications. Similar provision is made in Northern Ireland for the hearing of representations at public inquiries. For planning applications which do not give rise to public inquiries, the applicant has a right of appeal to the independent Planning Appeals Commission.

The Secretaries of State can direct that a planning application be referred to them for decision. This power to 'call in' is generally exercised only for proposals which raise planning issues of national or regional importance. The applicant and the local planning authority have the right to be heard by a person appointed by the Secretary of State, and a public inquiry will normally be held. In Northern Ireland, major planning applications are dealt with under the Planning (NI) Order 1991, which allows for a public inquiry in certain circumstances.

Environmental Impact Assessment

Planning applications for certain types of development must be accompanied by an environmental impact assessment. This should describe the likely significant environmental effects and measures proposed to minimise adverse consequences. These statements are made available to the public and to statutory bodies such as the Countryside Commission and English Nature (see p. 343). The planning authority must take into consideration the environmental statement, and any representations received on it, before granting planning permission.

Architectural Standards

High standards in new building are welcomed by the Government, although it encourages local planning authorities not to impose their architectural tastes on developers. The Department of the Environment, in collaboration with the independent Royal Institute of British Architects (RIBA) and the National House-Building Council, sponsors the biennial Housing Design Awards Scheme for England and Northern Ireland, with categories for renovation and new building.

Scotland and Wales have similar award schemes. Royal Fine Art Commissions for England and Wales and for Scotland advise government departments, planning authorities and other public bodies on questions of public amenity or artistic importance. An Art for Architecture scheme, funded by the Department of National Heritage, is receiving £100,000 in 1993–94 to enable artists and craftspeople to be involved in the design of buildings from the planning stage.

The RIBA, the principal professional body for architects, together with the Architects Registration Council of the United Kingdom, exercises control over standards in architectural education and encourages high architectural standards in the profession. The Royal Incorporation of Architects in Scotland is allied to it, as is the Royal Society of Ulster Architects. Following a review of the arrangements for the registration of architects, the Government proposes to move to a system of self-regulation through the chartered professional institutions.

A major RIBA study of the architectural profession is being undertaken with government support of £20,000. The strategic study will lay the foundations of a new strategy for architects to meet the major changes taking place in the industry. Many ideas have already been generated.

Conservation

Britain has for many years had policies and laws designed to protect both its natural environment and built heritage. For example, the first Act of Parliament to protect old buildings, the Ancient Monuments Protection Act, was passed as long ago as 1882. A wide variety of designations are used to protect areas, sites and monuments that are of special interest to conservationists, and various organisations work towards the conservation of differing aspects of Britain's national heritage. Many of these groups have very large memberships.

Britain is also involved in international conservation efforts and has signed important agreements with other countries to protect wildlife, habitats and heritage sites. Britain participated fully in the United Nations Conference on Environment and Development (UNCED), popularly known as the 'Earth Summit', held in Rio de Janeiro in June 1992, and is committed to carrying the process forward. Among the agreements reached was a framework convention on climate change (see p. 356), a convention on biodiversity, 'Agenda 21' (an action framework for the 21st century), a declaration setting out clear principles for sustainable development, and a declaration for the management of forests. Britain played an active role in the first meeting of the United Nations Commission on Sustainable Development in June 1993 and will participate in its work.

Administrative Arrangements

The Department of the Environment is responsible for countryside policy and environmental protection in England; the Department of National Heritage has responsibility for the listing of buildings and for scheduled ancient monuments. The Welsh Office, The Scottish Office Environment Department and the Department of the Environment for Northern Ireland have broadly equivalent responsibilities. Agencies such as English Nature, English Heritage, the Countryside Commission and their equivalents carry out many functions on behalf of the Government. The present arrangements for the nature conservation and countryside agencies were largely established by the Environmental Protection Act 1990, the most recent piece of major environmental legislation, and, in Scotland, by the Natural Heritage (Scotland) Act 1991. In addition, the local authorities and a wide range of voluntary organisations are actively involved in environmental conservation and protection.

This Common Inheritance

The environment White Paper *This Common Inheritance*, published in September 1990, was the first comprehensive statement by the Government of its policy on issues affecting the environment. It summarised more than

350 proposals for tackling such diverse issues as global warming, pollution control, the regulation of land use and planning, the rural economy, the countryside and wildlife. Two anniversary progress reports have been published, which reviewed progress and set out commitments to many further actions to protect the environment. The Government has established an Environmental Action Fund (see p. 348) which is, among other things, helping voluntary groups in England take forward the initiatives in the White Paper.

The Government intends to establish a Millennium Fund, subject to parliamentary approval. This would be supported by the proceeds of the proposed National Lottery (see p. 482). Among the things which the Millennium Fund could support are:

- the restoration of the buildings that symbolise and enrich British life;
- help for local communities and voluntary groups to run their own Millennium projects for local restoration schemes; and
- Millennium bursaries for young or newly retired people offering their time to schemes designed to change the face of Britain by the year 2000.

Built Heritage

Lists of buildings of special architectural or historical interest are compiled by the Government, in England with the advice of English Heritage. It is against the law to demolish, extend or alter the character of any 'listed' building without special consent from the local planning authority or the appropriate Secretary of State. The local planning authority can issue temporary 'building preservation notices' to protect unlisted buildings that are in danger while consideration is given to listing. In Northern Ireland the Department of the Environment for Northern Ireland is directly responsible for the listing of buildings.

Ancient monuments are similarly protected through a system of scheduling. English Heritage, the government agency responsible for the conservation of historic remains in England, has embarked upon a programme to evaluate all known archaeological remains in

England. This is expected to result in a significant increase in the number of scheduled monuments.

Table 23.1: Scheduled Monuments and Listed Buildings

	Listed buildings	Scheduled monuments
England	441,000	13,800
Scotland	39,000	5,600
Wales	14,000	2,600
Northern Ireland	8,200	1,100

Sources: Department of National Heritage, The Scottish Office, Welsh Office, Department of the Environment for Northern Ireland.

Many of the royal palaces and parks are open to the public; their maintenance is the responsibility of the Secretaries of State for National Heritage and for Scotland. English Heritage manages some 400 properties on behalf of the Secretary of State for National Heritage, advises him on applications for consent to alter or demolish scheduled monuments and listed buildings, and gives grants for the repair of ancient monuments, historic buildings and buildings in conservation areas in England. Most of its monuments are open to the public. Government funding for English Heritage is £100 million in 1993–94.

English Heritage announced proposals for the future management of its historic properties in October 1992. This is an extension of an existing policy to encourage local management of some less complex sites by suitable local organisations where there is enthusiasm and expertise. Management agreements are proposed to protect individual monuments and monitor public access.

The environment White Paper also announced that the Government had invited English Heritage to prepare a register of historic landscapes and battlefields. Progress on these registers is now well under way. The registers, like the existing register of historic parks and gardens, will be without direct legal effect, but will alert the Government, local planning authorities and others to the significance of these sites when considering development plans and applications for planning permission.

In Scotland and Wales similar functions are performed by Historic Scotland, which cares for 330 monuments, and by Cadw: Welsh Historic Monuments, which manages 127, with advice from an Ancient Monuments Board for each country. Historic Scotland and Cadw are executive agencies within The Scottish Office and the Welsh Office respectively. The Department of the Environment for Northern Ireland has 173 historic monuments in its care, and is advised by a Historic Buildings Council and a Historic Monuments Council.

The National Heritage Memorial Fund helps towards the cost of acquiring, maintaining or preserving land, buildings, works of art and other items of outstanding interest which are also of importance to the national heritage. In 1992–93 the Fund assisted in the preservation of 81 heritage items.

Local planning authorities have designated 7,800 'conservation areas' of special architectural or historic interest in England; there are over 350 in Wales, 556 in Scotland and 40 in Northern Ireland. These areas receive special protection through the planning system. Grants and loans are available from the appropriate historic buildings and monuments body for works which make a significant contribution towards the preservation or improvement of a conservation area.

Industrial, Transport and Maritime Heritage

Britain was the first country in the world to industrialise on a large scale, and many advances in manufacturing and transport were pioneered in Britain. This has resulted in a large industrial heritage, the importance of which is being increasingly recognised. Important sites are scheduled or listed; one of the most important, the Ironbridge Gorge, where Abraham Darby (1677–1717) first smelted iron using coke, has been designated a World Heritage Site (see p. 348). Other museums have also been set up, devoted to the preservation of industrial buildings and equipment.

Britain, which pioneered railways, has a fine heritage of railway buildings and structures, and there is an active movement to preserve it. Volunteers are very active in this. A large number of disused railway lines have been bought by railway preservation societies and returned to operation, often using preserved steam locomotives, and several railway museums have been established.

Important reminders of Britain's maritime past are also preserved. The historic naval dockyard at Chatham has been opened to the public; at Portsmouth HMS *Victory*, Nelson's flagship, HMS *Warrior*, the world's first iron battleship, and the remains of *Mary Rose*, raised from the seabed in 1982, are open to the public. The Imperial War Museum has preserved the cruiser HMS *Belfast*, which is open to the public in the Pool of London. Isambard Kingdom Brunel's SS *Great Britain*, the world's first large screw-driven ship, is preserved in Bristol. A voluntary body, the Maritime Trust, has been established to preserve vessels and other maritime items of historic or technical interest. The Trust's vessels include the clipper *Cutty Sark* at Greenwich.

Voluntary Sector

The Government supports the work of the national amenity societies and others in the protection of Britain's heritage. In England the Department of National Heritage has offered to make grants totalling £422,000 to 23 such organisations in 1993–94.

Among the organisations which campaign for the preservation and appreciation of buildings are:
- the Society for the Protection of Ancient Buildings;
- the Ancient Monuments Society;
- the Georgian Group;
- the Architectural Heritage Society of Scotland;
- the Ulster Architectural Heritage Society;
- the Victorian Society; and
- the Council for British Archaeology.

While funded largely by private donations, the amenity societies have paid professional staff and statutory responsibilities, in recognition of which they receive government support.

The National Trust (for Places of Historic Interest or Natural Beauty), a charity with over 2 million members, owns and protects 229 historic houses open to the public, in addition to over 230,000 hectares (568,000 acres) of land in England, Wales and Northern Ireland. Scotland has its own National Trust. The Civic Trust makes awards for development and restoration work which enhances its surroundings. It undertakes urban regeneration projects and acts as an 'umbrella' organisation for nearly 1,000 local amenity societies. There are associate trusts in Scotland, Wales and north-east England.

The Countryside and Nature Conservation

Four government agencies are responsible for countryside policy and nature conservation in Great Britain:
- the Countryside Commission and English Nature, which act in England;
- the Countryside Council for Wales (CCW); and
- Scottish Natural Heritage (SNH).

A Joint Nature Conservation Committee (JNCC) has also been established as the mechanism through which the three nature conservation agencies in England, Wales and Scotland fulfil their responsibilities for international and Great Britain-wide nature conservation matters. The JNCC also undertakes research and sets standards for data, monitoring and other matters. It includes representatives from Northern Ireland and independent members, and has a supporting specialist staff.

The countryside agencies are complemented by the rural development agencies, the objective of which is to encourage diversification of rural enterprise and thereby ensure a prosperous countryside. In England the Rural Development Commission is responsible for the diversification of the rural economy. It gives assistance for converting redundant buildings into workspaces, which create job opportunities while avoiding the need for new building. It has also taken part in measures to promote 'green' tourism.

Countryside Agencies

The countryside agencies are responsible for enhancing the natural beauty and amenity of the countryside and encouraging the provision of facilities for open-air recreation as well as providing for the needs of those who live and work in the countryside. Activities aided by these bodies include the provision by local authorities (sometimes in association with other bodies) and private individuals of country parks and picnic sites, often within easy reach of towns; the provision or improvement of recreational paths; and the encouragement of amenity tree-planting schemes. Total funding in 1993–94 is over £40 million for the Countryside Commission, £19 million for the CCW and over £36 million for SNH. The countryside agencies undertake research projects and experimental schemes, often working in consultation with local authorities and voluntary organisations. They give financial assistance to public, private and voluntary organisations, and individuals carrying out countryside conservation, recreation and amenity projects.

The Countryside Commission runs the Countryside Stewardship scheme, launched in 1991, which offers incentives to farmers and other land managers to enhance or restore valuable landscapes and habitats and improve access to, and enjoyment of, the countryside. In 1991, 900 agreements were made covering 30,000 hectares (74,000 acres). For the second year a further 1,300 agreements, covering 31,000 hectares (77,000 acres), were reached. In Wales an equivalent scheme is being run on a pilot basis by the CCW. Called Tir Cymen, it adopts a slightly different approach in that it applies to entire farms. Under government proposals announced in August 1993, the Countryside Stewardship scheme is to become part of Britain's package of agricultural environment measures. Part of

the reform of the Common Agricultural Policy (see p. 235), the package has been sent to the European Commission for approval.

> The Government launched Rural Action, a joint scheme of English Nature, the Countryside Commission and the Rural Development Commission, in December 1992. The scheme, worth £3.2 million over the first three years, is designed to help communities in rural areas carry forward their own ideas on caring for and improving the environment.

The Countryside Commission recognises over 210 country parks and over 230 picnic sites in England. A further 24 country parks and about 30 picnic sites in Wales are recognised by the CCW. In Scotland there are 36 country parks, and many local authority and private sector schemes for a variety of countryside facilities have been approved for grant aid by SNH.

Nature Conservation Agencies

English Nature, the CCW and SNH are responsible for nature conservation in their areas. This includes:

● establishing and managing nature reserves;
● advising the Government;
● identifying and notifying Sites of Special Scientific Interest (SSSIs);
● providing general information and advice;
● giving grants; and
● supporting and conducting research.

English Nature's funding for 1993–94 is almost £38 million.

There are 245 national nature reserves covering some 168,000 hectares (415,000 acres) and two marine nature reserves, surrounding the islands of Lundy, off the Devon coast, and Skomer, off the coast of Dyfed. Some 5,650 SSSIs have been notified in Great Britain for their plant, animal, geological or physiographical features. Local authorities have declared about 280 local nature reserves in England alone.

County nature conservation trusts, urban wildlife trusts and the Royal Society for the Protection of Birds (RSPB) play an important part in protecting wildlife, having established between them some 1,800 reserves. The county and urban trusts are affiliated to a parent organisation, the Royal Society for Nature Conservation. The RSPB is the largest voluntary wildlife conservation body in Europe.

In Northern Ireland both nature and countryside conservation are the responsibility of the Department of the Environment for Northern Ireland through its Environment Service. In 1993–94 total funding for the Environment Service is some £19.7 million, including £6.9 million for pollution control measures. The Council for Nature Conservation and the Countryside advises the Department on nature conservation matters, including the establishment and management of land and marine nature reserves and the declaration of Areas of Special Scientific Interest. Some 44 national nature reserves have been established and 40 Areas of Special Scientific Interest declared.

Wildlife Protection

Wildlife in Great Britain is protected principally by the Wildlife and Countryside Act 1981. This has:

- extended the list of protected species;
- restricted the introduction into the countryside of animals not normally found in the wild in Britain; and
- afforded greater protection for SSSIs and introduced provision for marine nature reserves.

There is also provision for reviews of the list of protected species to be conducted by the three official nature conservation agencies, acting jointly through the JNCC, every five years and submitted to the Secretary of State for the Environment. In Northern Ireland separate legislation on species and habitat protection is in line with the rest of Britain.

Species Recovery and Reintroduction

Considerable research and management is carried out to encourage the recovery of populations of species threatened with extinction. The three nature conservation agencies have also set up recovery programmes for threatened species of plants and animals, such as the dormouse, the Plymouth pear and the fen raft spider. The aim is to ensure the survival of self-sustaining populations of these species in the wild.

In areas where species have become extinct, schemes can be devised to reintroduce them into areas which they used to inhabit. For example, the red kite had died out in England and Scotland, although it was still found in Wales and mainland Europe. An international project was therefore co-ordinated by the JNCC and the Royal Society for the Protection of Birds to bring adult birds from Sweden and Spain and release them into the wild in areas which the species no longer inhabited. Other species that have been reintroduced in recent years include the white-tailed sea eagle and the Large Blue butterfly. The Royal Botanic Gardens at Kew holds some 3,000 plant specimens which are extinct or under severe threat in the wild, and has had some success with reintroduction projects.

Reliable information on the numbers and distribution of species is important in planning conservation strategies. Much research work is therefore done by conservation organisations to record and monitor animal populations. There are both national and local recording schemes, the latter usually collecting information on a county basis. Table 23.2 shows statistically significant changes in the populations of British bird species identified in recent research.

Tree Preservation and Planting

Tree preservation orders enable local authorities to protect trees and woodlands in the interests of amenity. Once a tree is protected, it is in general an offence to cut down, reshape or generally wilfully destroy it without permission. The courts can impose substantial fines for breaches of such orders. Where protected trees are felled in contravention of an order or are removed because they are dying, dead or dangerous, a

Table 23.2: Population Trends in Bird Species

	Period covered	Number of species examined	Population trends		
			Decrease	*Little change*	*Increase*
Rare breeding birds	1973–89	25	4	10	11
Wildfowl	1960/61–89/90	19	1	4	14
Waders	1971–89	11	2	5	4

Source: *Key Indicators for British Wildlife*, York University.

replacement tree must be planted. Local authorities have powers to enforce this.

Tree planting is encouraged through various grant schemes. The planting of broadleaved trees has increased tenfold since 1985. Major new initiatives include a project to create a new national forest in the Midlands and 12 community forests near large towns and cities. These are aimed at enhancing the environment and providing new opportunities for leisure and recreation. In Scotland substantial areas of woodland are being planted between Edinburgh and Glasgow under the Central Scotland Woodland Initiative.

Hedgerows

In July 1992 the Government launched a hedgerow incentive scheme in England. Administered by the Countryside Commission, it provides grants for managing hedgerows in environmentally sensitive ways. The scheme has provision for payments of £4.3 million over the period 1993–94 to 1995–1996. The CCW launched a hedgerow renovation scheme in December 1992.

The Coast

Local planning authorities along the coastline are responsible for planning land use at the coast; they also attempt to safeguard and enhance the coast's natural attractions and preserve areas of scientific interest. The protection of the coastline against erosion and flooding is administered centrally by the Ministry of Agriculture, Fisheries and Food, the Welsh Office and The Scottish Office. Operational responsibility lies with local authorities and the National Rivers Authority

(see p. 227). Certain stretches of undeveloped coast of particular scenic beauty in England and Wales are designated as heritage coast; jointly with local authorities, the countryside agencies have defined 45 coasts, protecting 1,525 km (948 miles). There are 29 marine consultation areas in Scotland. Statutory bodies taking decisions that affect these areas will be asked to consult SNH.

The National Trust, through its Enterprise Neptune campaign, raises funds to acquire stretches of coastline of great natural beauty and recreational value. Some £18 million has been raised so far and the Trust now protects 861 km (535 miles) of coastline in England, Wales and Northern Ireland. The National Trust for Scotland also owns large parts of the Scottish coastline and protects others through conservation agreements.

National Parks, Areas of Outstanding Natural Beauty and National Scenic Areas

The Countryside Commission and the CCW can designate National Parks and areas of outstanding natural beauty (AONBs), subject to confirmation by the Secretaries of State for the Environment and for Wales respectively.

Ten National Parks have been established in England and Wales. Their aim is first to provide protection for the outstanding countryside they contain and secondly to provide opportunities for access and outdoor recreation. They are 'national' in the sense that they are of value to the nation as a whole. However, most of the land remains in private hands. Special National Park authorities have been set up, one for each park. Among other things, they:

● act as the development control authority for their areas;

345

- negotiate public access and land management agreements and encourage farmers to manage their land in the traditional way;
- plant trees and look after footpaths; and
- set up information centres and employ rangers.

The Norfolk and Suffolk Broads have their own independent authority and enjoy protection equivalent to that of a National Park. It is intended that the New Forest in Hampshire should enjoy similar protection.

A total of 39 AONBs have been designated, covering around 2 million hectares (4.8 million acres) in England and 83,000 hectares (205,000 acres) in Wales. They comprise parts of the countryside which lack extensive areas of open country suitable for recreation and hence National Park status, but which nevertheless have an important landscape quality. Local authorities are encouraged to give special attention to AONBs in their planning and countryside conservation work.

In Scotland there are four regional parks and 40 National Scenic Areas, covering more than 1 million hectares (2.5 million acres), where certain kinds of development are subject to consultation with SNH and, in the event of a disagreement, with the Secretary of State for Scotland. Working parties have made recommendations for the management of the Cairngorms and for Loch Lomond and the Trossachs, two areas of outstanding natural importance in Scotland. In the wider countryside SNH provides grants for a range of countryside projects.

In Northern Ireland the Council for Nature Conservation and the Countryside advises the Department of the Environment for Northern Ireland on the preservation of amenities and the designation of areas of outstanding natural beauty. Nine such areas have been designated, covering 285,000 hectares (705,000 acres); seven areas are being managed as country parks and one as a regional park.

There are 11 forest parks in Great Britain, covering some 244,000 hectares (603,000 acres) and administered by the Forestry Commission. There are nine in Northern Ireland, where they are administered by the Forest Service of the Department of Agriculture.

Public Rights of Way and Open Country

County and metropolitan district councils in England and Wales are responsible for keeping public rights of way signposted and free from obstruction. Public paths are usually maintained by these highway authorities, which also supervise landowners' duties to repair stiles and gates. In Scotland, planning authorities are responsible for asserting and protecting rights of way. Local authorities in Great Britain can create paths, close paths no longer needed for public use and divert paths to meet the needs of either the public or landowners. Farmers in England and Wales are required by law rapidly to restore public paths damaged by agricultural operations. In England and Wales there are some 225,000 km (140,000 miles) of rights

Table 23.3: National Parks and Other Designated Areas, March 1993

	National Parks[a] area (sq km)	Percentage of total area in region	Areas of Outstanding Natural Beauty[b] Area (sq km)	Percentage of total area in region
England	9,934	8	19,595	15
Wales	4,098	19	832	4
Scotland	–	–	10,173	13
Northern Ireland	–	–	2,849	20

Sources: Countryside Commission, Scottish Natural Heritage, Department of the Environment for Northern Ireland.
[a] Including the Norfolk and Suffolk Broads.
[b] National Scenic Areas in Scotland.

of way. There are 11 approved national trails in England and Wales, covering over 3,100 km (1,900 miles), and three approved long-distance routes in Scotland, covering some 580 km (360 miles). The Countryside Commission intends to help authorities bring all rights of way in England into good order by the end of the century, and a Parish Path Partnership scheme has been introduced, which is designed to stimulate local involvement and improvement. The CCW intends to establish a network of public rights of way by 1995.

There is no automatic right of public access to open country, although many landowners allow it more or less freely. Local planning authorities in England and Wales can secure access by means of agreements with landowners. If agreements cannot be reached, authorities may acquire land or make orders for public access. Similar powers cover Scotland and Northern Ireland; in Northern Ireland the primary responsibility lies with district councils. In Scotland there is a tradition of freedom to roam, based on tolerance between landowners and those seeking reasonable recreational access to the hills.

Common land totals an estimated 600,000 hectares (1.5 million acres) in England and Wales, but a legal right of public access exists to only one-fifth of this area. Common land is usually privately owned, but people other than the owner may have various rights over it, for example, as pasture land. Commons are protected by law and cannot be built on or enclosed without the consent of the Secretaries of State for the Environment or Wales; this consent is normally only given for minor public works. There is no common land in Scotland or Northern Ireland.

Voluntary Sector

Many voluntary organisations are concerned to preserve the amenities of the countryside, including the Council for the Protection of Rural England, the Campaign for the Protection of Rural Wales, the Association for the Protection of Rural Scotland and the Ulster Society for the Preservation of the Countryside.

International Action

Britain plays a full part in international action to conserve wildlife. Its international obligations include the Berne Convention on the conservation of European wildlife and natural habitats, and EC directives on the conservation of wild birds and of natural habitats and wild fauna and flora. The implementation of the latter directive, which was adopted in May 1992, entails the designation of Special Areas of Conservation (SACs). Together with Special Protection Areas (SPAs) designated under the birds directive, the SACs will contribute to a Community-wide network of protected sites to be known as 'Natura 2000'. Some 70 SPAs have already been designated.

Britain is also party to the Ramsar Convention on wetlands of international importance. Some 62 sites in Britain have been designated under this convention, together with a further site in one of Britain's dependent territories. Other conservation measures promoted by the Government have included a ban (in conjunction with other EC countries) on the import of whale products and harp and hooded seal pup skins, and stricter controls for the protection of wild birds. Britain is a party to the Convention on International Trade in Endangered Species of Wild Fauna and Flora, which prohibits international trade in endangered species and regulates trade in less threatened species by means of a permit system.

The Convention on Biological Diversity was signed by over 150 countries, including Britain, at the June 1992 'Earth Summit'. It requires countries to:

- identify and monitor their genetic resources;

- set up protected areas to safeguard these resources; and

- develop national strategies for the conservation and sustainable use of biological diversity.

A national action plan is due to be published by the end of 1993. Wide consultation has been held on this.

Environmental Improvement Schemes

The Government assists local voluntary
organisations to promote projects such as
creating parks, footpaths and other areas of
greenery in cities; conserving the industrial
heritage and the natural environment; and
recycling waste. The Department of the
Environment makes grants through the
Urban Programme (see p. 322) and the new
Environmental Action Fund, worth about
£4 million in 1993–94, to support projects
with either direct or indirect environmental
gains. The Civic Trust has been chosen to
manage a Local Projects Fund, from which
some £350,000 will be available in 1993–94.

The Welsh Office made £500,000 available
in 1992–93 to voluntary organisations under
its Environment Wales initiative. The
Scottish Office Environment Department is
making £334,000 available in 1993–94 to
environmental organisations under its Special
Grants (Environmental) Programme, and a
further £420,000 to UK2000 Scotland, a
partnership between central and local
government, voluntary bodies and the private
sector, which carries out practical
environmental improvements. Scottish
Enterprise and Highlands and Islands
Enterprise (see p. 147) are responsible for
environmental improvement and land
reclamation in Scotland. The Government's
programme of Environmentally Sensitive
Areas (see p. 238) supports environmentally
sensitive practices that protect and enhance
the countryside.

The Groundwork Foundation manages a
network of trusts which work in partnership
with public bodies, the private sector,
voluntary organisations and individuals, and
aims to tackle environmental problems arising
from dereliction and vandalism and to
increase public awareness of the opportunities
to change and improve local environments.
Government funding for England in 1993–94
for the Groundwork Foundation is £5.6
million; a target has been set of establishing
50 trusts in England and Wales by 1995.

World Heritage Sites

Britain is fully represented in the World
Heritage List, which was established under
the World Heritage Convention to identify
and secure lasting protection for those parts
of the world heritage of outstanding universal
value. So far 13 sites in Britain have been
listed. These are:

- Canterbury Cathedral, with St
Augustine's Abbey and St Martin's
Church, in Kent;

- Durham Cathedral and Castle;

- Studley Royal Gardens and Fountains
Abbey, in North Yorkshire;

- Ironbridge Gorge, with the world's first
iron bridge and other early industrial
sites, in Shropshire;

- the prehistoric stone circles at
Stonehenge and Avebury, in Wiltshire;

- Blenheim Palace, in Oxfordshire;

- the city of Bath, in Avon;

- Hadrian's Wall;

- the Tower of London;

- the Palace of Westminster, Westminster
Abbey and St Margaret's, Westminster,
also in London;

- the islands of St Kilda, in Scotland;

- the castles and town walls of King
Edward I, in north Wales; and

- the Giant's Causeway and Causeway
Coast, in Northern Ireland.

Support for these sites can be
considerable. For example, English Heritage
is proposing a scheme to integrate
Stonehenge with its historic landscape and
minimise 20th-century intrusions upon the
scene. The plans involve removing the
present unsightly visitor facilities and the
road which carries traffic close to the
monument. A new visitor centre would be
built some distance from the stones.

24 Control of Pollution

For more than a century Britain has been developing policies to protect the environment against pollution from industry and other sources. Laws were introduced at an early stage to control air and water pollution—for example, the Alkali Act 1863 and, more recently, the Clean Air Acts 1956 and 1968. Legislation has been revised regularly to meet changing circumstances. The Environmental Protection Act 1990, which applies to Great Britain, has strengthened the existing system of protection against pollution. Legislation sets out a wide range of powers and duties for central and local government, covering all types of pollution, from greenhouse gases to litter.

Introduction

Britain supports international co-operation on matters of environmental protection. Increasingly, much of Britain's legislation on pollution control is being developed in collaboration with other member states of the European Community and organisations such as the Organisation for Economic Co-operation and Development and the United Nations and its agencies. Britain is taking a leading position in the development of a European ecolabelling scheme. Recently, with increasing scientific understanding of global pollution problems, the Government has been considering how its own policies and actions can be further guided by the principle of 'sustainable development', the theme of a major United Nations conference in June 1992 (see p. 356). Assistance is also given to developing countries for environmental projects; an Environmental Know How Fund was set up in April 1992 to help Eastern Europe and the former Soviet Union.

Many environmental objectives were achieved during the British presidency of the European Community in the second half of 1992. These included agreement on:

● a regulation accelerating the phasing out of ozone-depleting substances;

● a common position on a new directive to extend stringent standards on exhaust pollutants;

● a regulation on waste shipments and a decision on ratification by the Community of the Basel Convention on transboundary movements of hazardous wastes;

- the formal adoption of a directive on the harmonisation of programmes for reduction of pollution caused by waste from the titanium dioxide industry; and

- a resolution responding to the European Commission's Fifth Environmental Action Programme, which sets out the strategy for the Community's environmental policy to the year 2000 and which came into effect from January 1993.

Broad agreement was also reached on a Community-wide eco-management and audit scheme.

Administration

Executive responsibility for pollution control is divided between local authorities and central government agencies. Central government makes policy, exercises general budgetary control, promotes legislation and advises pollution control authorities on policy implementation. The Secretary of State for the Environment has general responsibility for co-ordinating the work of the Government on environmental protection. In Scotland and Wales the respective Secretaries of State are responsible for pollution control co-ordination within their countries. In Northern Ireland, this responsibility rests with the Department of the Environment for Northern Ireland. Local authorities also have important duties and powers. They are responsible for matters such as:

- collection and disposal of domestic wastes;

- keeping the streets clean from litter;

- control of air pollution from domestic and from many industrial premises; and

- noise and general nuisance abatement.

The National Rivers Authority (NRA) is responsible for monitoring water quality and the control of water pollution in England and Wales, on which it is expected to spend £90 million in 1993–94. In Scotland, the river purification authorities have statutory responsibility for water pollution control; the seven mainland authorities forecast expenditure of over £12 million in 1993–94.

In Northern Ireland, water quality is monitored by the Environment Service of the Department of the Environment for Northern Ireland. In England and Wales Her Majesty's Inspectorate of Pollution (HMIP) has an important role in the control of emissions to land, air and water from certain industrial processes through the mechanism of 'integrated pollution control' (see p. 351). The Government is committed to bringing together the functions of HMIP and the NRA, together with those presently exercised by waste regulation authorities, into a single Environment Agency. A Scottish Environment Protection Agency, with broadly similar responsibilities, is also proposed.

A permanent network of the environmental enforcement agencies of EC member states was established in November 1992, during Britain's presidency of the Community. Its first meeting was hosted by HMIP.

An independent standing Royal Commission on Environmental Pollution advises the Government on national and international matters concerning the pollution of the environment, on the adequacy of research and on the future possibilities of danger to the environment. So far it has produced 17 reports.

An Environmental Partnership was announced in November 1992 as part of the Capital Partnership initiative (see p. 322). This supports local authority programmes for recycling, waste management and dealing with contaminated land and landfill gas.

Business and Consumer Involvement

The Government takes part in a number of initiatives to involve businesses in environmental matters and to help the consumer play a part.

Advisory Committee on Business and the Environment

The Advisory Committee on Business and the Environment consists of 25 business people appointed by the Government to serve in a personal capacity rather than as representatives of particular interests. It is charged, among other things, with providing advice to the Government on environmental issues relevant to business. It aims to help encourage best environmental practice within British businesses.

The Committee's main work is carried on through its working groups. These have so far examined global warming, recycling, environmental management, the financial sector, and commercial and export opportunities.

Other Business Initiatives

These include, for example:

- the *Chief Executive's Guide* and *DIY Workbook*, published by Business in the Environment, part of the voluntary group Business in the Community;

- the launch of an Environment Business Forum by the Confederation of British Industry (CBI), which is open to all businesses whether or not they are members of the CBI; and

- many local and supplier initiatives around the country.

Eco-audit

In June 1993 the European Community adopted regulations for a voluntary Community-wide scheme of eco-audits. This will initially be targeted at the manufacturing, power and waste disposal sectors. Registrations will apply to individual sites rather than to companies' entire operations, but each company will be required to establish an environmental policy before any of its sites can be registered. The company would then have to prepare an environmental statement, open to the public, for each site it wishes to register; this statement would have to be validated by an accredited independent verifier. A full cycle of environmental audits at each site would have to be conducted at least once every three years.

Each EC member state is required to have established a competent body to maintain a register of sites by July 1994. The scheme should be fully operational by April or May 1995.

British Standard on Environmental Management

The British Standards Institution (see p. 155) has published BS7750, a full standard for environmental management systems which can be used by any organisation and is compatible with the EC eco-audit scheme. Certification of management systems under BS7750 is one means by which companies can seek to satisfy the requirements of the EC scheme. BS7750 shares many features of the widely-used BS5750 quality management standard and is expected to be certified in a similar way.

Ecolabelling

Many consumers wish to take environmental considerations into account when buying goods. The Government has therefore taken a leading part in developing the European ecolabelling scheme, based on a common label across the Community. The scheme will be voluntary and will apply to all consumer goods except food and pharmaceuticals. Criteria will be developed for individual product groups to identify those products which are less harmful to the environment throughout their lifecycle. The aim is to encourage manufacturers to produce more products that are less harmful to the environment.

Integrated Pollution Control

Under the Environmental Protection Act 1990 a system of 'integrated pollution control' (IPC) is being phased in to control certain categories of industrial pollution. The potentially most harmful processes are specified for IPC, and require authorisation from HMIP. Less harmful air pollution is controlled under a system of local authority air pollution control. In granting authorisation for releases under IPC, the Inspectorate requires the use of the best available techniques not entailing excessive cost to prevent or minimise polluting emissions and to ensure that any releases are made harmless. The staff of HMIP has been increased considerably to allow the full implementation of IPC; staffing rose from 227 in April 1991 to 334 in February 1993. In England and Wales, the NRA is responsible for monitoring waters receiving discharges authorised under IPC.

Her Majesty's Industrial Pollution Inspectorate is the Scottish equivalent of HMIP, and administers IPC jointly with the river purification authorities. In Northern Ireland broadly similar controls are exercised by the Environment Service, and proposals are being formulated for the introduction of a system of air pollution control similar to IPC. The Government is pressing for the introduction of IPC on the British model within the EC.

The Land

Certain local authorities are designated as waste collection, waste disposal or waste regulation authorities, responsible for different parts of the process of dealing with controlled wastes. Legislation has also established a licensing system for waste disposal sites, treatment plants and storage facilities receiving controlled wastes. It provides for a more intensive control system for special wastes, namely those which contain or consist of substances dangerous to life. HMIP, the NRA and the Hazardous Waste Inspectorate for Scotland may advise local authorities on how to improve their control of waste management and on how to work towards environmentally acceptable standards for dealing with hazardous wastes. In Northern Ireland similar advice is offered to district councils by the Environment Service.

Part II of the Environmental Protection Act strengthens existing controls on waste disposal. Responsibility for proper handling of waste will be imposed on everyone who has control of it from production to final disposal or reclamation. Authorities will be able to refuse licences if the applicant is not a fit and proper person. Operators will now

remain responsible for their sites until the waste regulation authority is satisfied that no future hazard is likely to arise. In England and Wales local authorities' waste disposal operations are being transferred to 'arm's length' companies or private contractors so as to separate them from the authorities' other jobs of setting policies and standards, and enforcement. Subject to further legislation, the Government intends that its proposed Environment Agency would take over local authority waste regulation functions.

In Scotland, the responsibility for the collection and disposal of refuse and the regulation of waste management activities remains with the district and islands councils, whose waste management function is examined by the Hazardous Waste Inspectorate. In Northern Ireland responsibility for the collection, disposal and regulation of waste rests with the district councils.

Litter

It is a criminal offence to leave litter in any public place in the open air or to dump rubbish except in designated places. The maximum penalty for this, previously set at £400, was increased under the Environmental Protection Act to £1,000, and was raised again in October 1992 to £2,500. The Act also introduced new powers for the public to apply to the courts for litter abatement orders and new duties on local authorities to keep their public land as free of litter and refuse (including dog faeces) as practicable. Similar powers are due to come into force in Northern Ireland in 1994.

A Tidy Britain Group survey carried out one year after the implementation of the Environmental Protection Act 1990 showed that Britain's streets were about 13 per cent cleaner in 1992 than in 1991.

To help counteract the problem of litter, financial support—totalling £2.9 million in 1993–94—is given to the Tidy Britain Group, which is recognised as the national agency for litter abatement. It provides a comprehensive litter abatement programme in collaboration with local authorities and the private sector. The Group secures sponsorship from industry to undertake litter abatement promotions and programmes such as its Neighbourhood Care Scheme. The Group's activities were extended to Northern Ireland with the establishment in 1991 of Tidy Northern Ireland.

Recycling and Materials Reclamation

The Government encourages the reclamation and recycling of waste materials wherever this is practicable; its target is for half of all recyclable household waste to be reused by 2000. Under the Environmental Protection Act 1990, local authorities have to make plans for the recycling of waste. The Act also requires waste disposal authorities in England to pay 'recycling credits' to waste collection authorities to pass on the reduced costs of disposal where waste is recycled. From April 1994 the credit will be increased so that the full amount saved must be passed on. In Wales and Scotland, the same authorities handle waste collection and disposal.

The Government has supported pilot 'Recycling City' initiatives in Sheffield, Cardiff, Dundee and the county of Devon, which have tested a variety of collection and sorting methods. Trial collections of recyclable waste are being supported and monitored in these and other locations.

Members of the public can deposit used glass containers for recycling in bottle banks—there are over 8,000 such sites in Britain, and it is anticipated that there will be 10,000 by 1995. There are also similar 'can banks' and 'paper banks' and, in some cases, plastics or textiles banks to collect these materials for recycling. In addition, voluntary organisations arrange collections of waste material, and can be paid a recycling credit by the local authority for doing so. Discussions with industry aimed at improving markets for collected recyclable waste have led to voluntary targets, such as a 40 per cent recycled content of newspapers by 2000, and grant aid for research and new plant.

Water

In general, it is against the law to allow any polluting matter to enter water in Britain except in accordance with a legal authorisation. In England and Wales the NRA is responsible for protecting water quality. Its principal method of controlling water pollution is through the regulation of all effluent discharges into groundwaters, inland and coastal waters (except those releases subject to IPC, which are controlled by HMIP). Discharge consents issued by the NRA specify what may be discharged and set limits on the volume and content of effluent, in order to achieve appropriate water quality standards. The NRA maintains public registers containing information about discharge consents, authorisations from HMIP and water quality. HMIP maintains registers of authorisations and associated monitoring. Similar arrangements apply in Scotland, where control is exercised by the river purification authorities. The Department of the Environment for Northern Ireland's Environment Service is responsible for controlling water pollution in Northern Ireland.

Government proposals for statutory water quality objectives for England and Wales, together with a new system of classifying river quality, were published in a consultation paper in December 1992. The objectives, which would be phased in gradually, would specify for each individual stretch of water the standards that should be reached and the target date for achieving them. The system of statutory water quality objectives would provide the framework for the NRA to set consents.

Over the past 30 years, notable progress has been made in cleaning up the previously heavily polluted major estuaries of the east coast of England and Scotland—the Thames, Humber, Tees, Tyne and Forth—which now support varied populations of fish and other wildlife. A 25-year scheme, supported by the Government and the EC, aims to reduce river pollution and improve water quality throughout the Mersey river basin and estuary. Other major schemes in progress include programmes to improve water quality in the Clyde in Scotland and the Lagan in Northern Ireland.

More than 95 per cent of the population in Britain live in properties connected to a sewer, and sewage treatment works serve over 80 per cent of the population. In England and Wales the water industry is planning to spend some £14,000 million (at 1989 prices) up to the year 2000 on improving sewerage, sewage treatment and disposal. Progressively higher treatment standards for industrial waste effluents and new measures to combat pollution from agriculture are expected to bring further improvements in water quality. In Scotland, sewage treatment and disposal come within the water and sewerage programme, which will total more than £728 million in the three years to 1995–96.

The Government is committed to meeting the requirements of a number of EC directives for the protection and improvement of water quality, for example, on the quality of surface water for abstraction for drinking water supply, the quality needed to support freshwater fisheries, the quality of water for bathing areas (see below) and the treatment of urban waste water.

Bathing Waters and Coastal Sewage Discharges

The Government has announced investment of around £2,200 million by the water industry to provide treatment of coastal sewage discharges. A £2,000 million programme to improve the quality of Britain's bathing waters should be largely complete by the end of 1995. In the 1992 tests of bathing water quality, it was found that 79 per cent of identified bathing waters (358 out of 455) in Britain met the mandatory coliform bacteria standards of the EC bathing water directive, compared with 66 per cent of beaches in 1988. The Government expects all but a handful of bathing waters to meet the directive's standards by 1995. The NRA is responsible for monitoring compliance with the directive. In 1990 the Government announced that the sea dumping of sewage sludge would be terminated completely by the end of 1998.

Marine Environment

In September 1992 a new Convention for the Protection of the Marine Environment of the North East Atlantic was agreed in Paris. It covers both land and sea, sets targets for the introduction of additional safeguards for the area, and requires contracting parties to take all possible steps to prevent or eliminate pollution through an action plan subject to annual review. Britain is also a leading participant in the series of North Sea Conferences, an international forum of countries bordering the North Sea. Good progress is being made in meeting North Sea Conference targets for reducing the input of dangerous substances into the sea. For example, inputs of cadmium and mercury to the North Sea fell by 61 per cent and 52 per cent respectively between 1985 and 1990.

International action on the prevention of pollution by ships is taken through the International Maritime Organization (IMO). Britain applies all international requirements to all ships in British waters and to British ships wherever they are. Enforcement is undertaken by the Department of Transport. Work is continuing within the IMO on further measures.

The Marine Pollution Control Unit (MPCU), part of the Department of Transport, is responsible for dealing with major spillages of oil or other hazardous substances from ships at sea. The arrangements for dealing with pollution are set out in the national contingency plan developed by the MPCU. The Unit has at its disposal a variety of counter-pollution equipment, including:

● remote sensing surveillance aircraft;

● aerial and seaborne spraying equipment;

● stocks of dispersants; and

● mechanical recovery and cargo transfer equipment.

In January 1993 the MPCU co-ordinated counter-pollution operations following the grounding of the MV *Braer* in the Shetland Islands. After this incident the Government set up an inquiry to advise on whether any further measures were appropriate to protect the coast of Britain from pollution from merchant shipping.

In order to minimise the environmental effect of offshore oil and gas operations, special conditions designed to protect the environment are included in licences for oil and gas exploration. These conditions are set in consultation with a number of bodies with environmental interests, including the relevant government departments and the Joint Nature Conservation Committee (see p. 342). Before commencing offshore operations, the operators are required to have oil spill contingency plans drawn up. In addition, all discharges that contain oil are controlled under the Prevention of Oil Pollution Act 1971, and limits are set for the permissible level of oil discharged. In response to requests from the North Sea Conference, progressively tighter limits on oil discharged with drill cuttings have been set. This has resulted in the quantity of oil discharges from this source from installations in British waters falling from 18,500 tonnes in 1988 to 6,000 tonnes in 1992.

Britain ended the dumping of industrial waste at sea in 1992. Waste has not been licensed for incineration at sea since 1990. Under the North East Atlantic Convention, and the earlier convention it replaces, the dumping at sea of most types of waste will be phased out over the next few years.

Air

Responsibility for clean air rests primarily with local authorities. Under the Clean Air Act 1993[1] and the Clean Air (Northern Ireland) Order 1981 they may declare 'smoke control areas' within which the emission of smoke from chimneys is an offence. About two-thirds of the dwellings in conurbations are covered by smoke control orders—around 6,340 are in force. Those industrial processes with the greatest potential for harmful emissions are controlled under the Environmental Protection Act 1990, in England and Wales by HMIP, and are becoming subject to IPC. Processes with a

significant but lesser potential for air pollution require approval from local authorities. Also, under the Clean Air Act, local authorities control emissions of dark smoke from trade and industrial premises. The 1990 Act also provides local authorities in England and Wales with streamlined powers to deal with statutory nuisances, including smoke, dust and smells. Similar legislation is being introduced in Northern Ireland.

Air quality in Britain has improved considerably in the last 30 years. Total emissions of smoke in the air have fallen by over 85 per cent since 1960. The domestic smoke control programme has been particularly important in achieving this result. London and other major cities no longer have the dense smoke-laden 'smogs' of the 1950s and in central London winter sunshine has increased by about 70 per cent since 1958.

Since 1990, daily air pollution data from the British monitoring network has been made available to the public by the Department of the Environment's Air Quality Bulletins. These give the concentrations of three main pollutants—ozone, nitrogen dioxide and sulphur dioxide—and grade air quality on a scale between 'very poor' and 'very good'. The information features in television and radio weather reports, and appears in many national and local newspapers. The data are also available on a special free telephone number and on videotext systems.

A comprehensive government review of urban air quality was announced in January 1992. Three independent committees of experts have been established to advise on different aspects of the problem, and will set guidelines and targets for air quality. Britain's automatic air quality monitoring network is also being extended and upgraded at a cost of £10 million.

Climate Change

The greenhouse effect is a natural phenomenon which keeps the earth at a temperature that can sustain life. But increasing man-made emissions of 'greenhouse gases', such as carbon dioxide,

---

[1] This Act consolidated earlier legislation on air pollution, including the Clean Air Acts 1956 and 1968.

methane and nitrous oxide, are leading to greater concentrations of these gases in the atmosphere. In 1988 the United Nations Environment Programme and the World Meteorological Organisation established the Intergovernmental Panel on Climate Change to consider climate change and possible responses to it. Britain chairs the working group which assesses the scientific evidence on climate change. It has concluded that man-made emissions would lead to additional warming of the earth, and that, without any change in emissions, global average temperature would increase by 0.3°C a decade, which would be faster than at any time over the past 10,000 years. Such changes could have major effects on the world.

In December 1990 the United Nations set up an Intergovernmental Negotiating Committee to draw up a framework convention on climate change. Britain played a leading role in the negotiations towards the convention, which was opened for signature at the United Nations Conference on Environment and Development meeting in Rio de Janeiro in June 1992. This commits all signatories to devising and reporting on the measures that they propose to take to combat climate change. Britain sees the outcome of the negotiations as a significant first step in the global response to climate change; the review process incorporated into the convention is one of its most important aspects. Britain was one of over 150 countries that signed the convention at the UNCED meeting.

The Government has also announced that it is prepared to return Britain's carbon dioxide emissions to 1990 levels by 2000, provided other countries take similar action. To meet this target, energy efficiency measures are the first priority; further steps are likely in the longer term. Current measures to combat the problem include:

- an increased budget for the Energy Efficiency Office (see p. 208);
- a major three-year publicity campaign on the greenhouse effect and energy use in the home;
- tighter building regulations to promote the energy efficiency of new houses;

- a government pledge to achieve a 15 per cent improvement in the energy efficiency of its buildings over a five-year period;
- a review of the potential of renewable energy sources; and
- significant increases in the tax on domestic and vehicle fuels.

Britain is also making a major research effort into global warming. The Hadley Centre for Climate Prediction and Research was opened in 1990 to build on the climate modelling programme of the Meteorological Office. The Department of the Environment's total expenditure on research related to climate change will be over £14 million in 1993–94. A major venture to investigate the role of the ice-covered Southern Ocean in regulating levels of carbon dioxide in the atmosphere was launched by the British Antarctic Survey in September 1992. Data collected from two research vessels will be used to produce a mathematical model of carbon cycling at the ice edge.

Ozone Layer

The Government is committed to the earliest possible phasing out of all ozone-depleting substances. Britain was one of the first 25 signatories to the Montreal Protocol, which deals with the protection of the ozone layer, and hosted the second meeting of the parties in June 1990, which substantially strengthened the protocol. The protocol was further strengthened in November 1992. The supply of chlorofluorocarbons (CFCs), 1,1,1 trichloroethane and carbon tetrachloride is to be phased out by the end of 1995 and halons by the end of 1993. There is provision for exemptions for any essential uses. Controls were also introduced on methyl bromide and on hydrochlorofluorocarbons (transitional substances with less ozone-depleting capacity than CFCs, which are needed in a number of areas if industry is to move away from CFCs quickly). They are to be phased out by 2030. Tighter intermediate reductions for many substances were also agreed. European Community legislation requires CFCs and carbon tetrachloride to be phased out by the end of 1994, again with exemptions for any essential uses.

Emissions of Sulphur Dioxide and Oxides of Nitrogen

Sulphur dioxide and oxides of nitrogen are the main gases that lead to acid rain. The principal sources are combustion plants that burn fossil fuels, such as coal-fired power stations, and, for oxides of nitrogen, road transport. National sulphur dioxide emissions have fallen by over 40 per cent since 1970 and the Government has initiated a substantial programme to ensure that this fall continues. For example, under the EC directive on the control of emissions from large combustion plants, the Government has published a national plan setting out phased reductions in emissions from existing plants of oxides of nitrogen to 1998 and of sulphur dioxide to 2003.

Table 24.1: Sulphur Dioxide Emissions in Britain 1971–91	
	million tonnes
1971	6.057
1976	5.184
1981	4.436
1986	3.895
1991	3.565

Source: Department of the Environment.

The damaging effect of acid depositions from combustion processes on freshwaters and soils has been demonstrated by scientific research. The Government is spending about £10 million a year on an extensive research programme into the causes and effects of acid rain, and the likely results of possible abatement technologies. Lower emissions of sulphur dioxide over the past 20 years (see Table 24.1) have led to the first signs of a decrease in acidification in some lochs in south-west Scotland.

Vehicle Emissions

There are about 24 million vehicles on Britain's roads, contributing substantially to

Britain's total emissions of carbon dioxide, carbon monoxide, hydrocarbons and oxides of nitrogen. Since 1970 a series of increasingly stringent regulations on cars and light vans has been implemented by the Government to bring carbon monoxide emissions from each new car down by over 90 per cent and hydrocarbon and nitrogen oxide emissions by over 80 per cent. Strict new standards for these vehicles were brought into force in January 1993 throughout the EC. These will reduce emissions from new cars by approximately 60 per cent over the previous standards and require almost all new petrol-engined cars to be fitted with catalytic converters. Further limits are being considered for application in 1996. The Community is committed to looking into possible controls on carbon dioxide emissions from cars.

Britain has also pressed the Community to introduce very strict emission standards for heavy goods vehicles and buses starting in 1993, with a further, much stricter phase in 1996. This will introduce stricter limits for gaseous emissions and, for the first time, limits on particulate emissions. The Government has introduced checks on exhaust emissions into the annual test of vehicle roadworthiness, measuring carbon monoxide and hydrocarbons. These limits are also subject to enforcement at roadside spot-checks. The sulphur content of industrial gas oils and diesel fuel is also controlled by EC legislation and will be subject to a further reduction in the next few years.

The amount of lead in the air in Britain has fallen by 70 per cent since the permitted lead content in petrol was reduced in 1986 from 0.4 to 0.15 grammes a litre and unleaded petrol was introduced. Britain took a leading role in negotiating an EC directive which required unleaded petrol to be made available throughout the Community by October 1989. Practically all petrol stations in Britain now sell unleaded petrol, and since 1990 new cars must have been manufactured to be capable of running on it. The Government has encouraged the use of cleaner fuel by introducing a substantial tax differential in favour of unleaded petrol. Demand for it has risen rapidly, and unleaded petrol now accounts for over half of all petrol sold in Britain.

Internationally developed standards have also been introduced to control the emission from civil aircraft of smoke, vented fuel and unburned hydrocarbons. Current indications are that aircraft contribute only a small amount to overall pollution, although the Government is funding further research and taking a leading role in European studies on this issue.

Noise

Local authorities have a duty to inspect their areas for noise nuisance, except from aircraft noise, and to investigate complaints about it. They must serve a noise abatement notice where the noise is judged to be a statutory nuisance. They can also designate 'noise abatement zones', within which registered levels of noise from certain premises may not be increased without their permission. There are also specific provisions in law to:

- control noise from construction and demolition sites;
- control the use of loudspeakers in the streets; and
- enable individuals to take independent action through the courts against noise amounting to a nuisance.

Tougher measures against noise were proposed in the environment White Paper. Many of its commitments were endorsed by an independent working party. It reported in October 1990 with 33 recommendations, many of which have now been implemented. The Government also has an environmental noise research programme, spending on which is expected to be about £650,000 in 1993–94.

Transport is a major source of noise, and control measures are aimed at reducing it at source, through requirements limiting the noise that aircraft and motor vehicles may make, and at protecting people from its effects. Operational measures are also used to minimise the effects of aircraft noise. Regulations set out the permissible noise levels for various classes of new vehicle. Government research also looks at ways of

reducing noise, and has demonstrated the feasibility of tougher noise limits for heavy goods vehicles.

Compensation may be payable for loss in property values caused by physical factors, including noise from new or improved public works such as roads, railways and airports. Regulations also enable highway authorities to carry out or make grants for insulation of homes that would be subject to specified levels of increased noise caused by new or improved roads. Noise insulation may be provided where construction work for new roads may seriously affect nearby homes.

Britain has played a leading role in negotiations aimed at the gradual phasing out of older, noisier subsonic jet aircraft. Flying non-noise certificated aircraft has been banned in Britain, and since 1990 British operators have no longer been allowed to add to their fleets further 'Chapter 2' aircraft (noisier planes, as classified by international agreement). A complete ban on the operation of Chapter 2 aircraft will begin to be implemented in April 1995, and it is intended to phase out all these types by April 2002. Various operational restrictions have been introduced to reduce noise disturbance further at Heathrow, Gatwick and Stansted, where the Secretary of State for Transport has assumed responsibility for noise abatement. These measures include:

- restrictions on the type and number of aircraft operating at night;
- the routeing of departing aircraft on noise-preferential routes; and
- quieter take-off and landing procedures.

The population disturbed by aircraft noise[2] at Heathrow fell from 1.47 million in 1978 to 562,000 in 1989, even though the number of air transport movements increased. This was largely because of the phasing out of older, noisier aircraft. Under government proposals announced in March 1993, airfields will be given powers to enforce noise amelioration schemes. The Secretary of State would be given powers to compel the airfield authorities to prepare such a scheme. Local

---

2 That is, living within the 35 Noise and Number Index noise contour, which is regarded as the onset of disturbance.

authorities would have powers to act against the owner of an airfield who did not take reasonable steps to ensure that an agreed scheme was operated effectively.

Radioactivity

Man-made radiation represents only a small fraction of that to which the population is exposed; most is naturally occurring. A large proportion of the man-made radioactivity to which the public is exposed comes from medical treatments, such as X-rays. Nevertheless, the man-made fraction is subject to stringent control. Users of radioactive materials must be registered by HMIP in England and Wales, and equivalents in Scotland and Northern Ireland, and authorisation is also required for the accumulation and disposal of radioactive waste. The Health and Safety Executive (HSE—see p. 139), through its Nuclear Installations Inspectorate, is the authority responsible for the granting of nuclear site licences for major nuclear installations. No installation may be constructed or operated without a licence granted by the Executive.

The National Radiological Protection Board (NRPB) provides an authoritative point of reference on radiological protection. Following the accident at the Chernobyl nuclear power station in the then Soviet Union in 1986, the Government has set up a national radiation monitoring network and overseas nuclear accident response system (RIMNET). An interim version has been operating since 1988. This is being replaced during 1993 by a larger and more fully automated system with 92 monitoring stations across Britain.

In 1987 the Government announced measures to deal with the problem of radon, a naturally occurring radioactive gas which can accumulate in houses. These included a free survey by the NRPB for householders living in radon-affected areas. In 1990 the Government halved the level at which it is recommended that householders take action to reduce radon in their homes. The NRPB has designated Cornwall, Devon, Northamptonshire and parts of Derbyshire and Somerset as 'radon-affected areas' (areas

where more than 1 per cent of the houses exceed the action level). An updated edition of the Government's advice booklet for householders was published in October 1992.

Radioactive Waste Disposal

Radioactive wastes vary widely in nature and level of activity, and the methods of disposal reflect this. Some wastes can be disposed of safely in the same way as other industrial and household wastes. UK Nirex Ltd is responsible for developing a deep disposal facility for solid low-level and intermediate-level radioactive waste. It is currently concentrating its detailed geological investigations on an area near the British Nuclear Fuels site at Sellafield, in Cumbria. As part of these studies, Nirex intends to construct an experimental rock laboratory, known as a 'rock characterisation facility'.

> The 1992 results of monitoring foodstuffs show that radioactivity in foodstuffs remains well below levels that would pose a risk to the public. Over 6,000 samples of milk, fruit, vegetables and meat were analysed.

The Department of the Environment is sponsoring research, in collaboration with other countries, into disposal of high-level or heat-generating waste. This waste will first be stored in vitrified form for at least 50 years to allow the heat and radioactivity to decay. In September 1992 Britain agreed not to dispose of radioactive waste at sea in the north-east Atlantic for at least 15 years, and only thereafter under tight conditions. The Department of the Environment's 1992–93 budget for research into environmental radioactivity and radioactive waste was £7 million.

Genetically Modified Organisms

Genetically modified organisms (GMOs) have many potential beneficial uses. However, there are risks that their heritable genetic material might persist in the environment in harmful ways. The Environmental Protection Act 1990 and regulations which came into force in February 1993 contain powers to ensure that any risks to the environment, including human populations, from the release of GMOs are prevented or minimised. The new legislation sets up a consent system for experimental releases of GMOs and for the EC-wide approval of GMO products. The Department of the Environment acts as the administrative contact for those applying for consent. The Government hopes that, with further experience of releases, it will be able to agree simplified procedures for the clearance of low-risk GMOs so that their benefits may be enjoyed as soon as possible with the least burden on industry consistent with safety.

Environmental Research

Research into environmental protection is essential to the Government's environmental policies. It has been estimated that its total spending on environmental research and development in 1993–94 will be £300-£400 million, including work in areas such as renewable energy. The Department of the Environment expects to devote about £57 million in 1993–94 to research into subjects including:

● climate change;

● atmospheric pollution and its monitoring;

● toxic chemicals and GMOs;

● waste disposal; and

● water quality and health.

Other departments have substantial programmes, notably the Ministry of Agriculture, Fisheries and Food, The Scottish Office Agriculture and Fisheries Department and other official bodies such as the NRA and the Meteorological Office.

The European Network of Environmental Research Organisations was set up in March 1993, with British participation, to facilitate the exchange of environmental information between some 3,000 researchers.

Research Councils

Basic and strategic research is carried out by the government-funded research councils (see pp. 272–6). All have a role in environmental protection research, but particularly important is the Natural Environment Research Council (NERC), which has a science budget allocation of £140 million in 1993–94, plus expected receipts of about £42 million from commissioned research and other income. The NERC undertakes and supports research in the environmental sciences and funds postgraduate training. Its programmes encompass the marine, earth, terrestrial, freshwater, polar and atmospheric sciences. The NERC lays stress on international collaborative work on global environmental issues. For example, it is helping to develop global atmospheric climate models and strengthening atmospheric research in the Arctic. A major research programme, the Terrestrial Initiative in Global Environmental Research aims to assess the likely impact of climate change on Britain and elsewhere. The NERC also co-ordinates the development and operation of the Environmental Change Network.

Further Reading

Control of Pollution. Aspects of Britain series, HMSO, 1993.

Environment Protection and Water Statistics. Annual report. HMSO.

The UK Environment. HMSO, 1992.

CHARITIES

Sir Ranulph Fiennes (right) and Dr Mike Stroud at Gould Bay, at the start of their journey on foot to the South Pole. So far their record-breaking walk has raised over £800,000 for the Multiple Sclerosis Society.

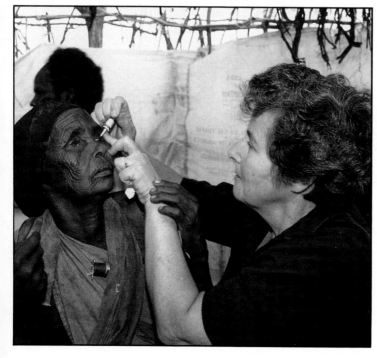

The charity Help the Aged works to improve the quality of life for elderly people both in Britain and internationally, offering practical assistance through, for example, clinics such as this one in Somalia.

CHILDREN

The 'hands-on' approach at Launch Pad, at London's Science Museum, makes learning fun. The interactive exhibits generate enthusiasm for science and technology, and provide experiences that underpin the formal teaching of science in schools.

Action for Sick Children has campaigned for 30 years to achieve accommodation in hospital for parents and carers of child patients. Most hospitals now have beds on children's wards, dormitories or flats so that children can receive the continual support of those closest to them.

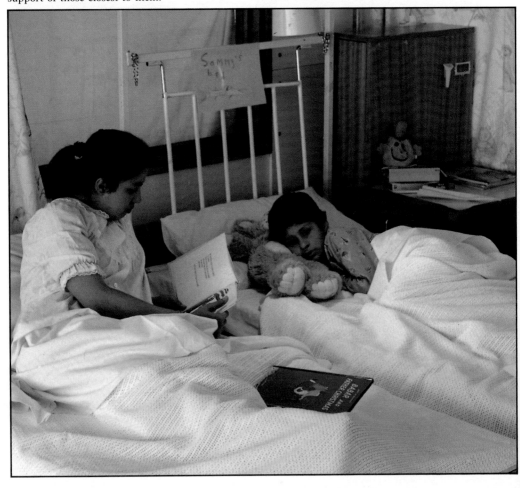

Young children all over Britain enjoy playing and socialising in groups formed under the auspices of the Pre-School Playgroups Association. It encourages the involvement of parents and carers and offers training for playgroup workers.

Football has become an increasingly popular sport for girls: several counties now have girls' football leagues, and girls can play in mixed teams at primary school.

RELIGION

The General Synod of the Church of England debating the ordination of women in November 1992. The Synod voted in favour of admitting women to the priesthood, and it is expected that the first ordinations could take place in 1994.

The Lord and Lady Provost of Glasgow examine a Sikh wedding sari at the opening of the St Mungo Museum of Religion in April 1993. The museum has displays on religions around the world and historical artefacts such as Egyptian mummy masks and bronze Buddha statuettes.

Social and
Cultural Affairs

25 Health and Social Services

Total spending on health and social services in 1993–94 is expected to be
£36,292 million: £36,000 million on health and £292 million on social services.
Recent developments include an increase in practice nurses at doctors'
surgeries, projects designed to improve health care in inner city areas and
among ethnic minorities, and new procedures for assessing the care needs for
individuals within the community.

The National Health Service (NHS) provides
a full range of medical services which are
available to all residents, regardless of their
income. Local authority personal social
services and voluntary organisations provide
help and advice to the most vulnerable
members of the community. These include
elderly, physically disabled and mentally ill
people, those with learning disabilities
(mental handicap) and children in need of
care.

Central government is directly responsible
for the NHS, administered by a range of
local health authorities and boards throughout
Britain acting as its agents, and for the social
security system. Personal social services are
administered by local authorities but central
government is responsible for establishing
national policies, issuing guidance and
overseeing standards. Joint finance and
planning between health and local authorities
aim to prevent overlapping of services and to
encourage the development of community
services.

Spending on the health service has
increased substantially in real terms since
1980, and is planned to grow further over the
next two years. More patients are being
treated than ever before. Spending on the
personal social services is determined by local
authorities. Central government has
restricted the total expenditure of individual
local authorities, but spending has risen
substantially in real terms since the late
1970s, reflecting the priority given to this
sector.

The NHS health programme consists of:

- Hospital and Community Health
Services (HCHS), providing all hospital
care and a range of community health
services;

- Family Health Services (FHS), providing
general medical, dental and
pharmaceutical services and some
ophthalmic services, and covering the
cost of medicines prescribed by general
practitioners (GPs);

- Central Health and Miscellaneous
Services (CHMS), providing services
most effectively administered centrally,
such as welfare food and support to the
voluntary sector; and

- the administrative costs of the health
departments.

Major Policy Developments

Reforms in Management

The NHS and Community Care Act 1990 introduced wide-ranging reform in management and patient care in the health and social care services. The NHS reforms, which came into effect in 1991, aim to give patients, wherever they live in Britain, better health care and greater choice of service, as follows:

1. Health authorities have been given a new role as purchasers of health care on behalf of their local residents, responsible for assessing local health care needs and ensuring the availability of a full range of services to meet identified health needs. They ensure that those needs are met within existing resources.

2. Each health authority is funded to buy health care for its local residents through arranging contracts with hospitals and other health service units in either the public or private sector. For the first time hospitals are directly funded for the number of patients they treat, making it easier for GPs to refer patients outside their area if treatment elsewhere is faster and better. However, powers exist for allocating resources where the urgent need for treatment does not allow NHS contracts to be arranged in advance.

3. The contracts agreed between health authorities and hospitals set out the quality, quantity and cost of the services to be delivered during the year. The contracts secured by each health authority are based on wide consultation with all local GPs.

4. Hospitals may apply to become self-governing NHS trusts (see p. 371), independent of local health authority control but remaining within the NHS. They are accountable to the relevant health department, treating NHS patients, and are funded largely through general taxation, under contracts with health authorities.

5. GPs from larger medical practices may apply to join the general practitioner fundholding scheme (see p. 370), under which they receive an annual budget directly from the health authority, enabling them to buy certain hospital services for their patients.

Health Service Expenditure in England

NHS Gross Expenditure 1992–93 (estimate)

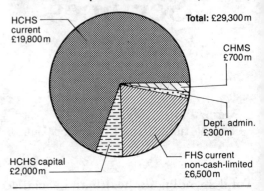

HCHS current £19,800m

Total: £29,300m

CHMS £700m

Dept. admin. £300m

FHS current non-cash-limited £6,500m

HCHS capital £2,000m

Hospital and Community Health Services Gross Current Expenditure by Sector 1990–91 (estimate)

Total: £14,746m

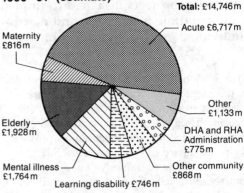

Maternity £816m

Acute £6,717m

Other £1,133m

DHA and RHA Administration £775m

Other community £868m

Elderly £1,928m

Mental illness £1,764m

Learning disability £746m

1. Other community services include health visiting, immunisation, screening, health promotion and community dental services.

2. Other services include ambulances, the blood transfusion service, mass radiography and the Service Increment for Teaching and Research (SIFTR).

Non-cash-limited Family Health Services Gross Expenditure 1991–92

Total: £5,983m

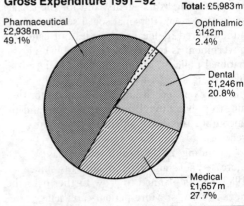

Pharmaceutical £2,938m 49.1%

Ophthalmic £142m 2.4%

Dental £1,246m 20.8%

Medical £1,657m 27.7%

Source: Department of Health. The Government's Expenditure Plans 1993-94 to 1995-96.

The reforms in community care provision, which came into force between April 1991 and April 1993, establish a new financial and managerial framework which aims to secure the delivery of good quality services in line with national objectives. They are intended to enable vulnerable groups in the community to live as independently as possible in their own homes for as long as they are able and wish to do so, and to give them a greater say in how they live and how the services they need should be provided. (For fuller details see p. 384.)

Broadly similar changes have been introduced under separate legislation in Northern Ireland, where health and personal social services are provided on an integrated basis by health and social services boards.

The Patient's Charter

Patient's Charters, which came fully into force in April 1992, are part of the health departments' response to the Citizen's Charter (see p. 64). Patient's Charters support the objectives of the NHS reforms: to improve standards of health care and sensitivity to patients in the NHS. They set out for the first time the rights of patients and the standards of care they can expect to receive from the NHS. The Government believes that patients should know what they can expect from the NHS and that the staff who provide services should understand what is expected of them. The responsibility for implementing the Patient's Charters rests with all parts of the NHS, English regions, purchasers and providers, and is carried out mainly through contract arrangements.

As well as restating the existing rights that patients have under the NHS, the Patient's Charter in England introduced three new rights. These are that patients must:

- be given detailed information on local health services, including quality standards and maximum waiting times;

- be guaranteed admission for treatment no later than two years from the date of being placed on a waiting list; and

- have any complaint about NHS services investigated, and receive a full reply as soon as possible.

In England the Patient's Charter also sets national charter standards. These are not legal rights but specific standards of service which the NHS aims to provide. These include respect for the individual patient; waiting times for ambulances, clinical assessment in accident and emergency departments and appointments in out-patient clinics; and cancellation of operations. Also included are local charter standards of service which health authorities aim to provide (see below).

Separate Patient's Charters have been developed for Scotland, Wales and Northern Ireland.

As a result of the Charter initiative, many local projects have been put into operation to help improve NHS services. There are now initiatives on every aspect of the Patient's Charter—from setting up translation services in 140 languages to encourage access to services, to asking patients for their views on improving services.

From April 1993 every family health services authority must have its own charter setting out the new national standards which it must meet and giving details of targets and local standards. In addition, family health services authorities are working with and supporting GPs and primary health care teams to produce local GP practice charters.

In response to the Charter Right to Information, English regions have set up health information services. These can provide details of the times people have to wait for treatment for all specialties in local hospitals, as well as information from hospitals further afield (see p. 371).

Developing Health Strategies

The Government emphasises the importance of promoting health as well as treating illness. Preventive health services such as health education, and the responsibility that individuals have for their own health, play a major part in this. While great progress has been made in eliminating infectious diseases such as poliomyelitis and tuberculosis, there is still scope for greater success in controlling the major causes of early death and disability.

The White Paper *The Health of the*

Nation, published in 1992, sets out a strategy for improving health. This is the first time a strategy has been developed for health in England and its long-term aim is to enable people to live longer, healthier lives. It sets targets for improvements in the following areas:

- coronary heart disease and stroke (the major cause of premature death in England);
- cancers (the second biggest cause of premature death);
- accidents (the commonest cause of death in those under 30);
- mental illness (a leading cause of ill-health and, through suicides, of death); and
- HIV/AIDS and sexual health (HIV/AIDS is perhaps the greatest new public health threat this century—see p. 379—and there is much scope for reducing sexually transmitted diseases and unwanted pregnancies).

Targets are set for reducing death rates (for example, from coronary heart disease and stroke in those under 65 by at least 40 per cent by the year 2000), for reducing ill-health (such as the incidence of invasive cervical cancer by at least 20 per cent by 2000) and for reducing risk behaviour (for example, the percentage of smokers to no more than 20 per cent of the population by 2000). While the NHS will have a central role in working towards the targets, the strategy also emphasises that there is a role for everyone in improving the nation's health.

The White Paper also sets out the Government's objective of ensuring the provision of effective family planning services for those people who want them. The conception rate for those under 16 years is a matter of particular concern.

Strategies have also been developed for Scotland, Wales and Northern Ireland. In Wales, where the first of Britain's four national health strategies was published in 1990, areas for improvement include, among others: cancers; cardiovascular disease; maternal and early child health; physical disability; mental handicap and mental health; and injuries. Scotland's national strategy,

published in 1992, places special emphasis on smoking, alcohol misuse, coronary heart disease, and cancer.

National action is under way in these areas. It includes interdepartmental taskforces, work with professional and voluntary bodies and the provision of guidance setting out a range of possible actions for each tier of the NHS. At local level, the NHS is being encouraged to form 'healthy alliances' for joint working with agencies ranging from the voluntary sector through to industry and the media. Progress towards the targets will be monitored regularly and formally reviewed, and periodic progress reports will be published.

The Government's health strategy has been welcomed by the World Health Organisation, which described it as a model that other countries might follow.

Improving London's Health Services

Proposals to improve the standard of London's health services were announced in February 1993. These include:

- developing better, local and accessible primary and community health services;
- providing a better-balanced hospital service, on fewer sites;
- streamlining specialist services; and
- consolidating medical education and research, chiefly through mergers of free-standing undergraduate medical colleges with multifaculty colleges of London University.

The National Health Service

The NHS is based upon the principle that there should be a full range of publicly provided services designed to help the individual stay healthy. The services are intended to provide effective and appropriate treatment and care where necessary while making the best use of available resources. All taxpayers, employers and employees contribute to its cost so that those members of the community who do not require health care help to pay for those who do. Some forms of treatment, such as hospital care, are provided free; others (see p. 368) may be charged for.

Growth in real spending on the health service is being used to meet the needs of increasing numbers of elderly people and to take full advantage of advances in medical technology. It is also used to provide more appropriate types of care, often in the community rather than in hospital, for priority groups such as elderly and mentally ill people and those with learning disabilities (mental handicap). Increased spending has, in addition, been allocated to combat the growing problems arising from alcohol and drug misuse; and to remedy disparities in provision between the regions of Britain.

The Government stresses the need for collaboration between the public and private health sectors and for improving efficiency in order to secure the best value for money and the maximum patient care. Measures to achieve more effective management of resources in the NHS have included:

- appointing at regional, district and unit levels general managers drawn from inside and outside the health service;

- improving the accountability of health authorities for the planning and management of their resources;

- increasing the proportion of total staff who provide direct patient care, such as doctors and nurses; and

- introducing a range of programmes to provide services at lower cost.

Considerable savings have been made through competitive tendering for hospital cleaning, catering and laundry services. At the end of 1992 the Government announced that total annual savings from competitive tendering up to 1990–91 were estimated at £626 million.

Economies are also made in prescribing by restricting the use of expensive branded products in favour of cheaper but equally effective equivalent medicines.

ADMINISTRATION

The Secretary of State for Health in England and the Secretaries of State for Scotland, Wales and Northern Ireland are responsible for all aspects of the health services in their respective countries. The Department of Health is responsible for national strategic planning in England. The Scottish Office Home and Health Department, the Welsh Office and the Department of Health and Social Services in Northern Ireland have similar responsibilities.

District health authorities in England and Wales and health boards in Scotland are responsible for securing hospital and community health services in their areas. England, because of its greater size and population, also has regional authorities responsible for regional planning, resource allocation, major capital building work and certain specialised hospital services best administered on a regional basis. The authorities and boards co-operate closely with local authorities responsible for social work, environmental health, education and other services. Family health services authorities (health boards in Scotland) arrange for the provision of services by doctors, dentists, pharmacists and opticians, as well as administering their contracts. Community health councils (local health councils in Scotland) represent local opinion on the health services provided.

In Northern Ireland health and social services boards are responsible for all health and personal social services in their areas. The representation of public opinion on these services is provided for by area health and social services councils.

Finance

Over 80 per cent of the cost of the health service in Great Britain is paid for through general taxation. The rest is met from:

- the NHS element of National Insurance contributions, paid by employed people, their employers, and self-employed people (13.9 per cent);

- charges towards the cost of certain items such as drugs prescribed by family doctors, and general dental treatment (3.9 per cent); and

- other receipts, including land sales and the proceeds of income generation schemes (1.4 per cent).

Health authorities may raise funds from voluntary sources. Certain hospitals increase their revenue by taking private patients who pay the full cost of their accommodation and treatment.

Almost 80 per cent of medical prescription items are supplied free. Prescription charges do not apply to the following:

- children under 16 years (or students under 19 and still in full-time education);
- expectant mothers and women who have had a baby in the past year;
- women aged 60 and over and men aged 65 and over;
- patients suffering from certain medical conditions;
- war and armed forces disablement pensioners (for prescriptions which relate to the disability for which they receive a war pension);
- people who are receiving income support or family credit (see p. 397); and people or families with low incomes.

There are proportional charges for all types of general dental treatment, including dental examination. However, women who were pregnant when the dentist accepted them for treatment or who have had a baby in the past year, anyone under the age of 18 (or 19 if in full-time education), people receiving income support or family credit, and families on low incomes, do not have to pay. Sight tests are free to children, those on low incomes and certain other priority groups. Some disadvantaged groups receive help with the purchase, repair and replacement of spectacles.

Hospital medical staff are salaried and may be employed full time or part time. Family practitioners (doctors, dentists, opticians and pharmacists) are self-employed and have contracts with the NHS. GPs are paid by a system of fees and allowances designed to reflect responsibilities, workload and practice expenses. Dentists providing treatment in their own surgeries are paid by a combination of capitation fees for treating children,

continuing care payments for adults registered with the practice, and a prescribed scale of fees for individual treatments. Pharmacists dispensing from their own premises are refunded the cost of the items supplied, together with professional fees. Ophthalmic medical practitioners and ophthalmic opticians taking part in the general ophthalmic service receive approved fees for each sight test carried out.

Staffing

The NHS is one of the largest employers in the world, with a workforce of nearly 1 million people. During the past ten years there has been a rise in the numbers of 'direct care staff' and a fall in the numbers of support staff. The sharp fall in the numbers of directly employed ancillary staff and of maintenance and works staff reflects the continuing effect of competitive tendering (see p. 367). Staff costs account for two-thirds of total NHS expenditure and 70 per cent of current expenditure on hospitals and community health services. For example, between 1981 and 1991:

- the number of medical and dental staff in England rose by 18 per cent to 48,600, while in Scotland the increase was 38 per cent to 7,890;
- the number of nursing and midwifery staff, who make up 50 per cent of the workforce, increased in England by 1 per cent (including agency staff) to 396,200; in Scotland the rise was 6 per cent to 75,068; and
- the number of scientific, professional and technical staff in England rose by 33 per cent; in Scotland this increase was 32 per cent.

The Government's aim throughout the service is progressively to introduce greater pay flexibility in order to allow managers to relate pay to local markets and reward individual performance. A number of measures are being taken to provide a more effective workforce through better management development, education and training (see p. 382).

Health Service Commissioners

There are three posts of Health Service
Commissioner (one each for England,
Scotland and Wales) for dealing with
complaints from members of the public about
the health service. The three posts are held
by the same person, who is also the
Parliamentary Commissioner for
Administration (Ombudsman), reporting
annually to Parliament (see p. 58).

The Health Service Commissioner can
investigate complaints that a person has
suffered injustice or hardship as a result of:

- a failure in a service provided by an
  NHS authority;
- a failure to provide a service which an
  NHS authority has a duty to provide; or
- a maladministration connected with
  action taken by or on behalf of an NHS
  authority.

The Health Service Commissioner's
jurisdiction does not extend to complaints
about clinical judgment, GPs, personnel
matters and the use of a health authority's
discretionary powers; separate procedures
exist for these. In Northern Ireland the
Commissioner for Complaints has a similar
role. An independent review of all aspects of
NHS complaints procedures is in progress.

FAMILY HEALTH SERVICES

The family health services are those given to
patients by doctors, dentists, opticians and
pharmacists of their own choice. They remain
the first point of contact most people have
with the NHS. Every year there are about
200 million consultations with family doctors
and about 30 million visits to the dentist.
Many of those who visit their family doctor
or dentist need no clinical treatment but
instead healthy lifestyle counselling and
preventive health care advice. The
Government's longstanding policy has been
to build up and extend these services in order
to improve health and relieve pressure on the
far more costly secondary care sector.

GPs provide the first diagnosis in the case
of illness and either prescribe a suitable
course of treatment or refer a patient to the

more specialised services and hospital
consultants. About four-fifths of GPs in
Britain work in partnerships or group
practices, often as members of primary
health-care teams. The teams also include
health visitors and district nurses, and
sometimes midwives, social workers and other
professional staff employed by the health
authorities. About a quarter of GPs in Great
Britain and about half in Northern Ireland
work in health centres, where medical and
nursing services are provided. Health centres
may also have facilities for health education,
family planning, speech therapy, chiropody,
assessment of hearing, physiotherapy and
remedial exercises. Dental, pharmaceutical
and ophthalmic services, hospital out-patient
and supporting social work services, may also
be provided.

There have been substantial increases in
primary health care staff in recent years. For
example, in England between 1978 and 1991,
the number of GPs increased by 22 per cent
(to 25,700), and average patient list size fell
by 16 per cent (to over 1,900), while the
number of family dentists increased by 27 per
cent (to 15,000). The number of GP practice
nurses increased almost ninefold—to 8,800 in
1991.

Special funds have been earmarked by the
Government for improving the quality of
primary health care in inner city areas.
Efforts have also been made to improve
health services for black and ethnic minority
groups. These include new health projects in
Britain's Chinese communities, a project in
Cardiff for the Somali refugee community,
and increased central funding for health
information material to be produced in many
minority languages.

The Government has welcomed a recent
report which recommends ways in which the
role of community pharmacists could be
developed to increase their contribution to
health care.

Eye Services

Entitlement to free NHS sight tests is
restricted to people on low incomes, children,
and those with particular medical needs.
Spectacles are supplied by registered

ophthalmic and dispensing opticians but unregistered retailers may also sell spectacles to most adults. Children, people on low incomes and those requiring certain complex lenses receive a voucher towards the cost of their spectacles.

Recent Developments

GP Fundholders

GP practices with 7,000 patients or more (6,000 in Scotland) may apply for fundholding status. This is a voluntary scheme which gives larger medical practices the opportunity to manage sums of NHS money for the benefit of their patients. It aims to improve services for patients and enable GPs to explore more innovative methods of providing health care. GP fundholders are responsible for part of their own NHS budgets, enabling them to buy certain non-urgent hospital services. Prescription charges and part of the cost of running the practice are also covered. Fundholders may negotiate for services directly with hospitals from both public and private sectors in any district or regional health authority in Britain. The scheme was expanded in April 1993 to enable GP fundholders to buy NHS community nursing services for their patients, including district nursing and health visiting services and community psychiatric and community mental handicap nursing.

By April 1993 over 6,700 GPs in more than 1,340 practices in Great Britain had become fundholders. Around a quarter of the population are now registered with a fundholding GP.

Contracts

The performance-related contract for GPs, which came into effect in 1990, was the first major reform of the family doctor service for over 20 years. It is designed to raise standards of care, extend the range of services available to patients and improve patient choice. The changes are intended to make it easier for patients to see their GP at times convenient to them; easier for patients to

change doctors; and to encourage doctors to practise more preventive medicine.

The new contract for dentists, introduced in 1990, aims at improving care and providing more information to patients about general dental services. As a result NHS dental care now includes preventive care as well as restorative treatment. All adult patients are now offered 'continuing care', and dentists are encouraged to practise more preventive dentistry for children. There are also incentives for dentists to undertake further training.

Clinical Audit

Clinical audit has been introduced in all health authorities. This is the systematic, critical analysis by doctors at all levels in the health service of the quality of the clinical care they give their patients, including the procedures used for diagnosis and treatment, the use of resources and the resulting outcome. In 1993–94 the Government is allocating almost £52 million to continue to develop clinical audit in the hospital and community health services.

Health Visitors, District Nurses and Midwives

Health visitors are responsible for the preventive care and health promotion of families, particularly those with young children. They have a public health role identifying local health needs and working closely with GPs, district nurses and other professions. District nurses give skilled nursing care to people at home or elsewhere outside hospital; they also play an important role in health promotion and education.

Midwives give care, support and teaching to women throughout pregnancy and birth and for up to 28 days after the baby is born. They work in hospital maternity units, health centres and GP surgeries and in the woman's home. Almost all babies are born in hospital but some antenatal care and most postnatal care is given in the community. The care given may be from a midwife, an obstetrician or a GP, depending on the woman's need and preferences.

HOSPITAL AND SPECIALIST SERVICES

A full range of hospital services is provided by district general hospitals. These include treatment and diagnostic facilities for in-patients, day-patients and out-patients; maternity departments; infectious diseases units; psychiatric and geriatric facilities; rehabilitation facilities; and other forms of specialised treatment. There are also specialist hospitals or units for children, people suffering from mental illness, those with learning disabilities, and elderly people, and for the treatment of specific diseases. Examples of these include the world-famous Hospital for Sick Children, Great Ormond Street, and the Royal Brompton National Heart and Lung Hospital, both in London. Hospitals designated as teaching hospitals combine treatment facilities with training medical and other students, and research work.

Many of the hospitals in the NHS were built in the 19th century; some, such as St Bartholomew's and St Thomas' in London, trace their origins to much earlier charitable foundations.

Much has been done to improve and extend existing hospital buildings and many new hospitals have been or are being opened. Since 1979 in Great Britain over 700 health building schemes, each costing £1 million or more, have been completed. A further 371 schemes are at various stages of development. This is the largest sustained building programme in the history of the NHS.

Recent policy in England and Wales has been to provide a balanced hospital service centred around a district general hospital, complemented as necessary by smaller, locally based hospitals and facilities.

A new development in hospital planning in England and Wales is the nucleus hospital. This is designed to accommodate a full range of district general hospital facilities and is capable of being built in self-contained phases or as an extension to an existing hospital. By mid-1993, 84 nucleus hospitals had been completed. A further 39 are at various stages of construction or planning. Those already open have proved economical to build and are providing high-quality and cost-effective services to patients.

The world's first low-energy nucleus hospital, which is expected to use less than half the energy of a conventional nucleus hospital, opened on the Isle of Wight in 1991. A second, in Northumberland, is expected to open later in 1993.

The hospital service is now treating more patients a year than ever before. Between 1978 and 1991–92 lengths of stay for in-patients declined and the number of people treated as day patients more than trebled, to 1.5 million.

Newer forms of treatment and diagnosis are being made more widely available. These include kidney dialysis, hip replacements, laser treatment and body scanning.

In 1986 the Government launched a drive to reduce hospital waiting lists and times. In England and Wales in 1993–94 nearly £42 million is being invested in a variety of projects, including mobile operating theatres, to improve waiting times for patients. In England in 1992–93 the number of patients waiting over a year for hospital treatment fell by 45 per cent to a record low of 56,000 (and by almost 20 per cent to 7,000 in Wales), while the number of patients waiting more than two years fell from 51,000 to fewer than 1,700. Regions no longer have any patients waiting more than two years for in-patient or day-case treatment. Since April 1993 there has been a new guarantee that no one should wait more than 18 months for a hip or knee replacement or a cataract operation.

Community services such as the psychiatric nursing service, day hospitals, and local authority day centres have expanded so that more patients remain in the community and others are sent home from hospital sooner.

NHS Trusts

Under the NHS and Community Care Act 1990 hospitals and other health service units (for example, ambulance services and community health services) may apply to become independent of local health authority control and establish themselves as self-governing NHS Trusts. The Trusts remain within the NHS, accountable through the NHS Management Executive to the Secretary of State and finally to Parliament. NHS Trusts are required to publish their business plans and annual reports and accounts, and to hold at least one public meeting a year.

Each NHS Trust is run by a board of directors. Trusts are free to employ their own staff and set their own rates of pay, although staff transferring to Trust employment retain their existing terms and conditions of service. Trusts are also free to carry out research and provide facilities for medical education and other forms of training. They derive their income mainly from NHS contracts to provide services to health authorities and GP fundholders. They may treat private patients and generate income provided this does not interfere with NHS obligations. By April 1993, 323 NHS Trusts were operational in Great Britain, delivering over two-thirds of NHS hospital and community health services.

Private Medical Treatment

The Government's policy is to welcome cost-effective co-operation between the NHS and the independent sector in meeting the nation's health needs. It believes that this will benefit the NHS by adding to the resources devoted to health care and offering flexibility to health authorities in the delivery of services. Some health authorities share expensive facilities and equipment with private hospitals, and NHS patients are sometimes treated (at public expense) in the private sector to reduce waiting lists. The scale of private practice in relation to the NHS is, however, very small.

It is estimated that about three-quarters of those receiving acute treatment in private hospitals or NHS hospital pay-beds are covered by health insurance schemes, which make provision for private health care in return for annual subscriptions. Over 3 million people subscribe to such schemes, half of them within group schemes, some arranged by firms on behalf of employees. Subscriptions often cover more than one person (for example, members of a family)

and the total number of people covered by private medical insurance in Britain is estimated at over 7 million. The Government has introduced tax relief on private health insurance premiums paid by people aged 60 and over to encourage the increased use of private health facilities.

Many overseas patients come to Britain for treatment in private hospitals and clinics, and Harley Street in London is an internationally recognised centre for medical consultancy.

There is a growing interest in alternative therapies such as homoeopathy and acupuncture, which are mainly practised outside the NHS. Under legislation passed in 1993 osteopathy became the first complementary therapy to achieve statutory regulation.

Organ Transplants

Over the past 25 years there have been significant developments in transplant surgery in Britain. The United Kingdom Transplant Support Service Authority provides a centralised organ matching and distribution service. During 1992, 1,642 kidney transplants were performed. A similar service exists for corneas and, in 1992, 2,423 were transplanted.

Heart transplant operations have been conducted at Papworth Hospital in Cambridgeshire and Harefield Hospital in London since 1979. There are six other designated heart transplant centres in England, while Scotland's first unit opened in Glasgow in 1991.

A programme of combined heart and lung transplants is in progress and in 1992, 325 heart, 89 lung, and 53 heart-lung transplants were performed. The world's first combined heart, lungs and liver transplant operation was carried out at Papworth in 1987.

There are six designated liver transplant units in England and 506 liver transplants were performed in 1992. Scotland's first liver transplant centre opened in Edinburgh in 1992. A voluntary organ donor card system enables people to indicate their willingness to become organ donors in the event of their death. Commercial dealing in organs for transplant is illegal.

Blood Transfusion Services

Blood transfusion services are run by the National Blood Authority in England, the Scottish National Blood Transfusion Service and the Common Health Services Agency in Wales.

Around 2.5 million donations are given each year by voluntary unpaid donors and separated into many different life-saving products for patients. Red cells, platelets and other products with a limited 'shelf life' are prepared at regional transfusion centres and the more complex processing of plasma products is undertaken at the Bio Products Laboratory in Elstree (Hertfordshire) and the Protein Fractionation Centre in Edinburgh.

Each of the three national bodies co-ordinates programmes for donor recruitment, retention and education, and donor sessions are organised regionally, in towns, villages and workplaces. Donors are normally aged between 18 (17 in Scotland) and 70. Regional transfusion centres are responsible for blood collection, screening, processing and regional blood banks. They also provide wide-ranging laboratory, clinical, research, teaching and advisory services and facilities. These are subject to nationally co-ordinated quality audit programmes.

Britain is completely self-sufficient in 'fresh' blood products and the National Blood Authority aims to meet fully the demand for plasma products in England. Scotland is already self-sufficient in all blood products.

Ambulance and Patient Transport Services

NHS emergency ambulances are available free of charge for cases of sudden illness or collapse, and for doctors' urgent calls. Rapid response services, in which paramedics use cars and motor cycles to reach emergency cases, have been introduced in a number of areas, particularly London and other major cities with areas of high traffic density. Helicopter ambulances serve many parts of England and an integrated air ambulance service is available throughout Scotland.

Non-emergency patient transport services are available to NHS patients considered by their doctor (or dentist or midwife) to be medically unfit to travel by other means. The principle applied is that each patient should be able to reach hospital in a reasonable time and in reasonable comfort, without detriment to his or her medical condition. In many areas the ambulance service organises volunteer drivers to provide a hospital car service for non-urgent patients.

Patients on income support, family credit or with low incomes may have their travelling expenses reimbursed. (In Scotland this also applies to patients in the Highland and Islands Development Area who travel 30 miles or more by land or five or more miles by sea to hospital.)

Rehabilitation

Rehabilitation services are available for elderly, young, disabled and mentally ill people, and those with learning disabilities who need such help to resume life in the community. These services are offered in hospitals, centres in the community and in people's own homes through co-ordinated work by a range of professional workers.

Medical services may provide free artificial limbs and eyes, hearing aids, surgical supports, wheelchairs, and other appliances. Following assessment, very severely physically disabled patients may be provided with environmental control equipment which enables them to operate devices such as alarm bells, radios and televisions, telephones, and heating appliances. Nursing equipment may be provided on loan for use in the home.

Local authorities may provide a range of facilities to help patients in the transition from hospital to their own homes. These include the provision of equipment, care from home helps, and professional help from occupational therapists and social workers. Voluntary organisations also provide services, complementing the work of the statutory agencies and widening the range of services.

Hospices

A number of hospices provide care for terminally ill people (including children), either directly in in-patient or day-care units or through nursing and other assistance in the patient's own home. Control of symptoms and psychological support for patients and their families form central features of the modern hospice movement, which started in Britain and is now worldwide. Some hospices are administered entirely by the NHS; the rest are run by independent charities, some receiving support from public funds. The number of voluntary hospices has more than doubled in the past ten years. There are about 200 hospices in England, providing almost 3,000 beds; and in Scotland 13 independent voluntary hospices providing almost 230 beds.

The Government is seeking to provide a level of public funding for the hospice movement which matches voluntary donations. In 1993–94, £32.3 million is being allocated to health authorities to enable them to offer increased support to hospices and similar organisations, while a further £5.6 million has been allocated to enable them to arrange for drugs to be supplied to hospices without charge. An extra £5 million is to be given to health authorities to help them pay for hospice care as part of the community care changes (see p. 384). In Scotland health boards have been allocated £2.7 million for 1993–94 to cover 50 per cent of the running costs of hospices in their areas and £400,000 has been provided for hospice pharmaceutical services. The National Council for Hospice and Specialist Palliative Care Services, which covers England, Wales and Northern Ireland, was launched in 1992. Its Scottish counterpart is the Scottish Partnership Agency for Palliative and Cancer Care, established in 1991.

Parents and Children

Special preventive services are provided under the health service to safeguard the health of expectant mothers and of mothers with young children. Services include free dental treatment, dried milk and vitamins; health education; and vaccination and immunisation of children against certain infectious diseases (see p. 379). Pregnant women receive antenatal care from their GPs and hospital clinics, and women in paid employment have the right to visit the clinics during working hours. Some 99 per cent of women have their babies in hospital, returning home shortly afterwards to be attended by a midwife or health visitor and, where necessary, their GP.

The Government attaches great importance to improving the quality of maternity services, and to making them more responsive to women's wishes on how care is provided. A government report published in August 1993 recommends giving women greater choice over the care they receive during pregnancy and childbirth.

A comprehensive programme of health surveillance is provided for pre-school children in clinics run by the community health authorities, and increasingly by GPs. This enables doctors, dentists and health visitors to oversee the physical and mental health and development of pre-school children. Information on preventive services is given and welfare foods are distributed. The school health service offers health care and advice for schoolchildren, including medical and dental inspection and treatment where necessary.

Child guidance and child psychiatric services provide help and advice to families and children with psychological or emotional problems.

In recent years special efforts have been made to improve co-operation between the community-based child health services and local authority social services for children. This is particularly important in the prevention of child abuse and for the health and welfare of children in care.

Human Fertilisation and Embryology

The world's first 'test-tube baby' was born in Britain in 1978, as a result of the technique of *in vitro* fertilisation. This opened up new horizons for helping with problems of infertility and for the science of embryology. The social, ethical and legal implications were examined by a committee of inquiry under Baroness Warnock (1984) and led eventually to the passage of the Human Fertilisation and Embryology Act 1990.

This Act set up the Human Fertilisation and Embryology Authority (HFEA) to control and license centres providing certain infertility treatments and centres undertaking human embryo research and storage of gametes and embryos.

It also:

- permitted research to be carried out on embryos for up to 14 days after fertilisation;

- defined the legal status and rights of children born as a result of *in vitro* fertilisation and techniques involving donation; and

- clarified the legal position on surrogate motherhood (the practice where one woman bears a child for another).

The HFEA maintains a code of practice giving guidance about licensed centres and reports annually to Parliament. These provisions constitute one of the most comprehensive pieces of legislation on assisted reproduction and embryo research in the world.

Legislation to ban commercial surrogacy agencies, and advertising of or for surrogacy services, was passed in 1985.

Family Planning

Free family planning advice and treatment are available to women from family doctors and from health authority family planning clinics, which also make services available to men. The *Health of the Nation* White Paper (see p. 365) recognises the need for providing effective family planning services for people who want them.

Abortion

The Abortion Act 1967, as amended in 1990, allows the ending of a pregnancy of up to 24 weeks by a doctor if two doctors consider that continuing the pregnancy would involve greater risk of injury to the physical or mental health of the woman (or to any existing children of the family) than having an abortion. There are three categories in which no time limit applies: where there is a risk of grave permanent injury to the physical or mental health of the woman; where there is a substantial risk of fetal handicap; or where continuing the pregnancy would involve a risk to the life of the pregnant woman greater than that of the pregnancy being terminated. The Act does not apply in Northern Ireland.

In 1991, 179,522 legal abortions were performed in England and Wales, compared with 186,912 in 1990, a decrease of 4 per cent. This was the first decrease in the annual number of abortions since 1983.

Drug Misuse

The misuse of dangerous drugs, such as heroin, cocaine and amphetamines, is a serious social and health problem, and the Government has made the fight against such misuse a major priority. Its strategy comprises action to reduce the supply of illicit drugs from abroad; to promote more effective law enforcement by the police and Customs services; and to maintain tight controls on medicinal drugs that can be misused. It also includes action to maintain effective deterrents against misuse; to develop effective programmes to treat and rehabilitate misusers; and to prevent people who are not misusers from starting, through educational programmes and publicity campaigns.

Research on various aspects of drug misuse is funded by several government departments. The Government is advised on a wide range of matters relating to drug misuse and connected social problems by the Advisory Council on the Misuse of Drugs.

Drug Statistics

Recent drug statistics show that between 1991 and 1992:

- the number of notified drug addicts increased by 19 per cent (to 24,700)—in line with the prevailing upward trend—while the number of new addicts notified increased by 21 per cent to 9,700.

- the proportion of those notified who are addicted to heroin, the most frequently reported drug, fell to below 70 per cent but this is balanced by an increase in notifications of addiction to methadone, which now accounts for over 40 per cent of notifications.

- fewer than 10 per cent were reported to be addicted to cocaine although the proportion is increasing;

- in general the highest numbers of all categories of notified addicts are to be found in London and the north west of England; and

- the proportion of addicts injecting drugs continues to fall and now represents 54 per cent of the total.

Prevention

The Government began a major national publicity campaign in 1985 to persuade young people not to take drugs, and to advise parents, teachers and other professionals on how to recognise and combat the problem. Subsequent phases of the campaign have warned of the dangers of heroin misuse and of the risks of transmitting HIV, the virus which causes AIDS (see p. 379), through the sharing of injecting equipment. Since 1991–92 the focus of the campaign has changed to give greater emphasis to locally-based campaigns.

A major initiative in November 1992, during Britain's presidency of the European Community, was European Drug Prevention Week. This was marked by events throughout Europe, including a range of activities in Britain at European, national and local levels, where the week focused on raising awareness among young people of the dangers of drug and solvent misuse.

The Drugs Prevention Initiative provides funding for local drug prevention teams in 20 areas in England, Scotland and Wales. Their task is to strengthen community resistance to drug misuse. The total budget for the

initiative is £5.8 million in 1993–94. Separate measures have been introduced in Scotland to discourage drug misuse through publicity campaigns and action in the education service and the community. A recent initiative has been the establishment of Drugline Scotland, a free government-funded telephone line, giving confidential advice.

The Government continues to make funds available for local education authorities in England and Wales to appoint staff to promote and co-ordinate preventive work in their areas, especially for anti-drug misuse work in schools. As part of the National Curriculum (see p. 408), children in primary and secondary schools receive education on the dangers of drug misuse.

Treatment and Rehabilitation

Funds have been made available to health authorities since 1986–87 for developing and expanding services for drug misusers. Further funding has also been allocated to help prevent the spread of HIV among and from injecting drug misusers. This includes schemes providing counselling and the exchange of clean for used injecting equipment—£2.7 million is being allocated in 1993–94 to expand the provision of needle exchange schemes within pharmacies.

The total amount available to health authorities in 1993–94 is over £24 million. In addition, a grant was introduced in 1991–92 to help local authorities develop voluntary sector services for alcohol and drug misusers. The grant (£3.3 million in 1993–94) has been successful in encouraging the involvement of local authorities in the provision of social care for drug users and increased local collaboration between agencies. Similar projects are in progress in Wales and in Scotland, where over £3 million and £2.4 million respectively is made available each year for the support of drug misuse services.

The *Health of the Nation* White Paper (see p. 365) set out targets for reducing by at least 75 per cent by the year 2000 the percentage of injecting drug misusers who report having shared needles in the previous four weeks.

Treatment for drug dependence is provided mainly on an out-patient basis.

Many hospitals provide specialist treatment for drug misusers, mainly in psychiatric units, or have special drug treatment units. An increasing number of GPs also treat drug misusers, but only certain specialist doctors are licensed to prescribe heroin, cocaine and dipipanone (Diconal). All doctors must notify the authorities of any patient they consider to be addicted to certain controlled drugs, and guidelines on good medical practice in the treatment of drug misuse are issued to doctors.

Other Sources of Provision

A number of non-statutory agencies work with and complement the health service provision. Advice and rehabilitation services including residential facilities, for example, are provided mainly by voluntary organisations. Support in the community is provided by the probation service and local social services departments (and in Scotland by social work departments).

Solvent Misuse

Action is also being taken by the Government to curb solvent misuse (the breathing in of vapour from glue, lighter fuel and other substances to achieve a change in mental state) by young people. There were 122 deaths as a result of solvent abuse in Britain in 1991. In England and Wales it is an offence to supply such substances to children under 18 if the supplier knows or has reason to believe they are to be used to cause intoxication. In Scotland proceedings can be taken under the common law. Government policy is directed towards preventing solvent misuse through the education of young people, parents and professionals and, where practicable, restricting the sales of solvent-based liquefied gas and aerosol products to young people. In 1992 the Government launched a national publicity campaign on solvent misuse intended to raise parental awareness of the problem.

Smoking

Cigarette smoking is the greatest preventable cause of illness and death in Britain. It accounts for around 110,000 premature deaths and an estimated 50 million lost working days each year, and costs the NHS an estimated £500 million a year for the treatment of diseases caused by smoking (for example, heart disease, lung cancer and bronchitis). In addition, smoking by pregnant women can cause low birth weight in infants. The Government is following an active health education policy supported by voluntary agreements with the tobacco industry aimed at reducing the level of smoking.

Health Education

The Government aims to reduce adult smoking in England from the present 30 per cent to 20 per cent by the year 2000. A further aim is to reduce smoking by young people by one-third between 1988 and 1994. Smoking is also being tackled as a priority in Wales, Scotland and Northern Ireland and similar targets have been set for the year 2000.

A five-year programme, costing £2.6 million a year, started in 1989; in late 1991 the Government launched a programme costing £500,000 a year to alert women to the dangers of smoking during pregnancy. Education on the harmful effects of smoking is included in the National Curriculum for all pupils in publicly maintained schools in England and Wales.

The Government also supports the work of the voluntary organisation Action on Smoking and Health (ASH), whose services include a workplace services consultancy, offering advice and help to employers in formulating smoking policies. The Government is committed to creating a smoke-free environment, with facilities where appropriate for those who wish to smoke. In 1991 it published a code of practice on smoking in public places. Health authorities have been asked to promote non-smoking as the normal practice in health service buildings and to give help and advice to people who want to give up smoking. The Independent Scientific Committee on Smoking and Health estimated that 'passive smoking', especially in the workplace and the home, may cause several hundred deaths through lung cancer every year.

Voluntary Agreements

Voluntary agreements between the Government and the tobacco industry regulate the advertising and promotion of tobacco products, and sports sponsorship by the industry. The agreement on tobacco advertising provides for the use on posters of six different health warnings about the dangers of smoking and contains measures to protect groups at particular risk, such as children, young people and women in early child-bearing years. Under the revised agreement, which came into force in 1992, new tougher health warnings now appear on tobacco advertising, and shopfront advertising is to be reduced by 50 per cent by 1996. The voluntary agreement on sports sponsorship covers levels of spending, restrictions on sponsorship of events chiefly for spectators under 18 years and controls over the siting of advertising at televised events.

Legislative Measures

It is illegal to sell any type of tobacco product to children; the maximum fine is £2,500. All tobacco advertising is banned on television and cigarette advertisements are banned on radio. Oral snuff products have been banned since January 1993.

Alcohol Misuse

Alcohol is consumed by over 90 per cent of the population. About 28 per cent of men and 11 per cent of women drink to an extent that may put their health at risk. An estimated 8 million working days each year are lost through alcohol-related absenteeism. The total cost to society of alcohol misuse has been estimated at £2,500 million.

The Government's view, as set out in the *Health of the Nation* White Paper (see p. 365), is that the consumption of alcohol in sensible quantities and in appropriate circumstances provides many people with enjoyment. Drinking fewer than 21 units of alcohol a week by men and 14 units a week by women is unlikely to damage health. (A unit is 8 grammes of pure alcohol, roughly equivalent to half a pint of ordinary strength beer or lager; or a glass of wine; or a pub measure of spirits.) The British medical profession advises that sustained drinking above these levels progressively increases the health risk, and that drinking over 50 units a week by men and over 35 units by women is definitely dangerous.

The White Paper includes targets for reducing the proportion of people drinking over sensible limits by the year 2005 and sets out a programme of action by government departments, health and local authorities, the independent sector, employers and the alcohol industry.

Part of the funds of the Health Education Authority (see p. 380) are for promoting the sensible drinking message in England, and equivalent bodies are similarly funded in other parts of Britain. At local level this requires co-ordinated action by a wide range of organisations with an interest in the use or misuse of alcohol. In England regional health authorities are funded to employ alcohol misuse co-ordinators to develop this work.

Treatment and rehabilitation within the NHS include in-patient and out-patient services in general and psychiatric hospitals and specialised alcoholism treatment units. Primary care teams (GPs, nurses and social workers) and voluntary organisations providing treatment and rehabilitation in hostels, day centres and advisory services, also play an important role.

The development of services to help problem drinkers and their families is being taken forward within the framework of community care. Local authorities are required to identify the need for alcohol misuse services in their area, and to list the services provided in their community care plans (see p. 384). They are then responsible for arranging for the needs of individuals with alcohol problems to be assessed, and for buying an appropriate course of care.

There is close co-operation between statutory and voluntary organisations. In England the voluntary agency Alcohol Concern, which is receiving a government grant of £612,000 for 1993–94, plays a prominent role in training for professional and voluntary workers, and improving the network of voluntary agencies and their collaboration with statutory bodies in the prevention of misuse.

In 1990 Alcohol Concern launched a workplace advisory service as part of a campaign to persuade companies that alcohol misuse is an industrial as well as a social problem. Between 1991–92 and 1995–96 a total government contribution of £6 million is being allocated to Alcohol Concern for improving and extending the network of care, advisory and counselling services. In addition, a grant of £2.3 million is being paid to local authorities during 1993–94 to assist voluntary agencies in improving and extending provision for alcohol and drug misusers. The Scottish Council on Alcohol undertakes similar work in Scotland, with the help of a government grant (£135,000 in 1993–94). Research and surveys on various aspects of alcohol misuse are funded by several government departments.

AIDS

Up to the end of June 1993 a total of 7,699 cases of AIDS had been reported in Britain, of whom 4,794 (62 per cent) had died; the total number of recognised HIV infections was 20,035. While this is recognised as a considerable underestimate of the true numbers of infections, attempts to contain the spread of HIV infection have nevertheless been successful and Britain now has one of the lowest estimated rates of HIV prevalence in Western Europe.

Government Strategy

The Government considers that the momentum of HIV prevention work must be sustained if this relatively favourable position is to be maintained. The latest medium-term predictions show that new cases of AIDS among homosexual men are levelling out and declining among injecting drug misusers, but there is a steady increase in cases of HIV infection through heterosexual contact.

Key elements of the Government's strategy for dealing with the disease include:

- encouraging appropriate behaviour change by increased targeting of sections of the population at particular risk, including homosexual and bisexual men and drug misusers;
- sustaining and improving general public awareness;
- continuing to make HIV testing facilities more widely known, and encouraging health authorities to commission additional accessible HIV testing sites; and
- continued funding for the voluntary sector.

The Government's commitment to policies in this area is demonstrated by its inclusion of HIV/AIDS with sexual health as one of the five key areas in the *Health of the Nation* White Paper (see p. 365). A concerted approach is being maintained, spanning government, the NHS, local authorities and the voluntary sector (including women's groups, Britain's faith communities and organisations working with ethnic minorities).

Details of Britain's contribution to international co-operation on AIDS are given in Chapter 20.

Voluntary Organisations

Voluntary agencies concerned with HIV/AIDS include the Terrence Higgins Trust, London Lighthouse and Scottish AIDS Monitor, which promote knowledge about the disease and help people with AIDS and HIV. Both London Lighthouse and the Mildmay Mission Hospital, in London, provide hospice care and community support. The Government will continue distributing grants on a yearly basis taking into account developing health priorities and the ability of voluntary bodies to raise funds from other sources for HIV/AIDS work.

Infectious Diseases

District health authorities (health boards in Scotland and Northern Ireland) carry out programmes of immunisation against diphtheria, measles, mumps, rubella, poliomyelitis, tetanus, tuberculosis and whooping cough. A new immunisation, 'Hib', was introduced in 1992, offering protection against invasive haemophilus disease, a major cause of meningitis in children under five years. More than 5 million doses are being made available during the first year of the campaign, sufficient to immunise every child under four with the appropriate dose.

Immunisation is voluntary, but parents are encouraged to protect their children. The proportion of children being vaccinated has been increasing since the end of 1978. In 1990 the Government introduced special payments to GPs who achieve targets of 70 and 90 per cent uptake of child immunisation. The response has been encouraging in many areas and the Government estimates that almost 90 per cent of GPs now earn bonus payments for meeting such targets.

The Public Health Laboratory Service provides a network of bacteriological and virological laboratories throughout England and Wales which conduct research and assist in the diagnosis, prevention and control of communicable diseases. Similar facilities are provided in Scotland by the Communicable Diseases (Scotland) Unit and, as in Northern Ireland, in some hospital laboratories.

Cancer Screening

Breast cancer is recognised as a major health problem in Britain. Some 13,000 women die from it each year and 1 in 14 women in England will develop it. To help combat this, the Government has set up a national screening programme under which women aged between 50 and 64 are invited for mammography (breast X-ray) every three years by computerised call and recall systems.

Nearly 1,900 women die each year in Great Britain from cancer of the cervix, and the Government has, similarly, set up a nationwide cervical screening programme. All district health authorities in England and Wales have computerised call and recall systems which enable all women aged between 20 and 64 to be invited at least every five years to have a smear test. Similar arrangements apply in Scotland (where the age range is 20 to 60) and in Northern

Ireland. Special payments are made to GPs who achieve uptake targets for smear tests of 50 and 80 per cent.

The reduction of deaths and illness from cancer is a key area in the Government's *Health of the Nation* White Paper (see p. 365). The targets set are:

- to reduce breast cancer deaths among women invited for screening by at least 25 per cent by the year 2000; and

- to reduce the incidence of invasive cervical cancer by at least 20 per cent by the year 2000.

Health Education

In England health education is promoted by the Health Education Authority, a part of the NHS. Its functions are to:

- advise the Government on health education;

- plan and carry out health education programmes in co-operation with health authorities and other bodies; and

- sponsor research and evaluation.

In addition, the Authority has the major executive responsibility for public education in Britain about AIDS. It also assists in the provision of training, and provides a national centre of information and advice on health education. Major campaigns carried out by the Authority include those focusing on coronary heart disease (represented by the 'Look After Your Heart' initiative), smoking and alcohol misuse. The Government has allocated some £36 million to the Authority for health education in England for 1993–94.

In Wales health education is undertaken by the Welsh Health Promotion Authority. The Health Education Board for Scotland and the Northern Ireland Health Promotion Agency are responsible for health education in their areas.

Almost all health authorities have their own health education service, which works closely with health professionals, health visitors, community groups, local employers and others to determine the most suitable local programmes. Increased resources in the health service are being directed towards health education and preventive measures. Since July 1993 GPs have received special annual payments for health promotion programmes.

Healthier Eating

There has been growing public awareness in recent years of the importance of a healthy diet. The *Health of the Nation* White Paper (see p. 365) followed the recommendations of the Committee on Medical Aspects of Food Policy (COMA) that people should reduce their average intakes of total fat and saturated fatty acids in order to reduce the burden of cardiovascular disease. Dietary targets have been set and a Nutrition Task Force has been established to advise on the most effective means of achieving them.

Nutritional labelling indicating the energy, fat, protein and carbohydrate content of food is being encouraged on a voluntary basis. Some supermarket chains have already introduced voluntary labelling schemes. To help people reduce their fat intake, the Government has issued guidelines on the labelling of food to show nutrient content in a standard format.

Current work by COMA includes a review of the relationship between diet and cardiovascular disease and between diet and cancer; and matters relating to the nutrition of infants and children. Its recent reports have included comprehensive information on dietary reference values for food energy and nutrients (1991); and the nutritional needs of elderly people (1992).

The Health Education Authority in England and its counterparts in Scotland, Wales and Northern Ireland, have all run public information campaigns promoting healthy eating.

ENVIRONMENTAL HEALTH

Environmental health officers employed by local authorities are responsible for a range of functions, including the control of air pollution and noise, and food hygiene and safety. Their duties also cover the occupational health and safety aspects of a variety of premises, including offices and shops; the investigation of unfit housing; and in some instances refuse collection and home safety.

Doctors who specialise in community medicine and are employed by the health authorities advise local authorities on the medical aspects of environmental health, infectious diseases and food poisoning. They may also co-operate with the authorities responsible for water supply and sewerage. Environmental health officers at ports and airports carry out duties concerned with shipping, inspection of imported foods, and disease control. In Northern Ireland district councils are responsible for noise control; collection and disposal of refuse; clean air; and food composition, labelling and hygiene.

Safety of Food

It is illegal to supply food unfit for human consumption or to apply any treatment or process to food which makes it harmful to health. Places where food or drink is prepared, handled, stored or sold must comply with certain hygiene provisions. Environmental health officers may take away for examination samples of any food intended for sale or human consumption. Specific regulations control the safety of particular foods such as milk, meat, ice-cream and shellfish. The Food Safety Directorate within the Ministry of Agriculture, Fisheries and Food ensures the safety and quality of Britain's food. The Directorate works closely with the health departments, which are responsible for the public health aspects of food safety. A consumer panel gives consumers a direct means of conveying their views on food safety and consumer protection issues to the Government.

Expert committees advise the Government on microbiological and chemical food safety, novel foods and processes, and veterinary products. The independent Advisory Committee on the Microbiological Safety of Food, for example, assesses the risks to human health from micro-organisms in food and drink and advises Ministers where appropriate.

The Food Safety Act 1990 emphasises the importance of food safety and consumer protection throughout the food chain. The Act applies to England, Wales and Scotland and introduced wider powers and greatly increased penalties for offenders. As a defence, food companies may show that they have taken all reasonable precautions to avoid committing an offence. Specific regulations govern the temperatures at which foods such as cooked meats should be stored. Separate, but similar, legislation exists in Northern Ireland.

A new public body, the Institute for Environment and Health, is to be established by the Medical Research Council (see below). This will be concerned mainly with chemical hazards to which people may be exposed through the environment.

SAFETY OF MEDICINES

The health and agriculture ministers are responsible for the licensing of medicines for human and veterinary use. The Medicines Commission advises the ministers on policy. The Committees on Safety of Medicines and on Dental and Surgical Materials advise on the safety and quality of medicinal products for human use. Both committees also monitor adverse reactions to drugs. Legislation also controls the advertising, labelling, packaging, distribution, sale and supply of medicinal products.

RESEARCH

In 1992–93 the Department of Health in England spent about £25 million on health and personal social services research, in addition to expenditure by the Medical Research Council (the main government agency for the support of biomedical and clinical research—see Chapter 19). Priority areas include research into health promotion and the prevention of ill health, environmental health, adult health and child care.

In England the Director of Research and Development at the Department of Health advises ministers on all aspects of health research; Wales also participates in the Department of Health's programme of centrally commissioned research. In Scotland

the directly funded programme is administered by the Chief Scientist of the Scottish Office Home and Health Department.

The strategy for the NHS research and development programme aims to ensure that health service care is based on high-quality research relevant to improving the health of the nation. The programme is managed by the regional health authorities, which are developing their own research plans. It is intended that up to 1.5 per cent of NHS expenditure will be used for research and development by 1997.

The Department of Health is involved in international research and development, and takes part in the European Community's medical and public health research programme.

THE HEALTH PROFESSIONS

Doctors and Dentists

Only people on the medical or dentists' registers may practise as doctors or dentists in the NHS. University medical and dental schools are responsible for teaching; the NHS provides hospital facilities for training. Full registration as a doctor requires five or six years' training in a medical school and hospital, with a further year's experience in a hospital. For a dentist, five years' training at a dental school is required.

An extensive review of postgraduate medical education was carried out in 1992–93 and is expected to lead to considerable improvements in junior doctors' education and training, including a significant reduction in the time which individual doctors spend in the training grades.

The regulating body for the medical profession is the General Medical Council and, for dentists, the General Dental Council The main professional associations are the British Medical Association and the British Dental Association.

Nurses

The minimum period of training required to qualify for registration as a first level nurse is general, mental health, mental handicap, or children's nursing is normally three years. Midwifery training for registered general nurses takes 18 months, and for those entering midwifery directly, three years. Health visitors are registered general nurses who have completed a one-year course in health visiting. District nurses are registered general nurses who practise within the community. They must complete a six-month course (nine months in Northern Ireland) followed by a period of supervised practice in district nursing.

Project 2000 is a new system for training nurses, designed to make nursing education more attractive and to give nurses a broader based education, enabling them to work in hospitals or the community without extensive further training. In 1993–94 the Government is allocating £114 million to fund the scheme in England, where nearly all nursing schools are now approved to offer Project 2000 courses; comparable arrangements are being made in other parts of Britain.

The United Kingdom Central Council for Nursing, Midwifery and Health Visiting is responsible for regulating and registering these professions.

Pharmacists

Only people on the register of pharmaceutical chemists may practise as pharmacists. Registration requires three or four years' training in a school of pharmacy, followed by one year's practical experience in a community or hospital pharmacy approved for training by the Royal Pharmaceutical Society of Great Britain or the Pharmaceutical Society of Northern Ireland (regulatory bodies for the profession).

Opticians

The General Optical Council regulates the professions of ophthalmic optician and dispensing optician. Only registered ophthalmic opticians (or registered ophthalmic medical practitioners) may test sight. Training of ophthalmic opticians takes four years, including a year of practical experience under supervision. Dispensing opticians take a two-year full-time course with a year's practical experience or follow a part-time day-release course while employed with an optician.

Other Health Professions

State registration may also be obtained by chiropodists, dietitians, medical laboratory scientific officers, occupational therapists, orthoptists, physiotherapists and radiographers. The governing bodies are seven boards, corresponding to the professions, under the general supervision of the Council for Professions Supplementary to Medicine. Training lasts one to four years and only those who are state registered may be employed in the NHS and some other public services.

Dental therapists (who have taken a two-year training course) and dental hygienists (with a training course of about a year) may carry out some simple dental work under the supervision of a registered dentist.

In 1990 a new group of NHS staff—health care assistants—began work in hospitals and the community. They are intended to support the work of more highly qualified staff.

National and Scottish Vocational Qualifications (NVQs and SVQs—see p. 415) have been developed for health care support workers, ambulance personnel, operating department practitioners, physiological measurement technicians and administrative and clerical staff. In addition, a new NVQ in Care has been launched for staff in social services and health care.

HEALTH ARRANGEMENTS WITH OTHER COUNTRIES

The member states of the European Community have special health arrangements under which Community nationals resident in a member state are entitled to receive emergency treatment, either free or at a reduced cost, during visits to other Community countries. There are also arrangements for referral for specific treatment in certain circumstances and to cover people who go to work or live in other Community countries. In addition, there are reciprocal arrangements with some other countries under which medical treatment is available to visitors to Britain if required immediately. Visitors are generally expected to pay if the purpose of their visit is to seek medical treatment. Visitors who are not covered by reciprocal arrangements must pay for any medical treatment they receive.

Personal Social Services

Personal social services assist elderly people, disabled people and their carers, children and young people, people with mental illness or learning disabilities, and families. Major services include skilled residential and day care, help for people confined to their homes, and the various forms of social work. The statutory services are provided by local government social services authorities in England and Wales, social work departments in Scotland, and health and social services boards in Northern Ireland. Alongside these providers are the many and varied contributions made by independent private and voluntary services. Much of the care given to elderly and disabled people is provided by families and self-help groups.

Demand for these services is rising because of the increasing number of elderly people, who, along with disabled and mentally ill people, or those with learning disabilities, can lead more normal lives in the community, given suitable support and facilities. The share of health authority resources devoted to community care services increased from 8.4 per cent in 1978–79 to just over 13 per cent in 1990–91.

The shift away from long-term hospital care to care in the community is reflected in recent hospital statistics. Average length of stay in the geriatric hospital sector has declined by around 9 per cent a year since 1978 and the numbers of occupied bed days in the mental health and learning disabilities sectors fell by 30 and 50 per cent respectively between 1978 and 1990–91. Personal social services staff increased by some 25 per cent between 1978–79 and 1990–91, the most significant increases being

in social work staff, day care and home helps. In the residential care group, increases in staff in adult services have been offset by reductions in the staff in children's homes.

Management Reforms

New policies on community care in England, Wales and Scotland have been implemented in stages under the NHS and Community Care Act 1990. In Northern Ireland similar arrangements were introduced in April 1993 under equivalent legislation. Many of the procedures which local authorities are implementing correspond to similar procedures being introduced in the NHS (see p. 364). Local authorities increasingly act as enablers and commissioners of services on an assessment of their populations' needs for social care.

- Since April 1991 inspection units have been responsible for inspecting local authority as well as private and voluntary sector residential care homes, and local authorities have had to have procedures for dealing with complaints about their social services.

- Since April 1992 local authorities have been obliged to produce community care plans after wide consultation with the NHS and other interests.

- Since April 1993 new procedures for assessing individuals' care needs and commissioning services to meet them have been introduced.

Local authorities are now responsible for funding and arranging social care in the community for people who require public support. This includes the provision of home helps or home care assistants to support people in their own homes, and making arrangements for residential and nursing home care for those no longer able to remain in their own homes. Previously, residents of these homes who obtained public funding received help principally through special higher levels of income support (see p. 396). To accompany their new responsibilities the Government has transferred resources from the Department of Social Security to local authorities for three years (1993–94 to

1995–96). In 1993–94 the transfer in England amounts to £399 million; in Scotland it is £41 million; in Wales £27.5 million; and in Northern Ireland £24.6 million.

Elderly People

Between 1981 and 1991:

- the number of people over 60 in Great Britain increased by about 500,000; little change is expected over the period 1991 to 1996;

- the number of people aged over 75 grew to nearly 4 million (an increase of about one-fifth) and this will be reflected in a future increase in the number aged over 80.

Between 1978–79 and 1990–91 total spending on health services for elderly people increased by 41 per cent and net spending on social services by 52 per cent in real terms. About 5 per cent of those aged 65 or over live in residential homes.

Services for elderly people are designed to help them live at home whenever possible. These services may include advice and help given by social workers, domestic help, the provision of meals in the home, sitters-in, night attendants and laundry services as well as day centres, lunch clubs and recreational facilities. Adaptations to the home can overcome a person's difficulties in moving about, and a wide range of equipment is available for people with difficulties affecting their hearing or eyesight. Alarm systems have been developed to help elderly people obtain assistance in an emergency. In some areas 'good neighbour' and visiting services are arranged by the local authority or a voluntary organisation.

Many local authorities provide free or subsidised travel for elderly people within their areas. Local authorities also provide residential care for elderly people and those in poor health.

As part of their responsibility for public housing, local authorities provide homes designed for elderly people; some of these developments have resident wardens. Housing associations and private builders also build such accommodation.

Disabled People

Britain has an estimated 6 million adults with one or more disabilities, of whom around 400,000 (7 per cent) live in communal establishments. Over the past ten years there has been increasing emphasis on rehabilitation and on the provision of day, domiciliary and respite support services to enable disabled people to live independently in the community wherever possible.

Local social services authorities help with social rehabilitation and adjustment to disability. They are required to identify the number of disabled people in their area and to publicise services, which may include advice on personal and social problems arising from disability, as well as occupational, educational, social and recreational facilities, either at day centres or elsewhere. Other services provided may include adaptations to homes (such as ramps for wheelchairs, and ground-floor toilets); the delivery of cooked meals; and help in the home. In cases of special need, help may be given with installing a telephone or a television. Local authorities and voluntary organisations may provide severely disabled people with residential accommodation or temporary facilities to allow their carers relief from their duties. Specially designed housing may be available for those able to look after themselves.

Some authorities provide free or subsidised travel for disabled people on public transport, and they are encouraged to provide special means of access to public buildings. Special government regulations cover the provision of access for disabled people in the construction of new buildings.

The Independent Living Fund was set up in 1988 to provide financial help to very severely disabled people who need paid domestic support to enable them to live in their own homes. During 1992–93 an estimated 22,000 people received help from the Fund. The Fund, for which the Government provided £77 million in 1992–93, ceased to operate in April 1993. People needing such help are now catered for under the mainstream arrangements for community care.

The Government introduced two trusts from April 1993:

- the first continues to support those people receiving help from the Fund at the time of its closure and ensures continuity in the care arrangements of all existing beneficiaries; and
- the second helps the most severely disabled people of working age to live independently in the community. It works in partnership with local authorities, which are expected to make a contribution in the form of services equivalent to what they would have spent on residential or nursing care.

In 1991 the Government committed £3 million for a pilot scheme in England—the National Disability Information Project—designed to improve information services for disabled people, their carers and service providers. Twelve projects are being funded until 1994 to explore ways in which the voluntary and statutory agencies can work together to provide information services aimed at satisfying the needs of users. Similar projects are being supported in Wales.

People with Learning Disabilities (Mental Handicap)

The Government's policy is to encourage the development of local services for people with learning disabilities and their families through co-operation between health and local authorities, and voluntary and other organisations.

Local authority social service departments are the lead statutory agency for planning and arranging services for people with learning disabilities. They provide such services as short-term care, support for families in their own homes, residential accommodation and support for various types of activities outside the home. The main aims are to ensure that as far as possible people with learning disabilities can lead full lives in their communities and that no one is admitted to hospital unless it is necessary on health grounds.

The NHS provides specialist services where the general health needs of people with learning disabilities cannot be met by ordinary NHS services, and residential care for those with severe disabilities or whose needs can only effectively be met by the NHS.

Mentally Ill People

Government policy aims to ensure that people with mental illnesses should have access to all the services they need as locally as possible. These services should be based on a comprehensive network of health and social services facilities in each district. They should be community based and easily accessible.

In England between 1981 and 1991 the number of community psychiatric nurses more than trebled (to 3,600); places in day hospitals increased by 75 per cent (to 22,700). Between 1979 and 1991 places in local authority residential homes grew by over 25 per cent (to 4,500); local authority day centre places more than doubled to 15,100.

Arrangements made by social services authorities for providing preventive care and after care for mentally ill people in the community include day centres, social centres and residential care. Social workers help patients and their families with problems caused by mental illness. In some cases they can apply for a mentally disordered person to be compulsorily admitted to and detained in hospital. The Mental Health Act Commission aims to provide improved safeguards for such patients. Similar arrangements apply in Wales, Scotland and Northern Ireland.

Since April 1991 district health authorities (health boards in Scotland) have been required to plan individual health and social care programmes for all patients leaving hospital and for all new patients accepted by the specialist psychiatric services. Other measures include a review of public funding of voluntary organisations concerned with mental health and a new grant (some £51 million for 1993–94) to local authorities to encourage them to increase the level of social care available to mentally ill patients, including those with dementia who need specialist psychiatric care in the community.

The Government plans to introduce legislation to provide a new power of supervised discharge for mentally ill patients who need special support after they leave hospital.

The first government-backed national survey of mental illness began in April 1993 and will be completed in 1995. The survey, which covers adults aged 16 to 64 living in communal establishments as well as those living in private households, will estimate the prevalence of different types of mental illness and will identify the resulting social disabilities. It will also examine the varying use of health, social and voluntary care services, and the risk factors associated with mental illness. A review of mental health nursing was announced in April 1992 and is expected to report in late 1993.

There are many voluntary organisations concerned with mental illness and learning disabilities, and they play an important role in providing services for both groups of people.

Help to Families

Social services authorities, through their own social workers and others, give help to families facing special problems. This includes services for children at risk of injury or neglect who need care away from their own families, and support for family carers who look after elderly and other family members in order to give them relief from their duties. They also help single parents. There are now many refuges run by local authorities or voluntary organisations for women, often with young children, whose home conditions have become intolerable. The refuges provide short-term accommodation and support while attempts are made to relieve the women's problems. Many authorities also contribute to the cost of social work with families (such as marriage guidance) carried out by voluntary organisations.

The Self-help and Families Project provides funding for nine voluntary agencies to assist groups of families to help themselves.

Child Care

Day care facilities for children under five are provided by local authorities, voluntary agencies and privately. In allocating places in their day nurseries and other facilities, local authorities give priority to children with special social or health needs. Local authorities also register childminders, private day nurseries and playgroups in their areas and provide support and advice services.

In April 1993 the Government launched a £45 million scheme to help create childcare facilities for children over five after school hours and during the holidays. The scheme, which will be operated through Training and Enterprise Councils and Local Enterprise Companies (see p. 143), will cover the whole of Great Britain from April 1994. These organisations will develop local partnerships in the community with employers, schools, parents, local authorities and voluntary organisations.

The authorities can offer advice and help to families in difficulties to promote the welfare of children. The aim is to act at an early stage to reduce the need to put children into care or bring them before a court.

Child Abuse

Cases of child abuse are the joint concern of many authorities, agencies and professions. Local review committees provide a forum for discussion and co-ordination and draw up policies and procedures for handling these cases. The Government established a central training initiative on child abuse in 1986. This consists of a variety of projects, including training for health visitors, school nurses, and local authority social services staff. Training packs have been drawn up for those concerned with implementing the Children Act 1989 (see p. 388).

In England, Wales and Northern Ireland children under the age of 14 in child abuse cases are able to give evidence to courts through television links, thus sparing them from the need to give evidence in open court.

Children in Care

Local government authorities must provide accommodation for children in need in their area who require it because they have no parent or guardian, have been abandoned, or when parents are unable to provide for them. The number of children in the care of local authorities continues to decline. Provisional statistics show that:

● the total number of children in care fell from 92,300 in 1981 to 59,800 in 1991;

● the proportion in care placed with foster parents increased from 39 per cent in 1981 to 57 per cent in 1991; and

● between 1990 and 1991 the number in residential care fell from 12,670 to under 12,000.

The Children Act 1989, which came into effect in England and Wales in 1991, recasts the legislative framework for children's services, care and protection into a single coherent structure. It lays new duties on local authorities to safeguard and promote the welfare of children. Under the Act parents of children in care retain their parental responsibilities but act as far as possible as partners with the authority. There is a new requirement to prepare a child for leaving the local authority's responsibility and to continue to advise him or her up to the age of 21. Local authorities are required to have a complaints procedure with an independent element to cover children in their care.

In England and Wales a child may be brought before a family proceedings court if he or she is neglected or ill-treated, exposed to moral danger, beyond the control of parents, or not attending school. The court can commit the child to the care of a local authority under a care order. Under the Children Act 1989 certain preconditions have to be satisfied to justify an order. These are that the child is suffering or is likely to suffer significant harm because of a lack of reasonable parental care or is beyond parental control. However, an order is made only if the court is also satisfied that this will positively contribute to the child's well-being and be in his or her best interests. In court proceedings the child is entitled to separate legal representation and the right to have a guardian to protect his or her interests.

All courts have to treat the welfare of the child as the paramount consideration when reaching any decision about his or her upbringing. The family proceedings court consists of specially trained magistrates with power to hear care cases as well as all other family and children's cases.

Recent concerns over standards of care in certain local authority residential care and children's homes have prompted a number of official inquiries whose recommendations are now being implemented. They include:

● Sir William Utting's inquiry into training, service planning, inspection and management (1990);

● Norman Warner's inquiry into the selection of staff in children's homes and the support and guidance available to them after appointment (1992);

● the Howe inquiry into staff conditions, management and training for all residential care staff in adult and children's homes (1992);

● the Skinner review of residential child care in Scotland (1992); and

● the Social Services Inspectorate review of children's homes in Wales (1991).

In Scotland children in trouble or in need may be brought before a children's hearing, which can impose a supervision requirement on a child if it thinks that compulsory measures are appropriate. Under these requirements most children are allowed to remain at home under the supervision of a social worker but some may live with foster parents or in a residential establishment while under supervision. Supervision requirements are reviewed at least once a year until ended by a children's hearing. A review of child care legislation in Scotland has been conducted and its results are under consideration.

In Northern Ireland the court may send children in need or in trouble to a training school, commit them to the care of a fit person (including a health and social services board), or make a supervision order. Children in trouble may be required to attend an attendance centre or may be detained in a remand home. New child care legislation is being prepared in Northern Ireland. Where appropriate it will reflect the changes introduced in England and Wales and will make a distinction between the treatment of children in need of care and young offenders.

Fostering and Community Homes

When appropriate, children in care are placed with foster parents, who receive payments to cover living costs. Alternatively, the child may be placed in a children's home, voluntary home or other suitable residential accommodation. In Scotland local authorities are responsible for placing children in their care in foster homes, in local authority or voluntary homes, or in residential schools. In Northern Ireland there are residential homes for children in the care of the health and social services boards; training schools and remand homes are administered separately. Regulations concerning residential care and the foster placement of children in care are made by central government.

Adoption

Local authorities are required by law to provide an adoption service, either directly or by arrangement with a voluntary organisation. Agencies may offer adoptive parents an allowance in certain circumstances if this would help to find a family for a child. Adoption is strictly regulated by law, and voluntary adoption societies must be approved by the appropriate social services minister. The Registrars-General keep confidential registers of adopted children. Adopted people may be given details of their original birth record on reaching the age of 18, and counselling is provided to help them understand the circumstances of their adoption. An Adoption Contact Register enables adopted adults and their birth parents to be given a safe and confidential way of making contact if that is the wish of both parties. A person's details are entered only if they wish to be contacted.

The report of a government review on adoption, published in late 1992, makes suggestions to improve present arrangements and to emphasise the rights of the child. The Government is to propose legislation to ensure that children remain at the centre of decisions affecting them.

Social Workers

The effective operation of the social services depends largely on professionally qualified social workers. Training programmes in social work are provided by universities and colleges of higher and further education. The Central Council for Education and Training in Social Work is the statutory body responsible for promoting social work training and offers advice to people considering entering the profession. A programme to introduce two-year courses leading to a new professional qualification, the Diploma in Social Work (DipSW), is being implemented. National Vocational Qualifications are being developed for other staff, including those in residential day and domiciliary care services.

Professional social workers (including those working in the NHS) are employed mainly by the social services departments of local authorities. Others work in the probation service, the education welfare service, or in voluntary organisations.

The Government is committed to improving social work training. In England alone it is providing £31.8 million in 1993–94 (£6 million in Scotland) through its training support programme to assist local authorities to train staff. Over 140,000 staff are expected to benefit from training, of whom nearly half work in residential care.

Further Reading

The Health of the Nation: A Strategy for Health in England. Cm 1986. HMSO, 1992.

26 Social Security

Spending on social security is rising because of increased numbers of beneficiaries, especially retirement pensioners, and long-term sick and disabled people. The value of retirement and most other long-term benefits has also increased in real terms since 1980. Planned spending in 1993–94 is £61,500 million—the Government's largest expenditure programme.

The social security system is designed to secure a basic standard of living for people in financial need by providing income during periods of inability to earn (including periods of unemployment), help for families and assistance with costs arising from disablement. Nearly a third of government expenditure is devoted to the social security programme, which provides financial help for people who are elderly, sick, disabled, unemployed, widowed, bringing up children or on very low incomes.

Some benefits depend on the payment of contributions by employers, employees and self-employed people to the National Insurance Fund, from which benefits are paid. The Government also contributes to the Fund. The other social security benefits are non-contributory and are financed from general taxation; some of these are income-related (see p. 396). Appeals about claims for benefits are decided by independent tribunals.

ADMINISTRATION

Administration in Great Britain is handled by separate executive agencies of the Department of Social Security:

- the Benefits Agency, responsible for paying the majority of social security benefits;

- the Contributions Agency, responsible for handling National Insurance contributions;

- the Information Technology Services Agency, responsible for computerising the administration of social security;

- the Child Support Agency, responsible for collecting and enforcing maintenance payments for children; it was set up in April 1993 (see p. 394); and

- the War Pensions Unit, for delivering services to war pensioners; it was also set up in April 1993.

The housing and council tax benefit schemes are administered mainly by local government authorities, which recover most of the cost from the Government.

In Northern Ireland contributions as well as social security benefits are administered by the Social Security Agency. The housing benefit scheme is administered by the Northern Ireland Housing Executive and the Rate Collection Agency; council tax does not apply in Northern Ireland.

Anti-fraud Measures

Further measures are being introduced to improve the prevention and detection of social security fraud. These include:

- greater incentives to local authorities to prevent and detect fraud in the benefits they administer;
- better use of information technology; and
- better targeting of resources, and additional resources where necessary.

In 1993–94 the Benefits Agency is expected to save over £500 million through anti-fraud work.

Advice about Benefits

The demand for advice about benefits is partly met by the Freeline Social Security Service, which handles over 1 million calls each year. A complementary service, the Social Security Advice Line for Employers, handles some 3,500 calls a week. The Ethnic Freeline Service provides information on social security in Urdu, Punjabi and Chinese. There is also a freeline service in Welsh.

CONTRIBUTIONS

Entitlement to National Insurance benefits such as retirement pension, sickness and invalidity benefit, unemployment benefit, maternity allowance and widow's benefit, is dependent upon the payment of contributions. There are four classes of contributions; **the rates given are effective from April 1993 to April 1994:**

- *Class 1—paid by employees and their employers.* Employees with earnings below £56 a week do not pay Class 1 contributions. Contributions on earnings of £56 a week and over are at the rate of 2 per cent of the first £56 of total earnings and 9 per cent of the balance, up to the upper earnings limit of £420 a week. Employers' contributions are subject to the same threshold. On earnings above the threshold, contributions rise in stages from 4.6 per cent of total earnings up to a maximum of 10.4 per cent when earnings are £195

or more a week; there is no upper earnings limit. The contribution is lower if the employer operates a 'contracted-out' occupational pension scheme (see below).

- *Class 2—paid by self-employed people.* Class 2 contributions are at a flat rate of £5.55 a week. The self-employed may claim exemption from payment of Class 2 contributions if their profits are expected to be below £3,140 for the tax year. Self-employed people are not eligible for unemployment and industrial injuries benefits.

- *Class 3—paid voluntarily to safeguard rights to some benefits.* Class 3 contributions are at a flat rate of £5.45 a week.

- *Class 4—paid by the self-employed on their taxable profits over a set lower limit (£6,340 a year), and up to a set upper limit (£21,840 a year) in addition to their Class 2 contribution.* Class 4 contributions are payable at the rate of 6.3 per cent.

Employees who work after pensionable age (60 for women and 65 for men) do not pay contributions but the employer continues to be liable. Self-employed people over pensionable age do not pay contributions.

BENEFITS

For most benefits there are two contribution conditions. First, before benefit can be paid at all, a certain number of contributions have to be paid. Secondly, the full rate of benefit cannot be paid unless contributions have been paid or credited to a specific level over a set period. Benefits are increased annually in line with percentage increases in retail prices. The main benefits (payable weekly) are summarised below. **The rates given are those effective from April 1993 until April 1994.**

Retirement Pension

A state retirement pension is payable, subject to the satisfaction of contribution conditions, to women at the age of 60 and men at the

Social Security Expenditure: Great Britain 1992–93

Analysis of planned expenditure 1992–93

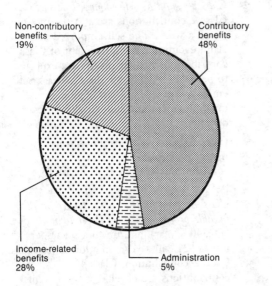

Non-contributory benefits 19%

Contributory benefits 48%

Income-related benefits 28%

Administration 5%

Percentage of expenditure by broad groups of beneficiaries 1992–93

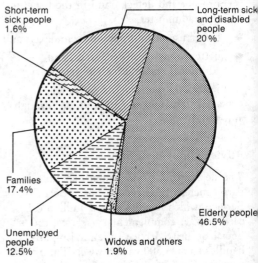

Short-term sick people 1.6%

Long-term sick and disabled people 20%

Families 17.4%

Elderly people 46.5%

Unemployed people 12.5%

Widows and others 1.9%

Source: *Social Security. The Government's Expenditure Plans 1993-94 to 1995-96.*

age of 65. The Sex Discrimination Act 1986 protects employees of different sexes in a particular occupation from being required to retire at different ages. This, however, has not affected the payment of the state retirement pension at different ages for men and women. The Government is committed to the equalisation of the state pension age for men and women and in 1991 published a discussion document setting out some of the issues involved. Comments and views on various approaches to equalisation, including differing common pension ages and models for a flexible pension age, were invited and responses are now being considered.

The state pension scheme consists of a basic weekly pension of £56.10 for a single person and £89.80 for a married couple, together with an additional earnings-related pension. Pensioners may have unlimited earnings without affecting their pensions. Those who have put off their retirement during the five years after state pension age may earn extra pension. A non-contributory

retirement pension of £33.70 a week is payable to people over the age of 80 who meet certain residence conditions, and who have not qualified for a contributory pension. People whose pensions do not give them enough to live on may be entitled to income support. Nearly 10 million people in Great Britain received a basic state pension in 1991.

Rights to basic pensions are safeguarded for mothers who are away from paid employment looking after children or for people giving up paid employment to care for severely disabled relatives. Men and women may receive the same basic pension, provided they have paid full-rate National Insurance contributions when working. From April 1999 the earnings-related pension scheme will be based on a lifetime's revalued earnings instead of on the best 20 years. It will be calculated as 20 per cent rather than 25 per cent of earnings, to be phased in over ten years from 1999. The pensions of people retiring this century will be unaffected.

Table 26.1: Estimated Number of Recipients of Benefits in Great Britain 1992–93[a]

Benefit	Contributory (C) or non-contributory (NC)	Thousands
Retirement pension	C	10,000
Widows' benefits	C	340
Unemployment benefit	C	715
Sickness benefit	C	135
Statutory sick pay	NC	330
Invalidity benefit	C	1,490
Maternity allowance	C	15
Statutory maternity pay	NC	85
Non-contributory retirement pension	NC	30
War pension	C	270
Attendance allowance	NC	765
Disability living allowance	NC	935
Disability working allowance	NC	5
Invalid care allowance	NC	195
Severe disablement allowance	NC	320
Industrial injuries disablement benefit	NC	295
Industrial death benefit	NC	25
Income support	NC	5,320
Child benefit	NC	
—numbers of children		12,485
—numbers of families		6,895
One parent benefit	NC	895
Family credit	NC	457
Housing benefit	NC	
—rent rebate		3,105
—rent allowance		1,210
Community charge benefit	NC	6,655

[a] Average number of people receiving benefit at any one time.

Occupational and Personal Pensions

Employers may 'contract out' their employees from the state scheme for the additional earnings-related pension and provide their own occupational pension instead. Their pension must be at least as good as the state additional pension. Joining an employer's contracted-out scheme is voluntary: employers are not free to contract out employees from the earnings-related pension scheme without the employees' consent. The state remains responsible for the basic pension.

Occupational pension schemes cover about half the working population and have over 11 million members. The occupational pension rights of those who change jobs before pensionable age, who are unable or who do not want to transfer their pension rights, are now protected against inflation up to a maximum of 5 per cent. Workers leaving a scheme have the right to a fair transfer value. The trustees or managers of pension schemes have to provide full information about their schemes. Some 67 per cent of recently retired people now have an occupational pension of over £58 a week, a sum greater than their basic state pension.

As an alternative to their employers' scheme or the state additional earnings-related pension scheme, people are entitled to choose a personal pension available from a bank, building society, insurance company or other financial institution. Some 5 million people have contracted out of the state earnings-related pension scheme and taken out personal pensions. A review of occupational pension law was published in September 1993. The Government is considering its recommendations.

A Pensions Ombudsman deals with complaints about maladministration of pension schemes and adjudicates on disputes of fact or law. A pensions registry helps people trace lost benefits.

Parents and Children

Most pregnant working women receive their statutory maternity pay directly from their employer for a maximum of 18 weeks. There are two rates:

- where a woman has been working for the same employer for at least two years, she is entitled to 90 per cent of her average weekly earnings for the first six weeks and to the lower rate of £47.95 a week for the remaining 12 weeks;

- where a woman has been employed for between 26 weeks and two years, she is entitled to payments for up to 18 weeks at the lower rate.

Women who are not eligible for statutory maternity pay because, for example, they are self-employed, have recently changed jobs or given up their job, may qualify for a weekly maternity allowance of £43.75, which is payable for up to 18 weeks.

A payment of £100 from the social fund (see p. 397) may be available if the mother or her partner are receiving income support, family credit or disability working allowance. It is also available if a woman adopts a baby.

Non-contributory child benefit of £10 for the eldest and £8.10 weekly for each other child is the general social security benefit for children. Tax-free and normally paid to the mother, it is payable for children up to the age of 16 and for those up to 19 if they continue in full-time non-advanced education. In addition, one-parent benefit of £6.05 a week is payable to certain people bringing up one child or more on their own, whether as their parents or not. A non-contributory guardian's allowance of £10.95 a week for an orphaned child is payable to a person who is

entitled to child benefit for that child. This is reduced to £9.80 if the higher rate of child benefit is payable for the child. In exceptional circumstances a guardian's allowance may be paid on the death of only one parent.

In 1992 the European Council of Ministers adopted a directive aimed at improving health and safety at work for pregnant women and nursing mothers. The directive provides maternity leave for 14 weeks with maternity pay equivalent to what the woman would receive if she were unable to work because of sickness. Legislation in Britain will be brought into line with the directive by October 1994.

Child Support Agency

An estimated 1.3 million lone parents bring up over 2 million children in Britain. Fewer than one in three receive regular maintenance payments for their children. The Government has set up the Child Support Agency, which takes over from the courts the main responsibility for obtaining maintenance for children. The Agency, which started work in April 1993, is responsible for tracing absent parents and collecting, enforcing and receiving child maintenance payments. Assessments are made using a formula which takes into account each parent's income and essential outgoings.

Widows

Widows under the age of 60, or those over 60 whose husbands were not entitled to a state retirement pension when they died, receive a tax-free single payment of £1,000 following the death of their husbands, provided that their husbands had paid a minimum number of National Insurance contributions. Women whose husbands have died of an industrial injury or prescribed disease may also qualify, regardless of whether their husbands had paid National Insurance contributions. A widowed mother with a young family receives a widowed mother's allowance of £56.10 a week with a further £9.80 for a child for whom the higher rate of child benefit is payable and £10.95 for each subsequent child. A widow's basic pension of £56.10 a week is payable to a widow who is 55 years or over when her husband dies or when her entitlement to widowed mother's allowance ends. A percentage of the full rate is payable to widows who are aged between 45 and 54 when their husbands die or when their entitlement to widowed mother's allowance ends. Special rules apply for widows whose husbands died before 11 April 1988. Entitlement continues until the widow remarries or begins drawing retirement pension. Payment ends if she lives with a man as his wife. Widows also benefit under the industrial injuries scheme.

A man whose wife dies when both are over pension age inherits his wife's pension rights just as a widow inherits her husband's rights.

Sick and Disabled People

Statutory Sick Pay and Sickness Benefit

A large variety of benefits is available for people unable to work because of sickness or disablement. Employers are responsible for paying statutory sick pay to employees for up to a maximum of 28 weeks. There are two weekly rates—£46.95 or £52.50—depending on average weekly earnings. Employees who are not entitled to statutory sick pay can claim weekly state sickness benefit of £42.70 instead, as can self-employed people. Sickness benefit is payable for up to 28 weeks.

Invalidity Pension and Allowance

A weekly invalidity pension of £56.10—with additions of £33.70 for an adult dependant, £9.80 for the eldest child and £10.95 for each other child—is payable when statutory sick pay or sickness benefit ends. For the period to count towards receiving invalidity pension the contribution condition for sickness benefit must be satisfied. An invalidity allowance of up to £11.95 a week, depending on the age when incapacity began, may be paid, but this is offset by any entitlement to an additional invalidity pension.

Severe Disablement Allowance

A severe disablement allowance of £33.70 plus an age-related addition of up to £11.95 a week may be payable to people under pensionable age who are unable to work and do not qualify for the National Insurance invalidity pension because they have not paid sufficient contributions. Additions for adult dependants and for children may also be paid.

Industrial Injuries Disablement Benefits

Various benefits are payable for disablement caused by an accident at work or a prescribed disease. The main benefit is industrial injuries disablement benefit; disablement benefit of up to £91.60 a week is usually paid after a qualifying period of 15 weeks if a person is 14 per cent or more physically or mentally disabled as a result of an industrial accident or a prescribed disease. During the qualifying period statutory sick pay or sickness benefit may be payable if the person is incapable of work. The degree of disablement is assessed by an adjudicating medical authority and the amount paid depends on the extent of the disablement and how long it is expected to last. Except for certain progressive respiratory diseases, disablement of less than 14 per cent does not attract disablement benefit. In certain circumstances disablement benefits may be supplemented by a constant attendance allowance. An additional allowance may be payable in certain cases of exceptionally severe disablement.

Other Benefits

Disability living allowance (which replaced attendance allowance for people disabled before the age of 65, and mobility allowance) was introduced in 1992. It is a tax-free benefit with two components for people under the age of 65 who need help with personal care or with mobility. The care component has three weekly rates— £44.90, £30 and £11.95. The mobility component has two rates—£31.40 and £11.95.

An independent organisation called

Motability helps disabled drivers and passengers wanting to use the higher mobility component to obtain a vehicle or wheelchair.

A non-contributory, tax-free *attendance allowance* of £30 or £44.90 a week may be payable to people severely disabled at or after age 65, depending upon the amount of attention they require. The higher rate of attendance allowance and/or disability living allowance is paid to people who are terminally ill.

A non-contributory *invalid care allowance* of £33.70 weekly may be payable to people between 16 and pensionable age who cannot take up a paid job because they are caring for a person receiving either the higher or middle rate of disability living allowance care component or attendance allowance; an additional carer's premium may be paid if the recipient is also receiving income support, housing benefit or council tax benefit. It is estimated that some 1.4 million adults in Great Britain care for a disabled person for at least 20 hours a week.

Disability working allowance is a new income-related tax-free benefit introduced in 1992. It provides help for some disabled people aged 16 or over who are working at least 16 hours a week but have a mental or physical illness which puts them at a disadvantage in getting work. Awards are for fixed periods of six months. To qualify a person must be receiving disability living allowance or have recently received a long-term incapacity benefit or a disability premium with an income-related benefit. The rate payable depends on the person's income and size of family.

Unemployment Benefit

Unemployment benefit of £44.65 a week for a single person or £72.20 for a couple is payable for up to a year in any one period of unemployment. Periods covered by unemployment or sickness benefit, maternity allowance or some training allowances which are eight weeks or less apart, are linked to form a single period of interruption of work. Everyone claiming unemployment benefit has to be available for work, but unemployed people wishing to do voluntary work in the community may do so in some cases without losing entitlement to benefit. People seeking unemployment benefit are expected to look for work actively and must have good reasons for rejecting any job that is offered.

Income Support

Although about half of fresh claims from unemployed people result in payment of unemployment benefit (see above), a large proportion of those on the unemployment register at any one time rely partly or wholly on income support. This is either because they have not paid sufficient contributions to qualify for unemployment benefit, or because their entitlement to it has run out, or because they are entitled to income support as well as unemployment benefit.

Income support is payable to people who are not in work, or who work for less than 16 hours a week, and whose financial resources are below certain set levels. It consists of a personal allowance ranging from £26.45 weekly for a single person or lone parent aged under 18 to £69 for a couple, at least one of whom is aged over 18. Additional sums, known as premiums, are available to families, lone parents, pensioners, long-term sick and disabled people, and those caring for them who qualify for the invalid care allowance.

The income support scheme sets a limit to the amount of capital a person may have and still remain entitled. People with savings or capital worth more than £8,000 are ineligible; savings between £3,000 and £8,000 will reduce the amount received.

Housing Benefit

The housing benefit scheme assists people who need help to pay their rent (rent and/or domestic rates in Northern Ireland), using general assessment rules and benefit levels similar to those for the income support scheme. People whose net income is below certain specified levels may receive housing benefit equivalent to 100 per cent of their rent.

As with income support (see above), the housing benefit scheme sets a limit of

£8,000 on the amount of capital a person may have and still remain entitled.

Council Tax Benefit

Council tax benefit, which replaced community charge benefit in Great Britain in April 1993, helps people to meet their council tax payments. The scheme offers help to those claiming income support and others with low incomes. Subject to rules broadly similar to those governing the provision of income support and housing benefit (see p. 396), people may receive rebates of up to 100 per cent of their council tax. A person who is liable for the council tax may also claim benefit (called 'second adult rebate') for a second adult who is not liable to pay the council tax and who is living in the home on a non-commercial basis.

Family Credit

Family credit is payable to employed and self-employed working families with children on modest incomes. It is payable to couples or lone parents. At least one parent must work for a minimum of 16 hours a week. The amount payable depends on a family's net income (excluding child benefit) and the number and ages of the children in the family. A maximum award, consisting of an adult rate of £42.50 weekly, plus a rate for each child varying with age, is payable if the family's net income does not exceed £69 a week. The award is reduced by 70 pence for each pound by which net income exceeds this amount. Family credit is not payable if a family's capital or savings exceed £8,000.

Social Fund

Discretionary payments, in the form of loans or grants, may be available to people on low incomes for expenses which are difficult to meet from their regular income. There are three types:

budgeting loans to help meet important occasional expenses;

crisis loans for help in an emergency or a disaster; and

- community care grants to help people re-establish themselves or remain in the community and to ease exceptional pressure on families.

The total discretionary budget of £340 million for 1993–94 is almost 12 per cent higher than in the previous year.

Payments are also made from the social fund to help with the costs of maternity or funerals or with heating during very cold weather. These payments are regulated and are not subject to the same budgetary considerations as other social fund payments.

War Pensions and Related Services

Pensions are payable for disablement or death as a result of service in the armed forces or for certain injuries received in the merchant navy or civil defence during war, or to civilians injured by enemy action. The amount paid depends on the degree of disablement: the maximum disablement pension for a private soldier is £97.20 a week.

There are a number of extra allowances. The main ones are for unemployability, restricted mobility, the need for constant attendance, the provision of extra comforts, and as maintenance for a lowered standard of occupation. An age allowance of between £6.50 and £20 is payable weekly to war pensioners aged 65 or over whose disablement is assessed at 40 per cent or more. Pensions are also paid to war widows and other dependants. (The standard rate of pension for a private's widow is £72.90 a week.)

The Department of Social Security maintains a welfare service for war pensioners, war widows and other dependants. It works closely with ex-Service organisations and other voluntary bodies which give financial aid and personal support to those disabled or bereaved as a result of war.

Concessions

Other benefits for which unemployed people and those on low incomes may be eligible include exemption from health service

Table 26.2: Tax Liability of Social Security Benefits

Not Taxable	Taxable
Attendance allowance	Income support paid to
Child benefit	unemployed people
Child's special allowance	Industrial death benefit
Disability living allowance	pensions
Disability working allowance	Invalid care allowance
Family credit	Retirement pension
Guardian's allowance	Statutory maternity pay
Housing benefit	Statutory sick pay
Income support [a]	Unemployment benefit
Industrial disablement benefit	Widowed mother's allowance
Invalidity benefit	Widow's pension
Maternity allowance	
One-parent benefit	
Severe disablement allowance	
Sickness benefit	
Social fund payments	
War widow's pension	

[a] Income support is taxable when paid to unemployed people who have to sign on, or to strikers or those directly interested in a trade dispute.

charges (see p. 368), grants towards the cost of spectacles, free school meals and free legal aid.

Reduced charges are often made to unemployed people, for example, for adult education and exhibitions, and pensioners usually enjoy reduced transport fares.

Taxation

The general rule is that benefits which replace lost earnings are subject to tax, while those intended to meet a specific need are not (see Table 26.2). Various income tax reliefs and exemptions are allowed on account of age or a need to support dependants.

ARRANGEMENTS WITH OTHER COUNTRIES

As part of the European Community's efforts to promote the free movement of labour, regulations provide for equality of treatment and the protection of benefit rights for employed and self-employed people who move between member states. The regulations also cover retirement pensioners and other beneficiaries who have been employed, or self-employed, as well as dependants. Benefits covered include child benefit and those for sickness and maternity, unemployment, retirement, invalidity, accidents at work and occupational diseases.

Britain also has reciprocal social security agreements with a number of other countries, which also provide cover for some National Insurance benefits and family benefits.

At the end of 1991 over 600,000 British national insurance pensions were paid overseas, at a cost of some £675 million during 1991–92.

Further Reading

Social Welfare. Aspects of Britain series, HMSO, 1993.

27 Education

Some 9 million pupils attend Britain's 34,600 state[1] and private schools and are taught by just over half a million teachers. The average pupil–teacher ratio is about 17:1, compared with 22:1 in 1970–71. The proportion of young people entering higher education in universities and colleges rose from one in eight in 1980 to one in five by 1990. It is now over one in four and is expected to reach one in three by the year 2000 (over two in five in Scotland). Continuing education for adults is provided by further education institutions, adult colleges and centres, and by universities, which have seen an increase in older students in recent years.

INTRODUCTION

History

Although government grants for education were first made in 1833, it was the 1870 Education Act in England and Wales which originally enshrined the idea of compulsory elementary education with government aid. There were two types of elementary school— church voluntary schools and state schools provided by school boards. Attendance at school became compulsory in 1880 for children aged between five and ten and the school leaving age was progressively raised to 14 by 1918.

A co-ordinated national system of education was introduced for the first time by the 1902 Education Act, under which local government became responsible for state education and for helping to finance the voluntary schools. The system was supervised by the Board of Education.

In 1944 a new Education Act raised the school leaving age to 15 and schools were divided into primary and secondary schools. All children were given a secondary education and the newly created Ministry of Education was empowered to develop a national education policy. Local government remained responsible for administering the system. Children were allocated to different secondary schools on the basis of selection tests taken at the age of 11. In the 1960s and 1970s this system was gradually replaced by comprehensive schools taking pupils of all abilities. The school leaving age was raised to 16 in 1972–73.

In Scotland an Act passed in 1872 transferred responsibility for education from the churches to elected school boards which provided education for children between the ages of 5 and 13. In 1901 the school leaving age was raised to 14. An Act passed in 1918 replaced the boards by local government authorities and made the provision of secondary education mandatory for all children wanting it. Church schools were

---

For ease of reference the term 'state school' is used to cover all types of school maintained from public funds.

399

transferred to education authorities, while preserving their denominational character. The school leaving age was raised to 15 in 1947 and to 16 in 1972–73.

Education in Northern Ireland was brought into a single system by legislation passed in 1923 under which local government took over responsibility for its administration, supervised by the Ministry of Education. Secondary education remained largely in the hands of voluntary bodies, with assistance provided from public funds. Education was made compulsory for pupils between the ages of 5 and 14. The school leaving age was raised to 15 in 1947 and to 16 in 1972–73. In the 1970s responsibility for the education system was transferred to five area education and library boards.

During the 1970s concern arose about the quality of education provided by Britain's schools and the lack of a formal national school curriculum. As a result the three education systems are undergoing the most far-reaching reforms since 1945.

Administration

The Secretary of State for Education has overall responsibility for school and post-school education in England. The Secretaries of State for Scotland, Wales and Northern Ireland exercise similar responsibilities in their countries.

The government education departments are the Department for Education in England, the Welsh Office Education Department, The Scottish Office Education Department and the Department of Education for Northern Ireland. They formulate education policies and are also responsible for the supply and training of teachers.

Most publicly financed school education is the responsibility of local education authorities (LEAs) which are part of the elected local government system; the rest is provided by self-governing grant-maintained state schools (see p. 402). In Northern Ireland the education service is administered locally by five education and library boards.

LEAs pay teachers and other staff, provide and maintain buildings and supply equipment and materials. Governing bodies in self-governing state schools are responsible for these functions. In England and Wales LEAs award grants to students progressing to further and higher education.

Post-school education establishments— universities, other higher education colleges and further education institutions—are self-governing.

Finance

Estimated spending on education in Britain in 1991–92 was £29,300 million. There are three separate elements of general government expenditure on education:

- Central government in England and Wales is responsible for direct funding of parts of the education service; most of this is devoted to further and higher education and allocated by the various funding councils (see p. 401). The Government also funds directly the current and capital costs of self-governing state schools and of city technology colleges (see p. 404).

- The second element is central government grants supporting expenditure made by LEAs on projects of particular importance to the Government. Projects assisted include the National Curriculum (see p. 408), local management of schools, teacher recruitment, support for information technology and health education in schools. Grants are made to self-governing state schools to support similar activities. Finance also goes to inner city schools facing particularly severe problems. In 1993–94 some £195 million is being allocated towards expenditure of £320 million in England.

- Additional direct grants are made for capital expenditure at voluntary-aided schools and in support of capital expenditure on schools by LEAs. These are also used to reimburse LEAs for expenditure on mandatory student grants (see p. 416).

LEAs in England and Wales are responsible for the remaining educational expenditure, most of which goes to schools; a large amount of this is indirectly funded by the Government through the Revenue Support Grant made to local government councils by the Department of the Environment. Councils are free to decide how much of this grant should be distributed to education and the other services for which they have responsibility.

The rest of local authority expenditure on education is met by local taxes and by the non-domestic rates paid by business and commerce. Local authorities are accountable to their electorates for spending decisions. Most schools are responsible for their budgets under schemes of devolved local management (see p. 402).

In Scotland education is financed on a similar basis.

In Northern Ireland the costs of the education and library boards are met in full by the Department of Education.

The Departments of Employment and of Trade and Industry also fund educational programmes; the former, for example, finances the Technical and Vocational Education Initiative (see p. 412) and Compacts (see p. 412).

Higher and Further Education

Higher education is largely financed by public funds, tuition fees for students paid through the awards system and income charged by institutions for research and other purposes.

Government finance for universities and other higher education institutions in England, Scotland and Wales is distributed by higher education funding councils in these countries. In Northern Ireland grant is paid directly to the universities by the Department of Education, following advice from the Northern Ireland Higher Education Funding Council. The private University of Buckingham receives no public grant.

In addition to teaching students, universities and other higher education institutions undertake training, research, or consultancy for commercial firms. The Government is encouraging them to secure a larger flow of funds from these sources. Many educational establishments have endowments or receive grants from foundations and benefactors.

The Government reimburses in full the amount spent by local authorities on mandatory student grants and fees (see p. 416).

Further education colleges are self-governing institutions, government funds being distributed to them by further education funding councils in England and Wales. The Scottish Office Education Department distributes funds to colleges in Scotland. In Northern Ireland further education colleges are financed by the Department of Education.

SCHOOLS

Parents are required by law to see that their children receive efficient full-time education, at school or elsewhere, between the ages of 5 and 16 in Great Britain and 4 and 16 in Northern Ireland. About 93 per cent of pupils receive free education financed from public funds, while the others attend independent schools paid for by fees from parents.

Boys and girls are taught together in most primary schools. More than 80 per cent of pupils in state secondary schools in England and Wales and about 66 per cent in Northern Ireland attend mixed schools. In Scotland nearly all secondary schools are mixed. Most independent schools (see p. 406) for younger children are co-educational; the majority providing secondary education are single-sex, although the number of mixed schools is growing.

School Management

England and Wales

There are three kinds of state school which are wholly or mainly supported from public funds:

- county schools are owned and funded by LEAs;
- voluntary schools, mostly established by religious denominations, are also financed by public funds, the governors of some types of voluntary school contributing to capital costs; and
- self-governing grant-maintained state schools (see p. 402).

Each LEA maintained county and voluntary school has a governing body which includes governors appointed by the LEA, elected teacher and parent representatives and people co-opted from the local community. Voluntary schools also have governors from the church associated with the school. The Government provides information to governors about education legislation. Many large firms recognise that school governorship is an important part of the links between business/commerce and the education system; they therefore give governors time off with pay during working hours.

By April 1994 all county and voluntary schools will be responsible for managing their budgets. In April 1991, 40 per cent of these schools in England had delegated budgets and this had risen to almost 70 per cent by April 1992. Under these arrangements, LEAs allocate funds—largely on the basis of pupil numbers—to the schools. The school governing body then becomes responsible for managing the school budget and for most aspects of staffing, including numbers, appointments and dismissals. From April 1994 LEAs will be funding special schools (see p. 405) by means of a formula designed to give the schools full control over their budgets.

Self-governing (Grant-maintained) State Schools

The Government expects that more of state schools will become self-governing, following an affirmative ballot by parents of the children in the school. Some 15 per cent of secondary schools in England are self-governing state schools.

The governing body for these schools consists of parents, teachers and people from the community served by the school. The five parent governors are elected by the parents of pupils at the school and the one or two teacher governors by the school's teachers. Governors take all decisions about school management, employ and pay staff, are responsible for school premises and may acquire or dispose of land.

Under the 1993 Education Act, a new statutory body, the Funding Agency for Schools, is being set up to calculate and pay grant to self-governing schools from public funds and be responsible for financial monitoring. LEAs will continue to be responsible for funding those state schools which do not become self-governing.

Once 10 per cent of pupils in either the primary or secondary schools in an LEA are being educated in self-governing schools, the Funding Agency will take responsibility, in tandem with the LEA, for provision of enough primary or secondary places in that sector. When 75 per cent of either primary or secondary children are educated in self-governing schools, the Agency will take full responsibility for providing school places in that sector.

Scotland

In Scotland most schools supported from public funds are provided by education authorities and are known as public schools. School boards play a significant part in the administration and management of these schools. The boards consist of elected parent and staff members as well as co-opted members. The Government has issued guidelines under which schemes of devolved management will be in place in primary and secondary schools by April 1996 and in special schools by April 1997.

Parents of children at public schools can opt for self-governing status following approval by a ballot; such schools receive funding directly from central government instead of the local education authority.

Northern Ireland

The main categories of school supported by public funds are:
- controlled schools, provided by the education and library boards and managed through boards of governors;
- maintained schools, managed by boards of governors with overall general management from the Council for Catholic Maintained Schools;
- voluntary grammar schools, which may be under Roman Catholic management or non-denominational boards of governors; and

- grant-maintained integrated schools, taking Protestant and Roman Catholic pupils.

All publicly financed schools include elected parents and teachers on their boards of governors.

Although all schools must be open to pupils of all religions, most Roman Catholic pupils attend Catholic maintained schools or Catholic voluntary grammar schools and most Protestant children are enrolled at controlled schools or non-denominational voluntary grammar schools.

The Council for Catholic Maintained Schools has responsibility for maintained schools under Roman Catholic management. Its main objective is to promote high standards of education in these schools. The Council's membership consists of trustees appointed by the Northern Irish bishops, of people appointed by the Department of Education in consultation with the bishops, and of parents and teachers.

The Government has a statutory duty to encourage integrated education as a way of breaking down sectarian barriers. There are 21 integrated schools, with 3,500 pupils.

New integrated schools receive immediate government funding. Existing controlled, maintained and voluntary grammar schools can also apply to become integrated following a majority vote by parents. There are two categories of integrated schools. Grant-maintained integrated status can be applied for by new and independent schools as well as those already receiving public funds. Once approved by a ballot of parents, the school is funded directly by the Department of Education and run by a board of governors. Controlled integrated status can be sought by voluntary and controlled schools; education and library boards can also apply to set up such schools. The boards provide funding for and supervise controlled integrated schools.

Secondary school governors have delegated responsibility for managing school budgets and staff numbers. Primary and nursery school governors have delegated responsibility for managing non-staff costs only.

Nursery and Primary Schools

Although there is no statutory requirement to educate under-fives, successive governments have enabled nursery education to expand. One-half of three- and four-year-olds receive education in nursery schools or classes or in infants' classes in primary schools; part-time pupils make up nearly half of under-fives in education. In addition, many children attend pre-school playgroups, most of which are organised by parents and incorporated in the Pre-School Playgroups Association.

Compulsory education begins at five in Great Britain and four in Northern Ireland, when children go to infant schools or departments; at seven many go on to junior schools or departments. The usual age for transfer from primary to secondary schools is 11 in England, Wales and Northern Ireland, but some local authorities in England have established first schools for pupils aged 5 to 8, 9 or 10, and middle schools for age-ranges between 8 and 14. In Scotland primary schools take children from 5 to 12, when they transfer to secondary schools.

Secondary Schools

Around nine-tenths of the state secondary school population in Great Britain attend comprehensive schools. These take pupils without reference to ability or aptitude and provide a wide range of secondary education for all or most of the children in a district. English and Welsh schools can be organised in a number of ways. They include:

- those that take the full secondary school age-range from 11 to 18;
- middle schools (see above); and
- schools with an age-range of 11 or 12 to 16, combined with a sixth-form or a tertiary college for pupils over 16.

Sixth-form colleges are schools which may provide non-academic in addition to academic courses. Tertiary colleges offer a range of full-time and part-time vocational courses for students over 16, as well as academic courses.

Most other children attend grammar or secondary modern schools, to which they are allocated after selection procedures at the age of 11.

There are 15 city technology colleges in England and Wales. While fulfilling the National Curriculum requirements of breadth and balance, the colleges emphasise science, technology and business understanding. They are a partnership between the Government and private sponsors and are expected to find a substantial proportion of the initial capital costs.

The Government is supporting technology specialisation in over 200 secondary schools in England. These receive capital grants to help develop technology teaching with a strong vocational emphasis.

Scottish secondary education is almost completely non-selective; the majority of schools are six-year comprehensives covering the age-range 12 to 18. The Government is committed to the principle of setting up technology academies in Scotland with a role similar to that of city technology colleges.

In Northern Ireland secondary education is organised largely along selective lines, based on a system of testing. However, there are some secondary schools run on a non-selective basis.

Rights of Parents

Under the various Parents' Charters, parents must be given general information about a school through a prospectus and the school's annual report or, in Scotland, the school's handbook. They also have a statutory right to express a preference for a particular school for their child, and there is an appeal system if their choice is not met. A school's admission limits must be designed to reflect its physical capacity in order to maximise parents' chances of securing a place for their child at their preferred school.

In England and Wales parents choosing among local secondary schools have the right to see:

- comparative tables showing the latest public examination results, school by school; and
- information in each school's prospectus on public examination results, vocational qualification results, truancy rates and the destinations of school leavers.

All local secondary schools, including independent ones, in England and Wales have to be included in national tables providing information about public examination results, vocational qualification results and truancy rates. Similar information is to be published about Scottish secondary schools. Information is also given to parents on the findings of school inspection reports (see p. 411).

Under the Parents' Charter, all state schools in England and Wales have to give parents a written annual report on their child's achievements, containing details about:

- the child's progress in all subjects and activities;
- the child's general progress and attendance record;
- the results of National Curriculum assessments and of public examinations taken by the child;
- comparative results of pupils of the same age in the school and nationally; and
- information about the arrangements for discussing the report with teachers at the school.

When a pupil transfers to another school, a record of his or her academic achievements, other skills, abilities and progress in school is sent to the new school on request. Information about the pupil's latest assessments and examination results is sent automatically.

The Government is also taking steps to enable schools to inform parents in jargon-free language about their policy regarding classroom organisation, curriculum planning and teaching methods.

In Scotland guidance has been issued to education authorities and schools on reports to parents. The new report provides information about attainment in the various subjects studied. Included are teachers' comments on pupils' progress and details about steps to build on success or overcome difficulties. There is one main school report each year and one brief update report. Parents have the opportunity to respond to the report and discuss the next steps at parent/teacher meetings.

The Northern Ireland reporting system to parents is broadly similar to that in England and Wales.

Failing Schools

Proposals designed to deal with schools performing badly in England and Wales are contained in the 1993 Education Act. If school inspectors identify a school failing to give its pupils an acceptable standard of education, the LEA will be able to appoint new governors and withdraw delegated management from the school. Should these measures fail to work, central government is empowered to bring in an Education Association to put the school under new management until its performance reaches a satisfactory level. The new management will be financed from central government. After further advice from the schools inspectorate (see p. 411), the Secretary of State for Education or the Secretary of State for Wales will decide whether to end the Association's period of care for the school and to consider the school for self-governing status.

Ethnic Minority Children

Most school-aged children from ethnic minorities were born in Britain and tend to share the interests and aspirations of children in the population at large. Nevertheless, a substantial number still have particular needs arising from cultural differences, including those of language, religion and custom.

The education authorities have done much to meet these needs. English language teaching continues to receive priority, with a growing awareness of the value of bilingual support in the early primary years. Schools may teach the main ethnic minority community languages at secondary level in England and Wales as part of the National Curriculum. Emphasis has been placed on the need for schools to take account of the ethnic and cultural backgrounds of pupils, and curricula should reflect ethnic and cultural diversity. Measures have been taken to improve the achievement of ethnic minority pupils, and to prepare all children, not just those of ethnic minority origin, for living in a multi-ethnic society.

Special Educational Needs

Special educational needs comprise learning difficulties of all kinds, including mental and physical disabilities which hinder or prevent learning. In the case of children whose learning difficulties are severe or complex, LEAs are required to:

- identify, assess and secure provision for their needs; and

- give parents the right to be involved in decisions about their child's special education.

If the education authority believes that it should determine the education for the child, it must draw up a formal statement of the child's special educational needs and the action it intends to take to meet them. Parents have a right of appeal if they disagree with the contents of the statement.

Wherever possible, children with special educational needs are educated in ordinary schools, provided that the parents' wishes are taken into account. Placement in an ordinary school must be compatible with the needs of the child and with the provision of efficient education for the other children in the school.

Because of concern about the way these arrangements are working in England and Wales, the 1993 Education Act will:

- set statutory time limits within which the education authority must carry out procedures for making assessments and statements;

- require the education authority to comply with parents' choice of school unless this is inappropriate for the child or involves an inefficient use of resources; and

● establish an independent tribunal to hear appeals against education authority decisions. The tribunal's decisions will be binding on all parties to the case.

The Government is also changing the law in England and Wales to ensure that a state school named in a statement of special educational needs should be required to admit the child. The education authority will have to consult the governors before naming the school.

The Act provides for a code of practice offering practical guidance to all state schools on early action to identify, assess and monitor pupils in order to ensure that all children requiring an assessment and, later, a statement are properly safeguarded. LEAs and schools will have to take account of the code.

The 1993 Education Act also deals with pupils with special educational needs who do not have statements. All state schools will have to provide details about their policy regarding the needs of all these pupils, including assessment.

In Scotland the choice of school is a matter for agreement between education authorities and parents.

There are 1,830 special schools (both day and boarding) for pupils with special educational needs who cannot be educated at ordinary schools. Some of these are run by voluntary organisations and some are established in hospitals. They cater for about 110,800 pupils. Developments in information technology (see p. 411) are increasingly leading to better quality education for these children.

Health and Welfare of Schoolchildren

Physical education, including organised games, is part of the curriculum of all maintained schools, and playing fields must be available for pupils over the age of eight. Most secondary schools have a gymnasium.

Government health departments are responsible for the medical inspection of schoolchildren and for advice on, and treatment of, medical and dental problems associated with children of school age. The education service seeks to help prevent and

deal with juvenile drug misuse and to assist prevention of the spread of AIDS. In England and Wales government funds have supported the appointment in most LEAs of drugs and health education co-ordinators for schools, colleges and the youth service. In Scotland this is an education authority responsibility.

LEAs and self-governing state schools are responsible for providing school meals for pupils. They are free to decide the nature of the services, taking account of local circumstances. They must provide meals free of charge to pupils whose parents receive a social security benefit called income support (see p. 396). Although LEAs do not have to provide milk to any pupil, they can decide to give free milk to pupils of parents in receipt of income support.

Under certain conditions LEAs must supply free school transport and have discretionary powers to help with the cost of travel to school.

In Northern Ireland school meals must be provided for primary, special and grant-aided nursery school pupils.

Corporal punishment is prohibited by law in state schools in Britain and for pupils in independent schools whose fees are met wholly or partly from public funds.

Independent Schools

Fee-paying independent schools must register with the appropriate education department and are open to inspection. They can be required to remedy serious shortcomings in their accommodation or instruction, and to exclude anyone regarded as unsuitable to teach in or own a school. About 7 per cent of schoolchildren attend independent schools.

There are 2,447 independent schools educating 603,000 pupils of all ages. They charge fees varying from around £300 a term for day pupils at nursery age to £4,000 a term for senior boarding pupils. Many offer bursaries to help pupils from less well-off families. Such pupils may also be helped by LEAs—particularly if the authorities' own schools cannot meet the needs of individual children—or by the Government's Assisted Places Scheme, under which financial assistance is given according to parental income. Over 37,000 places are offered in England, Wales and Scotland under the scheme. The Government also gives income-related help with fees to 500 pupils at five music schools and the Royal Ballet School; in 1991 this scheme was extended to provide a limited number of scholarships at cathedral choir schools.

Independent schools range from small kindergartens to large day and boarding schools and from new and, in some cases, experimental schools to ancient foundations. The 600 boys', girls' and mixed preparatory schools prepare children for entry to senior schools. The normal age-range for these preparatory schools is from seven-plus to 11, 12 or 13, but many have pre-preparatory departments for younger children. A number of independent schools have been established by religious orders and ethnic minorities.

Independent schools for older pupils—from 11, 12 or 13 to 18 or 19—include about 550 which are often referred to as public schools. These belong to the Headmasters' Conference, the Governing Bodies Association, the Society of Headmasters and Headmistresses of Independent Schools, the Girls' Schools Association and the Governing Bodies of Girls' Schools Association.

Teachers

Teachers in state schools in England and Wales are appointed by LEAs or school governing bodies. They must hold qualifications approved by the Department for Education.

Formal teacher appraisal is being introduced in English and Welsh schools. By 1995 all teachers will have completed the first year of their two-year appraisal cycle, which is intended to assist professional development, strengthen the management of schools and improve the quality of education provided to pupils.

Consideration is being given to ways of ensuring that teachers' pay is more closely related to performance.

Almost all entrants to teaching in state schools in England and Wales complete an approved course of teacher training. These courses are offered by university departments of education as well as other higher education establishments (see p. 415).

Non-graduates usually qualify by taking a four-year Bachelor of Education (BEd) honours degree. There are also specially designed two-year BEd courses—mostly in subjects where there is a shortage of teachers at the secondary level—for suitably qualified people. Graduates normally take a one-year Postgraduate Certificate in Education (PGCE) course.

Reform of Initial Teacher Training

Under new government reforms in England and Wales, schools will play a much larger part in initial teacher training as full partners of higher education institutions. Graduates on a 36-week one-year PGCE course who wish to become secondary school teachers, for instance, will train in schools for at least 24 weeks.

The Government expects that schools will take on more responsibility for planning and managing courses and for the selection, training and assessment of students, usually in partnership with institutions. Schools will train students to teach their specialist subjects, assess pupils and manage classes; they will also supervise students and assess their competence.

Higher education institutions will be responsible for ensuring that courses meet requirements for academic validation, presenting courses for accreditation and awarding qualifications to successful students. The schools will perform this role where there is no institution partner.

Accreditation

A system of approving institutions, rather than individual courses, is being introduced; course approval will continue during the transition to the new system. Higher education institutions will have to submit a five-year development plan to the Council for the Accreditation of Teacher Education (CATE) for approval. An inspection by the schools inspectorates in England and Wales will then take place, followed by a response from the institution. CATE will consider the inspectorate's report and the response and then make a recommendation to the Secretary of State, who will take the final decision on accreditation.

Other Training

Under the Licensed Teacher Scheme, a trainee teacher is appointed to the school, which provides training and pays a salary; on completion of a two-year period of in-service training, qualified teacher status is granted.

A recent report from OFSTED (see p. 411) indicates that licensed teachers are generally achieving satisfactory levels of teaching competence.

Qualified teachers from other European Community countries are usually granted qualified teacher status.

Scotland

All teachers in education authority schools must be registered with the General Teaching Council (GTC) for Scotland. The GTC is responsible for disciplinary procedures under which teachers guilty of professional misconduct may be removed permanently or temporarily from the register. Advice is given by the GTC to the Secretary of State for Scotland on teacher supply and the professional suitability of teacher-training courses.

All entrants to the teaching profession are graduates. New primary teachers qualify either through a four-year BEd course or a one-year postgraduate course at a higher education teacher-training institution. In addition, the University of Stirling offers courses which combine academic and professional training for intending primary and secondary teachers. Teachers of academic subjects at secondary schools must hold a degree containing two passes in the subjects which they wish to teach. Secondary teachers must undertake a one-year postgraduate training course. For music and technology, four-year BEd courses are also available, and for physical education all teachers take BEd courses.

Under new guidelines on initial teacher-training courses, students on the one-year postgraduate course for secondary teachers spend 22 weeks in school during their courses. In addition, the overall school placement for the undergraduate BEd degree for primary school teachers is 30 weeks over the four-year period of the course. The one-year postgraduate course for primary teachers remains unchanged; students will continue to spend 18 weeks in school and 18 weeks in college-based study.

All new pre-service and major in-service courses provided by teacher-training institutions must be approved by The Scottish Office Education Department and a validating body.

Education authorities have developed schemes to implement national guidelines for staff development and appraisal. Schemes must ensure that all teachers have been appraised at least once by the end of the 1995–96 school session.

Northern Ireland

Teacher training is provided by Queen's University Belfast, the University of Ulster and two colleges of education. The principal courses are BEd Honours (four years) and the one-year Postgraduate Certificate of Education. Education and library boards have a statutory duty to ensure that teachers are equipped with the necessary skills to implement education reforms and the Northern Ireland Curriculum.

Curriculum

England and Wales

The Government is introducing a broad and balanced curriculum designed to meet the individual needs of pupils and to be relevant to the responsibilities and experiences of adult life.

The National Curriculum consists of the core subjects of English, mathematics and science, as well as the other foundation subjects of history, geography, technology, music, art, physical education and, for secondary school pupils, a modern foreign language. The scope of these subject areas is defined and amended through parliamentary Orders. National Curriculum subjects are being introduced progressively; by 1996–97 the entire National Curriculum will be taught to all pupils.

The National Curriculum is being reviewed to see whether it can be made more manageable.

The Government has asked primary school head teachers in England to consider possible changes in teaching methods and organisation which would allow the grouping of pupils by ability and more use of specialist subject teaching for older children.

In Wales the Welsh language constitutes a core subject in Welsh-speaking schools and a foundation subject elsewhere under the National Curriculum. The National Curriculum requirements for Welsh were introduced in 1990. Some 80 per cent of primary schools either use Welsh as a teaching medium or teach it as a second language, while nearly 90 per cent of secondary schools teach Welsh as a first or second language.

There are statutory attainment targets specifying the knowledge, skills and understanding expected of children at the ages of 7, 11, 14 and 16. National statutory assessments of pupils' performance in reaching these targets in English, mathematics and science are gradually being implemented. These are a combination of tests for pupils and assessment by teachers of their classroom work; equal status is being given to test results and teacher assessment.

From 1994 the General Certificate of Secondary Education (GCSE) will be the main means for assessing attainment of 16-year-old pupils in National Curriculum subjects. GCSE examinations are usually taken after five years of secondary education and can lead on to more advanced education and training (see p. 413). The structure of the exam is being adapted in accordance with National Curriculum requirements. The results of assessments are given to parents.

Consideration is being given to extending the study of National Curriculum subjects, particularly technology, into vocational and practical areas for 14- to 16-year-old pupils whose aptitudes lie in this direction.

Scotland

The content and management of the curriculum are the responsibility of education authorities and head teachers, though guidance is provided by the Scottish Secretary of State and the Scottish Consultative Council on the Curriculum. The Council has recommended that secondary level pupils should follow a broad and balanced curriculum consisting of English, mathematics, science, a modern European language, social studies, technological activities, art, music or drama, religious and moral education, and physical education.

A major programme of curricular review and development is in progress for the 5 to 14 age-range. The Government has issued new guidance on English language, mathematics, expressive arts, Latin, modern languages, environmental studies and religious and moral education. This is intended to help schools design, plan and implement policies and programmes which will give all pupils a balanced and worthwhile experience in these subjects. Under new arrangements, standardised tests in English and mathematics are given to primary school pupils whenever they complete one of five levels. A major programme to extend modern language teaching to primary schools is in process, including pilot studies.

Provision is made for teaching in Gaelic in Gaelic-speaking areas.

Pupils take the Scottish Certificate of Education (SCE) at Standard grade at the end of their fourth year of secondary education at the age of 16. The Higher grade is taken in the fifth and sixth year. Some pupils also sit examinations for the Certificate of Sixth Year Studies or take vocational National Certificate units (see p. 414).

Northern Ireland

The common curriculum in all publicly financed schools is based on six broad areas of study: English, mathematics, science and technology, the environment and society, creative and expressive studies, and, for secondary schools, language studies. Religious education is obligatory at all stages. The curriculum will be fully implemented by September 1994.

Attainment targets, programmes of study and methods of assessment—at ages 8, 11, 14 and 16—are specified for all compulsory subjects. The first assessments were piloted in the school year 1992–93 for pupils at the ages of 11 and 14 who had followed programmes of study in English, mathematics and science for three years. Eight-year-old pupils will be assessed on a pilot basis in 1993–94 and the first assessments for 16-year-olds will be in 1994–95. As in England and Wales, the GCSE examination will be used to assess 16-year-old pupils.

The school curriculum includes six compulsory cross-curricular themes: cultural heritage, education for mutual understanding, health education, information technology, and, in secondary schools, economic awareness and careers education. The first theme is designed to help overcome distrust between Protestants and Roman Catholics by enabling them to understand the common and distinctive elements of their cultural heritage. The second is meant to teach them how to understand the other person's point of view and appreciate the benefits of resolving conflicts by non-violent means. Pupils are studying a common history curriculum in the environment and society area of study.

Religious Education and Collective Worship in Schools

In England and Wales maintained schools must provide religious education and a daily act of collective worship. Since the 1988 Education Reform Act, some local authorities have reviewed their agreed syllabuses for religious education to take account of the fact that religious traditions in Great Britain are in the main Christian. Syllabuses, however, also cover the teachings of the other main religions represented in the country.

The Government is proposing that those authorities which have not reviewed their syllabuses should be required to do so in a specified period. Each local education authority area has a standing council which gives advice on the development of religious education.

All voluntary schools provide the opportunity for denominational religious education.

Parents have the right to withdraw their children from religious education classes and from collective worship.

Scottish education authorities are required to see that schools practise religious observance and give pupils religious instruction; parents may withdraw their children if they wish. Certain schools provide for Roman Catholic children but in all schools there are safeguards for individual conscience.

In Northern Ireland, too, schools are obliged to offer religious education and collective worship, although parents have the right to withdraw their children from both. In controlled schools clergy have a right of access which may be used for denominational instruction. In voluntary schools collective worship and religious education are controlled by the management authorities. It is intended that religious education will have an agreed core syllabus which grant-aided schools can expand according to their own needs and wishes.

Curriculum Development and Assessment

In England the School Curriculum and Assessment Authority is responsible for:

- reviewing the school curriculum;
- advising the Government on content;
- carrying out programmes of research and development; and
- publishing information about the curriculum.

All GCSE and other qualifications offered to pupils of compulsory school age in state schools in England and Wales must be approved by the Government. Associated syllabuses and assessment procedures must comply with national guidelines and be approved by the Authority. The aim is to secure a reasonably wide choice of qualifications and syllabuses which support the National Curriculum.

The Authority will keep under review all aspects of examinations and assessment and will maintain links with the Curriculum and Assessment Authority for Wales.

In Scotland curriculum development is undertaken by the Scottish Consultative Council on the Curriculum. The Scottish Examination Board liaises with the Council on links between the curriculum and assessment.

Northern Ireland has two organisations, one responsible for the curriculum and the other for assessment. Both will be replaced in April 1994 by the Northern Ireland Council for Curriculum, Examinations and Assessment.

Information Technology

The National Curriculum places a strong emphasis on the use of information technology (IT) to enhance teaching and learning and ensure that all children are well versed in the new technologies. In England the average number of pupils per microcomputer in primary schools is 25, compared with 107 in 1984-85. The figure for secondary schools is 13, compared with 60 in 1984-85. Two-thirds of secondary schools use central computing facilities. In Wales the average number of pupils per microcomputer in primary schools went down from 68 to 34 between 1988 and 1991; in secondary schools over the same period the average number decreased from 30 to 14.

Department for Education grants are available to increase microcomputer provision, help secondary schools buy CD-ROM (compact disc—read only memory) drives and discs, and continue the programme of teacher training in the effective use of IT.

The Government also helps finance the National Council for Educational Technology, which encourages the use of microcomputers, electronic systems and other aspects of IT in education and training. The corresponding body in Scotland is the Scottish Council for Educational Technology.

Other government projects include funding for:

- the development of CD-ROM discs to support the National Curriculum;

- help for teacher-training institutions to purchase CD-ROM drives and discs;

- investigating the potential of interactive multimedia technology as a teaching aid and assessing its full use for curriculum development in schools; and

- assessing the value of portable computers and calculators in schools and the implication for teacher training.

In Wales the Welsh Office has financed the provision of satellite receiving equipment for secondary schools throughout the country.

In Northern Ireland, IT is one of the six compulsory educational themes forming part of the curriculum for all pupils of statutory school age in grant-aided schools.

Other Educational Aids

Teachers and pupils use a range of other aids in the classroom. Most schools have audio-visual equipment such as slide projectors and overhead projectors. The BBC (British Broadcasting Corporation) and the independent broadcasting companies transmit radio and television programmes designed for schools. Teachers' notes, pupils' pamphlets and computer software accompany many broadcast series.

The government-funded National Educational Resources Information Service enables schools to find out about teaching aids.

School Inspections

Various inspectorates report to the Government on the quality of education provided by schools.

In England the independent Office for Standards in Education (OFSTED) advises the Education Secretary on quality, standards and efficiency in school education and regulates a new system of school inspections. The inspection cycle began in

September 1993 for secondary schools and will start in September 1994 for primary and other schools.

Every school has to be inspected by a team of independent inspectors—headed by a registered inspector—containing educationists and lay people. Inspections take place according to agreed national standards monitored by OFSTED. Some 6,000 schools in England will be examined annually over a four-year period and this work will continue in four-yearly cycles. Parents are sent a summary of the full inspection report, which is published. School governing bodies have to prepare action plans to follow it up and then report back to parents on their progress.

OFSTED is headed by Her Majesty's Chief Inspector of Schools.

In 1992 a new and independent office of Her Majesty's Chief Inspector of Schools for Wales was established with similar functions to those of OFSTED. All schools will be inspected on a regular cycle, set at five years in the first instance.

In Scotland HM Schools Inspectorate is responsible for independent and objective evaluation of education standards and for advising the Scottish Secretary. During inspections, the views and concerns of parents are ascertained so that these can be taken into account by the inspectors. Full reports on inspections are published and a short summary given to parents. From 1994–95, each inspection team will contain lay people. The Inspectorate's Audit Unit collects, analyses and publishes evidence about the performance of schools and education authorities. Evidence is published on a comparative basis and recommendations are made for action and improvement.

School inspections in Northern Ireland are carried out by the Education and Training Inspectorate. The Government is planning to introduce from September 1993 a cycle of school inspections so that each school will be inspected every five years.

Schools, Careers and Business

One of the Government's key objectives is to help young people achieve their full potential and develop the skills the economy needs.

This requires close working relationships between industry and education.

The Technical and Vocational Education Initiative (TVEI), applicable in England, Scotland and Wales, is designed to ensure that the school curriculum for 14- to 18-year-olds is made more relevant to adult and working life in a modern technological society. It is financed and administered by central government, working in close co-operation with LEAs. Over 1 million students are benefiting from TVEI in England.

Education Business Partnerships, consisting of representatives from industry, education and the wider community, aim to bring about closer links between education and industry and ensure that young people develop the skills and attitudes to help them succeed in the labour market. They are supported by Training and Enterprise Councils (see p. 143) and LEAs.

One of the main schemes managed by the Partnerships is the Teacher Placement Service (TPS), funded by the Department of Employment. The objective of the TPS is to organise placements in business for teachers each year in order to extend their professional and personal development, improve learning opportunities for young people, and provide better careers education services. Since 1989 some 90,000 teachers have been on placements.

Compacts bring together employers, young people, schools, colleges and other bodies involved in training in order to help young people achieve more at school and continue education and training after the age of 16. Under Compact schemes young people agree to work towards agreed goals; in return for achieving them, employers provide a number of incentives including, in inner city areas, a job with training or training leading to a job.

Careers

Careers guidance helps individuals achieve their potential and closer links are being nurtured between schools and employers. LEAs are currently responsible for the Careers Service. This responsibility is being passed to central government under the 1993 Education Act. Once the change takes effect, the Government will be able to contract a range of organisations to provide a Careers Service which will be more responsive to the needs and demands of local communities.

Careers services in schools and colleges are supported by materials produced by the Careers and Occupational Information Centre.

In Northern Ireland careers education is one of the six compulsory education themes forming part of the school curriculum.

All state secondary schools in England and Wales have to provide leavers with a National Record of Achievement setting out their school attainments, including public examination and National Curriculum assessment results. The Record is designed to give people a simple record of achievement in education and training throughout working life. In Scotland the record is not compulsory but it is available to all education authorities for issue to school leavers.

In Northern Ireland all pupils are issued with a record of achievement on leaving primary and secondary education.

POST-COMPULSORY EDUCATION

Post-compulsory education takes place in school sixth forms, sixth form colleges, further education colleges, universities and other higher education institutions.

Recent reforms in England, Wales and Scotland have ended the distinction between universities, polytechnics and other higher education establishments. The present close relationship with Northern Ireland's existing unitary structure will continue. Degree-awarding powers have been extended to major institutions and there are new quality assurance arrangements. All the former polytechnics and one college have become universities.

In 1991–92 there were some 5.3 million people in Britain in post-compulsory education—547,000 in schools, 3.6 million in further education and 1.2 million in higher education.

In the 1980s the number of part-time students in universities, including the Open University (see p. 417), rose by 47 per cent and in the former polytechnics and colleges by 50 per cent.

By the mid-1990s, every 16- and 17-year-old leaving full-time education in Great Britain will be encouraged to undertake vocational education or training by the offer of a Youth Credit (see p. 128), enabling them to buy training from the establishment of their choice.

Credit accumulation and transfer schemes are in use in many English and Welsh post-school establishments. In Scotland a credit accumulation scheme covers courses in all further and higher education. Opportunities for further and higher education and training are publicised by national information services, such as the Educational Counselling and Credit Transfer Information Service, which is funded by the Department for Education.

In September 1993 the Government published charters for the users of further and higher education in England, chiefly students, parents and employers. These set out the standards of service which users should expect, including information about courses, financial support for students and complaints procedures if things go wrong. A similar charter has been published in Scotland.

Schools and Sixth-form Colleges

Having taken the GCSE examination (see p. 409) at the age of 16, students in England, Wales and Northern Ireland can stay on at school or, in the case of England and Wales, be educated in a sixth-form college. They study for examinations which are the main standard for entry to higher education or professional training. These include the academic General Certificate of Education (GCE) Advanced (A) level, an examination which is taken at the age of 18 or 19 after two years' study; part of the qualification is based on course work and the rest on written test papers. Advanced Supplementary (AS) levels enable sixth-form pupils to study a wider range of subjects. Students specialising in the arts and humanities, for example, can continue to study mathematics and technological subjects at the new level.

Requiring the same standard of work as A levels, an AS level occupies half the teaching and study time of an A level.

The Government is promoting equality of status for academic and vocational qualifications in England, Wales and Northern Ireland. For example, it is developing a system of new General National Vocational Qualifications (GNVQs) for young people in full-time education between the ages of 16 and 18. These provide a broad-based preparation for a range of occupations and higher education and are designed to have parity of esteem with GCE A levels. There are three GNVQ levels—Advanced, Intermediate and Foundation. An Advanced GNVQ, called the 'vocational A level', requires a level of achievement equal to two GCE A levels. Young people will be able to choose a combination of GCE A levels and GNVQ Advanced level.

Students wishing to continue in full-time education for a year after the age of 16 can study courses leading to the City and Guilds Diploma of Vocational Education.

Scotland

Pupils staying on at school after the end of compulsory education study for the Higher Grade Scottish Certificate of Education exam at the age of 16–18; passes at this grade are the basis for entry to higher education or professional training. However, entry is becoming more flexible as wider access to under-represented groups with non-standard qualifications is encouraged. The Certificate of Sixth Year Studies (CSYS) is for pupils who have completed their Higher grade main studies and who wish to continue studies in particular subjects.

A flexible system of vocational courses for 16- to 18-year-olds has been introduced in schools and colleges in disciplines such as business and administration, engineering and industrial production. These courses are also intended to meet the needs of many adults entering training or returning to education. The courses lead to the award of the non-advanced National Certificate, intended for students over 16 who have successfully completed a programme of vocational courses

based on short study units. Similar unit-based courses are also available at advanced levels.

General Scottish Vocational Qualifications (General SVQs) are designed to meet the needs of 16- to 19-year-olds at school or in further education colleges. Similar to the GNVQs in the rest of Britain, General SVQs are designed as a stepping-stone to higher education or further training.

Further Education

People over the age of 16 can also take courses in further education institutions. These cover courses up to and including GCE A level or GNVQ Advanced level. Much further education is work-related and vocational. The system is flexible and enables the student to acquire qualifications according to his or her abilities. Further education institutions supply much of the education element in government-sponsored training programmes such as Youth Training and Training for Work (see Chapter 11).

Many students on further education courses attend part time, either by day release or block release from employment or during the evenings. The system has strong ties with commerce and industry, and co-operation with business is encouraged by the Government and its agencies. Employers are normally involved in designing courses.

Courses are run by over 500 institutions of further education, many of which also offer higher education courses (see p. 415). In England, Wales and Scotland each is controlled by an autonomous further education corporation and governing body with substantial representation from business. Funds are allocated to institutions by further education funding councils in England and Wales; part of the funding is not cash limited and is directly related to student numbers. The councils have appointed quality assurance committees to help them assess the quality of education provided.

In Scotland funds are distributed to colleges by The Scottish Office Education Department.

Institutions are obliged to publish information about the way they use their financial and other resources. Expenditure plans provide for a record 25 per cent rise in full-time equivalent student numbers in England and a 28 per cent rise in Wales over the three-year period from 1993–94.

Vocational Qualifications

In the past the nature and standing of the many vocational qualifications were unclear and uncertain. The system was also difficult to understand for employers and those seeking training.

The National Council for Vocational Qualifications (NCVQ) is simplifying the system by establishing a new framework of National Vocational Qualifications (NVQs) in England, Wales and Northern Ireland. These are based on national standards defining the competence, knowledge and understanding that employers need. Awarding bodies have been reforming their qualifications for accreditation by the National Council.

The following five levels of NVQs have been established:

Level 1—Foundation
Level 2—Basic craft
Level 3—Technician, advanced craft, supervisor
Level 4—Higher technician, junior management
Level 5—Professional, middle management.

NVQs are made up of units. Performance of candidates is assessed in workplace conditions and the NVQ is a guarantee of competence to do a particular job. NVQs are designed mainly for people in work, although they can also be studied in colleges and some schools.

By the end of 1992, the NCVQ had accredited NVQs covering 83 per cent of the workforce at levels 1 to 4. The Government wants 50 per cent of young people to have reached NVQ level 3 by the year 2000.

In Scotland there is a similar system of Scottish Vocational Qualifications (SVQs), which are accredited and awarded by the Scottish Vocational Education Council (see below).

NVQs and SVQs have equal recognition throughout Britain. The General NVQ and General SVQ system for full-time students in education is described on p. 414.

Examining Bodies

About 90 per cent of vocational qualifications in England, Wales and Northern Ireland are assessed by three examining bodies and accredited by the NCVQ.

The Business and Technology Education Council (BTEC) plans and administers a unified national system of courses at all levels; the most popular subjects are business, engineering and construction.

The City and Guilds of London Institute provides mostly part-time qualifications in areas such as engineering, construction, catering, hairdressing and community care.

The RSA Examinations Board is the largest provider of information technology qualifications throughout Britain and offers NVQs in areas ranging from management/customer service to retailing and wholesaling.

Other vocational qualifications are awarded by a large number of professional bodies.

The Scottish Vocational Education Council (SCOTVEC) is the main accreditation and awarding body in Scotland.

Higher Education

Higher education consists of degree and other courses of a standard higher than the GCE A level or its equivalent. These include the four-year BEd courses for trainee teachers (see p. 407). The Government wishes to see an increase in the proportion of students in engineering and technology and on sub-degree courses such as two-year full-time vocational diplomas.

Access and foundation courses provide a preparation and an appropriate test before enrolment on a course of higher education for prospective students who do not possess the standard entry qualifications (GCE 'A' levels and equivalent qualifications). Many are from the ethnic minority communities. The growth of access courses has been very rapid in recent years; about 600 are now available nationwide.

The Scottish Wider Access Programme (SWAP) is designed to promote greater participation in higher education, especially by mature students and those without the normal entry requirements. Successful completion of a SWAP course guarantees a higher education place.

> Some 30 per cent of first-year undergraduate students in 1991 were aged 21 or over.

In order to maintain British expertise in technology, recent government schemes have sought to expand higher education and research in electronics, engineering and computer science by making available extra student places, and additional staff and research fellowships. A Graduate Enterprise Programme offers 450 places on management training courses for recently qualified graduates.

The Higher Education Quality Council, financed by subscriptions from universities and higher education colleges, is responsible for ensuring that institutions provide high-quality education.

The various higher education funding councils have responsibility for financing teaching, research and related activities in all publicly funded universities and colleges of higher education (see below).

Student Grants and Loans

Over 90 per cent of full-time students resident in England and Wales on first degree and other comparable higher education courses are eligible for mandatory awards covering tuition fees and maintenance. Contributions from parents are assessed according to their income. Awards are made by LEAs in England and Wales. Grants for other courses are given at the discretion of an LEA. Similar schemes are administered by The Scottish Office Education Department and the Northern Ireland education and library boards.

Grants for postgraduate study are offered by the government education departments and by the research councils (see Chapter 19). Some scholarships are available from endowments and also from particular industries or companies.

Most students on courses of full-time, non-postgraduate higher education can get a top-up student loan to help pay their maintenance costs. Loans are not means tested and repayments are indexed to inflation. The scheme is designed to share the cost of student maintenance more equitably between students, parents and the taxpayer. In 1991–92 loans worth £139 million were made to 261,000 students in Britain, representing 36 per cent of those eligible. Loans are administered by the Student Loans Company in Glasgow.

Limited access funds administered by universities and colleges are available to people in cases where access to higher education might be inhibited by financial considerations or where students face real financial difficulties. In 1993–94, for example, there is provision of £23.8 million in England for this purpose.

Universities

There are 83 universities (12 in Scotland), including the Open University. They are governed by royal charters or by Act of Parliament and enjoy academic freedom. They appoint their own staff, decide which students to admit, provide their own courses and award their own degrees. The universities of Oxford and Cambridge date from the 12th and 13th centuries, and the Scottish universities of St Andrews, Glasgow, Aberdeen and Edinburgh from the 14th and 15th centuries. All the other universities in Britain were founded in the 19th and 20th centuries. The 1960s saw considerable expansion in the number of new universities. The number of universities also increased considerably in 1992, when polytechnics and some other higher education establishments were given the freedom to become universities

Applications for first degree courses are usually made through the Universities and Colleges Admission Service (UCAS) in Cheltenham. Forms are completed and received at UCAS by 15 December in the year before courses begin. UCAS then sends them to the institutions selected by the applicant. People applying for places at Oxford and Cambridge universities have to submit an additional form to the university.

First degree courses are mainly full time and usually last three years in England and

Wales. However, there are some four-year courses, and medical and veterinary courses normally require five years. All first degree courses in Scotland require four years of study. The ratio of staff to full-time students is about 1 to 12.5.

Universities offer courses in a wide range of subjects, including traditional arts subjects and science and technology. Some courses lead to the examinations of the chief professional bodies, and to qualifications such as those of the BTEC.

Many universities have close links with commerce and industry, with some students having a job and attending on a part-time basis.

Degree titles vary according to the practice of each university. In England, Wales and Northern Ireland the most common titles for a first degree are Bachelor of Arts (BA) or Bachelor of Science (BSc) and for a second degree Master of Arts (MA), Master of Science (MSc), and Doctor of Philosophy (PhD). In the older Scottish universities Master is used for a first degree in arts subjects. Uniformity of standards between universities is promoted by employing external examiners for all university examinations.

The Open University and other universities are responsible for validating degrees at higher education institutions without degree-awarding powers.

Most staff combine research with their teaching duties and about half of postgraduate students are engaged on research projects. The Government is encouraging universities to co-operate closely with industry on research. Over 40 science parks have been set up by higher education institutions in conjunction with industrial scientists and technologists to promote the development and commercial application of advanced technology.

The Open University

The Open University is a non-residential university offering degree and other courses for adult students of all ages in Britain and the other member countries of the European Community. It uses a combination of specially produced printed texts, correspondence tuition, television and radio broadcasts, audio and video cassettes, and residential schools. There is also a network of study centres for contact with part-time tutors and counsellors, and with fellow students. No formal academic qualifications are required to register for most courses, but the standards of the University's degrees are the same as those of other universities. Its first degrees are the BA (Open) or the BSc (Open), which are general degrees awarded on a system of credits for each course completed. In 1993 there were some 86,000 registered undergraduates, and in all some 122,000 first degrees have been awarded since the University started its courses in 1970.

The University has a programme of higher degrees. The Bachelor of Philosophy (BPhil), Master of Philosophy (MPhil) and PhD are research degrees and the MA, MSc and Master of Business Administration (MBA) are awarded after successful completion of taught courses. About 9,000 students were registered on higher degree courses in 1993.

There are also programmes for professionals in education and the health and social welfare services, and for updating managers, scientists and technologists. Some of these are multi-media courses taught in a similar way to those in the undergraduate programme, and others are in the form of self-contained study packs. In 1992 about 39,000 students were following courses in these areas and 82,000 study packs were sold.

The University has advised many other countries on setting up similar institutions. It has made a substantial contribution to the new Commonwealth of Learning project, which brings together distance-teaching establishments and students throughout the Commonwealth, and to the European Distance Education Network. It is financed by the higher education funding councils.

Continuing Education for Adults

Continuing education for adults is provided by further education institutions, adult colleges and centres, and by voluntary bodies such as the Workers' Educational Association. The duty to provide it is shared by the new further education funding councils and by LEAs.

In addition to cultural and craft pursuits, students follow courses leading to academic and vocational qualifications, and courses which provide access to higher education. Adults' special educational needs for literacy and numeracy are also met, and there is provision for those seeking proficiency in English as a second language.

ALBSU

The Adult Literacy and Basic Skills Unit (ALBSU) is concerned with adult literacy, numeracy and related basic skills in England and Wales. It provides consultancy and advisory services, organises staff training and produces materials for teachers and students. Government funding was worth £3.2 million in 1992–93. Another programme is Basic Skills at Work, with government funding of £3 million; it is targeted at unemployed people and those in work who cannot progress without better basic skills.

Open College

Open learning opportunities have been extended with the formation in 1987 of the Open College, an independent company set up with government support. The College brings together broadcasters, educationists and sponsors, and provides vocational education and training courses below degree level. Programmes are broadcast by independent television's Channel 4. The Open College of the Arts, also launched in 1987, offers an arts foundation course to those wishing to study at home.

National Institute of Adult Continuing Education

The National Institute of Adult Continuing Education represents adult interests in education and training in England and Wales. It is a centre for information, research, development work and publication.

Scottish Community Education Council

The Scottish Community Education Council advises the Government and promotes all community education matters, including adult literacy and basic education, and youth work.

EDUCATIONAL RESEARCH

Educational research is supported financially by government departments, the Economic and Social Research Council (see Chapter 19), philanthropic organisations, higher education institutions, teachers' associations and other agencies.

The major research institutions outside the universities are the autonomous National Foundation for Educational Research in England and Wales and the Scottish Council for Research in Education.

EDUCATIONAL LINKS OVERSEAS

Large numbers of people come to Britain from overseas to study, and British people work and train overseas. The British aid programme encourages links between educational institutions in Britain and developing countries.

There has been an expansion of interest in European studies and languages, with exchanges of teachers, schoolchildren and students taking place. Exchange of students is promoted by a European Community scheme (ERASMUS), under which grants are provided to enable Community students and those from countries belonging to the European Free Trade Association to study in other states. Over 25,000 students from Britain have benefited from the scheme.

The Community's LINGUA programme seeks to improve and widen competence in the use of foreign languages. It gives grants towards in-service training for teachers, study abroad for language students, joint educational projects and exchanges for young people undergoing professional, vocational and technical education; it also covers measures to develop language training materials for business.

The Action Programme for Education and Training for Technology (COMETT) aims to foster co-operation between higher education establishments and industry in the Community by training personnel, especially in small and medium-sized enterprises, in the application of advanced technology.

The EC's PETRA vocational training programme for young people organises training and work experience placements in other member states.

Community member states have created nine European schools, including one at Culham, Oxfordshire, to provide a multinational education for the children of staff employed in Community institutions.

Overseas Students in Britain

British universities and other further and higher education establishments have built up their strong reputation overseas by offering tuition of the highest standards, maintaining low student-to-staff ratios, and offering the most relevant courses and qualifications.

In 1991 the number of overseas students attending publicly funded universities and other post-school institutions in Great Britain was 92,100. Some 30,000 came from other EC states. About 40 per cent of all overseas students were from the Commonwealth and Britain's dependent territories.

Some 36 per cent of students enrolled for full-time postgraduate study or research come from overseas.

In general, overseas students following courses of higher or further education pay fees covering the full cost of their courses. Nationals of other member countries of the European Community generally pay the lower level of fees applicable to British students; if their courses are designated for mandatory awards, they may be eligible for fees-only awards from LEAs.

Government Scholarship Schemes

The Government makes considerable provision for foreign students and trainees under its overseas aid programme and through other award and scholarship schemes. In 1991–92 some 22,000 overseas students were supported at a cost of £138 million.

The Foreign & Commonwealth Office

Scholarships and Awards Scheme, which operates in some 140 countries, offers study opportunities in Britain for present and future leaders, decision-makers and opinion formers. Some of the awards are jointly financed by the Foreign & Commonwealth Office, the private sector and academic institutions. The Department of Trade and Industry also finances a trade-related scholarship scheme in partnership with British industry.

Outside the aid programme, the Overseas Research Students Awards Scheme, funded by the Department for Education, provides assistance for overseas full-time postgraduate students with outstanding research potential; these awards meet the difference between the home/European Community and overseas student fee levels.

Other Schemes

Many public and private scholarships and fellowships are available to students from overseas and to British students who want to study overseas. Among the best known, and open to men and women from all walks of life, are the British Council Fellowships, the Commonwealth Scholarship and Fellowship Plan, the Fulbright Scholarship Scheme, the Marshall Scholarships, the Rhodes Scholarships, the Churchill Scholarships and the Confederation of British Industry Scholarships. Most British universities and colleges offer scholarships for which graduates of any nationality are eligible.

English as a Foreign Language

About 250 private English language schools in Britain are recognised by the British Council (see p. 420.). The Council has its own English-language teaching centres in other countries and runs a programme for teaching English related to specific jobs and skills. Other British language schools also enable people to learn English in their own countries.

The Government's aid programme supports the teaching of English in many developing countries. Publications and other material relating to English language teaching are a large component in many publishers' lists, constituting an important export.

BBC English offers a worldwide facility for the individual learner at home using BBC World Service radio and television broadcasts.

Educational Exchanges

British Council

The British Council promotes cultural and educational relations with other countries. It plays an important part in the management of the aid programme to education. The Council:

- recruits teachers for work overseas;
- organises short overseas visits by British experts;
- encourages cultural exchange visits; and
- fosters academic interchange between British higher education institutions and those in other countries.

Co-operation between higher education in Britain and developing countries is promoted with funding from the Overseas Development Administration. It includes:

- recruiting staff for overseas universities;
- the secondment of staff from British higher education establishments;
- interdepartmental faculty links; and
- short-term teaching and advisory visits, and general consultancy services.

Central Bureau for Educational Visits and Exchanges

The Central Bureau for Educational Visits and Exchanges provides information and advice on all forms of educational visits and exchanges. In addition, it:

- administers and develops a wide range of curriculum-related exchange schemes;
- links educational establishments and LEAs with their counterparts in other countries; and
- organises meetings, workshops and conferences related to professional international experience.

The Bureau administers teacher exchanges in Europe and the United States, short courses for language teachers, and international study visits. Opportunities for young people include school and class links and English language summer camps. For the post-16 age group, there are work placements and English language assistants' posts, as well as other exchange programmes.

Association of Commonwealth Universities

The Association of Commonwealth Universities promotes contact and co-operation between hundreds of member universities in Commonwealth countries or regions. It assists student and staff mobility by administering award schemes, including, for Britain, the Commonwealth Scholarship and Fellowship Plan and the Overseas Development Administration Shared Scholarship Scheme. An academic appointments service is also operated. The Association publishes information about Commonwealth universities, courses and scholarships, and organises meetings in different parts of the world.

THE YOUTH SERVICE

Britain's youth service—a partnership between local government and voluntary organisations—is concerned with informal social education of young people and with promoting their personal development.

Many of the voluntary organisations were established at the end of the 19th century and in the first decade of the 20th. In 1939 the Government first recognised the need for a youth service forming part of education and supported through LEAs. In 1944 the Education Act provided for the development of a service by LEAs, in partnership with the voluntary organisations.

There are some 5,600 full-time staff, about 31,500 full-time equivalent part-time workers and around 500,000 volunteers. Local authorities maintain their own youth centres and clubs and provide most of the public support for local and regional voluntary organisations. The service is said to reach around 5 million young people, the voluntary organisations contributing a significant proportion of overall provision.

The Department for Education's Youth Service Unit gives grants to the national voluntary youth organisations to meet 50 per cent of the cost of programmes designed to promote access to the youth service, support training for voluntary youth workers and help improve the efficiency and effectiveness of the organisations.

Funded primarily by central government, England's National Youth Agency provides:

- support for those working with young people;
- information and publishing services; and
- support for curriculum development.

It is also responsible for the accreditation of training and staff development for youth workers.

The Welsh Office provides grant aid to national youth service bodies with headquarters in Wales and has established a Wales Youth Agency similar to the one in England.

In Scotland the youth service forms part of community education, which is promoted by the Scottish Community Education Council (see p. 418). The Scottish Office gives grants to voluntary youth organisations to assist them with their headquarters expenditure and training of staff.

The Youth Council for Northern Ireland advises the education system on the development of the youth service, promotes provision of facilities and encourages cross-community activity among young people. It also helps co-ordinate youth service resources and provides funds for voluntary youth organisations' headquarters.

Voluntary Youth Organisations

National voluntary youth organisations undertake a significant share of youth activities through local groups, which raise most of their day-to-day expenses by their own efforts. Many receive financial and other help from LEAs, which also make available facilities in many areas. The voluntary organisations vary greatly in character and include the uniformed organisations such as the Scouts and Girl Guides. Other organisations are church-based. Some also represent Jews and Muslims. Sport and the arts are catered for by various bodies.

There are about 6,500 youth clubs which encourage their members to participate in sport, cultural and other creative activities. Some youth clubs provide information, counselling and advice.

Many local authorities and voluntary youth organisations have responded to new needs in society by making provision, for example, for the young unemployed, young people from the ethnic minorities, young people in inner cities or rural areas and those in trouble or especially vulnerable. Other areas of concern are homelessness and provision for handicapped young people.

Many authorities have youth committees on which official and voluntary bodies are represented. They employ youth officers to co-ordinate youth work and to arrange in-service training. There are also youth councils, which are representative bodies of young people from local youth organisations.

Youth Workers

In England and Wales a two-year training course at certain universities and higher education colleges produces qualified youth and community workers; several undergraduate part-time and postgraduate courses are also available. In Scotland one-, two- and three-year courses are provided at colleges of education. Students from Northern Ireland attend courses run in universities and colleges in Great Britain and the Irish Republic.

Other Organisations Concerned with Young People

Finance is provided by many grant-giving foundations and trusts for activities involving young people. The Prince's Trust and the Royal Jubilee Trust provide grants and practical help to individuals and organisations; areas of concern include urban deprivation, unemployment, homelessness, and young offenders. Efforts are also made to assist ethnic minorities.

The Duke of Edinburgh's Award Scheme challenges young people from Britain and other Commonwealth countries to gain bronze, silver or gold medals by meeting certain standards in activities such as community service, expeditions, the development of personal interests, social and practical skills and physical recreation.

Voluntary Service by Young People

Thousands of young people voluntarily undertake community service designed to help those in need, including elderly and disabled people. Organisations responsible for community service, such as Community Service Volunteers, International Voluntary Service and the British Trust for Conservation Volunteers, receive grants from the Government. Many schools also organise community service work as part of the curriculum, and voluntary work in the community is sponsored by a number of churches.

Youth Exchanges

The Youth Exchange Centre, managed by the British Council (see p. 420), gives advice, information, training and grants to British youth groups involved in international exchanges. The Centre is the national agency for the EC-sponsored exchange scheme Youth for Europe.

Further Reading

Choice and Diversity: A New Framework for Schools. Cm 2021. HMSO, 1992.

Department for Education and Office for Standards in Education. The Government's Expenditure Plans 1993–94 to 1995–96. Cm 2210. HMSO, 1993.

The National Curriculum and its Assessment: An Interim Report. July 1993. Available free from School Curriculum and Assessment Authority, Newcombe House, 45 Notting Hill Gate, London W11 3JB.

28 Religion

Everyone in Britain has the right to religious freedom—in teaching, worship and observance—without interference from the community or the State. Religious organisations and groups may own property, run schools, and promote their beliefs in speech and writing. There is no religious bar to the holding of public office.

INTRODUCTION

Most of the world's religions are represented in Britain, including large Hindu, Jewish, Muslim and Sikh communities, but Britain is predominantly Christian. Non-religious alternatives for humanists and atheists are offered by organisations such as the British Humanist Association and the National Secular Society.

Religious Freedom

Britain has a long tradition of religious tolerance. Freedom of conscience in religious matters was achieved gradually from the 17th century onwards. The laws discriminating against minority religious groups were gradually administered less harshly and then finally repealed. Heresy ceased to be a legal offence with the passage of the Ecclesiastical Jurisdiction Act 1677, and the Toleration Act 1688 granted freedom of worship to Protestant minority groups.

In 1828 the repeal of the Test and Corporation Acts gave nonconformists full political rights, making it possible for them to be appointed to public office. Roman Catholics gained political rights under the Roman Catholic Relief Act 1829, and the Jewish Relief Act 1858 enabled Jews to become Members of Parliament. In addition, the religious tests imposed on prospective students and academic staff of the universities of Oxford, Cambridge and Durham were successively abolished by Acts of 1854, 1856 and 1871. Similar restrictions on the staff of Scottish universities were formally removed in 1932.

The past 30 years have seen the acceptance of a wide variety of religious beliefs and traditions of large numbers of immigrants of different nationalities. Arrangements are made at places of work to allow the members of non-Christian religions to follow their religious observances.

Relations with the State

There are two established churches in Britain, that is, churches legally recognised as official churches of the State: in England the Church of England, and in Scotland the (Presbyterian) Church of Scotland. Ministers of the established churches, as well as clergy belonging to other religious groups, work in services run by the State, such as the armed forces, national hospitals and prisons, and are paid a salary for such services by the State.

Voluntary schools provided by religious denominations may be wholly or partly maintained from public funds. Religious education in publicly maintained schools is required by law throughout Britain, as is a daily act of collective worship (see p. 410). Religious broadcasting is subject to some legislative controls (see p. 424).

The Government contributes towards the upkeep of about 270 redundant Church of England churches for which no alternative use can be found but which are of architectural or historic importance. The contribution for the period 1989 to 1994 will be about £8.7 million. In June 1993 the Government launched the Historic Chapels Trust, which aims to preserve the redundant chapels and places of worship of other denominations and faiths.

The State makes no direct contribution to church expenses, although since 1977 limited state aid has been given for the repair of historic churches; in 1992–93 English Heritage grants to churches totalled £9.2 million. In 1991 the Government announced that new money would be made available to assist with the cost of repairs to cathedrals and comparable buildings; an additional £4 million will be made available each year in 1994–95 and 1995–96. Such funding is not restricted to Church of England buildings.

Involvement in Social Issues

Religious involvement in broader social issues was highlighted in the Church of England report *Faith in the City: A Call for Action by Church and Nation*, published in 1985. This made recommendations for improving conditions in the inner cities and other socially deprived areas, and led to the establishment in 1988 of the Church of England's Church Urban Fund, which aims to raise money for the Church's work in inner city and other priority areas. By June 1993 it had raised over £24.5 million and given grants to over 550 inner city projects. Two further reports, *Living Faith in the City* and *Faith in the Countryside*, were published in 1990. Organisations belonging to other churches and religious groups are also closely involved with a wide range of social issues.

The Inner Cities Religious Council has been meeting since 1992 under the chairmanship of a government minister at the Department of the Environment. Members are drawn from the Christian, Hindu, Jewish, Muslim and Sikh faiths. It aims to provide faith communities with a new and effective way of working together in the inner cities and deprived urban areas in order to bring about real and lasting change.

Statistics on Religious Affiliation

There is no standard information about the number of members of religious groups since questions are not normally asked about religious beliefs in censuses or for other official purposes, except in Northern Ireland. Each group adopts its own way of counting its members, and membership figures are therefore approximate.

There has been a fall in recent years in both the number of full-time ministers and the number of adults recorded as members of most of the larger Christian churches. At the same time there has been significant growth in a range of independent churches, and in new religious movements. Surveys have also revealed that many people who do not belong to religious groups claim to be religious and say they believe in God.

THE ESTABLISHED CHURCHES

The Church of England

The Church of England, founded by St Augustine in AD 597, became the established church of the land in the Reformation in the 16th century. Its form of worship was set out in the Book of Common Prayer, dating from 1549. The Church of England's relationship with the State is one of mutual obligation— the Church's privileges are balanced by certain duties it must fulfil. The Sovereign is the 'Supreme Governor' of the Church of England and must always be a member of the Church, and promise to uphold it. Church of England archbishops, bishops and deans are appointed by the Sovereign on the advice of the Prime Minister, although the Crown Appointments Commission, which includes

DANCE

Adzido Pan African Dance Ensemble promotes the richness and diversity of African culture while placing it in a contemporary context. The ensemble tours throughout the country, performing at major venues, but also running workshops for people of all ages and abilities.

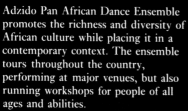

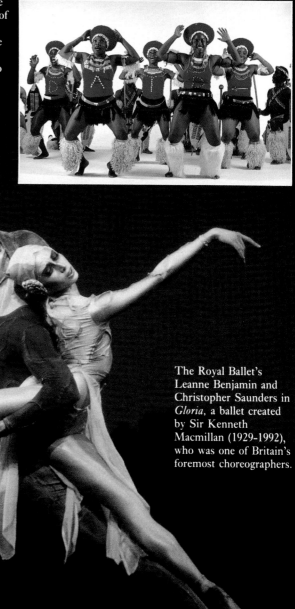

The Royal Ballet's Leanne Benjamin and Christopher Saunders in *Gloria*, a ballet created by Sir Kenneth Macmillan (1929-1992), who was one of Britain's foremost choreographers.

TREASURES OF BRITAIN

The Middleham Jewel is the finest piece
of medieval jewellery to have been
discovered in recent years. It was acquired
for the Yorkshire Museum for £2 million,
which included a grant of £180,000 from
the National Art Collections Fund.

A 15th century German tapestry, *The
Pursuit of Fidelity*, is among the items
on display at the Burrell Collection, in
Glasgow. The Collection ranges widely
over three continents, and in date from
the fourth millennium BC to the
19th century.

Jean François Millet's *Bergère Assise* was bought by the
Welsh art collectors Gwendolen and Margaret Davies in 1913.
Margaret Davies gave it away shortly before her death,
but it has now been reunited with the Davies sisters' collection
of French paintings in the National Museum of Wales, Cardiff.

The Ulster Museum, in Belfast, houses
this Belleek greyhound group. Belleek, the
most famous manufacturer of porcelain in
Ireland, was at its height at the end of the
19th century. The greyhound group was
modelled by the Reverend Halahan
Dunbar around 1890.

SPORT

Neil Thomas became the first British medallist ever in world-class gymnastics when he won a silver medal in the floor exercise at the World Gymnastics Championships in Birmingham in April 1993.

Wales's Colin Jackson wins a gold medal for Britain in the 110-metre hurdles at the World Athletics Championships in Stuttgart, Germany, in August 1993, setting a new world record of 12.91 seconds.

lay and clergy representatives, plays a decisive part in the selection of archbishops and diocesan bishops. All clergy swear their allegiance to the Crown. The Church can regulate its own worship. The two archbishops (of Canterbury and York), the bishops of London, Durham and Winchester, and 21 other senior bishops sit in the House of Lords. Clergy of the Church, together with those of the Church of Scotland, the Church of Ireland and the Roman Catholic Church, may not sit in the House of Commons.

The Church has two provinces: Canterbury, comprising 30 dioceses, including the Diocese in Europe; and York, which has 14 dioceses. The dioceses are divided into deaneries, which are in turn divided into about 13,000 parishes. There are, altogether, about 10,250 ordained stipendiary Church of England clergymen, and about 700 stipendiary women deacons, working within the diocesan structure, excluding Europe. It was estimated that in 1990, in the two provinces (excluding the Diocese in Europe), some 229,000 people were baptised into the Church; of these, 184,000 were under one year old, representing nearly 29 per cent of live births. In the same year there were 59,600 confirmations. Attendances at services on a normal Sunday are around 1.1 million. In 1990, 115,328 marriages were solemnised in the Church of England and the Church in Wales. These accounted for 66.2 per cent of all marriages with religious ceremonies, and 34.8 per cent of all marriages in England and Wales. Many people who rarely, if ever, attend services still regard themselves as belonging to the Church of England.

The central governing body is the General Synod, which comprises separate houses of bishops, clergy and lay members. Lay people are also concerned with church government in the parishes. The Synod is the centre of an administrative system dealing with such matters as missionary work, inter-church relations, social questions, and recruitment and training for the ministry. It also covers other church work in Britain and overseas, the care of church buildings and their contents, church schools (which are maintained largely from public funds), colleges and institutes of higher education,

voluntary and parish education, and centres for training women in pastoral work.

The Church's investment income is managed mainly by the Church Commissioners. Most of the remainder of the Church's income is provided by local voluntary donations.

> The average annual stipend of a Church of England clergyman is about £12,800; the average value of additional benefits, including free accommodation and a non-contributory pension, is estimated to be £7,100.

At present, only men may join the priesthood of the Church of England, but in November 1992 the General Synod voted to approve legislation which would allow the ordination of women to the priesthood. The measure requires the approval of both Houses of Parliament before receiving the Royal Assent. It is expected that the first women could be ordained to the priesthood in 1994.

The Deacons (Ordination of Women) Measure 1986 made it possible for women to become deacons.

The Church of Scotland

The Church of Scotland has a presbyterian form of government, that is, government by ministers and elders, all of whom are ordained to office. It became the national church following the Scottish Reformation and legislation of the Scottish Parliament, consolidated in the Treaty of Union 1707 and the Church of Scotland Act 1921, the latter confirming its complete freedom in all spiritual matters. It appoints its own office bearers, and its affairs are not subject to any civil authority.

The adult communicant membership of the Church of Scotland is about 790,000; there are about 1,250 ministers. Both men and women may join the ministry. About 1,500 churches are governed locally by Kirk Sessions, consisting of ministers and elders. Above the Kirk Session is the Presbytery, then the Synod, and finally the General Assembly, consisting of elected ministers and elders. This meets annually under the presidency of an elected moderator, who serves for one year. The Sovereign is normally represented at the General Assembly by the Lord High Commissioner.

There are also a number of independent Scottish Presbyterian churches, largely descended from groups which broke away from the Church of Scotland.

WALES

The Church in Wales became part of the Anglican Church at the Reformation. The Bible was translated into Welsh by Bishop Morgan in 1588. During the 18th and 19th centuries a powerful nonconformist (or Free Church—see below) movement developed throughout Wales: a census of religion in 1851 found that over 80 per cent of those at worship attended a nonconformist chapel. This strength was reflected in the disestablishment of the Church in Wales in 1920. There are about 220,000 members of the Free Churches in Wales, while the Church in Wales has some 108,000 members. The Church in Wales is responsible for the care of the country's medieval churches and cathedrals.

THE ANGLICAN COMMUNION

The Anglican Communion comprises 31 autonomous Churches in Britain and abroad, and three regional councils overseas with a total membership of about 70 million. In the British Isles there are four Anglican Churches: the Church of England (established), the Church in Wales, the Scottish Episcopal Church, and the Church of Ireland.

Every ten years the Lambeth Conference meets for consultation between all Anglican bishops. The last Conference was held in Canterbury in 1988. Presided over by the Archbishop of Canterbury, the Conference has no executive authority, but enjoys considerable influence. The Anglican Consultative Council, an assembly of lay people and clergy as well as of bishops, meets every two or three years and is intended to allow consultations within the Anglican

Communion. The Primates Meeting brings together the senior bishops from each Church at similar intervals.

THE FREE CHURCHES

The term 'Free Churches' is often used to describe some of the Protestant churches in Britain which, unlike the Church of England and the Church of Scotland, are not established churches. Free Churches have existed in various forms since the Reformation, developing their own traditions over the years. Their members have also been known as dissenters or nonconformists. All the major Free Churches allow both men and women to become ministers.

The Methodist Church, the largest of the Free Churches, with over 430,000 adult full members and a community of more than 1.3 million, originated in the 18th century following the evangelical revival under John Wesley (1703–91). The present church is based on the 1932 union of most of the separate Methodist Churches. It has 3,514 ministers and 7,207 places of worship.

The Baptists first achieved an organised form in Britain in the 17th century. Today they are mainly organised in groups of churches, most of which belong to the Baptist Union of Great Britain (re-formed in 1812), with about 165,000 members, 2,500 ministers and 2,300 places of worship. There are also separate Baptist Unions for Scotland, Wales and Ireland, and other independent Baptist Churches.

The United Reformed Church, with some 117,000 members, 995 ministers and 1,808 places of worship, was formed in 1972 following the merger of the Congregational Church in England and Wales (the oldest Protestant minority in Britain, whose origins can be traced back to the Puritans of the 16th century) with the Presbyterian Church of England, many of whose members are descended from Scottish Presbyterians. This was the first union of two different churches in Britain since the Reformation in the 16th century. In 1981 there was a further merger with the Reformed Association of the Churches of Christ.

The Salvation Army was founded in the

East End of London in 1865 by William Booth (1829–1912). Within Britain there are 55,000 members, 1,800 active full-time officers (who are ordained ministers) and more than 900 centres of worship. The Army is well known for its social work, which ranges from 50 hostels for the homeless to nearly 40 homes for the elderly, and for its nationwide prison chaplaincy service.

> The Salvation Army family tracing service, which seeks to restore family relationships, takes on 5,000 new cases each year.

Among the other Free Churches are the Presbyterian Church in Ireland, the Presbyterian (or Calvinistic Methodist) Church of Wales, the Union of Welsh Independents and the Afro-Westindian United Council of Churches.

THE ROMAN CATHOLIC CHURCH

The formal structure of the Roman Catholic Church in England and Wales, which ceased to exist after the Reformation in the 16th century, was restored in 1850. The Scottish Church's formal structure went out of existence in the early 17th century and was restored in 1878. However, throughout this period Catholicism never disappeared entirely. There are now seven Roman Catholic provinces in Great Britain, each under an archbishop, and 29 dioceses, each under a bishop (22 in England and Wales and seven in Scotland, independently responsible to the Pope). There are almost 3,300 parishes and about 7,300 priests (only men may become priests). Northern Ireland has six dioceses, some with territory partly in the Irish Republic. About one British citizen in ten claims to be a Roman Catholic. The Pope is represented diplomatically in Britain by an Apostolic Pro-Nuncio.

The Roman Catholic Church attaches great importance to the education of its children and requires its members to try to bring up their children in the Catholic faith. Almost 5 per cent of the teachers in Britain's 2,500 Catholic schools are members of religious orders. These orders also undertake other social work; about 250 Roman Catholic religious orders, congregations and societies are represented in Britain, as are congregations representing about 25 different nationalities who live in Britain. Most Catholic schools are maintained out of public funds.

OTHER CHRISTIAN CHURCHES

Other Protestant Churches include the Unitarians and Free Christians, whose origins are traceable to the Reformation, and the Pentecostalists, whose movement began in the early 20th century. The two main Pentecostalist organisations operating in Britain are the Assemblies of God and the Elim Pentecostal Church, many of whose members are of West Indian origin.

The Religious Society of Friends (Quakers), with about 18,000 adult members in Britain and 450 places of worship, was founded in the middle of the 17th century under the leadership of George Fox (1624–91). Silent worship is central to its life as a religious organisation.

The Christian Brethren is a Protestant body organised in its present form by J. N. Darby (1800–82). There are two branches: the Open Brethren (with an estimated 43,500 members) and the Closed or Exclusive Brethren (with an estimated 7,600 members).

A recent development in Christian worship has been the 'house church movement' (or 'new churches'), which began in the early 1970s and now has an estimated membership of almost 110,000. Services were originally held in private houses but now groups use a variety of hired buildings. These non-denominational congregations may come together as 'streams', of which some of the better known are New Frontiers, Pioneer and Ichthus.

Many Christian communities of foreign origin, including the Orthodox, Lutheran and Reformed Churches of various European countries, and the Coptic Orthodox Church and the Armenian Church, have established their own centres of worship, particularly in London. All these churches operate in a variety of languages.

There are also several other religious organisations in Britain which were founded in the United States in the last century. These include the Jehovah's Witnesses, the Church of Jesus Christ of the Latter-Day Saints (the Mormon Church), the Christian Scientists and the Spiritualists.

OTHER RELIGIONS

The Jewish Community

Jews first settled in England at the time of the Norman Conquest and remained until banished by royal decree in 1290. The present community in Britain dates from 1656, having been founded by those of Spanish and Portuguese origin, known as Sephardim. Later more settlers came from Germany and Eastern Europe; they are known as Ashkenazim.

The present Jewish community in Britain, numbering about 300,000, is the second largest in Europe.

The Jewish community is divided into two main groups. Some 77 per cent of the majority Ashkenazi Jews are Orthodox and most acknowledge the authority of the Chief Rabbi. The Sephardi Orthodox element follow their own spiritual head. The recently established Masorti movement, the Reform movement, founded in 1840, and the Liberal and Progressive movement, established in 1901, account for most of the remaining 23 per cent.

Jewish congregations in Britain number about 350. About one in three Jewish children attend Jewish schools, some of which are supported by public funds. Several agencies care for elderly and handicapped people.

The officially recognised representative body is the Board of Deputies of British Jews, which was established in 1760.

The Muslim Community

The most recent estimates suggest that Britain's Muslim population is around 1 million. The largest number originate from Pakistan and Bangladesh, while sizeable groups have come from India, Cyprus, the Arab world, Malaysia and parts of Africa. A growing community of British-born Muslims, mainly the children of immigrant parents, includes an increasing number of converts to Islam.

There are some 450 mosques and numerous Muslim prayer centres throughout Britain. Mosques are not only places of worship; they also offer instruction in the Muslim way of life and facilities for educational and welfare activities.

The first mosque in Britain was established at Woking, Surrey, in 1890. Mosques now range from converted houses in many towns to the Central Mosque in London and its associated Islamic Cultural Centre, one of the most important Muslim institutions in the Western world. The Central Mosque has the largest congregation in Britain, and during festivals it may number over 5,000. There are also important mosques and cultural centres in Liverpool, Manchester, Leicester, Bradford, Edinburgh and Glasgow.

Many of the mosques belong to various Muslim organisations, and both the Sunni and the Shia traditions within Islam are represented among the Muslim community in Britain. Members of some of the major Sufi traditions have also developed branches in British cities.

The Sikh Community

A large British Sikh community, comprising over 300,000, originates mainly from India. The largest groups of Sikhs are in Greater London, Manchester, Birmingham, Nottingham and Wolverhampton. Sikh temples or gurdwaras cater for the religious, educational, social welfare and cultural needs of their community. The oldest gurdwara in London was established in 1908 and the largest is in Southall, Middlesex. There are over 140 gurdwaras in Britain.

The Hindu Community

The Hindu community in Britain comprises around 320,000 members and also originates largely from India. The largest groups of Hindus are to be found in Leicester, different areas of London, Birmingham and Bradford. The first Hindu temple or mandir was opened in London in 1962 and there are now over 150 mandirs in Britain.

Buddhism

The Buddhist community in Britain consists largely of adherents of British or Western origin. There are about 150 Buddhist groups in Britain and some 50 centres, with at least 20 monasteries and a number of temples. All the main schools of Buddhism are represented. The Buddhist Society promotes the principles of Buddhism; it does not belong to any particular school of Buddhism.

Other Religious Communities

Other religious communities include about 30,000 Jains, whose religion is of ancient Indian origin. A deresar, or Jain temple, opened in Leicester in 1988. The Zoroastrian religion, or Mazdaism, originated in ancient Iran. It is mainly represented in Britain by the Parsi community, who are by origin from the South Asian sub-continent. The Baha'i movement, which originated in 19th-century Iran, regards all the major religions as divine in origin; there are an estimated 5,000 Baha'is in Britain.

New Religious Movements

A large number of new religious movements or cults, mainly established since the Second World War and often with overseas origins, are active in Britain. Examples include the Church of Scientology, the Transcendental Meditation movement and the Unification Church (popularly known as the 'Moonies'). In response to public concern about the activities of some of these cults the Government provided funding in 1987 for the Information Network Focus on Religious Movements, which is a group supported by the main churches. It seeks to provide objective information about new religious movements.

CO-OPERATION BETWEEN FAITHS

A number of organisations exist which seek to develop relations between different religions in Britain. They include the Inter-Faith Network for the United Kingdom, which links a wide range of organisations with an interest in inter-faith relations, including representative bodies from the Baha'i, Buddhist, Christian, Hindu, Jain, Jewish, Muslim and Sikh faith communities. Other organisations include the Council of Christians and Jews, which works for better understanding among members of the two religions and deals with issues in the educational and social fields. Religious leaders belonging to different faiths have also officiated jointly at a number of important public occasions. Christians, Muslims, Sikhs, Hindus, Jews and Buddhists, for example, have taken part together in the annual religious observance to mark Commonwealth Day, which has been attended by the Queen.

Co-operation among the Churches

The Council of Churches for Britain and Ireland was established in 1990, replacing the former British Council of Churches and taking over its role as the main overall body for the Christian churches in Britain. The Council co-ordinates the work of its 30 member churches, which are also grouped in separate ecumenical bodies for England, Scotland, Wales and Ireland.

The Free Church Federal Council includes most of the Free Churches of England and Wales. It promotes co-operation among the Free Churches and is a channel for communication with government. Inter-church discussions about the search for unity now take place through international as well as national bodies. The Roman Catholic, Orthodox and Lutheran Churches are represented on some of these, as are the Anglican and some of the Free Churches.

The Anglican Churches, the Church of Scotland and the main Free Churches are also members of the World Council of Churches. This organisation links some 310 churches in over 100 countries around the world.

Further Reading

Religion. Aspects of Britain series, HMSO, 1992.

29 The Arts

Artistic and cultural activity in Britain ranges from the highest professional standards to a wide variety of amateur performances and events. The arts also represent a major sector of economic activity. They contribute an estimated £6,000 million a year to Britain's balance of payments.

INTRODUCTION

Britain's artistic and cultural heritage is one of the richest in the world. The origins of English literature can be traced back to medieval times, while over the centuries Britain has amassed some of the finest collections of works of art of all kinds. The performing arts also have a long and distinguished history.

London is one of the leading world centres for the arts. Other large cities, including Birmingham, Sheffield, Manchester, Edinburgh, Glasgow and Cardiff, have also sustained and developed their reputations as centres of artistic excellence in recent years. Arts festivals attract wide interest. Many British artists of all kinds enjoy international reputations. Television and radio bring a wide range of arts events to a large audience. Arts activities introduced and developed by the ethnic minorities are also thriving. At an amateur level, numerous groups and societies for the arts make use of local talent and resources.

Department of National Heritage

The Secretary of State for National Heritage, who is a member of the Cabinet, is responsible for general arts policy. The office was created in 1992 and its holder heads the Department of National Heritage (see p. 499), which replaced the Office of Arts and Libraries as well as taking on a range of responsibilities from other departments. The Department determines government policy and administers government expenditure on national museums and art galleries in England, the Arts Council of Great Britain, the British Library and other national arts and heritage bodies. This includes responsibilities for listing and scheduling buildings and for royal parks and palaces (which includes the work of the Department's executive agency, Historic Royal Palaces). Other responsibilities include the regulation of the film industry, broadcasting, press regulation, the national lottery and the export licensing of antiques. The Secretaries of State for Wales, Scotland and Northern Ireland are responsible for the national museums, galleries and libraries in their countries, and for other cultural matters.

Government Policies

The Government's arts policies aim to:

- develop a high standard of artistic and cultural activity throughout Britain;

- encourage innovation; and

- promote public access to, and appreciation of, the arts, crafts and the cultural heritage.

The Department of National Heritage provides funds and advice, and encourages partnership with the private sector, including business sponsorship. National museums and galleries are given an incentive to increase their resources, for example, through trading and other activities. An important concept in funding policy is the 'arm's length' principle, by which government funds are distributed to arts organisations indirectly, through bodies such as the Arts Council of Great Britain and the British Film Institute. This principle helps to avoid undue political influence over funding decisions by ensuring that funds are allocated by those best qualified to do so.

Local Authorities

Local authorities maintain more than 1,000 local museums and art galleries and a network of some 4,000 public libraries. They also support many arts buildings, arts organisations and artistic events in their areas, providing grant aid for professional and voluntary organisations, including orchestras and theatre, opera and dance companies, although there is no statutory obligation for them to do so. They undertake direct promotions and contribute to the cost of new or converted buildings for the arts. In England this support is estimated to be about £200 million a year. Arts education in schools, colleges, evening institutes and community centres is the responsibility of central government education departments, in partnership with local education authorities and voluntary bodies.

Finance

Planned central government expenditure through the Department of National Heritage, excluding sport, amounts to £926 million in 1993–94, of which £226 million is channelled through the Arts Council to support the performing and visual arts throughout England, Scotland and Wales; over £72 million goes to the British Library. Grants are also made to the British Film Institute, the Crafts Council, certain other museums and arts bodies, and to the

National Heritage Memorial Fund. The Fund helps organisations wishing to acquire, for the public benefit, land, buildings, works of art and other objects associated with the national heritage. In Scotland The Scottish Office provides £28 million to the National Galleries and Museums and £21 million to the National Library.

Business Sponsorship

Industrial and commercial concerns offer vital sponsorship to a wide range of arts. The Business Sponsorship Incentive Scheme was introduced in Great Britain in 1984 in co-operation with the Association for Business Sponsorship of the Arts (ABSA), with the aim of raising the overall level of business sponsorship. (A similar scheme was set up in Northern Ireland in 1987.) Since its inception the scheme has brought over £60 million into the arts (including a government contribution of over £19 million) and has attracted over 2,780 first-time sponsors. An estimated 80 per cent of the awards have been made to arts organisations outside London. In 1993–94 the Government is making available £4.5 million to match new sponsorships.

Further support is encouraged by tax concessions which allow companies and individuals to obtain tax relief on donations to arts charities. For example, under the Gift Aid scheme, announced in 1990, single gifts of £250 and over in any one year qualify for tax relief.

Foundation for Sport and the Arts

The Foundation for Sport and the Arts was set up in 1991 by the Pool Promoters Association, with grants expected to total £60 million a year. About two-thirds of the revenue is used to benefit sport and the remainder to benefit the arts.

National Lottery

The new National Lottery (see p. 482) is expected to generate substantial funds for the arts, heritage, sports, charities and for a millennium fund to celebrate the year 2000.

Arts Councils

The independent Arts Council of Great Britain, established in 1946 by Royal Charter, is the main channel for government aid to the performing arts. Its chief aims are to:

- develop and improve the knowledge, understanding and practice of the performing and visual arts;
- increase their accessibility to the public; and
- advise and co-operate with government departments, local authorities and other organisations.

The Council gives financial help and advice to organisations ranging from the major opera, dance and drama companies; orchestras and festivals; to small touring theatres and experimental groups.

The Council also provides funds for the training of arts administrators and helps arts organisations to develop other sources of income, including box-office, trading profits, sponsorship and local authority support. It encourages contemporary dance, mime, jazz, literature, photography and art films, and helps professional creative writers, choreographers, composers, artists and photographers. The Council also promotes art exhibitions and tours and makes funds available for some specialist training courses in the arts. Emphasis is being placed on obtaining funds through partnership arrangements with local authorities and other agencies, and from commercial sources. As an extension of its responsibilities for funding the arts and arts organisations, the Arts Council promotes the arts through broadcasting, film and video (see p. 441).

Organisations in Scotland and Wales receive their subsidies through the Scottish and Welsh Arts Councils, which are committees of the Arts Council of Great Britain. The Government has announced plans for responsibility for the Scottish and Welsh Arts Councils to be transferred from the Department of National Heritage to the Scottish and Welsh Offices respectively from April 1994. Northern Ireland has an independent Arts Council with aims and functions similar to those of the Arts Council of Great Britain.

A review of the structure, organisation and staffing of the Arts Council was published in June 1993 (see p. 433). Following this, the Government has reaffirmed its commitment to the 'arm's length' principle for arts funding but will be exploring ways in which the Council's accountability can be improved. It has also stated that the different roles of the Government and the Arts Council should not obscure the fact that there are objectives which they share, for example, encouraging the widest possible access to the arts.

Developments in Arts Funding

In 1991 ten Regional Arts Boards were created to replace the 12 Regional Arts Associations in England. They are financed mainly by the Arts Council, with smaller sums from the British Film Institute and Crafts Council. Through forward planning and budgeting, the Boards are subject to a more clearly focused system of financial accountability to their national funders. One-third of the members of each Board are nominated by local authorities. Boards also include representatives of the regional business community as well as others with expertise and interest in the arts. The Boards offer financial assistance to artists and arts organisations and advise on, and sometimes help to promote, arts activities.

In 1992 the Arts Council delegated responsibility for funding 22 of its clients to the new Boards. In April 1994, a further 42 clients will be delegated. However, the Arts Council will retain funding responsibility for the four national companies—the Royal Opera House, the English National Opera, the Royal Shakespeare Company and the Royal National Theatre—as well as for the South Bank Centre. It will also remain responsible for publishing, touring companies without a regional base and all other arts organisations best assessed on a national level.

The National Arts and Media Strategy

To make the best use of the restructured system, the Government asked the Arts Council, with assistance from the British

Film Industry and the Crafts Council, to develop a medium-term strategy for the arts and associated activities. After a wide consultation process, the final strategy, entitled *A Creative Future*, was published in January 1993. This suggests new emphases in arts funding and outlines new priorities and activities. The Arts Council will be responsible for overseeing the strategy's implementation within the limits of the funds available. Similar strategies have been published in Scotland and Wales.

The Arts and Minority Communities

The arts activities undertaken by Britain's diverse communities embrace both traditional and new forms of artistic expression. In seeking to reflect and encourage this the Arts Council has, over the last five years, devoted particular attention to black and Asian dance and drama. In 1990 ADiTi, a development organisation for South Asian dance, was launched in Bradford. The Council has expanded its training to include arts administration and technical skills. The Commonwealth Institute arranges a varied programme of artistic events, and the Minorities Arts Advisory Service is an independent organisation which provides information on, and training in, the arts of these communities.

Arts and People with Disabilities

In *A Creative Future* (see above), the Arts Council expressed concern that the buildings where arts activities take place often fail to meet the needs of people with various types of disability, despite sensitive planning of new buildings and a considerable amount of work undertaken by local authorities and arts venues.

ADAPT, a voluntary organisation set up in 1989, contributes towards the cost of making new facilities accessible to disabled people. Its funds are raised from government and private sector sponsorship, administered by the Carnegie Trust, which has made the biggest contribution to the organisation. ADAPT has so far raised over £1 million.

In 1991 the Arts Council launched an Arts and Disability Directory, which provides information on all aspects of arts and disability. In March 1993 it published the *Report on the Initiative to Increase the Employment of Disabled People in the Arts*, which outlines an action plan.

Arts Centres

More than 200 arts centres in Britain provide opportunities for enjoying and taking part in a range of activities, with educational projects becoming increasingly important. Nearly all arts centres are professionally managed and most are supported by volunteer groups. Most arts centres are converted buildings, including former churches, warehouses, schools, town halls and private houses. The centres are assisted mainly by Regional Arts Boards and local authorities, while the Arts Council funds two large centres in London— the South Bank Centre and the Institute of Contemporary Arts. Many theatres and art galleries also provide a focal point for the community by making available facilities for other arts.

British Council

The British Council (see p. 290) promotes a knowledge of British culture overseas and maintains libraries (including film libraries) in many of the 100 countries in which it is represented. The Council initiates or supports overseas tours by British theatre companies, orchestras, choirs, opera and dance companies, and jazz, rock and folk groups, as well as by individual actors, musicians and artists. It also arranges for directors, designers, choreographers and conductors to work with overseas companies, orchestras and choirs. The Council organises and supports fine arts and other exhibitions overseas as well as British participation in international exhibitions and film festivals, and encourages professional interchange between Britain and other countries.

Visiting Arts Office

The Visiting Arts Office, an autonomous body administered by the British Council, promotes foreign arts in Britain. It provides a clearing house for British and overseas arts organisations, advises on touring matters and makes awards for projects.

Broadcasting

Both BBC radio and television and the independent companies (see Chapter 30) broadcast a wide variety of drama (including adaptations of novels and stage plays), opera, ballet, and music; and general arts magazine programmes and documentaries. These have won many international awards at festivals such as the Prix Italia and Montreux International Television Festivals. Independent television companies also make grants for arts promotion in their regions.

Broadcasting is thus a major medium for making the arts available to the general public and is a crucial source of work for actors, musicians, writers, composers, technicians and others in the arts world. It has created its own forms—nothing like arts documentaries or drama series, for instance, exists in any other medium. Broadcasters commission and produce a vast quantity of new work. Television and radio provide critical debate, information and education about the arts.

The BBC also has six orchestras, which employ many of Britain's full-time professional musicians. Each week it broadcasts about 100 hours of classical and other music (both live and recorded) on its Radio 3 FM channel. BBC Radio 1 broadcasts rock and pop music 24 hours a day and a large part of the output of BBC Radio 2 is popular and light music. There are at present two national commercial radio stations: Classic FM, which broadcasts mainly popular classical music; and Virgin, which plays broad-based rock music. Much of the output of Britain's local radio stations consists of popular and light music.

The BBC regularly commissions new music, particularly by British composers, and sponsors concerts, competitions and festivals. Each summer it presents and broadcasts the BBC Promenade Concerts (the 'Proms'), the world's largest music festival, at the Royal Albert Hall.

The Press

Many national and local newspapers devote considerable space to coverage of the arts, and developments in the arts are also covered in the ethnic minority press and in periodicals such as the *Spectator* and *New Statesman and Society* (see Chapter 30). Weekly 'listings' magazines, including *Time Out*, provide details of cultural and other events in London and other large cities.

There are also a large number of specialist publications which cover specific aspects of the arts, including the *Times Literary Supplement*, *Film Monthly*, *Antique* and *Opera Now*. A number of publications publish original literature, including the *London Magazine*, and *Granta*, which publishes fiction as well as cultural journalism. *New Musical Express (NME)* and *Melody Maker* cover rock and pop music. The newspaper *Stage and Television Today* is directed at professional actors and others in the industry.

Festivals

Some 650 professional arts festivals take place in Britain each year. The Edinburgh International Festival, featuring a wide range of arts, is the largest of its kind in the world. Other annual festivals held in the Scottish capital include International Folk and Jazz Festivals and the Film and Television Festival. The Mayfest, the second largest festival in Britain, takes place in Glasgow. Some well-known festivals concentrating on music are the Three Choirs Festival, which has taken place annually for 260 years in Gloucester, Worcester or Hereford; the Cheltenham Festival, largely devoted to contemporary British music; and the Aldeburgh festival. Among others catering for a number of art forms are the Royal National Eisteddfod of Wales, the National Gaelic Mod in Scotland, and the festivals in Belfast, Brighton, Buxton, Chichester, Harrogate, Malvern, Pitlochry, Salisbury, and York. Many much smaller towns also hold arts festivals. Other events include the Notting Hill Carnival in London, in which the Afro-Caribbean community plays a prominent part.

Arts 2000

Arts 2000 is an Arts Council initiative which celebrates the approach of the millennium. During each year between 1992 and 2000, a city, town or region in Britain will be nominated to celebrate a particular art form, concluding with the Year of the Artist in 2000. The East Midlands was the Region of Dance in 1993, Manchester is the City of Drama in 1994, and Swansea the City of Literature in 1995. The years 1997–99 have been nominated, respectively, as the year of opera and musical theatre; the year of photography and the electronic image; and the year of architecture and design.

Arts 2000 is a competitive process judged by an expert Arts Council panel. Winners are offered £250,000 from Arts Council funds, and are expected to make substantial contributions of their own to create a wide-ranging and imaginative programme with a strong European context.

DRAMA

Professional Theatre

Britain is one of the world's major centres for theatre, and has a long and rich dramatic tradition. There are many companies based in London and other cities and towns, as well as numerous touring companies which visit theatres, festivals and other venues, including arts and sports centres and social clubs. There are 66 companies in receipt of subsidies from the Arts Council.

Contemporary British playwrights who have received international recognition include:

- Harold Pinter—*The Caretaker, The Homecoming*;
- Tom Stoppard—*Rosencrantz and Guildenstern are Dead, Jumpers*;
- Caryl Churchill—*Serious Money, Top Girls*; and
- Peter Shaffer—*Equus, Amadeus*.

The musicals of Sir Andrew Lloyd Webber have been highly successful both in Britain and overseas; well known examples include *Jesus Christ Superstar, Evita* and *Cats*.

Among the best-known directors are Sir Peter Hall, Trevor Nunn, Adrian Noble, Jonathan Miller, Terry Hands and Deborah Warner, while the many British performers who enjoy international reputations include Sir John Gielgud, Sir Alec Guinness, Vanessa Redgrave, Sir Ian McKellen, Derek Jacobi, Albert Finney, Dame Judi Dench, Jonathan Pryce, Brian Cox, Juliet Stevenson and Dame Maggie Smith. British stage designers such as John Bury, Ralph Koltai and Carl Toms are internationally recognised.

Britain has about 300 theatres intended for professional use which can seat between 200 and 2,300 people. Some are privately owned, but most are owned either municipally or by non-profit-distributing organisations. Over 40 of these house resident theatre companies receiving subsidies from the Arts Council and Regional Arts Boards. In summer there are also open air theatres, including one in London's Regent's Park and the Minack Theatre, which is on an open cliffside near Land's End in Cornwall.

London has about 100 theatres, 15 of them permanently occupied by subsidised companies. These include:

- the Royal National Theatre, which stages a wide range of modern and classical plays in its three auditoriums on the South Bank;

- the Royal Shakespeare Company, which presents plays mainly by Shakespeare and his contemporaries, as well as some modern work, both in Stratford-upon-Avon and in its two auditoriums in the City's Barbican Centre; and

- the English Stage Company at the Royal Court Theatre in Sloane Square, London, which stages the work of many talented new playwrights.

The largest concentration of London's commercial theatres is around Shaftesbury Avenue. West End theatre attendances reached almost 11 million in 1992.

Most theatres are commercially run and self-financing, relying on popular shows and musicals to be profitable. By contrast, companies funded by the Arts Council tend to offer a variety of traditional and experimental or innovative productions. Experimental or innovative work is often staged in 'fringe' theatres in London and other cities; these are smaller theatres which use a variety of buildings, such as rooms in pubs.

The Theatres Restoration Fund is providing £4 million in 1992–94 for renovating and repairing theatres. It focuses on backstage projects for which no other funds are likely to be available. The Fund is financed jointly by the Government and the Wolfson Foundation and Family Charitable Trust.

In 1989 the partial remains of the Globe Theatre, where Shakespeare acted, and the Rose Theatre, where his plays were performed during his lifetime, were excavated on the south bank of the Thames; both have since been listed as ancient monuments. A modern reconstruction of the Globe Theatre, near its original site, is in progress.

Regional Theatres

Outside London most cities and many large towns have at least one theatre. Older theatres which have been restored include the Theatre Royal, Newcastle upon Tyne, which dates from the 18th century, and the Alhambra, Bradford, the Lyceum, Sheffield, and the Haymarket Theatre, Basingstoke, all dating from the 19th century. Others, such as the West Yorkshire Playhouse, Leeds, and the Theatre Royal, Plymouth, have been built to the latest designs. Major rebuilding schemes in progress include the restoration of Edinburgh's old Empire Theatre (to be renamed the Edinburgh Festival Theatre), with £1.7 million of public funds, to provide an international venue for large-scale productions. Several universities have theatres which house professional companies playing to the general public.

Most regional repertory companies mount about eight to ten productions a year; several have studio theatres in addition to the main auditorium, where they present new or experimental drama and plays of specialist interest. Repertory theatres also often

function as social centres by offering concerts, poetry readings and exhibitions, and by providing restaurants, bars and shops.

Regional theatre companies with major reputations include the Citizens' Theatre, Glasgow; the Royal Exchange, Manchester; Bristol Old Vic; the Liverpool Playhouse (the oldest surviving repertory theatre in Britain); and Nottingham Playhouse, one of the first modern regional theatres. Successful productions from regional theatre companies often transfer to London's West End, while the largest regional theatres receive visits from the Royal National Theatre or the Royal Shakespeare Company. The English Shakespeare Company tours the English regions and worldwide.

Theatre for Young People

Unicorn Theatre for Children and Polka Children's Theatre, both in London, present plays specially written for children; and the Whirligig Theatre tours throughout Britain. The Young Vic Company in London and Contact Theatre Company in Manchester stage plays for young people. Numerous Theatre-in-Education companies perform in schools. Some of these companies operate independently—Theatre Centre, for example, plays in London and tours further afield. Others are attached to regional repertory theatres such as the Belgrade in Coventry and the West Yorkshire Playhouse in Leeds. Most regional repertory theatres also mount productions for younger audiences, and concessionary ticket prices are generally available for those at school, college or university. There are also a number of puppet companies.

There has been a marked growth in youth theatres, which number more than 500 in England alone; both the National Youth Theatre in London and the Scottish Youth Theatre in Glasgow offer early acting opportunities to young people.

Dramatic Training

Training for actors, directors, lighting and sound technicians and stage managers is provided mainly in drama schools, among them the Royal Academy of Dramatic Art (RADA), the Central School of Speech and Drama, the London Academy of Music and Dramatic Art, and the Drama Centre (all in London); the Bristol Old Vic School, the Royal Scottish Academy of Music and Drama (Glasgow) and the Welsh College of Music and Drama (Cardiff). Theatre design courses, often based in art schools, are available for people wanting to train as stage designers. A number of universities and colleges offer degree courses in drama.

Amateur Theatre

There are several thousand amateur dramatic societies throughout Britain. They use a variety of buildings, including schools and public halls. Their work is encouraged by a number of organisations, such as the Central Council for Amateur Theatre, the National Drama Conference, the Scottish Community Drama Association and the Association of Ulster Drama Festivals. A nationwide umbrella body, the Voluntary Arts Network, has recently been established. Amateur companies sometimes receive financial support from local government, Regional Arts Boards and other bodies.

MUSIC

People in Britain are interested in a wide range of music, from classical to different forms of rock and pop music. Jazz, folk, world and light music, and brass bands also have substantial followings.

The first National Music Day was held in June 1992. Over 1,500 separate events were organised, ranging from large open-air concerts in Birmingham, Bath and London to many small events given by church choirs, school bands and folk groups. This is intended to become an annual event; a second National Music Day was held on 26–27 June 1993.

Orchestral and Choral Music

Seasons of orchestral and choral concerts are promoted every year in many large towns and cities. The principal concert halls in central

London are the Royal Festival Hall in the South Bank Centre, next to which are the Queen Elizabeth Hall and the Purcell Room, which accommodate smaller-scale performances; the Barbican Hall (part of the Barbican Centre for Arts and Conferences in the City of London); the Royal Albert Hall in Kensington; the recently-refurbished Wigmore Hall, a recital centre; and St John's, Smith Square. A major new concert hall, the Symphony Hall, opened in Birmingham in 1991, and a new 2,400-seat international concert hall is to be built for Manchester's Hallé Orchestra; the Government is to contribute £22 million, about half the expected cost.

The leading symphony orchestras are the London Philharmonic, the London Symphony, the Philharmonia, the Royal Philharmonic, the BBC Symphony, the Royal Liverpool Philharmonic, the Hallé (Manchester), the City of Birmingham Symphony, the Bournemouth Symphony, the Ulster and the Royal Scottish Orchestras and the BBC Welsh Symphony Orchestra. The BBC's six orchestras provide broadcast concerts which are often open to the public. There are also chamber orchestras such as the English Chamber Orchestra, the Academy of St Martin-in-the-Fields, the Bournemouth Sinfonietta, City of London Sinfonia, and the Scottish Chamber Orchestra. Specialised ensembles include the Orchestra of the Age of Enlightenment, the English Baroque Soloists and the English Concert. The London Sinfonietta and the Birmingham Contemporary Music Group specialise in contemporary music.

British conductors such as Sir Colin Davis, Sir Neville Marriner, Simon Rattle, Andrew Davis, Jane Glover, Sian Edwards and Jeffrey Tate reach a wide audience through their recordings as well as by their performances. The works of living composers such as Sir Michael Tippett, Sir Peter Maxwell Davies and Sir Harrison Birtwistle enjoy international acclaim. Other well-established composers include George Benjamin, John Tavener, Oliver Knussen, Colin Matthews, Nigel Osborne, Robert Saxton, Mark-Antony Turnage and Judith Weir. The Master of the Queen's Music,

Malcolm Williamson, holds an office within the Royal Household with responsibility for organising and writing music for state occasions.

The principal choral societies include the Bach Choir, the Royal Choral Society, the Huddersfield Choral Society, the Cardiff Polyphonic Choir, the Edinburgh International Festival Chorus and the Belfast Philharmonic Society. Almost all the leading orchestras maintain their own choral societies. The English tradition of church singing is represented by choirs such as those of King's College Chapel, Cambridge, and Christ Church Cathedral, Oxford, while other choirs such as the Roman Catholic Westminster Cathedral choir are also well known. There are many male-voice choirs in Wales and in certain parts of England.

Pop and Rock Music

Hundreds of hours of pop and rock music are broadcast through BBC and independent radio stations every week, while pop and rock magazine programmes and occasional live or recorded concerts on television further promote pop and rock, which is by far the most popular form of musical expression in Britain.

In the 1960s and 1970s groups such as the Beatles, the Rolling Stones, Led Zeppelin and Pink Floyd achieved international success. British groups continue to be popular throughout the world and are often at the forefront of new developments in music.

Some of the more recent groups, with examples of their recordings, include the Cure (*Wish*), Def Leppard (*Adrenalize*), the Pet Shop Boys (*Discography*), Right Said Fred (*Up*), Simply Red (*Stars*) and Wet Wet Wet (*High on the Happy Side*).

Well-known performers, with examples of recent recordings, include Phil Collins (*Serious Hits Live!*), Peter Gabriel (*Us*), Elton John (*The One*), Annie Lennox (*Diva*), Mike Oldfield (*Tubular Bells II*), Sting (*The Soul Cages*) and Lisa Stansfield (*Real Love*).

In recent years young black artists, including Seal, and Roland Gift of the group Fine Young Cannibals, have furthered the development of popular music.

The pop and rock music industry continues to contribute significantly to Britain's overseas earnings through the sale of recordings, concert tours, and promotional material including clothing and books. The recording industry in Britain has an estimated annual turnover of £1,000 million.

Jazz

Jazz has a large following in Britain and is played in numerous clubs and pubs. British musicians such as Barbara Thompson, Stan Tracey, Andy Sheppard and Courtney Pine have established strong reputations throughout Europe. Festivals of jazz music are held annually in Soho (London), Glasgow, Crawley (West Sussex) and at a number of other places. Jazz Services provides a national touring network.

Jazz FM, Britain's first radio station dedicated to jazz, was launched in the London area in 1990.

Training

Professional training in music is given mainly at colleges of music. The leading London colleges are the Royal Academy of Music, the Royal College of Music, the Guildhall School of Music and Drama, and Trinity College of Music. The City University's music industry course provides training in business practice aimed specifically at musicians and music administrators. Outside London the main centres are the Royal Scottish Academy of Music and Drama in Glasgow, the Royal Northern College of Music in Manchester, the Welsh College of Music and Drama, Cardiff, and the Birmingham Conservatoire.

Other Educational Schemes

Many children learn to play musical instruments at school, and some take the examinations of the Associated Board of the Royal Schools of Music. Music is one of the foundation subjects in the National Curriculum (see p. 408). The National Youth Orchestras of Great Britain, of Scotland and of Wales and other youth orchestras have established high standards. Nearly a third of the players in the European Community Youth Orchestra come from Britain. There is also a National Youth Jazz Orchestra.

OPERA AND DANCE

Interest in opera has increased greatly in the last ten years, while an estimated 6 million people take part in dance, making it one of Britain's leading participatory activities, and audiences are attracted to a widening range of professional dance.

Regular seasons of opera and ballet are held at the Royal Opera House, Covent Garden, London. The Royal Opera, Royal Ballet and the Birmingham Royal Ballet, which rank among the world's leading companies, are supported by professional orchestras, as are English National Ballet and Northern Ballet Theatre. Seasons of opera in English are given by the English National Opera at the London Coliseum. Scottish Opera has regular seasons at the Theatre Royal in Glasgow, and tours mainly in Scotland and northern England. Welsh National Opera presents seasons in Cardiff and other cities. Opera North, based in Leeds, tours primarily in the north of England and Opera Factory stages experimental work in opera and music theatre. English Touring Opera takes opera to towns throughout England. Opera Northern Ireland presents seasons at the Opera House, Belfast, and tours in Northern Ireland.

An opera season for which international casts are specially assembled is held every summer at Glyndebourne in East Sussex. This is followed by an autumn tour by Glyndebourne Touring Opera, often using casts drawn from the chorus of the festival season. Work on a new opera house to be built on the same site at Glyndebourne, costing £33 million, is due to be completed in May 1994. All the funding will come from private sources.

Subsidised Dance Companies

Subsidised dance companies include the Birmingham (formerly Sadler's Wells) Royal Ballet, which tours widely in Britain and overseas; English National Ballet, which divides its performances between London and the regions; Northern Ballet Theatre, which is based in Halifax and also tours; and Scottish Ballet, based in Glasgow. Other companies are Rambert Dance Company (Britain's oldest ballet company, which re-formed in 1966 as a leading contemporary dance company); London Contemporary Dance Theatre, which provides regular seasons in London besides touring extensively; Adzido Pan African Dance Ensemble; Shobana Jeyasingh; and the Green Candle and Phoenix Dance Company. The Arts Council also supports Dance Umbrella, an organisation which promotes an annual festival of contemporary dance. In addition, the three Arts Councils and the Regional Arts Boards support individual artists and offer project grants to several small groups.

Lloyd Newson, Christopher Bruce, Richard Alston and Siobhan Davies are among the foremost British choreographers, and Michael Clark and Darcey Bussell among the leading dancers.

Training

Professional training for dancers and choreographers is provided mainly by specialist schools, which include the Royal Ballet School, the Rambert Dance School and the London Contemporary Dance School. These, together with many private schools, have helped to raise British dance to its present standard. Dance is a subject for degree studies at a number of institutions, including the Laban Centre, the University of Surrey, Dartington College of the Arts in Devon and Middlesex University.

Courses for students intending to work with community groups are available at three institutions. In 1991 the Royal Ballet announced a scheme to widen access to ballet training for children from a broader range of backgrounds, including ethnic minorities.

The National Opera Studio in London provides advanced training.

National Dance Agencies

Six national dance agencies have been set up in Birmingham, Leeds, the East Midlands,

London, Newcastle upon Tyne and Swindon. The agencies, which receive Arts Council support, offer classes, provide information and advice, help to co-ordinate activities, and commission dance artists to create work.

Other Educational Schemes

The Arts Council runs Taped, a scheme to finance dance videos for use in education, while the Video Place provides a library of videotape documentation of dance performances for viewing by promoters, choreographers, dancers, teachers and students.

The Performing Arts and Technology School, which opened in Croydon, Surrey, in 1991, offers studies in drama, music and dance to pupils aged from 14 to 18, with the emphasis on the application of technology to the performing arts. The capital cost of £5.9 million is being shared between the Government (60 per cent) and the British phonographic industry (40 per cent).

Youth and Music, an organisation affiliated to the international Jeunesses Musicales, encourages attendance by young people at opera, dance and concert performances. All dance companies in receipt of funding from the Arts Council provide dance workshops and education activities. English National Ballet has created ballets designed for 4- to 8- and 10- to 14-year-olds; Ludus Dance Company, based in Lancaster, works mainly with young people; and Scottish Ballet Steps Out works in schools throughout Scotland.

The National Youth Music Theatre, which is based in London, gives young people between 11 and 18 the opportunity to perform music theatre under the guidance of professional directors and choreographers. All the work takes place in the school holidays.

The National Youth Dance Company and Yuva, the National South Asian Dance Youth Company, provide opportunities for young dancers to work with professionals and to create and perform dance.

FILMS

British films, actors, and the creative and technical services supporting them are widely acclaimed. In March 1993 Emma Thompson won an Oscar as the best film actress for her role in *Howard's End*. Other British performers who enjoy international reputations include Sir Dirk Bogarde, Michael Caine, Sir Anthony Hopkins, Kenneth Branagh, Jeremy Irons, Dudley Moore, Michael York, Gary Oldman, Bob Hoskins, Alan Rickman, and Greta Scacchi.

There are approximately 1,800 cinema screens in Britain and estimated attendances are currently running at about 1.9 million a week. Seating capacity in cinemas increased during the late 1980s, due almost entirely to the rise in the number of multi-screen cinema complexes to 60 from just one in 1985. Cinemas with five or more screens accounted for 29 per cent of all screens in Britain in 1992, compared with 12 per cent in 1988.

Cinema admissions in 1992 totalled an estimated 102.5 million—compared with 58.4 million in 1984. In London and other large cities there are a number of art or repertory cinemas showing films which have not been more widely distributed. These include low budget films from Britain and abroad; other foreign films, often with English subtitles; and older films which are being shown again, sometimes in a newly edited form. Arts centres often include cinemas, and film societies use a range of buildings including, for example, public libraries.

Animation

The recent resurgence of interest in the cartoon film in Britain is due in part to the pioneering work of British animators, who have created 3D animation and computer animation. Television has proved an important source of production finance and has fostered the work of Nick Park, Peter Lord, David Sproxton, Tim Burton and David Anderson. Two British films, *Creature Comforts* by Aardman Animation, and *Manipulation*, directed by Daniel Greaves, won Oscars in 1991 and 1992 respectively.

Government Support for the Film Industry

An annual government grant (almost £15 million for 1993–94) is made to the British

Film Institute and one of £1.3 million to the Scottish Film Council and the Scottish Film Production Fund. Since April 1993 Britain has been a member of Eurimages, the Council of Europe's film co-production support scheme, contributing approximately £5.5 million over the first three years of membership. Eurimages aims to develop the European cinema and audio-visual industry by providing financial support for feature length fiction films, creative documentaries and distribution.

In 1991 the British Film Commission was launched, with government funding of £3.5 million over four years. The Commission aims to attract film productions from overseas by offering a service to assist film-makers.

British Screen Finance, a private sector company, provides a source of finance for new film-makers with commercially viable productions who have difficulty in attracting funding. The company, investing its own money together with contributions from the Government, part-finances the production of low- and medium-budget films involving largely British talent. It encourages the early stages of film project development and the production of short films. In 1992 the Government agreed to provide funding of £6 million over three years from 1994.

British Film Institute

The development of film, video and television as art forms is promoted by the British Film Institute (BFI), founded in 1933, and in Scotland by the Scottish Film Council. The Institute offers some direct financial and technical help through its Production Board.

It runs the National Film Theatre in London and the National Film Archive, and has the world's largest library of information on film and television. The Institute holds extensive international collections of books, periodicals, scripts, stills and posters. Its Education Department aims to enable as many people as possible to discover new ways of appreciating film, video and television.

The National Film Archive contains over 200,000 films and television programmes, including newsreels, dating from 1895. BFI

South Bank comprises the Museum of the Moving Image, which traces the history of film and television, and the National Film Theatre. The latter has three cinemas showing films of historical, artistic or technical interest, and is unique in offering regular programmes unrestricted by commercial considerations. In November each year it hosts the London Film Festival, at which some 250 new films from all over the world are screened.

The BFI promotes, and helps to fund, a network of some 40 regional film theatres; and is involved in establishing film and television centres with a range of activities and facilities. It also co-operates with the Regional Arts Boards and grant-aids their film activities. In 1992 the Institute raised almost £13 million—nearly half its income—from its operations.

The Welsh Arts Council acts as the Institute's agent in Wales. In Scotland the Scottish Film Council supports regional film theatres, administers the Scottish Film Archive, and promotes and provides material for media education. Together with the Scottish Arts Council, it has set up the Scottish Film Production Fund. The BFI's charter was recently extended to Northern Ireland, where the BFI works with the Northern Ireland Film Council (NIFC). The NIFC receives funds from the Arts Council of Northern Ireland.

Children's Film

The Children's Film and Television Foundation produces and distributes entertainment films for children, shown largely through video and television.

The Children's Film Unit, which has received funding from the Children's Film and Television Foundation, was founded in 1981. The Unit makes feature films for children and runs weekly workshops for children on all aspects of film-making. The unit caters for about 50 children at any time and has produced 14 feature films.

Training in Film Production

The National Film and Television School is

financed jointly by the Government and by the film, video and television industries. It offers postgraduate and short course training for directors, editors, camera operators, animators and other specialists. The School enrols about 30 full-time students a year and about 500 on short course programmes. In 1993–94 it is receiving a government grant of £1.9 million.

The London International Film School, the Royal College of Art, and some universities and other institutions of higher education also offer training in film production.

Cinema Licensing and Film Classification

Cinemas showing films to the public must be licensed by local authorities, which have a legal duty to prohibit the admission of children under 16 to unsuitable films, and may prevent the showing of any film. In assessing films the authorities normally rely on the judgment of an independent non-statutory body, the British Board of Film Classification (BBFC), to which films must be submitted. The Board was set up on the initiative of the cinema industry to ensure a proper standard in films shown to the public. It does not use any written code of censorship, but can require cuts to be made before granting a certificate; on rare occasions, it refuses a certificate.

Films passed by the Board are put into one of the following categories:

- U, meaning universal—suitable for all;
- PG, meaning parental guidance, in which some scenes may be unsuitable for young children;
- 12, 15 and 18, for people of not less than 12, 15 and 18 years of age respectively; and
- Restricted 18, for restricted showing only at segregated premises to which no one under 18 is admitted—for example, licensed cinema clubs.

Videos

The BBFC is also legally responsible for classifying videos under a system similar to

that for films. It is an offence to supply commercially a video which has not been classified or to supply it in contravention of its classification—for example, to sell or hire a video classified 18 to a person under the age of 18.

VISUAL ARTS

State support for the visual arts consists largely of funding for the national museums and galleries, purchase grants for municipal museums and galleries, and funding through local authorities, the Museums and Galleries Commission and the area museum councils. It also includes funding for living artists channelled through the Arts Councils, the Crafts Council and the Regional Arts Boards, and grants towards the cost of art education. The Government encourages high standards of industrial design and craftsmanship through grants to the Design Council (see p. 155). All national museums and galleries are financed chiefly from government funds. They may charge for entry to their permanent collections and special exhibitions. All the national collections are managed by independent trustees.

Museums and art galleries maintained by local authorities, universities, independent museums and private funds may receive help in building up their collections through grants administered by the Museums and Galleries Commission (for England and Wales) and the Scottish Museums Council. Financial and practical assistance to both national and local museums and galleries is also given by the Arts Council and by trusts and voluntary bodies, including the Calouste Gulbenkian Foundation and the National Art Collections Fund.

Pre-eminent works of art accepted by the Government in place of inheritance tax are allocated to public galleries. Financial help may be available from the National Heritage Memorial Fund (see p. 431), which is being allocated £12 million by the Department of National Heritage in 1993–94. In recent years the Fund has made important contributions towards pictures bought by the Birmingham, Leeds and Manchester City Art Galleries, and by the national galleries and museums.

In co-operation with the Regional Arts Boards, the Arts Council makes grants towards the public display of the visual arts, especially contemporary and experimental works, and the publication of books and magazines. It also encourages the commissioning of works of art in public places. The South Bank Board maintains the Arts Council's collection of contemporary British art and organises touring exhibitions on behalf of the Council. The Council supports a number of galleries in London, including the Hayward Gallery, Photographers' Gallery and Whitechapel Art Gallery; and in the regions, the Arnolfini in Bristol and the Ikon Gallery in Birmingham. It also provides support for artists and photographers through purchasing and commissioning fellowships and residencies. Similar support is given by the Scottish Arts Council to galleries in Scotland. The Welsh and Northern Ireland Arts Councils have galleries in Cardiff and Belfast respectively.

A number of modern British sculptors and painters have international reputations, and have received international prizes and commissions for major works in foreign cities. Among the best known are David Hockney, Lucian Freud and Sir Eduardo Paolozzi. Younger artists who have achieved international reputations include Richard Deacon, Tony Cragg and Anish Kapoor.

Museums and Art Galleries

About 100 million people a year, across all social groups, attend some 2,000 museums and galleries open to the public, which include the major national collections and a wide variety of municipally and independently or privately owned institutions.

Government provision for the national museums and galleries is £220 million in 1993–94. The Museums and Galleries Improvement Fund, which is jointly financed by the Government and the Wolfson Charities, is providing an annual budget of £4 million over five years from 1991–92 for refurbishment. The Fund is already supporting over 100 projects at national and other museums and galleries, including work in Glasgow, Merthyr Tydfil, Newcastle upon Tyne and Liverpool.

The Government takes advice on policy matters from the Museums and Galleries Commission. The Commission also promotes co-operation between national and provincial institutions. Ten area museum councils supply technical services and advice on conservation, display, documentation and publicity.

The Government encourages the loan of objects from national and provincial collections so that works of art can be seen by as wide a public as possible. It provides funds for promoting the touring of exhibitions and for facilitating the loan of items between institutions.

The Museum Training Institute is responsible for developing training standards and programmes.

Museums Association

The independent Museums Association, to which many museums and art galleries and their staffs belong, and which has many overseas members, facilitates exchange of information and discussion of matters relating to museums and galleries. It provides training, seminars and research; its publications include the monthly *Museums Journal*.

National Collections

The national museums and art galleries, many of them located in London, contain some of the world's most comprehensive collections of objects of artistic, archaeological, scientific, historical and general interest. They are:

- the British Museum (including the ethnographic collections of the Museum of Mankind);
- the Natural History Museum;
- the Victoria and Albert Museum (the V&A, which displays fine and decorative arts);
- the Science Museum;
- the National Gallery (which houses western painting from around 1260 to 1920);

- the Tate Gallery (British painting and modern art);
- the National Portrait Gallery;
- the Imperial War Museum;
- the National Army Museum;
- the Royal Air Force Museum;
- the National Maritime Museum;
- the Wallace Collection (which includes paintings, furniture, arms and armour; and objets d'art); and
- the National Museums and Galleries on Merseyside.

An extension to the National Gallery, the Sainsbury Wing, opened in 1991. It provides a venue for major international touring exhibitions and other events.

Some of the museums in London have branches in the regions. Examples are the National Railway Museum (York) and the National Museum of Photography, Film and Television (Bradford), which are part of the Science Museum. The Tate Gallery opened a branch in Liverpool in 1988, and another in St Ives, Cornwall, in June 1993, while the V&A plans to open a branch in Bradford.

In Scotland the national collections are held by the National Museums of Scotland and the National Galleries of Scotland. The former include the Royal Museum of Scotland and the Scottish United Services Museum, both in Edinburgh; the Museum of Flight, near North Berwick; and the Scottish Agricultural Museum. A new Museum of Scotland is to be built next to the Royal Museum to house the National Museums'

Scottish collection. The National Galleries of Scotland comprise the National Gallery of Scotland, the Scottish National Portrait Gallery and the Scottish National Gallery of Modern Art.

The National Museum of Wales (where a major expansion scheme is in progress), in Cardiff, has a number of branches, including the Welsh Folk Museum at St Fagans and the Industrial and Maritime Museum in Cardiff's dockland.

Northern Ireland has two national museums: the Ulster Museum in Belfast and the Ulster Folk and Transport Museum in County Down.

Other Collections

Other important collections in London include the Royal Armouries, Britain's oldest museum, which has been housed in the Tower of London for 900 years; the Museum of London; Sir John Soane's Museum; the Courtauld collection; and the London Transport Museum. The Queen's Gallery in Buckingham Palace has exhibitions of pictures from the extensive royal collections.

Most cities and towns have museums devoted to art, archaeology and natural history, usually administered by the local authorities but sometimes by local learned societies or by individuals or trustees. Both Oxford and Cambridge are rich in museums. Many are associated with their universities, such as the Ashmolean Museum in Oxford, and the Fitzwilliam Museum in Cambridge.

Table 29.1: Estimated Attendance at National Museums and Galleries in England in 1992

British Museum	6,725,000
Imperial War Museum	1,141,000
National Gallery	4,300,000
Natural History Museum	1,612,000
National Maritime Museum	532,000
National Museums and Galleries on Merseyside	1,207,000
National Portrait Gallery	796,000
Science Museum	2,579,000
Tate Gallery	2,151,000
Victoria and Albert Museum and branches	1,526,000
Wallace Collection	200,000

Source: *Department of National Heritage Annual Report 1993.*

Many private collections of art and antiques in historic family mansions, including those owned by the National Trusts and English Heritage (see p. 341), are open to the public.

An increasing number of open air museums depict the regional life of an area or preserve early industrial remains. These include the Weald and Downland Museum in West Sussex, and the Ironbridge Gorge Museum in Shropshire. Skills of the past are revived in a number of 'living' museums, such as the Gladstone Pottery Museum near Stoke-on-Trent and the Quarry Bank Mill at Styal in Cheshire.

Among the more recent museums are the Museum of Science and Industry in Manchester; the Jorvik Viking Centre, a reconstruction of the Viking settlement in York; the Mary Rose Museum in Portsmouth, housing the restored wreck of the flagship of Henry VIII, which sank in 1545; and Eureka!, the first museum designed specifically for children, which opened in Halifax, West Yorkshire, in 1992. The Burrell Collection in Glasgow houses world-famous tapestries, paintings and objets d'art. The Design Museum, which opened in London's Docklands in 1990, houses exhibits charting changes in design and technology.

There are also a number of national art exhibiting societies, the most famous being the Royal Academy of Arts at Burlington House. The Academy holds an annual Summer Exhibition, where the works of hundreds of professional and amateur artists can be seen, and important exhibitions during the rest of the year. The Royal Scottish Academy holds annual exhibitions in Edinburgh. There are also children's exhibitions, including the National Exhibition of Children's Art.

Crafts

Government aid for the crafts, amounting to £3.1 million in 1993–94, is administered in England, Wales and Scotland by the Crafts Council. The Council supports craftsmen and women by promoting public interest in their work, and encouraging the creation and conservation of works of contemporary craftsmanship. Grants are available to help with setting up workshops and acquiring equipment. The Crafts Council runs the national centre for crafts in London, which houses a gallery, a reference library, a picture library, and a gallery shop. It organises the annual Chelsea Crafts Fair, and co-ordinates British groups at international trade fairs. Crafts Council exhibitions tour nationally and internationally, and grants are made to encourage exhibitions, projects and organisations. It also runs a craft shop at the Victoria and Albert Museum. Funding is given to the English Regional Arts Boards and the Scottish and Welsh Arts Councils for the support of crafts, and to Contemporary Applied Art, a membership organisation that holds exhibitions and sells work through its London gallery.

Funding is passed to the English Regional Arts Boards and to the Scottish and Welsh Arts Councils for the development of craft.

In 1992 Britain's crafts economy had an estimated annual turnover of £250 million.

Training in Art and Design

Most practical education in art and design is provided in colleges of art (among the best known of which are the Slade School, Goldsmith's College and the Royal College of Art, all in London), further education colleges and private art schools, many of which award degrees at postgraduate level. Art is also taught at an advanced level at the four Scottish Central (Art) Institutions.

Courses at universities concentrate largely on academic disciplines such as the history of art. The leading institutions include the Courtauld and Warburg Institutes of the University of London and the Department of Classical Art and Archaeology at University College, London. Art is one of the foundation subjects in the National Curriculum; and the Society for Education through Art encourages, among other activities, the purchase by schools of original works of art by organising an annual Pictures for Schools exhibition.

The Open College of the Arts offers

correspondence courses in art and design, painting, sculpture, textiles, photography and creative writing to people wishing to study at home.

Export Control of Works of Art

London is a major centre for the international art market, and sales of works of art take place in the main auction houses (two of the longest-established being Sotheby's and Christie's), and through private dealers. Certain items are covered by export control. These are:

- works of art and collectors' items over 50 years old and worth £20,000 or more (£5,000 or more in the case of British historical portraits);

- photographic material over 50 years old and valued at £500 or more an item; and

- documents, manuscripts and archives over 50 years old, irrespective of value.

A licence from the Department of National Heritage is required before such items can be exported. If the Department's advisers recommend withholding a licence, the matter is referred to the Reviewing Committee on the Export of Works of Art. If the Committee considers a work to be of national importance it can advise the Government to withhold the export licence for a specified time to give a public museum, art gallery, or private collector an opportunity to buy at a fair price. In 1991 the Committee published a review of the present system of export control, following which the Government decided against listing important paintings and other heritage objects to prevent them from being exported.

With the completion of the single European market in January 1993, there is concern that the removal of customs barriers for intra-community trade may facilitate the illicit export of national treasures. Discussions on methods of preventing this are in progress.

LITERATURE AND LIBRARIES

A number of literary activities receive public subsidy through the Arts Council. In 1990, for example, the Council sponsored its first international writers' tour, and contributed to an innovative television series on modern poetry. It continues to foster an interest in writing from diverse cultures through its support for translations and black publishing.

There are free public libraries throughout Britain (see p. 449), private libraries and several private literary societies. Book reviews are featured in the press and on television and radio, and numerous periodicals concerned with literature are published (see p. 455). Recognition of outstanding literary merit is provided by a number of awards, some of the most valuable being the Booker, National Cash Register and Whitbread prizes. In March 1993 V. S. Naipaul was awarded the first David Cohen British Literature Prize for a lifetime's achievement by a living British writer. The prize will be awarded every two years. Awards to encourage young writers include those of the Somerset Maugham Trust Fund and the E. C. Gregory Trust Fund. Many British writers are internationally recognised.

Well-known living novelists, with examples of their works, include

- Sir Kingsley Amis—*Lucky Jim, Stanley and the Women;*

- Anthony Burgess—*A Clockwork Orange, The End of the World News;*

- A. S. Byatt—*Possession: A Romance;* and

- Fay Weldon—*Praxis, The Cloning of Joanna May.*

Many writers from overseas, often from Commonwealth countries, also live and work in Britain, writing books in English which have a wide circulation in Britain and overseas.

Distinguished British poets include Ted Hughes, the Poet Laureate (the Poet Laureate is a member of the Royal Household who receives an annual stipend from the Civil List—see p. 46; he may write commemorative verse if he wishes); Geoffrey Hill; Tony Harrison; James Berry; Gavin Ewart; Wendy Cope; and Elizabeth Jennings.

English literature is taught extensively at schools, colleges and universities throughout

Britain. Creative writing is also taught at a wide variety of institutions; one of the best known centres is at the University of East Anglia, in Norwich, which also houses the British Centre for Literary Translation.

Authors' Copyright and Performers' Protection

Original literary, dramatic, musical or artistic works, films, sound recordings and broadcasts are automatically protected by copyright in Britain. This protection is also given to works from countries party to international copyright conventions. The copyright owner has rights against unauthorised reproduction, public performance, broadcasting and issue to the public of his or her work; and against dealing in unauthorised copies. In most cases the author is the first owner of the copyright, and the term of copyright is the life of the author and a period of 50 years after death (50 years from the year of release for films and sound recordings and 50 years from the year of broadcast for broadcasts).

The Copyright, Designs and Patents Act 1988 reformed copyright law and introduced the concept of moral rights, whereby authors have the right to be identified on their works and to object to derogatory treatment of them. The Act also updated the rights which protect performers against making and trading in unauthorised recordings of live performances, the term of protection for these rights being 50 years from the year in which the performance is given.

Literary and Philological Societies

Societies to promote literature include the English Association and the Royal Society of Literature. The leading society for studies in the humanities is the British Academy for the Promotion of Historical, Philosophical and Philological Studies (the British Academy).

Other specialist societies are the Early English Text Society, the Bibliographical Society and several societies devoted to particular authors, the largest of which is the Dickens Fellowship. Various societies, such as the Poetry Society, sponsor poetry readings and recitals.

Libraries

The British Library

The British Library, the national library of Britain, is one of the world's greatest libraries. Its collections comprise over 18 million items—monographs, manuscripts, maps, newspapers, patents, stamps and recorded sound. Publishers must deposit there a copy of most items published or available in Britain.

The National Bibliographic Service processes material legally deposited at the Library for inclusion in catalogues and maintains a machine-readable database of bibliographical records from which is derived the British National Bibliography (a list of new and forthcoming British books) and a range of automated bibliographical services.

The Research and Development Department is a major source of funding for research and development in library and information services.

The Library's Document Supply Centre at Boston Spa (West Yorkshire) is the national centre for inter-library lending within Britain and between Britain and countries overseas. It supplies 3.5 million requests a year, mostly from its own stock of 7 million documents.

In 1990 the Library set up the self-supporting Centre for the Book, to promote awareness of books and their role in British life.

The British Library's new London headquarters at St Pancras is being built at a cost of £450 million, and will be open to the public by 1996. It will provide reading rooms for most of the Library's London-based collections—humanities, science, technology and industry—and also specialist reading areas. The new Library aims to offer greatly improved services, including exhibition galleries, a bookshop, a lecture theatre and a conference centre.

Other Libraries

The National Libraries of Scotland and Wales, the Bodleian Library of Oxford University and the Cambridge University Library can also claim copies of all new

British publications under legal deposit. The first phase of a new building for the National Library of Scotland was opened in 1989, providing 49 km (30 miles) of storage shelving and accommodating a map library, lending services and the Scottish Science Library. The second stage is due to be completed in 1994.

Some of the national museums and government departments have important libraries.

- The Public Record Office in London and in Kew, Surrey, is an executive agency of the Lord Chancellor's Department. It houses the records of the superior courts of law of England and Wales and of most government departments, as well as famous historical documents. The Office has many millions of documents, dating from the time of the Norman Conquest to the present day. Public records, with few exceptions, are available for inspection by members of the public 30 years after the end of the year in which they were created.

- The Scottish Record Office in Edinburgh and the Public Record Office of Northern Ireland, Belfast, serve the same purpose.

Besides a number of great private collections, such as that of the London Library, there are the libraries of the learned societies and institutions. Examples are the Royal Institute of International Affairs, the Royal Geographical Society and the Royal Academy of Music. The Poetry Library in the South Bank Centre in London, owned by the Arts Council, is a national collection of 20th-century poetry written in or translated into English.

University Libraries

The university libraries of Oxford and Cambridge are unmatched by those of the more recent foundations. However, the combined library resources of the colleges and institutions of the University of London total 9 million volumes, the John Rylands University Library in Manchester contains 3.4 million volumes, Edinburgh 2 million, Leeds 1.8 million, and Birmingham, Glasgow,

Liverpool and Aberdeen each have over 1 million volumes. Many universities have important research collections in special subjects; examples include the Barnes Medical Library at Birmingham and the British Library of Political and Economic Science at the London School of Economics. University libraries also have on-line access to library information worldwide.

Special Libraries

Numerous associations and commercial and industrial organisations run library and information services. Although most are intended primarily for use within the organisation, many can be used, by arrangement, by people interested in the area covered, and the specialist publications held are often available for inter-library lending.

Public Libraries

Local authorities in Great Britain and education and library boards in Northern Ireland have a duty to provide a free lending and reference library service, and Britain's network of public libraries has a total stock of about 130.2 million books. In 1991–92 public libraries added nearly 13 million books to their stock; actual expenditure on new stock totalled £105.8 million. Public libraries issue an average of ten books a year for every person in Britain. Of these, 56 per cent are works of fiction for adults. Over half of the total population are members of public libraries. Some areas are served by mobile libraries, and domiciliary services cater for people unable to visit a library.

Many libraries have collections of compact discs, records, audio- and video-cassettes, and musical scores for loan to the public, while a number also lend from collections of works of art, which may be originals or reproductions. Most libraries hold documents on local history, and nearly all provide children's departments, while reference and information sections and art, music, commercial and technical departments meet the growing demands in these fields. The information role is one of increasing importance for many libraries, and greater use is being made of information technology, including microcomputers and reference databases.

The Government remains committed to providing a free basic library service—the borrowing and consultation of printed materials—but believes there is scope for greater private sector involvement. It makes available £250,000 a year to encourage new developments and increase efficiency. Priority is given to projects involving collaboration with other libraries and the private sector.

Public libraries charge for some services, such as research services and the lending of non-printed materials.

The Government is advised on library and information matters by four library and information services councils or committees, representing England, Wales, Scotland and Northern Ireland.

A government review of the scope and value of services provided by public libraries in England is in progress. The Government has also announced plans to carry out an investigation of the feasibility of contracting out the delivery of some parts of the public library service.

The Library Association

The Library Association is the principal professional organisation for those engaged in library and information services. Founded in 1877, the Association has 25,000 members. It maintains a Register of Chartered Librarians and publishes books, pamphlets and an official journal.

The Library Association is the designated authority for the recognition of qualifications gained in other EC member states.

Public Lending Right Scheme

The Public Lending Right Scheme, introduced in 1979, gives registered authors the right to receive payment from a central fund (totalling £5 million in 1993–94) for the loans made of their books from public libraries in Britain. Payment is made in proportion to the number of times the authors' books are lent out. In 1991–92, 97 authors received the maximum payment of £6,000.

Books

In 1992 British publishers issued some 79,000 separate titles, of which just over 59,000 were new titles and the remainder reprints and new editions. The British publishing industry devotes much effort to developing overseas markets, and in 1992 the value of exports of British books amounted to £773 million.

Among the leading organisations representing publishing and distribution interests are the Publishers Association, which has 160 members, representing over 262 separate publishing companies; and the Booksellers' Association, with 3,300 members. The Publishers Association, through its International Division, promotes the export of British books.

Historical Manuscripts

The Royal Commission on Historical Manuscripts is the central investigatory and advisory body on manuscripts, records and archives other than the public records. It maintains the National Register of Archives and advises owners, custodians and government; assists researchers; and co-ordinates the activities of bodies working in the field. It also publishes a series of *Guides to Sources for British History*.

The National Manuscripts Conservation Trust provides grants to record offices, libraries and other owners of manuscripts and archives accessible to the public.

Further Reading

The Arts. Aspects of Britain series, HMSO, 1993.

Department of National Heritage Annual Report 1993. Department of National Heritage.

30 The Media

More daily newspapers, national and regional, are sold for every person in Britain than in most other developed countries. On an average day 62 per cent of people over the age of 15 read a national morning newspaper; about 71 per cent read a Sunday newspaper. However, television viewing is by far Britain's most popular leisure pastime: 95 per cent of households have a colour television set and over two-thirds a video recorder. People spend an average of nearly four hours a day watching television, including video playbacks.

The Press

There is no state control or censorship of the press, but it is subject to the general laws on publication (see p. 459). Following publication of an independent review of the effectiveness of press self-regulation in January 1993, the Government has stated that it considers that the present arrangements for self-regulation are unsatisfactory, and has announced a number of steps to tackle intrusions into personal privacy (see p. 458). The press has since announced changes in response to the Government's comments (see p. 458).

Three out of four adults regularly read a paid-for regional or local newspaper as well as a free local paper. National papers have a total circulation of 14 million on weekdays and 16.1 million on Sundays, although the total readership is considerably greater.

Men are more likely to read newspapers than women (66 per cent against 57 per cent) and more people in the 45–64 age group read a daily newspaper than in any other age group.

There are about 125 daily (Monday to Saturday) and Sunday newspapers, some 2,000 weekly paid-for and free newspapers (including business, sporting and religious newspapers), and 7,000 periodical publications.

Several newspapers have had very long and distinguished histories. The *Observer*, for example, first published in 1791, is the oldest national Sunday newspaper in the world, and *The Times*, Britain's oldest daily national newspaper, began publication in 1785. The weekly *Berrow's Worcester Journal* claims to be the world's oldest newspaper in continuous circulation, having been established in 1690.

The press caters for a variety of political

views, interests and levels of education. Newspapers are almost always financially independent of any political party. Where they express pronounced views and show obvious political leanings in their editorial comments, these derive from proprietorial and other non-party influences. Nevertheless, during general election campaigns many newspapers recommend their readers to vote for a particular political party. Even newspapers which adopt strong political views in their editorial columns include feature and other types of articles by authors of a variety of political persuasions. In order to preserve their character and traditions, some newspapers and periodicals are governed by trustee-type arrangements. Others have management arrangements to ensure their editors' authority and independence.

In recent years working practices throughout the newspaper industry have undergone major changes in response to the challenges posed by computer-based technology and the need to contain costs. Newsprint, about three-quarters of which is imported, forms about a quarter of average national newspaper costs; labour represents over half. In addition to sales, many newspapers and periodicals earn considerable amounts from their advertising. Total yearly spending of around £4,000 million on press advertising makes the press by far the largest advertising medium in Britain. Unlike most of its European counterparts the British press receives no subsidies and relatively few tax and postal concessions.

In discussions on a 'new world information and communication order' Britain has opposed measures designed to increase governmental regulation of the media or limit the free flow of information. At the same time, it has reaffirmed its willingness to support efforts to improve communications systems in the developing world.

New Printing Technology

Publishers have been able to reduce production costs, often by using advanced systems for editing and production processes. The 'single keying' system, for example, allows journalists or advertising staff to input 'copy' directly into a computer terminal, and then to transfer it electronically into columns of type. Although it is possible to arrange page layouts on screen, and to have these made into plates for the printing press, at present very few such systems are in operation. Most involve the production of bromides from the computer setting; these are then pasted up into columns before being placed in a plate-making machine.

News International, publisher of three daily and two Sunday papers, has at its London Docklands headquarters more than 500 computer terminals, one of the largest systems installed at one time anywhere in the world. The *Financial Times* opened a new printing plant in Docklands in 1988 with about 200 production workers, compared with the 650 formerly employed in the City of London. The new Docklands plant of the Associated Newspapers Group uses flexography, an advanced printing process. Other papers have also set up computerised printing plants outside Fleet Street.

Newspaper Ownership

Ownership of the national, London and regional daily newspapers lies in the hands of a number of large press publishing groups (see Table 30.1). There are also some 100 independent regional and local newspaper publishers.

Although most enterprises are organised as limited liability companies, individual and partner proprietorship survives. The large national newspaper and periodical publishers are major corporations; many are involved in the whole field of publishing and communications. Some have shares in independent television and radio companies, while others have industrial and commercial interests.

The law provides safeguards against the risks inherent in undue concentration of ownership. Government consent is needed to transfer a newspaper or newspaper assets to a proprietor whose newspapers have an average daily circulation amounting, with that of the newspaper to be taken over, to 500,000 or more copies. Except in certain limited cases, consent may be given only after the President

Table 30.1: National Newspapers

Title and foundation date	Controlled by	Circulation[a] average February–July 1993
National dailies		
'Populars'		
Daily Mirror (1903)	Mirror Group Newspapers (1986)	2,670,396
Daily Star (1978)	United Newspapers	679,861
The Sun (1964)	News International	3,526,532
'Mid market'		
Daily Mail (1896)	Associated Newspapers Group	1,771,620
Daily Express (1900)	United Newspapers	1,489,108
Today (1986)	News International	543,718
'Qualities'		
Financial Times (1888)	Pearson	289,826
The Daily Telegraph (1855)	The Daily Telegraph	1,021,550
The Guardian (1821)	Guardian Newspapers Ltd	411,981
The Independent (1986)	Newspaper Publishing	343,308
The Times (1785)	News International	363,799
National Sundays		
'Populars'		
News of the World (1843)	News International	4,605,932
Sunday Mirror (1963)	Mirror Group Newspapers (1986)	2,661,721
The People (1881)	Mirror Group Newspapers (1986)	2,011,615
'Mid market'		
The Mail on Sunday (1982)	Associated Newspapers Group	1,991,151
Sunday Express (1918)	United Newspapers	1,716,633
'Qualities'		
Sunday Telegraph (1961)	The Daily Telegraph	579,504
The Independent on Sunday (1990)	Newspaper Publishing	379,317
The Observer (1791)	Guardian Newspapers Ltd	503,192
The Sunday Times (1822)	News International	1,224,472

[a]Circulation figures are those of the Audit Bureau of Circulations (consisting of publishers, advertisers and advertising agencies) and are certified average daily or weekly net sales for the period.

of the Board of Trade has referred the matter to the Monopolies and Mergers Commission and received its report.

Under the Broadcasting Act 1990 (see p. 462) no proprietor of a national newspaper or local newspaper is allowed more than a 20 per cent interest in direct broadcasting by satellite channels, independent television Channels 3 and 5, and national and local radio within its circulation area. (A local newspaper can own a local radio station if the station does not serve an area overlapping that served by the newspaper.)

The National Press

The national press consists of 12 daily morning papers and nine Sunday papers (see Table 30.1). Formerly they were produced in or near Fleet Street in London with, in some cases, northern editions being printed in Manchester. All the national papers have now moved their editorial and printing facilities to other parts of London or away from the capital altogether; some use contract printing. The *Independent*, for example, is printed in Bradford, Northampton and Portsmouth. Scottish editions of the *Sun*, *The Times*, the *News of the World* and the *Sunday Times* are printed in Glasgow.

In order to improve distribution and sales overseas, editions of the *Financial Times* are printed in Frankfurt, Roubaix (northern France), New Jersey and Tokyo, while the *Guardian* prints an international edition in Frankfurt. The *European*, a weekly English-language international newspaper, is printed in Britain, France, Germany and Hungary.

National newspapers are often described as either 'quality', 'popular' or 'mid-market' papers on the basis of differences in style and content. Five dailies and four Sundays are usually described as 'quality' newspapers, which are directed at readers who want full information on a wide range of public matters. Popular newspapers appeal to people wanting news of a more entertaining character, presented more concisely. 'Mid-market' publications cover the intermediate market. Quality papers are normally broadsheet (large-sheet) in format and mid-market and popular papers tabloid (small-sheet).

Many newspapers are printed in colour and most produce colour supplements as part of the Saturday or Sunday paper, with articles on travel, food and wine, and other leisure topics.

The leading Scottish papers, the *Scotsman* and the *Herald*, have considerable circulations outside Scotland.

There is a growing market for news and information in the electronic media, and quality papers such as the *Financial Times* provide material for use on databases and videotext services. *The Times* supplies a news service to British Sky Broadcasting (BSkyB), a direct satellite broadcasting company under the same ownership.

Regional Newspapers

There are about 100 morning, evening and Sunday newspapers and some 2,000 weekly paid-for and free distribution newspapers, publishing mainly regional and local news.

England

Of the morning papers the *Yorkshire Post* (Leeds), the *Northern Echo* (Darlington) and the *Eastern Daily Press* (Norwich), each has a circulation of over 82,000, and two provincial Sunday papers—the *Sunday Mercury* (Birmingham) and the *Sunday Sun* (Newcastle upon Tyne)—sell 152,000 and 120,000 copies respectively. Circulation figures of evening papers start at about 10,000 and most are in the 20,000 to 100,000 range. Those with much larger sales include the *Manchester Evening News* (222,000), Wolverhampton's *Express and Star* (218,000) and the Birmingham *Evening Mail* (206,000). Paid weekly papers have a mainly local appeal and most have circulations in the 5,000 to 60,000 range.

London has one evening paper, the *Evening Standard*, with a circulation of 476,400. It covers national and international news as well as local affairs. A number of evening papers are published in the outer metropolitan area. Local weeklies include papers for every district in Greater London, which are often local editions of individual papers.

Wales

Wales has one daily morning newspaper, the *Western Mail*, with a circulation of 71,800, and *Wales on Sunday*, with a circulation of 54,000. Both are published in Cardiff. Evening papers published in Wales are the *South Wales Echo*, Cardiff; the *South Wales Argus*, Newport; the *South Wales Evening Post*, Swansea; and the *Evening Leader*, Wrexham. Circulations range from 32,600 to 77,600. North Wales is served by the *Daily Post*, published in Liverpool, and the *Liverpool Echo*.

The weekly press (79 publications) includes English-language papers, some of which carry articles in Welsh; bilingual papers; and Welsh-language papers. Welsh community newspapers receive an annual grant as part of the Government's wider financial support for the Welsh language.

Scotland

Scotland has six morning, five evening and three Sunday newspapers. Local weekly newspapers number 118. The daily morning papers, with circulations of between 9,800 and 757,000, are *The Scotsman* (published in Edinburgh); the *Herald*; the *Daily Record* (sister paper of the *Daily Mirror*); the *Dundee Courier and Advertiser*; the *Aberdeen Press and Journal*; and the *Paisley Daily Express*. The daily evening papers have circulations in the range of 21,000 to 150,400 and include the *Evening News* of Edinburgh, Glasgow's *Evening Times*, Dundee's *Evening Telegraph* and Aberdeen's *Evening Express*.

The Sunday papers are the *Sunday Mail*, the *Sunday Post* and a quality broadsheet paper, *Scotland on Sunday*. The national *Sunday Express* has a Scottish edition (printed in Manchester) and the *Observer* and the *Sunday Times* carry Scottish supplements.

Northern Ireland

Northern Ireland has two morning newspapers, one evening and two Sunday papers, all published in Belfast, with circulations ranging from 19,600 to 131,000. They are the *News Letter* (unionist), the *Irish News* (nationalist), the evening *Belfast Telegraph*, *Sunday Life* and *Sunday World* (Northern Ireland edition).

There are about 50 weeklies. Newspapers from the Irish Republic, as well as the British national press, are widely read in Northern Ireland.

Free Distribution Newspapers

More than 1,000 free distribution newspapers, mostly weekly and financed by advertising, are published in Britain; over half are produced by established newspaper publishers. They have enjoyed rapid growth in recent years and now have an estimated total weekly circulation of about 35 million.

Ethnic Minority Publications

Over 70 newspapers and magazines in Britain are produced by members of the ethnic minorities. Most are published weekly, fortnightly or monthly. Two Chinese newspapers, *Sing Tao* and *Wen Wei Po*, the Urdu *Daily Jang* (see below) and the Arabic *Al-Arab*, however, are dailies.

The *Asian Times* and *Indiamail* are English language weeklies for people of Asian descent; the *Sikh Messenger* and *Sikh Courier* are produced quarterly. Afro-Caribbean newspapers include the *Weekly Gleaner*, a local edition of the long-established *Jamaican Gleaner*, and *West Indian Digest*. The *Voice* and *Caribbean Times*, both weeklies, are aimed at the black population in general. The *Weekly Journal*, the first 'quality' broadsheet aimed at Britain's black community, was launched in 1992. Leading ethnic language newspapers include the Urdu *Daily Jang*, an offshoot of the largest circulation paper in Pakistan, and the weekly *Gujarat Samachar*, a Gujarati tabloid. Publications also appear in Bengali (examples are the weeklies *Jagoran* and *Janomot*); in Hindi (the weeklies *Amar Deep*, *Hind Samachar* and *Navin Weekly*); and in Punjabi (the weeklies *Des Pardes* and *Punjab Darpan* and the monthlies *Rachna* and *Perdesan*).

Many provincial papers print special editions for their local populations. The *Leicester Mercury*, for example, publishes a daily Asian edition, incorporating news from the South Asian sub-continent.

The Periodical Press

The 7,000 periodical publications are classified as 'consumer general interest', 'special interest' and 'business-to-business'. There are also several hundred 'house magazines' produced by businesses or public services for their employees and/or clients. Directories and similar publications number more than 2,000. The 'alternative' press comprises a large number of titles, many of them devoted to radical politics, community matters, religion, the occult, science or ecology.

Consumer general and specialist periodicals comprise magazines for a wide range of interests. These include women's magazines; publications for children; religious periodicals; fiction magazines; magazines dealing with sport, motoring, gardening, youth interests and music; humour; retirement; and computer magazines. Learned societies, trade unions, regiments, universities and other organisations also produce publications.

Weekly periodicals with the highest sales are those which carry full details of the forthcoming week's television and radio programmes, including the satellite schedules. *What's on TV* has a circulation figure of 1.5 million, followed by the *Radio Times* with 1.4 million and *TV Times* with 1 million.

Woman's Weekly, Woman's Own, Woman, Weekly News (which sells mainly in Scotland), *Woman's Realm, My Weekly* and *Me* have circulations in the 355,000 to 689,000 range. In recent years several women's magazines from overseas have achieved large circulations: *Prima* and *Best*, for instance, each sell over 560,000 copies, while *Bella* and *Hello!* are also widely read. *Smash Hits*, with a circulation of 312,000, is a fortnightly magazine dealing with pop music and teenage lifestyles. *Viz*, a cartoon comic aimed at young adults, sells 869,000 copies. Of monthly magazines, *Reader's Digest* has the highest circulation (1.6 million).

The leading journals of opinion include *The Economist*, an independent conservative publication covering a wide range of topics. The *New Statesman and Society* reviews social issues, politics, literature and the arts from an independent socialist point of view, and the *Spectator* covers similar subjects from an independent conservative standpoint.

New Scientist reports on science and technology in terms that the non-specialist reader can understand. *Private Eye*, a satirical fortnightly, also covers public affairs. Weekly 'listings' magazines, such as *Time Out*, provide details of cultural and other events in London and other large cities.

Literary and political journals, and those specialising in international and Commonwealth affairs, appear monthly or quarterly, and generally appeal to a more academic readership. Many of the business, scientific and professional journals, whose publication ranges from twice weekly to quarterly, have a considerable circulation overseas. There are about 4,600 publications covering business and industrial affairs.

News Agencies

The principal news agencies in Britain are Reuters, based in London, the Press Association and Extel Financial.

Reuters

Reuters is a publicly owned company, employing over 10,000 staff in 79 countries. It has more than 1,200 staff journalists and photographers. The company serves subscribers in over 140 countries, including financial institutions; commodities houses; traders in currencies, equities and bonds; major corporations; government agencies; news agencies; newspapers; and radio and television stations.

Reuters has developed the world's largest private leased communications network to transmit its services. It provides the media with a wide range of news, news pictures and graphics. Services for business clients comprise constantly updated financial news, historical information, facilities for computerised trading, and the supply of communications and other equipment for financial dealing rooms. Information is distributed through video terminals and teleprinters. Reuters owns Reuters Television, a television news agency (see p. 471).

The Press Association

The Press Association—the British and Irish national news agency—is co-operatively owned by the principal daily newspapers of Britain outside London, and of the Irish Republic. It offers national and regional newspapers and broadcasters a comprehensive range of home news and provides regional papers with the world news from Reuters and Associated Press.

News is sent by satellite from London by the Press Association, certain items being available in Dataformat, as camera-ready copy. Its 'Newsfile' operation provides general news, sports and foreign news on screen by means of telephone and viewdata terminals. The photographic department offers newspapers and broadcasters a daily pictures service. The NewsFeatures service supplies reports of local or special interest and grants exclusive rights to syndicated features. It also offers a dial-in graphics facility, as well as extensive cuttings and photograph libraries.

Extel Financial

Extel Financial supplies information and services to financial and business communities throughout the world. Based in London, it has a network of offices in Europe, the United States and in the Asia Pacific region. Data is collected from all the world's major stock exchanges, companies and the international press. The company is a major source of reference material on companies and securities, and supplies up-to-the-minute business and company news.

Other Agencies

News services are also provided by Associated Press and United Press International, which are British subsidiaries of United States news agencies. A number of other agencies and news services have offices in London, and there are minor agencies in other cities. Syndication of features is not as common in Britain as in some countries, but a few agencies specialise in this type of work.

Training and Education

The National Council for the Training of Journalists (NCTJ), which represents many regional newspaper publishers, sets and conducts examinations, and organises short training courses for journalists.

The two main methods of entry into newspaper journalism are selection for a one-year NCTJ pre-entry course at a college of further or higher education or direct recruitment by a regional or local newspaper. Both types of entrant take part in 'on-the-job' training. Block-release courses, preceded by a period of distance learning, are provided for those who have not attended a pre-entry course. Similar courses exist for press photographers.

The first undergraduate courses in journalism in Britain started in 1991 at City University, London, at the University of Central Lancashire and at the London College of Printing, which also provides GCE (General Certificate of Education) Advanced ('A') level courses in journalism. Postgraduate courses in journalism are available at the University of Wales College of Cardiff; City University, London; the London College of Printing; Strathclyde University/Glasgow Caledonian University; and the Universities of Central Lancashire and Bournemouth.

Courses for regional newspapers in such subjects as newspaper sales, advertising, and management are provided by the Newspaper Society's training service. Some newspaper publishers carry out journalist training independently of the NCTJ, awarding their own certificates or diplomas. New National Vocational Qualifications (see p. 415) are now available in newspaper journalism.

Specialist training courses for journalists and news media managers from developing countries and from Eastern Europe are offered by the Thomson Foundation in Cardiff. The Foundation also runs training courses overseas and provides consultants to assist newspapers, news agencies and magazines in editorial advertising, management, circulation and the use of new technology. It runs an international journalism training centre in collaboration with Xinhua News Agency in Peking.

Through its charitable trust, the Reuter Foundation, Reuters offers assistance to overseas journalists to study and train in Britain and other parts of the world. The Foundation awards fellowships to journalists from developing nations to spend up to one year at Oxford University. It also runs shorter practical training programmes in London for journalists from Eastern and Central Europe.

The Periodicals Training Council is the official training organisation in periodical publishing. It offers a range of short courses covering management, editorial work, advertisement sales and circulation sales. It has special responsibility for editorial training and administers an editorial training scheme for those already in employment.

Newspapers in Education

Newspapers in Education, a worldwide scheme using newspapers to improve standards of literacy among young people, is run in Britain by the Newspaper Society. The scheme involves using newspapers in schools for teaching a wide range of subjects at all levels of education. Launched in Birmingham in 1984, the scheme has over 300 projects operated by regional newspapers in partnership with local schools.

Press Institutions

Employers' organisations include the Newspaper Publishers Association, whose members publish national newspapers, and the Newspaper Society, which represents regional and local newspapers in England, Wales and Northern Ireland. The Scottish Daily Newspaper Society represents the interests of daily and Sunday newspapers in Scotland; the Scottish Newspaper Publishers' Association acts on behalf of the owners of weekly newspapers in Scotland; and

Associated Northern Ireland Newspapers is made up of proprietors of weekly newspapers in Northern Ireland. The membership of the Periodical Publishers Association includes most independent publishers of business, professional and consumer journals.

Organisations representing journalists are the National Union of Journalists, with around 25,000 members, and the Chartered Institute of Journalists, with about 1,500 members. The main printing union is the Graphical, Paper and Media Union, with a membership of around 270,000.

> The Foreign Press Association was formed in 1888 to help the correspondents of overseas newspapers in their work by arranging press conferences, tours, briefings, and other services and facilities.

The Guild of British Newspaper Editors is the officially recognised professional body for newspaper editors. It has approximately 360 members and aims to maintain the professional status and independence of editors, defend the freedom of the press, and improve the education and training of journalists. The British Association of Industrial Editors is the professional organisation for editors of house journals. The Association of British Editors represents the whole range of media, including radio, television, newspapers and magazines.

Press Conduct

Readers' representatives have been appointed by most national papers to handle complaints. They also help to guarantee standards of accuracy, fairness and good behaviour on the part of journalists.

The Press Complaints Commission

The Press Complaints Commission, a non-statutory body, was set up in 1991, following recommendations in the report by the independent Committee on Privacy and Related Matters chaired by Mr (now Sir) David Calcutt, QC. The Commission was set up by the newspaper and periodical industry in a final attempt to make self-regulation of the press work properly. It is funded by PRESSBOF (the Press Standards Board of Finance), which was set up in 1990 to co-ordinate and promote self-regulation within the industry. These measures were prompted by growing criticism of press standards, with allegations of unjustified invasion of privacy and inaccurate and biased reporting, among other abuses, resulting in calls for government regulation of the press.

The Commission's membership is drawn from newspaper and magazine editors and from people from outside the industry. It deals with complaints by members of the public about the contents and conduct of newspapers and magazines, and advises editors and journalists. It operates a code of practice agreed by editors governing respect for privacy, opportunity to reply, corrections, journalists' behaviour, references to race and religion, payments to criminals for articles, protection of confidential sources and other matters. The Commission publishes regular reports of its findings.

Proposed Changes

In 1990 the Government indicated that it would review the effectiveness of press self-regulation once the Press Complaints Commission had been in operation for 18 months, and in 1991 it asked Sir David Calcutt to assess the effectiveness of the present arrangements. Sir David's report, *Review of Press Self-Regulation*, was published in January 1993 and recommended—among other things—the introduction of a statutory complaints tribunal.

In its initial response, the Government has stated that it agrees that the Commission is not an effective regulator of the press and recognises the argument for a statutory tribunal. However, the Government considers that introducing a statutory body would be a significant departure from the traditional approach to press regulation, and it would be extremely reluctant to take such action.

The Government accepts the report's recommendations on protecting personal privacy. It intends to bring forward proposals to create new criminal offences in England

and Wales to deal with intrusion on private property and the use of surveillance devices, photographs and recordings to obtain personal information for publication. Similar changes for Scotland will be considered.

In May 1993 the industry and the Press Complaints Commission announced steps to strengthen voluntary regulation. These include measures to increase the number of independent members of the Commission to ensure a lay majority; a strengthening of the code of practice; and the setting up of a helpline service for members of the public who fear the code of practice has been, or is about to be, breached.

Advertising Practice

Advertising in all non-broadcast media, such as newspapers, magazines, posters, cinema and direct mail, is regulated by the Advertising Standards Authority, an independent body funded by a levy on display advertising expenditure. The Authority aims to promote and enforce the highest standards of advertising in the interests of the public through its supervision of the British Code of Advertising Practice.

The Code's basic principles are to ensure that advertisements:

- are legal, decent, honest and truthful;
- are prepared with a sense of responsibility to the consumer and society; and
- conform to the principles of fair competition as generally accepted in business.

The Authority monitors advertisements to ensure their compliance with the Code and investigates any complaints received.

The advertising industry has agreed to abide by the Code and to back it up with effective sanctions. Free and confidential pre-publication advice is offered to assist publishers, agencies and advertisers. The Authority's main sanction is the recommendation that advertisements considered to be in breach of the Code should not be published. This is normally sufficient to ensure that an advertisement is withdrawn or amended. The Authority also publishes monthly reports on the results of its investigations.

The Authority is recognised by the Office of Fair Trading as the established means of controlling non-broadcast advertising. The Authority can refer misleading advertisements to the Director General of Fair Trading, who has the power to seek an injunction to prevent their publication.

The Press and the Law

The press generally has the same freedom as the individual to comment on matters of public interest. No laws governing the content of the press are in operation, but certain statutes include sections which apply to the press.

There are laws governing:

- the extent of newspaper ownership in television and radio companies (see p. 462);

- the transfer of newspaper assets (see p. 451); and

- the right of press representatives to be supplied with agenda and reports for meetings of local authorities and reasonable facilities for taking notes and telephoning reports.

There is a legal requirement to reproduce 'the printer's imprint' (the printer's name and address) on all publications, including newspapers. Publishers are legally obliged to deposit copies of newspapers and other publications at the British Library (see p. 447).

Publication of advertisements is governed by wide-ranging legislation, including public health, financial services and fraud legislation. Legal restrictions are imposed on certain types of prize competition; copyrights come under various copyright laws.

Laws on contempt of court, official secrets and defamation are also relevant to the press. A newspaper may not publish comments on the conduct of judicial proceedings which are likely to prejudice the reputation of the courts for fairness before or during the actual proceedings, nor may it publish before or during a trial anything which might influence the result. The unauthorised acquisition and publication of official information in such areas as defence and international relations are offences under the Official Secrets Acts 1911 to 1989, where unauthorised disclosure would be harmful. However, these are restrictions on publication, that is, on dissemination to the public by any means, not just through the printed press.

Most legal proceedings against the press are libel actions brought by private individuals. In such cases, the editor, proprietor, publishers, printer and distributor of the newspaper, as well as the author, may all be held responsible.

Defence Advisory Notices

Government officials and representatives of the media form the Defence, Press and Broadcasting Advisory Committee, which has agreed that in some circumstances the publication of certain categories of information might endanger national security. Details of these categories are contained in Defence Advisory Notices (D Notices) circulated to the media, whose members are asked to seek advice from the Secretary of the Committee, a retired senior military officer, before publishing information in these areas. Compliance with any advice offered by the Secretary is expected but there is no legal force behind it and the final decision on whether to publish rests with the editor, producer or publisher concerned.

The Notices were published for the first time in July 1993 to promote a better understanding of the system and to contribute to greater openness in government.

Television and Radio

Broadcasting in Britain has traditionally been based on the principle that it is a public service accountable to the people through Parliament. While retaining the essential public service element, it now embraces the principles of competition and choice.

Three public bodies have the main

responsibility for television and radio services to which nearly everyone has access throughout Britain:

- the BBC (British Broadcasting Corporation) broadcasts television and radio programmes;
- the ITC (Independent Television Commission) licenses and regulates non-BBC television services, including cable and satellite services; and
- the Radio Authority licenses and regulates all non-BBC radio services, including cable and satellite.

These authorities work to broad requirements and objectives defined by Parliament, but are otherwise independent in their day-to-day conduct of business.

The government department responsible for overseeing the broadcasting system is the Department of National Heritage. The Secretary of State for National Heritage is answerable to Parliament on broad policy questions.

Television

There are four terrestrial television channels, offering a mixture of drama, light entertainment, films, sport, educational, children's and religious programmes, news and current affairs, and documentaries.

The BBC provides two complementary national networks—BBC 1 and BBC 2—which are financed almost exclusively by licence fees. The ITC regulates two television services: ITV (Channel 3) and Channel 4, which are expected to complement each other and are largely funded by advertising. In Wales S4C (Sianel Pedwar Cymru) broadcasts programmes on the Welsh fourth channel. All four channels broadcast on 625 lines UHF (ultra-high frequency) and over 99 per cent of the population live within range of transmission.

British television productions continue to win many international awards, and in 1991 television companies received £132 million in export earnings.

Radio

Practically every home has a radio, and the widespread ownership of portable sets (including personal stereos) and car radios means that people can listen to radio throughout the day. Almost half the population listen to the radio on a normal day and 76 per cent do so over the week. Average listening time is around an hour and a half a day.

The BBC has five national networks, which transmit all types of music, news, current affairs, drama, education, sport and a range of features programmes. The Radio Authority regulates two national commercial radio stations; a third station is planned.

There are 39 BBC local radio stations serving England and the Channel Islands, and regional and community radio services in Scotland, Wales and Northern Ireland. Some 150 independent local radio (ILR) services are also in operation. More local stations are planned. Stations supply a comprehensive service of local news and information, sport, music and other entertainment, education and consumer advice. 'Phone-in' programmes allowing listeners to express their views on air are popular. About 90 per cent of the population can receive BBC or ILR stations.

Government Approach to Broadcasting

During the last few years broadcasting in Britain has seen radical changes. The availability of more radio frequencies, together with satellite, cable and microwave transmissions, has made a greater number of local, national and international services possible. Moreover, the technical quality of sound and pictures is improving. In response to rapidly developing technology and rising public demand for a wide choice of programmes and services, the Government introduced the Broadcasting Act 1990 with the aim of making the regulatory framework for broadcasting more flexible and efficient and giving viewers and listeners access to a wider range of services. At the same time the Act aimed to promote competition and to maintain high standards of taste and decency.

The 1990 Act takes full account of the need for programme quality and diversity, regional links, widespread ownership of broadcasting companies and proper geographical coverage, and makes provision for 'sharply focused statutory safeguards' backed by enforcement sanctions, including financial penalties.

Changes Introduced by the Broadcasting Act

The Broadcasting Act 1990 overhauled the regulation of independent television and radio and opened the way for many more services.

In 1991 the IBA (Independent Broadcasting Authority) was replaced by the ITC (Independent Television Commission), the Radio Authority and a new transmission and engineering company, National Transcommunications Limited (see below). At the same time the Cable Authority was made part of the ITC and the Radio Authority.

The ITC and the Radio Authority issue licences to commercial broadcasters and enforce rules to ensure diversity of ownership:

- The ITC awards major broadcasting licences by competitive tender to the highest bidders satisfying stipulated quality tests.

- The Radio Authority awards national radio licences by competitive tender to the highest cash bidders. Local radio licences are not allocated by competitive tender; the success of licence applications is in part determined by audience demand, and the extent to which prospective stations would increase variety.

The ITC does not have the former IBA's detailed involvement in scheduling but has wider powers than the IBA to enforce licence conditions and ownership rules. Both organisations were initially able to take out government loans, but are obliged to repay these and to support themselves from licence fees at the earliest possible date.

The 1990 Act made provision for setting up a new national independent television station, Channel 5, and three national commercial radio stations (see p. 466). Opportunities now also exist for launching hundreds of independent local radio and television channels.

The Broadcasting Act also provided for the former IBA's television and radio transmission networks to be privatised. In 1991 the IBA networks and other facilities were transferred to a new public company— National Transcommunications Limited (NTL). NTL was then sold for £70 million to a company formed for the purpose by Mercury Asset Management. NTL transmits television services for the independent television companies, Channel 4, S4C, and radio services for about 50 independent local radio stations.

Programming Obligations

The Government recognises the importance of public service broadcasting. Hence:

- the 1990 Act made no change to the BBC's 'cornerstone' public service role of providing high-quality programming throughout the full range of public tastes and interests; the essential programming remits of all BBC domestic services remain unchanged.

- Channel 4—in addition to retaining public service obligations—is, as before, required to be innovative and distinctive, and to cater for tastes and interests not adequately met by ITV and its successor Channel 3 (see p. 464). Three of the four current terrestrial television channels have, therefore, the same basic programming obligations as before the passage of the Act.

- Licence-holders of the independent television Channel 3 (and the proposed Channel 5) need to pass demanding quality tests (see p. 465). ITC regulations place a limit on the proportion of non-European material broadcast.

- Since January 1993 both the BBC and commercial television licensees have been required to ensure that at least 25 per cent of their original programming comes from independent producers. The system whereby major sporting occasions ('listed events'), such as the Grand National steeplechase and the Olympic Games, are made generally available to television audiences on the main terrestrial channels has been retained.

Ownership Rules

The Broadcasting Act 1990 established clearer and more extensive ownership rules. These are designed to enable the ITC and the Radio Authority to keep ownership of the broadcasting media widely spread and to prevent unhealthy concentrations and cross-media ownership. Controlling ownership from outside the European Community is largely prohibited, and national newspapers are allowed relatively small stakes in direct broadcasting by satellite (DBS) channels (see p. 468), Channels 3 and 5, and national and local radio. Public telecommunications operators are not allowed to have controlling interests in any Channel 3, Channel 5, national radio or domestic satellite licence; and political bodies and local authorities are barred from holding licences.

Programme Standards

Recognising that broadcasting is an extremely powerful medium with the potential to offend, exploit and cause harm, the Act contains guarantees on programme standards which are extended to all British-based broadcasters. These guarantees cover taste, decency, accuracy and balance. Under the 1990 Act the Government can proscribe unacceptable foreign satellite services receivable in Britain. Anyone in Britain supporting such a service can now be prosecuted for a criminal offence. The Act also gives the Broadcasting Standards Council a key role (see p. 469).

The BBC

The constitution, finances and obligations of the BBC are governed by a Royal Charter, which expires in December 1996, and by a Licence and Agreement. The Corporation's board of 12 governors, including the chairman, vice-chairman and a national governor each for Scotland, Wales and Northern Ireland, is appointed by the Queen on the advice of the Government. The board of governors is ultimately responsible for all aspects of broadcasting on the BBC. The governors appoint the Director-General, the Corporation's chief executive officer, who heads the board of management—the body in charge of the daily running of the services.

The BBC has a strong regional structure. The three English regions—BBC North, BBC Midlands & East and BBC South—and the Scottish, Welsh and Northern Ireland national regions, make programmes for their local audiences as well as contributing to the national network.

The National Broadcasting Councils for Scotland, Wales and Northern Ireland advise on the policy and content of television and radio programmes intended mainly for reception in their areas. Local radio councils representative of the local community advise on the development and operation of the BBC's local radio stations.

Finance

The domestic services of the BBC are financed almost wholly from the sale of television licences. Households with a television must buy an annual licence costing £83 for colour and £27.50 for black and white. Over 20.1 million licences were current in June 1993; of these some 19.1 million were for colour. More than two-thirds of expenditure on domestic services relates to television.

Licence income is supplemented by profits from trading activities, such as television programme exports, sale of recordings and publications connected with BBC programmes, hire and sale of educational films, film library sales, and exhibitions based on programmes. BBC World Service Radio is financed by a grant-in-aid from the Foreign & Commonwealth Office (£176 million in 1993–94), while BBC World Service Television is self-funding.

In 1991 the BBC took over from the Home Office responsibility for administering the licence fee system. TVL, a subsidiary company of the Post Office, undertakes the licence administration on behalf of the BBC. Since 1988 annual rises in the licence fee have been linked to the rate of inflation; this is intended further to improve the BBC's efficiency and encourage it to continue to develop alternative sources of revenue. An independent review to assess progress began in June 1993. The longer-term future of the TV licence fee will be considered as part of the review of the BBC's Royal Charter.

The Future of the BBC

A government discussion paper, *The Future of the BBC*, was published in November 1992. This sets out the framework for a debate on the future of the BBC, covering all aspects of its work and structure. At the same time the BBC published a discussion document, *Extending Choice*, on the future of the organisation. This details areas in which the BBC can make a special contribution in extending choice for viewers and listeners.

BBC Television

The two channels, BBC1 and BBC 2, are scheduled in a complementary way to cater simultaneously for people of different interests. Although both services cover the whole range of television output:

- BBC 1 presents a wide range of programmes, including news and current affairs, major documentaries, sport, popular drama and light entertainment, and children's programmes.
- BBC 2 presents music and the arts, new talent, innovative documentaries, sport, international films and serious drama, and is a forum for debate.

> Apart from a break during the Second World War, the BBC has been providing regular television broadcasts since 1936. Together, BBC 1 and BBC 2 transmit over 17,000 hours of programmes a year for national and regional audiences.

Programmes for both networks are produced mainly in London; a third of all programmes shown nationally are made in the regions. Both the BBC and the commercial television companies enter into agreements with overseas television corporations in order to make new programmes economically.

BBC Subscription Television Ltd

In 1990 the BBC set up a subsidiary to run subscription-financed television services in the night hours under the name BBC SELECT. Broadcasting is between 2.00 and 6.00 hours on BBC1, when the BBC is off the air. Programmes, transmitted in scrambled form, are designed to be video-recorded and watched at a time to suit the individual viewer. Initially BBC SELECT has been broadcasting professional, training and educational services but consumer interest services are also planned.

BBC Network Radio

BBC Network Radio serves an audience of 27 million in Britain, broadcasting around 35,000 hours of programmes each year on its five networks:

- BBC Radio 1 broadcasts rock and pop music 24 hours a day;.
- BBC Radio 2 (on FM only) transmits popular music and light entertainment, also for 24 hours a day;.
- BBC Radio 3 (also on FM only) broadcasts mainly classical music, but presents jazz, drama, poetry, short stories and talks as well;.
- BBC Radio 4 is the main speech network, providing the principal news and current affairs service, together with drama, comedy, documentaries and panel games; it also carries parliamentary coverage; and
- BBC Radio 5 (on medium wave only) is dedicated chiefly to sport, education and speech programmes for young people, and a selection of programmes from the World Service (see p. 470).

The BBC has announced plans for a 24-hour news and sport network from April 1994 to replace the existing Radio 5.

Independent Broadcasting

Independent Television Commission

Like the Radio Authority and S4C, the ITC's constitution and finances are governed by the

Broadcasting Act 1990. The ITC is responsible for licensing and regulating non-BBC television services operating in or from Britain. These include:

- ITV (Channel 3);
- Channel 4;
- the proposed Channel 5;
- cable and other local delivery services;
- independent teletext services; and
- domestic and non-domestic satellite services available to viewers in Britain.

Since January 1993, when the new Channel 3 licences came into effect, the ITC has ceased to broadcast programmes. These responsibilities have now passed to the new licensees (see p. 465). The ITC monitors the licences and licence conditions but is not involved in detailed scheduling of programmes.

The ITC is advised by committees on educational broadcasting, religious broadcasting, charitable appeals and advertising. Ten viewer consultative councils also comment on the commercial services' programmes.

ITV Programmes

The first regular ITV (independent television) programmes began in London in 1955. ITV programmes are broadcast 24 hours a day throughout the country. About one-third of the output comprises informative programmes—news, documentaries and coverage of current affairs, education and religion. The remainder covers sport, comedy, drama, games shows, films, and a range of other programmes with popular appeal. Over half the programmes are produced by the programme companies and ITN (Independent Television News— see below).

ITV (Channel 3) Programme Companies

ITV is made up of 15 regionally based television companies which are licensed to supply programmes in the 14 independent television geographical regions. Two companies share the contract for London, one providing programmes during weekdays and the other at the weekend. An additional ITC licensee provides a national breakfast-time service, transmitted on the ITV network.

The licensees operate on a commercial basis, deriving most of their revenue from selling advertising time. The financial resources, advertising revenue and programme production of the companies vary considerably, depending largely on the population of the areas in which they operate. Although newspapers may acquire an interest in programme companies, safeguards exist to ensure against concentration of media ownership, thereby protecting the public interest.

Each programme company plans the content of the programmes to be broadcast in its area. These are produced by the company itself, or by other programme companies or bought from elsewhere.

A common news service is provided 24 hours a day by ITN. ITN has been appointed to supply a service of national and international news to the ITV network for a ten-year period from January 1993.

ITV Network Centre

The ITV Network Centre, which is wholly owned by the ITV companies, independently commissions and schedules those television programmes which are shown across the ITV network. Programmes are commissioned from the ITV companies as well as from independent producers. The Centre also promotes the ITV network and co-ordinates developments in technology and training.

Licences

The ITV licences for Channel 3, which came up for renewal at the end of 1992, were awarded by the ITC in October 1991. Twelve existing franchise holders and four new companies were awarded licences.

Channel 3 licences are awarded for a ten-year period by competitive tender to the highest bidder who has passed a quality threshold. In exceptional cases a lower bid can be selected, for instance, where an applicant is able to offer a significantly better quality of service than that offered by the highest bidder.

There are safeguards for quality programming. Licensees are required to offer a diverse programme service, a proportion of good-quality programmes, as well as high-quality regional and national news and current affairs programmes, and children's and religious programmes. There is for the first time a statutory duty to present programmes made in and about the region. There is also a requirement for district and regional programming to be aimed at different areas within regions. Channel 3 licensees are obliged to operate a national programme network. Networking arrangements are subject to government approval so that anti-competitive practices are avoided.

Channel 4 and S4C

Channel 4, which began broadcasting in 1982, provides a national television service throughout Britain, except in Wales, which has a corresponding service— S4C (Sianel Pedwar Cymru). In January 1993 Channel 4 became a public corporation, licensed and regulated by the ITC, selling its own advertising time and retaining the proceeds. It was previously a public limited company owned by the ITC. The service, including that in Wales, was financed by annual subscriptions from the former ITV programme companies in return for advertising time in fourth channel programmes shown in their own regions.

Channel 4's remit is to provide programmes with a distinctive character and to appeal to tastes and interests not generally catered for by Channel 3. It must present a suitable proportion of educational programmes and encourage innovation and experiment. Channel 4 commissions programmes from the ITV companies and independent producers and buys programmes from overseas. It broadcasts for around 139 hours a week, about half of which are devoted to informative programmes.

In Wales programmes on the fourth channel are run and controlled by S4C. Its members are appointed by the Government. S4C is required to see that a significant proportion of programming, in practice 23 hours a week, is in the Welsh language and that programmes broadcast between 18.30 and 22.00 hours are mainly in Welsh. At other times S4C transmits national Channel 4 programmes.

Like Channel 4, S4C has sold its own advertising since January 1993. S4C is expected to cover only 10 per cent of its costs from advertising, with the remainder financed by the Government.

Gaelic TV Fund

The Gaelic Television Committee, appointed by the ITC, was set up under the Broadcasting Act 1990 to administer government finance for making television programmes in Gaelic. A fund of £9.5 million has been created and programmes thus financed came on screen from January 1993. The Fund aims to increase the output of Gaelic television programmes from 100 to about 300 hours each year.

Channel 5

A new national terrestrial television channel— Channel 5—was advertised in April 1992 and was intended to come into operation in late 1994. The new channel was to be financed through advertising, subscription or sponsorship, or a combination of all three.

The ten-year licence was to be awarded by competitive tender, with applicants having to pass a quality threshold similar in scope to that for Channel 3. The licensee would be required to retune domestic electronic equipment (for example, video recorders) which might suffer interference from Channel 5 transmission.

In December 1992 the ITC announced its decision not to award a licence. It had received only one bid and was not satisfied that the applicant would be able to maintain its proposed service throughout the period of the licence. The ITC is reviewing the future options for the Channel 5 licence.

Local Television

The Broadcasting Act 1990 makes provision for the further development of local television services. Local delivery licences are awarded by competitive tender and there is no quality threshold. ITC licence-holders can supply national and local television channels using both cable and microwave transmission systems. Services delivered could be aimed at communities such as ethnic minorities.

The Radio Authority

Independent local radio (ILR) is based on principles similar to those of ITV (see p. 464). The programme companies operate under licence to the Radio Authority and are financed mainly by advertising revenue. Licences for existing operators will expire between 1994 and 1996.

The Radio Authority, which took over responsibility for independent radio from the IBA in 1991, is required to ensure that licensed services, taken as a whole, are of a high quality and offer a range of programmes calculated to appeal to a variety of tastes and interests. Powers to deter 'pirate' or illegal broadcasters have been strengthened.

The Authority awards national radio licences by competitive tender to the highest cash bidder. The licence for the first independent national radio service (INR1) was awarded to *Classic FM* in 1991. The new station, which broadcasts mainly popular classical music, together with news and information, began operating in September 1992. The licence for the second independent national service (INR2) was awarded in 1992 to *Virgin 1215*. This station began broadcasting in April 1993, playing broad-based rock music. The third national service (INR3), which must be speech-based, is to be advertised in late 1993.

In the course of the 1990s more local radio stations will come on the air, some of which could be neighbourhood and 'community of interest' stations. Areas to be covered will initially be those not at present adequately served by independent local radio. Local radio licences are not allocated by competitive tender; the success of licence applications is

in part determined by the extent to which applicants meet the needs and interests of the people living in the area and whether they have the necessary financial resources to sustain programme plans for the eight-year licence period.

Some of the locations have been selected with small-scale 'community radio' in mind. As part of its brief to develop a wide range of radio services, the Authority aims to establish a number of more specialist stations.

The Radio Authority also issues restricted service licences. These are issued on demand (subject to certain conditions and frequency availability), usually for a maximum of 28 days. They enable local events—such as sports events, arts festivals and conferences—to be covered by a temporary radio service in a limited area, for example, part of a city or town or an arena.

Teletext

The BBC and independent television each operate a teletext service, offering constantly updated information on a variety of subjects, including news, sport, travel, weather conditions and entertainment. The teletext system allows the television signal to carry additional information which can be selected and displayed as 'pages' of text and graphics on receivers equipped with the necessary decoders. Both the BBC and Channels 3 and 4 have a subtitling facility for certain programmes for people with hearing difficulties. These services are available whenever the transmitters are on the air. Nearly 40 per cent of households in Britain have teletext sets and over 7 million people turn to the service daily—more than the circulation figures for daily newspapers.

Licences

The Broadcasting Act 1990 introduced a new regulatory system for licensing spare capacity within the television signal. This allows more varied use of spare capacity—data transfer, for instance—but the position of teletext and subtitling on commercial television is safeguarded.

At the end of 1991 the ITC advertised three teletext licences—a single public service licence for teletext on Channels 3 and 4 (and S4C) and two separate licences for commercial additional services to subscription or closed user groups, using three lines of spare capacity on each channel. These ten-year licences are awarded by competitive tender, with applicants having to satisfy certain statutory requirements before their cash bid can be considered. The ITC awarded the main teletext licence to UK Teletext Ltd, which replaced Oracle in January 1993, and awarded one of the commercial additional service licences on Channel 3 to the only bidder, Data Broadcasting International. The other commercial additional service licence on Channel 4 remains unallocated.

Channel 3 is obliged to offer a subtitling service for at least 50 per cent of its programmes by 1998, with further increases after that.

Cable Services

Cable services are delivered to consumers through underground cables and are paid for by subscription. These responsibilities are now carried out by the Cable and Satellite Division of the ITC and by the Radio Authority, which issues cable radio licences.

'Broadband cable', the cable systems currently being designed and built, can carry between 30 and 45 television channels, including terrestrial broadcasts, satellite television, and channels delivered by videotape. Cable systems usually carry a local channel. Interactive services such as home shopping, home banking, security and alarm services, electronic mail and remote meter readings are also possible. Franchises have already been granted covering areas which include two-thirds of all homes and nearly all urban areas in Britain—around 14.5 million households in total. In April 1993, 58 broadband cable franchises were in operation in Britain, seven of which had been set up within the past year. Regulation is as light as possible to encourage the development of a

wide range of services, and flexible enough to adapt to new technology. The ITC is continuing the Cable Authority's practice of awarding only one broadband cable franchise in each area so that the new franchisee is protected from direct competition in the early stages. At present over 2 million homes are able to receive broadband cable services and there are almost 500,000 subscribers.

Licences are granted on a non-competitive basis to programme services which are likely to meet consumer protection standards and are run by suitably qualified people. ITC licences are required for systems capable of serving more than 1,000 homes. Systems extending beyond a single building and up to 1,000 homes require only an individual licence from OFTEL (see p. 264). Cable investment must be privately financed.

Direct Broadcasting by Satellite

Direct broadcasting by satellite (DBS), by which television is transmitted directly by satellite into people's homes, has been available throughout Britain since 1989. The signals from satellite broadcasting are received through specially designed aerials or 'dishes'.

Several British-based satellite television channels have been set up to supply programmes to cable operators and viewers with dishes in Britain and, in some cases, throughout Europe. While some offer general entertainment, others concentrate on specific areas of interest, such as sport, music and children's programmes.

The largest satellite programmer is BSkyB (British Sky Broadcasting), which provides 15 channels devoted to light entertainment, news, feature films, sport and home shopping transmitted from the Astra satellite.

Other satellite channels available to British viewers include Eurosport (sport), CNN (news), MTV (pop videos), and TV Asia (for Asian viewers). The choice available to viewers is expanding steadily.

In November 1992 BBC Enterprises and Thames TV (one of the former ITV franchisees) launched a joint entertainment satellite channel—UK Gold—on the Astra satellite. Programmes include drama, soaps, comedy, children's television and quizzes.

Educational Broadcasting

Both the BBC and Channel 4 broadcast educational programmes for schools and continuing education programmes for adults. Broadcasts to schools deal with most subjects of the National Curriculum (see p. 408), while programmes for adults cover many areas of learning and vocational training. Books, pamphlets, filmstrips, computer software, and audio and video cassettes, are produced to supplement the programmes. Around 90 per cent of primary schools and 93 per cent of secondary schools in Britain use schools television. The ITC has a duty to ensure that schools programmes are presented on independent television.

The BBC broadcasts around three hours of radio and 22 hours of television each week on behalf of the Open University (see p. 417).

Advertising and Sponsorship

The BBC must have the consent of the Secretary of State for National Heritage before broadcasting any commercial advertisement. It may not broadcast any sponsored programme. The policy of the BBC is to avoid giving publicity to any firm or organised interest except when this is necessary in providing effective and informative programmes. It does, however, cover sponsored sporting and artistic events.

Advertising and sponsorship are allowed on independent television and radio subject to controls. The ITC and the Radio Authority operate codes of advertising standards and programme sponsorship.

Advertisements on independent television and radio are broadcast between programmes as well as in breaks during programmes. Advertisers are not allowed directly to influence the content of programmes. Advertisements must be distinct and separate from programmes. The time given to them

must not be so great as to detract from the value of the programmes as a medium of information, education or entertainment. Television advertising is limited to an average of seven minutes an hour during the day and seven and a half minutes in the peak evening viewing period. Advertising is prohibited in religious services and in broadcasts to schools. Teletext UK Ltd (see p. 467) carries advertisements.

The ITC and the Radio Authority's codes governing standards and practice in advertising give guidance on the forms of advertisement which are prohibited.

Prohibited advertising includes political advertising, advertisements for betting and for cigarettes and cigarette tobacco, and—on television only—for cigars and pipe tobacco. (Advertisements for the last two are permitted on radio.)

The Radio Authority and, since January 1993, ITV and Channel 4 are permitted to screen religious advertisements, provided they comply with the guidelines issued by the ITC and the Radio Authority.

Both the ITC and the Radio Authority can impose severe penalties on any television or radio company failing to comply with their codes. The Broadcasting Standards Council's code of practice (see p. 469) covers advertisements.

Sponsorship in Independent Broadcasting

In Britain sponsorship is a relatively new way of helping to finance commercial broadcasting, although the practice has long been established in other countries. In return for their financial contribution, sponsors receive a credit associating them with a particular programme.

The ITC's Code of Programme Sponsorship and the Radio Authority's Advertising and Sponsorship Code aim to ensure that sponsors do not exert undue influence on the editorial content of programmes and that sponsorships are made clear to viewers. News and current affairs programmes may not be sponsored. Potential sponsors for other categories of programme may be debarred if their involvement could constrain in any way the editorial independence of the programme maker. References to sponsors or their products must be confined to the beginning and end of a programme and around commercial breaks; they must not appear in the programme itself. All commercial radio programmes other than news bulletins may be sponsored.

Government Publicity

Government publicity material to support non-political campaigns may be broadcast on independent television and radio. This is paid for on a normal commercial basis. Short public service items, concerning health, safety and welfare, are produced by the Central Office of Information for free transmission by the BBC and independent television and radio.

British Satellite News is an international satellite news service produced for the Foreign & Commonwealth Office by a private sector company, WTN (see p. 471). The service, under the editorial control of the Foreign & Commonwealth Office, transmits programmes five days a week. These are distributed, mainly by satellite, free to television stations throughout Eastern Europe, the Middle East and Southern Africa for use in news bulletins.

Broadcasting Standards

The independence enjoyed by the broadcasting authorities carries with it certain obligations over programme content. Programmes must display, as far as possible, a proper balance and wide range of subject matter, impartiality in matters of controversy and accuracy in news coverage, and must not offend against good taste. Broadcasters must also comply with legislation relating to obscenity and incitement to racial hatred.

The BBC, the ITC and the Radio Authority apply codes providing guidance on violence and standards of taste and decency in television programmes, particularly during hours when children are likely to be viewing.

Broadcasting Standards Council

The Broadcasting Standards Council (BSC) was set up by the Government in 1988 to act as a focus for public concern about the portrayal of violence and sex, and about standards of taste and decency. Its remit covers television and radio programmes and broadcast advertisements and includes monitoring programmes broadcast into Britain from abroad.

Under the Broadcasting Act 1990 the Council was granted statutory powers requiring the codes of practice of the BBC and other broadcasting regulatory bodies to reflect the BSC's own code. The BSC monitors programmes, examines complaints from the public and undertakes research. In 1992–93 the Council received 2,023 complaints, of which 1,355 fell within its remit. It has already published the results of several public attitude surveys.

Broadcasting Complaints Commission

The Broadcasting Complaints Commission, an independent statutory body, deals with complaints of unfair treatment in broadcast programmes and of unwarranted infringement of privacy in programmes or in their preparation. In 1992–93 it received 928 complaints, 115 of which fell within its jurisdiction. Details of complaints made and decisions reached are published annually.

Parliamentary and Political Broadcasting

The proceedings of both Houses of Parliament may be broadcast on television and radio, either live, or more usually in recorded and edited form on news and current affairs programmes.

The BBC and the commercial services provide time on radio and television for an annual series of party political broadcasts. Party election broadcasts are arranged following the announcement of a general election. In addition, the Government may make ministerial broadcasts on radio and television, with opposition parties also being allotted broadcast time.

Audience Research

Both the BBC and the independent sector are required to keep themselves informed on the state of public opinion about the programmes and advertising that they broadcast. This is done through the continuous measurement of the size and composition of audiences and their opinions of programmes. For television, this work is undertaken through BARB (the Broadcasters' Audience Research Board), owned jointly by the BBC and the ITV Network Centre. For radio, joint research is undertaken for BBC radio and for commercial radio by RAJAR (Radio Joint Audience Research).

Both the BBC and the independent sector conduct regular surveys of audience opinion on television and radio services. Public opinion is further assessed by the BBC and ITC through the work of their advisory committees, councils and panels. Regular public meetings are also held to debate services, and consideration is given to letters and telephone calls from listeners and viewers.

Training

The BBC provides some non-financial technical assistance, particularly in training the staff of overseas broadcasting organisations. The Government finances overseas students on broadcasting training courses at the BBC, the British Council and the Thomson Foundation; the Foundation also conducts courses overseas in broadcast journalism, media management, radio and television production, and technology.

INTERNATIONAL SERVICES

BBC World Service Radio

The BBC World Service broadcasts by radio worldwide, using English and 39 other languages. Output amounts to 873 hours weekly of direct language transmissions. The main objectives are to give unbiased news, reflect British opinion and project British life, culture and developments in science and industry. News bulletins, current affairs programmes, political commentaries and topical magazine programmes form the main part of the output. These are supplemented by a sports service, music, drama and general entertainment. Regular listeners are estimated to number 124 million.

The languages in which the World Service broadcasts and the number of hours devoted to each are prescribed by the Government. Otherwise the BBC has full responsibility and is completely independent in determining the content of news and other programmes.

> The BBC World Service broadcasts by radio for 24 hours a day in English, supplemented at peak listening times by programmes of special interest to Africa, East Asia, South Asia, Europe, the Caribbean and the Falkland Islands.

BBC World Service news bulletins and other programmes are re-broadcast by some 630 radio and cable stations in over 90 countries, which receive the programmes by satellite. Two World Service departments also specialise in supplying radio material for re-broadcast. *BBC Transcription* sells BBC radio programmes to overseas broadcasters in over 100 countries, while *BBC Topical Tapes* airmails some 250 tapes of original programmes to subscribers in over 50 countries each week.

BBC English is the largest language-teaching venture in the world. Lessons are broadcast daily by radio with explanations in some 30 languages, including English, and re-broadcast by many radio stations. BBC English television programmes are also shown in more than 90 countries. A range of printed, audio and video material accompanies these programmes.

Another part of the World Service, *BBC Monitoring*, listens to and reports on foreign broadcasts, providing a daily flow of significant news and comment from overseas to the BBC and the Government. This information is also sold to the press, businesses, academic staff and public bodies.

BBC World Service Television

BBC World Service Television was set up in 1991 to establish a worldwide television service. The company is a wholly self-funding subsidiary of the BBC and receives no revenue from either the TV licence fees or from the Government. The company at present provides services to three continents:

- a subscription channel in Europe, based on a mixture of BBC 1 and BBC 2 programmes, news bulletins, and weather and business reports. Viewers receive the service by cable or direct to their homes, using special decoders.

- a 24-hour news and information channel available throughout Asia. Funded by advertising, the service is one of the channels offered throughout Asia by the commercial company STAR TV. The channel is compiled by the BBC and transmitted by satellite to Hong Kong, where advertising is added by STAR TV before distribution.

- a news and information channel shown throughout Africa, launched in April 1992. The service is available to viewers who have the appropriate satellite reception equipment and in countries where national broadcasters make the service part of their regular output.

COI Overseas Radio and Television Services

The Central Office of Information (COI), which provides publicity material and other information services on behalf of government departments and other public agencies, produces radio programmes for overseas. Recorded material is sent to radio stations all over the world. COI television services also make available material such as documentary and magazine programmes.

News Agencies

Reuters Television, the largest international television news agency in the world, supplies news pictures to over 200 broadcasters and their networks in 84 countries. Reuters Television is a wholly-owned subsidiary of Reuters (see p. 455) and uses 120 Reuters bureaux and a global satellite network to gather and distribute its material.

WTN (Worldwide Television News), owned by ITN, ABC (the American Broadcasting Corporation), and Channel 9 in Australia, supplies news and a wide range of television services to some 1,000 broadcasters in 93 countries, as well as to governments and international corporations.

Both agencies provide services through the Eurovision network (see below) and by satellite.

International Relations

European Agreements

In 1991 Britain implemented two important European agreements on cross-border broadcasting: the European Community Directive on Broadcasting and the Council of Europe Convention on Transfrontier Television. Under these, countries have to remove restrictions on the retransmission of programmes originating from other participating countries. They must also ensure that their own broadcasters observe certain minimum standards on advertising, sponsorship, taste and decency, and the portrayal of sex and violence on television.

European Broadcasting Union

The BBC and the Radio Authority are members of the European Broadcasting Union, which manages Eurovision, the international network of television news and programme exchange. The Union is responsible for co-ordinating the exchange of programmes and news over the Eurovision network and intercontinental satellite links. It also maintains a technical monitoring station where frequency measurements and other observations on broadcasting stations are carried out. The Union provides a forum linking the major public services and national broadcasters of Western Europe and other parts of the world, and co-ordinates joint operations in radio and television.

International Telecommunications Union

The BBC takes part in the work of the International Telecommunications Union, the United Nations agency responsible for regulating and controlling all international telecommunications services, including radio and television. The Union also allocates and registers all radio frequencies, and promotes and co-ordinates the international study of technical problems in broadcasting.

Other International Bodies

The BBC is an associate member of the Asia-Pacific Broadcasting Union and also belongs to the Commonwealth Broadcasting Association, which meets every two years to discuss public service broadcasting issues.

TECHNICAL DEVELOPMENTS

One of the most important recent developments in television has been in news coverage, where compact electronic cameras have replaced film cameras, eliminating the need for film processing and enabling pictures to be transmitted directly to a studio.

Other recent advances in television broadcasting include:

- adoption of digital video tape recorders;
- increasing use of computer-aided digital equipment for picture generation and manipulation;
- use of portable satellite links to transmit pictures from remote locations to studios; and
- the introduction of stereo sound on the NICAM 728 digital system, developed by the BBC.

Both the BBC and the independent sector are developing further digital techniques for studio applications and inter-studio links; in early 1993 such digital links began operating in the independent sector.

The BBC and the IBA co-operated in the development of teletext, and teletext sets in some 30 countries are based on the British system.

In satellite broadcasting, the MAC transmission format was developed by IBA engineers, who went on to devise refinements for the MAC system compatible with widescreen television.

Both the BBC and the ITC are undertaking projects in a number of important areas of long-term research. These include:

- the development of a 1,250-line wide-screen high definition television (HDTV);
- enhancements to the PAL colour television system;
- digital terrestrial television broadcasting;
- data transmission studies; and
- digital audio broadcasting.

Further Reading

Broadcasting. Aspects of Britain series, HMSO, 1993.

Extending Choice: The BBC's Role in the New Broadcasting Age. BBC, 1992.

The Future of the BBC: A Consultation Document. CM 2098. HMSO, 1992.

Review of Press Self-Regulation. HMSO, 1993.

31 Sport and Active Recreation

There is widespread participation in sport in Britain, with the most popular activities ranging from swimming to snooker. Internationally British sportsmen and women compete in some 70 different sports, many of which were invented by the British, and Britain currently has more than 80 world champions in over 30 sports.

INTRODUCTION

Many sports attract large crowds for the major sporting events throughout the year, including the FA (Football Association) Challenge Cup Final, the Wimbledon lawn tennis championships and the Open Golf Championship. An even greater number of people watch these events on television, with many sports receiving extensive television coverage. The sports attracting the largest television audiences include football, athletics, snooker and boxing. Following the introduction of direct broadcasting by satellite (DBS) and the greater availability of cable, the amount of televised coverage has increased substantially. Important sporting occasions ('listed events'), such as the Olympic Games, may not be shown exclusively by DBS or cable and must be made generally available to television viewers.

As well as being a popular pastime, sport is a major industry in Britain. In addition to the professional sportsmen and women, over 450,000 are employed in the provision of sports clothing, publicity, ground and club maintenance and other activities connected with sport. In total an estimated £9,750 million is spent on sport annually in Britain.

PARTICIPATION

Participation in sport continues to rise, due mainly to an increase in leisure time and an improvement in facilities. A growing awareness of the importance of regular exercise for good health has contributed to an upsurge of interest in keep fit and other forms of aerobic exercise.

It has been estimated that 29 million people over the age of 16 regularly take part in sport or exercise. The 1990 General Household Survey found that almost two-thirds of those interviewed had taken part in at least one sporting activity during the four weeks before interview and that men were more likely than women to have participated in sport. The most popular participation sports are walking (including rambling and hiking), swimming, snooker/pool, keep fit/yoga and cycling.

Women and Sport

A major effort was made in the 1980s to narrow the gap between men's and women's participation in sport and active recreation. This effort resulted in an increase of about 1 million in the number of women taking part in sport between 1987 and 1990. The numbers participating in 'physical contact' sports, such as football and rugby, are also increasing, and more women now play traditionally male-dominated sports, such as snooker and billiards. Sports and physical activities particularly favoured by women include swimming, keep fit and aerobics.

During the 1990s emphasis has switched to encouraging women to adopt leadership roles, such as coaches, officials and administrators. Projects to promote coaching opportunities have been established by the Sports Councils (see p. 475) in partnership with the National Coaching Foundation (see p. 477) and the Women's Sports Foundation (WSF).

Women's Sports Foundation

The WSF is a voluntary organisation, which aims to represent the views of the many women involved in sport. With Sports Council funding, the WSF promotes the establishment of women and sports groups throughout Britain and co-operates with sports and education organisations. In 1986 it initiated the Sportswomen of the Year Awards and in 1992 it launched a new nationwide awards scheme for girls and young women between the ages of 11 and 19.

Ethnic Minorities

The Sports Council is encouraging local authorities to become more sensitive to the needs of minority groups in their communities. For example, in Yorkshire a network of contacts has been created within the black communities to involve ethnic minorities in cricket. This has increased the number of black cricket coaches and the numbers of young black people taking part in the game. The project is now being extended to other sports.

Many sports, such as athletics, boxing, football, rugby union and rugby league, have already been successful in attracting large numbers of participants from the ethnic minorities.

Young People

Special programmes of activity for young people are run by the governing bodies of individual sports, and the four Sports Councils organise local and national initiatives to encourage more young people to take part in sport. In March 1993 the Sports Council launched a new policy document—*Young People and Sport*—which sets out a number of objectives to ensure a co-ordinated development of sport for young people.

Government's Objectives

The Government's priorities for sport were outlined in December 1991 in a policy statement—*Sport and Active Recreation*. The Government's primary objectives are to:

- promote physical exercise and participation in sport and active recreation;
- help participants in sport achieve higher standards of performance;
- promote partnerships with the private sector in the provision and management of sports facilities (see p. 475); and
- promote sport for people with disabilities (see p. 480).

ORGANISATION AND ADMINISTRATION

Responsibility for government policy on sport and active recreation in England has rested with the Secretary of State for National Heritage since the creation of the Department of National Heritage in April 1992. The Secretaries of State for Wales, Scotland and Northern Ireland are responsible for sport in their countries. In Northern Ireland the Department of Education makes direct grants towards the capital cost of facilities to local authorities and voluntary sports bodies.

Responsibility for the organisation and promotion of sport is largely decentralised, and many sport and recreation facilities are provided by local authorities. The main mechanism by which the Government directly channels financial assistance to sport is through the Sports Councils. This 'arm's length' principle of funding safeguards the long-established independence of sports organisations in Britain.

Sports Councils

The Sports Councils, appointed and directly funded by the Government, are the Government's principal advisers on sporting matters. The Government works closely with them in implementing its sports policies.

There are four Councils:

- the Sports Council—for general matters affecting Great Britain and specifically English matters;
- the Sports Council for Wales;
- the Scottish Sports Council; and
- the Sports Council for Northern Ireland.

The Councils make grants for sports development, coaching and administration to the governing bodies of sports and other national organisations, and administer the National Sports Centres (see p. 478). Grants and loans are also made to voluntary organisations, local authorities and commercial organisations to help them provide sports facilities. In 1993–94 the Councils are allocating government funds amounting to approximately £67 million.

Support for Facilities

Facilities receiving support from the Sports Councils include sports halls, indoor swimming pools, intensive-use pitches, indoor tennis halls and school facilities.

One of the Sports Council's most significant schemes is the Indoor Tennis Initiative, which aims to establish a network of 50 local indoor tennis centres, through grant-aid of up to one-third of capital costs. Twenty-one centres have already been developed in England.

A Sports Council grant of £3 million contributed towards the costs of building the National Indoor Arena in Birmingham, which was formally opened in autumn 1991. In 1993 the arena staged the World Badminton Championships and in 1995 the World Netball Championships will be held there.

The Council has agreed to provide £1.5 million towards the development of a National Hockey Stadium at Milton Keynes.

The Scottish Sports Council contributed £150,000 towards Scotland's first specialist equestrian centre, which was established in 1992 at Devon Park, Central Region.

Development of Sport

Strategies for the development of sport have been drawn up by the four Sports Councils. The aims are broadly to ensure that:

- all young people have the opportunity to acquire basic sports skills;
- everyone has the opportunity to take part in sport and active recreation of their choice;
- everyone with the interest and ability has the opportunity to improve their standard of performance in sport and fulfil their potential; and
- everyone with the interest and ability has the opportunity to reach the highest standards of sporting excellence.

Much of the Sports Councils' budget is directed at increasing participation by the general public. The Councils are concentrating in particular on raising participation rates among the young, inner city dwellers and people with disabilities (see p. 480).

In May 1993 the Sports Council launched a new document—*Sports in the Nineties: New Horizons*—which sets out its vision for sport for the next five years.

A national strategic approach for Scottish sport was recently set out by the Scottish Sports Council. *Sport 2000* aims to introduce 250,000 people to sport by the end of the decade.

Local Authorities

Local authorities are the main providers of basic sport and recreation facilities for the local community. In England local authorities manage over 1,500 indoor centres, largely built in the last 20 years, as well as numerous outdoor amenities. The facilities provided include parks, lakes, playing fields, sports halls, tennis courts, golf courses, swimming pools, gymnasiums and sports centres catering for a wide range of activities.

There has been a rapid growth in the provision of artificial pitches—largely for hockey—and a similar increase in the number of leisure pools, which offer wave machines, waterfalls, jacuzzis and other leisure equipment. Gross annual expenditure by local authorities on sport and recreation amounts to over £1,000 million in England alone.

National Sports Associations

The Central Council of Physical Recreation (CCPR) is a non-governmental voluntary association in England whose membership consists of governing bodies of sport and other organisations with an interest in sport and physical recreation. Similar bodies in Scotland, Wales and Northern Ireland are the Scottish Sports Association, the Welsh Sports Association and the Northern Ireland Council of Physical Recreation (NICPR). The primary aim of these bodies is to represent the interests of their members to the appropriate national and local authorities, including the Sports Councils, from which they receive funding. Award schemes run by the associations include the CCPR's Community Sports Leaders Award Scheme and the NICPR's Service to Sport Awards.

The largest of the four associations is the CCPR, which comprises 200 British bodies and over 60 English associations. In recent years the CCPR has set up a number of sports bodies, including the Institute of Sports Sponsorship (ISS), which comprises some 80 major British companies that sponsor sport. The ISS aims to develop sponsorship at local, national and international level.

British Sports Forum

The sports associations of Wales, Scotland and Northern Ireland, the CCPR and the British Olympic Association have recently come together in the British Sports Forum. The purpose of this body is to present the united voice of the non-governmental sports sector, both domestically and internationally.

Sports Governing Bodies

Individual sports are run by over 400 independent governing bodies, whose functions usually include drawing up rules, holding events, regulating membership, selecting and training national teams and promoting international links. There are also organisations representing people who take part in more informal physical recreation, such as walking and cycling. The majority of the sports clubs in Britain belong to the appropriate governing body.

Sports Clubs

A wide variety of recreational facilities are provided by local sports clubs. Some cater for indoor recreation, but more common are those providing sports grounds, particularly for cricket, football, rugby, hockey, tennis and golf. There are approximately 150,000 sports clubs in Britain, with about 6.5 million members. Many clubs linked to business firms cater for sporting activities. Commercial facilities include tenpin bowling centres, ice and roller-skating rinks, squash courts, golf courses and driving ranges, riding stables, marinas and, increasingly, fitness centres. In all, the private sector owns and runs some 500 major sports facilities.

Countryside Bodies

The Countryside Commission (for England), the Countryside Council for Wales and Scottish Natural Heritage are responsible for conserving and improving the natural beauty and amenity of the countryside, and for encouraging the provision of facilities for open-air recreation. The three bodies assist in the provision or improvement of recreational parks, country parks and picnic sites and the opening up of rights of way and National Trails.

In Northern Ireland the Ulster Countryside Committee advises the Department of the Environment on the preservation of amenities and the designation of 'areas of outstanding natural beauty'.

British Waterways Board

The British Waterways Board is a publicly owned body responsible for managing and developing much of Great Britain's inland waterways. Many leisure and recreational pursuits, such as angling and various types of sailing and boating, are enjoyed on waterways and reservoirs. The Board, which is responsible for approximately 2,000 miles (3,220 km) of canals and water navigations, actively promotes water safety and organises community activities.

National Coaching Foundation

The National Coaching Foundation (NCF) aims to provide educational and advisory services for coaches in all sports. The Foundation works in partnership with the Sports Councils, and its work complements and supports the coaching development carried out by sports governing bodies. Sixteen national coaching centres provide locally accessible services in coach education, information and advice as well as research and consultancy.

In 1991–92 the Sports Council provided a grant of £700,000 to the NCF to enable it to set up Champion Coaching, a pilot after-school coaching scheme for those aged 11 to 14. Following a £1.3 million grant from the Foundation for Sport and the Arts, the pilot scheme has been developed into a three-year programme which will involve about 40,000 children and some 4,000 coaches.

British Olympic Association

The British Olympic Association (BOA) is the National Olympic Committee for Britain and comprises representatives of the 31 governing bodies of those sports in the programme of the Olympic Games (summer and winter). Its primary function is to organise the participation of British teams in the Olympic Games, but it is also responsible for nominating British cities for staging the Olympics.

The BOA determines the size of British Olympic teams and sets standards for selection, raises funds and makes all necessary arrangements. It also makes important contributions in the fields of coaching, drug testing and control, and sports medicine. The Association's British Olympic Medical Centre at Northwick Park Hospital in north London supplies a medical back-up service for competitors before and during the Olympic Games.

The BOA is supported by sponsorship and by donations from commerce and industry and from the public.

National Playing Fields Association

The National Playing Fields Association is a charity whose purpose is to promote the provision of recreation and play facilities for all age groups. It aims to ensure that there are adequate playing fields and playspace available for use by the community. There are affiliated associations in the English and Welsh counties and independent organisations in Scotland and Northern Ireland.

The Government has awarded a grant of £500,000 to the Sports Council, in conjunction with the National Playing Fields Association and the CCPR, to compile a register of recreational land in England as part of a strategy to safeguard playing fields.

Sports Medicine and Sports Science

Sports medicine and sports science are increasingly being acknowledged as important areas for assisting the improvement of performance and the achievement of excellence. In order to provide a more co-ordinated service to sportsmen and women, the Sports Council has established a National Sports Medicine Institute, based at St Bartholomew's Hospital, London.

The Institute's main function is to provide clinical services aimed at assessing and improving fitness, and treating and preventing medical disorders related to sport. Work is in progress to develop a network of regional centres to provide both clinical and educational services, which will be linked with new support services at the National Sports Centres. The Sports Council is allocating £500,000 towards sports medicine in 1993–94. In Scotland a network of some

30 sports medicine centres has been created.

The development of sports science support services for the national governing bodies of sport is currently being promoted by the Sports Council, in collaboration with the BOA and the NCF, in order to raise the standards of performance of national squads. In 1993–94 the Sports Council is contributing £550,000 in support of science studies. The Sports Council for Wales received £250,000 from the Welsh Office in 1992–93 to establish a sports science unit in Wales.

Olympic Bid by Manchester

Manchester's bid to stage the 2000 Olympic Games failed to win sufficient support from the International Olympic Committee (IOC), which announced in September 1993 that the Games would be held in Sydney.

However, the construction in east Manchester of two major new facilities which would have been used for the Games will still be completed. These comprise an indoor arena, which will be used for a wide range of sports, including boxing, football, ice skating and ice hockey, and Britain's first indoor velodrome. When completed in 1994, the velodrome will become Britain's National Cycling Centre. Construction of these facilities has been assisted by government grants of £35 million towards the arena and £8 million towards the velodrome.

NATIONAL SPORTS CENTRES

The four Sports Councils operate a total of 12 National Sports Centres, which provide world-class facilities for training and competition at the highest level. First priority at the Centres is given to the governing bodies of sport for national squad training and for the training of coaches. However, the Centres also make their facilities available to top sportsmen and women for individual training and to the local community. All of the Centres provide residential facilities.

England

In England the Sports Council operates four major National Centres and a minor National Centre for climbers at Harrison's Rocks in Kent.

Crystal Palace

Crystal Palace in London is a leading competition venue for a wide range of sports and a major training centre for national squads, clubs, schools and serious enthusiasts. Its facilities are used by some 22 separate governing bodies of sport, and the Centre is a regional centre of excellence for athletics, netball, weightlifting and swimming. Crystal Palace stadium is Britain's major international athletics venue, with a capacity for 17,000 spectators. Other facilities include an Olympic-size swimming pool and a Sports Injury Centre.

Bisham Abbey

Bisham Abbey in Berkshire caters for a number of sports, including tennis, football, hockey, weightlifting, squash, rugby and golf. The England football, rugby and hockey squads undergo regular preparation work at the Centre. Bisham Abbey has long-standing partnerships with the British Amateur Weightlifters Association and the Lawn Tennis Association, which has helped to develop the Abbey as the National Tennis Training Centre.

Lilleshall

Lilleshall National Sports Centre in Shropshire offers extensive sports facilities, which are used by a variety of national teams. Facilities include a world-class gymnastic training centre, regularly used by the British gymnastic squads, and extensive playing fields for football and hockey. The Football Association uses Lilleshall as its base for major coaching activities and has established a training school there.

Holme Pierrepont

The National Watersports Centre at Holme Pierrepont in Nottinghamshire is one of the most comprehensive water sports centres in the world, with facilities for rowing, canoeing, water skiing, powerboating, ski-racing, angling and sailing. It's main feature is a 2,000 metres regatta course.

Wales

The Sports Council for Wales runs two National Sports Centres: the Welsh Institute of Sport and the National Watersports Centre. A further Centre—Plas y Brenin—is run by the Sports Council.

The Welsh Institute of Sport in Cardiff is the country's premier venue for top-level training and for competition in a large number of sports. Facilities include a world-standard gymnastics hall, a sports science unit and a sports injury clinic. In 1991–92 a £1.25 million refurbishment was started.

The National Watersports Centre at Plas Menai in north Wales is primarily a centre of excellence for sailing and canoeing but also stages mountain activities in nearby Snowdonia. Its extensive range of activities include dinghy and catamaran sailing, offshore cruising and powerboat training.

Plas y Brenin National Mountain Centre, situated in Snowdonia National Park in north Wales, offers a variety of courses in rock climbing, mountaineering, sea and river canoeing, orienteering, skiing and most other mountain-based activities.

Scotland

Scotland has three National Sports Centres, which are operated by the Scottish Sports Council.

The National Outdoor Training Centre at Glenmore Lodge near Aviemore caters for a wide range of activities, including hill walking, rock climbing, mountaineering, kayaking, skiing and canoeing. The Centre is undergoing a £1.6 million redevelopment programme with the help of an £800,000 government grant.

The Inverclyde National Sports Training Centre at Largs has a large number of facilities, including a gymnastics hall, a purpose-built golf training facility and a laboratory for fitness assessment. The Centre also acts as an important competition

venue for major national and international championships.

The Cumbrae National Water Sports Training Centre on the island of Great Cumbrae in the Firth of Clyde offers an extensive range of courses catering for all levels of ability. The Centre has a comprehensive range of modern craft for a wide variety of sailing activities, as well as sub-aqua diving equipment.

Northern Ireland

The Northern Ireland Centre for Outdoor Activities in County Down, run by the Sports Council for Northern Ireland, offers courses in mountaineering, rock climbing, canoeing and outdoor adventure. Also available are leadership and instructor courses leading to nationally recognised qualifications.

SPORT FOR PEOPLE WITH DISABILITIES

Associations for People with Disabilities

The key organisations for people with disabilities are the British Sports Association for the Disabled (BSAD), the United Kingdom Sports Association for People with Mental Handicap, the British Paralympic Association (BPA) and a range of bodies concerned with individual disabilities and single sports. These include the Riding for the Disabled Association, which caters for some 25,000 riders.

British Sports Association for the Disabled

The BSAD is a national body working across all the disabilities. It promotes the development of sport for people with disabilities at local level, and organises regional and national championships in a range of sports.

The Scottish Sports Association for the Disabled, the Federation of Sports Associations for the Disabled (Wales) and the Northern Ireland Committee on Sport for Disabled People have similar co-ordinating roles.

United Kingdom Sports Association for People with Mental Handicap

The United Kingdom Sports Association for People with Mental Handicap is a co-ordinating body with a membership of over 20 national organisations. The Association promotes and supports the work of its members and provides training. It also works closely with the BPA in co-ordinating the participation of people with learning difficulties in the Paralympics. The first-ever Paralympic Games for people with learning difficulties were held in Madrid in September 1992.

National Disability Sports Organisations

There are six national disability sports organisations concerned with individual disabilities. These organisations provide coaching and help to organise national competitions in conjunction with the national governing bodies of sport and the BSAD. They comprise:

● the British Amputee Sports Association;
● British Blind Sport;
● the British Deaf Sports Council;
● the British Wheelchair Sports Foundation;
● Cerebral Palsy Sport; and
● the British Les Autres Sports Association, which caters for those whose disabilities are not covered by other organisations.

British Paralympic Association

Britain's participation in the Paralympics is organised by the BPA, which liaises closely with the BOA. The BPA assists in the preparation and training of Paralympic and other international teams, and advises the Sports Council on the distribution of grants for all international disabled sports events.

Government Report

In 1989 the Government published a report on sport for people with disabilities—*Building on Ability*. Its main recommendation was that sport for disabled and able-bodied people should be increasingly integrated, with athletes with disabilities being encouraged to participate in sporting events either in direct competition with able-bodied athletes or in parallel events.

Following publication of the report, the Government provided the BPA with £500,000 for the establishment of a trust fund to support a variety of disabled sport initiatives. Additional funds were also given in 1991 to the Sports Council and to the Scottish Sports Council to help implement the report's recommendations.

The governing bodies of sport are increasingly taking responsibility for both able-bodied participants and those with disabilities. Close liaison takes place between individual sports and the Sports Council, which provides advice to governing bodies on encouraging the integration of people with disabilities.

SPONSORSHIP AND OTHER FUNDING

The private sector makes a substantial investment in sports sponsorship, contributing some £230 million a year. This involves more than 2,000 British companies.

Sponsorship may take the form of financing specific events, or of grants to individual sports organisations or sportsmen and women. Investment includes sponsorship of cricket and football leagues, sporting events such as horse races, and of individual performers. Motor sport and football receive the largest amounts of private sponsorship.

Sponsorship of sport is encouraged by a number of bodies, including the Institute of Sports Sponsorship (ISS—see p. 476), the Scottish Sports Council's Sponsorship Advisory Service, which has raised almost £3 million directly for Scottish sport over the last ten years, and the Sports Council for Wales' Sponsorship Advisory Service, which in its first two years of operation has helped generate £140,000 for Welsh sport.

Successive governments have negotiated voluntary agreements with the tobacco industry to regulate tobacco companies' sponsorship of sport.

Business Sponsorship Scheme

In an effort to increase the current levels of sports sponsorship, the Government has established a business sponsorship incentive scheme for sport targeted at the 'grass roots' level.

> The 'Sportsmatch' scheme was launched at the end of 1992 and assists local sport by providing government funds to match those from business sponsors. Sportsmatch will provide funding of over £3.7 million a year in Great Britain.

In England the scheme is managed as a joint venture between the Department of National Heritage and the ISS. Under the scheme, local sport can gain up to £75,000 a project from the Government if the same amount is secured in business sponsorship. Sportsmatch intends to concentrate on local amateur sport and to encourage firms which have not used sponsorship before.

Similar arrangements have been announced for the new scheme in Scotland and Wales, where it is administered by the appropriate Sports Councils in association with the ISS. Northern Ireland has its own sports sponsorship incentive scheme, which is currently being reviewed.

Sports Aid Foundation

The Sports Aid Foundation raises and distributes funds from industry, commerce and private sponsors in order to assist the training of talented individuals. Grants are awarded on the recommendation of the appropriate governing bodies of sport to British competitors who need help preparing for Olympic, World and European championships. The Scottish and Welsh Sports Aid Foundations and the Ulster Sports and Recreation Trust have similar functions.

Foundation for Sport and the Arts

The Foundation for Sport and the Arts was set up by the pools promoters in 1991 to channel funds into sport and the arts. The pools promoters are providing the Foundation with some £43.5 million a year. A further £21.8 million a year is received as a result of the 2.5 per cent reduction in pool betting duty in the 1990 Budget. About £43.5 million a year is available for sport.

The Foundation works closely with the Sports Councils and other sports bodies, and makes numerous grants to sports clubs and sporting organisations.

Recent assistance includes:

- a contribution of £1 million towards the proposed Northern Ireland Sports Training Centre; and

- £200,000 to Yorkshire & Cleveland Riding for the Disabled to assist with the cost of providing a major centre for disabled riders.

Horserace Betting Levy

Most betting in Britain takes place on horse racing and greyhound racing. Bets may be made at racecourses and greyhound tracks, or through over 10,000 licensed off-course betting offices, which take about 90 per cent of the money staked. A form of pool betting —totalisator betting—is organised on racecourses by the Horserace Totalisator Board (the Tote). Racecourse bets may also be placed with independent on-course bookmakers.

Bookmakers and the Tote contribute a levy—a fixed proportion of their profits—to the Horserace Betting Levy Board. The amount of levy payable is decided by the racing and bookmaking industries. The Levy Board promotes the improvement of horse breeds, advancement of veterinary science and better horse racing.

In 1991–92 the total money staked in all forms of gambling, excluding gaming machines, was estimated at £24,594 million.

National Lottery

In March 1992 the Government set out its proposals for a new national lottery in a White Paper—*A National Lottery Raising Money for Good Causes*. This recommended that sport should be one of the main beneficiaries of such a lottery, which could be in operation by late 1994. The main provisions of the National Lottery etc. Act 1993, which paves the way for the introduction of the Lottery, are that:

- the Lottery should be run by the private sector; and
- a National Lottery Distribution Fund will be established, with the proceeds being divided equally between arts, sports, the national heritage, charities and the Millennium Fund.

The money for sport will be split between the four Sports Councils. Once fully operational, the National Lottery could raise up to £1,500 million a year.

SPORT AND EDUCATION

All schools (except those solely for infants) are expected to have a playing field or the use of one, and most secondary schools have a gymnasium. Some have other amenities such as swimming pools, sports halls and halls designed for dance and movement.

National Curriculum

The Government believes that all young children should have the opportunity to learn basic sports skills. It has therefore made physical education (PE), which includes sport, a compulsory subject in the National Curriculum (see p. 408) for all pupils aged 5 to 16 in state-maintained schools in England and Wales. Pupils will also be required from autumn 1994 to have been taught to swim at least 25 metres by the age of 11.

In Scotland the Secretary of State for Scotland has issued National Guidelines which contain programmes of study and attainment targets for physical activity for pupils aged 5 to 14.

Partnerships with the Local Community

The Government is encouraging stronger links between schools and the wider community to ensure that children have access to the sports amenities which clubs and associations can make available outside school hours.

In Scotland an initiative aimed at

strengthening the links between schools, clubs and the community was launched by the Scottish Sports Council in 1991. 'Team Sport Scotland' seeks to promote the development of school-aged team sport and was made possible through a Scottish Office grant of £400,000 in the first year, with a commitment to further funding for the following two years.

In 1991 the Government launched a new guide—*A Sporting Double: School and Community*—to encourage and assist the sharing of school facilities between schools and the local community. The Education Act 1993 includes provisions to allow school governors to enter into agreements for the joint management of school premises for community purposes.

SPECTATOR SAFETY AT SPORTS GROUNDS

Safety at sports grounds is governed by legislation. The main instrument of control is a safety certificate which is issued by the relevant local authority. When determining the conditions of a safety certificate, the local authority is expected to comply with the Guide to Safety at Sports Grounds. This was revised in 1990 to include the relevant safety recommendations of the Taylor Report on the Hillsborough stadium disaster in Sheffield in 1989, which resulted in the death of 96 spectators.

The Taylor Report

The Taylor Report, published in 1990, contained a wide range of recommendations for promoting better and safer conditions at all sports grounds. The report's major recommendation was that sports grounds designated under the Safety of Sports Grounds Act 1975 should become all-seated under a phased programme.

The Government accepted most of the report's recommendations for making sports stadiums safer and agreed the timetables for the introduction of all-seater stadiums for football (see p. 483).

Under the Football Spectators Act 1989 the Government established a Football

Licensing Authority (FLA), which is responsible for assisting in the implementation of the all-seating policy in England and Wales. The FLA operates a licensing system for grounds on which designated football matches are played.

Football Grounds

In 1992 the Government reviewed its policy on requiring all League football grounds to have seated accommodation only. Clubs in the Premier League, First Division clubs in the Football League and national stadiums are still required to have all-seated accommodation by August 1994. However, this requirement has been relaxed for the Second and Third Divisions of the Football League, providing that the terracing is safe. In Scotland Premier Division clubs and national stadiums must meet the 1994 deadline, but First and Second Division clubs may retain the use of standing accommodation.

The Football Trust

The Football Trust 1990 was established by the pools promoters. Its income is over £32 million a year and it is funded partly by the pools promoters from their spotting-the-ball competition and partly from a 2.5 per cent reduction in pool betting duty to run for five years, announced in the 1990 Budget. This concession will provide more than £100 million to football on the understanding that the money made available must be used to assist football clubs and the national stadiums to fund capital works for the comfort and safety of spectators and, in particular, all-seater stadiums in line with the recommendations of the Taylor Report.

In August 1993 the Government agreed to extend the concession for a further five years in order to help clubs in the lower divisions of the Football League to ensure that any terracing retained at their grounds meets the required safety standards.

Crowd Control

The Government has worked closely with the police, football authorities and the governments of other European countries to implement crowd control measures.

Legislation has made it an offence in England and Wales to throw objects at football matches, run onto the playing area or chant indecent or racist abuse. There are also controls on the sale and possession of alcohol at football grounds and on transport to and from grounds.

Courts in England and Wales have the power to prohibit convicted football hooligans from attending football matches. They also have powers to impose restriction orders on convicted football hooligans to prevent them travelling abroad to attend specified matches. Closed-circuit television has greatly assisted the police in controlling crowds. The National Criminal Intelligence Service Football Unit co-ordinates police intelligence about football hooligans and liaises with overseas police forces.

DRUG ABUSE IN SPORT

National Action

The Sports Council introduced a new independent drug testing regime in 1988. This provides for random testing in and out of competition by independent sampling officers, and the publication of adverse findings. The Council also funds the IOC-accredited laboratory at King's College, London University, which carries out analysis and research into methods of detection for new drugs which unfairly aid performance. The Government is currently considering the possibility of strengthening legal controls on anabolic steroids.

In 1992–93 the Sports Council intensified its drugs-testing programme, with greater emphasis being placed on out-of-competition tests. There were 48 positive reports in 1992–93, compared with 53 in 1991-92.

Sports Council funding in Britain for the programme exceeded £820,000 in 1992–93.

International Action

In 1990 the Council of Europe developed an Anti-Doping Convention to tackle the problem of drug abuse in sport, the main aim of which is to provide an international framework within which national anti-doping campaigns can work effectively. Britain has already implemented the provisions of the convention.

World Conference on Anti-doping in Sport

The Fourth Permanent World Conference on Anti-doping in Sport took place in London in September 1993. The Conference was organised by the Sports Council in association with the IOC Medical Commission and brought together more than 200 experts on drugs in sport from 60 countries. The three-day conference examined current anti-doping developments throughout the world, why competitors take drugs and how they obtain them, and the views of the next generation of competitors on drug abuse.

A TO Z OF POPULAR SPORTS

Some of the major sports in Britain are described below. Additional information on these and other sports not covered here can be found in *A Digest of Sports Statistics for the UK*, published by the Sports Council.

Angling

One of the most popular countryside sports is angling, of which there are three main types: coarse, game and sea.

Angling is an overwhelmingly male sport, with an estimated ten times as many male as female participants among Britain's 4 million anglers. Many fish for salmon and trout, particularly in the rivers and lochs of Scotland and in Wales. In England and Wales the most widely practised form of angling is for coarse fish. Separate organisations represent game, coarse and sea fishing clubs in England, Wales, Scotland and Northern Ireland.

The National Federation of Anglers in England organises national championships for coarse fishing and enters a team in the world angling championships.

Association Football

Association football is controlled by separate football associations in England, Wales, Scotland and Northern Ireland. In England 340 clubs are affiliated to the English Football Association (FA) and more than 42,000 clubs directly through regional or district associations. The FA, founded in 1863, and the Football League, founded in 1888, were both the first of their kind in the world.

In England and Wales a major change occurred in August 1992 when a new FA Premier League was started, comprising 22 clubs. The remaining 70 full-time professional clubs play in three main divisions run by the Football League. In Scotland there are three divisions, with 38 clubs, which play in the Scottish Football League. In Northern Ireland, 16 semi-professional clubs play in the Irish Football League. During the season, which lasts from August until May, over 2,000 English League matches are played; total attendances reached over 20 million in 1991–92.

The major annual knock out competitions are the FA Challenge Cup and the Coca-Cola Cup (the League Cup) in England, the Tennents Scottish Cup, the Scottish League Cup, the Irish Cup and the Welsh FA Cup.

England is to host the European Championships finals in 1996.

Athletics

Amateur athletics is governed in Britain by the British Athletic Federation (BAF), which is affiliated to the International Amateur Athletic Federation. The BAF is responsible for the selection of British teams for international events, and also administers coaching schemes. For the Olympic Games and the World and European championships one team represents Britain.

Athletics is attracting increasing numbers of participants. In recent years there has been a significant growth in mass participation events, such as marathons and half marathons. The London Marathon, which takes place every spring, attracted over 25,000 runners in 1993.

Recent successes at international level include two gold medals at the 1993 World Indoor Athletics Championships in Toronto, Canada—Yvonne Murray in the 3,000 metres and Tom McKean in the 800 metres—and three gold medals at the 1993 World Athletics Championships in Stuttgart. Britain's gold medallists were Linford Christie in the 100 metres, Colin Jackson in the 110 metres hurdles (in a new world record) and Sally Gunnell in the 400 metres hurdles, also in a world record. Britain won a total of ten medals in Stuttgart and finished fourth in the overall medals table.

Badminton

Badminton is organised by the Badminton Association of England and the Scottish, Welsh and Irish (Ulster branch) Badminton Unions. Around 5 million people play badminton in Britain and there are over 5,000 clubs. Most clubs do not own their own facilities but hire courts from local authority sports centres, schools and churches.

In 1992 badminton was introduced into the Olympics.

Basketball

In Britain over 750,000 people participate in basketball. The English Basket Ball Association is the governing body in England, and there are similar associations in Wales, Scotland and Northern Ireland. All of the associations are represented on the British and Irish Basketball Federation, which acts as the co-ordinating body for Britain and the Irish Republic.

The leading clubs play in the National Basketball Leagues. Mini-basketball and micro-basketball are versions of the game which have been developed for players under the age of 13.

Wheelchair basketball is played under the same rules, with a few basic adaptations, and in the same court as the running game. Over 30 teams play in the National League.

Bowls

The two main forms of bowls are lawn (flat green and crown green) and indoor bowls. The game is increasingly enjoyed by adults of all ages. In recent years the most notable increases have been in the number of women taking part. Bowls is also popular among people with disabilities.

About 4,000 lawn bowling clubs are affiliated to the English, Scottish, Welsh and Irish (Northern Ireland Region) Bowling Associations, which, together with Women's Bowling Associations for the four countries, play to the rules of the International Bowling Board. The British Crown Green Bowling Association is the governing body of crown green bowls, and the indoor game in England is administered by the English Indoor Bowling Association. Similar associations exist for Scotland, Wales and Northern Ireland and there are separate women's associations in each country.

At the world outdoor championships in 1992 Tony Allcock won the singles gold and Scotland won the Leonard Trophy (the team title), together with gold medals in the pairs and the fours. In 1993 Richard Corsie won the world indoor singles championships for the third time in five years.

Boxing

Boxing in Britain is both amateur and professional, and in both strict medical regulations are observed.

All amateur boxing in England is controlled by the Amateur Boxing Association. There are separate associations in Scotland and Wales, and Northern Ireland forms part of the Irish Boxing Association. The associations organise amateur boxing championships as well as training courses for referees, coaches and others. The wearing of headguards is now compulsory in all British amateur competitions.

Professional boxing is controlled by the British Boxing Board of Control. The Board appoints inspectors, medical officers and representatives to ensure that regulations are observed and to guard against overmatching and exploitation. Britain currently has five world champions: Chris Eubank (World Boxing Organisation—WBO— super-middleweight champion), Nigel

Benn (World Boxing Council—WBC—super-middleweight), Steve Robinson (WBO featherweight), Paul Weir (WBO straw-weight) and Lennox Lewis (WBC heavyweight).

Cricket

Both the Marylebone Cricket Club (MCC), which frames the laws of the game, and the Test and County Cricket Board (TCCB—representing first-class cricket) are based at Lord's cricket ground in north London, the administrative centre of the world game. Men's cricket in Britain is governed by the Cricket Council, consisting of representatives of the TCCB, the National Cricket Association (representing club and junior cricket), the Minor Counties Association, the Scottish Cricket Union, the Irish Cricket Union and the MCC.

Cricket is played in schools, colleges and universities, and amateur teams play weekly games in cities, towns and villages from late April to the end of September. Throughout Britain there is a network of league cricket, minor counties and club games.

The main competition in professional cricket is the Britannic Assurance County Championship, played by 18 first-class county teams in four-day matches. There are also three one-day competitions: the Benson and Hedges Cup, the National Westminster Trophy and the AXA Equity & Law Sunday League.

Every year there is a series of five-day Cornhill Insurance Test matches played between England and a touring team from Australia, India, New Zealand, Pakistan, South Africa, Sri Lanka or the West Indies. A team representing England usually tours one or more of these countries in the British winter. A World Cup competition takes place every four years, and England were runners-up to Pakistan in the 1992 final.

Cricket is also played by women and girls, the governing body being the Women's Cricket Association. Women's cricket clubs have regular local fixtures and there are regular county matches as well as an area championship. Test match series

and a World Cup competition are also played. In 1993 England won the Women's World Cup for the second time.

Cycling

Cycling is one of Britain's fastest growing sports. Cycling activities include road and track racing, cycle speedway, time-trialling, cyclo-cross (cross country racing), touring and bicycle moto-cross (BMX). In recent years there has been a significant growth in the use of all-terrain or mountain bikes.

The British Cycling Federation is the governing body for cycling as a sport, with over 17,600 members. The Cyclists' Touring Club has 40,000 members and is the governing body for recreational and urban cycling and represents cyclists' interests in general. The Scottish Cyclists Union controls the sport in Scotland. In Northern Ireland the sport is controlled by the Ulster Cycling Federation and the Northern Ireland Cycling Federation.

In July 1993 Chris Boardman set a new one-hour world record at the Bordeaux velodrome, when he became the first man to break through 52 km (32 miles). Another world record was broken by Graeme Obree, who lowered the 4,000 metres record when winning the world 4,000 metres pursuit title at Hamar, Norway, in August 1993.

Major cycling events in Britain include the Milk Race and the Kelloggs Tour of Britain, which take place annually. In 1994 Britain is to host two stages of the Tour de France.

Equestrianism

Equestrian activities include recreational riding, endurance riding, carriage driving, one- and three-day eventing and show jumping. The arts of riding and driving are promoted by the British Horse Society, which is concerned with the welfare of horses, road safety, riding rights of way and training. It runs the British Equestrian Centre at Stoneleigh in Warwickshire. With some 60,000 members, the Society is the parent body of the Pony Club and the Riding Club movements, which hold rallies, meetings and competitions culminating in annual national championships.

Leading horse trials, comprising dressage, cross-country and show jumping, are held every year at a number of locations, including Badminton (Avon) and Gatcombe Park (Gloucestershire).

Show jumping is regulated and promoted by the British Show Jumping Association. The major show jumping events each year include the Royal International Horse Show at Hickstead (West Sussex) and the Horse of the Year Show at Wembley in London.

The authority responsible for equestrian competitions (other than racing) at international and Olympic level is the British Equestrian Federation, which co-ordinates the activities of the British Horse Society and the British Show Jumping Association.

Golf

The Royal and Ancient Golf Club (R & A), situated at St Andrews in Scotland, is the ruling authority of the sport for most of the world. The Golfing Union of Ireland and parallel unions in Wales, Scotland and England are the national governing bodies for men's amateur golf. These bodies co-operate with the R & A and are represented on the Council of National Golf Unions, which is the British co-ordinating body responsible for handicapping and organising international matches. Women's amateur golf is governed by the Ladies' Golf Union.

Club professional golf is governed by the Professional Golfers' Association (PGA) and the Women's PGA. For tournament professionals the governing bodies are the PGA European Tour and the Women Professional Golfers' European Tour Ltd. There are about 1,900 golf courses in Britain.

The main event of the British golfing year is the Open Championship, one of the world's leading tournaments. Other important events include the Walker Cup and Curtis Cup matches for amateurs, played between Great Britain and Ireland and the United States, and the Ryder Cup match for professionals, played between Europe and the United States. Among the leading British professional players are Nick Faldo and Ian Woosnam. Nick Faldo won the Open in 1992 for the second time and is currently ranked number one in the world.

Greyhound Racing

Greyhound racing is one of Britain's most popular spectator sports and takes place at 37 major tracks. Meetings are usually held three times a week at each track, with at least ten races a meeting. The rules for the sport are drawn up by the National Greyhound Racing Club, the sport's judicial and administrative body. The representative body is the British Greyhound Racing Board.

There are about 50 mainly small tracks which operate independently. Like the major tracks, they are licensed by local authorities.

Gymnastics

Gymnastics is divided into four main disciplines: artistic (or Olympic) gymnastics, rhythmic gymnastics, sports acrobatics and general gymnastics. Both men and women compete in artistic gymnastics, although the apparatus used differs. Rhythmic gymnastics is for women only and consists of routines performed to music with ribbon, balls, clubs, hoop and rope. Sports acrobatics is gymnastics with people rather than apparatus. General gymnastics is non-competitive and is available to all age groups and to people with special needs.

The governing body for the sport is the British Amateur Gymnastics Association (BAGA). Over the past decade the number of clubs affiliated to the BAGA has nearly doubled. The sport is particularly popular with schoolchildren and young adults, and it has been estimated that between 3 and 4 million schoolchildren take part in some form of gymnastics every day.

At the 1993 World Gymnastics Championships in Birmingham Neil Thomas became the first Briton to win a gymnastics medal at world level when he won the silver medal in the floor exercise.

Highland Games

Scottish Highland Games cover a wide range of athletic competitions in addition to activities such as dancing and piping competitions. The main events include running, cycling, throwing the hammer, tossing the caber and putting the shot.

Over 70 gatherings of various kinds take place throughout Scotland, the most famous of which include the annual Braemar Gathering and the Argyllshire and Cowal Gatherings.

The Scottish Games Association is the official governing body responsible for athletic sports and games at Highland and Border events in Scotland.

Hockey (Field and Indoor)

The modern game of hockey was started by the Hockey Association (of England), which acts as the governing body for men's hockey. Parallel associations serve in Scotland, Wales and Ireland.

Levels of sponsorship and participation have increased in recent years following British success at the 1988 and 1992 Olympics. Cup competitions and leagues exist at national, divisional or district, and club levels, both indoors (six-a-side) and outdoors, and there are regular international matches.

The controlling body of women's hockey in England is the All England Women's Hockey Association; separate associations regulate the sport in Scotland, Wales and Ireland. League, county, club and school championships for both outdoor and indoor hockey are played annually in England. Regular international matches are played.

Traditionally hockey has been played on grass pitches, but recently there has been an increase in the use of artificial pitches, which allow a faster, more free-flowing game. All major competitions are now played on an artificial surface.

Horse Racing

Horse racing takes two forms—flat racing, and National Hunt (steeplechasing and hurdle racing). The main flat race season runs from late March to early November, but following the introduction of all-weather racing in 1989 flat race meetings now take place throughout the year. The Derby, run at Epsom, is the outstanding event in the flat racing calendar. Other classic races are: the Two Thousand Guineas and the One Thousand Guineas, both run at Newmarket; the Oaks (Epsom); and the St Leger (Doncaster).

The National Hunt season runs from late July/early August to early June. The most important meeting is the National Hunt Festival held at Cheltenham in March, which features the Gold Cup and the Champion Hurdle. The Grand National, run at Aintree, near Liverpool, is the world's best-known steeplechase and dates from 1837. In 1993 the race was declared void for the first time in its history following two false starts and the failure to recall all the runners. The Jockey Club subsequently set up a working group to consider improvements to the starting procedure, and has accepted the recommendations made by the group.

In June 1993 overall responsibility for the control of racing was passed from the Jockey Club to a new body—the British Horseracing Board, which consists of representatives of the racing industry. The Jockey Club retains an administrative role and is responsible for licensing, discipline, security and anti-doping measures.

Britain has 59 racecourses and about 12,000 horses currently in training.

Ice Skating

Ice skating takes three main forms: figure skating (solo and pairs), ice dancing and speed-skating (indoor and outdoor). The governing body is the National Ice Skating Association of Great Britain.

Participation in ice skating is concentrated among the under-25s, and is one of the few sports that attracts more female than male participants. There are over 70 rinks in Britain; almost half have opened since 1985.

British couples have won the world ice dance championship 17 times. Britain's most recent success in this event was achieved by Jayne Torvill and Christopher Dean, who won four consecutive world championships between 1981 and 1984. The couple intend to return to international competition in 1994 following a rule change which permits professional skaters to return to amateur competition.

Judo

Judo, an individual combat sport derived from the ancient Japanese art of ju-jitsu, is popular not only as a competitive sport and self-defence technique, but also as a means of general fitness training. An internationally recognised grading system is in operation through the sport's governing body, the British Judo Association.

In the 1992 Olympics women's judo was included for the first time, and Britain won a total of four medals in the women's and men's events. Britain has won medals for judo at every Olympic Games since 1972.

At the 1993 World Judo Championships Nicola Fairbrother won a gold medal in the under 56 kg category.

Keep Fit

Various forms of movement and fitness activities are practised in Britain that include elements of eurhythmics, dance and aerobic exercise. The Keep Fit Association receives funding from the Sports Council to promote physical fitness and a positive attitude to health in England. Its national certificated training scheme for keep fit teachers is recognised by local education authorities throughout Britain. Autonomous associations serve Scotland, Wales and Northern Ireland.

The Sports Council plans to launch a new governing body for England—the National Exercise and Fitness Association.

Martial Arts

A broad range of martial arts, mainly derived from Japan, the People's Republic of China, Taiwan, Hong Kong and Korea, has been introduced into Britain during the 20th century. There are recognised governing bodies responsible for their own activities in karate, ju-jitsu, aikido, Chinese martial arts, kendo, taekwondo and tang soo do. The most

popular martial art is karate, with over 100,000 participants.

A review of martial arts organisations was undertaken in 1990 by the Sports Council. The review recommended the establishment of an Advisory Group on Martial Arts, which has since been set up by the Sports Council, to provide a forum for discussing martial arts issues.

Motor-car Sports

The main four-wheeled motor sports include motor racing, autocross, rallycross, rallying and karting. In motor racing the Formula One Grand Prix competition is the major form of the sport.

The governing body for four-wheeled motor sport is the RAC (Royal Automobile Club) Motor Sports Association. The Association issues licences for a variety of motoring competitions and organises the Network Q RAC Rally, an event in the contest for the World Rally Championship, and the British Grand Prix, which is held at Silverstone as part of the Formula One World Motor Racing Championship. In 1993 Britain also staged the Formula One European Grand Prix at Donington Park.

British car constructors, including Lotus, McLaren and Williams, have enjoyed outstanding successes in Grand Prix racing, and Britain has had seven world champion motor racing drivers.

In 1993 Nigel Mansell won the IndyCar World Series Championship, which takes place in the United States and Australia. In so doing he became the first man to win the IndyCar title in his debut year and the only driver to win the Formula One world championship and IndyCar titles in successive years.

In 1993 Damon Hill recorded three consecutive Grand Prix victories in his first full season of Formula One racing.

Motor-cycle Sports

Motor-cycle sports include road racing,

moto-cross, grass track, speedway, trials, drag racing and sprint. It is estimated that there are between 40,000 and 50,000 competitive motor cyclists in Britain.

The governing bodies of the sport are the Auto-Cycle Union in England and Wales, the Scottish Auto-Cycle Union and the Motor Cycle Union of Ireland (in Northern Ireland). The major events of the year include the Isle of Man TT races and the British Road Race Grand Prix. The Auto-Cycle Union provides off-road training by approved instructors for riders of all ages.

Mountaineering

All forms of mountaineering, which includes hill-walking and rock-climbing, are growing in popularity. There are around 100,000 rock-climbers and 700,000 hill-walkers, whose representative body is the British Mountaineering Council; separate bodies serve Scotland and Ireland.

British mountaineers have played a leading role in the exploration of the world's great mountain ranges. The best-known is Chris Bonington, who has climbed Everest and led many other successful expeditions. In May 1993 Rebecca Stephens became the first British woman to climb Everest.

Netball

More than 60,000 adults play netball regularly in England and a further 1 million participants play in schools. The sport is played almost exclusively by women and girls both indoors and outdoors.

The All England Netball Association is the governing body in England. Scotland, Wales and Northern Ireland have their own governing bodies. The number of clubs affiliated to the All England Association has more than doubled in recent years.

Rowing

Rowing is taught in many schools, colleges and rowing clubs throughout Britain. The main types of boats are single, pairs and double sculls, fours and eights. The governing body in England is the Amateur Rowing Association; similar bodies regulate the sport in Scotland, Wales and Northern Ireland.

The University Boat Race, between eight-oared crews from Oxford and Cambridge, has been rowed on the Thames almost every spring since 1836. The Head of the River Race, also on the Thames, is the largest assembly of racing craft in the world, with more than 420 eights racing in procession. At the Henley Regatta in Oxfordshire crews from all over the world compete each July in various kinds of race over a straight course of 1 mile 550 yards (about 2.1 km).

At the World Rowing Championships in September 1993 Britain won four gold medals: Gregory Searle, Jonathan Searle and Garry Herbert (coxed pairs); Steven Redgrave and Matthew Pinsent (coxless pairs); Peter Haining (lightweight single sculls); and the women's lightweight fours (Alison Brownless, Jane Hall, Annemarie Dryden and Tonya Williams).

Rugby Football

Since the end of the 19th century rugby football has been played according to two different codes: rugby union (a 15-a-side game) is played by amateurs and rugby league (a 13-a-side game) by professionals as well as amateurs.

Rugby union is played under the auspices of the Rugby Football Union in England and parallel bodies in Wales, Scotland and Ireland. Important domestic competitions include the divisional and county championships in England; the league and national club knock-out competitions in England and Wales; and the National League and Inter-District Championships in Scotland.

The Five Nations Tournament between England, Scotland, Wales, Ireland and France is contested each year. Overseas tours are undertaken by the national sides and by the British Lions, a team representing Great Britain and Ireland.

Seven-a-side rugby union has a strong following. Tournaments include the Middlesex Sevens, which is held every year at Twickenham, and every four years there is a World Cup. The inaugural World Cup was held in Edinburgh in April 1993 and was won by England.

Rugby league has its own distinct set of rules, but it has kept many of the features of the union game. However, unlike rugby union, which is played nationally, it is concentrated in the north of England.

The governing body of the professional game is the Rugby Football League, which sends touring teams representing Great Britain to Australia, New Zealand and Papua New Guinea; annual matches are also played against France. The Challenge Cup Final, the major club match of the season, is played at Wembley Stadium in London.

The amateur game is governed by the British Amateur Rugby League Association. Matches between England and France are held each year and tours are arranged to Australia and New Zealand. A national league consisting of ten leading clubs was formed in 1986, and a second division in 1989.

Skiing

Skiing takes place in Scotland from December to May and also at several English locations when there is sufficient snow. The five established winter sports areas in Scotland are Cairngorm, Glencoe, Glenshee, the Lecht and Aonach Mor, all of which have a full range of ski-lifts, prepared ski runs and professional instructors.

There are over 150 artificial or dry ski-slopes located throughout Britain, and it is estimated that 1.5 million people in Britain take part in the sport. The governing body of the sport is the British Ski Federation.

Snooker and Billiards

Snooker has greatly increased in popularity in recent years and become a major spectator sport as a result of heavy television coverage of the professional tournaments. It is estimated that between 7 and 8 million people now play the game.

British players have an outstanding record in snooker and have dominated the major professional championships. The main tournament is the annual Embassy World

Professional Championship, held in Sheffield. In the 1980s Steve Davis won the world title six times and in 1993 Stephen Hendry became world champion for the third time.

The controlling body for the non-professional game in England is the English Association for Snooker and Billiards. Scotland, Wales and Northern Ireland have separate associations. The World Professional Billiards and Snooker Association is responsible for professional players, organises all world-ranking professional events and holds the copyright for the rules.

A growing number of women play snooker and billiards. Their representative body is the World Ladies Billiards and Snooker Association, with around 250 members. A women's world snooker championship is played every year in London. The Embassy World Professional Championship was opened to women in 1992.

Squash

The governing body for squash in England is the Squash Rackets Association; there are separate governing bodies in Wales, Scotland and Northern Ireland. The main tournament is the British Open Championship.

There are nearly 9,000 squash courts in England, and the estimated number of players in Britain is almost 1 million. The main providers of facilities are member clubs, commercial organisations and local authorities.

Swimming

Swimming is considered to be one of the most beneficial forms of exercise and attracts people with a wide range of abilities from all age groups. It is enjoyed by millions of people both as a popular recreational activity and as a competitive sport.

All forms of competitive swimming are governed by the Amateur Swimming Association (ASA) in England and by similar associations in Scotland and Wales. These three associations combine to form the Amateur Swimming Federation of Great Britain, which acts as the co-ordinating body for the selection of Great Britain teams and the organisation of international competitions. Northern Ireland forms part of the Irish Amateur Swimming Association.

Instruction and coaching are provided by qualified teachers and coaches who hold certificates awarded mainly by the ASA.

The most advanced aquatic facility in the world was opened in 1991 at Ponds Forge, Sheffield. The pool hosted the 1993 European Championships, at which Britain won a total of 12 medals including a gold medal for Nick Gillingham in the 200 metres breaststroke.

Table Tennis

Table tennis is played by a broad range of adults, with men far outnumbering women. The sport is particularly popular in schools and youth clubs, and is also a major recreational and competitive sport for people with disabilities.

The governing body in England is the English Table Tennis Association. There are separate governing bodies in Scotland, Wales and Northern Ireland. Table tennis became an Olympic sport in 1988.

Tennis

The controlling body for tennis in Great Britain is the Lawn Tennis Association (LTA), to which the Welsh and Scottish LTAs are affiliated. Northern Ireland forms part of Tennis Ireland. Tennis was incorporated into the Olympics in 1988.

The main tournament is the annual Wimbledon fortnight, one of the four tennis 'Grand Slam' tournaments. This draws large crowds to the All England Club, and the tournament is covered extensively on television. Prize money has increased dramatically over the last decade and totalled £5 million in 1993. Since 1980 the All England Club has donated £81.5 million to the LTA.

There are national and county championships and national competitions for boys' and girls' schools. Short tennis to encourages children aged five and over to take part in the sport. The game uses a court of similar size to a badminton court and is played in over 3,000 schools and in leisure

centres. In all, some 3 million people play tennis in Britain. The last decade has seen a big increase in the number of indoor courts.

British tennis recently showed signs of a revival when James Baily won the 1993 junior singles championship at the Australian Open, becoming the first British male to win a singles Grand Slam title for 28 years.

Tenpin Bowling

The first tenpin bowling centre in Britain opened in 1960. It is estimated that there are now some 4.8 million people who take part in tenpin bowling every year in Britain. There are over 200 national tournaments and an annual National Championship.

Britain has 200 indoor bowling centres and more than 30,000 people belong to the sport's governing body, the British Tenpin Bowling Association.

Volleyball

Volleyball is played both indoors and outdoors, and is particularly popular among schoolchildren and university and college students. Mini-volley is a version of the game adapted for children under 13.

The English Volleyball Association and parallel associations in Scotland, Wales and Northern Ireland act as the sport's governing bodies. The British Volleyball Federation meets regularly to discuss interests of common concern and to draw up policies.

Yachting

Yachting comprises sailing, powerboating and windsurfing on both inland and offshore waters. Offshore racing takes place between one-design classes or under handicap, which provides level racing for boats of different size and shape. The most well-known ocean races include the Whitbread Round The World Yacht Race and the Fastnet Race. Powerboating has two main forms: inland circuit racing and offshore racing.

The Royal Yachting Association is the governing body for all yachting in Britain. It is estimated that about 3 million people participate in the sport.

Appendices
and Index

Government Departments and Agencies

An outline of the principal functions of the main government departments and executive agencies (see p. 66) is given on the following pages.

Each section is divided into Cabinet ministries and other departments. Executive agencies are normally listed under the relevant department, although in some cases they are included within the description of the departments' responsibilities.

The work of many of the departments and agencies listed on pp. 495–500 covers Britain as a whole. Where this is not the case, the following abbreviations are used:

- (GB) for functions covering England, Wales and Scotland;

- (E,W & NI) for those covering England, Wales and Northern Ireland;

- (E & W) for those covering England and Wales; and

- (E) for those concerned with England only.

The principal address and telephone number of each department are given. For details of the addresses of executive agencies see the *Civil Service Year Book*.

The Cabinet Office and the responsibilities of the Office of Public Service and Science— OPSS—are described on p. 60.

Cabinet Office (Office of Public Service and Science)
70 Whitehall, London SW1A 2AS Tel: 071 271 1234

Executive Agencies
Central Office of Information (see p. 500)
Chessington Computer Centre
The Civil Service College
HMSO (see p. 500)
Occupational Health Service
Recruitment and Assessment Services

Economic Affairs

CABINET MINISTRIES

Ministry of Agriculture, Fisheries and Food
Whitehall Place, London SW1A 2HH
Tel: 071 270 3000
Policies for agriculture, horticulture, fisheries and food; responsibilities for related environmental and rural issues (E); food policies.

Executive Agencies
Agricultural Development and Advisory Service
Central Science Laboratory
Central Veterinary Laboratory
Pesticides Safety Directorate
Intervention Board for Agricultural Produce
Veterinary Medicines Directorate

Department of Employment
Caxton House, Tothill Street, London SW1H 9NF Tel: 071 273 3000
The Employment Service; employment; training, youth education and business start up; vocational qualifications; health and safety at work; industrial relations; equal opportunities; co-ordinating government policy on issues of particular concern to women; statistics on labour and industrial matters (GB); the Careers Service (E); international representation on employment and training matters.

Executive Agency
Employment Service

Department of Trade and Industry
Ashdown House, 123 Victoria Street, London SW1E 6RB Tel: 071 215 5000
Industrial and commercial affairs; promotion of new enterprise and competition; information about new business methods and opportunities; investor protection and consumer affairs. Specific responsibilities include innovation policy; regional industrial policy and inward investment promotion; small businesses; management best practice and business/education links; deregulation; international trade policy; commercial relations and export promotion; competition policy; company law; insolvency; radio regulation; patents and copyright protection (GB); the development of new sources of energy and the Government's relations with the energy industries.

Executive Agencies
Accounts Services Agency
Companies House
Insolvency Service
Laboratory of the Government Chemist
National Engineering Laboratory
National Physical Laboratory
National Weights and Measures Laboratory
Patent Office
Radiocommunications Agency

Department of Transport
2 Marsham Street, London SW1P 3EB Tel: 071 276 3000
Land, sea and air transport; domestic and international civil aviation; international transport agreements; shipping and the ports industry; marine pollution; regulation of drivers and vehicles (including road safety); regulation of the road haulage industry; transport and the environment. Motorways and trunk roads; oversight of local authority transport (E). Sponsorship of London Transport (E), British Rail (GB) and the Civil Aviation Authority.

Executive Agencies
Vehicle Inspectorate Executive Agency
Driver and Vehicle Licensing Agency
Driving Standards Agency
Vehicle Certification Agency
Transport Research Laboratory

HM Treasury
Parliament Street, London SW1P 3AG Tel: 071 270 3000
The formulation and implementation of economic policy; the planning of spending and taxation; and the central framework of Civil Service management and pay. General oversight of the financial system.

OTHER DEPARTMENTS

HM Customs and Excise
New King's Beam House, 22 Upper Ground, London SE1 9PJ Tel: 071 620 1313
Collecting and accounting for Customs and Excise revenues, including value added tax; agency functions, including controlling certain imports and exports and compiling trade statistics.

ECGD (Export Credits Guarantee Department)
2 Exchange Tower, Harbour Exchange Square, London E14 9GS Tel: 071 512 7000
Provision of insurance for project exporters against the risk of not being paid for goods and services; access to bank finance for exports; insurance cover for new investment overseas.

Board of Inland Revenue
Somerset House, London WC2R 1LB Tel: 071 438 6622
Administration and collection of direct taxes; valuation of property (GB).

Office of HM Paymaster General

Sutherland House, Russell Way, Crawley, West Sussex RH10 1UH Tel: 0293 560999
An executive agency providing banking services for government departments other than the Boards of Inland Revenue and Customs and Excise, and the payment of public service pensions.

Central Statistical Office

Great George Street, London SW1P 3AQ Tel: 071 270 3000
An executive agency preparing and interpreting key economic statistics needed for government policies; collecting and publishing business statistics; publishing annual and monthly statistical digests.

REGULATORY BODIES

The Office of Electricity Regulation (OFFER)

Hagley House, Hagley Road, Birmingham B16 8QG Tel: 021 456 2100
Regulating and monitoring the electricity supply industry; promoting competition in the generation and supply of electricity; ensuring that companies comply with the licences under which they operate; protecting customers' interests (GB).

Office of Gas Supply (OFGAS)

Southside, 105 Victoria Street, London SW1E 6QT Tel: 071 828 0898
Regulating and monitoring British Gas to ensure value for money for customers, and granting authorisations to other suppliers of gas through pipes; enabling development of competition in the industrial market.

Office of Telecommunications (OFTEL)

Export House, 50 Ludgate Hill, London EC4M 7JJ Tel: 071 634 8700
Monitoring telecommunications operators' licences; enforcing competition legislation; representing users' interests.

Office of Water Services (OFWAT)

Centre City Tower, 7 Hill Street, Birmingham B5 4UA Tel: 021 625 1300
Monitoring the activities of companies appointed as water and sewerage undertakers (E & W); regulation of prices and representing customers' interests.

Legal Affairs

CABINET MINISTRY

The Lord Chancellor's Department

Trevelyan House, 30 Great Peter Street, London SW1P 2BY Tel: 071 210 8500
Administration of the Supreme Court (Court of Appeal, High Court and Crown Court), the county courts, and the magistrates' courts (E & W), together with certain other courts and tribunals and the Council on Tribunals. Responsibility for the Northern Ireland Court Service; national archives (maintained by the Public Record Office—see below); the Public Trust Office and the Official Solicitor's Department.

All work relating to judicial and quasi-judicial appointments (see p. 98). Overall responsibility for civil and criminal legal aid, for the Law Commission and for the promotion of general reforms in the civil law. (The Home Office has important responsibilities for the criminal law.) Lead responsibility for private international law. The Legal Services Ombudsman and the Advisory Committee on Legal Education and Conduct are independent of the Department but report to the Lord Chancellor. Except for the Northern Ireland Court Service, the Lord Chancellor's remit covers England and Wales only.

Executive Agencies
HM Land Registry
Public Record Office

OTHER DEPARTMENTS

Crown Prosecution Service

50 Ludgate Hill, London EC4M 7EX Tel: 071 273 8000
An independent organisation responsible for the prosecution of criminal cases resulting from police investigations, headed by the Director of Public Prosecutions and

accountable to Parliament through the Attorney General, superintending minister for the service (E, W & NI).

Legal Secretariat to the Law Officers
9 Buckingham Gate, London SW1E 6JP
Tel: 071 828 7155
Supporting the Law Officers of the Crown (Attorney General and Solicitor General) in their functions as the Government's principal legal advisers (E, W & NI).

The Attorney General, who is also Attorney General for Northern Ireland, is the Minister responsible for the Treasury Solicitor's Department (see below), and has a statutory duty to superintend the Crown Prosecution Service (see above), the Serious Fraud Office (see below), and the Director of Public Prosecutions for Northern Ireland.

Parliamentary Counsel
36 Whitehall, London SW1A 2AY Tel: 071 210 6633
Drafting of government Bills (except those relating exclusively to Scotland); advising departments on parliamentary procedure (E, W & NI).

HM Procurator General and Treasury Solicitor's Department
Queen Anne's Chambers, 28 Broadway, London SW1H 9JS Tel: 071 210 3000
Provision of a legal service for a large number of government departments. Duties include instructing Parliamentary Counsel on Bills and drafting subordinate legislation; providing litigation and conveyancing services; and giving general advice on interpreting and applying the law (E & W).

Executive Agency
Government Property Lawyers

Lord Advocate's Department and Crown Office (see p. 502)

Serious Fraud Office
Elm House, 10-16 Elm Street, London WC1X 0BJ Tel: 071 239 7272
Investigating and prosecuting serious and complex fraud under the superintendence of the Attorney General (E, W & NI).

External Affairs and Defence

CABINET MINISTRIES

Ministry of Defence
Main Building, Whitehall, London SW1A 2HB Tel: 071 218 9000
Defence policy and control and administration of the armed services.

Executive Agencies
Military Survey
Naval Aircraft Repair Organisation
Maintenance Group
Service Children's Schools (North West Europe)
Defence Research Agency
Duke of York's Royal Military School
Meteorological Office
Queen Victoria School

Defence Support Agencies
Chemical and Biological Defence Establishment
Defence Analytical Services Agency
Defence Operational Analysis Centre
Defence Postal and Courier Service
Director General Defence Accounts
Hydrographic Office

Foreign & Commonwealth Office
King Charles Street, London SW1A 2AH
Tel: 071 270 3000
Conduct of Britain's overseas relations, including advising on policy, negotiating with overseas governments and conducting business in international organisations, promoting British exports and trade generally; administering aid (see below). Presenting British ideas, policies and objectives to the people of overseas countries; administering the remaining dependent territories; and protecting British interests abroad and British nationals overseas, including the provision of consular facilities to British citizens overseas.

OTHER DEPARTMENTS

Overseas Development Administration
94 Victoria Street, London SW1E 5JL Tel: 071 917 7000
Responsibility for Britain's overseas aid to developing countries, for global environmental assistance, and also for the joint administration, with the Foreign & Commonwealth Office, of assistance to Eastern Europe and the countries of the former Soviet Union. Responsibility for overseas superannuation.

Executive Agency
Natural Resources Institute

Social Affairs, the Environment and Culture

CABINET MINISTRIES

Department for Education
Sanctuary Buildings, Great Smith Street, London SW1P 3BT Tel: 071 925 5000
Formulates and promotes policies for education (E); responsibility for the Government's relations with universities (GB).

Executive Agency
Teacher's Pensions Agency

Department of the Environment
2 Marsham Street, London SW1P 3EB Tel: 071 276 4438
Policies for local government finance and structure, housing, construction, inner cities, environmental protection, water industry, energy efficiency, the countryside and rural areas, land use planning and the Government estate, including the Property Services Agency (GB).

Executive Agencies
Building Research Establishment
Ordnance Survey (see p. 500)
Planning Inspectorate
Queen Elizabeth II Conference Centre
The Buying Agency

Department of Health
Richmond House, 79 Whitehall, London SW1A 2NS Tel: 071 210 3000
National Health Service; personal social services provided by local authorities; and certain aspects of public health, including hygiene (E).

Executive Agencies
Medicines Control Agency
National Health Service Pensions Agency
NHS Estates

Home Office
50 Queen Anne's Gate, London SW1H 9AT Tel: 071 273 3000
Administration of justice; criminal law; treatment of offenders, including probation and the prison service; the police; crime prevention; fire service and emergency planning; licensing laws; regulation of firearms and dangerous drugs; electoral matters and local legislation (E & W). Gaming (GB). Passports, immigration and nationality; race relations; royal matters. Responsibilities relating to the Channel Islands and the Isle of Man.

Executive Agencies
Fire Service College
Forensic Science Service
HM Prison Service
United Kingdom Passport Agency

Department of National Heritage
2-4 Cockspur Street, London SW1Y 5DH Tel: 071 270 3000.
The arts (GB); public libraries; local museums and galleries; tourism; sport; heritage—including listing and scheduling buildings, and royal parks and palaces (E); broadcasting; press regulation; film industry; export licensing of antiques; the National Lottery.

Executive Agencies
Historic Royal Palaces
Royal Parks

Department of Social Security
Richmond House, 79 Whitehall, London SW1A 2NS Tel: 071 210 3000
The social security system (GB). Four

executive agencies cover the main aspects of the Department's work: the Benefits Agency; the Contributions Agency; the Child Support Agency; and the Information Technology Services Agency. A fifth agency, the Resettlement Agency, runs residential units designed to help single homeless people and a War Pensions Unit provides services to war pensioners and their widows.

OTHER DEPARTMENTS AND AGENCIES

Central Office of Information
Hercules Road, London SE1 7DU Tel: 071 928 2345
An executive agency providing publicity material and other information services for government departments and publicly funded organisations.

HMSO (Her Majesty's Stationery Office)
St Crispins, Duke Street, Norwich NR3 1PD and Sovereign House, Botolph Street, Norwich NR3 1DN Tel: 0603 622211
An executive agency providing stationery, office machinery and furniture, printing and related services to Parliament, government departments and other public bodies. Publishing and selling government documents.

Ordnance Survey
Romsey Road, Maybush, Southampton SO9 4DH Tel: 0703 792000
An executive agency providing official surveying, mapping and associated scientific work covering Great Britain and some overseas countries (see p. 499).

Office of Population Censuses and Surveys
St Catherine's House, 10 Kingsway, London WC2B 6JP Tel: 071 242 0262
A department responsible for administration of the marriage laws and local registration of births, marriages and deaths; provision of population estimates and projections and statistics on health and other demographic matters; Census of Population (E & W). Surveys for other government departments and public bodies (GB).

Office for Standards in Education (OFSTED)
Elizabeth House, York Road, London SE1 7PH Tel: 071 925 6773
Monitoring standards in English schools; regulating the work of independent registered schools inspectors (E) (see p. 411).

Northern Ireland

CABINET MINISTRY

Northern Ireland Office
Stormont, Belfast BT4 3ST Tel: 0232 763255
Whitehall, London SW1A 2AZ Tel: 071 210 3000

NORTHERN IRELAND DEPARTMENTS

Department of Agriculture for Northern Ireland
Development of agricultural, forestry and fishing industries; rural development; veterinary, scientific and advisory services; administration of European Community support and other arrangements.

Department of Economic Development for Northern Ireland
Development of industry and commerce, as well as administration of government policy on tourism, energy, minerals, industrial relations, employment equality, consumer protection, health and safety at work and company legislation. Administration of an employment service and training schemes through the Training and Employment Agency and assistance to industry through the Industrial Development Board for Northern Ireland.

Department of Education for Northern Ireland
Control of the five education and library boards and education as a whole from nursery to higher and continuing education;

youth services; sport and recreation; cultural activities and the development of community relations within and between schools.

Department of the Environment for Northern Ireland

Environmental protection; housing; planning; roads; transport and traffic management; vehicle licensing and taxation (including the Driver and Vehicle Testing Agency); harbours, water and sewerage; Ordnance Survey (an executive agency); maintenance of public records; certain controls over local government; and the Rates Collection Agency, an executive agency.

Department of Finance and Personnel

Control of public expenditure; liaison with HM Treasury and the Northern Ireland Office on financial matters, economic and social research and analysis; European Community co-ordination; charities; Valuation and Lands Agency (an executive agency); policies for equal opportunities and personnel management; and management and control of the Northern Ireland Civil Service.

Department of Health and Social Services for Northern Ireland

Health and personal social services; social legislation; and the Office of the Registrar-General. It is responsible for the Northern Ireland Child Support Agency.

The Social Security Agency has responsibility for the administration of all social security benefits and the collection of National Insurance contributions.

Scotland

CABINET MINISTRY

The Scottish Office

St Andrew's House, Edinburgh EH1 3DG
Tel: 031 556 8400
Dover House, Whitehall, London SW1A
2AU Tel: 071 270 3000
The Scottish Office's responsibilities are

discharged principally through its five departments (which include four executive agencies). There are also four smaller departments: the Registers of Scotland (an executive agency); the Scottish Record Office (an executive agency); the General Register Office for Scotland; and the Scottish Courts Administration.

An outline of the functions of the main Scottish departments is given below:

The Scottish Office Agriculture and Fisheries Department

Promotion and regulation of the agricultural and fishing industries; safeguarding public, plant and animal health welfare; and enforcement of fisheries laws and regulations through the Scottish Fisheries Protection Agency.

The Scottish Office Environment Department

Environment, including environmental protection, nature conservation and the countryside; land use planning; water supplies and sewerage; local government, including finance; housing; building control; protection and presentation to the public of historic buildings and ancient monuments through Historic Scotland, an executive agency.

The Scottish Office Education Department

Education (excluding universities); student awards; the arts, libraries, museums and galleries; Gaelic language; sport and recreation.

The Scottish Office Home and Health Department

Central administration of law and order (including police service, criminal justice, legal aid and the Scottish Prison Service, an executive agency); the National Health Service; fire, home defence and civil emergency services; social work services.

The Scottish Office Industry Department

Industrial and regional economic development matters; co-ordination of

Scottish Office European interests; employment; training; energy; tourism; urban regeneration; new towns; roads and certain transport functions, particularly in the Highlands and Islands.

Central Services
Services to the five Scottish departments. These include the Office of the Solicitor to the Secretary of State, The Scottish Office Information Directorate, Finance, Personnel Management and Office Management Divisions.

Proposed Changes
The Government has announced plans to transfer responsibility for training policy in Scotland and the Scottish Arts Council to The Scottish Office from April 1994. In addition, ownership of Highlands and Islands Airports would be transferred to The Scottish Office and the Government would also review the scope for transferring to The Scottish Office responsibilities for encouraging industrial innovation.

The following are directly responsible to the Law Officers and are not part of The Scottish Office:

Lord Advocate's Department and Crown Office
Fielden House, 10 Great College Street, London SW1P 3SL Tel: 071 276 3000
Provision of legal advice to the Government on issues affecting Scotland; responsibility for drafting government primary legislation relating to Scotland and adapting for Scotland other primary legislation. Provision of advice on matters of parliamentary procedure affecting Scotland.

Crown Office
5-7 Regent Road, Edinburgh EH7 5BL Tel: 031 557 3800
Control of all prosecutions in Scotland.

Wales

CABINET MINISTRY

Welsh Office
Cathays Park, Cardiff CF1 3NQ Tel: 0222 825111
Gwydyr House, Whitehall, London SW1A 2ER Tel: 071 270 3000
Many aspects of Welsh affairs, including health, community care and personal social services; education, except for terms and conditions of service, student awards and the University of Wales; the Welsh language and culture; agriculture and fisheries; forestry; local government; housing; water and sewerage; environmental protection; sport; land use, including planning; countryside and nature conservation; ancient monuments and historic buildings (through CADW, an executive agency).

The Department's responsibilities also include roads; tourism; enterprise and training; selective financial assistance to industry; the Urban Programme and urban investment grants in Wales; the operation of the European Regional Development Fund in Wales and other European Community matters; women's issues; non-departmental public bodies; civil emergencies; all financial aspects of these matters, including Welsh revenue support grant; and oversight responsibilities for economic affairs and regional planning in Wales.

Recent Legislation

The public Acts of Parliament passed since autumn 1992 are listed below. Thirteen Acts were introduced by private members: these are indicated by asterisks. All are available from HMSO.

Boundary Commissions Act 1992. Makes further provision regarding the membership of the Boundary Commissions, the timing of their reports and the local government boundaries of which account is to be taken in their reports. Ch 55. £1.45.

Car Tax (Abolition) Act 1992. Ch 58. £1.05.

Civil Service (Management Functions) Act 1992. Allows the Government to devolve to departments and agencies many detailed matters concerning the management of their staff. Ch 61. 65p.

Consolidated Fund (No 3) Act 1992. Authorises sums to be issued out of the Consolidated Fund to meet the Government's expenditure requirements. Ch 59. 60p.

Maintenance Orders (Reciprocal Enforcement) Act 1992. Enables orders by magistrates' courts to be enforced where one party is resident in Britain and the other party is resident in a country with which Britain has a reciprocal agreement. Ch 56. £3.20.

Sea Fish (Conservation) Act 1992. Provides for the conservation of fish stocks by restricting the number of days that fishing vessels may spend at sea. Ch 60. £2.30.

Sporting Events (Control of Alcohol Etc) (Amendment) Act 1992. Ch 57. 60p.

Agriculture Act 1993. Ends the milk marketing schemes (see p.235) in Great Britain and the wool and potato guarantees. Ch 37. £9.25.

Appropriation Act 1993. Gives authority for sums to be issued out of the Consolidated Fund to meet the Government's expenditure requirements. Ch 33. £7.

Asylum and Immigration Appeals Act 1993. Provides for an acceleration and simplification of decision-making in asylum cases and a streamlining of the immigration appeals system (see p. 29). Ch 23. £3.80.

Bail (Amendment) Act 1993. Grants the prosecution a right of appeal against decisions to grant bail. Ch 26. 65p.

Bankruptcy (Scotland) Act 1993. Amends 1985 Act to improve the conduct of sequestrations. Ch 6. £5.90.

British Coal and British Rail (Transfer Proposals) Act 1993. Gives British Coal and British Rail powers to take any steps necessary to prepare for privatisation. Ch 2. £1.10.

Carrying of Knives Etc. (Scotland) Act 1993. Makes it an offence in Scotland to carry an article with a blade or point in a public place. Ch 13. £1.10.

Charities Act 1993. Consolidates legislation on charities. Ch 10. £11.

Clean Air Act 1993 (see p. 355). Ch 11.£7.70.

Consolidated Fund Act 1993. Authorises sums to be issued out of the Consolidated Fund to meet the Government's expenditure requirements. Ch 4. 60p.

Consolidated Fund (No 2) Act 1993. Ch 7. 65p.

Criminal Justice Act 1993. Toughens the sentencing powers of courts in England and Wales, and sets out measures to deal with the financing of terrorism and the proceeds of drug trafficking, money laundering, insider dealing and fraud. Ch 36. £11.

Damages (Scotland) Act 1993. Clarifies the law in Scotland on the right of certain relatives of a deceased person, and the right of executors, to claim damages in respect of the death of the deceased from personal injuries. Ch 5. £1.50.

Disability (Grants) Act 1993. Authorises payments to the Independent Living (Extension) Fund, the Independent Living (1993) Fund and Motability. Ch 14. 65p.

Education Act 1993. Introduces measures designed to improve the quality of education, to enhance diversity and parental choice, and to encourage school autonomy and accountability. Ch 35. £19.90.

European Communities (Amendment) Act 1993. Provides for Britain's ratification of the Maastricht Treaty on European Union (see p. 295). Ch 32. 65p.

Finance Act 1993 (see Chapter 10). Ch 34. £20.95.

Foreign Compensation (Amendment) Act 1993. Extends the powers to make Orders in Council under the Foreign Compensation Act 1950. Ch 16. £1.10.

*Gas (Exempt Supplies) Act 1993. Allows gas to be supplied through pipes more readily, but just as safely, by simplifying the procedures required by the Gas Act 1986. Ch 1. £1.10.

Judicial Pensions and Retirement Act 1993. Makes further provision with respect to judicial pensions. Ch 8. £11.

Leasehold Reform, Housing and Urban Development Act 1993 (see p. 330). Ch 28. £19.65.

*Licensing (Amendment) (Scotland) Act 1993. Amends the Licensing (Scotland) Act 1976 in relation to certain planning certificates. Ch 20. 65p.

*Local Government (Overseas Assistance) Act 1993. Clarifies the powers of local authorities to provide technical assistance overseas. Ch 25. £1.10.

*Merchant Shipping (Registration Etc) Act 1993. Amends and restates the law on the registration of merchant vessels. Ch 22. £7.

National Lottery etc. Act 1993 (see p. 482). Ch 39 £7.70.

Non-domestic Rating Act 1993. Limits increases in non-domestic rates for 1993–94. Ch 17. £1.10.

*Osteopaths Act 1993. Establishes the General Osteopathic Council for developing, promoting and regulating the profession. Ch 21. £6.30.

Prisoners and Criminal Proceedings (Scotland) Act 1993. Amends the law of Scotland relating to the early release of prisoners and that governing criminal evidence and procedure. Ch 9. £7.70.

*Protection of Animals (Scotland) Act 1993. Increases penalties for certain acts of cruelty to animals in Scotland. Ch 15. 60p.

Radioactive Substances Act 1993. Consolidates legislation on radioactive substances. Ch 12. £7.

Reinsurance (Acts of Terrorism) Act 1993. Relates to the financing of reinsurance obligations of the Government in respect of loss or damage to property resulting from acts of terrorism. Ch 18. 65p.

Representation of the People Act 1993. Allows home service personnel of the Royal Irish Regiment to register as civilian voters for elections in Northern Ireland. Ch 29. 60p.

*Road Traffic (Driving Instruction by Disabled Persons) Act 1993. Enables people with certain physical disabilities to be authorised in certain circumstances to give paid driving instruction. Ch 31. £3.30.

*Sexual Offences Act 1993. Abolishes the presumption of criminal law that a boy under the age of 14 is incapable of sexual intercourse. Ch 30. 60p.

Social Security Act 1993. Introduces a 1 per cent additional rebate for personal pension holders aged 30 and over and provides for a Treasury grant to be paid into the National Insurance Fund. Ch 3. £1.10.

Trade Union Reform and Employment Rights Act 1993 (see p. 136). Ch 19. £11.95.

*Video Recordings Act 1993. Introduces a system of titles and numbers for video works assigned by the British Board of Film Classification and extends the limit for starting proceedings for prosecuting alleged offenders under the Video Recording Act 1984. Ch 24. £1.10.

Welsh Language Act 1993. The Bill (see p. 23) received Royal Assent on 21.10.93. Ch 38. £4.30

Britain's Economy: Statistical Annex

All the following statistics, apart from some relating to the labour market and retail sales, cover England, Wales, Scotland and Northern Ireland. Some figures may be subject to revision at a later stage.

Gross Domestic Product (GDP)				
				£ million
	1985	1990	1991	1992
GDP at market prices[a]	357,344	551,118	573,645	596,165
GDP at factor cost[b]	307,902	478,886	494,824	514,594
GDP at factor cost at 1990 prices	407,844	478,886	467,720	465,646
Value indices at current prices —GDP at factor cost (1990 = 100)	64.3	100.0	103.3	107.5
Percentage change since previous year	*+9.7*	*+0.4*	*+3.3*	*+4.1*
Volume indices at 1990 prices—GDP at factor cost	85.2	100.0	97.7	97.2

[a] Market prices are the prices people pay for goods and services.
[b] Factor cost is the cost of goods and services before adding taxes and subtracting subsidies.

Output				
	1985	1990	1991	1992
Output of production[a] industries (1985 = 100)	100.0	109.3	106.1	105.8
Output per person employed (1985 = 100)				
Whole economy	100.0	107.4	107.7	110.2
Percentage change since previous year	*–*	*-0.1*	*+0.3*	*+2.3*
Manufacturing	100.0	122.8	124.6	130.9
Percentage change since previous year	*–*	*+1.6*	*+1.5*	*+5.1*

[a] Consists of the mining and quarrying, manufacturing and electricity, gas and water supply industries.

Labour Market[a]

Thousands

	1985	1990	1991	1992	June 1993
Employees in employment	21,414	22,913	22,251	21,835	21,324
Self-employed	2,614	3,298	3,143	2,989	2,978
Unemployment	3,028	1,663	2,287	2,767	2,912
Percentage of workforce	10.9	5.8	8.1	9.8	10.4
Percentage increase in earnings on previous year	n.a.	+9.7	+8.0	+6.1	+3.4

[a] Figures for employees in employment and self-employment are for June each year and the former are seasonally adjusted. Other figures are annual averages, except for June 1993. The figures for unemployment are seasonally adjusted, while those for earnings are not seasonally adjusted and are for Great Britain.
n.a. = not available.

Retail Sales[a]

	1988	1990	1991	1992
Volume index (average 1990 prices) 1990 =100	97.3	100.0	98.9	99.5
Percentage change since previous year	–	*+0.7*	*-1.1*	*+0.6*
Value in current prices (1990 = 100)	87.6	100.0	104.7	108.5
Percentage change since previous year	–	*+7.0*	*+4.7*	*+3.6*

[a] Figures are for Great Britain.

Prices

	Jan 1987	1990	1991	1992	June 1993
Retail Prices Index (RPI) (Jan 1987 = 100)	100.0	126.1	133.5	138.5	141.0
Percentage change since previous year	–	*+9.5*	*+5.9*	*+3.7*	*+1.2*
RPI excluding mortgage interest payments	100.0	122.1	130.3	136.4	141.0
Tax and price index[a]	100.0	119.9	126.5	130.2	131.7

[a] This measures the change in gross income, in June of each year, needed for taxpayers to maintain their purchasing power, allowing for changes in the RPI.

506

Overseas Trade

				£ million
	1985	1990	1991	1992
Visible trade:				
Exports (fob)[a]	77,991	101,718	103,413	107,047
Imports (fob)[a]	81,336	120,527	113,697	120,453
Visible balance	-3,345	-18,809	-10,284	-13,406
Invisibles balance	+5,583	+541	+2,632	+4,786
Current balance	+2,238	-18,268	-7,652	-8,620

[a] Free on board, that is, all costs accruing up to the time of placing the goods on board the exporting vessel having been paid by the vendor.

Sources

The following Central Statistical Office publications:
United Kingdom National Accounts 1993 Edition
United Kingdom Balance of Payments 1993
Monthly Digest of Statistics
CSO press notices
Department of Employment *Employment Gazette*

The Citizen's Charter Initiative

A detailed account of the Citizen's Charter initiative is given on pp. 64–5. The White Paper which launched the initiative in July 1991 and a follow-up report, published in November 1992, are:

The Citizen's Charter. Raising the Standard. Cm 1599. HMSO, £8.50. ISBN 0 10 115992 7. (See p. 64.)

The Citizen's Charter First Report: 1992. Cm 2101. HMSO, £8.50. ISBN 0 10 121012 4. (See p. 64.)

A White Paper on Open Government was published in July 1993—see p. 65. (*Open Government.* Cm 2290. HMSO, £11. ISBN 0 10 122902 X.)

INDIVIDUAL CHARTERS

The 37 Charters published as part of the Citizen's Charter initiative, with the name of the department or organisation responsible in brackets,[1] are:

Benefits Agency Customer Charter (Social Security Benefits Agency)

Charter for Further Education—see p. 413 (Department for Education)

Charter for Higher Education—see p. 413 (Department for Education)

Contributor's Charter (Social Security Contributions Agency)

Child Support Agency Charter (Child Support Agency)

Courts Charter—see p. 84 (Lord Chancellor's Department, Home Office, Crown Prosecution Service)

Employer's Charter (Social Security Contributions Agency)

Jobseeker's Charter—see p. 130 (Employment Service)

London Underground Customer's Charter (London Underground Ltd)

Parent's Charter—see p. 404 (Department for Education)

Passenger's Charter—see p. 254 (British Rail)

Patient's Charter—see p. 365 (Department of Health)

Redundancy Payments Service Charter (Department of Employment)

Taxpayer's Charter—see p. 117 (Inland Revenue)

Taxpayer's Charter (HM Customs and Excise)

Tenant's Charter—see p. 333 (Department of the Environment)

Traveller's Charter (HM Customs and Excise)

Northern Ireland

Northern Ireland Charter (Northern Ireland Office—Department of Finance and Personnel)

Bus Passenger's Charter (Ulsterbus)

Charter for Patients and Clients (Northern Ireland Office—Department of Health and Social Services)

Charter for Social Security Agency Clients (Northern Ireland Social Security Agency)

Child Support Agency Charter (Northern Ireland Child Support Agency)

Northern Ireland Tenant's Charter (Northern Ireland Housing Executive)

---

[1]The addresses and telephone numbers of government departments are given on pp. 495–502.

Parent's Charter (Northern Ireland Office—Department of Education)

Railway Passenger's Charter (Northern Ireland Railways)

RUC Charter (Royal Ulster Constabulary)

Training and Employment Agency Customer's Charter (Training and Employment Agency, Northern Ireland)

Scotland

Further and Higher Education Charter for Scotland

Justice Charter for Scotland

Parent's Charter for Scotland

Patient's Charter for Scotland

Tenant's Charter for Scotland

(All published by The Scottish Office)

Wales

Charter for Further Education

Charter for Higher Education

Parent's Charter for Wales

Patient's Charter for Wales

Tenant's Charter for Wales

(All published by the Welsh Office; all are bilingual in English and Welsh)

Further Information

Information about the charters, including telephone numbers and addresses, can be obtained by calling 0345 300130 (all calls are charged at local rates). The service is available 24 hours a day. For copies of the guide to the Charter Mark awards (see p. 65), ring 071 270 6304.

Obituaries

Marshal of the Royal Air Force Sir Dermot Boyle, GCB, KCVO, KBE, AFC
Chief of the Air Staff 1956–59
Born 1904, died May 1993

Les Dawson
Comedian, actor, writer
Born 1934, died June 1993

Dame Elisabeth Frink, CH
Sculptor
Born 1930, died April 1993

Sir William Golding, CBE
Author, winner of the Nobel Prize for Literature, 1983
Born 1911, died June 1993

Stewart Granger
Stage and film actor
Born 1913, died August 1993

Cardinal Gordon Gray
Roman Catholic Archbishop of St Andrews and Edinburgh 1951–85
Born 1910, died July 1993

Lord Grimond of Firth (formerly Jo Grimond)
Liberal MP 1950–83. Leader of the Liberal Party 1956–67 and May–July 1976
Born 1913, died October 1993

James Hunt
World motor racing champion, 1976
Born 1947, died June 1993

Sir Kenneth Macmillan
Principal Choreographer to the Royal Ballet from 1977
Born 1929, died October 1992

Ian Mikardo
Labour MP 1945–59, 1964–87
Born 1908, died May 1993

Bobby Moore, OBE
Professional footballer, captained England's football team when it won the World Cup in 1966
Born 1941, died May 1993

Sir John Moores, CBE
Businessman, founder of the Littlewoods Organisation, art patron
Born 1896, died September 1993

Professor C. Northcote Parkinson
Author, historian and journalist
Born 1909, died March 1993

Dr Magnus Pyke, OBE
Scientist and broadcaster
Born 1908, died October 1992

Lord Ridley of Liddesdale (formerly Nicholas Ridley)
Conservative MP 1959–92 and Government minister 1970–72, 1979–90
Born 1929, died March 1993

Dame Freya Stark
Traveller and writer
Born 1893, died May 1993

E. P. Thompson
Writer, historian and peace campaigner
Born 1924, died August 1993

Sir Roy Watts
Chief Executive of British Airways 1979–82, Chairman of Thames Water 1983–93
Born 1925, died April 1993

Lord Zuckerman OM, KCB (formerly Solly Zuckerman)
Scientist; Chief Scientific Adviser to the Government 1964–71
Born 1904, died April 1993

Index

Items are indexed under England, Northern Ireland, Scotland or Wales only where they are matters peculiar to these countries; otherwise they are indexed under the relevant subject headings.

Acknowledgments for photographs
Cover: Milepost 92½, COI Pictures, Press Association; **Citizen's Charter** (photographs in colour sections listed top to bottom and left to right): United Bristol Healthcare NHS Trust, Inland Revenue; **Conserving Britain's Heritage**: National Trust, COI Pictures, Northern Ireland Tourist Board, COI Pictures; **National Hyperbaric Centre**: COI Pictures; **Pollution Control**: COI Pictures; **Waterways**: Wales Tourist Board, Northern Ireland Tourist Board, Still Moving Picture Company, COI Pictures; **Aerospace**: COI Pictures, Rolls-Royce; **Small Businesses**: COI Pictures, Mercury Communications Ltd; **Exports**: Academy of St Martin-in-the-Fields, Financial Times, BCB Ltd, Churchill; **New Technology**: COI Pictures, BT; **Agriculture**: COI Pictures, Reed Farmers Publishing Group; **Tourism**: Still Moving Picture Company, Northern Ireland Tourist Board, Madam Tussauds, Wales Tourist Board; **Health**: COI Pictures; **Charities**: Multiple Sclerosis Society, Help the Aged; **Children**: COI Pictures, Action for Sick Children, Pre-School Playgroups Association, Eileen Langsley/Supersport; **Religion**: Keith Ellis, Glasgow Museums; **Dance**: Adzido Pan African Dance, Royal Ballet; **Treasures of Britain**: Yorkshire Museum, Glasgow Museums: The Burrell Collection, National Museum of Wales, Ulster Museum; **Sport**: Press Association.

Cover illustration by Davide de Angelis

Printed in the United Kingdom for HMSO
Dd 297023   C21   12/93

Main Railway Passenger Routes

Electrified InterCity
and Express Routes

Other InterCity
and Express Routes

Other routes

Inverness

Aberdeen

Dundee

Perth

Stirling

Edinburgh

Glasgow

Berwick

Newcastle upon Tyne

Londonderry   Larne

Carlisle

Belfast

Darlington   Middlesbrough

Scarborough

Harrogate

York

Leeds   Hull

Blackpool   Bradford

Preston

Manchester   Doncaster   Grimsby

Liverpool

Sheffield

Holyhead

Nottingham

Crewe   Derby

Stafford   King's Lynn

Shrewsbury   Leicester   Peterborough   Norwich

Birmingham

Coventry

Worcester   Cambridge   Ipswich

Hereford   Colchester   Harwich

Fishguard

Gloucester   Oxford

Swansea   Newport   Swindon   London   Margate

Cardiff   Bristol   Bath   Reading   Ashford   Dover

Gatwick   Folkestone

Salisbury   Hastings

Taunton   Southampton   Portsmouth   Brighton   Eastbourne

Bournemouth

Exeter   Weymouth

Newton Abbot

Plymouth

Penzance

0   20   40   60   80   100 km

0   20   40   60 miles